Consumer ADR in Europe

This is the first systematic comparative study into how consumer ADR systems (usually ombudsmen and *médiateurs*) work, the differing national architectures within which they operate and how they can be improved. It describes ADR schemes in Belgium, France, Germany, Lithuania, the Netherlands, Poland, Slovenia, Spain, Sweden and the United Kingdom as well as emerging pan-EU dispute resolution schemes. Use of the techniques of mediation, conciliation and adjudication are noted. It also covers EU measures on consumer ADR, and 2011 proposals for legislation on ADR and ODR. Data on volumes, cost and duration of ADR schemes are compared, both between different systems and with courts. The authors' findings underpin EU and national developments, and outline options for future policy. Findings and proposals are included for the functions, scope, performance, essential requirements, architecture and operation of ADR systems. The relationships between ADR, courts and regulators are discussed, and need for reforms are noted. This is a ground-breaking work that will have a major impact on European legal systems.

Civil Justice Systems

Series General Editor, Chris Hodges, Director, CMS Programme, CSLS, University of Oxford

This series covers new theoretical and empirical research on the mechanisms for resolution of civil disputes, including courts, tribunals, arbitration, compensation schemes, ombudsmen, codes of practice, complaint mechanisms, mediation, and various forms of Alternative Dispute Resolution. It examines frameworks for dispute resolution that comprise combinations of the above mechanisms, and the parameters and conditions for selecting certain types of techniques and procedures rather than others. It also evaluates individual techniques, against parameters such as cost, duration, accessibility, and delivery of desired outcomes, and illuminates how legal rights and obligations are operated in practice.

Also in this series:

The Costs and Funding of Civil Litigation
A Comparative Perspective

Edited by
Christopher Hodges, Stefan Vogenauer and Magdalena Tulibacka

Consumer ADR in Europe

Christopher J S Hodges

MA (Oxon), PhD (Lond), FSALS
Head of the CMS Research Programme on Civil Justice Systems,
Centre for Socio-Legal Studies,
University of Oxford
Erasmus Professor of the Fundamentals of Private Law,
Erasmus University
Life member, Wolfson College, Oxford
Solicitor

Iris Benöhr

M Res and PhD (European University Institute, Fiesole)
Licence en Droit (University of Neuchâtel, Switzerland)
Post-Doctoral Researcher, Centre for Socio-Legal Studies, University of Oxford
Admitted to the Brussels Bar (2009–2011)
Attorney admitted to the Bar (Supreme Court Zurich)

Naomi Creutzfeldt-Banda

MA (USQ Australia), PhD (Georg-August-Universität Göttingen)
Post-Doctoral Researcher, Center for Socio-Legal Studies, University of Oxford

·HART·
PUBLISHING

OXFORD AND PORTLAND, OREGON
2012

Published in the United Kingdom by Hart Publishing Ltd
16C Worcester Place, Oxford, OX1 2JW
Telephone: +44 (0)1865 517530
Fax: +44 (0)1865 510710
E-mail: mail@hartpub.co.uk
Website: http://www.hartpub.co.uk

Published in North America (US and Canada) by
Hart Publishing
c/o International Specialized Book Services
920 NE 58th Avenue, Suite 300
Portland, OR 97213-3786
USA
Tel: +1 503 287 3093 or toll-free: (1) 800 944 6190
Fax: +1 503 280 8832
E-mail: orders@isbs.com
Website: http://www.isbs.com

British Library Cataloguing in Publication Data
Data Available

ISBN: 978-1-84946-348-5 (Hart Publishing)
978-3-8329-7260-8 (Verlag CH Beck)

Typeset by Criteria International
Printed and bound in Great Britain by
CPI Group (UK) Ltd, Croydon, CR0 4YY

In Memoriam
Malcolm Carlisle OBE
(1947 – 2011)

SUMMARY CONTENTS

Detailed Contents		ix
List of Tables and Figures		xv
Contributors		xix
Interviewees		xxi
Abbreviations		xxv
Introduction Christopher Hodges, Iris Benöhr, Naomi Creutzfeldt-Banda		xxix
Consumer ADR at EU Level		
1. Alternative Dispute Resolution for Consumers in the EU	Iris Benöhr	1
Consumer ADR in Selected Member States		
2. Belgium	Stefaan Voet	25
3. France	Christopher Hodges, Iris Benöhr, Naomi Creutzfeldt-Banda	37
4. Germany	Iris Benöhr, Christopher Hodges, Naomi Creutzfeldt-Banda	73
5. Lithuania	Christopher Hodges	117
6. The Netherlands	Franziska Weber, Christopher Hodges	129
7. Poland	Magdalena Tulibacka	167
8. Slovenia	Aleš Galič and Christopher Hodges	197
9. Spain	Iris Benöhr, Franziska Weber	209
10. Sweden	Franziska Weber, Christopher Hodges, Naomi Creutzfeldt-Banda	229
11. The United Kingdom	Naomi Creutzfeldt-Banda, Christopher Hodges, Iris Benöhr	253
12. Best Practice in Customer Care in the UK	Christopher Hodges	339
13. Cross-border Consumer ADR	Christopher Hodges, Naomi Creutzfeldt-Banda, Iris Benöhr	355
Findings		
14. Empirical Findings	Naomi Creutzfeldt-Banda	367
15. Findings and Conclusions	Christopher Hodges, Iris Benöhr, Naomi Creutzfeldt-Banda	389

Appendices

1. Commission Recommendation of 30 March 1998 on the principles applicable to the bodies responsible for out-of-court settlement of consumer disputes (98/257/EC) 455
2. Commission Recommendation of 4 April 2001 on the principles for out-of-court bodies involved in the consensual resolution of consumer disputes (2001/310/EC) 463
3. European Code of Conduct for Mediators 471
4. French Charter of Consumer Mediation 475

DETAILED CONTENTS

Summary Contents	vii
List of Tables and Figures	xv
Contributors	xix
Interviewees	xxi
Abbreviations	xxv
Introduction	**xxix**
Consumer ADR	xxix
The Different Meanings of ADR	xxix
The World of CADR	xxx
Policy Decisions	xxxi
The Research Question and Approach	xxxii
Plan of the Book	xxxiii
Methodology	xxxiv
Consumer ADR at EU level	
1. Alternative Dispute Resolution in the EU	**1**
Introduction	1
Access to Justice and ADR at the International and Regional Level	2
Historic overview of key ADR Related Actions in the EU	3
Competences of the EU in Civil Justice and Consumer ADR	5
Specific EU Measures Regarding ADR	7
EU Cross-border Networks	13
EU-Wide Complaints Reporting	18
The European Commission's Proposals on Consumer ADR and ODR	20
Conclusions	23
Consumer ADR in Selected Member States	
2. Belgium	**25**
The New FPS Economy and its Mediation Task	25
Creation of Belmed	26
Information	27
Online Application	29
CADR Agencies	34
3. France	**37**
Overview	37

The Institutional Landscape for Consumer Issues 38
Consumer Claims and Mediation within the Court System 39
Consumer Complaints Boards 41
Types of Médiateur 43
Banking 46
Insurance 51
Energy 56
Transport 62
Electronic Communications 65
Internet 68
Doctors 69
Evaluation 70

4. Germany **73**
The National Context 73
Privatised Enforcement of Consumer Law 82
Overview of Consumer ADR Bodies 87
Chambers of Commerce 89
The Insurance Ombudsman 90
Doctors 94
Transport 96
Online Travel 99
Financial Services 100
Telecoms 108
Lawyers 112
The Failed 'Ombudsman.de' Scheme 113
Energy 114
Conclusions 115

5. Lithuania **117**
Overview 117
Courts 117
Public Sector Ombudsman 121
Integrated Regulatory and ADR System 121
Conclusion 128

6. The Netherlands **129**
Summary 129
National Culture of Negotiated Settlement 130
The *Geschillencommissie* Structure 135
ANVR: Travel Sector 149
Thuiswinkel: Web Traders 152
Financial Services: KiFid 153
Discussion 159
Overall 164

7. Poland **167**
Introduction 167
Forms of ADR in Poland 168
ADR Bodies 178
Summary and Assessment of Lingering Problems 194
Evaluation 196

8. Slovenia **197**
Mediation in Business Sectors 197
General Consumer Arrangements 199
Courts and ADR 201
Small Claims Procedure in Regular Courts 204
Evaluation 206

9. Spain **209**
Introduction 209
The Legal Framework and Consumer Claims within the Court System 209
Overview of the ADR System in Spain 212
ADR in Specific Sectors 219
Conclusions 227

10. Sweden **229**
Introduction 229
The Policy of Prioritising Consumer Advice 229
Private Sector ADR 231
The National Board for Consumer Disputes 239
Courts 246
The Consumer Agency 248
Group Claims 249
Cross-border Claims 250
Evaluation 251

11. The United Kingdom **253**
Introduction 253
Courts and Mediation 254
The Wide Culture of ADR 257
Models of Consumer ADR 258
ADR within Consumer Regulation 261
Private Sector ADR Bodies 266
Financial Services 272
Finance & Leasing Association 282
Pensions 284
The Legal Ombudsman 289
Telecoms 291
Energy 307
General Consumer Trading Sectors: Resolution of Disputes under Codes of Business Practice 312

Motor Codes 320
Travel Disputes: The ABTA Code and Schemes 328
Estate Agents 334
Evaluation 338

12. Best Practice in Customer Care in the UK **339**
Introduction 339
Boots 341
British Telecom 348
Procter & Gamble 350

13. Cross-border Consumer ADR **355**
European Car Rental Conciliation Service 355
SELDIA: The European Direct Selling Association 356
European Energy Ombudsman Group 358
ODR 358
ODR for Domain Names 360
EU ODR 364
UNCITRAL 365

Findings

14. Empirical Findings **367**
Incidence of Claims 368
By Country 369
By Sector 377
Thresholds and Limits 379
Case Fee for Consumers 380
Levels of Loss and Detriment 381
The Cost of Major CADR Schemes 382
WIPO 384
Cost per Inquiry 384
Duration 385
EU Consumer Complaint Data 386

15. Findings and Conclusions **389**
Findings of the State of CADR in the EU 389
The Unique Concept of CADR 389
The Extent of CADR 389
Coverage 390
Knowledge of CADR 391
The National Context of CADR schemes 392
The Historical Development of CADR Models and Techniques 394
Market Regulation, Reducing Cost and Maintaining Business Reputation as Drivers for CADR 395
CADR in the Context of DR 398
Models of CADR 400
Ombudsmen 401

CADR with Business Codes of Practice 402
Modes and Techniques of Dispute Resolution in CADR Systems 403
The Sequencing of Dispute Resolution Pathways 405
The First Stage; Direct Contact with Traders 407
Advice, Information and Dispute Resolution 408
CADR and Collective Redress 409
Variations in Effect: Persuasive or Binding? 411
Conceptual issues with CADR 412
The Basis of CADR Decisions: Law and Fairness 412
Should CADR or Courts Decide the Law? 415
Binding and Non-binding Decisions 416
Compliance 417
Due Process Issues for CADR 418
The Purpose and Nature of CADR 420
ADR as an Essential Aspect of Regulation and Behaviour Control 422
Capturing and Using Market Information 423
What Criteria Should Apply to CADR? 425
Proposed Essential Requirements and KPIs 426
Architectural Issues 429
Centralised and Sectoral Schemes 429
Maximising Usage: Unified Architecture, Visibility, Consistency and Trust 430
Filling Gaps to Extend Coverage 433
Best Operating Procedures 437
Confidence and Trust 437
Accessibility 437
Language 438
Access Cost 439
Efficiency 439
Independence and Impartiality 440
Transparency 445
Factors Affecting Cost, Efficiency and Incidence 446
Conclusions 448
A Model for a National Consumer ADR Architecture 449

Appendices

1. Commission Recommendation of 30 March 1998 on the principles applicable to the bodies responsible for out-of-court settlement of consumer disputes (98/257/EC) 455
2. Commission Recommendation of 4 April 2001 on the principles for out-of-court bodies involved in the consensual resolution of consumer disputes (2001/310/EC) 463
3. European Code of Conduct for Mediators 471
4. French Charter of Consumer Mediation 475

LIST OF TABLES AND FIGURES

Chapter **Page**

3 France

Figure 3.1 List of French mediation organisations 43
Table 3.1 Inquiries and mediations 2010 50
Table 3.2 Inquiries and mediation requests by subject area 2010 50
Table 3.3 Types of issues raised with ASF 2007-2010 51
Figure 3.2 Mediation Charter of the FFSA 53
Figure 3.3 Code of Good Conduct for the insurance societies that are members of the FFSA or GEMA 54
Figure 3.4 Overview of insurance mediation applications 55
Table 3.4 Percentage of *médiateur's* recommendations followed by companies in 2010 58
Table 3.5 Complaints received by the EDF *médiateur* 2006-2010 60
Table 3.6 Responses by consumers 60
Table 3.7 Processes and main reasons for complaints 61
Table 3.8 Website contacts to FNAUT in 2010 62
Table 3.9 Response times for the SNCF *médiateur* 63
Table 3.10 Types of infringements 64
Table 3.11 Sources of referrals since 2006 65
Table 3.12 Number of applications received and opinions given 2005-2010 68
Table 3.13 Type of complaints in 2010 68
Table 3.14 Complaint figures 2010 70
French Charter of Consumer Mediation 475

4 Germany

Table 4.1 Complaints data 2006-2010 93
Table 4.2 Complaints to Insurance Ombudsman 2006-2010 93
Table 4.3 Subject matter of complaints, by percentages 93
Table 4.4 Percentages of outcomes of complaints 94
Table 4.5 Decisions in matters concerning doctor liability 2008 96
Table 4.6 Amount of court cases avoided: Evaluation June 2007 96
Table 4.7 Categories of complaints 100
Figure 4.1 Details that should be included in a complaint to BaFin 102
Table 4.8 Complaint areas 2006-2010 108
Table 4.9 Overview of number and outcome of complaints received annually 2006-2010 108
Table 4.10 Fees charged by BnetzA 110
Table 4.11 Claims statistics of BnetzA 111
Table 4.12 Areas of complaints and inquiries 2010 111

5 Lithuania

Table 5.1 Court stamp duty charges in civil disputes 118
Table 5.2 Litigation rates in Lithuania 120
Table 5.3 Complaint data for communications 125
Table 5.4 Air Transport Passenger Complaints handled by the Lithuanian Civil Aviation Administration 127
Table 5.5 Complaints upheld and dismissed 127

6 The Netherlands

Table 6.1 The 50 Sectoral Complaints Commissions 136
Figure 6.1 Total company costs for *Geschillencommissie* cases in 2007 139
Table 6.2 General statistics 146
Table 6.3 Cases against ANVR members 151
Table 6.4 Cases received by KiFid 155
Table 6.5 Outcome of Financial Services Ombudsman cases in 2010 155
Table 6.6 Cases received by the Financial Services *Geschillencommissie in 2010* 156
Table 6.7 Outcome of *Geschillencommissie* cases in 2010 156
Table 6.8 Outcome of Financial Services *Geschillencommissie* cases in 2010 156
Table 6.9 Financial Services Appeal Committee, 2009 and 2010 156

7 Poland

Table 7.1 Cases referred to mediation 2006-2009 172
Table 7.2 Claims data from Tribunals in Szczecin 1991-2009 182
Table 7.3 Fees for the Arbitration Tribunal of the Polish Banks Association 188
Table 7.4 Fees for the Arbitration Tribunal of the Financial Supervision Commission 189
Table 7.5 Fees for the Arbitration Tribunal of the Insurance Ombudsman 192

8 Slovenia

Table 8.1 Statistics for ECC Slovenia in 2010 200
Table 8.2 Statistics for civil litigation cases in all country courts in Slovenia 206

9 Spain

Figure 9.1 The mediation process managed by OCU 218
Table 9.1 Processed complaints by type of resolution 224

10 Sweden

Table 10.1 Types of patient insurance claims: average 1997-2001 235
Figure 10.1 Contacts received by Telecom Advisers 2007-2011 237
Figure 10.2 Contacts received by Telecom Advisers 2005-2011 238
Table 10.2 ARN's departments 240
Table 10.3 Cases received by ARN 2008-2011 245
Table 10.4 Total number of cross-border cases handled by ARN 2006-2010 245
Table 10.5 Type of decision in cross-border disputes 2008-2010 246
Table 10.6 Compliance rates 2008-2010 246

The United Kingdom

Table 11.1 Summary typology of Consumer ADR Schemes in UK 259
Table 11.2 Major sectors, regulatory authorities and consumer ADR providers 259
Figure 11.1 Level of satisfaction with how a complaint was handled 266
Table 11.3 Allocation of Ombudsman Service costs between service sectors 272
Table 11.4 FOS budget figures 280
Table 11.5 Complaints types 2007-2010 281
Table 11.6 Total number of complaints to Ofcom 2007/8 to 2009/10 291
Table 11.7 Number of complaints closed under the Broadcasting code 293
Figure 11.2 Awareness of official dispute resolution bodies 297
Table 11.8 OFCOM's key criteria for an ADR scheme 298
Figure 11.3 The outcome of consumer complaints 299
Figure 11.4 The OFCOM Approved Code of Practice for Complaints Handling 300
Table 11.9 Contacts received by OS:C 2007/08-2010/11 304
Figure 11.5 CISAS enquiries and valid applications 2005-2010 304
Table 11.10 Number of complaints 2009-2010 304
Table 11.11 Reasons for OS:C accepting a complaint 2009-2010 305
Table 11.12 OS:C Complaint Data 2009-10 and 2010-11 305
Table 11.13 Ranges of awards made by OS:C 2009-10 and 2010-11 305
Table 11.14 Nature of complaints to OS:C and CISAS 306
Table 11.15 Performance against OS:C Key Performance Indicators 306
Table 11.16 Energy Ombudsman complaints 2008/09 to 2010/2011 310
Table 11.17 Reasons for accepting a complaint 2010-2011 311
Table 11.18 Reasons for the complaint 2010-2011 311
Figure 11.6 Overview of the core CCAS criteria 313
Table 11.19 Cost to the consumer and fees for businesses of accessing ADR for the OFT approved codes 317
Table 11.20 Code sponsor complaint information 319
Table 11.21 Code membership statistics 2010 322
Table 11.22 Complaint statistics 326
Table 11.23 Code subscription costs 327
Figure 11.7 ABTA complaint statistics 2000/01-2008/09 333
Table 11.24 Subject matter of complaints to OS:P in 2010-2011 336
Figure 11.8 Summary of OFT's criteria for approval of the schemes 337

12 Customer Care

Figure 12.1 The complaint journey process 347
Figure 12.2 Boots Retail Issue management process 348

13 Cross Border

Table 13.1 Total number of WIPO cases 1999-2011 363
Table 13.2 Outcomes of WIPO cases 1999-2011 363

14 Empirical Findings

Figure 14.1 Total number of contacts per sector divided into proportions of redirected contacts and those categorized as complaints 369

Table 14.1 Details of complaints by scheme 370
Figure 14.2 Total number of contacts per sector divided into proportions of redirected contacts and those categorized as complaints 370
Table 14.2 Details of complaints per scheme 371
Table 14.3 Total number of contacts (if available) by sector showing accepted and resolved cases 372
Figure 14.3 *De Geschillencommissie* number of contacts per year showing the proportions of initiated and processed claims 372
Figure 14.4 ECC NET Slovenia proportion of complaints and request for information 373
Figure 14.5 Spanish arbitration system for consumer disputes *Sistema Arbitral de Consumo* proportion of complaints and redirected contacts 373
Table 14.4 Details of categorized complaints 374
Figure 14.6 Total number of contacts per sector divided into proportion of redirected contacts and those categorized as complaints 374
Figure 14.7 ARN proportion of complaints dealt with and those dismissed 375
Table 14.5 Details of categorized complaints 376
Figure 14.8 Total number of contacts per sector showing proportions of redirected/inquiries and complaints 376
Table 14.6 Total number of contacts telecoms by country 378
Figure 14.9 Total contacts in 2010 378
Figure 14.10 Total contacts in 2010 378
Table 14.7 Total number of contacts financial services by country 379
Figure 14.11 Total number of contacts without FOS 379
Table 14.8 Overview of cost to consumer by country and scheme 381
Table 14.9 Allocation of Ombudsman Service costs between service sectors 384
Table 14.10 Average duration per case in months by country and scheme 385

15 Conclusions

Figure 15.1 Integrated use of techniques by CADR providers 406
Figure 15.2 More sophisticated model for escalated use of techniques 406
Figure 15.3 Escalation model with an outsourced function of binding decision-making 407
Figure 15.4 The Netherlands Model 430

CONTRIBUTORS

Aleš Galič is an associate professor at the Faculty of Law in Ljubljana, his main interests in teaching and research are Civil Procedure, International and European Civil Procedure, Arbitration Law and Alternative Dispute Resolution. He has participated in numerous expert groups for drafting legislation in Slovenia and also in Montenegro.

Magdalena Tulibacka is an independent researcher whose published research work covers Polish law and civil procedure, Central and East European product liability law, European Union law, Europeanization of law, and EU civil justice. She is Associate Research Fellow of the Centre for Socio-Legal Studies' Programme in European and Comparative Civil Justice. Dr Tulibacka taught European Union law, comparative law, and product liability law at the University of Westminster and the University of Oxford. She spoke at numerous academic and legal practitioners' conferences on European law and civil procedure. She cooperated with BEUC on designing training courses in EU consumer law for personnel of European consumer organisations and civil servants. She co-edited and contributed chapters to other books published by the European and Comparative Civil Justice Systems Programme: *Costs and Funding of Litigation: Comparative Review* (Hart, 2010), and *The Globalization of Class Actions* (The American Academy of Political and Social Science, 2009).

Stefaan Voet is a research and teaching assistant at the Institute for Procedural Law at Ghent University, and an attorney at the bar of Bruges. In 2011, he obtained his PhD in Law on complex litigation in Belgium. He was a visiting scholar at the Law Center of the University of Houston, and SMU Dedman School of Law in Dallas. He frequently speaks at national and international conferences, and regularly publishes in the field of civil procedure.

Franziska Weber is a final year PhD student at the Erasmus University of Rotterdam. Within the European Doctorate of Law and Economics program she carries out research on consumer law enforcement in various European countries. She completed her LL.M. 'Master European Law School' at the University of Maastricht *cum laude* in 2008 and registered with the Madrid Bar Association as a Spanish lawyer in 2011.

INTERVIEWEES

Netherlands

Professor Willem van Boom of Erasmus University
Paulien van der Grinten and Neils Frenk of the Ministry of Justice
Dr Alex Brenninkmeier, the National Ombudsman
Herman Schilperoort of Raad voor Rechtsbijstand (the Legal Aid Authority)
Dries Cuijpers and Bob Boelema of the Netherlands Consumer Authority
Bregje Krainen of Consumentenbond
Hubert van Breemen of VNO-NCW
Peter Moerkens and Koos Nijgh of De Geschillencommissie Stichtung
Peter Beatson
Professor T Jongbloed, of Utrecht University
AC Oosterholt of KiFiD
AC Monster, Financial Services Ombudsman
Prisca Ancion-Kors and Fabian Bloem of the Dutch Advertising Council
Léon Mölenberg of Thuiswinkel
Gerard de Vries Lentsch of ANVR
Leonard Böhmer of CMS Dirks Star Busman

Germany

Dr Jens Wagner, Dr Tim Reher, of CMS Hasche Sigle
Professor Reinhard Zimmermann, Dr Felix Steffek, Liane Schmiedel of the Max Planck Institute for Comparative and International Private Law
Petra Sandvoss of HandelsKammer Hamburg
Dr Daniela Strauss, Birgitt Maasch-Wiesel Bundesnetzagentur
Professor Günter Hirsch Insurance Ombudsman
Edgar Isermann, Christof Berlin of söp
Dr Georg Starke of BMELV
Dr Heiko Willems, Dr Ulrike Suchsland-Maser of BDI
Natasha Sassenrath-Alberti Domenik Wendt of GDV
Professor Jürgen Basedow, Max Planck Institute for Comparative and International Private Law
RA Katrin Upmeier of Bundesverband deutscher Banken e.V.
Jana Brockfeld Federation of German Consumer Organisations
Bernadette Zawal-Pfeil of Kundenbeschwerdestelle beim Bundesverband der Deutschen Volksbanken und Raiffeisenbanken - BVR
Herr J Neu of Schlichtungsstelle für Arzthaftpflichtfragen der norddeutschen Ärztekammern
Prof Schmid of Reiseschiedsstelle

Denmark

Ole Hasselgaard and Dr Ketilbjørn Hertz of the Ministry of Justice
Jens Olsen of the Ombudsman
Henrik Saugmandsgaard Øe, the Consumer Ombudsman and Tina Emilie Pedersen
Peter Jacobsen of Patientforsikringen
Jan Erik Svensson of Gorrissen Federspiel

France

Xavier Beaud, Service de la médiation Autorité des marchés financiers (AMF)
Mr Constans, Médiateur du ministère de l'Économie, de l'Industrie et de l'Emploi
Francis Frizon, Médiateur auprès de la Fédération française des sociétés d'assurances
Madame Letzeler, Fédération française des sociétés d'assurances
Cédric Musso, UFC-Que Choisir
Nicolas Godfroy, UFC-Que Choisir
Bernard Cieutat, Médiateur de SNCF
Leila Schwartzenbart, Déléguée générale, AMCE
Patricia Foucher, Service juridique et économique, Institut National de la Consommation
Michel Astruc, Médiateur GDF-SUEZ
Stéphane Mialot, Directeur des services energy Médiateur
Bernard Dreyfus, of Défenseur des Droits
Elyane Zarine, présidente, Commission de la Médiation de la Consommation (CMC)
Joëlle Simon, MEDEF
Loïc Armand, L'Oréal

Lithuania

Dr Rimantas Simaitis, Associate Professor, Vilnius University
Raidla Lejins & Norcous
Renata Juzikienė, Director, Law Systems Department, Ministry of Justice
Feliksas Petrauskas, General Director of the State Consumer Rights Protection Authority
Aida Gasiūnaitė, Head of the International and EU Affairs Coordination Division, State Consumer Rights Protection Authority
Aivė Čeponienė, Head of Division, State Consumer Rights Protection Authority
Virginija Žegunytė, Head of Air Transport Division, Civil Aviation Administration
Lina Rainienė, Acting Deputy Director, Communications Regulatory Authority
Eugenijus Žvalionis, Director of Communications Department, Communications Regulatory Authority
Saulius Linkevičius, Director, European Customers Centre

Slovenia

Jana Huč Uršič, Director of ECC Slovenia
Professor Dr Ernest Petrič, President of the Constitutional Court
Andrej Friedl and Marko Djinović, Chamber of Commerce of Slovenia
Natasha Stanič

Spain

José Domingo Gómez Castallo, General Director, Autocontrol
Alejandro Perales, President of AUC (Asociación de Usuarios de la Comunicación)
Rocío Algeciras, Member of the Legal Service, FACUA-Consumers in Action
Emilio Lizarraga Bonelli, Secretary of the Ethical Commission, ICOMEM (Medical Association Madrid)
Enric Brazis Caubet, ENDESA, Energy Ombudsman, Office Manager
Professor Fernando Esteban de la Rosa, Universidad de Granada.
Alicia Menéndez González, Director of the Arbitration Department at the Spanish National Institute on Consumer Affairs and Secretary of the National Arbitration Board
Begoña Outomuro Pérez, Área de Consultas y Reclamaciones Dirección General de Seguros y Fondos de Pensiones, Ministerio de Economía y Hacienda
David Ortega from OCU (Organización de Consumidores y Usuarios;
Cristina Menéndez de Luarca, Servicio de Reclamaciones, Banco de España
Ignacio Pérez Pérez, Jefe de Servicios de Juntas Arbitrales

Sweden

Professor Ulf Bernitz, Stockholm University
Gunnar Larsson, Swedish Consumer Agency
Jolanda Girzl, Konsument Europa/ECC Sweden
Torsten Palm, Allmänna reklamationsnämnden
Anna Lefevre Skjöldebrand, SwedishMedtech
Tomas Tetzel and Marie-Louise Ulfward, Swedish Bankers' Association
Marie Lüning, SEB
Anna Montelius, Swedish Post and Telecom Agency
Mattias Grafström, The Swedish Telecom Advisers
Staafan Löfgren, Insurance Sweden
Carl Espersson and Agneta Karlbom, The Swedish Patient Insurance Association
Peter Rigling and Elisabeth Ekwall, Road Traffic Injuries Commission
Peder Hammarskiold, Hammarskiold & Co
Henrik Bellander, Uppsala University
Philip Rämsell, Stockholm University

UK

T Hardy and F Thomas of CMS Cameron McKenna LLP
Heidi Munn, Stella d'Italia, Duncan Lawson, John Madill of BIS
Monica Arino, Marc Caines, Ian Blair, Claudio Pollack, Jeff Loan, Alan Pridmore of OFCOM
Donna Davis, Kate Damania of OFT
Clive Gordon, Jamie Kerr, Matthew Horne, Nick Walker and Marie Bogdan of FSA
David Baker, Paul Bentall, Laura Layfield, Maria White and Adrian Dally of the FOS
Joanne Milligan of Consumer Focus
Deborah Prince and Chris Warner of Which?
Tony King, Pensions Ombudsman
Megan Charles of the Finance and Leasing Association
Gregory Hunt of CEDR Disputes Group
Alan Connarty and Veena Kanda, both formerly of IDRS

Lewis Shand Smith of The Ombudsman Service
Charles Fachiri, Daryl Nurthen and Simon Bunce of ABTA
Christine Francis of Cosmos Travel
Seftton Samuels and Melanie Wiseman of SMMT
Tristan Holland of Motor Codes Limited
Madeleine Campbell-Barker and David Moran of RMIF
Ian Larkins of Daimler Chrysler UK
Keith Richards of Raleo Ltd
Michael Todd of the Advertising Standards Authority
Heather Simmons of the Prescription Medicines Code of Practice Authority
Adrian Booth and Graham Hardy of Boots plc
Lesley Atkinson, Claire Dodgeon and Andrew McCarthy of Procter & Gamble
Chris Holland and Tim Liddell of BT
Craig Berry of RBS
Jonathan Peddie of Barclays
Robert Lane CBE, Ben Holland, Chris Watson, Simon Morris, Mark Grant, Mark Atkinson, Susan Barty, Guy Pendell and David Marks of CMS Cameron McKenna

International

Brigitte Acoca, OECD
Peter Avery, Head, Consumer Policy Unit, OECD
Richard Knubben, Leaseurope
Mauritz Bruggink, Executive Director, Seldia – the European Direct Selling Association
Erik Wilbers, WIPO

European Commission

Rossella Delfino, European Commission
Maria-Cristina Russo, European Commission
Sebastian Bohr, European Commission
Eleni Tampaki, European Commission
Nicole Scourti, European Commission
Tamás András Molnár, Head of Unit, European Commission
David Mair, European Commission
Marilena Di Stasi, European Commission

ABBREVIATIONS

ABTA	The Travel Association (formerly Association of British Travel Agents)
ADNRC	Asian Domain Name Dispute Resolution Centre (cross-border)
ADR	alternative dispute resolution
AFM	*Autoriteit Financiële Markten* - Financial Markets Authority (Netherlands)
AMCE	*L'Association de Médiation des Communications Electroniques* - the Electronic Communications Mediation Association (France)
AMF	*l'Autorité des Marchés Financiers* - Financial Markets Authority (France)
ANVR	*Algemene Nederlandse Vereniging van Reisondernemingen* - Dutch Association of Travel Agents and Tour Operators (Netherlands)
ANWB	*Koninklijke Nederlandse Toeristenbond* – Royal Dutch Tourist Board (Netherlands)
APN	Board for Personal Injury Liability Insurance (Sweden)
ARN	*Allmänna reklamationsnämnden* - National Board for Consumer Disputes (Sweden)
ASF	*l'Association des Sociétés Financières*, ASF (Financial Companies Association (France)
AUC	*Asociación de Usuarios de la Comunicación* – Consumer Association for Communication (Spain)
BaFin	*Bundesanstalt für Finanzdienstleistungsaufsicht* - Federal Financial Supervisory Authority (Germany)
BAFM	*Bundes-Arbeitsgemeinschaft für Familien Mediation* - Federal Association for Family Mediation (Germany)
BGB	*Bürgerliches Gesetzbuch* - German Civil Code (Germany)
BMELV	*Bundesministerium für Ernährung, Landwirtschaft und Verbraucherschutz* - Federal Ministry of Food, Agriculture and Consumer Protection (Germany)
BnetzA	*Bundesnetzagentur* - Federal Network Agency (Germany)
BVL	*Bundesamt für Verbraucherschutz und Lebensmittelsicherheit* - Federal Office of Consumer Protection and Food Safety (Germany)
C2B	consumer-to-business (dispute)
CAC	Czech Arbitration Court (cross-border)
CCAS	Consumer Code Approval Scheme (OFT UK)
CEDR	Centre for Effective Dispute Resolution
CISAS	Communications and Internet Services Adjudication Scheme
CMC	*Commission de la médiation de la consommation* - Commission of Consumer Mediation (France)
CNMV	*Comisión Nacional del Mercado de Valores* - National Stock Exchange Commission (Spain)

Commission	European Commission
CRLC	*Commissions de Règlement des Litiges de Consommation* - Consumer Complaints Boards (France)
DIS	*Deutsche Institution für Schiedsgerichtsbarkeit* - German Institution of Arbitration (Germany)
DR	dispute resolution
EC	European Community
ECHR	European Convention of Human Rights
ECJ	European Court of Justice
ECODIR	Electronic Consumer Dispute Resolution (cross-border)
ECRCS	European Car Rental Conciliation Service (cross-border)
ECT	European Community Treaty
EEC-NET	European Consumer Centre Network (EU)
EEJ-NET	Extra-Judicial Network (EU)
EGZPO	*Einführungsgesetz zur Zivilprozeßordnung* - Code of Civil Procedure (Germany)
EUCFR	EU Charter of Fundamental Rights
FBF	*Fédération Bancaire Française* - French Banking Federation (France)
FFSA	*Fédération Française des Sociétés d'Assurances* - French Federation of Insurance Companies (France)
FI	*Finansinspektionen* - Swedish Financial Supervisory Authority (Sweden)
FIDIC	International Federation of Consulting Engineers
FIN-NET	Financial Services Complaints Network
FLA	Finance & Leasing Association (UK)
FNAUT	*Fédération Nationale des Associations d'Usagers des Transports* – National Federation of Associations of Transport Users (France)
FNR	The Board for Legal Protection Issues (Sweden)
FOS	Financial Ombudsman Service (UK)
FPSs	Federal Public Services (Belgium)
FSA	Financial Services Authority (UK)
GC	*Geschillencommissie* - ADR Board (Netherlands)
GDV	*Gesamtverband der Deutschen Versicherungswirtschaft* - German Insurance Association (Germany)
ICANN	Internet Corporation for Assigned Names and Numbers (cross-border)
ICT	Information and communications technology (cross-border)
IDRS	IDRS Limited (UK)
INC	*Instituto Nacional del Consumo* - National Consumer Institute (Spain)
IPF	Insurance and Pension Funds (Spain)
KiFiD	*Klachteninstituut Financiële Dienstverlening* - Financial Services Complaints Institute Foundation (Netherlands)
KFB	Swedish Consumers Insurance Bureau
KO	*Konsumentombudsman*, Swedisch Consumer Ombudsman (Sweden)
LEC	*Ley de Enjuiciamiento Civil* - code of civil procedure (Spain)
LEI	Legal expenses insurance (Netherlands)
MCL	Motor Codes Limited (UK)
MEDEF	Mouvement des Entreprises de France - principal business association (France)

MKB	*Brancheorganisatie voor het midden- en kleinbedrijf* - Employers Association for SMEs (Netherlands)
NAF	National Arbitration Forum (cross-border)
NMa	*Nederlandse Mededingingsautoriteit* - Dutch Competition Authority
NMI	Nederlands Mediation Instituut (Netherlands)
OCU	*Organización de Consumidores y Usuarios* - Organization of Consumers and Users (Spain)
ODR	online dispute resolution
OECD	Organisation for Economic Co-operation and Development
OFCOM	Office of Communications (UK)
OFGEM	Office of the Gas and Electricity Markets (UK)
OFT	Office of Fair Trading (UK)
OFWAT	Water Services Regulatory Authority (UK)
OKN	The Attorney Cost Board (Sweden)
OLC	Office for Legal Complaints (UK)
ONIAM	*L'Office National d'Indemnisation des Accidents Médicaux* – The National Compensation Body for Medical Accidents (France)
OPAS	Occupational Pensions Advisory Service (UK)
ORR	Office of Rail Regulation (UK)
OS	Ombudsman Services (UK)
OTELO	Office of the Telecoms Ombudsman (now OS:C)
PFN	Board for Insurance of Persons (Sweden)
POL	The Insurance Appeal procedure concerning an attorney's suitability (Sweden)
PPI	Payment Protection Insurance (UK)
PPSs	Federal Public Planning Services (Belgium)
PRS	Premium rate services (UK)
S	§ - section (Germany)
SELDIA	Direct Selling Association (cross-border)
SER	*Sociaal-Economische Raad* - Social and Economic Council (Netherlands)
SGC	*Stichting Geschillencommissie* - Consumer Complaint Commissions (Netherlands)
SGR	*Stichting Garantiefonds Reisgelden* - Travel Refund Guarantee Fund (Netherlands)
SMMT	Society of Motor Manufacturers and Traders
Söp	*Schlichtungsstelle für den öffentlichen Personenverkehr e.V* - Conciliation Body for Public Transport of Passengers (Germany)
TFEU	Treaty on the Functioning of the European Union
TPAS	Pension Advisory Service (UK)
TPO	The Property Ombudsman (UK)
TPR	Pensions Regulator (UK)
UDRP	Uniform Domain Name Dispute Resolution Policy (cross-border)
UNCITRAL	United Nations Commission on International Trade Law
VBI	*Verband Beratender Ingenieure* - Association of Consulting Engineers (Germany)
VEH	*Vereniging Eigen Huis* - sectoral consumer associations (Netherlands)

VNO-NCW	*Verbond van Nederlandse Ondernemingen-Nederlands Christelijk Werkgeversverbond* - Confederation of Netherlands Industry and Employers (Netherlands)
VZBV	*Verbraucherzentrale Bundesverband e.V* - Federation of German Consumer Organisations
WBZ	*Wettbewerbszentrale* - Centre for Protection against Unfair Competition (Germany)
WCAM	*Wet Collectieve Afwikkeling Massaschade* - Act on the Collective Settlement of Mass Claims (Netherlands)
WIPO	World Intellectual Property Organization (cross-border)

INTRODUCTION

Christopher Hodges, Iris Benöhr, Naomi Creutzfeldt-Banda

Consumer ADR

This book examines the recent phenomenon of Alternative Dispute Resolution (ADR) for disputes between consumers and businesses in the context of a European-wide debate on methods of dispute resolution. By ADR we mean *any* 'alternative dispute resolution' mechanism, that is, any mechanism that is 'alternative' to the traditional model of civil proceedings issued in the courts. However, this book is about the specific area of *consumer* ADR, which is distinct from other manifestations of ADR. Many are familiar in Europe with ADR in the form of mediation, frequently in the context of resolving disputes that are, or would otherwise be, proceeding in court. However, consumer ADR occupies a different context, and one that is currently far less well known, at least to many lawyers and judges, and many consumers. Indeed, the world of consumer ADR is so distinct that we propose to coin a new acronym for it in this book: CADR.

The Different Meanings of ADR

There is nothing new about ADR: the Chinese were using it to resolve disputes three thousand years ago[1] and it has existed in North America for some decades.[2] ADR has a number of different meanings in different contexts. The traditional way to examine ADR is as a range of possible *techniques*. The following list was published in 2010:[3]

a. **In-house complaints procedures**: many ADR schemes stipulate that individuals must have exhausted the company's in-house complaints procedures before using the ADR mechanism.
b. **Mediation**: mediation is conducted confidentially and consists of an independent third party actively assisting the parties in working towards a negotiated agreement of a dispute.

[1] S Roberts and M Palmer, *Dispute Processes. ADR and the Primary Forms of Decision-Making* (Cambridge: Cambridge University Press, 2005).

[2] M Shapiro, *Courts. A Comparative and Political Analysis* (Chicago, University of Chicago Press, 1981).

[3] *Mapping UK consumer redress. A summary guide to dispute resolution systems* (Office of Fair Trading, May 2010), available at http://www.oft.gov.uk/shared_oft/general_policy/OFT1267.pdf.

c. **Conciliation**: this is a process similar to mediation but in which the neutral third party takes a more active role in putting forward terms of settlement or an opinion on the case.
d. **Arbitration**: in arbitration an independent third party considers both sides in a dispute, and makes a decision that resolves the dispute. In most cases the arbitrator's decision is legally binding on both sides.
e. **Adjudication**: like arbitration, adjudication involves an independent third party considering the claims of both sides and making a decision. This usually produces a decision that is binding on the company but not on the consumer.
f. **Ombudsman schemes**: ombudsmen are independent, impartial intermediaries who consider complaints. The particular mechanisms of ombudsman schemes vary but they often combine neutral fact-finding, mediation and adjudication in various tiers.
g. **Legal mechanisms**: formal legal action is usually the last resort employed by consumers to obtain redress. Consumers can, however, take legal action without going through other mechanisms if they wish.

Different combinations of the above techniques can often be found to exist in practice. For example, a combination of different techniques can be used sequentially, so as to encourage parties to deal with disputes in simple and cheap ways first, through direct negotiation, before escalating unresolved disputes into other techniques involving third parties. Hence, some business sectors have tiers of approaches, starting with direct negotiation, ending with the courts, and in between involving one or more other techniques.

The World of CADR

All of the above techniques share the meaning that they are dispute resolution procedures that are outside of, but closely linked to, the court process, and take place within its shadow. In this meaning, ADR is a technique, such as mediation that is used in conjunction with a claim that is being brought, or potentially brought, in the court system. Such mediation might precede the issue of court proceedings, or occur after proceedings have commenced so as to try to reach resolution of the proceedings through negotiated or other means as an alternative to final adjudication by the judge. This ADR process (direct negotiation assisted by mediation, or early neutral evaluation of the merits of a claim) might or might not result in resolution of the dispute by agreement between the parties. If no agreement is reached, the ADR process may, nevertheless, have been valuable in clarifying the issues in dispute and the strength of the arguments of the parties involved.

In the wider sense, however, CADR might not be associated with court proceedings at all. All that is required is that a dispute exists, and any technique, or combination of techniques, may be used in order to resolve it, whether this involves a court at some stage or some other technique. In the context of consumer-to-business (C2B) disputes, dispute resolution takes place within a different architectural structure that is entirely separate from courts. It may be that the dispute could end up being taken to the court process, but this rarely happens. The important point is that CADR structures have emerged that operate wholly separately from courts, and process many disputes with no reference to courts.

This book is concerned with CADR in this wider, non-court sense. We seek to uncover the new universe of CADR systems, to find out how they operate, to evaluate them, and determine how they might be extended and improved.

The starting point is that many sectoral ADR systems exist in EU Member States, and the national architectures differ significantly. CADR schemes have emerged piece-meal over the past forty years, and in many Member States within only the last decade. But they are now a major phenomenon. CADR systems need to be examined in relation to both courts and regulators in order to see whether their functions are in competition or synergistic.

This book seeks to analyse some of the major existing national models. The facts and analysis presented here are far from complete, and no claim is made that this work is comprehensive. The diversity of CADR systems that currently exist is considerable, and may surprise many readers. CADR has expanded significantly in recent years, and is clearly still expanding: a state of stability has not yet been reached, so it is premature to propose final conclusions or standard models. But the current analysis should provide a useful starting point.

Policy Decisions

CADR is important and topical at EU level. On 29 November 2011, the European Commission adopted two legislative proposals on CADR (one being on the related area of online dispute resolution, ODR). Many people may be unclear exactly what CADR is, and frequently confuse it with court-related mediation, especially since they may only be familiar with the EU Mediation Directive, adopted in 2009 for implementation in 2011.

The European Commission has sponsored three studies on CADR in preparing for its 2011 proposals, which provide a highly important map of CADR across the 27 Member States. Professor Stuyck's study of the position within the Member States[4] reveals that there is a huge variation in national mechanisms for collective redress. It has been noted that 'redress' is itself a wide concept, and can encompass mechanisms that operate both within and outside traditional court-based litigation, such as arbitration, small claims procedures, mediation and other 'alternative dispute resolution' techniques, public oversight of restoration and compensation (such as ombudsmen, public enforcement activities, *partie civile* piggy-back claims, recovery of the proceeds of crime) and self-regulatory or voluntary mechanisms (such as no fault schemes, codes of conduct and other informal mechanisms).[5]

We pay tribute to the excellent work done in those studies by Professor Stuyck and his Leuven team and to Dr Alleweldt and his Civic Consulting team.[6] It is always a challenge to obtain such a vast amount of data on a new subject from 27 Member States, and to present the information and the picture coherently, particularly within the methodological, time and budgetary constraints that arise in connection with any such Commission or

[4] J Stuyck, E Terryn, V Colaert, T Van Dyck, N Peretz, N Hoekx and P Tereszkiewicz, *Study on alternative means of consumer redress other than redress through ordinary judicial proceedings* (Catholic University of Leuven, 17 January 2007), published April 2007, para 384, the Comparative Report and the 28 National Reports are available at ec.europa.eu/consumers/redress/reports_studies/index_en.htm.

[5] See European Commission, *Green Paper on consumer collective redress*, COM(2008) 794 final, 27 November 2008, available at ec.europa.eu/consumers/redress_cons/greenpaper_en.pdf.

[6] *Study on the use of Alternative Dispute Resolution in the European Union*, (Brussels, Civic Consulting, 2009).

governmental study. Nevertheless, a number of questions remained after reading those studies—and it is an unfortunate fact that not many people do in fact read such long and detailed studies.

Hence, we set out to try to illuminate further the world of CADR in Europe, and how it actually works. We wished to have this book available at the time that European Member States and the European Parliament would be considering the Commission's CADR proposals, so as to inform their deliberations. Whatever the outcome of those deliberations, however, it is clear that national and individual CADR systems will continue to spread and evolve. Hence, this book should intend to inform discussions about how that might best happen.

It is important to understand that this book is not about the various mechanisms that might be used to seek or deliver consumer redress. CADR systems are, of course, primarily intended to deliver consumer redress, but they are not the only possible pathway. Various other public or private systems, whether individually or in combination with themselves and/or with CADR systems, may also deliver consumer redress. CADR systems are certainly emerging as one of the most important and promising possible pathways for consumer redress, and this book seeks to illuminate them. But a comprehensive picture of all the possible pathways, and an evaluation of them, must await another occasion.

The Research Questions and Approach

This book is primarily concerned with the following issues:

- What is the current state of CADR in Europe? What systems currently exist? How do they work? How extensively are they used? How much do they cost, how long do they take, and so on? These are micro-level empirical issues.
- How might European governments and those providing or wishing to use CADR best extend and improve their CADR systems? What are the best national or international architectures for CADR? This involves examining CADR systems at their macro levels, and comparing different architectures.
- How can individual CADR systems be improved? This is a micro level issue, with a comparative perspective. This involves examining a number of current CADR systems, preferably those that differ significantly, together with any formal criteria that are applied to them, so as to be able to answer the question: What is, or should be, current best practice for CADR systems?

Accordingly, in order to answer the above questions, we designed a research project with the following main elements. It is necessary to examine a number of differing CADR systems, so as to identify the current phenomenon of CADR, and to have a sufficient range of models from which to draw comparative conclusions. It transpires that there are many different models of ADR and CADR. It would not be practical for us to have undertaken research into the position in all 27 Member States, given firstly that we wanted to go to a certain level of detail and depth and, secondly, that we wanted to finish this project so that this book could be available soon after the publication of the Commission's proposals. Accordingly, we have selected ten Member States, which we believe give a sufficiently wide spectrum of the current European phenomenon of CADR. The States selected are: Belgium (albeit not in the same format as other chapters, but to highlight the important development of Belmed), France, Germany, Lithuania, Poland, Slovenia, Spain, Sweden, the Netherlands, and the United Kingdom.

We are well aware that this list omits Member States that have interesting CADR schemes. We are grateful for discussions with experts from, for example, Denmark, Italy and Portugal. Regrettably, constraints of time and space have not permitted us to include those and other countries in this book. However, we continue to research ADR and dispute resolution systems, and hope to include those and other countries in our future work. CADR is clearly a developing phenomenon, and current EU-level debates will only encourage further swift development.

Since the goal is to examine both national architectures of CADR systems and the modes of operation of leading CADR models, this project has not attempted to give a complete picture of CADR in every Member State. It would simply not be feasible to examine every single CADR scheme that exists in even the ten Member States that we selected. Therefore, we may have inadvertently omitted some important schemes, but we believe that the picture that we have painted is, nevertheless, sufficiently robust and accurate for the purposes of this project. At the least, our work will have illuminated a number of leading CADR systems.

For reasons of limiting the scale of this project, so that it could be accomplished within around eighteen months, we have limited the focus to CADR models as defined in the Commission's proposals, namely contractual disputes between consumers and businesses (what are known as B2C issues: business-to-consumer). This omits a number of other important ADR models, notably those for personal injury claims. There are notable examples of personal injury compensation schemes, especially in Nordic States and France, but consideration of these will have to await another occasion.

Although, for the same reason, consideration of court-annexed mediation and similar models are outside the scope of this analysis, it is, nevertheless, necessary to say something about such matters for some jurisdictions. This is because both the historical development and current operation of CADR models are often strongly influenced by both the pre-existing court systems and regulatory systems of a state that cover private and public enforcement of consumer law. Hence, we aim to give a brief indication of why national CADR systems have developed the way they have, highlighting influences from civil procedure, regulatory and cultural systems.

CADR systems are often found clustered in particular industry sectors. This may have occurred because of market conditions in particular sectors, or specifically because legislators have encouraged or required CADR systems to be introduced within them. There is little consistency across different Member States of those business sectors that do, or do not, have CADR systems. However, we have tried to focus on the position in the Member States covered here of national models for financial services, telecoms, energy, and general consumer trading, so that comparisons can be made across countries.

Plan of the Book

The first chapter examines the development and current status of CADR at EU level. This is followed by ten chapters that describe the architecture of CADR systems in ten selected Member States, and illustrate the current modes of operation of important schemes. The state of best practice in relation to the important topic of companies' in-house customer care functions is then illustrated with selected examples from the United Kingdom (chapter 12). Chapter 13 then examines some examples of cross-border dispute resolution schemes, both at EU and global levels.

We then draw together the findings of the preceding chapters on national CADR systems, so as to examine the policy issues that arise, based on a comparative empirical analysis of the information from the status of CADR systems in the ten Member States. Some of the most important statistics collected during this study are presented in chapter 14. We finally set out our findings and conclusions in chapter 15. It reviews the following main points: the factual findings on the state of CADR in Europe; the conceptual issues that arise; the issues that arise for the architecture of national systems; and best practice for CADR schemes. Based on the information collected, we return to consider the three central questions posed, namely:

- What is the current state of CADR in Europe?
- How might the architecture of CADR systems be improved?
- How might individual CADR systems be improved?

We conclude by setting out a suggested model for how CADR schemes should be designed, both in relation to general coordinated architecture and general mode of operation.

It must be repeated that it has only been possible, for reasons of time and space, to include ten Member States in this study. There may be useful information from other States. In addition, many—but not all—of the CADR systems and techniques are relatively new and as yet undeveloped. For both these reasons, sufficient experience and data on which to found a mature evaluation of CADR and its models may not yet be available. Accordingly, the findings are preliminary. There is undoubtedly scope for further research. Nevertheless, it will be seen that a wealth of material has been assembled in this book.

Methodology

The information and findings presented here are some of the fruits of the ongoing CMS Research Programme on Civil Justice Systems at the Centre for Socio-Legal Studies at the University of Oxford.[7] This research has also been carried out in collaboration with colleagues at the Behavioural Approaches to Contract and Tort (BACT) Programme at the Law Faculty of Erasmus University, Rotterdam.

Consideration of the various options for dispute resolution prior to 2008 had led us to various conclusions: that far more dispute resolution options exist than are widely known; that there has been no systematic overview of all the options, no evaluation of them, or coherent plan for how they might be used or prioritised within a contemporary civil justice system; that some ADR pathways might be extremely useful for certain types of disputes; and that previous policy assumptions (notably that courts and lawyers are not only the principal dispute resolution option but also always the preferable one), need to be robustly tested. In short, it is time for a comprehensive review of the options for dispute resolution,

[7] For details of the Programme and its various constituent projects see http://www.csls.ox.ac.uk/european_civil_justice_systems.php.

without pre-conceived notions. This work on CADR therefore fits into a far wider ongoing research agenda.

In 2009, Dr Magdalena Tulibacka, in conjunction with the United Kingdom's consumer association *Which?*, carried out an internet-based survey of how many ADR pathways could readily be identified in the United Kingdom, and found some 130 mechanisms.[8] Since January 2010, we have undertaken more detailed research into CADR in the ten Member States noted above. The first stage was to draw up a list of questions to be asked about individual schemes, such as: what are the rules, what is the governance, how transparent is the scheme, how much does it cost (both to participants and overall), how long do disputes take to be processed, what outcomes occur, and so on.

The second stage was to answer as many of those questions as possible from materials on the websites or elsewhere. The third stage was to interview CADR providers, users, and representatives of government, consumers and business, to check the facts but more importantly to gain an understanding of the history and context of CADR at both micro and macro levels. It is, of course, that third stage that has taken most time.

We are very grateful to colleagues who have collaborated in the research and writing of various chapters. Franziska Weber of Erasmus University has worked on the Netherlands, Spain and Sweden. Dr Magdalena Tulibacka has looked at Poland. Dr Stefaan Voet of Ghent University has looked at Belgium. Professor Aleš Galič has produced a chapter on Slovenia in record time.

We have undertaken around 100 interviews. We are most grateful to many who have made themselves available for interview, frequently at short notice, whose names are listed at the end of this chapter (and we apologise if we have inadvertently omitted anyone from that list). Many have also provided considerable assistance with insights and arrangements. We are also grateful to Professor Lisa Webley and Dr Angus Nurse, who contributed respectively draft chapters on mediation in family law in England and Wales and the UK Local Government Ombudsman, and for kindly agreeing to hold those pieces over to a future publication.

Special thanks are due to our colleagues Dr Rebecca Money-Kyrle, Andres Gonzalez-Watty for assistance with research and references, and Katie Orme for cool and wonderfully efficient administration. Various friends have kindly commented on drafts of national chapters, notably Professor Ulf Bernitz, Zbynek Loebl, Patricia Foucher and Dr Felix Steffek.

We are also grateful to the funders of the CMS Research Programme on Civil Justice Systems: the international law firm CMS and the European Justice Forum. They have been exemplary in providing research funds with no strings attached, and have allowed us complete freedom to select what we wanted to research, how we wanted to do it, and what we have said about our findings. Such enlightened support is all too rare, and greatly appreciated.

Finally, we warmly thank all at Hart Publishing who have provided wonderful professional support at great speed.

Oxford, February 2012

[8] An updated list is at http://www.csls.ox.ac.uk/AlternativeDisputeResolution.php.

1

Alternative Dispute Resolution for Consumers in the European Union

IRIS BENÖHR

Introduction

In an enlarged European market, consumers move increasingly across the European Union and engage in online transactions. This has led to a higher number of cross-border purchases and complaints, requiring new means of dispute resolution. Alternative Dispute Resolution (hereafter ADR) is regarded as an important element in the attempt to provide simple and efficient redress at EU level.[1]

This chapter refers to consumer ADR mechanisms which are designed as an alternative to resolving a conflict in a court. They cover out-of-court schemes that lead to the settling of a dispute through the intervention of a third party, such as an arbitrator, mediator or an ombudsman. This third party can propose or impose a solution, or merely bring the parties together to assist them in finding a solution.[2]

ADR schemes aim at facilitating speedy and low cost solutions that are more time efficient and flexible than ordinary procedures before the court.[3] They have been growing in popularity in Europe and in the Member States[4] and are particularly useful for consumer related disputes involving small monetary claims.[5]

The European Commission has been active in promoting the development of ADR. Two Recommendations have established quality criteria in the EU that each ADR scheme should offer to its users.[6] In addition, a Directive on Mediation in Civil and Commercial Matters aims to ensure a sound relationship between the mediation process and judicial

[1] See OECD, *Recommendation on Consumer Dispute Resolution and Redress* (Paris, OECD, 2007).

[2] See the ADR definition applied in the European Commission's Consultation Paper 'On the Use of Alternative Dispute Resolution as a Means to Resolve Disputes Related to Commercial Transactions and Practices in the European Union,' 2011, para 6.

[3] http://ec.europa.eu/consumers/redress/out_of_court/index_en.htm.

[4] M Tulibacka and C Hodges, *English Justice System – Beyond the Courts: Mapping out the Non-judicial Civil Justice Mechanisms* (Research Report of the Centre for Socio-Legal Studies, Oxford, 2009), at http://www.csls.ox.ac.uk/european_civil_justice_systems.php. At international level, see also United Nations Commission on International Trade law Model Law on ADR.

[5] HW Micklitz, N Reich, P Rott, *Understanding EU Consumer Law* (Intersentia, Antwerp, 2009) 341.

[6] Commission Recommendation of 30 March 1998 on the principles applicable to the bodies responsible for out-of-court settlement of consumer disputes OJ 115, 17/04/1998, 31 – 34; Commission Recommendation (EC) 2001/310 on the principles for out-of-court bodies involved in the consensual resolution of consumer ADR, OJ L 109, p 56.

proceedings by establishing common EU rules on key aspects of civil procedure.[7] A number of networks were also created to facilitate finding extra-judicial solutions to cross-border consumer disputes.[8]

At the Member State level, a large number of ADR mechanisms exist, which comply with the European Commission's Recommendations.[9] Many of these schemes focus on sectors presenting a high number of disputes, such as the telecommunications sector.

While ADR systems have developed considerably during the last decade, a number of shortcomings prevail in the current framework. The European Commission published an ADR consultation paper in 2011, highlighting that the existing ADR procedures do not cover all fields of consumer sectors and are often inconvenient for cross-border cases.[10]

This chapter describes the emergence of ADR as part of the access to justice movement in Europe. It then analyzes the competences of the EU in ADR, and describes specific measures and key ECJ cases within this field. Finally, it outlines the recent proposals by the European Commission on Consumer ADR.

Access to Justice and ADR at the International and Regional Level

The importance of ADR procedures was highlighted by the global access to justice movement in the late 1970s. One of the leading scholars in this field, Mauro Cappelletti, helped to broaden the concept of access to justice beyond courts, including alternative dispute resolution as a significant part of civil procedure.[11] In a seminal work in 1978, Cappelletti and Garth enumerated three phases (or waves) of legal innovations fostering access to justice:[12]

1. the reform of institutions for delivering legal services to the poor;
2. the strengthening of the representation of diffuse interests, such as those of consumers and environmentalists;
3. a shift in focus to a broader conception of access to justice.

The last point may also include dispute-processing and less formal alternatives to courts. According to Cappelletti, alternative dispute resolution mechanisms are essential to make access to justice available to a wider group of citizens.[13] He describes ADR as a means that can provide high quality dispute resolution solutions. In particular, it provides the opportunity to find an amicable solution between the parties, which 'has the potential to preserve the relationship (…), rather than a final break of the relationship.'

[7] Directive 2008/52/EC of 21 May 2008 on certain aspects of mediation in civil and commercial matters.

[8] For example, the European Consumer Centres Network and FIN-NET.

[9] At least 750 national ADR schemes, according to the 2009 DG SANCO, *Study on the use of Alternative Dispute Resolution in the European Union* (Berlin, Civil Consulting 2009) at http://ec.europa.eu/consumers/redress_cons/adr_study.pdf.

[10] European Commission's Consultation Paper 'On the Use of Alternative Dispute Resolution as a Means to Resolve Disputes Related to Commercial Transactions and Practices in the European Union,' 2011.

[11] Mauro Cappelletti, 'Alternative Dispute Resolution Processes within the Framework of the World-Wide Access-to Justice Movement' (1993), 3 *The Modern Law Review* 56, 287 ff.

[12] Mauro Cappelletti & Bryant G Garth, 'Access to Justice: The Newest Wave in the Worldwide Movement to Make Rights Effective' (1978), 27 *Buffalo Law Review* 181.

[13] Mauro Cappelletti, 'Alternative Dispute Resolution Processes' (1993).

Subsequently, access to justice has played an increasingly central role in Europe and has been recognised as a human right. The right to access to justice and to a fair trial are guaranteed under Article 6 of the European Convention on Human Rights. Furthermore, The Charter of Fundamental Rights of the EU provides for the 'right to an effective remedy and to a fair trial' (Article 47 EUCFR).[14]

ADR has also gradually been promoted at the international and regional policy level.[15] The Council of Europe adopted a number of recommendations to promote ADR and mediation:

- Recommendation on alternatives to litigation between administrative authorities and private parties (2001);[16]
- Recommendation on mediation in civil matters (2002).[17]

The second Recommendation is particularly important for consumer-related disputes. It provides a definition of mediation and describes the scope, organisation and procedure of mediation that member states should apply. Furthermore, it also advises states among others to provide training to mediators and to inform the public about mediation options.

More recently, at the international level, the UN Commission for International Trade Law (UNCITRAL) is in the process of developing procedural rules for online dispute resolution (ODR), to resolve dispute arising from e-commerce.[18] ODR is often defined as a form of ADR which takes advantage of the speed and convenience of the Internet.[19] It is an effective redress tool for consumers, as it can resolve high volume and low value cross-border cases cheaply.

Finally, finding specific ADR mechanisms for consumers has increasingly been debated in the Organisation for Economic Co-operation and Development (OECD). In 2006 the OECD adopted a report on *Consumer Dispute Resolution and Redress in the Global Marketplace*.[20] This report provides an overview of OECD member countries' mechanisms for consumer dispute resolution and evaluates the different existing approaches. In particular, it highlighted the importance to foster cross-border dispute resolution mechanisms and find suitable funding solution for ADR.[21]

Historic Overview of Key ADR Related Actions in the EU

In the EU, the number of ADR schemes has increased considerably since the global access to justice movement. ADR mechanisms are used to resolve disputes between citizens and

[14] See a detailed report on fra.europa.eu/fraWebsite/attachments/report-access-to-justice_EN.pdf.

[15] There is also a growing trend by private entities to adopt cross-border ADR mechanisms, eg the European Car Rental Conciliation Service adopted in 2010, helps customers with unresolved complaints concerning cross border vehicle rentals within Europe: www.leaseurope.org/index.php?page=consumer-redress-service.

[16] Recommendation of the Committee of Ministers on alternatives to litigation between administrative authorities and private parties, Rec (2001) 9, 5 September 2001.

[17] See wcd.coe.int/ViewDoc.jsp?id=306401&Site=COE&BackColorInternet=DBDCF2&BackColorIntranet=FDC864&BackColorLogged=FDC864.

[18] See www.uncitral.org/uncitral/commission/working_groups/3Online_Dispute_Resolution.html.

[19] See more on ODR in Pablo Cortes, 'Developing Online Dispute Resolution for Consumers in the EU: A Proposal for the Regulation of Accredited Providers' (2010), *International Journal of Law and Information Technology*.

[20] OECD, *Consumer Dispute Resolution and Redress in the Global Market Place* (Paris, OECD, 2006): www.oecd.org/dataoecd/26/61/36456184.pdf.

[21] ibid, 58.

administrations,[22] in working relationships, in commercial relations, consumer disputes and family matters.

The importance of ADR for consumer protection has been debated for some time. In 1998 the Commission published a communication on 'out-of-court settlement of consumer disputes.'[23]

Furthermore, in the European Council on Justice that took place in Tampere in October 1999, EU leaders drew attention to how much importance they placed on the role of ADR in cross-border disputes.[24] In March 2000, at the Lisbon Summit on employment and the information society, EU leaders asked the European Commission and the EU Council of Ministers to reflect upon ways of applying ADR methods to resolve conflicts in the area of e-commerce with the aim of promoting consumer confidence.[25]

In April 2002 the Commission launched a Green Paper on ADR so as to initiate a debate on a certain number of legal issues that were raised with regard to ADR in civil and commercial law.[26] As a result of the Green Paper the EU adopted a voluntary European Code of Conduct for Mediators launched in July 2004[27] and a Mediation Directive in 2008.[28] The aim was to promote the application of mediation as a cheap and fast alternative to court procedures in commercial cross-border disputes.

Furthermore, on 13 June 2007 the EU adopted a Regulation establishing a European Small Claims Procedure.[29] Although the small claim procedure is not an ADR mechanism as such, it provides an alternative to the usual court procedures. It aims to improve access to justice by simplifying cross-border small claims litigation in civil and commercial matters, and by reducing costs.[30] 'Small claims' are defined as cases concerning sums under EUR 2,000, excluding interest and expenses.[31] This regulation also reduces the length of procedures, as it eliminates the intermediate step of requiring the recognition of the case and its enforcement in another state. It is of particular importance for consumers, as they often refrain from taking actions because of low damages claims and high court-costs. However,

[22] For example, the European Ombudsman was established by the Maastricht Treaty to investigate maladministration complaints in the EU institutions; more at: www.ombudsman.europa.eu/home.faces.

[23] See ec.europa.eu/consumers/redress/out_of_court/commu/index_en.htm.

[24] See also a 1999 follow-up paper on a Consumer Policy Action Plan of 1998, where the Commission mentioned prioritising consumer access to justice ADR of consumer disputes, requiring the establishment of out-of-court settlement bodies, *Report on the communication from the Commission on the Consumer Policy Action Plan 1999–2001* (COM(98)0696-C4-0035/99).

[25] The EU also established a European Judicial Network, see Council Decision of 28 May 2001 establishing a European Judicial Network in civil and commercial matters, [2001] OJ L 174/25.

[26] Commission (EC) 'Green Paper on alternative dispute resolution in civil and commercial law', COM (2002) 196, final, 19 April 2002, para 10. In the green paper the importance of ADR as a means of achieving social harmony was highlighted, by which the parties do not engage in a process of confrontation but rather in a process of rapprochement, thereby themselves achieving a consensual solution that maintains their commercial or other relations.

[27] See europa.eu.int/comm.justice_home/ejn/adr_ec_code_conduct_en.pdf.

[28] Directive (EC) 2008/52 concerning certain aspects of mediation in civil and commercial matters [2008] OJ L136/3.

[29] Regulation (EC) 861/2007 establishing a European small claims procedure, [2007] OJ L199/1.

[30] ibid.

[31] G Haibach, 'The Commission Proposal for a Regulation Establishing a European Small Claims Procedures: an Analysis' (2005) *European Review of Private Law,* 593–601; E Hondius, 'Towards a European Small Claims Procedure' in L Thévenoz & N Reich (eds), *Liber Amicorum Bernd Stauder, Consumer Law* (Geneva, Schulthess, 2006), 131 ff; J Baldwin, 'Is there a limit to the expansion of small claims?' in MDA Freeman (ed), *Current Legal Problems*, vol 56, (Oxford, Oxford University Press, 2004), 313–343; CJ Whelan (ed), *Small claims courts – A comparative study*, (Oxford, Clarendon, 1990), 253 ff.

a study in 2007 has shown that the cost, length or complexities of these procedures are still too high to allow effective access to justice.[32]

In 2010 the EU launched a 'European e-Justice portal'[33] to facilitate access to justice contributing to the creation of a single area of justice. This portal provides information to citizens, business and practitioners on legislation and case law in all Member States promoting understanding of different legal systems. Among information on legal aid and courts, it also provides a useful general overview on mediation systems in the Member States.[34]

At the Member State level various important national reforms of civil procedure during the past decade have also encouraged the development of ADR schemes.[35] They have established different out-of-court models varying extensively across the EU.[36] While some ADR schemes are supported by public initiatives, such as the consumer complaints boards in Scandinavian countries, others rely rather on self-regulation, as in Germany. The legal effect of the decisions adopted by ADR schemes also differ considerably, as some are merely voluntary recommendations whereas others are only binding for the professional.[37]

The EU recently commissioned several studies on the effectiveness of ADR mechanisms in the EU and in the Member States.[38] These studies showed that, while ADR has been efficient in special sectors various shortcomings prevail, such as a lack of information about available schemes, wide diversity and a lack of general coverage. Therefore, the European Commission proposed two new legislative measures in 2011 to strengthen the efficiency of ADR and ODR throughout the EU.[39] These are described at the end of this chapter.

Competences of the EU in Civil Justice Matters and Consumer ADR

The growing interest of the EU in ADR mechanisms raises the question of its competences to adopt measures in this field. The following section will analyse the Treaty provisions that deal with civil justice and ADR.

Originally, the EU did not enjoy express power in the area of ADR and therefore applied soft law instruments to determine minimum-quality criteria of ADR schemes.[40]

[32] The University of Leuven conducted a study in 2007 on alternative means of consumer redress. It consists of a comparative report and 28 national reports (hereafter 'Leuven Study'), p 10: also available at: ec.europa.eu/consumers/redress/reports_studies/index_en.htm (accessed in July 2009).

[33] See the webpage at e-justice.europa.eu/home.do?action=home&plang=en.

[34] See e-justice.europa.eu/content_mediation-62-en.do.

[35] E Blankenburg, 'The Infrastructure for Avoiding Civil Litigation: Comparing Culture of Legal Behaviour in The Netherlands and West Germany' (1994) 28 *Law & Society Review* 4, 789–808. E Blankenburg, 'Civil Litigation Rates as Indicators for Legal Cultures', in D Nelken (ed) *Comparing Legal Cultures*, (Sudbury, Dartmouth Publishing Co, 1997), 41.

[36] AAS Zuckerman, *Civil Justice in Crisis, Comparative Perspectives of Civil Procedures* (Oxford, Oxford University Press, 1999) 3 ff; C Hodges, S Vogenauer and M Tulibacka (eds), *The Costs and Funding of Civil Litigation: A Comparative Perspective* (Oxford, Hart Publishing, 2010).

[37] ec.europa.eu/consumers/redress/out_of_court/index_en.htm.

[38] DG SANCO. Study on the use of Alternative Dispute Resolution in the EU (Berlin, Civic Consulting 2009 and Leuven Study).

[39] Commission (EC) 'Proposal for a Directive on Alternative Dispute Resolution for Consumer Disputes (Directive on consumer ADR)', COM (2011) 793/2, final, 29 November 2011 and Commission (EC) 'Proposal for a Regulation on online dispute resolution for consumer disputes (Regulation on consumer ODR)', COM (2011) 794/2, final, 29 November 2011.

[40] For example, Commission Recommendation (EC) 98/257 on the principles applicable to the bodies responsible for the out-of-court settlement of consumer disputes [1998] OJ L 115, 31; see also N Reich, 'More

Extension of the competence of the European Community into the area of civil justice systems began in 1999, when the objective of establishing 'an area of freedom, security and justice' was included in the Treaty of Amsterdam.[41] The Commission has since sought to simplify the legal context within the EU to improve access to justice.[42] There has also been a slow trend towards a stronger harmonisation of legislation in the EU.[43]

Within litigation systems, developments have taken place in the context of a European Judicial Network in civil and commercial matters (EJ-NET),[44] and a Community framework of activities to facilitate the implementation of judicial cooperation in civil matters.[45] There has also been emphasis on ADR, since this can avoid or shorten legal processes, and save money.

Since the Lisbon Treaty in 2009 the EU has a wider competence to adopt civil justice measures. Article 81 of the Treaty on the Functioning of the European Union (TFEU) broadened the competences of the EU in the field of civil justice and could serve as a general basis for cross-border ADR measures.[46]

The pre-Lisbon Treaty Article 65 EC stated that improving measures which have cross-border implications could be taken 'in so far as necessary for the proper functioning of the internal market'.[47]

The new Article 81 (2) TFEU on civil procedure now provides the possibility for the EU to adopt civil justice measures without requiring a market-making objective.[48] This provision would allow legislation on, *inter alia*:

> (...)
> (e) effective access to justice;
> (g) the development of alternative methods of dispute settlement;(…).

Thus, the EU can adopt ADR measures on the basis of this Article. This competence is nonetheless generally restricted to cross-border matters, so that purely Member States procedures may remain unaffected.[49]

Clarity after Claro?, Arbitration clauses in consumer contracts as an ADR (alternative dispute resolution) mechanism for effective and speedy conflict resolution, or as '*deni de justice*?' 3 *European Review of Contract Law* 1, 41–61.

[41] See more in Eva Storskrubb, *Civil Procedure and EU Law: A Policy Area Uncovered* (Oxford, Oxford University Press, 2008).

[42] Giuseppe Gargani, *Explanatory Statement: Report on the Prospects for Approximating Civil Procedural Law in the European Union* (Committee on Legal Affairs and the Internal Market, 30 January 2004).

[43] C Hodges, 'Europeanisation of Civil Justice: Trends and Issues' (2006) 1 *Civil Justice Quarterly*, 96–123, see also the European Parliament 'Resolution on the prospects for approximating civil procedural law in the European Union' COM(2002) 654 + COM(2002) 746 – C5-0201/2003 – 2003/2087(INI), 30 January 2004.

[44] Council Decision (EC) 2001/470 establishing a European Judicial Network in civil and commercial matters, [2004] OJ L 174/25.

[45] Council Regulation (EC) 743/2002 establishing a Community framework of activities to facilitate the implementation of judicial cooperation in civil matters, [2002] OJ L 115/1.

[46] E Storskrubb, *Civil Procedure and EU Law, A Policy Area Uncovered*, Studies in European Law (Oxford, Oxford University Press, 2008), 184; C Hodges, *The Reform of Class and Representative Actions in European Legal Systems* (Oxford, Hart Publishing, 2008), 95.

[47] Art 65 ECT stated: 'Measures in the field of judicial cooperation in civil matters having cross-border implications, to be taken (...) in so far as necessary for the proper functioning of the internal market, shall include: (...) (c) eliminating obstacles to the good functioning of civil proceedings, if necessary by promoting the compatibility of the rules on civil procedure applicable in the Member States.'

[48] M Tulibacka, 'Europeanization of Civil Procedures: In Search of a Coherent Approach' (2009) 46 *Common Market Law Review*, 1527–1565.

[49] D Fairgrieve and G Howells, 'Collective Redress Procedures: European Debates' (2009), 58 *International and Comparative Law Quarterly*, 406 ff.

However, the EU could adopt broader measures by relying in addition on sector specific provisions, such as Article 169 TFEU regarding consumer protection.

According to Article 169 (1) TFEU, the EU aims to promote the interests of consumers and ensures a high level of consumer protection. The Union shall in particular: 'contribute to protecting the health, safety and economic interests of consumers, as well as to promoting their right to information, education and to organise themselves in order to safeguard their interests.' In order to attain these objectives the EU can adopt two types of measures (Article 169(2)):

(a) measures adopted pursuant to Article 114 TFEU in the context of the completion of the internal market;
(b) measures which support, supplement and monitor the policy pursued by the Member States.

The harmonisation measures adopted pursuant to Article 114 TFEU must have as their objective the establishment and functioning of the internal market. This requirement does however not apply to measures adopted according to Article 169 (2) (b).

Although the European Commission has the choice between the different legal provisions described above, most EU measures regarding consumer law have been adopted on the basis of Article 114 TFEU. The new 2011 Commission's proposal on consumer ADR is also based on this Article. It remains to be seen if this proposed, far-reaching measure complies with the requirement of Article 114 TFEU to foster market functioning. Article 169 (2) (b) might have been a more appropriate basis for the Draft Directive as it allows the EU to adopt measures that support and supplement ADR consumer schemes in the Member States, without requiring a market-building rationale.

Specific EU Measures Regarding ADR

Recommendations to Promote the Quality of Consumer ADR

Since 1998 the Commission has adopted two Recommendations to promote consumer ADR. They establish a number of minimum guarantees, such as independence and effectiveness, which ADR schemes should respect.

Recommendation 98/257/EC on the Principles Applicable to the Bodies Responsible for Out-of-Court Settlement of Consumer Disputes was adopted in 1998.[50] It applies to consumer ADR schemes which, no matter what they are called, either propose or impose a solution to resolve a dispute.

This Recommendation sets seven minimum guarantees in ADR proceedings:[51]

1. independence,
2. transparency,
3. adversarial principle,
4. effectiveness,
5. legality,

[50] Commission Recommendation (EC) 98/257/EC on the principles applicable to the bodies responsible for the out-of-court settlement of consumer disputes, [1998] OJ L 115.

[51] See Arts I–VII of the Commission Recommendation (EC) 98/257/EC on the principles applicable to the bodies responsible for the out-of-court settlement of consumer disputes, [1998] OJ L 115.

6. liberty, and
7. representation.

Recommendation 2001/310/EC,[52] adopted in 2001, applies to ADR schemes which involve a more consensual resolution of disputes. It targets out-of-court mechanisms where third party bodies responsible for consumer dispute resolution procedures: 'no matter what they are called, attempt to resolve a dispute by bringing the parties together to convince them to find a solution by common consent.'[53] However, the recommendation does not cover customer complaints services or such mechanisms provided by or on behalf of a business.[54] Part II of the Recommendation sets four minimum guarantees that such ADR schemes should respect:[55]

1. impartiality,
2. transparency,
3. effectiveness,
4. fairness.

Both Recommendations have positively influenced consumer ADR schemes in the Member States, which have often adopted the minimum quality guarantees in their procedures. The Commission has developed a database with more than 500 ADR schemes which, according to Member States, meet the Commission's quality criteria, complying with the Recommendations.[56]

Voluntary Code of Conduct and Mediation Directive

A Code of Conduct for Mediators was promoted by the European Commission and developed in conjunction with a large group of practitioners and mediation experts. This code was adopted by mediation experts in 2004 and sets out a number of principles to which individual mediators in civil and commercial matters can voluntarily decide to commit.[57] Mediation organizations can also adhere to the Code and promote the respect of its principles through information, training or monitoring of mediators.[58]

Under the Code of Conduct, mediation is defined as: 'any process where two or more parties agree to the appointment of a third-party – hereinafter "the mediator" – to help the parties to solve a dispute by reaching an agreement without adjudication and regardless of how that process may be called or commonly referred to in each Member State.'[59]

Adherence to the Code is without prejudice to national legislation or rules regulating individual professions.[60] The Organisations that apply the Code's mediation principles can

[52] Commission Recommendation (EC) 2001/310 on the principles for out-of-court bodies involved in the consensual resolution of consumer ADR, OJ L 109, p 56.

[53] Part I (1) of the Commission Recommendation (EC) 2001/310 on the principles for out-of-court bodies involved in the consensual resolution of consumer ADR, OJ L 109.

[54] Part I (2) of the Commission Recommendation (EC) 2001/310 on the principles for out-of-court bodies involved in the consensual resolution of consumer ADR, OJ L 109.

[55] See Part II (A–D) of the Commission Recommendation (EC) 2001/310 on the principles for out-of-court bodies involved in the consensual resolution of consumer ADR, [2001] OJ L 109.

[56] This database can be accessed at http://ec.europa.eu/consumers/redress_cons/schemes_en.htm.

[57] European Code of Conduct for Mediators promoted by the Commission and adopted by mediation experts in October 2004: see ec.europa.eu/civiljustice/adr/adr_ec_code_conduct_en.pdf.

[58] ibid.

[59] ibid.

[60] ibid.

notify the Commission in order to be added to a 'European Code of Conduct for Mediators' list.[61]

More recently, the EU also adopted a Directive in 2008 on certain aspects of mediation in civil and commercial matters, based on Article 61c and Article 67 (5) ECT.[62]

According to Article 1, the Directive aims to:

> (…) promote the amicable settlement of disputes by encouraging the use of mediation and by ensuring a balanced relationship between mediation and judicial proceedings.

The Directive harmonises national rules concerning mediation and some elements of national civil procedures in a relatively limited manner, and is confined to cross-border mediation only. However, Member States can also extend the application of the provisions implementing the Directive onto purely national mediation procedures.[63]

A cross-border dispute is defined in Article 2 as:

> (…) one in which at least one of the parties is domiciled or habitually resident in a Member State other than that of any other party on the date on which:
> (a) the parties agree to use mediation after the dispute has arisen;
> (b) mediation is ordered by a court;
> (c) an obligation to use mediation arises under national law; or
> (d) for the purposes of Article 5 an invitation is made to the parties.

The Directive promotes mediation as a viable alternative to court litigation to facilitate access to justice. It places an obligation on the Member States to provide the general public with information on how to contact mediators and organisations offering mediation services (Article 9). Furthermore, it aims at providing a harmonised approach to mediation – by requiring appropriate training for mediators and providing common definitions for both mediators and mediation.

According to Article 3 (b):

> Mediator means any third person who is asked to conduct mediation in an effective, impartial and competent way, regardless of the denomination or profession of that third person in the Member State concerned and of the way in which the third person has been appointed or requested to conduct the mediation.

The Directive refers to mediation as a voluntary process, but it does not prejudice national law provisions which provide for sanctions or incentives related to participation in mediation (Article 3 (a)). It also applies to cases where parties are referred to mediation by a judge and where mediation is prescribed by law (Article 3(a)).

Importantly, the Directive clarifies at Article 3 (a) (2) that it includes mediation conducted by a judge who is not responsible for any judicial proceedings concerning the dispute in question. However, it excludes attempts made by the court or the judge to settle a dispute in the course of judicial proceedings concerning the dispute in question.

At Article 4 the Directive requires Member States to strengthen the quality of mediation through control mechanisms and the promotion of training. In particular a high level of effective, impartial and competent mediation should be ensured at Member State level.

The Directive also states that courts before which cross-border disputes are brought may refer the parties to mediation schemes.

[61] The list is published at ibid.
[62] Directive (EC) 2008/52 on certain aspects of mediation in civil and commercial matters, [2008], OJ L 136/3.
[63] See ibid, Art 2 for the definition of a cross border dispute.

In addition, the Directive regulates the following aspects of mediation:

- enforcement of agreements resulting from mediation (Member States must in general ensure that agreements are enforced) (Article 6);
- the appropriate courts and authorities to make requests to must be communicated to the Commission which then makes the information available to the general public (Article 10);
- confidentiality of mediation (Article 7);
- and prescription and limitation periods (Member States must ensure that parties who refer their dispute to mediation are not prevented from later bringing the case to a court or using arbitration because of prescription or limitation periods) (Article 8).

The Directive had to be transposed by each Member State by 21 May 2011,[64] apart from Denmark, which opted out.[65] The mediation Directive makes cross-border dispute resolution in civil and commercial matters more effective. It establishes a coherent EU framework ensuring a balanced relationship between mediation and judicial proceedings.[66] The Directive also provides an incentive for Member States to go beyond the requirements in the Directive promoting mediation in a purely national context.

ADR in Sectoral EU Legislation

A number of sectoral EU directives in specific sectors *encourage* or *require* Member States to establish adequate and effective out-of court dispute resolution procedures.

Measures that *encourage* Member States to establish ADR schemes are the:

- Distance Marketing of Financial Services Directive[67]
- Timeshare Directive[68]
- E-commerce Directive[69]
- Postal Services Directive[70]
- Insurance Mediation Directive[71]
- Markets in Financial Instruments Directive (MiFID)[72]

[64] For a comparative study on mediation regulation and implementation of the Mediation Directive see Felix Steffek, 'Mediation in Europa und der Welt – Rechtvergleichende Forschung zur Umsetzung der Mediationsrichtlinie' (2009), 1 *Zeitschrift* für *Konflikt-Management*, 1–22; Felix Steffek, 'Rechtsvergleichende Erfahrungen für die Regelung der Mediation' (2010), 74 *The Rabel Journal of Comparative and International Private Law*, 841 ff.

[65] Press release from 2010 by the EU on the Mediation Directive: http://europa.eu/rapid/pressReleasesAction.do?reference=IP/10/1060&format=HTML&aged=0&language=EN&guiLanguage=en.

[66] For the impact of the Directive on Germany, see Jan-Bertram Hillig and Martin Huhn, 'Impact of the EU Mediation Directive on the German Construction Sector' (2010), 162 *Journal of Legal Affairs and Dispute Resolution in Engineering and Construction* 2.

[67] Directive 2002/65/EC concerning the distance marketing of consumer financial services, 9.10.2002, Art 14.

[68] Directive 2008/122/EC of 14 January 2009 on the protection of consumers in respect of certain aspects of timeshare, longterm holiday product, resale and exchange contracts (Art 14(2)), OJ L 33, 3.2.2009, Art 14.

[69] Directive (EC) 2000/31 on certain legal aspects of information society services, in particular electronic commerce, in the Internal Market (Directive on electronic commerce), [2000] OJ L 178/1.

[70] Directive (EC) 2008/6 amending Directive 97/67/EC with regard to the full accomplishment of the internal market of Community postal services, [2008] OJ L 52, 3.

[71] Directive 2002/92/EC on insurance mediation (Art 11(1)), OJ L 9, 15.1.2003, Art 11.

[72] Directive (EC) 2004/39 on markets in financial instruments amending Council Directives 85/611/EEC and 93/6/EEC and Directive 2000/12/EC and repealing Council Directive 93/22/EEC, [2004] OJ L 145/1, 33.

In turn, EU legislative frameworks that *require* that adequate and effective ADR schemes are put in place are:

- The telecom sector[73]
- The energy sector[74]
- The Consumer Credit Directive[75]
- The Payment Services Directive[76]

For example, the EU Consumer Credit Directive 2008/48/EC,[77] contains an ADR requirement at Article 24 entitled 'out- of-court resolution', which states:

> 1. Member States shall ensure that adequate and effective out-of-court dispute resolution procedures for the settlement of consumer disputes concerning credit agreements are put in place, using existing bodies where appropriate.

Article 24 (2) then continues:

> Member States shall encourage those bodies to cooperate in order to also resolve cross-border disputes concerning credit agreements.

Finally, the EU Directive 2006/123/EC on services in the internal markets contains a detailed provision on the settlement of disputes.[78] The Services Directive requires providers that are part of an ADR scheme to provide consumers with information on this scheme.

Article 27 (1) states that: '(…) Member States shall take the general measures necessary to ensure that providers respond to the complaints (…) in the shortest possible time and make their best efforts to find a satisfactory solution (…)'.

According to paragraph 4 providers that are subject to a code of conduct, or are members of a trade association or professional body offering recourse to an ADR means, have to inform their customers thereof.

These Directives show that there is an increasing trend in EU law to include provisions regarding alternative redress mechanisms in consumer-related measures. While the older consumer Directives rarely mentioned out-of-court dispute resolution, in the new Directive Member States are often encouraged to promote such schemes.

The European Court of Justice Case Law on Judicial Consumer Protection

The European Court of Justice (ECJ) has become more active in determining the judicial protection of consumers with regard to ADR related matters.

[73] Directive (EC) 2009/136 amending Directive 2002/22/EC on universal service and users' rights relating to electronic communications networks and services.

[74] Directive (EC) 2009/72 concerning common rules for the internal market in electricity and repealing Directive 2003/54/EC, [2009] OJ L211/55; and Directive (EC) 2009/73 concerning common rules for the internal market in natural gas and repealing Directive 2003/55/EC, [2009] OJ L211/94, p 55, 94.

[75] Directive (EC) 2008/48 on credit agreements for consumers and repealing Council Directive 87/102/EEC, [2008] OJ L 133/66, 66.

[76] Directive (EC) 2007/64 on payment services in the internal market amending Directives 97/7/EC, 2002/65/EC, 2005/60/EC and 2006/48/EC and repealing Directive 97/5/EC, [2007] OJ L319/1, 32.

[77] Directive (EC) 2008/48 on credit agreements for consumers and repealing Council Directive 87/102/EEC, [2008] OJ L 133/66.

[78] Directive (EC) 2006/123 on services in the internet market, [2006] OJ L376.

In a recent case *Alassini*[79] the ECJ had to decide whether Italian mandatory mediation rules are contrary to the principle of effective judicial protection.[80] This case concerned a 2003 national law that implemented the Universal Service Directive 2002/22/EC (USD) in Italy by introducing, among others, mediation rules.[81] In a preliminary ruling the ECJ had to determine whether an attempt to achieve out-of-court settlement can be made a mandatory condition in Italy for the admissibility before the courts of actions in disputes between providers and end-users under the USD.

In its assessment the ECJ examined the principle of effective judicial protection from a human rights perspective, which is included in Article 6 and 13 of the ECHR and confirmed by Article 47 of the European Charter of Fundamental Rights. It held that according to settled case-law these rights are not absolute but can be restricted by measures of general interest provided they are proportionate. [82]

In this particular case, the Court considered that the Italian law imposing a duty on the parties to attempt to find an amicable dispute resolution solution constituted a legitimate objective in the general interest which was not disproportionate. Therefore, the Court decided that the law complied with the principle of effective judicial protection and was not precluded by EU law.

In a number of cases the ECJ also had to decide on the conflict between consumer protection included in the Directive 93/13 on unfair terms and contractual arbitration clauses.

In *Claro v Centro Movil,* a company included the use of an arbitration tribunal, raising issues of fairness.[83] The ECJ ruled that the national court was required to assess whether a contractual arbitration clause was void even when the consumer has not raised the issue of unfairness in the arbitration proceedings but only in the action for annulment.[84]

A more recent judgment, *Asturcom Telecomunicaciones SL v Cristina Rodríguez Nogueira,*[85] concerned the enforcement of an arbitration award. In this case an unfair arbitration clause had been included in a mobile phone contract of a Spanish telecommunication company. The Court held that a national court:

> hearing an action for enforcement of an arbitration award which has become final and was made in the absence of the consumer is required, where it has available to it the legal and factual elements necessary for that task, to assess of its own motion whether an arbitration clause in a contract concluded between a seller or supplier and a consumer is unfair, in so far as, under national rules of procedure, it can carry out such an assessment in similar actions of a domestic nature.[86]

The ECJ went further than in *Claro v Centro Móvil* by stating that Article 6 of the Directive on unfair terms forms part of the rules of public policy.[87]

As a result of these cases the national courts have to become active under certain conditions and act of their own motion to verify the potential unfairness of standard terms

[79] *Alassini* (C-317/08, C-317/08, C-319/08 and C-320/08) March 18, 2010.

[80] See also J Davies and E Szyszczak, 'ADR: Effective Protection of Consumer Rights?' (2010) 35 *EL Rev* October 2010-11-19.

[81] Legislative Decree No 259 of August 1, 2003 relating to the Electronic Communications Code GURI No 214 of September 15, 2003, 3.

[82] *Alassini* (C-317/08, C-317/08, C-319/08 and C-320/08) March 18, 2010 at [63].

[83] C-168/05 Claro *v Centro Movil Milenium SL* [2006] *ECR* I-10421.

[84] The consumer often lacks legal knowledge and has limited power to change contractual arbitration clauses.

[85] Case C-40/08, *Asturcom Telecomunicaciones SL v Cristina Rodríguez Nogueira.* – ECR 2009, p I-9579.

[86] Case C-40/08, *Asturcom Telecomunicaciones SL v Cristina Rodríguez Nogueira.* – ECR 2009, p I-9579, para 59.

[87] Case C-40/08, *Asturcom Telecomunicaciones SL v Cristina Rodríguez Nogueira.* – ECR 2009, p I-9579, para 52.

or to annul an arbitration award if it is based on an unfair contract clause.[88] This might well influence EU Member States' practice to undertake stricter assessment of arbitral clauses in consumers' contracts.[89]

EU Cross-border Networks

In the last decade the EU has launched a number of networks in order to facilitate cross-border dispute resolution. These networks deal either with general cross-border consumer matters (such as the European Consumer Centres Network), or with specific fields (such as FIN-NET) that facilitate dispute resolution in cross-border cases between consumers and financial services providers.

The European Consumer Centres Network

In 2001, an Extra-Judicial Network (EEJ-NET) was launched by the EU[90] and a consumer claim form promulgated to facilitate consumers' access to ADR providers.[91] This EEJ-Net consisted of national 'clearing houses' that assisted consumers to settle possible cross-border disputes with companies by guiding them towards alternative dispute resolution mechanisms.[92]

The task of the network was to:

- inform consumers of the possibilities of recourse to alternative dispute resolution mechanisms;
- facilitate cross-border complaints, particularly by helping the complainants to overcome linguistic difficulties by providing practical assistance such as translating complaint forms;
- facilitate the lodging of complaints using the appropriate standard ADR form;
- follow-up resolution of complaints and action taken involving ADR within the network.[93]

In January 2005, this network was merged with the European Consumer Centres 'Euroguichets', which provided information and assistance on cross-border issues and became the 'European Consumer Centres Network' (ECC-Net).

The ECC-Net was established to assist consumers in the resolution of cross-border complaints and disputes.[94] It consists of a single European consumer centre in every Member State and in Iceland and Norway that function as contact points for consumers.

[88] Karin Sein, Protection of Consumers against Unfair Jurisdiction and Arbitration Clauses in Jurisprudence of the European Court of Justice, Juridica International XVIII/2011.

[89] B U Graf, A E Appleton, ECJ Case C 40/08 Asturcom – EU Unfair Terms Law Confirmed as a Mattter of Public Policy, ASA Bulletin, vol 28, No 2, 2010, 417.

[90] Council Resolution (EC) 2000/C on a Community-wide network of national bodies for the extra-judicial settlement of consumer disputes, OJ C 155/1.

[91] See www.eejnet.org/filing_complaint; ec.europa.eu/consumers/publications/factsheet-ECC-Net_en.pdf.

[92] See europa.eu/legislation_summaries/other/l32043_en.htm.

[93] See europa.eu/legislation_summaries/other/l32043_en.htm.

[94] See ec.europa.eu/consumers/publications/factsheet-ECC-Net_en.pdf.

The network is funded by both the European Commission and national governments and handles over sixty thousand cases every year.[95]

From an organizational point of view the host organization of the individual Consumer Centres must be a public or non-profit-making body selected by the Member State and approved by the European Commission.[96] For instance, in the UK the Consumer Center is hosted by the Trading Standards Institute and is co-funded by the European Commission and the UK Department for Business, Enterprise and Regulatory Reform.[97]

The objective of the ECC-Network is to ensure consumer confidence when purchasing cross-border.[98]

Its main tasks are:

- to inform consumers and to give them advice about their rights when shopping cross-border;
- to give advice and support to any consumer with a complaint related to a cross-border purchase;
- to provide easy access to ADR-bodies in situations where it has not been possible to solve a cross-border consumer complaint amicably and to assist in this process;
- to raise the awareness of the out-of-court resolution schemes among consumers and businesses and sharing best practices at national and EU level;
- to cooperate with other EU-networks which provide essential information on EU, national legislation and case-law, such as SOLVIT and FIN-NET.[99]

Case-handling procedures and key statistics

In the event that consumers cannot resolve a cross-border dispute they can contact the Consumer Centre in their country of residence for help.

This Consumer Centre, together with the Centre in the country where the dispute occurred, can support a consumer who has a complaint by contacting the affected business. Furthermore, they act as intermediaries between the consumer and the relevant ADR system.

In particular, the Consumer Centers have the following role:

1. to determine the appropriate out-of-court scheme;
2. to provide the consumer with detailed information about the relevant ADR bodies.
3. to inform the consumer of the advantages and disadvantages of ADR;[100]
4. to help consumers monitor their dispute, where necessary;
5. to provide access to translation services when required.[101]

In theory, the procedure consists of the following steps. The Consumer Centre is contacted by the consumer located in the same country. As a result, this Centre assists the consumer

[95] For example for the period 2007–2008 the Commission provided € 8.5 million of funding to the ECCs, see ec.europa.eu/consumers/redress_cons/docs/annual_report_ecc_2007.pdf.

[96] *Cross-border Dispute Resolution Mechanisms in Europe – Practical Reflections on the Need and Availability* (ECC-Net, 2009).

[97] The UK centre opened in August 2007 taking enquiries from consumers and handling cross border cases referred from other Member States. The centre is fully operational and staged an official launch on 14 November to raise awareness with consumers and stakeholders. www.ukecc.net/default.asp.

[98] ECC-Net, *Cross-border Dispute Resolution* (2009).

[99] ibid, 10–11.

[100] For instance the Centre will explain the advantages of ADR compared to other methods of redress, such as any time limits or cost issues.

[101] ECC-Net, Cross-border Dispute Resolution 2009, 11.

with an eventual translation and then transfers the case to the Consumer Centre where the business is located (hereafter the 'Business ECC'). The latter forwards the case to the appropriate ADR scheme, which then contacts the trader and tries to solve the case. After the dispute resolution procedure it informs the Business ECC of the outcome, which then informs the Consumer Centre where the consumer is located, which in turn lets the consumer know.[102]

In practice however, the procedure is often different from that described above because in a large number of cases appropriate ADR schemes are missing. In such cases, Business ECCs usually try to solve the cases directly without seeking the help of an ADR body.[103]

From 2006–2009, most complaints tackled by ECCs concerned products and services, and contract terms. The main sector concerned by far was air transport, and a large number of complaints also concerned on-line transactions (55%).[104]

The total number of complaints handled by ECCs has been between 50,000 and 60,000 annually. In 2008 and 2009 the volume of information requests and complaints split into around 25,000–30,000 information requests and 30,000–35,000 complaints.

The ECC-Net has provided consumers with valuable assistance in the resolution of cross-border disputes. This has been particularly useful in sectors where cross-border purchasing is common and will probably increase in the future, such as air transport and e-commerce. The mixture of Centre services providing both advice regarding rights and helping more concretely to settle the dispute is helpful, as consumers often do not know the relevant legal framework. However, the lack in coverage of ADR schemes in Member States has rendered effective dispute resolution difficult. As explained above in the Member States appropriate ADR schemes are often absent, so the ECC-Net tries to resolve the dispute directly with the traders.[105] These shortcomings might however be overcome if the new EU ADR Draft Directive was adopted, as it requires that ADR schemes will be available for all consumer disputes.

FIN-NET

For the financial services sector the Commission has set up a specific dispute resolution network of national ADR bodies, called FIN-NET (Financial Services Complaints Network). This network was established in 2001 and deals with ADR cross-border disputes between consumers and financial services providers, covering the European Union, Norway, Iceland and Liechtenstein.[106]

The objective of FIN-NET is to provide consumers with easier access to ADR schemes in cross-border cases through the cooperation and assistance of national ADR bodies.[107]

In particular, the network aims to:

- provide consumers with easy and informed access to out-of-court redress in cross-border disputes;

[102] ibid.

[103] ibid, 10–11.

[104] In 2011 FIN-NET had 55 Members, see the ECC Network website at: ec.europa.eu/consumers/ecc/key_facts_figues_en.htm.

[105] ECC-Net Cross-border Dispute Reolution 2009, 10–11.

[106] See ec.europa.eu/internal_market/finservices-retail/finnet/index_en.htm.

[107] DG Internal Market and Services, *Evaluation of FIN-NET* (2009, Centre for Strategy & Evaluation Services).

- ensure efficient exchange of information between European out-of-court complaint schemes;
- improve the quality of ADR schemes and ensure that they operate under a common set of principles;
- raise consumer confidence in financial services from other Member States.[108]

If a consumer has a complaint against a financial service provider from another country, the FIN-NET member in the consumers' country will help to identify the relevant complaint scheme in the financial services provider's country. Furthermore, it will provide information about the scheme and its complaint procedure.[109]

If the consumer then decides to file a complaint, the FIN-NET member will transfer it to the relevant scheme in the service provider's country or suggest to the consumer to file a complaint directly with the cross-border scheme.

A Memorandum of Understanding links FIN-NET Members, including a declaration of intent on cross-border co-operation between the parties. Amongst other things the Memorandum describes the procedure of cooperation and conditions of exchange of information in handling cross-border complaints. As the Memorandum is of a voluntary nature it does not create any legal rights or obligations.[110]

In order to be admitted as a member of FIN-NET a scheme must provide out-of-court settlement of disputes between consumers and service providers in financial services. In addition, it has to comply with the principles set out in Commission Recommendation 98/257/EC of 30 March 1998 on the principles applicable to the bodies responsible for out-of-court settlement of consumer disputes.[111] This means that a Member State authority has to certify to the Commission that it complies with all the seven principles of the Recommendation (ie independence, transparency, adversarial procedure, effectiveness, legality, liberty and representation). Details of organizations that have registered with FIN-NET can be found on its webpage.[112]

Key data and evaluation

The data from FIN-NET's activity reports[113] reveal a strong increase in the number of complaints handled from the initial annual total of 335 in 2001. In 2009, FIN-NET handled 1,542 cross-border cases, out of which 884 were in the banking sector, 244 in the insurance sector, 410 in the investment services sector, and four that cannot be attributed to one sector.[114] An important characteristic of FIN-NET's activity is the very uneven distribution among its member ADRs. For example, according to data from 2009, only five ADRs deal with over 85% of the total number of complaints handled. The other 20 have between five and twenty cases each and the remaining ADRs having no more than a few cases annually.[115]

[108] ibid.

[109] See ibid. The information provided by the FIN-NET member includes contact details, coverage, organisation, in which languages the scheme operates, whether there are any charges to be paid by the consumer, whether the decision of the scheme is binding and typical times for handling complaints.

[110] See ec.europa.eu/internal_market/fin-net/members_en.htm.

[111] Commission (EC) 98/257 on the principles applicable to the bodies responsible for out-of-court settlement of consumer disputes, [1998] OJ L 115/31.

[112] www.fin-net.eu.

[113] ibid.

[114] ibid.

[115] DG Internal Market and Services, Evaluation of FIN-NET (2009), 27.

The most active ADR scheme is by far the UK Financial Ombudsman Service that covers all types of financial services and in 2008 handled 842 cases – up from 444 in 2007 – representing 58% of the total 1,405 complaints reported. The Irish Financial Services Ombudsman Bureau is also quite active with 76 cases handled in 2008 – mainly insurance – and 186 in 2007. The high activity of the two ADRs is seen partly to be a reflection of the relatively increased cross-border trade of specific types of services between Ireland and the UK, but also, according to the ADRs representatives, the common language and the similar legal framework of the two countries makes it easier for consumers to file a complaint.[116]

An evaluation report from 2009 commissioned by DG Internal Market and Service showed that FIN-NET can work well in specific cases. However, the report also revealed significant gaps in the coverage of the network. For instance, some EU Member States had no ADR schemes for particular financial services sectors,[117] and a number of schemes were not members of FIN-NET.[118] Importantly, they were sometimes not members because they did not comply with the ADR principles set out in the Commission Recommendation 98/257/EC of 1998.[119]

In conclusion, the number of complaints has risen gradually so that FIN-NET provides useful assistance to cross-border consumer complaints. However, the evaluation report also indicates that the availability and quality of these schemes for consumers across the EU Member States differ considerably. The new EU proposals 2011 on consumer ADR described in the last section of this chapter might provide a solution to both of these problems.

SOLVIT

SOLVIT is an 'on-line problem solving network' which aims at solving conflicts out-of-court caused by the misapplication of Internal Market law by public authorities.[120] Established in July 2002, SOLVIT has a Centre in every EU Member State as well as in Norway, Iceland and Liechtenstein. These Centres cooperate to provide alternative dispute resolution for cross-border complaints from citizens and businesses. They are not responsible for disputes between consumers and businesses.[121] Consumers may however file cross-border complaints regarding the violation of EU consumer and market law by public authorities.[122] In practice this rarely occurs, as for instance in 2010 the largest number of cases regarded social security issues, residence rights and professional qualifications.[123]

The SOLVIT Centres are part of the national authority and try to find a solution free of charge usually within ten weeks. They are coordinated by the European Commission, which supports them with database facilities and helps to speed up the procedure. The Commission also refers relevant cases to the Centres.[124]

[116] ibid.

[117] Austria, Bulgaria, Cyprus, Estonia, Hungary, Latvia, Romania, Slovakia and Slovenia.

[118] Spain, France, Hungary, Lithuania, Latvia, Norway, Romania, Slovakia.

[119] Internal Market and Services, Evaluation of FIN-NET (2009), 19–20.

[120] See ec.europa.eu/solvit/site/about/index_en.htm.

[121] ECC-Net or FIN-NET are responsible for cross-border disputes between businesses and consumers depending on the type of cross-border case. For general citizens complaints about EU institutions the European Ombudsman is responsible: ombudsman.europa.eu.

[122] See ec.europa.eu/solvit/site/index_en.htm.

[123] See SOLVIT *Annual Report 2010* available at:ec.europa.eu/solvit/site/docs/solvit_2010_report_en.pdf.

[124] See ec.europa.eu/solvit/site/about/index_en.htm.

The procedure works as follows: a case is submitted to the local SOLVIT Centre, which checks that the formal requirements are met. The case is then entered into an on-line database and forwarded to the SOLVIT Centre in the Member State where the problem occurred. The latter confirms the acceptance of the case within a week, provided it is well founded and the misapplication of the internal market law can be resolved effectively. If the solution of a dispute requires the abrogation of a national rule a legal action might be more appropriate. Nevertheless, SOLVIT may instead convince a Member State to waive the rule that does not comply with EU law until it is annulled.[125]

The final suggested solution by SOLVIT does not need to be accepted by the claimants and cannot be challenged through SOLVIT.[126] However, if the claimants are not satisfied with the outcome they can file a legal action to the national court or bring a complaint before the European Commission.

In conclusion, SOLVIT is a useful network to solve cross-border claims of citizens and businesses against national authorities informally and expediently. This is also suggested by the high rate of solved cases.[127] In these cases a misapplication or wrong implementation of EU law has been redressed and the problem solved for the claimant or the Networks found that there was no violation of EU law.[128]

EU-Wide Complaints Reporting

The EU also took initiatives to promote publication of comparable consumer complaints information, including ADR data. This effort formed part of the EU Consumer Policy Strategy 2007–2013 which strives to empower EU consumers.[129]

In May 2010, the European Commission adopted a Recommendation introducing an EU-wide method for classifying and reporting consumer complaints. This initiative aims to harmonize the different complaint classifications in Europe and provide a Union-wide database of consumer complaints.[130] This complaints method can be applied on a voluntary basis by complaint bodies.[131]

Such a harmonized consumer complaint reporting method is particularly important to assess the effectiveness of the numerous out-of-court schemes in the EU. As they are of a more informal nature than court procedures, comprehensive data is not always made publicly available. As a result, evaluation and overview is sometimes difficult, even at national level. Thus, comparable form and regular publication of complaints can improve the transparency of ADR schemes and provide a better understanding of problematic cases in a sector. At the same time data has to be published in a way that does not violate the confidentiality requirements in ADR schemes.

The Commission's recommendation proposes a standardised way of collecting and reporting consumer complaints, using a common set of criteria. For instance, it proposes to

[125] See ec.europa.eu/solvit/site/about/index_en.htm#why.

[126] See ec.europa.eu/solvit/site/about/index_en.htm#why.

[127] For instance, in 2010 SOLVIT had 90 % success rate of the 1363 solved cases for which it was competent.

[128] SOLVIT *Annual Report 2010*.

[129] See ec.europa.eu/consumers/strategy/facts_en.htm.

[130] See the recommendation at ec.europa.eu/consumers/strategy/complaints_en.htm. See ec.europa.eu/consumers/strategy/complaints_en.htm.

[131] ec.europa.eu/consumers/strategy/complaints_en.htm.

distinguish complaints depending on product category (eg an airline ticket, electricity, or a bank account) and type of complaint (eg quality, price, safety, delivery).

According to paragraph 3 (a) of the Recommendation complaint handling bodies should collect and register at least the following information:

(i) country of the consumer;
(ii) country of the trader;
(iii) name of the complaint handling body;
(iv) reason for contact by the consumer, distinguishing between complaints and enquiries;
(v) date of receiving the complaint or enquiry;
(vi) selling method (...)

Furthermore, according to paragraph 4 (b) of the recommendation complaint handling bodies are encouraged to collect and register the following additional data:

(i) advertising method;
(ii) means of payment;
(iii) name of the trader;
(iv) value of the transaction;
(v) value of the loss incurred by the consumer;(...).

Organisations that deal with consumer complaints (ie authorities, consumer organisations or ombudsmen) can opt in to the system and to sending their data to the Commission. The Commission would then make the aggregate data public through the 'Consumer Markets Scoreboard.'

The Scoreboard evaluates key indicators to identify malfunctioning in EU consumer markets, including consumer satisfaction and complaints.[132] For example, the 5th Consumer Scoreboard (2011) included an analysis of ADR data in the EU.[133] The Scoreboard showed that whereas not many Europeans make use of ADR mechanisms or courts for settling their disputes, they seem to favour ADR. In particular, 48% of consumers agreed that it is easy to resolve disputes through ADR mechanisms compared to only 33% for courts. The countries which have the highest percentage of consumers who find it easy to resolve disputes through alternative mechanisms are Ireland, United Kingdom and Cyprus. 56% of retailers are aware of the existence of ADR. Nevertheless, the use of ADR is quite limited considering that only 10% of retailers have used this type of dispute resolution mechanism. Denmark and Ireland are the countries where ADR mechanisms are the most popular among retailers.[134]

The EU-wide complaints reporting classification provides evidence of market failures affecting consumers. This will assist the EU and Member State to determine targeted policy responses to overcome shortcomings, for instance by introducing legislative measures on consumer ADR.

[132] The Consumer Scoreboard was developed in 2008 by the Commission in conjunction with the Member States see: ec.europa.eu/consumers/strategy/facts_en.htm.

[133] 5th Consumer Scoreboard, 2011, 42–44.

[134] ibid.

The European Commission's Proposals on Consumer ADR and ODR

On 29 November 2011 the Commission issued two legislative proposals on the resolution of consumer-related disputes out-of-court: a draft Directive on ADR[135] and a draft Regulation on ODR.[136] The Commission's objective is 'to improve the functioning of the retail internal market and more particularly to enhance redress for consumers.'

Both proposals are based on Article 114 TFEU that requires a market-building rationale. The Commission mentioned in a communication on these proposals[137] that 'the diversity and uneven geographical and sectoral availability of ADR entities prevent consumers and businesses from fully exploiting their potential'. It assumes that the new ADR legislation for consumers can boost economic growth, by ensuring equal access to justice to consumers in all EU regions.

These ADR and ODR proposals have been developed as a result of a number of studies[138] that showed gaps in coverage of out-of-court schemes and insufficient awareness about these tools and their availability. The new proposals aim to overcome these challenges, while adapting the existing regulation to new contexts, characterized among other things by an increase in the use of the Internet.[139]

In a detailed impact assessment the Commission compared a number of policy options and concluded that only a combination of two instruments on ADR and ODR can ensure out-of-court dispute resolution. In particular, a Framework Directive was considered the most appropriate way to ensure full ADR coverage in all Member States, to inform consumers about ADR and to ensure quality principles.

The Proposed Directive on Consumer ADR

The Commission proposed a specific Directive on consumer ADR to ensure the quality and availability of such schemes for contractual disputes. According to Article 1, the objective of the Directive is : '(…) to contribute to the functioning of the internal market and to the achievement of a high level of consumer protection by ensuring that disputes between consumers and traders can be submitted to entities offering impartial, transparent, effective and fair alternative dispute resolution procedures.'

The proposal applies to procedures for the out-of-court resolution of consumer-related disputes. It regulates contractual disputes arising from the sale of goods or the provision of services by a trader established in the Union, to a consumer resident in the Union (Article 2). Hence, the draft Directive would cover both domestic and cross-border disputes whilst not

[135] Commission (EC) 'Proposal for a Directive on alternative dispute resolution for consumer disputes and amending Regulation (EC) No 2006/2004 and Directive 2009/22/EC (Directive on consumer ADR)', COM (2011) 793/2, final, 29 November 2011.

[136] Commission (EC) 'Proposal for a Regulation on online dispute resolution for consumer disputes (Regulation on consumer ODR)', COM (2011) 794/2, final, 29 November 2011.

[137] Commission (EC) 'Communication by the European Commission on Alternative Dispute Resolution for consumer disputes in the Single Market', COM (2011) 791, final, 29 November 2011.

[138] See Study on the Use of Alternative Dispute Resolution in the European Union of 16 October 2009 and the Leuven Study on alternative means of consumer redress other than redress through ordinary judicial proceedings (Leuven study).

[139] Commission (EC) 'Communication by the European Commission on Alternative Dispute Resolution for consumer disputes in the Single Market', COM (2011) 791, final, 29 November 2011, p 2.

applying to in-house dispute resolution services operated by traders, to direct negotiation, or judicial attempts at settlement.

This Draft Directive tackles in particular three key shortcomings,[140] which impede the effectiveness of consumer ADR:

(a) Gaps in the coverage of ADR entities at both sector-specific and geographical level;
(b) Lack of awareness and insufficient information preventing consumers and businesses from using ADR entities; and
(c) Variable quality of ADR: a significant number of ADR entities are not in line with the core principles laid down by the two Commission Recommendations.[141]

Consequently, the four main elements of the legislative proposal are:

1. Ensuring that ADR procedures exist for all consumer disputes

Member States under the proposed Directive have to ensure that disputes can be submitted to an ADR scheme for all consumer disputes. In addition, ADR schemes should provide the possibility to file a case online and exchange information via electronic means (Article 5 Draft Directive).[142]

2. Information on ADR and cooperation

According to the Draft Directive Article 10, traders must inform consumers about the relevant ADR schemes and whether or not they commit to use ADR in relation to complaints lodged against them. Member States have to ensure that consumers can obtain help regarding their cross-border complaints – an obligation that Member States can delegate to their ECC-Net offices (Article 11 Draft Directive). Moreover, the proposal encourages cooperation between ADR entities and national authorities entrusted with the enforcement of consumer protection legislation.

3. Quality of ADR entities

ADR schemes should respect the quality principles provided by the two Commission Recommendations. The Draft Directive also includes a number of quality requirements that an ADR scheme has to comply with: expertise, impartiality, transparency, effectiveness and fairness (Articles 6–9). In addition, the proposal states that disputes should be resolved within 90 days, and that ADR procedures should be free of charge or of moderate costs to consumers.

4. Monitoring

In each Member State, a competent authority will be in charge of monitoring the work of ADR entities established on its territory.

The Directive would enter into force in national law 18 months after adoption.

[140] See Study on the use of Alternative Dispute Resolution in the European Union of 16 October 2009, http://ec.europa.eu/consumers/redress_cons/adr_study.pdf, pp 56–63; 112–115; 120–121.

[141] Commission (EC) 'Communication by the European Commission on Alternative Dispute Resolution for consumer disputes in the Single Market', COM (2011) 791, final, 29 November 2011, 6.

[142] Commission (EC) 'Proposal for a Directive of the European Parliament and of the Council on alternative dispute resolution for consumer disputes and amending Regulation (EC) No 2006/2004 and Directive 2009/22/EC (Directive on consumer ADR)', COM (2011) 793/2, final, 29 November 2011, 4.

The ODR Regulation

The Draft Regulation on Consumer ODR, which aims at fostering the EU internal market, has a special focus on e-commerce. Recent data[143] showed that current ADR schemes for e-commerce are incomplete and only half of the existing schemes offer the possibility of submitting consumer complaints online while very few provide the option to deal with the entire process online.[144] Thus, a key element of the Draft Regulation addresses precisely this point, by proposing the establishment of a *European online dispute resolution platform* ('ODR platform').

ODR platform

The platform will consist of an interactive website offering a single point of entry to consumers and traders who seek to resolve disputes out-of-court. In the current proposal, this platform would apply to disputes arising from cross-border e-commerce transactions and would be free of charge. It could be accessible in all EU official languages. ADR schemes established in Member States, notified to the Commission in accordance with the 'Directive on consumer ADR' would be automatically registered electronically with the ODR platform.

Consumers and traders will be able to submit their complaints through an electronic form on the platform's website. The platform will then check if a complaint can be processed and will seek the agreement of the parties to transmit it to the competent ADR scheme. The chosen ADR scheme will in turn try to resolve the dispute, in accordance with its own rules of procedure, within 30 days from the date of receipt of the complaint. It will notify the platform of relevant information regarding the development of the dispute.

Moreover, the draft regulation proposes to establish a network of online dispute resolution facilitators ('ODR facilitators' network'). Such a network will have one contact point in each Member State, and will provide support to the resolution of disputes submitted via the platform.

Information about the ODR platform

Another important element of the proposal is that it requires EU traders engaged in cross-border e-commerce to inform consumers about the ODR platform. This information shall be made easily, directly, prominently and permanently accessible on the traders' websites, and will be provided again when the consumer submits a complaint to the trader.

Monitoring

The compliance by ADR schemes with the obligations set out in this Regulation will be monitored by the competent authorities to be established in the Member States, in accordance with the Directive on consumer ADR.

In conclusion, both legislative proposals are an ambitious and welcoming initiative to strengthen consumer ADR in the European Union. The mixture of ODR regulation and

[143] The 2010 report of the European Consumer Centre's Network indicates that more than half of complaints (56.3%) received by the ECC-Net were linked to e-commerce transactions. However, out of the 35.000 cross border complaints received by ECC network in 2010, 91% could not be referred to an ADR scheme in another Member State as no suitable ADR scheme existed (ec.europa.eu/consumers/ecc/docs/2010_annual_report_ecc_en.pdf).

[144] Commission (EC) 'Proposal for a Regulation of the European Parliament and of the Council on online dispute resolution for consumer disputes (Regulation on consumer ODR)', COM (2011) 794/2, final.

ADR framework Directive is a promising move towards a comprehensive solution for consumers to access out-of-court schemes. However, it remains to be seen how these proposals will be funded. As all Member States have to provide full coverage of consumer ADR, the establishment of such a system may turn out to be expensive.

Conclusions

This chapter discussed recent trends, at the international and European level, in the design and adoption of ADR schemes for consumers. Out-of-court redress mechanisms are increasingly recognized as an important element to strengthen access to justice. Consequently, a growing number of organizations adopted recommendations regarding ADR (eg, the Council of Europe) or are in the process of developing specific ODR procedures (eg, the UNCITRAL).

In the last decade, the EU has also become gradually more active in the regulation of consumer ADR. While this has been initially done through soft law recommendations, the latest trend is towards adopting binding measures for ADR. Initially, the Commission adopted non-binding Recommendations that influenced ADR schemes positively in the Member States to respect quality standards in their organization and procedures. Then, the mediation Directive (2008) harmonised national rules concerning cross-border mediation in a relatively limited, but *binding* manner. Finally, the most recent ADR and ODR legislative proposals include wide ranging measures obliging the Member States to ensure that ADR schemes are available for all consumer disputes and respect certain quality principles. At the same time, the proposal builds on existing ADR schemes, leaving Member States free to decide how to transpose the obligation.

This active approach by the Commission is supported by the broader competence that the EU received to legislate in cross-border civil justice matters, since the Lisbon Treaty. The new proposal is however not based on the civil justice provision, which is confined to cross-border issues, but on Article 114 TFEU, because the proposal goes beyond cross-border measures.

The new legislative proposals on consumer ADR and ODR are very welcome initiatives that can help to overcome problems of lack of information and lack of coverage which afflict current schemes. In particular, the ODR Regulation will facilitate processing consumer complaints in e-commerce matters.

2

Belgium

Stefaan Voet

The New FPS Economy and its Mediation Task

After the 1999 elections, the Belgian federal government made the modernization of public administration one of its main priorities. A major reform of the various administrations, aimed at restoring citizens' confidence in the public institutions, was announced. This program is known as the Copernicus reform.[1] The core of it was that the citizen is not there for the administration, but that the administration and its civil servants must be at the service for the citizen. The latter, and not the administration, is at the centre.

One of the aims of the Copernicus reform was to restructure the federal administrations.[2] The ministries were replaced by Federal Public Services (FPSs) and Federal Public Planning Services (PPSs).[3] The tasks entrusted to the former are the same as those given to the former ministries. The latter handle *ad hoc* matters associated with socially-based issues that require coordination between several FPSs, such as the policy on equal opportunity or sustainable development.

In 2002, and in this context, the Ministry of Economic Affaires was reformed to the FPS Economy, SMEs,[4] Self-Employed and Energy.[5] Its task is to create the conditions required for the competitive, sustainable and balanced operation of the goods and services market in Belgium. To achieve this aim, the FPS plays an active and effective part in controlling the overall standards framework of the country's economic and monetary union.

The Copernicus reform was extended to the Directorate-Generals of the Ministry. From then on, the Directorate-General responsible for enforcement was called the Directorate-General Enforcement and Mediation. In particular, the 'mediation part' was added. The reason for this is unclear. The content of the mediation task was totally left open, so the Directorate-General was given a free and broad discretion to interpret it.

[1] Copernicus proposed that the sun, and not the earth, is the centre of the solar system (the heliocentric system), and that the earth and other planets turn around the sun. See on the Belgian Copernicus reform: G Joris, C De Visscher & C Montuelle, 'Federal public administration reform in Belgium: new public management under deconstruction', www.congresafsp2009.fr/sectionsthematiques/st45/st45jorisdevisschermontuelle.pdf.

[2] Other aspects of the reform were the abolition of the ministerial cabinets (and the replacement by three new bodies: the strategic council, the management committee and the strategic cell), the reinforcement of the autonomy of the directorates of the FPSs and a new appointment procedure for managers.

[3] An overview can be found on www.belgium.be/en/about_belgium/government/federal_authorities/federal_and_planning_public_services/.

[4] Small, and Medium Enterprises.

[5] http://economie.fgov.be/en/.

From the beginning, one thing was clear: besides ethical objections, the Directorate-General did not have the financial resources and infrastructure to intervene or mediate in individual (consumer) cases. In the beginning of the new century, markets were liberalized (eg the energy and telecommunication market). This gave cause for a lot of consumer complaints. The first thing the Directorate-General did, under the mediation umbrella, was sectorial mediation. They invited the market players (business and consumer associations) and tried to solve complaints on a sectorial basis.

Because the Directorate-General is convinced of the fact that creating a favourable environment for consumer A(O)DR leads to a better functioning of the goods and services market,[6] it decided, still under the mediation umbrella, to promote A(O)DR. This led to the Belmed project.

Creation of Belmed

Belmed was created in three phases. First of all, a feasibility study was ordered on the introduction of an online mediation tool. The study was carried out in 2005–2006 by the Research Center on IT & Law of the University of Namur and the Brussels Management School.[7] The research explored the legal, economical and technical (IT) possibilities of online mediation. One of the conclusions was to establish a private – public partnership to create an ODR tool.

In a second phase, and on the basis of this study, a stakeholder consultation was organized with business associations, consumer associations, ombuds services, etc. The enthusiasm was great, except for the financial aspect. None of the stakeholders wanted to support the project financially.

In a third and final phase, a European tender was launched at the end of 2009 to develop the software. Eight companies were interested, including IBM. In January 2010, the tender was assigned to IRIS Solutions & Experts, an IT company from Louvain-la-Neuve.

Belmed, which is an abbreviation for *Bel*gian *Med*iation,[8] was presented in April 2011. It is a digital portal (platform) on ADR and ODR, which it wants to promote and make more accessible. Belmed consists of two pillars: on the one hand offering information on ADR, and on the other hand providing ODR for consumers and enterprises.

Belmed only applies to consumer disputes (non-commercial disputes are excluded) and disputes between a consumer residing in one of the 27 EU member states, and an enterprise that is registered in the Belgian Register for Companies, or *vice versa* (disputes between consumers and disputes between enterprises are excluded).

The website of Belmed is www.belmed.fgov.be, and is available in Dutch, French, German and English:

[6] At the launch of Belmed, the Belgian Economy Minister underlined that Belmed is a facilitating instrument for economic life, and not a control instrument.

[7] C Lazaro, J Gérard & Y Poullet (CRID) & I Choquet & A Ejzyn (ICHEC), 'Etude relative au marché et à la faisabilité quant à la mise en oeuvre d'un système alternatif de résolution en ligne des litiges (SPF Economie)', April 2006, 270 p. (the study can be consulted (in French) on www.crid.be/pdf/public/5593.pdf).

[8] The name 'Belmed' is protected in the Benelux, France, Germany, Italy, and Spain.

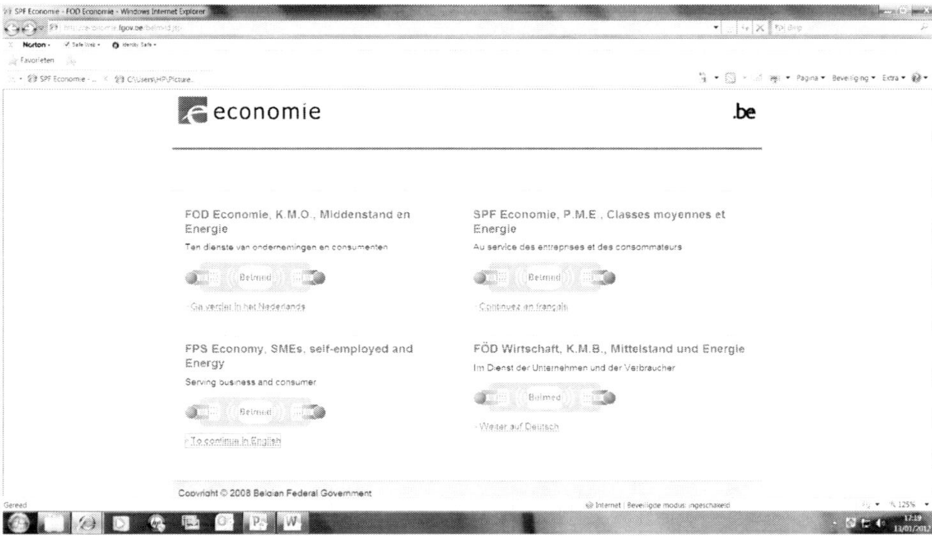

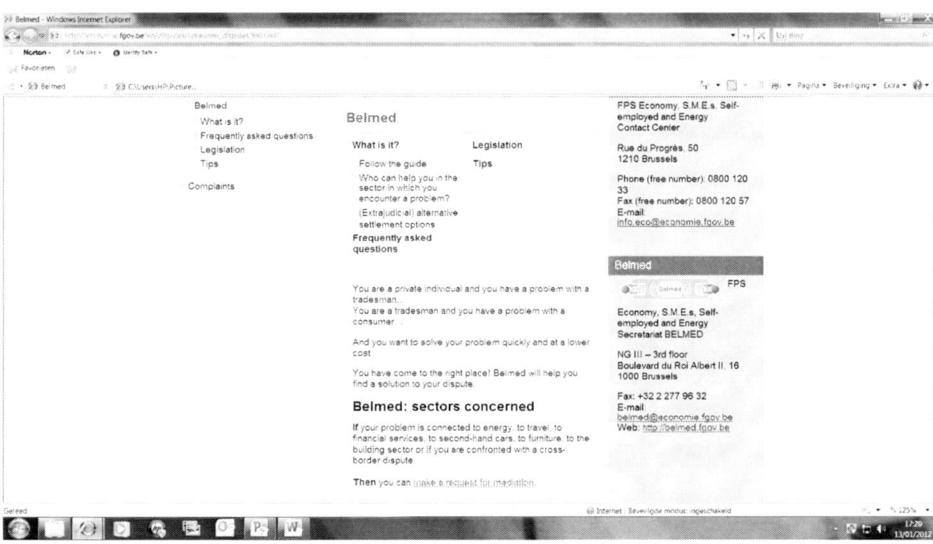

Information

On the one hand, the information part contains a guide on how to settle a dispute in an amicable way.[9] It not only explains what a formal notice,[10] a consumer dispute,[11] a third

[9] http://economie.fgov.be/en/disputes/consumer_disputes/Belmed/what/guide/.

[10] 'It is an official letter inviting the person it is addressed to (the debtor) to carry out within a fixed deadline an obligation that is his responsibility (solving a problem, paying a sum, respecting a contractual obligation, etc). This should preferably be sent by recorded delivery with an acknowledgement receipt, which makes it possible to prove that the formal notice has reached the person it was addressed to.'

party,[12] and alternative dispute resolution[13] are, but also offers concrete examples of eg a formal notice:

> Place and date
> Name and address of the sender
> Name and address of the addressee
>
> Dear Sir or Madam,
>
> Re: purchase of …… (description) – invoice/order form reference – … (date)
>
> I have bought the above-mentioned … from you on … (date).
> The contract (or order form) mentions a precise deadline (or date) for the delivery: .... This deadline (or date) is now over.
> As I still have not heard from you, I enjoin and ask you to take all the necessary measures to proceed to the delivery during the next … days.
> Yours faithfully,
>
> Signature

Other examples of letters can be found under 'Tips':[14] eg a general purpose registered letter, a registered letter dealing with a product breaking down, and a registered letter to terminate a contract.

On the other hand, the information part offers a convenient outline of all existing ADR tools in Belgium.[15] It gives an overview of all Belgian arbitration,[16] conciliation,[17] mediation,[18] and ombudsmen agencies.[19] All this information is also offered per sector[20] (consumer goods, general consumer services, financial services, postal services and electronic communications, transport services, leisure services, energy and water, health, education, and cross-border disputes) and subsector.[21] The information outline of each

[11] 'It is a problem that appears during a commercial transaction between a consumer and a tradesman. This is the type of disputes that Belmed handles, with the exception of disputes between private individuals or between consumers. Scams, fraud or disputes dealing with fiscal or social law are not concerned either.'

[12] 'The 'third party' is a person or authority entitled to lead an alternative dispute resolution process. Depending on his degree of involvement in the search for a solution, the third party leads: a mediation procedure, (…), a conciliation procedure, (…), an arbitration procedure, (…) a mediation procedure, (…). To carry out this mission, the 'third party' must respect several rules: independence (he has no interest in the parties' problem), impartiality and neutrality, confidentiality (he cannot reveal the content of the exchanges between the parties), and transparency (the parties are informed of the evolution of the process). Belmed collaborates with authorities that respect these rules and are notified to the European Commission or to the mediators approved by the FPS Justice.'

[13] 'Alternative' means that the search for a solution takes places out of court (one also talks about 'extrajudicial' resolution). Compared to a court action, this method has many advantages: it is fast; it is inexpensive (some authorities do not charge anything, and the fees for the intervention of an approved mediator are usually divided in equal parts); it is confidential (while court debates are public), and it maintains a good relationship between the parties (in case of agreement, there are two winners instead of a winner and a loser).'

[14] http://economie.fgov.be/en/disputes/consumer_disputes/Belmed/tips/.

[15] http://economie.fgov.be/en/disputes/consumer_disputes/Belmed/what/alternative_settlement_options. Another (more limited) overview can be found on the website of the European Judicial Network in civil and commercial matters (http://ec.europa.eu/civiljustice/adr/adr_bel_en.htm).

[16] Real Estate Conciliation, Arbitration and Mediation Board, Mediation and Arbitration Office, Arbitration Commission for Consumers and Textile Carers, Furniture Disputes Commission, and Travel Disputes Commission.

[17] Real Estate Conciliation, Arbitration and Mediation Board, Justices of the Peace, Second-hand Vehicle Reconciliation Commission, Travel Dispute Commission, and Construction Reconciliation Commission.

[18] Real Estate Conciliation, Arbitration and Mediation Board, Mediation and Arbitration Office, Federal mediation service 'Patient Rights', Mediation Service Banks – Credits – Investments, and an approved mediator

[19] Ombudsman Service for the Postal Sector, Insurance Ombudsman, The Mediator for rail passengers, Ombudsman Service for Energy, and Telecom Mediation Service.

[20] http://economie.fgov.be/en/disputes/consumer_disputes/Belmed/what/help/.

[21] eg the sector 'consumer goods' contains the following subsectors: food, clothing and footwear, furnishing, household appliances, audio and video equipment, new cars, second-hand cars, etc. The sector 'transport services'

agency is similar. At a single glance, all relevant information can be consulted: the address, the website, for which problems the agency is competent, the prerequisites for access, how the process works, a complaint form, the rules, and the costs.[22]

The information part finally contains some frequently asked questions,[23] an overview of relevant (Belgian and European) legislation and some tips.

All the aforementioned information is explained in a plain and accessible language, thereby avoiding legalese.

Online Application

On the other hand, and this is the second pillar, Belmed offers the possibility of making an online application for arbitration, conciliation, or mediation. The idea is to create one digital portal, or access point, for the consumer and tradesman. After an application is made, the Belmed system will automatically send it to the competent agency. So, the consumer or tradesman do not have to find out, in advance, which agency is competent for their dispute.

If a consumer or tradesman wants to make an application, he/she has to click on the 'make a request for mediation' link on the introductory webpage[24] (see the screenshot *supra*).

The consumer or tradesman who visits the Belmed platform for the first time, will be faced with two 'accessibility criteria'. On the one hand, an application can only be made when one has already contacted the other party to report the problem and try to solve it. If not, the applicant will be referred to the aforementioned guide in the information part, which contains an example of a formal notice. On the other hand, an application can only be made if there is no court proceeding pending. If so, the applicant will receive (albeit limited) information on how to mediate during a court proceeding.[25]

contains the following subsectors: railways, tramways, busses, subways, airlines, taxi, water transport, and rental services. The sector 'financial services' contains the following subsectors: payment accounts, credit/loans, payment services, investments, and insurances.

[22] One example: the 'Furniture Disputes Commission':
- Address: Kasteelstraat 1A B10, 1700 Dilbeek; Phone: +32 2 478 47 58; Fax: +32 2 478 37 66; e-mail: clmeubles@gcmeubelen.be; website: http://www.navem.be (available only in French or in Dutch)
- Prerequisites for access: the store must be a member of Navem and the standard contract must have been used (in French or in Dutch); you must have tried to solve the dispute directly with the company, to no avail; the damage must have taken place a month ago minimum.
- How does it work? See brochure (in French or in Dutch).
- Form. Form to download (in French or in Dutch), print and fill in or to be asked from the Commission + enclose a copy of any useful document.
- Rules. Rules defining the procedure to follow (in French or in Dutch).
- Fees. 100 euro as a guarantee if you are a member of Test-Achats, Navem or Arcopar. 150 euro if you are not a member of Test-Achats, Navem or Arcopar. If the intervention of an expert is needed, a deposit will have to be made. The losing party will have to pay for the expertise costs.

[23] http://economie.fgov.be/en/disputes/consumer_disputes/Belmed/questions/. The questions are: 'amicable dispute resolution, what does it mean?', 'if I do not have a computer, how can I contact Belmed?' (see *infra*), 'how long does a mediation procedure via Belmed take?', 'can I try mediation if I am already involved in a trial?', 'what is an approved mediator?', 'what is to authenticate a document?', 'what to do if the mediation attempt fails?'.

[24] http://economie.fgov.be/en/disputes/consumer_disputes/Belmed/.

[25] The applicant will see the text of Art 1730, §1 of the Belgian Judicial Code: 'any party can propose to the other parties, independently of any judicial or arbitral procedure, before, during or after a judicial procedure, to resort to the mediation process.'

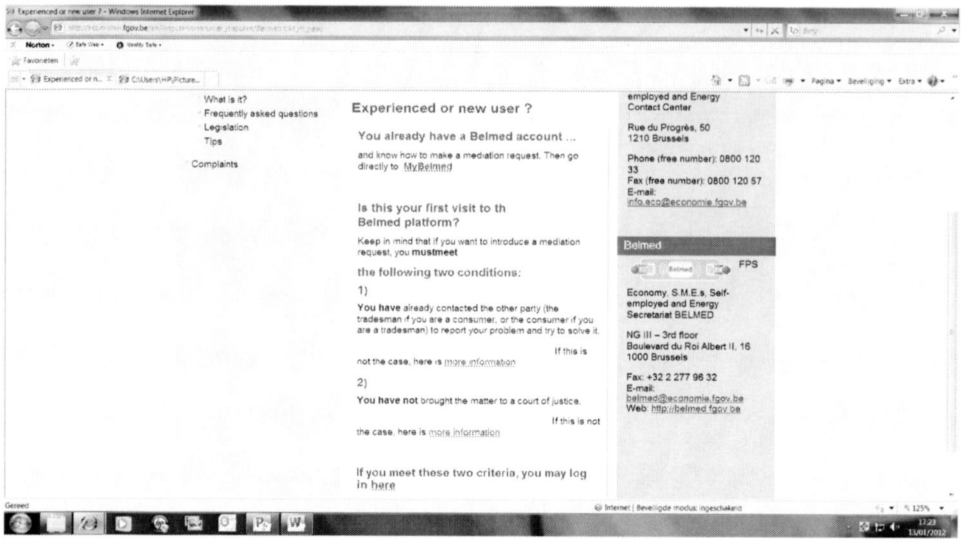

If the applicant has contacted the other party to no avail, and there is no court proceeding pending, he/she can log in and register.

There are two ways to register.[26] First of all, every Belgian resident can use his or her electronic ID card or token with the federal authentication portal to register. Secondly, every Belgian resident and every European consumer can create a personal Belmed account. All European consumers can use the system. For the moment, they can only do so when they have a dispute with a company that is registered in the Belgian Register for Companies (eg a German consumer who lives in Berlin and bought a second hand vehicle in Antwerp, or an Englishman who lives in Brussels and has a dispute with a real estate agency in Bruges).

Every private individual, or enterprise, can create a personal Belmed account. The applicant has to fill out the following information: email, password, name, first name, street, n°, zip code, city, country, phone, language (Dutch, French, German, or English), and gender. The applicant also has to agree with the terms of use.[27]

[26] https://belmed.economie.fgov.be/belmed/faces/login/login_form.jsf?belmed-user-language=EN.

[27] '1. Belmed offers a place where consumers and traders can talk freely – with the help of a mediator – to try and solve a commercial dispute amicably. 2. Each party can end this dialogue whenever they wish. 3. If mediation does not work, one or both parties concerned can try another type of amicable resolution (for instance, arbitration or conciliation with a justice of the peace), or can bring the dispute to a court of justice. 4. Belmed users promise not to use this space to denounce or criticize any person, company or institution. If such a negative behaviour or any exterior disruption renders dialogue impossible, the mediator will inform the Belmed manager and will, if necessary, suspend or even cancel the mediation procedure. 5. The Belmed platform is entirely secure and confidential, which implies only Belmed users and the mediator have access to it. Belmed also observes the loi du 8 décembre 1992 relative à la protection de la vie privée et à l'égard des traitements de données à caractère personnel (privacy act). This means that the Belmed manager as well as the mediator in charge of a mediation request promise not to divulge any data of a personal nature or pertaining to the dispute in question. Anyone can ask – in writing – a correction of his personal data from the person in charge of the processing: (…). 6. When a mediation request is made via the appropriate form, the applicant automatically receives an acknowledgement receipt that gives a reference number to the request. Within two working days, Belmed will indicate which amicable resolution options are possible. If there is a mediator in the specific sector, and if this mediator works with Belmed, the request will be automatically sent to him. He will then contact the applicant and the other party in the dispute and inform them on the process. 7. Since the Belmed platform is secure, users can only access it after registration and authentication – preferably with the electronic identity card or eID, or, failing that, a personal code (federal token for more information or to request a token, use the following link: https://www.belgium.be/usermgmt/

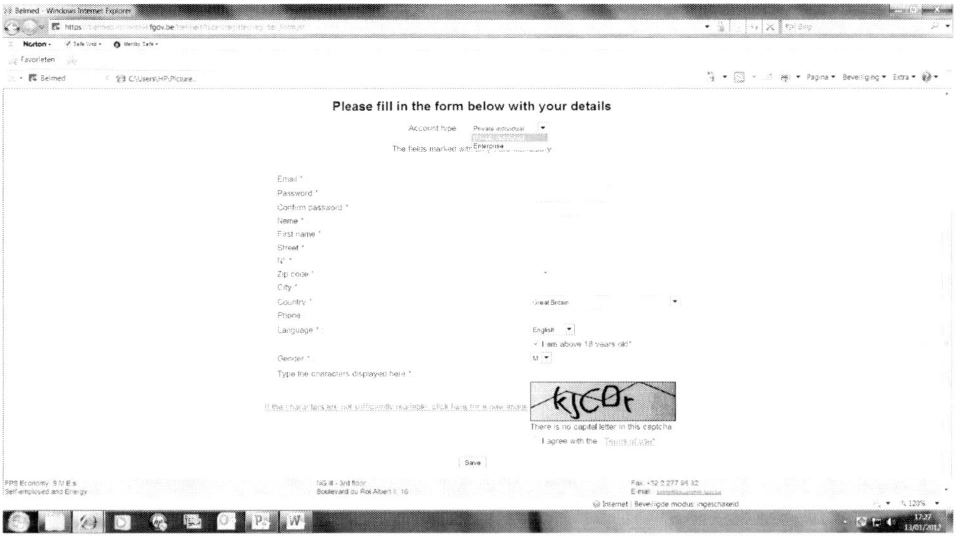

When the consumer or tradesman has registered, he/she receives a confirmation email with a link to validate the registration.

The Belmed account consists of different parts: making a new request, an overview of all (current and previous) applications ('my cases'), an email inbox ('my inbox'), a link to the account (where the applicant can edit his or her personal information) ('my account'), and a help link.

A new request can be made in three capacities: as a private individual consumer, as an intermediary for a private individual consumer (eg a son making an application for his 80-year old grandmother who has a problem with her electricity supplier, or a father making an application for his 15-year old son who has a problem with his new cell phone), and as an intermediary for a company (eg a lawyer or accountant).

eGovUserMgmtwebapp/public/RegistrationIntro.do) or a personal password. This access enables each party to talk to the mediator, to send him documents by e-mail, to correct/update personal data or to follow up the dispute online. 8. The Belmed space is available 24/7 (subject to technical or maintenance constraints). Any message sent to the mediator (secure space) will receive an answer as soon as possible, during office hours. 9. Before any mediation request, the applicant has to give his explicit consent to Belmed's terms of use. 10. As it does not play any part in the mediation process, the FPS Economy, SMEs, Self-employed and Energy cannot be held responsible for any direct or indirect harm resulting from the use of the Belmed space (08/11/2011).'

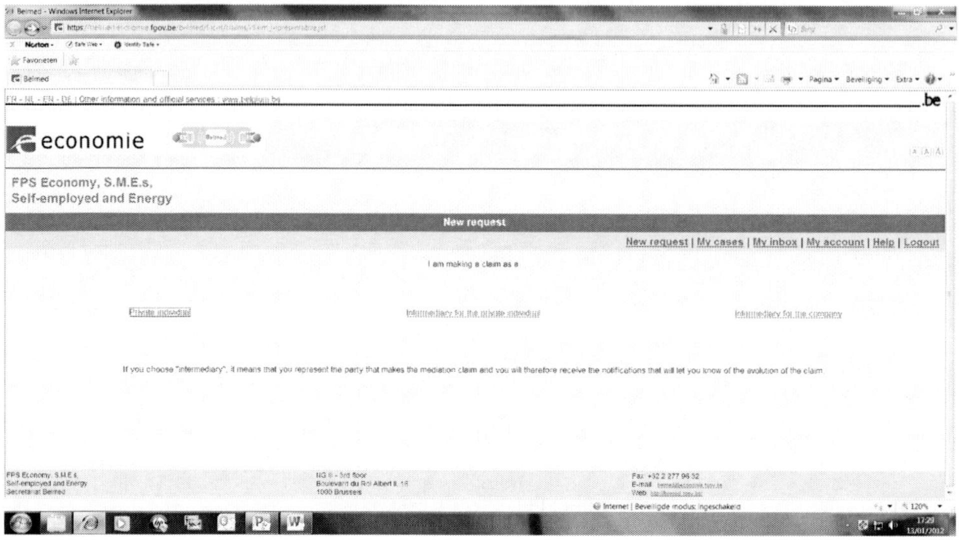

The structure of the online request is based on Commission Recommendation 2010/304/EU of 12 May 2010 on the use of a harmonised methodology for classifying and reporting consumer complaints and enquiries.[28]

Preliminarily, the applicant will be confronted, for the second time, with the two 'accessibility criteria': 'have you contacted the tradesman/consumer concerned to report your problem?' and 'did you take the matter to court?'. Then the applicant has to provide information about the provider, or supplier (there is a tool to search for the business number), or, if the application is done by a tradesman, information about the consumer who eg didn't pay an invoice. The request information itself is vital (see next screenshot), because the system will use this to send the application to the competent agency.

The applicant has to fill out:

- the sector (and subsector) where the problem has occurred: consumer goods, education, energy and water, financial services, general consumer services, health, leisure services, postal services and electronic communications, or other;
- the sales method: distance or face to face;
- the type of problem: contracts and sales, delivery of goods/provision of services, invoicing/billing and debt collection, price/tariff, privacy and data protection, provider change/switching, quality of goods and services, redress, safety (covers both goods (including food) and services), unfair commercial practices, warranty/statutory guarantee and commercial guarantees, or other issues;
- the value of the claim ('financial loss estimation'): between 500 and 1,800 euros, from 0 to 500 euros and over 1,800 euros.

Finally, there is an unlimited empty field ('description') where the applicant can provide additional information. It is also possible to add scanned documents (eg an invoice, pictures, a letter etc), that can also be send by regular mail.

[28] Official Journal L 136 of 2 June 2010.

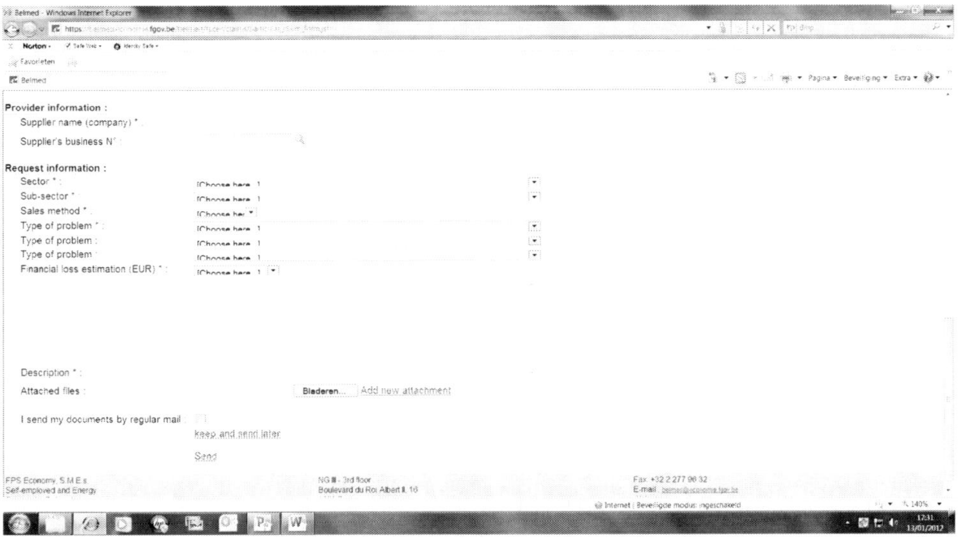

When the applicant clicks on 'send', the application will be sent, through the Belmed system, to the competent agency. From that moment on, this agency will deal with the case: they will contact the applicant, examine the admissibility of the application,[29] contact the opponent, explain the arbitration/conciliation/mediation process, etc). This entire process goes online.

Belmed only serves as an administrator, a 'serving-hatch'. The FPS doesn't see the identity of the applicant, nor does it read the application, nor does it interferes in the ADR process. This makes sense, because the FPS is the control agency of some of the arbitration/conciliation/mediation agencies that are using Belmed.

The FPS only collects statistical data (how many times the system is used, how many people clicked on the guide, how many people made an application for mediation with respect to a travel dispute, etc).[30] This data is vital for two reasons. One, if a lot of applications are made in a sector where there currently is no ADR agency (in which case the applicant receives general information on how to start an informal conciliation procedure with the Justice of the Peace), this is an objective policy argument for the FPS to persuade the sector to create such an agency.[31] Two, a lot of similar applications (eg with respect to a specific deficient product) can indicate a collective problem, which can be a trigger for a governmental (or other) body to act and seek collective redress.

At the end of 2011, six CADR agencies have signed a protocol to work with the Belmed system:

- Ombudsman Service for Energy;
- Mediation Service Banks – Credits – Investments;
- Second-hand Vehicle Reconciliation Commission;
- Travel Dispute Commission;

[29] If the agency is not competent (because the applicant has chosen the wrong sector), this will be communicated to the applicant, who will have to make a new application. In other words: the 'incompetent agency' will not send the application directly to the 'competent agency'.

[30] This statistical data will be published.

[31] This already seems to be the case with respect to consumer goods.

- European Consumer Centre;
- Furniture Disputes Commission.

In the near future, the Real Estate Conciliation, Arbitration and Mediation Board, and the Belgian Direct Marketing Association will join the Belmed system.

All Belmed partners must comply with the minimum guarantees of the two EU Recommendations of 1998 and 2001 to promote consumer ADR: Commission Recommendation 98/257/EC of 30 March 1998 on the principles applicable to the bodies responsible for out-of-court settlement of consumer disputes[32] (independence, transparency, adversarial principle, effectiveness, legality, liberty, and representation) and Commission Recommendation 2001/310/EC of 4 April 2001 on the principles for out-of-court bodies involved in the consensual resolution of consumer disputes[33] (impartiality, transparency, effectiveness, and fairness).

In the long run, the FPS wants to have agreements with *all* CADR agencies. If two or more agencies are competent in one sector, the consumer will be able to choose based on specific parameters (eg cost and speed). In other words, competition between the agencies will be tolerated.

Attention is also paid to consumers who do not have computer access.[34] A collaboration is established with non-profit organizations that help poor and socially excluded people, and with Public Computer Spaces (eg libraries and schools). In those Public Computer Spaces, and with the help of those organizations, consumers who don't have a computer, or don't have computer skills, also can make an application.

Finally, the Belmed site contains some success stories in the energy, financial services, second-hand cars and travel sector.[35]

CADR Agencies

The five Belgian ADR agencies that currently have signed the Belmed protocol, cover a wide range of consumer disputes.

For any problem arising between a consumer and a supplier within the framework of the electricity and natural gas market, the consumer can apply to the (public) *Ombudsman Service for Energy*.[36] There are two prerequisites: the consumer must have tried to solve the dispute directly with the company, to no avail; and the dispute cannot be more than

[32] Official Journal L 115 of 17 April 1998. See also appendices of this book.

[33] Official Journal L 109 of 19 April 2001. See also appendices of this book.

[34] One of the frequently asked questions is 'If I do not have a computer, how can I contact 'Belmed'?'. The answer is: 'you can go to a public computer room (PCR) where someone will help you browse the Belmed website. Info: PPS Social Integration, anti-Poverty Policy, Social Economy and Federal Urban Policy : tel. : +32 2 508 85 85 or +32 2 508 85 86.' For the visually impaired, it is always possible to enlarge the screen.

[35] http://economie.fgov.be/en/disputes/consumer_disputes/Belmed/success_stories. One example in the second-hand cars sector: 'Description of the dispute. A merchant from the region of Mons sold a BMW 318 from 2003 to a private individual residing in the province of Walloon Brabant. The sale took place in March 2011. Two months later, the engine started to stop at random due to a failure of the crankshaft and of the flow meter. At first, the seller refused to take action. Result : conciliation agreement. After many letters, the seller has accepted to cover parts of the repair costs as a gesture of reconciliation, which the customer accepted and which solved the problem. The customer has since then resold the vehicle.'

[36] www.mediateurenergie.be.

one year old. The Ombudsman will try to reach an amicable solution with the company in question. If this doesn't work, he will give a non-binding recommendation. If the request is considered admissible, the collection process carried out by the electricity or gas company will be suspended from the moment the request was made with the mediation service and until this service gives a recommendation or until the dispute is settled amicably. In case of failure, the parties can still try arbitration or take the matter to a court. The service of the ombudsman is for free.

For any problem related to a bank service, a credit, an investment, assets management, stocks, etc., one can apply to the (private) *Mediation Service Banks – Credits – Investments.*[37] There are some prerequisites. First of all, the applicant must have tried to solve the dispute directly with the company, to no avail. Secondly, the financial institution must be a member of the Belgian Banker's Association, the Professional Union of Credit Providers, the Belgian Association of Stock Exchange Members, or the Belgian Asset Managers Association. Thirdly, disputes concerning a trade decision (rate or credit refusal) or overindebtedness, are excluded. And fourthly, the applicant must act as a private individual. A legal person (company) can only appeal to the service if it concerns a cross-border payment of €12,500 maximum within the European Union. The mediator, helped by a consumer representative, will try to solve the problem and will propose a non-binding recommendation (unless the problem concerns a basis banking service, such as the opening of an account with withdrawal and payment possibilities, in which case the decision will be binding). In case of failure, the parties can still take the matter to a court. No fees have to be paid. Legal persons calling on the Mediation Service for a dispute dealing with a cross-border payment have to pay €50.

For any problem relating to the purchase of a second-hand vehicle, the consumer can go to the (private) *Second-hand Vehicle Reconciliation Commission.*[38] There are two prerequisites: the trader must be a member of Federauto and the standard contract must have been used, and the applicant must have tried to solve the dispute directly with the company, to no avail. A conciliation expert will first try to solve the problem with the parties. If he can find an agreement, he will write down an agreement report to be signed by the parties. If this doesn't work, he will send a notice (binding for the parties but only with respect to the technical aspect of the case) to the Commission, which will then gather a college made up of representatives for car drivers (Touring and VTB-VAB) as well as for the professional sector (Federauto) to make a unanimous decision. In case of disagreement, a lawyer (third party) intervenes to take a stand as an arbiter. A fee of €50 has to be paid. If the expert's mission must be extended or expanded, the parties must pay €100 plus €0.30 per Km (expert's travel allowance) each. For other possible charges, an estimate will be sent to the parties for approval.

The (private) *Travel Dispute Commission* handles disputes opposing a traveler and a tour operator and/or a travel agency.[39] The Travel Dispute Commission is qualified to handle disputes by way of conciliation or arbitration. It is not competent if the complaint concerns physical damage, the non-inclusion of a travel insurance or of an assistance insurance, etc. There are four prerequisites. First of all, the tour operator and/or travel agency must be registered with the Belgian Register for Companies. Secondly, the general terms included in the tour operator's brochure and/or on the travel agent (or travel agency)'s order form must

[37] www.ombfin.be.

[38] www.federauto.be.

[39] www.clv-gr.be.

correspond to the general terms of the Travel Dispute Commission. Thirdly, the applicant must have tried to solve the problem amicably with the tour operator and/or travel agent. And fourthly, the application must be made within specific time limits. After the parties have signed a conciliation agreement, a conciliator will be chosen. He will actively guide the parties to find a solution but will not impose any. In case of failure, the parties can still take the matter to a court. A fee of €50 has to be paid. In case of arbitration, a college made up of professional and consumer representatives will analyze the case, and make a definitive and binding decision. A 10 per cent guarantee of the sum the applicant claims as compensation (with a minimum of €100) has to be paid.

The (private) *Furniture Disputes Commission* deals with disputes concerning furniture.[40] There are three prerequisites: the store must be a member of Navem (the National Federation of Furniture Traders) and a standard contract must have been used; the applicant must have tried to solve the dispute directly with the company, to no avail; and the damages must have taken place no more than a month ago. If the applicant is a member of Test-Achats (Belgium's largest consumer organization), or Navem, a guarantee of €100 has to be paid. If the applicant is not a member, a fee of €150 has to be paid. If the intervention of an expert is needed, a deposit will have to be made.

[40] www.navem.be.

3

France

Christopher Hodges, Iris Benöhr and Naomi Creutzfeldt-Banda

Overview

Consumer ADR in France has distinct national characteristics. The existence of *médiateurs* is well established in a number of situations, as are many of the general principles. But the system is also in a state of transition.

The first point to make is linguistic. There are many *médiateurs* in France, and much discussion about *médiation*. The term 'ombudsman' is less known, but as will appear below, the French *médiateurs* function in almost identical fashion to what would be called an ombudsman in other Member States. This chapter uses the French words, and assumes that they have the same meaning as 'ombudsman'.

France has a tradition of mediation in disputes between citizens and public services. This is to a significant extent an expression of the Constitutional principle of solidarity between citizens and the State. There is a strong system of local conciliation through a court-annexed justice conciliator, who is highly accessible to those involved in litigation. A national network of consumer dispute settlement committees (CRLCs) is authorised to be created in each of the 96 *Départements*, but only three *Départements* currently fund a local CRLC.

Médiateurs began to appear within some larger companies in France around the early 1990s. They constitute what in other countries would be considered to be the top of the internal customer complaint department, but they have adopted an additional aura of independence from the company, whilst remaining part of it. Examples were AXA France (1993), GDF SUEZ (previously 'Gaz de France', 1999), BNP Paribas, 2002 (in the wake of the adoption of the so-called *loi Murcef*, passed in 2001). Sectoral *médiateurs* also appeared, notably in the postal sector (1992),[1] insurance (FFSA, 1993), financial services (ASF, 1995), direct selling (FVD as regards their *Commission paritaire de médiation de la vente directe*, 1995), and electronic communications.[2]

The appearance of *médiateurs* lay in the objectives of major businesses, partly to be able to maintain better and closer relations with their customers (which risked fracture if customers became unhappy with products and services, even if they were of acceptable quality), partly to avoid the costs, publicity and divisiveness of court proceedings, and partly as a response to the national debate on whether to introduce class actions to resolve mass consumer issues.

[1] Involving a protocol signed by national consumers organisations.

[2] see www.mediateur-telecom.fr/home: 2003.

The current state of evolution on mediation in France has been summarised by the *Médiateur national de l'énergie*, who is the only statutory *médiateur* in relation to consumer-to-business issues:

> French mediation is seeking its identity: mediation, namely an amicable way of settling disputes, is becoming increasingly popular in France, but consumer associations, enterprises, and public bodies have widely diverging views on its working principles. The national energy *médiateur* is championing the importance of independence and transparency.[3]

The position of *médiation* has crystalised in 2011 with the adoption of a national Charter for consumer disputes, which sets out important principles. It holds that mediation should not be binding on either party, and not involve binding recommendations. It should, however, be free to consumers.

Implementation of the EU Mediation Directive in 2011 introduced a definition of mediation in French law, and some criteria of what constitutes a 'good' *médiateur*, namely that the *médiateur* must accomplish his mission with impartiality, competence and diligence.[4] It is debatable whether the omission of a requirement for independence is significant, given the number of in-house *médiateurs* in French companies.

The Institutional Landscape for Consumer Issues

Consumer affairs are overseen by the Ministry for the Economy, Industry and Employment. Consumer policy is implemented by the Directorate-General for Competition, Consumer Affairs and Fraud Repression (DGCCRF),[5] which works together with a number of independent administrative authorities[6] and specialist agencies.[7] There are seventeen consumer associations, mainly with sectoral focus: the leading national associations are *Union Fédérale des Consommateurs* (*UFC – Que Choisir*)[8] and *Confédération de la Consommation, du Logement et du Cadre de Vie* (CLCV). All of the consumer associations try to assist with consumer complaints. The principal business association is *Le Mouvement des Entreprises de France* (MEDEF).[9] Formal discussion between consumers, businesses, the public services and the authorities responsible for consumer issues take place at the

[3] National Energy Ombudsman, *Activity Report* (2010), www.energie-mediateur.fr/fileadmin/user_upload/RapportMNE_2010_UK.pdf.

[4] www.legifrance.gouv.fr/affichTexte.do?cidTexte=JORFTEXT000025179010&fastPos=1&fastReqId=1554304886&categorieLien=id&oldAction=rechTexte. The amendment to the civil procedure code is: *Livre V: La résolution amiable des différends*, in which Arts 1542 and 1543 add an ADR procedure between parties in litigation with their lawyers.

[5] For its tasks and powers see www.dgccrf.bercy.gouv.fr. When appropriate, DGCCRF works with other authorities, in particular the Ministry of Justice, the Ministry of Agriculture and Fisheries, the Ministry of Health, Youth and Sports, and the Ministry of Sustainable Development.

[6] Such as the Competition Authority, the Financial Markets Watchdog (AMF), the Electronic Communications and Postal Services Watchdog (ARCEP), the Insurance and Mutual Societies Watchdog (ACAM), the National IT and Freedoms Watchdog (CNIL), and the Energy Watchdog (CRE).

[7] Notably the French Food Safety Agency (AFSSA) and the French Agency for the Safety of Health Products (AFSSAPS).

[8] See www.quechoisir.org; *Que Choisir*. The *Institut national de la consommation* (INC; see www.conso.net) publishes a monthly magazine *60 Millions de Consommateurs*.

[9] www.medef.fr MEDEF established a Commission on mediation, and published a *Guide to Mediation* in May 2009.

National Consumer Council (CNC),[10] chaired by the Consumer Affairs Minister. As alternatives to the courts, the DGCCRF sponsored the establishment of consumer dispute settlement committees (CRLCs).

Consumer Claims and Mediation within the Court System

Since its reformation after the 1789 Revolution, the French justice system has been based on fundamental principles that include access to justice for all, independence and neutrality of the courts.[11] The principle of free access to justice finds expression in the rule that litigants do not pay the costs of provision of courts and judges, and the fees (*dépenses*) that are payable[12] are comparatively low.[13] However, the loser pays rule applies to approved *dépenses*, on a tariff basis, and some part of any lawyer's fees incurred: the amounts recovered are usually modest.[14]

France has two separate but parallel systems of courts: the administrative courts and the ordinary courts.[15] Each system has a pyramid structure, with a single court at the top and various courts at the base. Litigants displeased with a court decision on one level can seek a review before a court on the next level of the hierarchy. In each order, a single court of last instance ensures that the lower courts apply the law in the same way.

The public authorities play an important role in French national life. The administrative courts settle disputes between private persons and public authorities.[16] For instance, for a claim for damages for breach of contract to which a public authority is a party the case must be brought to an administrative court. There are 42 local courts (*tribunaux administratifs*) and eight courts of appeal (*cours administratives d'appel*), which are subject to the appellate or cassation jurisdiction of the *Conseil d'Etat*.[17]

The ordinary courts ('judicial' courts) settle disputes in a wide range of areas, including civil, commercial and consumer issues.[18] For civil and commercial matters, the ordinary courts are organized on local and regional levels.[19] If both parties are professionals, the competent court is typically the Commercial Court. When one party is not a professional, the competent courts are the Tribunals of First Instance (*Tribunal d'instance* or *Tribunal de grande instance*, depending on the amount of the claim. The *Tribunal d'instance* is appropriate for claims under or equal to €10,000 and the *Tribunal de grande instance* for claims exceeding €10,000. The local magistrate (*Juge de proximité*), a non-professional

[10] www.minefi.gouv.fr/conseilnationalconsommation.

[11] French Ministry (2007), ambafrance-us.org/IMG/pdf/Justice_ag.pdf.

[12] Code of Civil Procedure, Art 695.

[13] Y Desdevises and A-L Villedieu, 'France' in C Hodges, S Vogenauer and M Tulibacka (eds), *The Costs and Funding of Civil Litigation. A Comparative Perspective* (Oxford, Hart Publishing, 2010).

[14] ibid.

[15] E Hayaux du Tilly, *European Civil Justice*, second edition, volume 2 (France, Sweet & Maxwell, 2004), 141.

[16] French Ministry (2007), ambafrance-us.org/IMG/pdf/Justice_ag.pdf.

[17] E Hayaux du Tilly, *France, European Civil Justice* (2nd edn, vol 2, 2004, Sweet & Maxwell) 141. French Ministry of Justice 2007, ambafrance-us.org/IMG/pdf/Justice_ag.pdf. See www.conseil-etat.fr/media/document/plaquette_ja_english.pdf.

[18] Hayaux du Tilly, *European Civil Justice* (2004), 141. Civil procedure in France has mainly been governed by the *Nouveau Code de Procedure Civile* (NCPC) since 1975. L Cadiet, *Code de procédure civil* (Paris, LexisNexis, 2012).

[19] Hayaux du Tilly (n 15), 147.

magistrate, introduced in October 2003 to deal with minor disputes, is appropriate for sums not exceeding €4000.[20] There are some special rules: for example trial about consumer credit are dealt with specifically by the *Tribunal d'instance*, which is also in charge of rental contracts. In January 2013, *juridictions de proximité* will be abolished, so consumer affairs will be treated by a *Tribunal d'instance*, and *juges de proximité* will be attached to the *Tribunal de grande instance*.[21]

The procedure before the *Tribunal d'instance* and before the *Juridiction de proximité* is oral and there is no need for the assistance of, or representation by, a lawyer. Plaintiffs can simply introduce their claims by filing a form at the court registry (*déclaration au greffe*),[22] which is then responsible for communicating the claim to the defendant. Consequently, the parties do not have to bear high costs, apart from those necessary for every trial.

Mediation can be used for cases in court, as regulated by sections 131–1 of the Code of Civil procedure. The judge will appoint a *médiateur* who is qualified, impartial and independent. The mediation process must not exceed three months, and confidentiality is guaranteed. The *médiateur*'s remuneration is set by the judge, and is payable by the parties, who must make an initial payment at the start, except in the case of an impecunious party.

Specific solutions have been introduced to facilitate dispute resolution for small claims procedures and consumer access to justice.[23] Firstly, a 'small claims' procedure was introduced in March 1988: the *declaration au greffe* and procedure of *injunction de faire*. Theses procedures were studied in Dijon and the Creusot, and found to be useful for consumers since they do not have to pay the bailiff in order to obtain a summons.

Secondly, Act 2002-1138 of 9 September 2002[24] was adopted to make justice more accessible to citizens and capable of dealing efficiently with small claims and minor offences. According to Article L. 331-2 modified by Act 2005-47, a network of local courts can rule on disputes by individuals, provided that they are unrelated to their profession and for a value not exceeding €4,000.[25]

Thirdly, parties can also use a legal conciliator (*conciliateur de justice*), who is appointed by a court of appeal judge to facilitate settlement of disputes out of court, in particular those involving a consumer and a trader and rental contract matters. If conciliation is successful, even partially, a statement of agreement signed by the professional and the consumer and the conciliator will be drawn up. If the agreement is approved by the judge, it has the authority of a ruling.[26]

Fourthly, a magistrate of first instance will also make a prior attempt at conciliation to help both the consumer and professional who wish to avoid court proceedings to come to an agreement.[27] The procedure is free of charge (except that since October 2011 there

[20] www2.economie.gouv.fr/directions_services/dgccrf/documentation/publications/depliants/litiges_anglais.pdf.

[21] www.legifrance.gouv.fr/affichTexte.do?cidTexte=JORFTEXT000024960344&fastPos=14&fastReqId=706671112&categorieLien=id&oldAction=rechTexte.

[22] The *declaration au greffe* is only for sums not exceeding €4000.

[23] C Montfort, France—National Report' in J Stuck et al, *An Analysis and Evaluation of Alternative Means of Consumer Redress other than Redress Through Ordinary Judicial Proceedings. Final Report* (Leuven, Katholieke Universiteit Leuven, 2006) (the Leuven Study). ec.europa.eu/consumers/redress_cons/collective_redress_en.htm.

[24] Loi n° 2002-1138 du 9 septembre 2002 d'orientation et de programmation pour la justice, available at http://www.legifrance.gouv.fr/affichTexte.do?cidTexte=JORFTEXT000000775140.

[25] Code de l'organisation judiciaire, Art L. 331–2 modified by Act n° 2005-47 du 26 janvier 2005 – Art 3 JORF 27 relative aux compétences du tribunal d'instance, de la juridiction de proximité et du tribunal de grande instance (1).

[26] Direction générale de la Concurrence, de la Consommation et de la Répression des Fraudes (2006) www2.economie.gouv.fr/directions_services/dgccrf/documentation/publications/depliants/litiges_anglais.pdf.

[27] ibid.

is a revenue stamp costing €35, introduced to finance the public legal aid service), but may only be used for disputes not exceeding €10,000 or disputes expressly attributed to the magistrates' court.[28] If an agreement is reached, a report is drawn up by the judge that has the force of an order that can be executed by a bailiff. Otherwise, the parties may take legal proceedings, some of which are free of charge.[29] In practice, however, the judge often convinces the parties to go to the legal conciliator (*conciliateur de justice).*

Fifthly, according to Articles 127 – 131 of the Code of Civil Procedure the parties can choose to conciliate before the judge or any third person of their choice during legal proceedings.[30]

Finally, Article L 331-1 of the Code de la Consommation includes a special procedure for cases regarding consumers' over-indebtedness that seems to work effectively.[31] It applies as a first step of the procedure an ADR conciliation scheme that, if it is not complied with, leads to a judicial scheme. To begin with, the debtor must make a request before a specialised conciliation commission (*Commission de surendettement des particuliers).*[32] The commission can then suggest to the creditors to suspend or stop the judicial actions against the debtor to conciliate an agreement between the parties by the proposal of a plan.[33] If the commission's recommendations are not followed by the creditors, the commission can issue non-compulsory awards.[34] After this, a single judge can start a hearing if the parties do not comply with these awards.[35]

Consumer Complaint Boards

A network of Consumer Complaints Boards (*Commissions de Règlement des Litiges de Consommation*: CRLC)[36] is approved across the country to facilitate consumer complaints arising from the sale of goods or the provision of services by businesses to natural persons for their private use. However, because of a lack of finance, only three *départements* currently have CRLCs.

The CRLC aims to resolve complaints arising from the sale of goods or the provision of services by businesses to natural persons for their private use within two months of a complaint being filed. The service is free, flexible and easily accessible. The CRLC looks at complaints not falling explicitly within the remit of any other specialised conciliation body. A CRLC may be established within each consumer committee at *département* level,[37] and consists of:

- The office of chairman of a CRLC that may be assumed by any person whose expertise in the legal and/or economic field and experience qualifies them for such a function. No functions may be assumed by any person acting on behalf of an organisation for the protection of consumers' interests or anyone active in the business, crafts or industrial sector.

[28] ibid.
[29] ibid.
[30] See also the Leuven Study, *An Analysis and Evaluation of Alternative Means of Consumer Redress* (2006).
[31] See the Leuven Study (n 23).
[32] ibid.
[33] Code de la Consommation, Art L 331–6.
[34] See the Leuven Study (n 23).
[35] ibid.
[36] Pursuant to the Decree of 20 December 1994; see www.conso.net.
[37] France is organised into 96 *Départements*, plus 5 overseas *Départements*.

- In each *département*, the chairman is appointed by the 'prefect' (*préfet*) for a renewable term of two years, subject to prior approval by the two assessors on the board.

The competent CRLC is that located in the *département* where the consumer is resident. The positions of regular and deputy assessors on a CRLC may be occupied by any persons whose experience and expertise in the fields of economics and/or consumer law qualifies them for such a function. The *préfet* of the *département* is to appoint two regular assessors and between two and six deputy assessors—with an equal number representing consumers and businesses respectively—for a period of three years.

Process

Complaints are submitted to the chairman of the CRLC. The secretariat registers these and notifies the parties which rapporteur is in charge of the case. For each complaint received, the chairman appoints a rapporteur, whose task is to try to bring about an amicable settlement between the parties within a period of two months. Before a rapporteur is appointed, the chairman must ensure that the consumer was able to contact the customer complaints department of the company concerned. The rapporteur deals with the case, acting under the authority of the chairman. The chairman may, subject to the agreement of the two regular assessors, relieve a rapporteur of his duties if there are serious and justifiable reasons for such a step.

The rapporteur investigates the case and draws up a brief report on each case being handled, stating the nature of the complaint, the names of the parties, their arguments and proposals for a negotiated settlement of the dispute. In the course of his investigation, the rapporteur may, subject to the prior approval of the chairman, use a simplified procedure.

Where necessary, the chairman requests the assessors' opinion on the proposal for a settlement drawn up by the rapporteur. If the rapporteur uses this procedure and a proposed settlement is submitted to the parties for their signature, they must be informed that the CRLC has given its prior approval. The parties must also be informed that use of the simplified procedure will enable the CRLC to draw up a conciliation report if the rapporteur merely sends on the agreement signed by them. If the simplified procedure is not used, the rapporteur submits his report to the CRLC's secretariat and asks for it to be put on the agenda of a future meeting of the CRLC.

Meetings of the board are called by the chairman. The secretariat informs the parties at least two weeks before the date scheduled for the meeting that their case is to be heard by the board. The letter of notification sent to the parties must indicate the date, place and time of the meeting, and must invite them to attend in person if possible. The parties are also informed that they may, if they wish, nominate a person of their choice to assist them at the meeting, or appoint a duly authorised representative.

The secretariat must also provide the parties with a list of accredited consumer associations and inform them that they may use the services of these organisations if they consider that this would be useful.

The number of cases handled by the boards, and their outcomes, are not published. Only one board, the MCE of Rennes (*Département 35*), publishes an annual report, which says its mediations are successful in 80 per cent of cases.[38]

[38] Annual Report, (*Commissions de Règlement des Litiges de Consommation*, 2010), available at www.mce-info.org/upload/documentation/fichier/332fichier1.pdf.

Types of *Médiateur*

Médiateurs in France fall into the following general categories:

- Public sector ombudsmen, principally *Le Défenseur des Droits*,[39] which was created in 2011 as a merger of four previous bodies.[40] Public sector dispute resolution is not considered further here. Other examples, who deal with administrative rather than consumer disputes, are *Le Médiateur du Ministère de l'Économie, de l'Industrie et de l'Emploi* (*Médiateur* of the Ministry for the Economy, Industry and Employment)[41] and *Médiation de la ville de Paris*.
- *Médiateurs* who are embedded within companies. These often exist in leading companies, and examples are: *Médiation d'Electricité de France*, *Médiateur de Gaz de France*, *Médiateur du Groupe La Poste*, *Médiateur de la SNCF* (*Médiateur* of the French railway company), *Médiateur de la RATP* (*Médiateur* of the Paris public transport company), *Médiateur des aéroports de Paris* (*Médiateur* of the Paris airport company).
- *Médiateurs* covering particular sectors. These are relatively recent in origin. Leading examples are: *Médiateurdunet.fr* (abolished since 2010), *Commission Paritaire de la Vente Directe* (Joint Committee for Direct Selling), *Médiateur de la Téléphonie* (*Médiateur* for Telecommunications), *Médiateur de la Fédération Française des Sociétés d'Assurances* (FFSA – French Federation of Insurance Companies), *Médiateur du voyage et du tourisme* (travel and tourism), and others in the water distribution and franchise sectors.[42] Only two are created by statute: MINEFI (Ministry of Economy, Finance and Industry[43]) and Energy.

Many different types of mediation exist, and particular approaches are promoted by bodies such as the National Association of Mediators (ANM). The extent to which mediation has spread in France over the past fifteen years can be seen from the list of organisations involved in mediation shown in Figure 3.1 with their dates of creation.

Figure 3.1: List of French mediation organisations

Institut National d'Aide aux Victimes et de Médiation (INAVEM),[44] 1986
Centre National de la Médiation (CNM),[45] 1988
Association Nationale des Médiateurs (ANM),[46] 1997
Association des Médiateurs Européens (AME),[47] 1999
Conseil National Consultatif de la Médiation Familiale (CNCMF),[48] 2001
Fédération Nationale des Centres de Médiation (FNCM),[49] 2001

[39] defenseurdesdroits.fr.

[40] The *Médiateur de la République*, created in 1973, the *Defenseur des enfants*, the High Authority against Discriminations and for Equality (HALDE), and the Deontology of the Security National Commission (CNDS).

[41] www.minefi.gouv.fr.

[42] For an overwiew see www.conso.net/page/bases.5_vos_droits.4_dossiers_juridiques.1_les_mediateurs.

[43] www.economie.gouv.fr/index.php.

[44] www.inavem.org.

[45] Association founded by Jean-François Six, editor of the *Cahiers de la Médiation*, and chaired by him since then.

[46] mediateurs.asso.fr.

[47] www.mediateurseuropeens.org. Formerly, Ombudsman Association of the Bar of Paris

[48] www.unaf.fr/spip.php?article151. This was dissolved in 2005.

[49] cnb.avocat.fr/Mediation.

Union Nationale des Médiateurs Chambre Syndicale de la Médiation (UnaM-CSM),[50] 2001
Fédération Nationale de la Médiation Familiale (FENAMEF),[51] 2002
Groupement Européen des Magistrats pour la Médiation (section français) (GEMME),[52] 2005
Chambre Nationale des Praticiens de la Médiation (CNPM),[53] 2006
Institut Français de la Médiation,[54] 2007
Union Professionnelle Indépendante des Médiateurs (UPIM), 2007
Chambre Professionnelle de la Médiation et de la Négociation (CPMN),[55] 2007
Office National des Médiateurs (ODM), 2008
Office National de la Médiation,[56] 2008
France Médiation,[57] 2008
Institut Français de Certification des Médiateurs (IFCM),[58] 2008
Agence Européenne d'Arbitrage, de Conciliation, d'Expertise et de Médiation (AEACEM), 2009

A key development was the creation in 2002 of the *Club des médiateurs*[59] to bring together mediators' organizations (companies, government, communities) that share the same values in mediation. The Club was originally 'Club of the Public Services Ombudsmen'. It developed a charter[60] in 2004, setting out the basis of values shared by its members and their shared vision of institutional mediation.

Working groups of the CNC deliberated in 2003–2004 and 2006–2007 on mediation and ADR, with the main objective of defining criteria for good mediation practice.[61] After the 2004 discussions, various public sector ombudsmen registered with the ECC-Net. Debates about ADR continued against the background of two factors: one was the negotiation at EU level of the Mediation Directive, passed in 2008 for implementation by 2011, and the other was a national debate about collective redress, in which political statements were made that unless business supported and underpinned effective consumer ADR structures, a law would be passed that introduced a generic class action. In response, MEDEF created a Consumer Committee in 2009, whose remit included to 'ensure that consumers' trust and the satisfaction of consumers' requirements again become central issues of the debates concerning the place of enterprises in society, in particular through the development of mediation in order to resolve consumer-related disputes'.

In 2010, the Club reorganised under the Mediators Association Act 1901 to strengthen its promotion and development of institutional mediation in France, welcoming new members. The Club now comprises government, institutions and companies.[62] In 2010 it established

[50] www.unam-csm.com/index0.html. This was replaced by FCNM at the end of 2007.

[51] www.mediation-familiale.org.

[52] www.gemme.eu/fr.

[53] www.cnpm-mediation.org. Association of a dozen mediators of the Loire *Département*.

[54] www.institut-français-mediation.com

[55] www.cpmn.info/wp. Substituted by UNAM-CSM, National Union of Mediators—Union Chamber of Mediation.

[56] www.formation-de-mediateur.fr.

[57] www.francemediation.fr.

[58] www.institut-francais-mediation.fr. The Association declared its closure at the end of 2008, and it occurred in June 2009.

[59] *Le Club des Médiateurs de Services Public* www.clubdesmediateurs.fr. In 2011 the President, was Emmanuel Constans, Ombudsman of the Ministry of Economy and Budget, and Vice-President was Jocelyne Canetti, Ombudsman of EDF. Not all ombudsmen have been invited to join.

[60] www.clubdesmediateurs.fr/la-charte.

[61] ec.europa.eu/consumers/empowerment/docs/FR_web_country_profile.pdf.

[62] The members as at January 2012 are AMF, *Caisse des Consignations*, EDF, the French Federation of Insurance, France 2, France3, France Television, GDF-Suez, La Poste, the Ministry of Economy, Finance and Industry, Ministry of Education, the Ombudsman, *Mutuelle Sociale Agricole*, RATP, SNCF, *Ville de Paris*.

a training module for employees of mediation services of its members, to understand the cultural and legal aspects of the activity of mediation, to master the basic principles that govern it, to identify the key steps its history, to identify the different types of mediation, and to understand the steps and methodology of investigation of a case.[63]

The *Commission de la Médiation de la consommation* (Commission of Consumer Mediation (CMC) was established on October 20, 2010,[64] to be 'responsible for issuing opinions and proposing measures of all kinds to assess, improve and disseminate best practices of mediation for non-court settlement in consumption'. It will audit the use of mediation devices and set ethical rules. It was charged with developing a charter of good mediation practice, which was published in 2011 (a translation can be found at the end of the chapter).[65]

The charter was influenced by a number of factors. Firstly, strong reliance on the principle that mediation should be free of charge to the consumer was influenced by the fact that access to the court is relatively cheap in France, and that it was wished to attract consumers into an ADR pathway. Secondly, the approach was influenced by the existence of many in-house company *médiateurs* and relatively few sectoral ones, in contrast to some other countries. Thirdly, the principle of access to the courts was upheld in the rule that mediation should be voluntary—for both consumer and company. It is rare to find in France a situation in which companies agree in advance to accept the recommendations of *médiateurs*. These considerations can be illustrated by the cultural approach to mediation included in statements by business bodies:

> Mediation is both an approach to social problems and a resolution method.[66]
>
> [Médiateurs] share a vision of citizens service, customers and users that emphasizes listening, dialogue and resolution through amicable settlement of disputes. They are widely known to their institutions and their public due to their transparency, the values that underpin their work, their role of being preventative guarantees impartiality and efficacy attached to their status and procedures they respect.[67]
>
> It is important to recall that mediation is a dispute settlement mode that relies on the parties' resolve and that cannot exist in the absence of such resolve.[68]

As recalled in paragraph (13) of the Recitals of Directive No 2008/52/EC of 21 May 2008 on certain aspects of mediation in civil and commercial matters: mediation 'should be a voluntary process in the sense that the parties are themselves in charge of the process and may organise it as they wish and terminate it at any time'.[69] An enterprise's decision to rely on mediation forms part of an approach for the continuous improvement of the complaint treatment process.

Mediation must be used after all remedies internal to the enterprise ('consumer unit' or 'client unit') have been exhausted. Most issues between sellers/suppliers and consumers are

[63] There is an associated website dedicated to the promotion of institutional mediation: www.clubdesmediateurs.fr.

[64] Under the Act of 1 July 2010 on reform of consumer credit. The CMC is chaired by Elyane Zarin, President of OR.GE.CO (General Organization of Consumers); the appointment of a senior consumer figure was seen as a strong political signal.

[65] www.mediation-conso.fr/doc/French_Charter_of_consumer_mediation.pdf.

[66] GDF SUEZ Mediator's report 2010, 15, available at: www.gdfsuez.com/fr/accueil/mediateur/le-mediateur-de-gdf-suez.

[67] ibid, 14.

[68] *MEDEF's response to the DG SANCO consultation concerning alternative dispute resolution means* (MEDEF, 2011), 2, available at http://ec.europa.eu/consumers/redress_cons/adr_responses/b_MEDEF_en.pdf.

[69] ibid.

settled at this stage. The large majority of disputes between consumers and sellers/suppliers originate from difficulties related to contracts, and not any unlawful conduct. A consumer survey in 2011[70] found that where consumers had had disputes with traders in the past year, the most related to telephony (24 per cent), general consumer trading (22 per cent) and information (12 per cent), with many other sectors at lower levels, including transport (5 per cent), banking and insurance (each 3 per cent) and energy (2 per cent). Almost all complaints made had been directed to the consumer service of the supplier (56 per cent) or the seller (38 per cent). Seventy-six per cent of consumers surveyed said they had previously heard of mediation, although only 50 per cent said they knew how to find a *médiateur*.

Banking

Legal Requirement for Banking *Médiateurs*

Banking mediation emerged in France in the late twentieth century in order to improve the relationship between banks and their clients. In 2001 a law dealing with urgent economic and financial measures (*Loi portant mesures urgentes à caractère économique*—Loi MURCEF),[71] established the basis for a mediation scheme for disputes rising between banks and consumers. It was intended to coordinate the several mediation offices that existed formerly in this area. Since the MURCEF law, banks must provide a mediation scheme and inform their customers about this alternative redress mechanism.[72] The *médiateur*'s range of tasks and how a case should be submitted to the *médiateur* are defined by the individual banks.[73] The *médiateurs* are selected on the basis of their expertise and impartiality and the procedure is free of charge.[74]

The *médiateur* has a relatively short period (approximately two months) to issue his recommendation.[75] However, if the disagreement persists at the end of mediation, the client or the banking institution remain free to initiate a legal proceeding.[76]

The means of contacting the *médiateur* and his contact details appear on the account statements sent to the customers, as well as on the account agreements. The recourse to a banking *médiateur* is voluntary and cannot exclude the possibility of a judicial proceeding.

The banks have the choice of establishing an in-house mediation service or using the mediation service provided by specific financial services organisations. In general, the larger banks have integrated their own mediation services.

[70] By *Crédoc*, a research centre for the study and observation of living conditions; www.credoc.fr.

[71] www.legifrance.gouv.fr/affichCode.do?idArticle=LEGIARTI000020874250&idSectionTA=LEGISCTA000020874252&cidTexte=LEGITEXT000006072026&dateTexte=20120209) and www.legifrance.gouv.fr/affichCode.do?idArticle=LEGIARTI000021979552&idSectionTA=LEGISCTA000021979561&cidTexte=LEGITEXT000006072026&dateTexte=20120209. For the annual report see www.banque-france.fr/la-banque-de-france/missions/protection-du-consommateur/infobanque-votre-banque-et-vous/mediation-bancaire.html.

[72] Monetary and Financial Code, Art L 312-1-3, now Art L. 315-1. In order to encourage good mediation, a *comité de la médiation bancaire* was created by Murcef Law: this is why the *Commission de la médiation de la consommation* does not deal with bank matters.

[73] Note by the European Consumer Centre *France, Mediation and consumption: How does it work.*

[74] Monetary and Financial Code, Art L 312-1-3.

[75] ibid.

[76] ibid.

For banks that do not have their own mediator specialized organizations have made a mediation service available to them and their customers:

- *l'Autorité des Marchés Financiers*, AMF (Financial Markets Authority);[77]
- *l'Association des Sociétés Financières*, ASF (Financial Companies Association); and
- *la Fédération Bancaire Française*, FBF (French Banking Federation).

The AMF is a public institution, whereas the two latter organisations are private professional associations offering mediation services. The *médiateurs* of the ASF and the AMF are described in detail below.

The Ombudsman of the *Autorité des Marchés Financiers*

The Autorité des Marchés Financiers (AMF) is an independent public agency with legal personality and financial autonomy, responsible for regulating and overseeing financial markets in France and protecting investors.[78] It was established by the French Financial Security Act of 1 August 2003 and was formed from the merger of various financial services commissions to improve the efficiency of France's financial regulatory system and to give it greater visibility.[79] Its remit is to:

- safeguard investments in financial instruments and in all other savings and investment issues
- ensure that investors receive information
- maintain orderly financial markets

The AMF also supports financial market regulation at the EU and international level and has four kinds of responsibilities: regulation, authorisation, supervision and enforcement.

The AMF is empowered to conduct inspections and investigations and its Enforcement Committee may impose penalties or sanctions to punish breaches of the AMF General Regulation or professional obligations.

The AMF has jurisdiction over:

- *Corporate Finance activities and disclosures*: The AMF regulates corporate finance activities and disclosures by listed companies.
- *Collective investment products*: The AMF authorises the creation of open-end and closed-end funds. It verifies the information set out in the simplified prospectuses that must be provided to customers before they invest in any product.
- *Market and infrastructure*: The AMF sets the principles of organisation and operation applicable to market operators and approves the rulebooks of clearing houses.
- *Services Providers*: The AMF sets conduct of business rules and other requirements applicable to professionals authorised to provide investment services.

[77] www.amf-france.com.

[78] www.amf-france.org/affiche.asp?id=7294.

[79] *Commission des opérations de bourse* (COB), *Conseil des marchés financiers* (CMF) and *Conseil de discipline de la gestion financière* (CDGF); www.amf-france.org/affiche_page.asp?urldoc=lesmissionsamf.htm&lang=en&Id_Tab=0.

The AMF's Ombudsman Service

The AMF houses an ombudsman scheme that provides assistance to non-professional investors (consumers and non-profit associations). It aims to promote understanding of financial markets, and handles complaints about financial information, order execution, transfers of securities accounts and asset managements. As part of the AMF, the ombudsman has its own budget, to enable him to carry out mediation in a neutral and impartial manner. The ombudsman cannot receive orders concerning the individual cases handled under its responsibility.

The Ombudsman's office has a two-fold remit: answering investors' queries and arranging out-of-court settlement. In its first function, the Ombudsman's Office deals mainly with queries from private investors, citizens' associations companies on a wide range of financial services issues. These include stock market mechanisms, disclosure requirements for publicly traded companies, rules and regulations for portfolio management, transmission and reception of trade orders, and custody.[80] Investors can call the ombudsman services through a telephone helpline.[81]

In the second function, the Ombudsman's Office can help parties that are in dispute to reach an out-of-court settlement and avoid legal action. It does not act as lawyer for either party or as a judge. A charter governs this procedure, which is free of charge, confidential and elective (requiring the consent of both parties).[82]

The dispute resolution function has a statutory basis. Pursuant to Article L. 621-19 of the French Monetary and Financial Code:

> The Authority shall be authorised to receive claims relating to matters within its jurisdiction from any interested party and to deal with them appropriately. When necessary, it shall propose out-of-court settlements of the disputes brought to its attention, via conciliation or mediation.
> Submitting a dispute to the Autorité des marchés financiers (AMF) to find an out-of-court settlement shall entail suspension of the statute of limitations for civil and administrative proceedings. The statute shall apply again once the AMF declares the mediation finished. The AMF shall cooperate with foreign authorities for out-of-court settlement of crossborder disputes.
> The Authority may propose amendments to laws and regulations dealing with disclosures to holders of financial instruments and the public, markets in financial instruments and the status of investment services providers.

The Ombudsman may be contacted by any person or legal entity involved in a dispute of an individual nature falling within AMF jurisdiction described above. The Ombudsman intervenes in disputes relating to investor information, order execution (lead-time, order content), portfolio management and custody. The Ombudsman's Office does not have jurisdiction in the field of taxation, life insurance or banking (interest charges, loans, overdrafts, etc). It also does not advise on individual investment opportunities and cannot intervene if an AMF audit or enquiry is underway or if legal proceedings have already been initiated.[83]

Before seeking assistance from the Ombudsman's Office, the investor must have contacted the financial intermediary or the company in which they are a shareholder. A claim may only be brought to the attention of the Ombudsman when a prior action has been taken against the investment services provider or issuer, and the complaint has remained unanswered or

[80] www.amf-france.org/affiche_page.asp?urldoc=mediateur.htm&lang=en&Id_Tab=0.
[81] ibid, Phone number +33 (0)1 5345-6464.
[82] ibid.
[83] ibid.

has been rejected either totally or partially. It is also a condition that no legal action or AMF investigation is in progress regarding the same facts.

The procedure

The AMF mediation procedure is free of charge. The Ombudsman may only undertake the mediation procedure with the consent of both parties. In principle, mediation lasts three months from the time when all useful evidence has been supplied to the Ombudsman by the parties.

The mediation procedure is an adversarial procedure. It is carried out in writing, but the Ombudsman may decide to hear the parties separately or together. Enquiries are sent through the post or filed using the three online forms (for enquiries, mediation requests and reports). Each party presents its position in the dispute and produces legible copies of supporting documents in their possession (eg account agreements, discretionary mandates, subscription forms, trade confirmations, account statements, management reports, letters, emails, screen shots, etc). Both parties are heard and a written record is kept of the procedure. The Ombudsman can ask the parties to meet and will seek to find a solution acceptable to both parties. The parties will then indicate whether they agree to it. If they do, the Ombudsman will see that it is put into effect. The parties can modify the solution or decide at any time to terminate the procedure.[84] The Ombudsman and the parties are bound by the strictest obligations of confidentiality.

The mediation procedure ends either by an out-of-court settlement, or by the statement of a persistent disagreement, the withdrawal of one of the parties, or by the start of legal action relating to the dispute. Whatever the outcome of the procedure, the Ombudsman informs the parties, in writing, of the end of his intervention.

Both parties retain the right to bring the dispute in front of the courts at any time. The submission of the dispute to the courts brings the intervention of the Ombudsman to an end.

The AMF cooperates with foreign stockmarket regulators in the resolution of cross-border disputes[85] and the ombudsman is member of the EU FIN-NET.

Statistics

According to AMF's Annual Report (2010), of the 1,397 queries received in 2010, 1,001 were inquiries (72 per cent) and 396 were mediation requests (28 per cent),[86] having fallen from 2009 (2,029, 1,249 and 735 respectively). Of these contacts, 686 (or 49 per cent) were made using online forms, showing a rising use of this method for submitting queries (35 per cent in 2009).[87]

The telephone helpline fielded 829 calls in 2010. Most queries were submitted by retail investors (individuals acting alone: 90 per cent), with 7 per cent from authorities and 3 per cent collectively from lawyers, associations and internet service providers. Further data is given the Tables 3.2 and 3.3.

Requests from other authorities or administrations rose from 5 per cent to 7 per cent, while requests from other sources remained constant.

[84] ibid.
[85] ibid.
[86] Annual Report of the AMF (2010).
[87] ibid, 4.

Table 3.1: Inquiries and mediations 2010[88]

Number of inquiries handled	1,041
Percentage of inquiries closed within one month of receipt	86%
Number of mediation requests	520
Percentage of cases closed within 6 months	74%
Percentage of cases considered on their merits in which agreements were reached	40%

Table 3.2: Inquiries and mediation requests by subject area, 2010[89]

	Inquiries and mediation requests	Mediation requests only
Issuers, corporate finance, general market matters, financial instruments	46%	–
Collective investment schemes, discretionary management	29%	59%
Order reception and transmission	14%	13%
Direct marketing, advice on asset management and financial investment	6%	–
Miscellaneous	–	15%
Account management – custody	–	13%

The *Médiateur* of the ASF

The French Association of Specialised Finance Companies (ASF)[90] established a mediation scheme in 1995, to which members of the ASF may voluntarily subscribe.[91] The ASF mediator provides out-of-court dispute resolution solutions for consumers and their brokers or financial service providers in the following areas:

- financial conventions concluded by individuals for their personal needs;
- the management of a deposit account for individuals;
- information precedent to the housing loan contract.

The mediation service is free of charge for consumers,[92] and is financed by the financial services providers that have subscribed to the scheme. According to Article 2 of ASF's mediation regulation the *médiateur* has the right to receive adequate funding by ASF, which is fully covered by the membership fees of the association. No specific standing fees or per case fees are published.

The *médiateur* must be independent. Pursuant to Article 2 of the mediation regulation the *médiateur* is chosen according to his skills and impartiality by the Board of the ASF and representatives of consumer organizations. He is appointed for a period of two years and is bound by confidentiality.[93] The ASF provides the *médiateur* with sufficient financial resources to work effectively and independently (Article 2 (2)).

[88] ibid, 5.

[89] ibid, 8.

[90] ASF is the professional organisation that represents institutions specialised in finance (consumer credit, house financing, leasing, factoring, guarantees and investment services). It was created under the regulatory framework of the banking act of 24 January 1984.

[91] www.asf-france.com/mediation.

[92] www.asf-france.com/Accueil/ASF-English-presentation.pdf.

[93] ibid.

A case may be submitted to the mediator only if the consumer first tried to contact the trader unsuccessfully. The mediator can then propose recommendations in order to try to resolve the dispute between the financial service provider and its costumer.

The mediator of the ASF organizes an annual meeting with financial institutions in order to discuss possible failures encountered in certain mediation cases. In the annual report the mediator then proposes specific measure in order to improve customer services and information.[94] The ASF ombudsman is a member of the EU FIN-NET.

In 2010 the *médiateur* received 1,656 cases, of which he admitted 1,076 cases (83 per cent) that were finalized by the end of the year. Of these, 84 concerned the provision of information or the analysis of specific laws or contracts without the resolution of a dispute. The *médiateur* decided 617 of the cases in favour of the debtor (62 per cent), and 375 (38 per cent) against the claimants. Of those not admitted, 123 (7.5 per cent) did not relate to ASF and 156 (9.5 per cent) related to another *médiateur*.[95] The breakdown of types of case are shown in Table 3.3.

Table 3.3: Types of issues raised with ASF 2007–2010 (Annual Report ASF (2010))

	2007 %	**2008 %**	**2009 %**	**2010 %**	**2010 number**
Entries FICP	13	10	10	13	158
Debt restructuring		11	16	13	157
Prepayments	9	9	8	12	139
Insurance problems	17	13	12	10	123
Litigation cases	6	7	5	7	81
Plans of over-indebtedness (establishment, management)	2	4	6	6	74
Accounts (objections or requests for explanation)	10	8	6	6	71
Workings of a revolving credit	3	3	3	4	49
Claims against solidarity among co-borrowers	3	2	2	3	38
Fraudulent use of cards	4	3	3	2	30
Established or operating levy	2	2	2	2	30
Litigation costs (delivery, operation)	3	2	2	2	29
Challenges to taking out loans	3	3	3	2	26
Requests for documents	3	2	2	2	24
Adjustable-rate real estate	6	11	4	1	13
Implementation of the loan		1	1	1	13
Miscellaneous	13	9	13	14	159
Total numbers of issues	**744**	**1,123**	**1,402**	**100%**	**1,214**

Insurance

In France, several *médiateurs* exist to deal with insurance complaints without being notified to the European Commission.[96] The *médiateur* of the French Federation of Insurance Companies is the only notified scheme and will be described below.

[94] www.asf-france.com/mediation.

[95] See the Annual Report of the ASF Médiateur for the year 2010, www.asf-france.com/mediation/Pages/Page-mediateur.aspx.

[96] The *médiateur du GEMA* (www.gema.fr), *médiateur de la Chambre Syndicale des Courtiers d'Assurances* (CSCA) (www.csca.fr), *médiateur du CTIP* (www.ctip.asso.fr), *médiateur de la Fédérale Mutualiste* (www.mutualite.fr); for more information regarding these schemes see: www.acam-france.fr/mediateurs.

The *Médiateur* of the French Federation of Insurance Companies

The *médiateur* of the French Federation of Insurance Companies (*Fédération Française des Sociétés d'Assurance)* (FFSA) is able to rule on disputes involving members that have signed its Mediation Charter (see Figure 3.2). The FFSA is the leading trade organisation in the insurance sector and represents 90 per cent of the insurance market.[97] The mediation scheme of the FFSA was established by members in 1993 and is private and voluntary. The Charter is intended to provide a framework whereby policyholders and third parties can benefit from mediation for the settlement of their disputes, without resorting to litigation.[98] Under the Charter, the insurer and the insured can seek advice from the in-house *médiateur* or refer the matter to the FFSA-appointed *médiateur*. Six companies have established their own in-house *médiateur*.

While mediation is particularly useful for dispute resolution between consumers and insurers arbitration has traditionally remained the most frequently used mechanism to resolve disputes between insurers and reinsurers or between reinsurers. An insurance and reinsurance arbitration centre (*Centre Français d'Arbitrage de Réassurance et d'Assurance*) (CEFAREA) was established in 1995 to facilitate arbitration. Rules on the conduct and arbitration procedure were adopted, a list of arbitrators established and model arbitration clauses proposed.[99]

The FFSA *médiateur* is appointed unanimously by a board comprising the Chairman of the National Consumer Institute of Consumption (*Institut National de la Consommation*), the Chairman of the Advisory Committee of the National Insurance Council (*Commission Consultative du Conseil National des Assurances*) and the Chairman of the FFSA. Its term of office is two years (renewable). Mr Francis Frizon is the current FFSA Mediator.

Legal framework regarding insurance mediation in France

French law transposing EU Directive 2002/92/EC on insurance mediation (Insurance Mediation Directive) treats any person conducting an insurance mediation activity in exchange for remuneration as an insurance or reinsurance intermediary.[100] Insurance mediation is defined as an activity that consists of introducing, proposing or facilitating the conclusion of insurance contracts.[101]

Furthermore, insurers must specify in information documents made available to prospective policy-holders the conditions in accordance with which complaints shall be processed.[102] These documents should also inform the policy-holder about dispute resolution mechanisms within the company and provide contact details of a mediator.

The *médiateur* of the FFSA is a member of the cross-border European network FIN-NET.

[97] www.ffsa.fr.

[98] A first mediation mechanism was put in place for insurance company members in 1989 by the French Insurance Mutual Undertakings Group (*Groupement des Entreprises Mutuelles d'Assurances*) (GEMA). GEMA is the trade organisation of insurance mutuals and their subsidiaries. Apart from its representative role of 50 entities, it also carries out studies on the evolution of insurance.

[99] In 2008 CEFAREA became member of the Paris Centre for Mediation and Arbitration (*Centre de Médiation et d'Arbitrage de Paris*) (CMAP).

[100] Insurance Code, Art L. 511-1.

[101] ibid.

[102] ibid, Art L. 112-2, inserted by Law No 94–5 of 4 January 1994.

Procedure

The mediation service is free of charge and there are no limits on the amount of the complaint to the *médiateur*. A request for mediation can only be accepted after all the internal, contractual or other means of redress made available by the insurance company in question have been exhausted. No time limit applies. The FFSA *médiateur* should deliver his opinion within three months. In practice, the average time taken to handle a complaint varies according to the individual files. If mediation does not give rise to an agreement, the *médiateur* issues a non-binding written opinion and the parties remain free to bring the matter before the courts.

Article 8 of the Mediation Charter provides that the *médiateur* should take into account elements of law and equity. However, the same Article states that the *médiateur* aims at achieving an amicable solution that cannot correspond to a judicial approach.

Figure 3.2: Mediation Charter of the FFSA

①A FFSA mediator shall be appointed unanimously by a board made up of the Chairman of the Institut national de la consommation [National Consumer Institution], the Chairman of the Comité consultatif du secteur financier [Consultative Committee for the Financial Sector] and the Chairman of the Fédération française des sociétés d'assurance. The period of his appointment shall be three (3) years and shall be renewable.
② The FFSA mediator shall carry out his task completely independently.
③The mediator shall receive all of the assistance, funds and powers necessary to carry out his task. Companies shall have a maximum period of six (6) weeks to respond to requests for information or documents issued by the FFSA mediator.
④ The task of the FFSA mediator shall be to investigate disputes in the insurance sector between an insured or a third party and an insurance company. Only disputes involving private individuals shall be subject to the jurisdiction of the FFSA mediator.
⑤ A matter may be submitted to the FFSA mediator by the insured, by a third party, or with the consent of such parties, by the insurance company, after the internal dispute resolution procedures of such company have been exhausted. In such a case, the limitation period shall be interrupted. No matter may be submitted to the FFSA mediator if litigation has been instigated or is underway.
⑥ After having investigated the matter with the assistance of the parties, the FFSA mediator shall issue a motivated advice within three (3) months. The advice shall not be binding on the parties. The decision on whether or not to implement the advice of the mediator must be taken by the directors of the company and notified to the FFSA mediator.
⑦The FFSA mediator shall inform the insured or the third party that they continue to be entitled to instigate proceedings before the Courts.
⑧It shall be stipulated in any advice issued by the FFSA mediator that it has been prepared taking into account elements of law and equity but also with the aim of achieving an amicable solution which cannot correspond to a judicial approach.
⑨ An insurance company may appoint a specific mediator as long as such person is an independent party, with whom the company may not have or have had any employment connection. Such company mediator shall then be substituted for the FFSA mediator; his intervention shall comply with the same formal conditions and time periods as the FFSA mediator, as defined in paragraphs 2, 3, 4, 5, 6, 7 and 8 above. The company mediator

shall co-ordinate with the FFSA mediator and shall ensure with him the harmonisation of the opinions handed down and shall keep him informed of his activities.
(10) The FFSA mediator shall publish an annual report which shall provide an account of his activities and of the activities of the company mediators who shall for such purpose submit to him a report on their interventions.Within the Association Française de l'Assurance, the FFSA and GEMA have collaborated on rules of good conduct for companies active in the personal insurance sector. This collaboration has led to the adoption of a Code of Good Conduct. The Code may be consulted in its entirety on the website of the Association Française de l'Assurance.

Figure 3.3: Code of Good Conduct for the insurance societies who are members of the FFSA or GEMA

Within the Association Française de l'Assurance, the FFSA and GEMA have collaborated on rules of good conduct for companies active in the personal insurance sector. This collaboration has led to the adoption of a Code of Good Conduct. The Code may be consulted in its entirety on the website of the Association Française de l'Assurance.

UNDERTAKING IN RELATION TO THE PUTTING IN PLACE OF MEDIATION MECHANISMS

Approved by the General Meeting of the FFSA on 15 December 2009 and by the Executive Committee of GEMA on 11 June 2009, this undertaking was confirmed by the General Meeting of the FFSA on 21 June 2011 and by the Executive Committee of GEMA on 12 May 2011.

Mediation mechanisms were put in place for insurance company members, in 1989 at GEMA and in 1993 at the FFSA.

It should be noted that Law No 94-5 of 4 January 1994 inserted into the Insurance Code an Article L112-2, which requires insurers to specify in information documents made available to prospective policy-holders the conditions in accordance with which complaints shall be processed, and the fact that there exists within the company a body entrusted with such task which is obliged, should a dispute not be settled, to provide the complainant with the contact details of the mediator.

This undertaking seeks to set out the minimum rules applicable to mediation.

The insurance companies which are members of the FFSA or GEMA must put in place a mediation mechanism available to all of their policy-holders which satisfies the following requirements at least:

- the mediators must be independent of the insurance companies for whom they intervene andmust perform their tasks entirely independently;
- the insurance companies must endeavour to respond promptly to requests for information and documents issued by mediators in the context of the requests submitted to such mediators;
- any insured holding insurance cover in a personal capacity shall be entitled to have free access to the mediator with jurisdiction, depending on his or her insurance company. This right shall however only vest after the policy-holder has exhausted all complaint procedures within the company;

- the instigation of a mediation procedure by the policy-holder or with his or her consent shall lead to the automatic suspension of any prescription periods which may have commenced until the mediator issues an opinion. At the end of the mediation, the policy-holder shall retain all of his or her rights to instigate any judicial proceedings.

Statistics

According to the Annual Report of the FFSA (2010): in 2010, 5,316 requests for mediation were made for companies affiliated to the FFSA, and 333 to the GEMA *médiateur*, making a total for all insurance companies in France of 5,649. The number of applications was relatively constant between 1995–2000 at around 500 cases per year, then rose to around 1,300 for 2001–2005, and has risen considerable since 2006, as shown in Figure 3.4. Of the FFSA cases in 2010, as many as 45.9 per cent of applications were rejected: 33 per cent (1,759) were referred to in-house procedures, 6.6 per cent were outside the *médiateur's* jurisdiction, and 6.3 per cent were returned for insufficient information. That year, 77 per cent of applications originated from individuals, 10 per cent from other *médiateurs*, and 2.7 per cent from a consumer organisation. Of the FFSA claims, 47 per cent related to property and liability insurance, 53 per cent to insurance of the person (23.8 per cent under individual policies and 29.2 per cent collective policies).

Figure 3.4: Overview of insurance mediation applications[103] 1995–2010

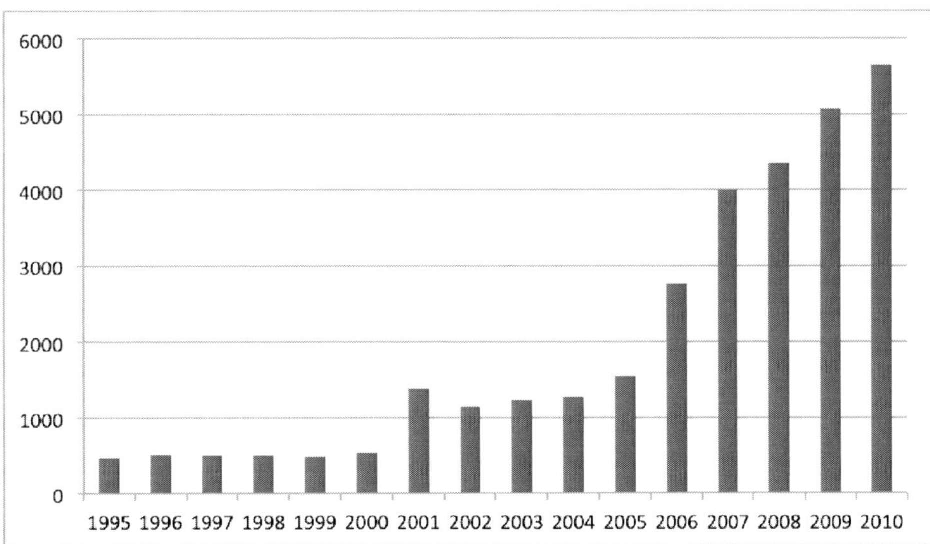

In 2010, the FFSA *médiateur* handled many cases involving small sums, often around €100 and as low as €15.[104]

[103] Annual Report of the FFSA 2010, 36.
[104] ibid, 41.

In 2010, formal recommendations were issued in 391 cases by the FFSA *médiateur* and 274 by the GEMA *médiateur*. Of the former 391, 54.7 per cent were in favour of companies, 26.9 per cent were favourable to applicants, and 18.4 per cent partly favoured applicants. The FFSA *médiateur* reported that his recommendations were not acted on by the parties in whole or in part in 2.5 per cent of cases in 2010.

Furthermore, the *médiateur* reported that companies were required to respond to his requests for information or documents within six weeks, and that almost 90 per cent of his opinions were delivered within three months.

Energy

The *Médiateur national de l'énergie*

The national energy *médiateur*[105] is the only *médiateur* in France established by statute apart from the *médiateur* of the French *Ministères de l'Economie et du Budget* (Minéfi).[106] The office is regulated by the law of 7th December 2006 on the energy market.[107] The *médiateur national* came into existence as part of an initiative to open up the energy market, proposed by the CNC in 2005 and implemented by DGCCRF, which recommended that a sectoral ombudsman should be created alongside the sectoral regulator. The new scheme was originally intended to operate from July 2007, and the new and innovative public office of *médiateur national* was created by December 2006 under the law on the energy market, but the appointment was delayed by elections in 2008, and the post was only filled in December 2008. Before the 2006 law, two companies, EDF and GDF-SUEZ, which together supply 95 per cent of the French energy market, each had their own in-house *médiateurs*, outlined below, whose existence was not affected by the introduction of the *médiateur national*. Companies are required to answer the *médiateur national*'s questions within a fixed timeframe (2 months), but may also retain their in-house *médiateurs*, and this may cause confusion.

The model for *médiateur national* was inspired by considerations of administrative justice and courts, so established strict rules on structures and procedures. The existence of fixed legal rules that govern the *médiateur*'s function have the advantage of giving clear legitimacy and a statutory framework but the disadvantage of impeding what might be regarded as a proper mediation function, as well as evolution in scope and processes. The law has been criticised as being too complex. For example, it requires the *médiateur* to write a formal and motivated recommendation to every complaint, but no precedents existed for this. The *médiateur* can only deal with 30 per cent of complaints received, and rules on admissibility had to be set up to filter the complaints. The *médiateur* finds that the rules can impede attempts to improve productivity.

[105] www.energie-mediateur.fr.

[106] *Décret n°2002-612 du 26 avril 2002 instituant un médiateur du ministère de l'économie, des finances et de l'industrie.*

[107] A further law reorganising the electricity market was published in the Official Gazette on December 7, 2010 and came into force in early 2011, known as the NOME Act. See Energy code, Art L. 122-1, available at www.legifrance.gouv.fr/affichCode.do;jsessionid=8F39C51D8791D78E5BAF40346397D755.tpdjo16v_3?idSectionTA=LEGISCTA000023985676&cidTexte=LEGITEXT000023983208&dateTexte=20120209.

The 2011 budget of the *médiateur nationale* was € 6.6 million,[108] which was partly financed out of a tax called CSPE that mainly funds social tariffs, renewable energy subsidies and equalization of regulated prices in islands.

Procedure

The *médiateur national* is an independent administrative authority responsible, under the 2006 law, for examining consumer complaints, recommending solutions to disputes relating to the performance of contracts for the supply of electricity or natural gas, and taking part in campaigns to inform consumers about their rights.[109] After examining the case the *médiateur* prepares a written recommendation supported by detailed arguments, which are designed to enable the dispute to be settled within two months of the case being brought before him.

The only admissible applications are those that have been subject to a prior written complaint to an electricity or natural gas supplier, who has two months in which to propose a solution to the consumer. If the consumer has not received a satisfactory reply from his supplier by the end of that period, or if the latter has not replied, the consumer can appeal to the *médiateur* within a maximum of two months.

All claims submitted to the national energy *médiateur* are examined case by case. All claims are subject to in-depth technical and legal investigations. The *médiateur* has 40 staff, ten case handlers, who are legally trained, and two team managers. Examination is based on consultation and cooperation between the parties. While a case is being examined the *médiateur* can hear the parties or ask them to produce comments within a set time. With the parties' agreement he can also hear consenting third parties.

After examining the case, the *médiateur* prepares a written recommendation for a solution to the dispute within two months of the case being brought before him, which is communicated in writing to each of the parties, who are free to follow the *médiateur*'s opinion or not. However, suppliers must inform the *médiateur* within two months of the follow-up made to his recommendation.

The drafting of the recommendations is subject to four key principles:

- Simplicity: the recommendations must be understandable by anybody without any special legal or technical knowledge;
- Fairness: the recommendations take account of every situation and restore the balance between the parties;
- Exemplarity: the recommendations can highlight opportunities for improvement by suppliers and network operators to avoid similar disputes arising in future;
- Pro-activeness: if necessary the examination of case files leads to an in-depth investigation of current rules and procedures and operator practices.

[108] *Journal officiel de la République française* – N° 20 du 25 Janvier 2011. For the 2012 budget see www.legifrance.gouv.fr/affichTexte.do?cidTexte=JORFTEXT000025242218&fastPos=1&fastReqId=1831877087&categorieLien=id&oldAction=rechTexte.

[109] Campaigns to inform consumers about their rights and available complaint procedures, located on the 'Energy info' information unit, are financed jointly by the *médiateur national* and the Energy Regulation Commission (CRE). The unit includes a call centre open from Monday to Friday between 08:30 a.m. and 6:00 p.m. (0800 112 212, a free number since January 2012) together with a web site: www.energie-info.fr. An example of a campaign with INC, a TV consumer programme, in 2011 is at www.conso.net/video/visionneuse_conso.php?videoDocIdy=23153.

Any recourse to the *médiateur* suspends the time allowed for applications through the courts.[110] When the *médiateur* has made his recommendations the time allowed for legal recourse continues from the point when the appeal was made, as if the mediation had not taken place.

The *médiateur* is required to report on his work to Parliament, and has chosen to publish on his website his most important recommendations, in view of his duty to look at wider market issues/trends and not just individual complaints. Individual recommendations publish the amounts awarded but not the name of the company, whereas, annual reports publish aggregated data that includes the names of companies, number of cases per company, answering delays, and follow up of the recommendations. On rare occasions, the ombudsman does publish the name of a company that does not comply with a recommendation, if any other option had been unsuccessful.

The *médiateur* seeks to identify wider problems in the relationship, such as incorrect tariffs or unfair terms, and this information is picked up by consumer associations and other commentators. The energy sector has complicated contracts, between consumer-supplier, supplier- distributor, and consumer–distributor. There is little judicial case law on energy law issues, so the *médiateur* tries to give clarity through his recommendations, working closely with the energy public authorities (they are in the same building) and responding to consultations.[111] An attempt was made to improve the quality and readability of contracts. A December 2010 report on billing by companies summarizes all the knowledge and recommendations of the *médiateur*, and similar guidelines are planned on other issues.

Statistics[112]

In 2010, 17,467 complaints were received (986 were online, 6,890 were by letter and 9,591 by phone). Sixty-eight per cent of the complaints within the competence of the *médiateur* were settled or were subject to a recommendation. That year, 802 recommendations were issued, of which 67 were published. The average award was €373, and average processing time of complaints was 183 days.

The referrals received by the *médiateur* in 2010 related to the following suppliers: 43 per cent GDF SUEZ, 38 per cent EDF, 12 per cent DIRECT ENERGY, 4 per cent POWEO, 3 per cent other. The admissibility of received referrals was 58 per cent potentially admissible, 35 per cent admissible and 7 per cent not admissible. The outcome of recommendations by the *médiateur* in 2010 is in Table 3.4.

Table 3.4: Percentage of *médiateur's* recommendations followed by companies in 2010

	Others	GDF/SUEZ	Direct energy	EDF	POWEO	ERDF	GrDF	TOUS
No information on the follow-up		3	6	9	3		4	4
Recommendations not followed		8	10	12	22	41	51	20

[110] Civil Code, Art 2038.

[111] The *médiateur* and the energy regulator are in the same building. Nevertheless, they do not always agree: an example of recent difference in opinion concerns smart metering. The *médiateur* does not always feel that companies listen to his recommendations, and has as a result become more assertive.

[112] Annual report (2010) www.energie-mediateur.fr/fileadmin/user_upload/RA_MNE_2010V2.pdf.

Recommendations followed in part	12	16	1	16	6	16	16	14
Recommendations followed	88	73	83	63	69	43	29	62

The Mediation at EDF (Electricité de France)

The EDF Group has had a *médiateur* since around 1999,[113] who acts as a last resort in the business, when all other avenues have been exhausted and were unsuccessful. The *médiateur* is the independent reviewer of appeals to the President of EDF arising out of any dispute over a contractual relationship with an affiliate of EDF (client, network user, supplier, or partner). The *médiateur* of the EDF Group leads the institutional relationship between the EDF Group and the consumer,[114] including bi-annual meetings with consumer associations, and annual meetings between the representatives and leaders of the Group.

During 2010, individuals within the Group's National Consumer Service have been identified on a regional basis to liaise with delegates of the *médiateur*, and regular exchanges between the two parties have been instituted, based on written principles of collaboration, which are being duplicated at regional entities of the Regional Services User Network (ERDF). This also strengthens relations between the Commerce Department, consumer associations and ERDF.

Process

Complaints must first be made to the relevant local contact between consumer and the Group. If they are not resolved, the consumer may complain to regional and national levels, and finally to the Group *médiateur*. Upon receipt of a complete complaint file, the *médiateur* sends an acknowledgment within 48 hours. He then analyses and investigates the case. If necessary, he contacts those involved in the dispute. He seeks an equitable solution, which is then presented in writing as a report, within two months, to all parties.

The *médiateur* states that he approaches solutions in accordance with a rigorous ethical approach, based on the following principles:

- *Independence and impartiality*: analysing the situation without favouring the interests of either party;
- *Respect people*: any criterion of personal opinion or position must be taken into account in the analysis of the case;
- *Equity*: applying the rule or practice that interferes the least with human situations;
- *Adversarial*: ensuring that each party communicates its views to the other;
- *Listen*: taking into account the particular circumstances of each party;
- *Balanced listening*: being available and attentive to the parties;
- *Privacy*: the ombudsman is bound to confidentiality regarding the names of parties, the information and evidence obtained during the investigation of the dispute;
- *Transparency*: the activity of the *médiateur* is presented in an annual report available to all.

[113] fr.edf.com/mediateur-du-groupe-edf/la-mediation-a-edf-48650.html.

[114] The current ombudsman, Jocelyne Canetti, who was appointed by the President of EDF in September 2009 for a period of three years, is also Vice-President of the Commission of Consumer Mediation, and has a high profile in promoting mediation nationally.

Statistics

In 2010, the EDF *médiateur* received 4,476 contacts, of which 3,808 were redirected elsewhere, for example back down the internal customer complaint structure, and 669 (17.5 per cent) were accepted.[115] As shown in Table 3.5, this situation has followed a similar pattern in recent years, although the volume of direct contacts has continued to increase.

Table 3.5: Complaints received by the EDF *médiateur* 2006–2010

	Redirected files	Admissible files	Total
2006	1202	215	1417
2007	1392	197	1571
2008	2116	316	2432
2009	2469	545	3014
2010	3808	668	4476

The number of admissible files has been rising, and in 2010 the EDF *médiateur* closed 634 of the outstanding 758 caseload.[116] The average amount in dispute in 2010 was €1,120: 50 per cent of cases involved over €1,000, and 23 per cent over €2,000. The *médiateur* achieved his goal of dealing with more than 80 per cent of the cases in two months. The average processing time was 52 days, and 45 per cent of cases were processed within 50 days. In 2010, the *médiateur* upheld applicants' complaints completely or partially in 61 per cent of cases. 16 per cent of cases in 2010 involved the *médiateur* reviewing cases where consumers wrote in again after receiving his initial recommendation. Responses by consumers were reported as shown in Table 3.6.

Table 3.6: Responses by consumers

Request further explanation	21%
Thank the *médiateur*	6%
Provides new evidence and requests a further recommendation	5%
Contests the recommendation	46%
Reject the recommendation/ confirmation of prior response given by the company at national level	23%

GDF SUEZ

GDF SUEZ mediation was established in March 1999, in partnership with consumer groups, after the creation of GDF SUEZ in 2008.[117] The *médiateur* of GDF SUEZ[118] resolves ongoing problems with any person or organization regarding the Group's activities, whether or not a client, through amicable settlement of disputes. The *médiateur*'s mission is to help to improve relationships with customers, through his recommendations and through the

[115] *Rapport du Mediateur EDF 2010* available at: http://fr.edf.com/fichiers/fckeditor/Commun/Edf_en_france/documents/rapport_mediateur_2010_vf.pdf.

[116] ibid.

[117] A merger between Gas de France and Suez.

[118] www.gdfsuez.com/fr/accueil/mediateur/le-mediateur-de-gdf-suez. The Mediator of GDF SUEZ is currently the spokesman of the EEOG.

development of mediation, and he has promoted methods of dispute resolution throughout the group's services and subsidiaries.

Procedure

Before approaching the *médiateur*, the consumer must have used the dispute resolution services of GDF SUEZ members and not be satisfied with the outcome. The applications must be sent in writing, either via letter or online form.

The *médiateur* will let the applicant know how the request will be handled. The complaint usually comes directly from a consumer, customer GDF SUEZ or its subsidiaries in France and Europe. The *médiateur* can also be addressed by a consumer association chosen by an individual. Similarly, a professional organization or a consular chamber can intervene on behalf of a professional or business. Within 48 hours the applicant receives information on treatment modalities of the application, and the next steps that are needed to resolve the problem exposed.

Statistics

In 2010, the *médiateur* received 6,351 complaints, of which 6,246 cases were reassigned to resolution teams operating within the Group for mediation with the client. The remaining 105 cases, which were more complex disputes, were dealt with by the *médiateur* as a last resort before court proceedings. The *médiateur* reported that:

- 90 per cent of clients had a response within 48 hours that indicated what processing method would be used;
- 66 per cent had a response from the service concerned within fifteen days;
- the cases of mediation as a last resort were closed within two months, with a success rate of 95 per cent, except for (an unknown number of) complex cases.

The reasons for complaints were stated as shown in Table 3.7.

Table 3.7: Processes and main reasons for complaints

Process		First reason	Second reason	Third reason
Energy billing	88%	Bill disputes Faults and changes of meter, estimates, contract changes	Cancellation of contract Billing, usage, payment reviews, direct debits, readings	Payments of bills Payment terms, dispute over direct debit
Gas distribution	4%	Disputes regarding costs of services	Unjustified disconnection of energy supply	Operations at the customer's home
Sales offers and tariffs	3%	Dissatisfaction with plan taken out	Dispute regarding the price of natural gas	Quality of information
Contact with GDF SUEZ	4%	Request for compensation	Personalized follow-up	Other
Quality and safety of interior equipment	0%	Quality of the service	Diagnosis quality Dual fuel	Other

Transport

FNAUT

The *Fédération Nationale des Associations d'Usagers des Transports* (FNAUT)[119] is a consumer association whose activities include[120] advice and representation to passengers[121] on legal claims involving violation of the rules of consumer protection. FNAUT acts as a filter in checking the validity of claims, as well as representative of travellers in pursuing them. It often brings claims to the mediation services of the SNCF and the RATP (see below), in order to resolve disputes out of court after solutions were not found through companies' customer services.[122] FNAUT also acts as a watchdog in monitoring the mediators' publications, so as to raise issues that companies should address. FNAUT charges fees for its services: for normal complaints, the fee is €16 for members and €34 for non-members,[123] and for airline issues €42 for members and €60 for non-members.[124] It requires that travellers contact the travel company first, and allows a month for them to respond. The 2010 website hits as at 1 December 2010 were as shown in Table 3.8.[125]

Table 3.8: Website contacts to FNAUT in 2010

Air travel	2,025
RATP travel	1,841
Passenger SNCF	9,106
Referral to local court	3,946
Plane flight cancellation	5,249
Plane – overbooking	4,401
Plane – death or injury	1,976
Plane – loss, damage or delay of baggage	11,795
Plane – civil liability of travel agencies	6,135
Plane – delay	4,492
SNCF – personal injury	8,656
SNCF – aggression	3,156
SNCF – delay of a train	70,564
SNCF – theft, loss or damage to luggage	14,775

[119] www.fnaut.asso.fr. FNAUT is a member of various European groupings of passengers and environment protection.

[120] The FNAUT was formed with two objectives: to facilitate the movement of all, especially non-motorized, and to promote transport policy for people and goods consistent with sustainable development. It publishes a monthly newsletter with updates about transport policy: www.fnaut.asso.fr/images/docs/publications/chartesncf.pdf.

[121] Pedestrians, cyclists, disabled, families of victims of road accidents, users of urban public transport, rail and road, river and urban transit corridors that face the nuisance of traffic, citizens concerned with global environment and regional planning.

[122] As with a number of other associations, the FNAUT signed agreements with SNCF and RATP allowing them to use their Mediateurs to resolve disputes between users and operators. The FNAUT takes care of all the steps to the Ombudsman and the transport service concerned. A request, supported by a consumer association will carry more weight.

[123] Membership of FNAUT (€ 18) + fees (€ 16); for those living in Ile de France, the fee is € 30 (membership of AUT Ile de France € 14 + fees € 16).

[124] Membership of FNAUT (€ 18) + fees (€ 42); for those living in Ile de France, the fee is € 56 (membership of AUT Ile de France € 14 + fees € 42).

[125] fnaut.asso.fr/index.php/voyagez-malin.html.

The *Médiateur de SNCF*

Since 1994, the institution of the *médiateur de SNCF*[126] allows travellers to seek a second opinion regarding their complaints. The *médiateur* is established as an independent person within the company, appointed by the President of SNCF, to examine issues with fairness and impartiality, according to a protocol signed with consumer protection associations.

The *médiateur* aims to respond to letters within 2 months. This is a considerable administrative challenge, as the *médiateur* answers every letter in person. On average it takes 2–4 months to deal with a claim. The *médiateur* has 4 people working with him and several interns that assist at the claim entry level. Additionally there are 2 people running the online system.

A change was instituted in 2009 to enable the *médiateur* to be contacted directly.[127] Information about this change was distributed widely to travellers, both by SNCF, including posters in stations, and the media. The result was a sharp increase in claims submitted to the *médiateur*: 746 in 2008, 2,485 in 2009, and 3,731 in 2010. This increase was due solely to claims brought directly by individuals: none in 2008, 2,066 in 2009, and 3,408 (92 per cent of the total) in 2010. Over the same period, the number of cases referred by associations declined.

The 2009 increase in caseload resulted in an increase in the length of time within which the *médiateur* was able to deal with cases, but this was addressed in 2010, as shown in Table 3.9, and has been maintained in 2011. In 2011 the target time to respond was within 50 days.

Table 3.9: Response times for the SNCF *médiateur*

	2009	2010	First 5 months of 2011
Less than 2 months	36%	53%	56%
2 to 4 months	34%	44%	44%
Over 4 months	34%	3%	0%
Average response time	81 days	59 days	57 days

In 2010, 20 per cent of applications received were not within the *médiateur's* competence. They were cases that either had not first been sent raised with after-sales services (12 per cent of cases), or fell outside the jurisdiction of the *médiateur*, since they related to matters such as accidental injury, identity theft, SNCF activities as a travel agent, business subject to a proceedings (8 per cent of cases). The *médiateur* gave his opinion in the two-thirds of claims brought before him. In 14 per cent of cases accepted in 2009 and 2010, the customer had obtained satisfaction with after-sales services before the *Médiateur* deliberated on the issue. The Protocol on Mediation provides that customers can make a complaint if they have not received a response from the service after a month.

The majority (70 percent) of claims submitted to the *médiateur* in 2010 were classified as 'commercial issues', and cover a wide range of matters. Requests for refunds of tickets, involving unused tickets or tickets lost or stolen, and not resulting from the commitment time guaranteed (EHG) represent 30 per cent of commercial claims. Complaints about consequences of delays and their impact on the rest of a trip account for 24 per cent of

[126] *Société National des Chemins de Fer* (French Railways). The current ombudsman is Bernard Cieutat, a former magistrate of the Court of Auditors.

[127] Annual report (2010), www.clubdesmediateurs.fr/sites/clubdesmediateurs.fr/files/upload/document/pdf/Mediation_der.pdf.

commercial disputes. Complaints about the website sncf.com have recently remained constant at 11 per cent.

The number of complaints to the *médiateur* about the Railway Police is stable and represented 30 per cent of referrals in 2010. Of those, 96 per cent related to tariff violations, 4 per cent to crimes of behaviour (such as improper use of the alarm signal, violating the ban on smoking): see Table 3.10.

Table 3.10: Types of infringements

No ticket	55%
Unjustified reduction	21%
Ticket does not consist	7%
Reservation is not valid	4%
Other infringements (long travel, upgrades, alarm signal, etc.)	13%

The opinion of the *médiateur* is not likely to be challenged, unless the client or the company provides new evidence, in which case the *médiateur* may review his opinion. In 2010, 257 people wanted to reject an opinion, and the *médiateur* upheld the client's request in 10 per cent of reviewed cases. A claimant who is not satisfied with the *médiateur's* view retains the ability to bring a claim in court.

The *médiateur* has no defined budget: he requests funding from the President of SNCF, who then grants funds. The online scheme had a budget of €120,000 in 2011.

The *Médiateur de RATP*

The RATP Group, which includes the Paris *Métro* and also extensive bus, RER, and tramway transport, carries 12 million people daily. It has an in-house *médiateur*, who accepts complaints after the consumer has first made a complaint to customer services.[128] The office was created in 1990 under an agreement made by the Directorate General with consumer associations, and extended in 2006.[129] If the consumer is disputing a reported offence, the complaint must be made within two months of that offence. Customers can complain themselves or through a consumer group.

The *médiateur* first assesses the admissibility of the complaint, and sends a letter in acknowledgement of acceptance or explaining the reasons for rejection. He may send the file to the relevant RATP service department himself if the customer has not first done this. The main reasons why cases are deemed inadmissible are that the complaint is made too early because customer service has not yet been contacted; the complaint is made too late, ie outside the two-month period following the offence; or the complaint falls outside the remit of the *médiateur*.

The *médiateur* then investigates the case based on the information provided, to examine, firstly, the grounds of the request and the relevance of the arguments and, secondly, the lawfulness and legitimacy of the company's position. He will ask the relevant RATP departments for any additional information he feels he needs to decide the case. The *médiateur* has 45 days to respond to a complaint. In particularly difficult cases, this time

[128] www.ratp.fr/fr/ratp/c_5032/saisir-le-mediateur.

[129] *La médiation à la RATP*, available at www.ratp.fr/fr/ratp/r_6176/la-mediation-a-la-ratp.

period may be extended to four months. Many complaints relate to fines imposed on travellers, in which cases the *médiateur* informs them that the fine recovery procedure is suspended while the *médiateur* investigates the case, and it will not be referred to the police court to start proceedings.

Once the investigation is complete, the *médiateur* informs the complainant of the outcome of the complaint by letter, explaining the reasons for his decision. A copy is also sent to the RATP department responsible for its implementation. He has power to decide that no further action will be taken on an infringement or fine, or that the fine remains partly or wholly valid. A decision by the *médiateur* cannot be appealed, but a customer can pursue a complaint in the courts.

The *médiateur*'s annual report is published, therefore providing the same information to both customers and RATP. The report also informs RATP management of some of the questions that have been raised by customers and publishes the answers that have been given to them. It therefore serves as an additional tool for dialogue between customers and the company.

Statistics

The *médiateur* received 294 referrals in 2010.[130] The number of complaints increased annually from inception in 2006 until 2009, with a 7 per cent fall in 2010, as shown in Table 3.11. The number of inadmissible cases has doubled in the previous two years.

Table 3.11: Sources of referrals since 2006

Year	Other	Médiateur de la Republique	Specific	Signatory associations
2006	23	17	94	39
2007	–	24	174	28
2008	8	16	233	14
2009	18	19	268	12
2010	11	21	255	7

Electronic Communications

Alternative methods for dispute resolution are mandated under EU directives, as discussed at chapter 1. The EU requirements were implemented by DGCCRF (Directorate General for Consumer Affairs, Competition and Repression of Fraud) and ARCEP (Regulatory Authority for Electronic Communications and Post). The electronic communications sector serves more than 106 million customers in France. Companies have customer service departments for questions and complaints. Dialogue between companies and consumer associations has helped to advance methods of handling complaints.

The *Médiateur des Communications Electroniques*[131] was created in 2003 as an industry initiative to consider disputes in the sector of fixed telephony, mobile telephony and internet. It is available for clients of the operators that have signed the charter of mediation and are

[130] Mediation Officer Report (2010), www.ratp.fr/fr/ratp/c_5032/saisir-le-mediateur.

[131] www.mediateur-telecom.fr.

members of the *Association Médiation des Communciations Electroniques* (AMCE: the Electronic Communications Mediation Association), which was established in July 2002 as an association under the Act of 1 July 1901 in order to provide administrative support to the *médiateur*. The members of AMCE comprise most of the French telecom operators and Internet Service Providers.[132]

The AMCE aims to be a free, fair and fast alternative dispute resolution service for small business and residential customers in France who have unresolved complaints about their telephone or internet service. The *médiateur* is impartial and neutral towards the industry, government and consumer organizations. The *médiateur* is appointed for a term of three years that is renewable once. He is chosen after consultation with the DGCCRF and consumer bodies on the basis that his skills, authority and independence are recognized. His mandate is irrevocable. Since March 2008 consumers can appeal to the *médiateur* online.

AMCE's current budget is €1.3 million, for 12 employees, (a mediator, 1 managing director, 8 legal counsel, and 2 assistants). Its fifteen members represent 98 per cent of the French telecom sector serving the general public (consumers), not the business sector: only a few small operators are not members. Every month AMCE charges its members an agreed fee for each case it has received involving that operator.

The system of mediation in the electronic communications sector is based on five fundamental principles:

Freedom
- The use of the *médiateur* of electronic communications is optional.
- The consumer is participating voluntarily in the mediation process and can terminate it at any time.
- The consumer can contact the *médiateur* directly or through representation of a consumer association, or a lawyer.
- The mediation is not binding on the consumer.

Free
- Contacting the *médiateur* is free and done by ordinary mail.
- All costs of processing the application as well as the involvement of phone operators and internet are the responsibility of the *médiateur's* independent experts.

Efficiency
- There is only one *médiateur* for the electronic communications sector (fixed and mobile telephony, Internet, television).
- The *médiateur* agrees to give his opinion within three months.
- A mediation charter, which defines the principles of the mediation is widely shared by operators to their customers.
- The *médiateur* is under an obligation of confidentiality, allowing parties to speak freely. In return, the opinions of the *médiateur* are confidential and cannot be used in court, unless agreed to by both parties.

Independence
- The *médiateur* is chosen, after consultation with the DGCCRF (Directorate General for Consumer Affairs, Competition and Repression of Fraud) and consumer groups, from candidates whose competence and authority are widely recognized.

[132] The current members are: Bouygues Telecom, France Télécom, Orange, Ten by Orange, SFR, Universal Mobile, Carrefour Mobile, Simplicime, Télé2 mobile, Numéricable, Free, Alice, NRJ Mobile.

- The *médiateur* is appointed for a term of three years.
- The *médiateur* investigates cases independently.

Transparency

- The Charter sets out the principles of mediation that are shared with clients.
- The *médiateur's* areas of responsibility are clearly indicated in the responses of consumer services operators, once the referral is made.
- Each year, the *médiateur* writes a report that assesses how he completed his mission and expresses his recommendations.

Procedure

A consumer who has a complaint about their telephone service, mobile or Internet Service Provider, or television, and who has tried to solve it with the service provider directly without success, can lodge a claim with the *médiateur* provided the service provider is a member of AMCE, and the consumer has not taken legal action. A claim must be lodged in writing (by post or website: in order to keep costs low, AMCE does not provide a telephone service). The application is free to the consumer. AMCE's case handler will first check that the complaint falls within its remit (admissability: this takes about 2 minutes on the website, by responding to simple questions like 'Who is your operator? What answer did they provide?'). Within 48 hours, the *médiateur* will inform the complainant what action to take. If the case proceeds, the complainant completes a written form giving the necessary information and attaching relevant documents. The form must be completed within 15 days. The *médiateur* is obliged to keep all information confidential: all documents submitted are destroyed after analysis. The *médiateur's* opinion is confidential: parties cannot produce it in a court proceeding, unless expressly agreed between them. Both parties retain the right to bring the dispute before the competent courts.

The *médiateur* then asks the operator to provide the documents in its possession and to state its position. The *médiateur* investigates the case independently, and may call on independent experts as he wishes. The *médiateur* bases his opinion on law and equity. It is communicated in writing to each party within three months. Each party is free to accept or reject the *médiateur's* opinion, and should present its position to the other party and to the mediator within one month.

Statistics[133]

The number of complaints received between 2005 and 2010, and associated outcomes, is shown in Table 3.12: there were 18,672 cases received in 2010, of which 3,554 were valid applications: 1,374 were received through the website and 2,180 were sent by post. Thus, 15,110 were redirected.

[133] Annual report (2010) www.mediateur-telecom.fr/ressources/media/files/Rapport_Mediateur_2010.pdf; the charter is at www.mediateur-telecom.fr/charte.html.

Table 3.12: Number of applications received and opinions given 2005–2010

Year	Received cases	Opinion given
2005	2,508	579
2006	3,723	680
2007	7,466	1,787
2008	20,076[134]	3,173
2009	17,252	3,302
2010	18,672	3,554

In 2010, the percentage of requests upheld was 87 per cent (3,104 satisfied queries). The total number of complaints resolved on the basis of a proposal from the operator increased in 2010 by 7 per cent. This represents 1,001 cases resolved satisfactory. Cases that result in compromise increased by 23 per cent (1,611 cases), reflecting the goal of mediation to find an acceptable solution for both sides. The total number of opinions that were not followed was 13.

The duration of the process has shortened: in 2010 the average decreased to 69 days from 75 in 2009. The increased pursuit of mediated solutions resulted in processing time ranging from 8 days to 2 ½ months. The mediator has set a goal of continuing to reduce processing time down to no more than 2 months.

The type of complaints received in 2010 is shown in Table 3.13.

Table 3.13: Type of complaints in 2010

	Number	Percentage
Technical problems	893	25.0
Billing	869	24.5
Contract	976	27.5
Cancellation	814	23.0

Internet

Le Forum des droites sur l'internet[135] (Forum of Internet Rights, FDI) was created in December 2000 under the 1901 Law on Associations on the initiative of the Prime Minister to reflect on questions of law and society related to the Internet, and to inform the public and foster dialogue between government, companies and users on such issues. In 2010, the Forum included nearly 70 members, public bodies, associations and private companies. In 2003 it launched a website information service *DroitDuNet.fr*, for which the most popular issues were protection of children (violent or pornographic content) (53 per cent), payment security (36 per cent) and computer security (viruses, hacking) (30 per cent).

Since 2004 it has also offered a mediation service for disputes related to the Internet. The service was piloted for a year before opening to the public, and showed a significant success rate: 75 per cent of the cases were settled out of court and 90 per cent of agreements

[134] This peak is a result of the extension of jurisdiction and the opening of an online referral line.
[135] www.foruminternet.org.

were met. A review in 2006 found that the mediation service had logged more than 5,400 applications, of which 3,200 were dealt with, with a resolution rate of 89 per cent for cases closed. 97 per cent of cases related to electronic commerce, of which non-receipt of goods and hidden defects made up the bulk. There was a satisfaction rate of over 73 per cent.

However, on December 7, 2010, the Association announced its dissolution, after the State did not renew its grant for 2011.[136]

Since 2006, a partnership between FDI and the AFNIC, deal with the extra-judicial settlement of disputes over domain names brought by individuals.

Doctors

L'ordre des médecins, the French Order of Physicians, was established by Government edict in 1945, to uphold medical ethics, and to be a self-regulatory and representative organisation.[137] It is financed by doctors, and has a network of councils in each *département*. Its functions include a mediation and conciliation role between physicians and patients and between physicians themselves.

Disciplinary chambers of first instance[138] have disciplinary powers (appeals can be made to the disciplinary section of the National Council, and ultimately to the *Conseil d'Etat*). They comprise nine regular members, and an equal number of substitutes, elected by the departmental councils for nine years, of whom a third are renewed every three years. Also present in an advisory capacity are a legal expert, the local Director of Public Health (DAS), a Professor of Medicine, a medical officer from the national health care insurance system (*Securité sociale*), and a representative of salaried doctors.

Cases can be submitted by the departmental councils, the minister, the departmental director of health, the prefect, the public prosecutor, doctors associations, or an individual doctor. Receipt of a complaint leads to investigation of medical records and review of cases by a panel that comprises a permanent doctor, a part-time doctor, nurses, five contractor doctors who are active in a hospital or clinic, an emergency physician, a general practitioner, and a surgeon along with ten other delegates, such as teachers, a radiation oncologist, or a judge. Possible sanctions are warning, censure, temporary or permanent suspension from a public medical post, temporary suspension or erasure from the Register.

On 7 September 2010 a partnership agreement was signed between the *Médiateur de la République* (now *Le Défenseur des Droits*)[139] and the National Council of the College of Physicians (CNOM),[140] concerning the reciprocal exchange of information to identify corrective and preventive actions that are best suited to improving quality and safety of care. The two institutions work closely on the treatment of individual claims, in addition to reviewing proposals for improvement of safety of care and quality of relations with users of the health system. The *Défenseur* now contacts the CNOM in any claim relating to ethics, ethics and professional practice. Statistics for 2010 are at Table 3.14.

[136] www.foruminternet.org/institution/espace-presse/communiques-de-presse/le-forum-des-droits-sur-l-internet-est-dissout-3118.html.

[137] www.conseil-national.medecin.fr.

[138] They also hear disputes over healthcare insurance claims.

[139] See above p 43. *Le Défenseur des Droits* is Jean-Paul Delevoye.

[140] www.conseil-national.medecin.fr/system/files/mediature.pdf.

Table 3.14: Complaint figures 2010[141]

Contacts to the call centre	11,880
Letters received during treatment	1,400
Web forms processed	282
Requests for a medical or surgical adverse events	39%
Requests reports of abuse or violence	20%

In 2010 almost 18 per cent of the requests came from professionals who were unable to resolve a dialogue with a patient, or felt professional isolation after undergoing a medical accident, or threatened in their work. Recognising these reasons for complaints, the *défenseur* raised the issue with the Department of Health, and created the *Pôle santé et sécurité des soins* (The Healthcare Division and Safety of Care) in 2009.[142] This introduced an assistance unit to support professionals involved in the management of post-traumatic stress, confronted with complex and sensitive situations, and associated with a collapse in dialogue with stakeholders with no prospect of solutions.

Complaints for compensation arising out of medical accidents are dealt with under the national medical compensation scheme operated by the *Office National d'Indemnisation des Accidents Médicaux* (ONIAM),[143] created by the Act of 4 March 2002. Details of that interesting and successful scheme are outside the scope of this book, but the procedure involves investigation by local *Commissions régionale de conciliation et d'indemnisation des accidents medicaux* (CRCI), which seek first to mediate a negotiated agreement between the victim and the insurer of the health professional.[144] If agreement is not reached, and the Commission reaches the conclusion that a healthcare provider was at fault, the provider or his insurer is informed and is expected to make an offer of compensation to the victim,[145] failing which ONIAM will itself make a payment and reclaim the money from insurers. ONIAM received 732 claims in 2010.[146]

Evaluation

Consumer ADR is an important subject in France, and there have recently been serious efforts to establish a consistent approach based on high standards of practice through the adoption of the general Charter. The spread of *médiation* has occurred on a sectoral basis, and is expected soon to be introduced in more sectors, although this leads to an organisationally disparate approach, as with the UK and Germany. The possibility that a unified national system might exist, through the CRLCs, has been undermined because of a lack of funding from *départements*. Business sectors are, therefore, establishing sectoral

[141] Annual report 2010 available at: www.mediateur-republique.fr/fic_bdd/pdf_fr_fichier/1295941775_Bilan_P3S.pdf.

[142] *Le Journal du Mediateur de la Republique*, Fevrier 2009, No 44. www.mediateur-republique.fr

[143] www.oniam.fr/oniam/presentation-oniam. Created under Code de la santé publique: see www.legifrance.gouv.fr/affichCode.do?cidTexte=LEGITEXT000006072665&dateTexte=20111107.

[144] See G Helleringer, 'Symposium on Medical Malpractice and Compensation in Global Perspective: Part I: Medical Malpractice and Compensation in France, Part II: Compensation based on National Solidarity' (2011) 86 *Chi-Kent L Rev* 3, 1125.

[145] Code la Santé Publique Art L 1142-14.

[146] Annual report ONIAM (2010), at www.oniam.fr/IMG/rapportsoniam/rapport2010.pdf.

consumer ADR systems. As with Germany and the UK, the sectoral approach can lead to a lack of consistency and clarity in how consumer ADR operates.

Some confusion arises from use of the name '*médiateur*' for both in-house company ombudsmen (where there are several leading and powerful figures) and external sectoral ombudsmen (where some are being established by trade associations but only two are so far established by law). This situation exists in some other countries, but the confusion is more acute in France, where the dominance of in-house *médiateurs* appears to have confused consumers and not encouraged an ideally high level of consumer confidence in the independence of such *médiateurs*, or of *médiateurs* in general. The position is not assisted by stories that some in-house customer complaint mechanisms involve several stages, which mean that customers may give up before reaching the end of what may be a long and complex process, and become disillusioned in the system, preferring to seek a court solution. There is, therefore, confusion over whether the function of *médiateurs* in general are sufficiently independent.

4

Germany

Iris Benöhr, Christopher Hodges and Naomi Creutzfeldt-Banda

The National Context

ADR in Germany is, from a comparative perspective, a prime example of the maxim that context is paramount. The concept of 'ADR' is frequently referred to in Germany, but has a particular meaning, essentially encompassing mediation associated with court proceedings, or arbitration. There are some limited examples of ADR that do not occur in the context of alignment to court proceedings, such as ombudsman procedures, but they are currently limited in scope and in usage. In this respect, the German ADR landscape resembles that of the United Kingdom as it was around 1995. However, there is no reason why the German ADR scene should not develop extra-court procedures that are highlighted in some other jurisdictions elsewhere in this book.

There are two essential features of the German dispute resolution system, which need to be understood both in order to describe it as it exists today and in order to explain its historical development. These features are the nature of the civil procedure system and the fact that lawyers have largely maintained a monopoly on giving legal advice.

Taken together, the features identified above produce a relatively high volume of litigation per head of population in Germany compared with many other jurisdictions.[1] In consequence, there is widespread use of, and familiarity with, the litigation system. Simply put, the court system works, and produces reliable results reasonably quickly and cheaply (especially when the wide availability of insurance is taken into account). Accordingly, there has historically been little social or cost pressure for alternatives to the courts to be developed. Lawyers, whose costs are comparatively low for litigation, have been able to maintain a monopoly on legal advice and representation in court, and therefore have kept the role of gatekeepers on disputes. Lawyers have directed disputes into the court system, thereby maintaining their monopoly and income stream. The costs of litigation have not been allowed to become so high and disproportionate as in some other jurisdictions, such as England, and therefore pressure by lawyers or parties to look for alternatives to courts has been kept in check.

Looking merely at the statistics on ADR in EU states, it appears that there are numerically more ADR bodies in Germany than in any other Member State.[2] Yet the statistics are misleading, since there is a comparability issue. As at February 2010, 203 German ADR

[1] E Blankenburg, 'Civil Litigation Rates as Indicators for Legal Cultures', in D Nelken (ed), *Comparing Legal Cultures* (Colorado, Dartmouth Publishing, 1997); *Justizbericht in Zivilsachen* (Bundesamt für Statistik, 2007).

[2] See ec.europa.eu/consumers/redress_cons/ecc_germany_en.htm, and ec.europa.eu/consumers/redress/out_of_court/commu/acce_just04_en_ccb_en.pdf.

schemes were registered with the European Commission—which was more than any other Member State.[3] The Civic Study in 2009 identified 223 ADR bodies in Germany.[4] However, the overwhelming majority of bodies are focussed on mediation of cases, either cases that are proceeding in court or that would be brought in court if the mediation does not succeed. They are not particularly focused on consumer claims.

The number of bodies that deal with consumer ADR issues by providing a completely non-court pathway is far more limited than appears from the overall statistics. Further, such bodies are relatively recent and have relatively low usage, although there is considerable scope for growth.

The Court System

The courts occupy a position in dispute resolution in Germany that is not only central but also highly dominant. For many years, that situation prevented, or made unnecessary, the development of alternative pathways. The courts have several clear advantages when compared with those of many other jurisdictions:[5] they are cheap, quick, efficient, and have costs that are predictable (both in relation to claimants' costs for court and lawyers fees, and potential liability under the loser pays rule). As a result of the predictability of costs, legal expenses insurance has developed, and is widely held for individual claimants, with third party funding for meritorious claims being available relatively cheaply from insurers on a case-by-case basis.

Maintaining the rule of law is a central principle enshrined in the German constitution (*Rechtsstaatsprinzip*), and requires not only that there should be free access to the courts, but also that litigation costs should be both predictable and reasonable.[6] The general rule is that the loser pays the costs.[7] The amounts reimbursable for both the court fees,[8] and fees of opponents' lawyers'[9] and experts are specified in tariffs, and are comparatively low amounts. The amounts in the tariff vary depending on (a) the sum in dispute and (b) the stage that a case reaches. The arrangements discourage plaintiffs from inflating the amount of a claim. They also encourage settlement, since the lawyer receives a higher fee (*Einigungsgebühr*) for the middle stage of the procedure if settlement is achieved than he would if the case had continued. This result is, again, intended to encourage settlement. Scale fees for lawyers and courts are maintained at modest levels partly because lawyers do less work than they would under a common law system, and partly as a result of a policy of cross-subsidisation (*Quersubventionierung*) between more and less remunerative cases.[10]

[3] ec.europa.eu/consumers/redress_cons/ecc_germany_en.htm.

[4] See ec.europa.eu/consumers/redress_cons/adr_study.pdf.

[5] See A Stadler & W Hau, 'The Law of Civil Procedure' in M Reimann, J Zekoll & W Ebke (eds.), *Introduction to German Law*, 2nd ed (The Hague, 2005).

[6] A cognate principle is reflected in the 'principle of equality' in Art 3 of the German Constitution, which means that every person is equal before the law.

[7] German Civil Procedure Code, (*Zivilprozessordnung* (ZPO)), s 91.

[8] By the German Court Fees Act, (*Gerichtkostengesetz* (GKG)). Certain other statutory provisions govern payment of court fees in certain cases (eg guardianship and probate cases). Undisputed debt claims may use an abbreviated procedure (*Mahnverfahren*), in which the costs are half of those that apply in the *Amtsgericht* or *Landgericht* courts.

[9] By the German Lawyers' Fees Act, the *Gesetz über die Vergütung der Rechtsanwältinnen und Rechtsanwälte* (RVG).

[10] However, a 2006 study revealed that 38% of participants believed that cross-subsidisation was 'not workable': C Hommerich and M Kilian, *Vergütungsvereinbarungen deutscher Rechtsanwälte* (Soldan Institute, 2006), 22, figure 1.

The predictability of costs to assert (and defend) a claim in the courts facilitated the development many decades ago of legal expenses insurance (LEI). LEI is widely held by individuals in Germany, and was held by 43 per cent of German households in 2006.[11] The predictability and comparatively low cost of litigation in Germany results in the German system producing a considerably higher level of smaller claims than most other European states.[12] However, a study comparing different types of litigation in the Netherlands with the German *Land North Rhine-Westphalia* found that low value consumer disputes were processed in both countries by 'pre-court institutions', ie ADR bodies, rather than through litigation, although there were more alternatives and more pre-court conflict institutions in the Netherlands than in Germany, with the Dutch managing to filter better in the first instance.[13]

Legal aid is available in court proceedings (*Prozesskostenhilfe*),[14] subject to an applicant proving to the court qualification under means and merits tests. Legal advice and assistance (*Beratungshilfe*) may be provided separately by a *Land* or a local Bar.

The average duration of cases that involve less than €5,000 is 4.7 months in the Amtsgericht, and if appealed a total of 16.7 months; and of cases over €5,000 8.1 months in the *Landgericht* and if appealed in the *Oberlandesgericht* a total of 24.6 months.[15] In both cases, any further appeals to the Supreme Court take on average a further two years.[16]

Small claims procedures are available across most of Germany, enacted by the various State legislatures (*Landesgesetzgebung*), which usually involve claims of less than €600, and endeavour to resolve such claims primarily by way of extra-judicial mediation. The small claims procedure is not widely used in practice, and does not operate so as to prevent a claimant from taking its case straight to court.[17] The European Small Claims Procedure[18] has also been available since 2009 in respect of cross-border claims of €2,000 or less.

The courts in Germany are bound by the Code of Civil Procedure to 'promote at every stage of the legal procedure a consensual settlement'. They are encouraged by scholarly writings to adopt a 'peace-making function' and in practice are pressured by heavy case loads to engage in settlement activities and avoid writing judgments.[19] Continental procedure permits the judge discretion to shift back and forth between his role as conciliator and his role as adjudicator.[20]

[11] C Hommerich, M Kilian and R Dreske, *Statistisches Jahrbuch der Anwaltschaft 2007/2008* (Soldan Institut für Anwaltmanagement, 2008), Tables 7.2. and 7.2.2. See also AAS Zuckerman, 'Lord Woolf's Access to Justice: Plus çà change…' (1996) 59 *Modern Law Review* 773, 791–795; M Kilian, 'Alternatives to Public Provision: the Role of Legal Expenses Insurance in Broadening Access to Justice: The German Experience' (2003) 30 *Journal of Law and Society* 31, also in R Moorehead and P Pleasance, *After Universalism: Re-engineering Access to Justice* (Blackwell Publishing, 2003).

[12] C Hommerich, M Kilian and R Dreske, *Statistisches Jahrbuch der Anwaltschaft 2007/2008* (Soldan Institut für Anwaltmanagement, 2008). E Blankenburg, 'Patterns of Legal Culture: The Netherlands compared to Neighbouring Germany' (1998) 46 *The American Journal of Comparative Law* 1, vol 46.

[13] Blankenburg, 'Patterns of Legal Culture', 1–26.

[14] Civil Procedure Code, ss 114–127a.

[15] StatistischesBundesamtRechtspflege 2010 available at: http://www.destatis.de/jetspeed/portal/cms/Sites/destatis/Internet/DE/Content/Publikationen/Fachveroeffentlichungen/Rechtspflege/GerichtePersonal/Zivilgerichte2100210107004,property=file.pdf.

[16] K J Hopt and F Steffek (eds), *Mediation – Rechtstatsachen, Rechtsvergleich, Regelungen* (Tübingen Mohr Siebeck, 2008), 81.

[17] If a claim for less than €600 is brought by way of court proceedings, the court has a broad discretion as to the conduct of the case: German Civil Procedure Code, section 495a. Such cases are conducted in an informal manner if the parties are unrepresented.

[18] Regulation (EC) 861/2007, establishing a European Small Claims Procedure [2007] OJ L 199/1. The procedure has been implemented in the German Civil Procedure Code, section 1097ff.

[19] KF Röhl, 'The Judge as Mediator', Dispute Processing Research Program, Working Paper 1983–89, University of Wisconsin-Madison Law School; see S Roberts and M Palmer, *Dispute Processes. ADR and the Primary Forms of Decision-Making* (Cambridge University Press, 2005).

[20] E Blankenburg, 'Patterns of Legal Culture: The Netherlands compared to Neighbouring Germany', in *The American Journal of Comparative Law*, (1998) vol 46, 1 at 17.

Settlement is regarded as being better than a court decision, since it brings the dispute to an end and is the appropriate social goal (*Rechtsfrieden*, literally: legal peace).

Various aspects of the system are directed at resolving cases through direct negotiation, thereby saving money and reinstating social relations. If a party institutes proceedings and the opponent immediately concedes liability, the claimant will be required to pay the costs. This rule is aimed at encouraging settlement through direct negotiation. There is no limit on the number of pre-action exchanges between the parties.

The Influence of Lawyers

For many decades, lawyers held a monopoly on legal advice, protected by law.[21] Blankenburg drew attention to the huge impact that that monopoly had in restricting the development of sources of legal information and advice by trade union, consumer, insurance and general civil society sources, and in particular on the development of ADR as opposed to court forms of dispute resolution.[22] The restriction has only recently begun to be liberalised, and German law now distinguishes between legal advice out-of-court and representation before the courts. Only in 2007 did the Legal Service Act (*Rechtsdienstleistungsgesetz*) allow 'non-lawyers' to provide free legal advice out-of-court, thereby enabling charities, consumer organisations and other associations to provide legal advice in the field of their expertise.

No legal representation of the parties is needed before the local courts (*Amtsgericht*), which are competent for claims up to €5,000.[23] However, before the German district courts and before all courts of higher instances, parties are obliged to be represented by a lawyer.[24]

Socio-Legal Culture

National character and culture can be seen in influencing attitudes to the courts and ADR. Given a 'national sense of internalized social order' and doing what people 'say they will do according to the recognized rules and nothing more',[25] the use of clear rules enforced by courts contrasts with the culture of negotiation in Holland. Public pressure to observe rules can be very powerful. Business practice rarely uses codes: there is a strong culture of compliance based on social norms. Landmark cases have considerable impact, and attract widely reported headlines in the media, and public attention.

It is relevant that the German language has a number of words for different concepts: *Schiedsgericht* (arbitration), *Mediation* (mediation), *Schlichtung* (conciliation), *Ombudsman* (ombudsman).

[21] See the German Legal Services Act (*Rechtsberatungsgesetz* (RBerG)), RGBl. I S. 1478 (BGBl. III 303–12) that was annulled in 2008. The objective of this law was to ensure a high quality of legal advice for the clients; see M Henssler and LS Terry, 'Lawyers Without Frontiers—a View From Germany', *Dickinson Journal of International Law*, Vol. 19:2, 2001, 304.

[22] E Blankenburg, 'Civil Litigation Rates as Indicators for Legal Cultures' in D Nelken, *Comparing Legal Cultures* (Aldershot: Dartmouth, 1997); E Blankenburg, 'Patterns of Legal Culture: The Netherlands Compared to Neighbouring Germany' (1998) 46 *American Journal of Comparative Law* 1, 1–41.

[23] *Gerichtsverfassungsgesetz* (German Courts Constitution Act) § 23 Nr. 1, 71 Abs. 1 GVG.

[24] s78 ZPO (Code of Civil Procedure Rules).

[25] B Tomalin, *The Essential Guide to Customs & Culture. Germany*, (UK, Kuperard, 2011).

Encouragement of ADR before Court Proceedings

Mediation in the German Introductory Law of the Code of Civil Procedure

German Law does not place a general duty on the contending parties to attempt to resolve their dispute extra-judicially before bringing their matter to court. However, pursuant to Section 15a(1) of the Act Introducing the Code of Civil Procedure (EGZPO),[26] a federal state can require by law that an action shall only be brought before a court once an attempt to achieve consensus has been made at a recognised conciliation office. This may apply, *inter alia*, to:

- financial disputes coming under the jurisdiction of a local court (*Amtsgericht*), where the amount of the claim in dispute does not exceed 750 euros,
- certain disputes relating to the law concerning neighbours, and
- disputes relating to defamation claims, where the derogatory remarks were not made via the press or broadcasting media.

Where a federal state makes the above provisions, an action of one of the above types brought without an attempt to reach a consensus would be dismissed as being inadmissible. Not all the federal states have so far availed themselves of the possibility to demand an extra-judicial attempt to achieve consensus. However, conciliation procedures are not necessary in the following cases:[27]

- Petitions to modify a judgment, supplementary actions for security deposits, actions relating to the recognition of judgments from abroad, cross-actions and actions which have to be filed within a statutory or judicial period of time,
- Motions for a new trial,
- Claims under deed or bill-enforcement proceedings,
- Litigious procedure, where a claim is being asserted under summary proceedings for the recovery of a debt, and
- Actions pertaining to enforcement measures.

Furthermore, conciliation procedures are not allowed if the parties do not live or have their registered office or branch in the same *Land*. The federal states can apply state laws to restrict the scope of application of section 15a(1) EGZPO and to extend the reasons for exclusion in section 15a(2) EGZPO.

For judicial proceedings at first instance, the Code of Civil Procedure (ZPO) provides for consensual discussions to precede the (contentious) court hearing in order to achieve an amicable settlement of the dispute.[28] This principle does not apply when discussions to

[26] This Act (*Einführungsgesetz zur Zivilprozeßordnung*: EGZPO) was adopted on 1 January 1999 and section 15a EGZPO (1) provides: 'The states can introduce the mandatory use of mediation schemes before a complaint can be admitted by the courts, if the case concerns:

1) financial disputes before the Magistrates Court up to a litigation value of € 750,
2) certain neighbourhood disputes,
3) defamation disputes where the alleged defamation has not occurred through the media,
4) disputes over claims under section 3 of the General Equal Treatment Act.'

Certain exceptions were specified in s 15 a (2) EGZPO. A discussion of the Bavarian mediation law is provided by K Funken, 'Comparative Dispute Management: Court-connected Mediation in Japan and Germany' (2002) 3 *German Law Journal*, see the German Law Journal webpage at: http://www.germanlawjournal.com/index.php?pageID=11&artID=130.

[27] EGZPO, s 15a(2).

[28] ZPO, s 278(2).

achieve a consensus have no prospect of success because an attempt to reach consensus had already been made at an extrajudicial conciliation office, eg under a federal state law pursuant to section 15a EGZPO, or it is obvious for other reasons that consensual discussions are hopeless. Instead of requiring consensual discussions according to section 278(2) ZPO, in suitable cases a court can also suggest that the parties resolve their dispute extrajudicially.[29]

Within the framework of mandatory conciliation proceedings (cf section 15a EGZPO), the failure of an attempt to reach a consensus is a precondition for the admissibility of an action. It is thus possible to bring the matter before a court if no solution to the dispute has been reached. If consensus proceedings pursuant to section 278(5) of the Code on Civil Procedure (ZPO) are unsuccessful, the proceedings are converted into contentious ones as a result. If there has been an attempt at extra-judicial dispute settlement before a private sector conciliation body in response to a customer complaint, the participants can bring the case before the court if they have not accepted the conciliation offer.[30]

During an attempt to settle a dispute extra-judicially, the statute of limitations is suspended with reference to the claims of the parties to the dispute.[31] This has the effect of not pressurising the parties into bringing their extra-judicial negotiations to a close before the period of limitation runs out.

Arbitration

One alternative to courts, arbitration, has long been used in Germany, in appropriate cases. The traditional circumstances in which arbitration is preferred are well-known and straightforward. The Arbitration Rules of the German Institute for Arbitration (*Deutsche Institution für Schiedsgerichtsbarkeit*: DIS) date from 1998,[32] and it introduced Supplementary Rules for Corporate Law Disputes, effective from 15 September 2009.[33] Arbitration has advantages in comparison with courts when parties need confidentiality (such as to preserve commercial secrets,[34] or even the fact that a dispute exists), or when an arbitrator can apply particular expertise that a normal judge does not posses (such as for complex construction, technical or maritime disputes), or in international contracts so as to overcome arguments over choice of jurisdiction and submission to unknown foreign legal systems. However, the costs in arbitration can be unpredictable and/or higher than in courts. Therefore, many straightforward commercial contracts for the sale of goods or services do not contain arbitration clauses, because the courts will usually be cheaper and otherwise comparable in expertise and duration.

A good example of the use of arbitration comes from the building and engineering sector. The German Association of Consulting Engineers (*Verband Beratender Ingenieure*: VBI)[35]

[29] ZPO, s 278(5) sentence 2.

[30] A conciliation offer is defined in the rules of procedure for conciliation boards, s 5(3) (*Schlichtungsstellenverfahrensordnung*).

[31] For consensus and arbitration proceedings before state-run or recognised consensus boards, this is a direct consequence of s 204(1) No 4 of the German Civil Code (BGB). For other forms of alternative dispute resolution, it is a consequence of s 203 sentence 1 BGB.

[32] www.dis-arb.de/scho/schiedsordnung98-e.html. The law was based on the UNCITRAL Model Law on International Commercial Arbitration – 1985, see www.unicitral.org.

[33] www.dis-arb.de/download/DIS_SRColD_%202009_Download.pdf

[34] Arbitration clauses are common in the constitutions of family-owned corporations, so as to keep disputes away from public scrutiny.

[35] See www.vbi.de/english/about-vbi.html. The association has around 3,000 member firms employing more than 45,000 consultants and engineers.

facilitates dispute adjudication as an ADR method for the settlement of disputes, especially for complex, large-scale and international construction projects. FIDIC, the International Federation of Consulting Engineers, introduced dispute adjudication as a dispute resolution process in its standard contractual terms since the mid-1990s. Dispute adjudication has been part of all standard sample contracts since 1999. Around 50,000 FIDIC contracts are awarded every year. The purpose of dispute adjudication is the prompt, cost-effective and conclusive resolution of disputes, while staff, equipment and building materials are still on the building site.

VBI has undertaken the task of training and examining German-speaking dispute adjudicators in accordance with FIDIC standards. It keeps records of German-speaking dispute adjudicators and acts as a nominating body for enquiries from parties wishing to involve a dispute adjudicator.

The parties to a contract agree to choose a board of up to three adjudicators (engineers or others) who then supervise the development and completion of the construction on site. By setting tight deadlines within which the dispute adjudication boards must make their decisions the procedure is accelerated. As a rule, the deadline is 84 days. Within this period, the parties have the opportunity to present the facts of the matter and to exchange their points of view. Following an oral hearing, the dispute adjudication board makes its decision. The decision is binding, but can be reviewed by the Court of Arbitration. The possibility to start a judiciary process in front of traditional courts also remains open.

As a result of good results in the engineering sector, the German Association for Construction Law, supported by the German Construction Industry Federation (HDB), commenced in January 2010 a new dispute resolution procedure for the building sector as a whole (*Streitlösungsordnung für das Bauwesen*), promoting dispute adjudication, arbitration and mediation.

The Mediation Phenomenon

In looking at ADR in Germany, the phenomenon of mediation will be apparent, and has been widely discussed. However, it is important to note that what has almost invariably been referred to is mediation associated with court-based claims, and discussion has only recently included mechanisms that stand entirely apart from courts as an integral dispute resolution procedure.

The adage about 'bargaining in the shadow of the law' is highly pertinent here: the usual situation is that parties may 'mediate in the shadow of the courts', whereas in some other Member States ADR pathways exist within their own firmament and are not as connected to the courts as mediation is in Germany.

In order to promote use of amicable dispute resolution, of which mediation is one example, and diminish the workload for the courts, a Federal law came into effect on 1 January 1999 that permitted the German states *(Länder)* to introduce compulsory mediation regarding specific civil disputes.[36] In those states that have implemented this law, a claimant must, on commencing a court claim, provide the certificate issued by the mediation board that proves the unsuccessful attempt at reconciliation by the parties.

[36] See Section 15a EGZPO (1) of the the Introductory Law of the Code of Civil Procedure (*Einführungsgesetz zur Zivilprozeßordnung*) (EGZPO), described on pp 77–78 of this chapter.

A number of organisations providing mediation services and training for mediators has arisen since the 1990s, notably *Bundesverband Mediation* (BM: The Federal Association of Mediation, created 1992),[37] *Bundesverband Mediation in Wirtschaft und Arbeitswelt* (BMWA: Federal Association of Mediation in Business and Workplace, created in 1996),[38] *Centrale für Mediation*[39] (CfM: the Centre for Mediation, created 1998), and *Bundes-Arbeitsgemeinschaft für Familien-Mediation*[40] (BAFM: Federal Association for Family Mediation, created 1992). The German mediation associations BAFM, BM and BMWA, the Swiss Confederation for mediation SDM-FSM and the Austrian Association for Mediation ÖBM have mutually recognized training regulations and guidelines. In 2008, a number of major businesses founded the *Round Table Mediation und Konfliktmanagement der deutschen Wirtschaft* (Round Table Mediation and Conflict Management),[41] to support the development of mediation in business disputes, with academic support from the European University Viadrina at Frankfurt (Oder). Their work has focused on developing principles on conflicts.[42]

The EU Mediation Directive[43] aroused considerable debate within Germany, leading up to its implementation in May 2011.[44] The Mediation Directive is viewed as the most significant development in civil procedure in Germany for many years. It is revolutionary in its impact. The existing procedure in the civil procedure code is based on a model of conflict between the parties, which is resolved by the judge, whereas mediation involves compromise by the parties themselves. The Directive not only introduces this change in culture but institutionalises it on a permanent basis.

The state of mediation in Germany remains patchy across the country, vividly described as 'a sea with islands'.[45] The sea is the all-pervasive court system, in which various islands of mediation have emerged comparatively recently, and are of differing size and disposition. Mediation has occurred where someone has fostered it, for example a local *Land* government or court President. In Lower Saxony, for example, some Court Presidents support mediation, some judges have been trained as mediators, and there are high usage and success rates as regards mediation within courts. In contrast in Baden-Württemberg, the government was for a long time not attracted to mediation, hence there was no boost to judicial careers to support it, and usage is still limited, although a few model projects have recently appeared. Germany is in a transitional period on the use of mediation. It is currently unclear whether or not the Mediation Directive will give the situation a boost.

The choice of mediator is a private matter for the parties. Competition has, therefore, developed between different suppliers, and a large number have emerged. Mediator

[37] www.bmev.de.

[38] www.bmwa.de/about.php?myOID=&myUID=.

[39] www.centrale-fuer-mediation.de.

[40] www.bafm-mediation.de.

[41] www.rtmkm.de.

[42] The motivation for companies is simply commercial: the costs of conflict resolution form part of the costs of a conflict, so firms have become more attuned to monitoring costs and have sought to reduce the transactional costs.

[43] Directive 2008/52/EC of the European Parliament and of the Council of 21 May 2008 on certain aspects of mediation in civil and commercial matters, available at eur-lex.europa.eu/LexUriServ/LexUriServ.do?uri=OJ:L:2008:136:0003:0008:EN:PDF.

[44] See F Steffek, 'Rechtsvergleichende Erfahrungen für die Regelung der Mediation' (2010) RabelsZ Bd. 74, 841–881; KJ Hopt, and F Steffek, *Mediation – Rechtstatsachen, Rechtsvergleich, Regelungen – Gutachten im Auftrag des Bundesministeriums der Justiz der Bundesrepublik Deutschland* (Tübingen 2008); H Eidenmüller and M Prause, 'Die europäische Mediationsrichtlinie – Perspektiven für eine gesetzliche Regelung der Mediation in Deutschland' (2008) *NJW*, 2737–2743.

[45] Dr F Steffek in a meeting with the authors in May 2011.

associations tend to organise themselves according to particular subject-matter, such as those who specialise in family law or commercial law.

An important issue in relation to future development of mediation is how the insurance sector will react. Who will pay for a mediation? Will insurers fund mediation? Insurers are now increasingly including the cost of mediation in their policies, and varying their requirements on quality of mediators. Two issues remain central to implementation of the Mediation Directive.[46] Insurers have asked for quality criteria to be included in the law.

The extent to which mediation develops will depend on comparative costs issues as between mediation and the courts system. Will the costs of a failed mediation be counted as costs, and recoverable costs, of the procedure? One of the situations in which mediation has been shown to be most successful is where a judge (who is not the judge who is in charge of the file) acts as mediator, and this situation currently triggers no additional court or lawyers costs to be paid. Accordingly, a key question is how large the market might be for mediation outside the courts, since the costs of not just the mediator but also the parties' lawyers will need to be funded. Insurers or parties who pay must perceive there to be a favourable cost-benefit balance if mediation is going to be preferred to the courts. It is also unclear whether court-provided mediation will save money for the courts: if it does not, then court costs can be expected to rise, either in general or through a specific charge for mediation. Current gaps in the mediation landscape could take a long time to fill.

There is no clearly accepted policy on what the state should provide in relation to dispute resolution, or in what form.

The German civil procedure rules inherently provide less pre-action information to be exchanged between parties than do the English rules. The English mediation model is supported precisely because of such pre- and early-action exchange of information. In Germany, a claim starts when a claimant sends a document to the court that is a statement of the facts and main evidence on which the party relies. A defendant then produces his statement of facts and the evidence that supports his case. Each party's statement is, therefore, inherently one-sided. The judge can only get an overview of what the case is about by carefully considering the statements of both sides at the first hearing, so as to form a comprehensive independent picture of the merits and which issues are agreed or are in contention. The stance of each party remains throughout one of asserting the facts and interpretation of law that he wants to put forward.

The draft Mediation Law will require people to state if they have tried mediation. The implication of this is that the lawyers on both sides will have to gain an understanding of the facts, real nature of the case and the legal position that is wider than has traditionally been the case, so as to assess the relative merits of each party's case. Not only is that a fundamentally new approach, it is an approach that is not catered for within the ongoing civil procedure rules, and it may also give rise to extra work that is not provided for under the costs tariff, which will have to be funded somehow. In contrast, when England and Wales made a similar revolutionary shift to introduce ADR,[47] both the philosophy and

[46] The government made early progress in considering how to implement the Directive, and commissioned a comparative study from the Max Planck Institute in 2007. Drafts of a law were presented and widely discussed. However, progress was interrupted by Federal elections, which resulted in a change of Justice Minister from an SDP to a Liberal politician, and the need for fresh ministerial briefings and obtaining full Cabinet approval, which was delayed by other pressing issues.

[47] Civil Procedure Rules (1999); Lord Woolf 'Access to Justice: Interim Report to the Lord Chancellor on the Civil Justice System in England and Wales', HMSO (Final Report).

rules of civil procedure underwent significant reform so as to align the operation of court procedure with the practicalities of negotiated settlements.

Privatised Enforcement of Consumer Law

The Limited Role of Public Authorities

The resolution of disputes involving consumers and businesses in Germany needs to be seen also in the context of the constitutional structure and the environment for enforcing consumer law.

Since Germany is a federal country, the Federal Government generally enacts legislation governing consumer protection within the scope of its constitutional competences. The 16 federal states, the *Länder*, are responsible for the enforcement of laws. Hence, there is no central supervisory authority for consumer protection in Germany, and neither federal nor state bodies are particularly active in enforcement of consumer law, save in relation to enforcing the safety and health protection of consumers, eg with regard to foodstuffs.

The Federal Ministry of Food, Agriculture and Consumer Protection (BMELV) is responsible for consumer policy, consumer protection and general matters regarding consumer information.[48] The Federal Office of Consumer Protection and Food Safety (BVL),[49] an independent higher federal authority within the BMELV, is responsible for cross-border violations of consumer rights, operating under the EU Consumer Protection Cooperation Regulation[50] and the German EC Act that implements it.

Enforcement of consumer law is privatised[51] in two ways.[52] Firstly, in the field of economic consumer protection, consumers concerned are themselves generally responsible for asserting private claims under civil law, eg if purchased products show material defects, they must take court action if necessary and there is no public enforcement authority that takes care of this for them. Secondly, private organisations are particularly active in enforcing unfair competition law (especially misleading advertising) and unfair consumer trading laws. Two types of private organizations are involved, one funded by business (the *Wettbewerbszentrale: WBZ*)[53] and others that are consumer organizations that are largely state-funded (the *Verbraucherzentralen*). Although individual consumers may pursue their own claims, these two types of bodies are the widely preferred mechanisms for enforcing both individual and collective issues.

[48] See www.bmelv.de/EN/ConsumerProtection/consumer-protection_node.html.

[49] www.bvl.bund.de/EN/Home/homepage_node.html.

[50] Regulation (EC) 2006/2004 on cooperation between national authorities responsible for the enforcement of consumer protection [2004] OJ L364/1.

[51] A structure that relies strongly on enforcing consumer law through private actors in the courts leads to a steady stream of cases in the Federal Supreme Court about contract and tort, including consumer protection law. This is not so in the UK, where such cases do not now reach the Supreme Court and they appear to have dried up, as they now seem to have diverted into other ADR systems. The authors are grateful to Professor Reinhard Zimmermann for this observation.

[52] See http://ec.europa.eu/consumers/redress_cons/ecc_germany_en.htm, andhttp://ec.europa.eu/consumers/redress/out_of_court/commu/acce_just04_en_ccb_en.pdf.

[53] Zentrale zur Bekämpfung gegen unlauteren Wettbewerb e.V. (Wettbewerbszentrale: WBZ); Centre for Protection against Unfair Competition, see www.wettbewerbszentrale.de/de/institution/profil/auftrag.

This system deals only with prevention, and not with redress. Seeking damages is a matter for the individuals affected to pursue personally. Both the WBZ and the consumer associations have the right to take action under the 'skimming off' law,[54] but the former does so rarely, typically only in hard core cases such as involving fraud. Unscrupulous traders can disappear quickly, in which case the private bodies try to involve prosecutors, who are far more effectively armed to take action against rogues.

Private Enforcement of Unfair Commercial Practices

Under the Act against Unfair Competition (*Gesetz gegen den unlauteren Wettbewerb*: UWG),[55] an advertisement or any kind of unfair commercial practice (ie misleading practices, unfair business terms, distance selling contracts, guarantees, e-commerce), independent of the media or business sector, can only be queried by civil action and are therefore dealt with before the civil courts. In addition to legislation, some codes exist covering questions of taste and decency. Specific types of advertising, such as concerning alcohol and cars, discrimination and the role of women in advertising, are dealt with by the German Advertising Council (*Deutscher Werberat*). However, most commercial practices are regulated by law, such as misleading statements, sales promotions, prize competitions, unfair marketing practices, medical and food advertising, price labelling and shop opening hours.

The UWG grants those whose rights have been infringed the right to apply to a court in civil proceedings for an injunction against others' unfair competition.[56] Such rights are also exercisable by the WBZ[57] and, since 1965,[58] by consumer associations. The system has been operating effectively, swiftly and cheaply for 100 years. The enforcement system is free to consumers: losers pay under the court costs rules. The establishment costs of the consumer associations are paid by the state, and those of the WBZ are paid for by businesses.

The *Wettbewerbszentrale*

The WBZ is a self-regulatory body of German business founded in 1912. It comprises all chambers of commerce, most trade and craft corporations, about 750 other industrial or commercial associations and approximately 1,300 companies. It deals with over 15,000 complaints a year at its head office in Bad Homburg and five regional branch offices (Berlin, Dortmund, Hamburg, Munich, and Stuttgart). Its total annual budget is not published. Infringement cases are handled by a team of in-house lawyers. Where court proceedings are instituted, cases are outsourced to a member of a panel of external law firms. The annual

[54] See the skimming-off procedure *(Gewinnabschöpfung)* according to s10 of the German Act Against Unfair Competition (*Gesetz gegen den unlauteren Wettbewerb: UWG*). This Act allows consumer or competition associations since 2004 to skim off unlawful gains. However, due to the complexity of the procedure, it has shown little practical effect. See information provided by the VZBV at: www.vzbv.de/cps/rde/xbcr/vzbv/rechtsdurchsetzung_broschuere_vzbv_2011.pdf.

[55] Originally introduced in 1909.

[56] UWG, s 8.

[57] See UWG, para 8.3 and the German Law on injunctions *(Unterlassungsklagengesetz (UklaG)). See also*, s 33 of the German Act Against Restraints on Competition (*Gesetzes gegen Wettbewerbsbeschränkungen*: *GWB*), para 33 regarding cartel damages.

[58] In order to implement Regulation (EC) 2006/2004 on consumer protection cooperation, in the *Verbraucherschutzdurchsetzungsgesetz* (the Law on Consumer Protection Enforcement).

budget for such external work is €750,000, although the court-specified level of costs is recovered in those cases that are won.

An important function of the WBZ is to provide information and advice to its members concerning advertising and marketing practices in the planning stage (copy advice), so as to prevent infringements from occurring. This *ex ante* function is effective and widely used by companies. Members of staff also give talks and seminars on current matters of interest concerning general and specific topics in competition law. The WBZ publishes a monthly journal, *Der Wettbewerb: Aus der Praxis – Für die Praxis*, which is addressed to its members and the public, to inform them of significant changes, developments and judgments in the area of unfair competition law. Furthermore, the WBZ publishes an analysis of the most important court decisions and essays concerning competition law on a monthly basis (*Urteils- und Literaturauswertung*). It also publishes an annual report, which gives an overview on developments in different branches of trade and industry (ie tourism, telecommunication, e-commerce, financial sector, health sector, energy sector) and outlines the most important cases dealt with by the WBZ. Press releases are issued regularly on selected current cases as well as on developments in legislation and jurisdiction. Information collected from court decisions around the country is widely relied on by other courts as well as by traders and others. Such decisions create an extensive legal framework for market activity, and legal commentaries.

Consumer Associations (*Verbraucherzentralen*)

Consumer organisations in Germany do not require any approval by the state, and operate at national and *Länder* levels. There are two large consumer organizations that operate throughout Germany and receive funding from the federal budget, the Federation of German Consumer Organisations (*Verbraucherzentrale Bundesverband e.V.*: VZBV)[59] and *Stiftung Warentest*, the premier consumer testing organisation. Forty-two other consumer organisations or consumer-policy oriented associations operate and are members of VZBV. Other consumers organisations also exist, such as the German Consumer Initiative (*Verbraucherinitiative e.V.*).

The VZBV[60] is a non-governmental, independent organisation that represents the political, economic and social interests of consumers, vis-à-vis policy-makers and the private sector.[61] The federation was established in 2000 as a result of the merger of three consumer-interest organisations[62] and has approximately 100 staff members working in the Berlin offices.[63] Registered as a non-profit association, it acts as an umbrella organization for the 16 consumer advice centres in the federal states and for 26 other consumer-policy oriented associations. These consumer bodies form an integrated system of advice, information, law enforcement and representation of political interests promoting consumer interests which has more than eight million individual members.[64] Consumers receive advice from a network of 190 advice centres dealing with around four million individual contacts with

[59] www.vzbv.de/go.
[60] www.vzbv.de/go.
[61] www.verbraucherzentrale.de/en/wir.php.
[62] The AgV, the VSV and the *Stiftung Verbraucherinstitut*.
[63] www.vzbv.de/go/wir/wir_ueber_uns/index.html.
[64] www.vzbv.de/go, See the note on Germany on the EU Commission website: http://ec.europa.eu/consumers/index_en.htm.

consumers per year. All advice centres have recourse to a database of 'advisory stances' (ie model answers for typical problems). The formulation of advisory stances is coordinated by the federal association and is subject to a uniform quality management. The individual advisory activities are stored in a central computer database. This constitutes the basis for, on the one hand, being able to systematically take action against recurring violations and, on the other hand, for obtaining a precise empirical picture of existing consumer problems.

The €8.7 million annual budget of VZBV is 90 per cent funded from annual institutional grants provided by the federal government,[65] together with contributions from public authorities, businesses, economic operators and civil society at national, European and international level.[66] At the federal state level, the consumer advice centres receive both institutional and project financing. The centres also contribute to this funding with consultation fees and the sale of consumer advice guides.

VZBV deals with a wide range of consumer topics such as sustainable consumption, financial services, health care and food law. Its tasks include enforcement through lawsuits, the development of standards and providing professional training for the staff of member organisations. VZBV is particularly active on three levels:

- consumer-policy lobbying and advising politicians and policy-makers to achieve rules that guarantee a transparent market;
- legal implementation, by highlighting irregularities and enforcing consumer rights in courts;
- promoting consumer advice services.[67]

Stiftung Warentest, a foundation established in 1964 under private law, is charged with the task of informing the public about the quality and environmental friendliness of goods and services on the basis of tests. Furthermore, the foundation is to provide general information about optimal private housekeeping and health- and eco-conscious behaviour. Around 88 per cent of the annual earnings of *Stiftung Warentest* or approximately €50 million come from the sale of its publications, eg the magazines *test* and *FinanzTest*. In addition, the foundation receives an annual grant from the federal budget as compensation for the fact that it waives income from advertisements in its publications in order to maintain its independence from suppliers.

Procedure

Consumer complaints that involve breaches of consumer law may be made to the WBZ or any consumer association. Those bodies are empowered to bring injunction proceedings to end the infringement, but do not have power to seek damages. Complaints are received from any source, including competitors, consumers, trade associations and public authorities such as the police, trade and health authorities. Business organisations and authorities provide 80 per cent of complaints to the WBZ, and the WBZ considers that a competitor is the best type of complainant, since it will have far greater technical and timely knowledge than most consumers or other outsiders.

[65] The Federal Ministry of Food, Agriculture and Consumer Protection (BMELV).

[66] The Federal Ministry funds also individual projects run by different consumer organizations, such as the German Nutrition Society and the Information Service for Consumer Protection, Food and Agriculture.

[67] www.verbraucherzentrale.de/en/wir.php.

In practice, enforcement cases are frequently resolved at an early stage. The body will usually first write to the trader asking him to sign an undertaking (*Abmahnung*) to amend or discontinue the advertising or commercial practice.[68] This declaration contains a penalty clause, so breach of which will give rise to a fine.[69] Legal action is threatened in the case of non-compliance. The threat of an injunction to protect the collective interests of consumers can be sufficiently powerful to result in swift settlement, although some cases are taken to the courts for wider market reasons, including setting a precedent.

In urgent cases, the body can seek a preliminary court injunction prohibiting the unfair commercial practice. Cases that involve unfair competition law usually satisfy the requirement for urgency. Therefore, many such cases are dealt with this way. The court will normally issue the preliminary injunction within a day by immediate order. In the case of contravention, the court can charge the opponent with an administrative fee of up to €250,000.

In non-urgent cases, before taking court action, the WBZ will—in appropriate cases—try to reach an amicable agreement, which may involve the complaint being brought before the Board of Conciliation of the regional Chamber of Commerce.[70] Court proceedings may be instituted in the *Landgericht*, and are subject to the normal loser pays rules. A claimant has to prove all details and facts in his claim, but the burden of proof rests on the defendant to produce the evidence that his advertising complies with the law, so firms usually can either produce such evidence or not, and that result determines the outcome of a challenge. If a case proceeds to the trial stage, the judge will often be faced with complex technical evidence.

The consumers associations and the WBZ liaise regularly, and sometimes institute cases against the same infringers. The WBZ's approach is to respond to individual complaints by instituting individual cases, finding solutions, and stopping unfair advertising. Consumer associations can, in addition, sometimes raise issues that have more political aspects, and seek media coverage aimed at highlighting issues. The WBZ considers that the Federal competition authority (*Bundeskartellamt*) is better equipped to obtain facts and market information in relation to competition law issues: the private bodies do not have power to inspect companies, and civil procedure law contains no general right to discovery of documents.

Statistics

The procedure is usually fast. On average, advertisements or unfair commercial practices are often withdrawn or amended within 1 to 2 weeks from receiving a complaint. If a preliminary injunction procedure is commenced before a civil court, a settlement can be achieved within a day by immediate order.

The WBZ receives around 14,000 complaints a year.[71] Of those, only around 50 per cent are well founded. Warning letters are sent out in roughly 6,000 to 7,000 cases a year, 80–90 per cent of which result in amicable settlement by the recipient. Around 600–700 cases are started in court every year.

[68] The WZB is authorised by s 13 *Unterlassungsklagengesetz* (Law on injunctions, implementing Directive 98/27 EG on Injunctions for the Protection of Consumers' Interests) to request information from postal and telephone authorities and companies on a customer's personal data. Thus, the WZB has the power to disclose the identity of the owner of a German P.O. Box or telecommunication service.

[69] See http://www.vzbv.de/cps/rde/xbcr/vzbv/rechtsdurchsetzung_broschuere_vzbv_2011.pdf, 7.

[70] http://www.wettbewerbszentrale.de/de/home.

[71] WBZ Annual Report 2010 available at: www.wettbewerbszentrale.de/media/getlivedoc.aspx?id=31254; In the mid-2000s when eBay was widely used, the number was considerably higher.

In 2010 the WBZ started to record the source of complaints. Of the overall 14000 contacts, 2500 are consumer complaints; all others are from businesses, official, legal or political authorities or associations.

Example of selected areas that are complained about to the WBZ in 2010:

Sector	**Amount of cases**
Health sector (Doctors, Chemists, Health insurance, pharma industry, optitians...	1368
Bidding platforms (ebay, my-hammer, ..)	1203
Trade	1044
stationary trade	950
Tourism / tavel	787
Car sector	764
Online trade	667
Driving schools	479
Security	480
Expert opinoins	362
Media / publishers	342
Finance (banks, insurance, insurance broker, financial services)	229
Telecoms	198
Lottery / gaming / mashines	170
Architects / engineers	161
Energy	153

Cross-border Cases

The *Bundesamt für Verbraucherschutz und Lebensmittelsicherheit* (BVL)[72] is the 'single liaison office' in Germany for the European cooperation in consumer protection and is the competent authority for cross-border enforcement of a large number of consumer rights.[73] The BVL can delegate foreign cases received to the WBZ or consumer associations.

In 2009, the WBZ received around 120 complaints from German competitors and consumers concerning marketing practices of companies abroad (mainly Austria, Switzerland and Great Britain). Enforcement abroad is based on the Brussels Regulation, and has been found to be difficult in practice.

Overview of Consumer ADR Bodies

A wide range of models of consumer ADR are found in Germany. The overall picture is confusing, and hides a number of important gaps. One source of confusion arises from the fact that the existing bodies can be categorised in different ways. If the bodies are categorised by source of funding, or whether they are public or private bodies, the following appears:

- ADR within public authorities, such as the *Bundesbank*, or *Bundesnetzagentur*;
- Private legal entity with state funding, such as *Schlichtungsstelle Mobilität*, now superceded;

[72] www.bvl.bund.de/EN/091_ConsumerProtection/01_Tasks/02_EuropeanConsumerProtectionCooperation/wvs_EuropeanConsumerProtectionCooperation_node.html

[73] Regulation (EC) No 2006/2004 on Consumer Protection Cooperation (CPC) and the EC Consumer Protection Enforcement Act.

- Privately funded ADR schemes, whether arbitration boards or ombudsman, such as *Reiseschiedsstelle*, *Versicherungsombudsman*, *Schlichtungsstelle für den Öffentlichen Personenverkehr* and the *Schlichtungsstellen für Arzthaftpflichtfragen*.

In contrast, if the bodies are categorised by type of technique, they are based on either conciliation or arbitration. Thus the Federal government states:

> There are in the Federal Republic of Germany many conciliation boards which deal with the amicable resolution of consumer-related conflicts before they reach the courts. The conciliation boards are mostly organised by professional bodies (associations and confederations) and therefore define their competence according to their line of business. Thus, conciliation boards exist in the field of vehicle repair, cleaning of textiles and other trades (building trade, radio and television engineers etc.) ...[74]

Further, within the private sector, arbitration tribunals and conciliation boards are part of the services offered by the chambers of industry and commerce in nearly all larger cities, as well as their chamber of handicrafts (*Handwerkskammer*). Some conciliation boards are run by sectoral trade bodies, such as the motor trade in relation to vehicle repairs and motor dealers for defects in second-hand vehicles, and by the liberal professions, such as the medical councils and architects' associations, organised in nearly every federal state. The professional associations of lawyers, patent agents, tax consultants and chartered accountants are bound to mediate, if called upon, in disputes between their members and their members' clients.

The Civic Consulting Report found:[75]

> The number and diversity of ADR schemes in Germany is very high. There are many schemes that are mostly organised by professional bodies (the Chambers of Industry and Commerce, the General Medical Councils) and the guilds of different crafts (vehicle repair, shoemakers, cleaning of textiles and other traders) aimed at using expert knowledge in a particular sector when a case arises. These schemes exist in larger cities as part of the services offered by their chamber of industry and commerce as well as by their chamber of handicrafts (*Handwerkskammern*). There are also ADR schemes run by the motor trade, by the motor dealers, by the liberal professions (medical councils architects' associations and associations of lawyers, patent agents, tax consultants and chartered accountants) that operate at local level.

ADR services are then offered by the ombudsmen, especially for disputes between providers of financial services and consumers: the Ombudsman for Private Health Insurance, the Ombudsman for Insurances, the Ombudsman for Disputes with Banking Houses, the Ombudsman of Building and Loan Associations and the Ombudsman for Disputes involving Online Trade. In addition, the *Schlichtungsstelle Mobilität* and *Reiseschiedsstelle* provide ADR services in transport and travel sector respectively.

The number of ombudsmen is currently small but growing. The first and most successful is the Insurance Ombudsman, whose model has been copied for Transport.

But the overall position on ADR within Germany is one of confusion of models and pathways. Some sectors have far more ADR opportunities than others. Different options exist within different sectors, such as for financial services and banks. The profile of different ADR schemes varies enormously, and so does the extent to which they are used:

[74] From http://ec.europa.eu/civiljustice/adr/adr_ger_en.htm#102.

[75] DG SANCO, *Study on the use of Alternative Dispute Resolution in the European Union* (Berlin, Civil Consulting 2009), at http://ec.europa.eu/consumers/redress_cons/adr_study.pdf.

some are prominent and others hardly known at all. There are also differences in relation to the powers of the various bodies, especially over whether outcomes are binding or not. Recommendations made by conciliation boards are not as a rule binding on the parties. However, the board's award sometimes places one-sided obligations on the business undertaking.

Thus, making generalisations about the state of ADR bodies in Germany is difficult, given their diversity. It would not be helpful to give details of the operation of every body. The position will be illustrated by summarising certain types and sectors.

Chambers of Commerce

Every major city has a chamber of commerce (*Handelskammer*), which almost always has a long-established arbitration court (*Schiedsgericht*), and more recently a mediation facility. The objective is to provide a forum for resolution of disputes that is more appropriate than courts, for example by providing expertise for various commercial sectors. They handle both B2B and B2C disputes, including allegations of infringing the unfair competition law UWG.

The Hamburg arbitration court, which with Munich is the largest chamber in Germany,[76] has 2,500 arbitrations per year, over half of which end in settlement. There are various specialist courts. The main court of arbitration has 5 to 10 cases per year, in more than 50 per cent of which one or both parties are international, and who choose Hamburg as a neutral place for the dispute. Arbitration cases valued under €25,000 are handled by a single arbitrator, whereas higher value cases have three arbitrators, although parties sometimes decide to accept one arbitrator to keep the cost down. There is no formal requirement for arbitrators, but most are legally qualified. The arbitration court that deals with grains and coffee has three arbitrators from within the professional membership plus a legal adviser. That court is too costly for consumers as the minimum fee is €1,000.

The Hamburg chamber of commerce has a mediation centre, which was one of the first to be established in Germany, and was intended to provide high quality mediation. (The main user in this centre is Airbus, which has operations in France and at Hamburg.) The general mediation centre has 20–25 cases per year. The chamber of commerce provides a forum to inform and facilitate mediation. Its website lists recommended mediators, which the public can contact free of charge. The chamber of commerce charges a fee to contact a mediator. The chamber of commerce also has conciliation centres. All the centres have their own rules.

The Hamburg chamber of commerce processes about 800 consumer cases a year against traders. The consumers contact the chamber by phone and then follow a formal process under the chamber's mediation rules. There is a high drop out rate after the initial phone conversation and after the request for a written explanation of the problem. The chamber does not charge a fee to the consumer. If the parties agree to appoint a mediator, they must agree a fee with the mediator, which is usually €150 to €350 per hour or €1,200 to €2,800 a day, plus VAT.

[76] The Hamburg chamber of commerce has 150,000 member businesses and around 250 staff.

The Insurance Ombudsman

The most established Ombudsman scheme in Germany is the Insurance Ombudsman, which was created on 1 October 2001 on the initiative of the German Insurance Association (*Gesamtverband der Deutschen Versicherungswirtschaft*: GDV).[77] The objective was to promote out-of-court dispute resolution between insurance companies and consumers and to enhance consumer protection.[78] ADR was thought to be of particular importance to facilitating redress in the insurance sector in Germany, which has a notably large number of contracts between consumers and insurance companies: there are more than 400 million insurance contracts, more than 90 million of which involve capital savings, financing of residential property and securing financial assistance in old age. Thus, insurance has been described as a 'service of general interest'.[79]

The founders were concerned to overcome 'structural asymmetry' between consumers and insurance companies.[80] Insurance contracts are often complex and difficult to understand for consumers, and providers have more legal expertise and financial resources to enforce their rights. The Ombudsman procedure was specifically intended to demonstrate the commitment of insurance providers to taking consumer issues seriously, and hence support confidence in the sector. The Ombudsman system helps to counterbalance imbalances and assists contracting parties to settle their disputes on an equal footing if a problem arises.[81] Insurers have an obligation to inform customers of the Ombudsman procedure in every contract and in any relevant discussion.[82]

The 2004 Insurance Intermediaries Directive[83] provided that an ADR body should exist for disputes, and the German Ministry of Justice awarded this competence to the Insurance Ombudsman.[84]

The Role and Independence of the Ombudsman

The Insurance Ombudsman is an independent private institution that provides alternative dispute resolution and forms part of FIN-NET. By this means, the funding and function of the Ombudsman is independent of the trade association. Approximately 95 per cent of private insurance companies are members of the Insurance Ombudsman Association (*Versicherungsombudsman e.V.*). The Ombudsman is funded by an annual contribution of the companies that are member of the Insurance Ombudsman Association and by case fees. The annual contribution by the companies varies depending on their gross premium income. Individual claims attract a case fee of €100 payable by companies, which is adjusted at the end of a claim.

[77] J Basedow, 'Small Claims Enforcement in a High Cost Country: The German Insurance Ombudsman' in P Wahlgren (ed), *What is Scandinavian Law? Social Private Law* (Stockholm Institute for Scandinavian Law, 2007), 54.

[78] www.versicherungsombudsmann.de/Navigationsbaum/WirUeberUns/AufgabenUndZweck/index.html.

[79] G Hirsch, The German Insurance Ombudsman, speech paper, 2011, 2.

[80] ibid.

[81] ibid.

[82] Solvency II Framework Directive (Directive 2009/138/EC), Art 185; Art 1 No 19 of the German Regulation on Information Obligations for Insurance Contracts *(VVG-InfoV)*.

[83] Directive (EC) 2002/92 on insurance mediation [2002] OJ L9/3.

[84] The Federal Ministry of Justice has recognized the Insurance Ombudsman as an arbitration board within the meaning of the EU Mediation Directive. See s 214 of the German Insurance Contract Act (VVG). For more

The dispute resolution service of the Ombudsman is free of charge to consumers. They retain the option either to file a claim with a state court or with the Insurance Ombudsman. The decision by the Ombudsman is legally binding for the insurance companies, while the recommendations are voluntary for consumers.[85] Even after the decision by the Insurance Ombudsman, the consumer can still lodge a claim with the ordinary court.[86]

Maintaining the independence of the insurance ombudsman is regarded as very important. The neutrality of the Ombudsman is ensured by his independent status. The Ombudsman is not an employee of the association and dismissal is only possible for obvious gross misconduct of his obligations. He is independent in his decision-making and is not subject to any instructions from other bodies. He has, however, to observe the law in his decision-making,[87] and in making recommendations in achieving voluntary settlements.

In order to be elected to the office of Ombudsman, the candidate has to show particular expertise in insurance matters and needs to be impartial. This means that he cannot take up assignments in the insurance sector that are incompatible with his function.[88] Furthermore, representatives of both the insurance companies and consumers have to agree with the election of the Ombudsman. The appointment decision is taken by the Advisory Council of the Ombudsman Association, where insurers and consumer organisations are represented equally. In addition, there are members from the supervisory authority, academia and the parliamentary groups of the political parties represented in the German Parliament.[89] The Ombudsman is elected for a period of five years and reports to the Membership Assembly and Advisory Council once a year.[90] The current Insurance Ombudsman is Professor Dr Günter Hirsch. He has a staff of 45, including eighteen lawyers and fourteen insurance salespeople.

Powers and Procedures

The Ombudsman procedure differs from state court procedures because it is more flexible and is limited to simple issues that can be decided expeditiously. The application can be made orally, in writing or in other forms, and the respondent usually has to reply within a month.[91] Before lodging a complaint the consumer must have contacted the insurer providing it with a deadline of at least 6 weeks for a reply.

The Ombudsman can accept complaints that are brought by a consumer against an insurer if the latter is a member of the Ombudsman Association. The procedural rules refer to the definition of a consumer that is used in EU law and included in section 13 of the German Civil Code (*Bürgerliches Gesetzbuch*: BGB). As a result, a natural person who concludes an insurance contract for a purpose that is outside his or her trade, business or profession, may lodge a complaint.[92] However, the Ombudsman is not competent, inter

information see the Article published by the German Ombudsman: Günter Hirsch, 'The German insurance Ombudsman' (2011) *ZVersWiss* 100, 566.

[85] s 11 para 1 code of procedure.

[86] s 11 para 1 code of procedure. See Basedow, *Small Claims Enforcement in a High Cost Country* (2007), 54.

[87] www.versicherungsombudsmann.de/Navigationsbaum/WirUeberUns/StellungUndKompetenz/index.html.

[88] Basedow (n 77), 55.

[89] See note by the Insurance Ombudsman, p 7.

[90] www.versicherungsombudsmann.de/Navigationsbaum/WirUeberUns/AufgabenUndZweck/index.html.

[91] Basedow (n 77), 56.

[92] See Insurance Ombudsman note, 8.

alia, in cases regarding healthcare insurance or if a case is already pending in a court or arbitration tribunal.[93]

The Ombudsman can refuse a complaint if it would use too much of his resources. Importantly, the Ombudsman is obliged to dismiss a case if it deals with a question of 'legal principles' that needs to be decided by the court.[94] The Insurance Ombudsman investigates the facts of the cases *ex officio*.[95]

He can take a legally binding decision up to a sum of €10,000. Above that threshold he may pronounce non-binding recommendations in disputes about claims of up to €100,000.[96]

The procedure is designed to be more informal than that of courts, and the Ombudsman assists consumers in making complaints. Lawyers are not required and are normally not used by the parties. The Ombudsman regards a particularly important aspect of his function as helping the parties to find a mutual understanding and solution to their problem. Accordingly, he usually adopts a conciliation function as a first step, prior to his decision-making function, and the former is often successful. If the Ombudsman thinks that he is likely to decide against an enterprise, he indicates this to the company so as to give it an opportunity to settle the case itself, thereby assisting it to re-establish its relationship with its customer. He considers that he has a particular opportunity to create flexible 'win-win' solutions for the parties that can decease tension between them, in contrast to the 'win-lose' decisions that are the outcome of court decisions. If the Ombudsman decides in favour of the insurer, he pays particular attention to providing the consumer with an explanation of his decision.

The Ombudsman applies the law, although he considers that there is a margin of interpretation of the legal rules, and where the facts are not clear. Since under the rules the insurance providers are prohibited from taking disputes to court, the Ombudsman considers that he should refrain from making a decision against an enterprise if a fundamental legal question is involved, since that should be decided by a court, although this situation arises only rarely.

Respondents may request at any stage of the proceedings that the Ombudsman withdraws from the case if they can show that it concerns a test case of fundamental importance.[97] This is however only possible provided that the respondents commit themselves, to reimburse the complainant the legal costs before the court of first instance, even if the respondent wins the case.

Where cases arise that involve important decisions, companies have the option of asking the Ombudsman to resolve them or of starting the test case procedure in court. If the Ombudsman handles the procedure, the enterprise will be liable for all the costs at first instance (the consumer not being liable). The Ombudsman is obliged to deal with mass issues as a test case, without discretion, and all similar cases are stayed pending the decision of the test case. The current Ombudsman considers that it would be an improvement to give the Ombudsman the power to declare a case to be a test case.

[93] s 2 para 3 code of procedure.
[94] s 8 para 2 of the code of procedure. See J Basedow (n 77), 58.
[95] J Basedow (n 77), 58.
[96] See section 2 of the Insurance Ombudsman procedural rules. Prior to November 2010 the limit was €80,000.
[97] Rule 8.4.

Statistics[98]

The number of complaints that the Insurance Ombudsman receives has increased considerably since the office began, and in 2010 stands at over 18,000 complaints a year. In 2010 about 12,720 complaints were admitted and 5,034 were not admitted. The claim success rate is around 38 per cent. Over 90 per cent of claims involve less than €10,000.

The majority of cases are decided within three months. The Ombudsman procedures have become more efficient with time and are shorter than the usual court procedures.

Table 4.1: Complaints data 2006–2010

	2006	2007	2008	2009	2010
Complaints made	18,451	17,592	18,837	18,145	18,357
Complaints concluded	17,038	16,889	18,801	18,261	18,609

The claims figures for 2006–2010 are at Table 4.1. Both the total number of complaints (around 18,000) and the percentage of admissible complaints (69 per cent) have been at consistent levels. The subject matter of complaints is indicated in Table 4.3. Of the 12,720 admissible complaints in 2010, 12,565 related to insurance companies and 155 to intermediaries. Complaints were received by letter (61 per cent), email (18 percent), telephone (11 per cent) and fax (9 per cent). Of the inadmissible complaints, 33 per cent related to facts prior to the period of jurisdiction, and 29 per cent had no connection with an intermediary. The success rate of admissible intermediary complaints was 22 per cent.

Table 4.2: Complaints to the Insurance Ombudsman 2006–2010

	2010	2009	2008	2007	2006
Total complaints	18,357	18,145	18,837	17,592	18,451
Admissible	12,720	12,371	13,375	11,583	12,768
Not admissible	5,034	5,045	4,740	5,302	5,043
No follow up	603	729	722	707	640

Table 4.3: Subject matter of complaints, by percentages

	2010	2009	2008	2007	2006
Life/pension	38.5	39.3	40.7	41.4	55.4
Legal insurance	15.2	13.9	13.1	12.1	10.1
Car insurance	7.1	5.6	6.4	5.9	4.9
Accident	4.1	3.6	3.6	2.6	1.7
Building	7.4	8.9	8.8	9.2	6.5
Home contents	7.0	6.9	5.0	5.6	4.1
Private insurance	4.9	4.9	4.5	4.7	3.7
Disability for work	3.2	2.9	2.7	3.0	2.6
Other	7.7	9.0	9.2	8.6	6.5

[98] *Annual report* Insurance Ombudsman *(2010)*. www.versicherungsombudsmann.de/Ressourcen/PDF/Jahresbericht-2010.pdf.

Table 4.4: Percentages of outcomes of complaints

	Finalised by the Ombudsman	Accepted by broker	Settlement	Withdrawn	Total
Justiciable	75.3	7.4	2.5	6.2	91.4
Not justiciable	3.1	0.6	0.0	4.9	8.6
Total	78.4	8.0	2.5	11.1	100.0

Eighty-six per cent of complaints were for under €5,000, although a small number reached the ceiling, which was €100,000 by late 2011. Admissible complaints took an average of 4.4 months to complete.

In 2010, the Insurance Ombudsman cost €3.2 million and had an income of €3.6 m which means a profit of €0.04 m.[99]

Evaluation

The Insurance Ombudsman has increasingly been recognized by both public bodies[100] and private actors as an effective dispute resolution provider. This ADR model was copied by the transport sector Ombudsman (see below) and has been considered by scholars to be successful and may inspire wider areas of consumer dispute resolution.[101] Insurers have applied this dispute resolution mechanism as a marketing advantage. The costs are lower than court proceedings and involve less potential for adverse publicity. Consumers, in turn, have an additional option to file a complaint without the financial risks that a court procedure would entail.

Doctors

Claims for medical negligence against physicians in Germany are handled by twelve specialist conciliation schemes, which are organized on a regional basis in the *Länder*, although some schemes cover more than a single *Land*. The largest scheme is in North Germany and is called *Schlichtungsstelle für Arzthaftpflichtfragen der norddeutschen Ärztekammern*[102] (conciliation scheme for medical liability disputes). It was established in 1976 and has handled a steadily increasing number of claims, totalling around 85,000 claims between 1976 and 2010, currently around 4,000 cases a year. The conciliation schemes were created as a response to a perception that valid claims in the courts were not succeeding, since medical experts appointed were reluctant to criticise their colleagues, and patient confidence was falling. The Federal medical association (*Ärztekammer*) wished to create a separate, more satisfactory and quicker dispute resolution service. However, the different regional conciliation schemes operate under different rules, established by the

[99] ibid.

[100] Several states provide that court claims can only be filed after an out of court mediation institution has tried to solve the dispute.

[101] J Basedow (n 77), 61.

[102] http://norddeutsche-schlichtungsstelle.de.

local medical chamber, and the result is confusing and makes comparisons challenging. However, it should be kept in mind that lawyers and other professionals are organised regionally as well. Some attempts have now been made to work towards a single national standard, bearing in mind that lawyers now operate across *Land* borders and bring claims in different *Länder*, under different procedures and rules, and subject to different relations with the local medical chamber.

The north German scheme in Hanover is organisationally independent of the nine medical chambers that it covers.[103] The chambers finance the scheme but they have no influence on the scheme. The chambers have the right to change the procedures but not to be involved in individual cases. The scheme only has the obligation to report back to the chambers on financial matters. The North German scheme costs €4.1 million per year. The advantage of being independent is that patient and doctor can be sure that their dispute will not be 'known' by the medical chambers: no 'name and shame' policy operates.

Mediation as a technique has been found to be unsuited to medical claims, since its aim is to bring the parties together and restore trust, whereas patients are generally unwilling to approach a medical problem in this way.[104] In addition, there is asymmetry of expertise between doctors and patients that hinders reaching consensus. However, in recent years the general aims of the scheme to improve the relationship between doctor and patient, and so keep the number of court cases low, have expended to encompass preventing future mistakes in treatment and improving patient safety.

The north German scheme has 55 doctors from all medical specialities with expert knowledge to draw upon. Every case is looked at by a lawyer and a doctor, who are in constant exchange with each other. The doctors have regular seminars to improve their expertise in medico-legal issues, and employees and independent experts are trained frequently. About 3,000 independent experts are consulted by the Hanover scheme per year throughout Germany (in contrast to courts, which only use local experts). The Hanover scheme's quality system has been approved since 2007 by the national standards body,[105] and is subject to regular inspections, which have proved high motivation for employees.

The scheme is free of charge for patients and doctors. The settlement process is aimed to be fair, transparent, free of barriers, with minimal formalities and fast. The scheme obtains the medical records, makes an assessment of the case, obtains comments from parties about the identity of the external expert to be consulted and the list of questions to be asked, and subsequently on the expert report, and reaches an internal decision on legal liability. The decision of the settlement is not legally binding. Any party can terminate the investigation process at any time. The time limits for the independent processes are usually two weeks to one month, but the parties can call and ask for an extension. The timing at court is very strict, if a document is submitted late then the case gets dismissed, the north German scheme is more lenient with timing. The average duration per case is 14 months.

The doctor's insurance company (*Haftpflichtversicherung*) is an equal player in the process, and takes the decision (without involving the doctor) whether to pay or not. The involvement of the insurance company in this process has been found to save a lot

[103] The following information was supplied by Johann Neu and Christine Wohlers of *Schlichtungsstelle für Arzthaftpflichtfragen der norddeutschen Ärztekammern*.

[104] See B K Hattemer, *Mediation bei Störungen des Arzt-Patient-Verhältnisses* (Springer, 2011). The book provides a detailed analysis of the possibilities and limitations of mediation in a variety of problems in the doctor-patient relationship.

[105] Under DIN EN ISO 9001:2008 TUV, www.tuevsued.de/management_systeme/qualitaet/iso_90012000.

of time and money (although this is not the same for all the dispute resolution schemes in Germany). The insurers pay a fixed rate for the service and pay for the external expert report. This makes it possible to pay the external independent evaluators the same rates as they receive from a court. The settlement decision has no impact on the doctor's insurance premium as it is seen as a good will decision of the insurers to be a part of this process.

The process will only go ahead if all parties agree. The consent can be withdrawn at any time by the parties.

The north German scheme finalizes a case with a decision that comments on the claims made in the process from a legal basis. This means that they decide if the claims are made rightfully or not. The damage is differentiated; if the conclusion is that a medical mistake caused the damage, with this documentation the patient can claim directly from the doctor's insurance, which is involved in the proceedings, without any further paperwork or time spent. Other schemes do not try to prove this information; they merely prove that a medical problem has occurred.

Statistics

Table 4.5: Decisions in matters concerning doctor liability 2008: 4,840

Landgerichte in North Germany, first instance	46%	2,230 decisions
North German out-of-court settlement Hanover	54%	2,610 decisions

Table 4.6: Amount of court cases avoided; Evaluation June 2007: 800 decisions from the year 2002

800 cases decided at out-of-court settlement Hanover	
court follow-up	Court avoided
73: 9%	727: 91%

Since 2000, anonymised data from cases has been entered into a Medical Error Reporting System (MERS), which the federal *Ärztekammer* decided in 2006 to operate throughout Germany.

Transport

Various regional Conciliation Boards[106] or *Ombudsstellen*[107] have been created in some *Länder*, which usually make non-binding recommendations for complaints involving bus, subway, tram and railway services. A publicly financed national pilot scheme for long distance travel, the *Schlichtungsstelle Mobilität*,[108] was discontinued in 2009. In its place,

[106] An example is Schlichtungsstelle Nahverkehr des Landes Nordrhein-Westfalen (Conciliation Board for Local Public Transport in North Rhine-Westphalia).

[107] Such as *Ombudsstelle Nahverkehr Bayern* (Ombudspoint for Local Public Transport Bavaria) and a similar one in Baden-Württemberg.

[108] www.schlichtungsstelle-mobilitaet.org. See case study at Civic Consulting 2009, pp 455–460.

the private transportation companies founded The Conciliation Body for Public Transport CBPT (*Schlichtungsstelle für den öffentlichen Personenverkehr* (söp)).[109,110]

Söp is an independent and neutral organization and offers its service throughout Germany to customers of train, bus, flight and ship companies that are members of its conciliation scheme. This process is free of charge for the consumer; the cost of the scheme is met by the transport companies. Söp evaluates the complaint and makes a settlement suggestion to resolve the dispute acceptable for both sides and outside of court. Söp can deal with cases of a value up to € 30,000: a normal claim is between €10 and €200. For example, a consumer can get help with a complaint about:

- Delays and missed connections,
- Cancellations,
- Damaged or lost luggage,
- Faulty information,
- Tickets and reservations,
- Bad service.

It is common for travellers to use more than one form of transport (eg train to plane), and investigating a complaint can take up a lot of time, involving a long chain of transport providers and contracted partners. The söp scheme aims to focus its expertise and contacts on dealing with that part of the chain that relates to the claim, thereby avoiding the need for a consumer to confront various different conciliation boards. Söp covers 99 per cent of long-distance rail travel and 95 per cent of regional travel. Söp is seeking to expand membership and offers a 'get to know' programme explaining the benefits of the service. The same approach is also applied to cross-border travel. Söp does only handle complaints against transport companies, ie, it does not cover conflicts related to the services of third online booking platforms, and refers such cases to the *Reiseschiedsstelle*. While the focus is currently on railway transport, söp aspires to become a ADR scheme covering all modes of transportation. It has the capacity to handle complaints in German, English and French. The main current challenge and coverage gap stems from the reluctance of airline companies to participate in ADR procedures. The German federal government is considering legislation to require airlines to subject themselves to ADR.

The Process

The customer must first contact the company concerned. Beside legal statutes of limitation, there are no time limits in which the consumer has to have complained to the company or approached söp. The consumer lodges his complaint in writing. Söp's approach is voluntary, so it first ensures that the travel company is a member of its scheme: this is the case if the company is a member of the trade association *Trägerverein der Schlichtungsstelle für den öffentlichen Personenverkehr e.V.*. After receipt of all the necessary documents, söp contacts the transport company to ask them for a statement. It does not hear witnesses, and makes its decision on the basis of the documents.

Söp produces a report with a recommendation for a consensual settlement on the basis of applying the law to the facts, as would occur in court. All the conciliators at söp are lawyers.

[109] Information below includes comments from Director Edgar Isermann and Christof Berlin of söp.

[110] www.soep-online.de/die-schlichtung.html. söp was listed as satisfying Recommendation 98/257/EC in June 2010.

The recommendation only becomes binding if both the traveler and the transport company agree to it, with any possible modifications. Each side can decide to take their case to court at any time of the process.

Söp aims to resolve the dispute by win-win solutions: It finds that there are many situations where the law has no good solution. For example, if a train breaks down during daytime and the passenger decides to take a taxi to his final destination, the rail company arguably has no obligation to pay for the taxi. The law does not cover this situation, so söp can make a suggestion to the company to resolve the dispute (such as involving vouchers or shared taxi cost) and the company has two weeks to reply. Söp can support a creative outcome and make good-will suggestions to the company. It seeks to reinforce the companies' motto 'more than satisfaction' for travellers. The main task of söp is to ensure out-of-court settlement of individual disputes between travellers and the transport companies helps to strengthen customer satisfaction with the travel companies. Both parties can take the case to court at any time and thereby end the settlement process.

The process usually is handled within 3 months. Söp has a 90 per cent success rate in settling rail disputes. It has a steady media presence, with over 3,000 mentions per year, and conveys its ability to solve disputes amicably. Söp is capable of processing mass problems, including an individual perspective and always tries to give the individual an answer to his particular problem. Successive complaints from the same person are rare.

Costs and Funding

The settlement process is funded by the transport companies. For the traveller as a complainant the conciliation is free. They carry only their own costs, for example for postage and copies, or the involvement of lawyers.

Every member company pays an annual fee (€1,000 for a single company but groups of companies like *Deutsche Bahn* pay €5,000 max) as well as a case fee (€25 for unjustified claims and €150, €200, €300, €400, €600 or €800 per case, depending on the time and expenditure involved). Although the scheme is privately founded and funded, its advisory council includes public authorities, which command about one-third of the votes, the other two-thirds representing associations that deal with consumer and travellers' rights and transportation companies.

During the first two years of work since December 2009, söp received around 6,800 individual cases, of which 4,500 related to rail disputes and 2,300 to air travel. Most of the rail disputes could be settled, whereas the majority of the flight cases is still pending, due to the lack of co-operation by many airlines. Complaints fall into the following types:

Rail

Customer rights	48%
Bahn card [rail discount card]	18%
Additional travel cost in retrospect	16%
Refunds	9%
Other	9%

Air

Delays	47%
Cancellations	31%
Luggage	8%
Tickets	5%
Being stranded	5%
Other	4%

Online Travel

In 2004 some of the larger companies that offer online travel founded the *Verband Internet Reisevertrieb* (VIR)[111] (association of online travel sales). One of the association's goals is to ensure that consumers have confidence in booking travel services on the Internet. In order to build such confidence, the association launched its travel arbitration scheme in March 2005, which aims at finding an amicable settlement to disagreement between online travel agents and their clients. This facility is the first of its kind in the travel industry and was one of the first in Germany to receive official EU certification.[112]

VIR provides customers (including those outside Germany), who have booked a trip online through a member of the scheme, with independent intermediaries ('arbitrators')[113] that can be invoked whenever the parties themselves do not manage to resolve the dispute. The arbitrator will then consider the complaint objectively and make a proposal on how a dispute can be resolved amicably, to the satisfaction of both parties. Companies that join the scheme are required to agree to try and solve any complaints with the customer before the scheme is approached. A complaint can be submitted in writing, as email, by online form, or phone. The complaint is dealt with according to the guidelines in the *Verfahrensordnung*,[114] based on the idea of voluntary participation and active support of the process by the parties. All the facts and circumstances of each individual case are evaluated with all submitted documents. Cases are handled in the German language, but can be dealt with in English. The *Reiseschiedsstelle* deals with online flight bookings only, an area that the söp does not cover, and the two bodies co-operate and refer cases to each other.

Arbitrators are required to be experienced lawyers with the qualification to hold a judicial office, and to have relevant work experience in the area of travel and aviation law: experience of the industry is deemed to be important, although the arbitrator must be neutral and independent of the parties. The arbitrator receives no salary from the scheme or parties, but a fee from the parties in any case of arbitration, regardless of whether the settlement recommendation is accepted or not. Arbitration is free to customers because the association and its affiliated companies meet the cost of the scheme and the process. Members pay an annual fee, which includes one free arbitration per month. Parties are not represented by a lawyer. Passengers must, however, pay only the costs of any lawyer from

[111] Members are Avigo, ebookers, Expedia, Holiday Autos, Opodo, Lastminute und Travel24: see www.reiseschiedsstelle.de.

[112] ec.europa.eu/consumers/redress/out_of_court/ecc_germany_en.htm.

[113] The leading arbitrator is Professor Schmid.

[114] For more detail see: www.reiseschiedsstelle.de.

whom they choose to obtain advice and their own expenses (such as telephone, postage and copying costs.)

The process lasts four weeks[115] from receipt of the complaint to the submission of a settlement recommendation. The scheme deals with 200 cases per year, and numbers are rising. In the first 12 months of operation, the *Reiseschiedsstelle* received 86 phone enquiries, in 30 of which the scheme had no jurisdiction because either the journey was not booked online or not booked through a VIR-member, or because it is quite clear that there was no fault by the travel intermediary. Of the remaining 56 cases accepted for arbitration, two proposals (3.5 per cent) were not accepted by the consumer, and one case had not concluded. In 96.5 per cent of those accepted cases, settlement was successfully reached. Under 2 per cent of cases end at court. The complaints for 2010 were categorized as shown in Table 4.7.

Table 4.7: Categories of complaints

Complaints about	Cases
Bookings[116]	10
Lack of information[117]	19
Travel problems[118]	15
Problems with air travel contracts[119]	12

VIR and its member companies see a number of benefits with the scheme: complaints are dealt with faster than the courts, much more cheaply, involving less complicated procedures and on an individual level. The debate is not conducted in public, so the companies' operational practices are not made public, which limits damage to the image of companies and the entire travel industry. The ombudsman, Professor Schmid, has noted a significant decline in the number of cases since the start of the scheme, which he attributes to companies learning from his decisions and changing their behavior.

Financial Services

A large number of financial services providers have voluntarily agreed to settle disputes with the help of private conciliators or ombudsmen. However, the ADR providers are fragmented since they have arisen within the confines of the main historical sectors, notably private banks, co-operative banks and building societies (savings and loan).[120] In addition, a

[115] In the first 12 months of the *Reiseschiedsstelle*, a settlement process took an average of 15.9 days.

[116] Typical cases: booked by accident, booked something else than intended (eg without rental car); double booking after a termination of the booking process; viewed the booking request as the confirmation; or booking by under-aged persons.

[117] Typical cases: no, wrong or misleading information, flight booking without information for the traveller, not received information regarding changes.

[118] Typical travel shortcomings like hotel overbooking, non-compliance with contractual obligations, double room instead of family room, wrong hotel.

[119] Typical cases: no on-board meal although it was booked, damage to baggage, long waiting for connecting flights, stressful transfer, etc.

[120] BaFin provides information about the procedures and contact points at www.bafin.de/cln_109/nn_723250/DE/Verbraucher/BeschwerdenAnsprechpartner/OmbudsBeschwerde/ombudsbeschwerde__node.html?__nnn=true.

complaints facility exists within the regulator, the Federal Financial Supervisory Authority (BaFin), and an arbitration board of the German Bundesbank (*Schlichtungsstelle bei der Deutschen Bundesbank*).

The first step in all of these complaint procedures usually requires the consumer to contact the company in order to try to solve the issue directly with the company before taking the matters further. If no solution is found, the consumer can lodge a complaint with a wide range of ADR schemes that are specialized in financial services or with the courts.

The Federal Financial Supervisory Authority (BaFin) and its Mediation Board

BaFin (*Bundesanstalt für Finanzdienstleistungsaufsicht*) is the supervisory authority of financial services providers, insurance undertakings and securities. It was established in May 2002[121] and is an independent public law institution that is subject to oversight by the Federal Ministry of Finance. BaFin is funded by fees and contributions from the institutions and undertakings that it supervises.

BaFin is a purely administrative authority and does not have an arbitration function. It cannot give binding rulings on individual disputes, because questions of law are a matter for the courts alone. It cannot provide expert opinions on general questions of law.[122]

BaFin can decide if a company is behaving in a legally correct manner and whether or not supervisory measures have to be taken against the company.[123] Complaints by individuals provide BaFin with an important source of information for its supervisory work and help to detect breaches, such as insider trading or price manipulation.[124] BaFin specifies the format for complaints: see Figure 4.1. Where complaints are well founded, BaFin contacts the institution concerned and follows it up. It deals with about 20,000 complaints regarding insurance undertakings and 5,000 complaints about banks and financial services institutions every year. If a complaint relates to insurance or banking, the complainant can use the online complaints form.[125] Importantly, the complaint has no bearing upon the expiry of legal or contractual deadlines (eg payment or registration dates or statutory limitation periods).

BaFin usually proceeds as follows:

- It evaluates whether the information and documentation provide basis on which to reach a final decision on a case.
- If not, it requests a statement from the company concerned.
- The company reports back to BaFin, explaining the reasons for its decision.
- If the outcome of the investigation is that the company's decision is not in breach of its statutory responsibilities it will let the complainant know.
- In the contrary case, it will pursue the matter further with the company.[126]

[121] www.bafin.de/cln_179/nn_720486/EN/BaFin/bafin__node.html?__nnn=true.

[122] BaFin can only assess a complaint if the company concerned is subject to its supervision, ibid.

[123] ibid.

[124] BaFin may then launch an investigation, and reports the case to the public prosecutor's office if the suspicion is substantiated. See ibid.

[125] ibid.

[126] ibid.

BaFin is not responsible for compensation complaints regarding securities transactions (eg shares purchased or sold). These kinds of complaints have to be addressed to the courts. However, BaFin can be contacted when:

- an individual feels badly advised with regard to the purchase of securities (eg equities, warrants) and have lost money as a result, or if an offer appears to be suspect. BaFin might then investigate a potential breach of the Securities Trading Act.
- unsolicited calls are made regarding investments.

Figure 4.1: Details that should be included in a complaint to BaFin

- Name and address.
- The name and address of the company concerned.
- If the complaint relates to an insurance policy, the type of policy, the policy number and, if applicable, the claim number.
- If the complaint relates to a credit or financial services institution, the type of product should be mentioned (safe custody account, current account, savings plan, etc.), the account or customer number, and the name of the account holder if it is someone else.
- If the complaint relates to the purchase of securities, the Security Identification Number (WKN or the new ISIN).[127]
- The problem has to be described as precisely as possible and enclose copies of any supporting documentation (eg contract, statements of account, insurance certificate, correspondence).

On 1 July 2011, BaFin established a mediation board for consumer disputes relating to provisions of the Investment Act (*Investmentgesetz* (InvG)).[128] The objective of the board is to provide consumers with an easily accessible, efficient and relatively fast means of dispute resolution that is free of charge.[129] On 28 June 2011 BaFin adopted a Regulation on the Mediation Board according to section 143c (3) of the Investment Act.[130]

The BaFin Mediation Board is a back-up mediation body, because it only applies to mediation cases against companies which either are not members of the *Bundesverband Investment and Asset Management e. V.* (BVI) or have not joined the Ombudsman scheme of the BVI.[131] The BVI established a specialized ombudsman scheme for disputes regarding investment matters.[132]

BaFin has appointed two mediators to its Mediation Board. The procedures take place before a single mediator. In order to be selected as a mediator, an employee of BaFin needs to be qualified to exercise the office of a judge, possess at least three years of legal professional experience, and should not supervise the companies subject to the Investment Act.[133] The BaFin and several other associations, such as the Federation of German Consumer Organization (VZBV) and the Central Credit Committee (ZKA) take part in the selection procedure of the Mediation Board.

[127] www.bafin.de/cln_179/nn_720486/EN/BaFin/bafin__node.html?__nnn=true.

[128] This ADR procedure constitutes a procedure before a conciliation body within the meaning of section 15 (3) sentence 1 off the Introductory Act of the German Code of Civil Procedure, see also BaFin Quarterly, Q3/11, pp 9 and 12.

[129] BaFin Quarterly, Q3/11, 9.

[130] (*Investmentschlichtungsstellenverordnung –InvSchlichtV*) BGB. I, 1299.

[131] www.ombudsstelle-investmentfonds.de/index.php/ombudsstelle/liste-der-teilnehmenden-gesellschaften.

[132] See more at www.ombudsstelle-investmentfonds.de/index.php/ombudsstelle/liste-der-teilnehmenden-gesel lschaften.

[133] BaFin Quarterly, Q3/11, 10.

The mediator is independent and not bound by instructions in his or her decision making. The BaFin mediation procedure takes into account the principles of procedure established in the Recommendation of the European Commission.[134]

The application for a mediation procedure must be submitted to the Mediation Board in writing. Applications are inadmissible if the case is already pending with a court or another alternative redress body.[135] The mediator aims at reaching an agreement between the parties providing an independent evaluation of the legal situation considering also aspects of equity and good faith. The procedure ends with a written proposal by the mediator. If the parties accept the proposal recourse to the courts is normally excluded.[136]

For the consumer the procedure is free of charge, whereas for the respondent a fee of EUR 200 applies.

The Arbitration Board at the Deutsche Bundesbank

The Arbitration Board at the German Central Bank[137] provides alternative dispute resolution in relation to payment services[138] and the distance marketing of financial services.[139] It was established in August 1999 in Frankfurt am Main by the German Central Bank and aims at improving access to justice for consumers.

For consumers the procedure is free of charge, whereas for the banks every case costs €200. While the parties do not need legal representation, they can be represented by a third party of their choice if they so wish. The banks have to inform their costumers about the Arbitration Board of the Central Bank.

The establishment and responsibilities of the Arbitration Board are set out in section 14 (1) of the German Prohibitory Injunctions Act (*Unterlassungsklagengesetz*).[140]

In particular, the Arbitration Board is responsible for complaints in connection with:

- Payment services;[141]
- Consumer credit;[142]
- The distance marketing of financial services,[143] with the exception of insurance services.

The Arbitration Board consists of the arbitrators and a support office, which is the contact point for complaints and provides administrative support to the arbitrators.[144] The arbitrators are qualified judges who act independently and impartially.[145] The current three arbitrators are all Directors of the Bundesbank, and serve part time on the Arbitration Board.

[134] German law Section 143c (5) sentence 2 of the InvG and Commission Recommendation of 30 March 1998 on the principles applicable to the bodies responsible for out-of-court settlement of consumer disutes (98/257/EC).

[135] BaFin Quarterly, Q3/11, 10–11.

[136] BaFin Quarterly, Q3/11, 10–12.

[137] That is the English title used by this body, although it is debatable whether 'conciliation' is a better translation than 'arbitration'.

[138] BGB s 675c to 676c.

[139] www.bundesbank.de/schlichtungsstelle/schlichtungsstelle.php.

[140] German Bundesbank, The Arbitration Board at the German Central Bank, leaflet, Frankfurt am Main, 2011, 2.

[141] ss 675c to 676c of the German Civil Code (*Bürgerliches Gesetzbuch*) and Council Regulation (EC) 924/2009 on cross-border payments in the Community and repealing Regulation (EC) No 2560/2001 [2009] OJ L266/1.

[142] ss 491 to 509 of the German Civil Code.

[143] ss 312b to 312d of the German Civil Code.

[144] German Bundesbank, *The Arbitration Board at the German Central Bank, leaflet* (Frankfurt am Main, German Bundesbank, 2011), 2.

[145] ibid.

Any customer may file a complaint directly with the Arbitration Board in connection with payment services, distance marketing of financial services and consumer credits. A large number of complaints are resolved by the support office at an early stage by providing consumers with further information. Cases are also often directly transferred to the private ombudsman schemes of the different banking associations.

Complaints against companies which are members of any of the associations below and which participate in the arbitration proceedings provided by these associations should in fact be addressed directly to the associations concerned:[146]

- Bundesverband Öffentlicher Banken Deutschlands;
- Bundesverband deutscher Banken;
- Bundesverband der Deutschen Volksbanken und Raiffeisenbanken;
- Sparkassenverband Baden-Württemberg;
- Rheinischer Sparkassen- und Giroverband;
- Deutscher Sparkassen- und Giroverband.

A complaint is inadmissible if:

- the matter of complaint is already pending before a court, has been brought before a court in the past or is brought before a court by the complainant during the arbitration proceedings;
- the dispute has been settled out of court;
- an application for legal aid has been rejected because the action intended to be brought offers no prospect of success;
- the matter is already the subject of an arbitration proposal or the arbitration proceedings of an arbitration body pursuant to section 14 (1) of the German Prohibitory Injunctions Act or of any other conciliation body which deals with the settlement of disputes;
- the claim had already become statute-barred when the customer complaint was lodged and the respondent pleads the defence of limitation.[147]

A complaint must be submitted to the Arbitration Board in writing with a brief description of the facts and problems together with the necessary documentation (eg correspondence, invoices from the enterprise, account statements etc). The procedure takes on average three to four months and is divided into a preliminary proceeding and arbitration proceeding.

Preliminary proceedings

If the support office receives a complaint, it confirms receipt of the statement and examines the documents submitted. Admissible complaints are passed on to the company concerned with a request to comment within one month.[148]

The support office forwards the company's comments to the complainant, who then has the opportunity to submit a written opinion within a month. If the complainant does not respond, the complaint is considered to be resolved and the proceedings are closed.[149]

[146] ibid, 4.
[147] ibid, 5.
[148] ibid, 7.
[149] ibid, 7.

Arbitration proceedings

If the customer complaint is not resolved, the matter is passed on to the responsible arbitrator, who makes his decision on the basis of the documents submitted in the proceedings.[150] He can ask the parties involved to provide additional comments or information, but cannot take evidence unless it can be supported through the presentation of documents. A hearing is not conducted.[151]

The arbitrator presents a written arbitration proposal, which is voluntary for the parties. Neither the proceedings nor the arbitrator's decision affect the party's right to bring the matter before the courts.[152]

The parties involved can announce whether they accept the arbitrator's decision within six weeks of receiving it. Once this deadline has expired, the support office informs the parties of the outcome.[153] If an agreement is not reached, an 'attestation of an unsuccessful conciliation attempt pursuant to section 15a (3) sentence 3 of the Act concerning the Introduction of the Code of Civil Procedure'[154] is issued.

All customer complaints are treated as strictly confidential and are therefore not published. The Arbitration Board meets the requirements of the Recommendations of the EU regarding ADR and is a member of FIN-NET.[155]

Data

In 2009, 93 consumers contacted the Arbitration Board with inquiries about information about the calculation of costs regarding cross-border transfer payments and online payments. During this period 174 written complaints were submitted to the board. 91 of the complaints could not be addressed by the Arbitration Board because of a lack of competence. Nine of the complaints were referred to private Ombudsman schemes.[156] 74 of the complaints were admissible and processed by the Arbitration Board. A large majority of these cases (54 complaints) were solved by providing the parties with detailed explanations about the legal framework.

The Ombudsman and Conciliation Services

Many banks and the majority of insurers in Germany have voluntarily agreed to settle possible disputes with the help of private conciliators and ombudsmen. The ombudsmen are appointed for a specific period and may not be dismissed prematurely simply because they have adjudged a case to the company's disadvantage.[157]

These ADR units have been established within the industry associations of the respective companies, and are usually independent and impartial.

[150] ibid, 8.
[151] ibid.
[152] ibid.
[153] ibid.
[154] s 15a Abs.3 Satz 3 des Gesetzes betreffend der Einführung der Zivilprozessordnung.
[155] the European network of complaints schemes for financial services launched by the European Commission.
[156] German Bundesbank, *Annual Report for the Arbitration Board of the German Bundesbank, for the whole year 2009*, 7–8.
[157] www.bafin.de/cln_179/nn_720486/EN/BaFin/bafin__node.html?__nnn=true.

Major financial services associations that provide ADR services are:

- Cooperative banks: *Kundenbeschwerdestelle beim Bundesverband der Deutschen Volksbanken* (BVR) (Federation of the German Credit Unions and Agricultural Banks, Customer Complaints Office);
- Public-sector banks: *Bundesverband* Öffentlicher *Banken Deutschlands e.V.* (VÖB) Kundenbeschwerdestelle (Association of German Public Sector Banks, Customer Complaints Office);
- Private Banks and Mortgage banks: *Kundenbeschwerdestelle beim Bundesverband deutscher Banken e.V.* (Association of German Banks, Customer Complaints Office);
- Private building and loan associations: *Ombudsfrau der privaten Bausparkassen e.V. and Verband der privaten Bausparkassen, Kundenbeschwerdestelle* (Federation of the Private Building Societies, Customer Complaints Office), and several regional conciliation bodies, for which the central contact point is *Deutscher Sparkassen- und Giroverband* (DSGV), *Kundenbeschwerden* (German Savings Bank Association, Customer complaints);
- Land building and loan associations: *Schlichtungsstelle der Landesbausparkassen* (Conciliation body of the Land building societies);
- Disputes concerning credit transfers or misuse of credit cards, if no other arbitration unit is responsible: *Schlichtungsstelle der Deutschen Bundesbank*.

In some cases, the decisions makers are highly qualified legal professionals, eg former federal judges. The procedural rules to be applied are similar between the respective ombudsmen.

The procedure is free of charge for the complainants. However, they will have to bear all costs they have incurred (postage, copies, telephone charges etc.) and possible legal advice fees for an attorney.

If a consumer would like an ADR body to assess a case, the first step is to ask the company in question whether it operates within the ADR system and, if so, which body is responsible for the case.

The Ombudsman Scheme of the Private Commercial Banks

The Ombudsman Scheme of the Private Commercial Banks is an out-of court conciliation procedure that was established in 1992 by the Private Commercial Banks in Germany.[158] The Ombudsman Scheme is a key part of the private commercial bank's consumer policy scheme, which includes four parts: consumer education, information, contract transparency and out-of-court dispute resolution facilities.[159] The establishment of this scheme reflected a new approach of the banks in order to build trust in their services and has been promoted by the EU. Consumers' complaints were also viewed as a tool of assessment of their services.[160] This scheme applies mainly to consumers, but also to companies and self-employed persons in the event of disputes relating to credit transfers or misuse of a payment card. Details of the procedure and the admissibility requirements are set out in the 'Rules of procedures

[158] *Bundesverband der Deutschen Banken, The Comprehensive Consumer Policy Scheme of the German Private Commercial Banks* (Berlin 2007), 44.

[159] *Obudsman Der Privaten Banken Tätigkeitsbericht 2009*, 104.

[160] *Bundesverband der Deutschen Banken*, The *Comprehensive Consumer Policy Scheme of the German Private Commercial Banks* (Berlin 2007), 44.

for the settlement of customer complains in the German banking sector' approved by the Federal Ministry of Justice.[161]

The Ombudsman is an independent and impartial person that can provide a binding decision on cases up to a €5000 specific amount. Above this amount; the rulings are not binding on the private commercial banks that are affiliated to the scheme. However, even in the latter case banks often comply with the recommendation of the Ombudsman.

The procedure is free of charge for consumers and provides them with a quick dispute resolution without any risks. The consumers can refuse a decision or recommendation issued by the ombudsman service if they are not satisfied with the outcome. In this case, they can subsequently approach a court of law. The customer's legal interest cannot be prejudiced by expiry of the statutory limitation period during the Ombudsman proceedings.[162]

A Customer Complaints Office was set up at the Association of German Banks to act as an interface between bank clients and the Ombudsman Scheme.[163] Costumers of a private commercial bank can contact this office in writing and have to describe the problem, the history of the case and the desired outcome, adding any relevant documents. A large number of cases are already solved through information and negotiation before they reach the Ombudsman.

The Ombudsman Scheme of the Private Commercial Banks has been recognized by banks and costumers as an effective dispute resolution solution. Many banks have as a consequence introduced their own in-house complaint settlement schemes in order to solve a problem informally. Furthermore, a large number of banking associations have been inspired by the Ombudsman Scheme of the Private Commercial Banks and have set up their own Ombudsman system. For example the Association of German Public Sector Banks has an Ombudsman since May 2001. An important difference is however that their decisions are only voluntary for the banks.

Also at the government level the Ombudsman has been recognized as an ADR scheme. For instance, for disputes between retail or corporate customers and private commercial banks relating to credit transfer law, distant financial services and misuse of payment cards the Ombudsman replaces the ADR body set up at the *Deutsche Bundesbank* under the German Prohibitory Injunction Act.[164]

Furthermore, if the regional law uses the possibility under section 15 of the Act introducing the Code of Civil Procedure, a complainant must apply an ADR body before taking a legal action, provided that the amount of dispute does not exceed €750. This obligation can be met by the costumer by contacting the private commercial banks' Ombudsman, which is considered equivalent to a government dispute settlement body.[165]

The Ombudsman is part of FIN-NET that helps complainants in cross-border cases.

The failure of Lehman Brothers in 2008 triggered a rise in the number of complaints, which continued throughout 2009. [166] In 2009, the number of complaints received totalled over 6,500, which was an increase of around 35 per cent compared with 2008.

[161] ibid.

[162] ibid, 45.

[163] Bundesverband der Deutschen Banken, The Comprehensive Consumer Policy Scheme of the German Private Commercial Banks, Berlin 2007, 45.

[164] The Federal Ministry has given the Ombudsman Scheme the public dispute-settlement mandate for these areas, see Bundesverband der Deutschen Banken, The Comprehensive Consumer Policy Scheme of the German Private Commercial Banks, Berlin 2007, 47.

[165] *Bundesverband der deutschen Banken* (Berlin 2007) 48.

[166] *Bundesverband der Deutschen Banken* (Berlin 2010), 106–112.

Tables 4.8 and 4.9 show a five year comparison of the trend in complaints, broken down into individual lines of business.[167]

Table 4.8: Complaint areas 2006–2010[168]

Area	**2006**		**2007**		**2008**		**2009**		**2010**	
Securities business	725	19.3%	796	22.0%	1,867	38.6%	3,104	47.7%	3,186	49.1%
Lending business	1,006	26.8%	898	24.9%	1,000	20.7%	1,072	16.5%	1,038	16.0%
Payments business	1,234	32.9%	1,172	32.5%	1,252	25.9%	1,516	23.3%	1,462	22.5%
Basic account	431	11.5%	386	10.7%	354	7.3%	358	5.5%	396	6.1%
Savings business	300	8.0%	272	7.5%	254	5.3%	348	5.3%	351	5.4%
Guarantees/third party security	19	0.5%	18	0.2%	11	0.2%	12	0.2%	13	0.5%
Miscellaneous	38	1.0%	68	1.9%	99	2.0%	104	1.5%	48	0.7%
Total	3,753	100%	3,610	100%	4,837	100%	6,514	100%	6,494	100%
Source: Association of German Banks, 30 June 2011										

Table 4.9: Overview of number and outcome of complaints received annually 2006–2010[169]

Area	**2006**	**2007**	**2008**	**2009**	**2010**
Total number of complaints	3,753	3,610	4,837	6,514	6,494
Complaints not followed up by customer	607	617	744	1,030	1,234
Inadmissible/unsuitable complaints	598	385	743	1,184	1,036
Admissible complaints	2,548	2,608	3,350	4,300	4,224
Complaints resolved in favour of customer (also partly)	1,423	1,403	1,824	2,260	1,716
Compromise proposed by ombudsman	51	68	89	229	178
Complaints resolved in favour of bank	1,074	1,137	1,437	1,811	1,048
Source: Association of German Banks, 30 June 2011					
1) Admissible complaints under the Rules of Procedure which the ombudsman nevertheless declines to resolve as further evidence-taking would be necessary.					
2) Of the 4,224 admissible complaints, 1,282 are still being processed.					

Telecoms

Bundesnetzagentur (BnetzA) is the federal agency that regulates electricity, gas, telecommunications, post and railway network services.[170] Since 1999 it has operated a statutory settlement procedure that aims to find solutions for disputes between consumers

[167] *Bundesverband der Deutschen Banken*, (Berlin 2011).
[168] ibid.
[169] ibid.
[170] Information kindly supplied by Dr Daniela Strauss and Birgitt Maasch-Wiesel of *Bundesnetzagentur*.

and providers in the telecoms sector. One of the main objectives is to operate quickly, since court cases can take one to two years. The scheme was notified by the European Commission in October 2010,[171] after undergoing a complex assessment procedure by the Ministry of Justice and the European consumer centre in Kehl, to ensure it complies with the EU ADR standards.

The legal basis for consumer protection is set out in the *Telekommunikationsgesetz* (TKG) (telecommunications law), section 47a which deals with settlement. The consumer can start the settlement process with the BnetzA if the telecoms provider has not met one of the specified laws.[172] BnetzA listens to both parties, following public settlement rules (*SchliO2008*).[173] The process ends if the parties decide not to go ahead or if the BnetzA decides that no settlement can be reached. The scheme does not award compensation: it tries to solve the problem.

Consumers usually submit their complaints in writing, and can do so online, but oral complaints are accepted. Parties and conciliators are expected to maintain the privacy of parties, so that business secrets do not become publicly available. The arbitrators are bound to secrecy. The rules state that all parties have to be treated equally, and all written documents are to be presented to both parties. It is possible to be represented by a lawyer or by a representative of a consumer association: this happens in about 10 per cent of cases.

The settlement body meets once a week and comprises three officials within the BnetzA, one acting as rapporteur. There has never been a complaint about possible prejudice in recruiting the settlement board from within the regulator.

The settlement body checks the claim (this takes about 1–2 weeks), which is then sent to the telecom provider, which has 4 weeks to respond. There is no collection of evidence by the scheme, but the body can request further details from the parties. The consumer then has 3 weeks to respond to the company's statement, after which the company has a further 3 weeks to respond. The service submits a proposal to the parties, giving a brief explanation in plain language, which is not legally binding and which the parties have three weeks to accept, although the period can be extended. If the proposal is accepted, it constitutes an amicable agreement, and is contractually enforceable. If there is no agreement, the parties can take the dispute to the civil court, after which it is not possible to go back to the scheme.

Telecom providers have an obligation to tell their customers about the BnetzA settlement scheme. No details are made public about individual cases, but the BnetzA as regulator maintains an internal case database, which assists in identifying trends on which it may need to act.

[171] http://ec.europa.eu/consumers/redress_cons/ecc_germany_en.print.htm.

[172] ss 43a, 43 to 46 /2 and §84 of Council Directive (EC) 2007/717 about roaming in public mobile phone nets in the Union and the amendment of the Directive 2002/21/EC [2007] OJ L171, 32. The investigations catalogue includes: inclusion of the interests of persons with disabilities, use of properties, fault repair, standards-based technical service, network access, right to itemised billing, prepaid services, connection charge, content of bills, part payment, billing objections, liability to pay in the case of incorrectly established charges, disconnection, continuing obligations for short code services, entry in public directories, publication requirements, number misuse, right to information on additional services.

[173] www.bundesnetzagentur.de/SharedDocs/Downloads/DE/BNetzA/Verbraucherservice/Telekommunikation/Schlichtungsstelle/Schlichtungsordnung2008ID17039pdf.pdf?__blob=publicationFile.

Cost

The process is at a cost to both parties according to section 145 TKG, which is a tariff based on the amount in dispute. Where the dispute resolution service submits a proposal for resolution, it shall rule on the costs as appears fair, having regard to the findings of fact and the matter in dispute. Each party shall bear the costs it has incurred from participating in the proceedings. The fee is a minimum of € 25 and increases in line with the value of the matter in dispute. The fees charged are shown in table 4.10:

Table 4.10: Fees charged by BnetzA

Value of matter in dispute up to ... euro	Fee ... euro
300	25
600	35
900	45
1200	55
1500	65
2000	73
2500	81
3000	89
3500	97
4000	105
4500	113
5000	121
6000	136
7000	151
8000	166
9000	181
10.000	196
13.000	219
16.000	242
19.000	265
22.000	288
25.000	311

In 2010[174] the number of complaints reaching the consumer service at the BnetzA has risen 21% compared to 2009. Most of the 69.886 complaints were received by telephone. However a trend can be seen that more consumers contact the BnetzA by email. Details of the sectors complained about are in tables 4.11 and 4.12.

Table 4.11: Claims statistics of BnetzA

Telecommunication	2010
Overall claims applications	703
Cases resolved; of which 9% withdrawn cases, of the remaining cases 46% were rejected as not complying with TKG	679

[174] BnetzA anuual report (2010), www.bundesnetzagentur.de/SharedDocs/Downloads/DE/BNetzA/Presse/Berichte/2011/Jahresbericht2010pdf.pdf?__blob=publicationFile.

Number of cases that were re-directed (additional to the 703)	174
Finalized and admissible cases	
Success rate [settlement reached]	66%
Discontinued cases by complainant	5%
Cases discontinued by company	29%
Post	
Overall claims applications	10
Successfully completed	3
Unresolved as no settlement reached	3
Rejected case	1

Table 4.12: Areas of complaints and inquiries 2010 [total 69,886 complaints]:

Complained about	Amount
Telekom	54,880
Electricity	10,400
Gas	2,401
Post	2,161
Trains	44

Telecom

Complaint	2010	2009
Contracts	14,505	13,429
Number misuse	10,964	6,955
TK bill	10,408	6,721
Change of provider	7,448	5,524
Number queries	4,049	3,262
General services	1,697	1,605
Other	5,809	8,268

Electricity

Complaint	2010	2009
Bills	2,083	1,963
Contracts	1,736	1,397
Renewable energy	1,670	1,006
Delay in change of provider	1,428	926
Change of provider	918	585
Electricity prices / tariffs	550	458
Meters	365	263
Other	1,623	1,204

Gas

Complaint	2010	2009
Bill	587	181
Delay in provider change	516	1.053
Contract	411	236
Change of provider	259	237
Gas prices / tariffs	126	150
Insolvency of gas provider	58	2
Other	444	377

Post

Complaint	2010	2009
Delivery and receipt	1,188	1,13
Service	239	142
Accessibility of postal services	66	197
Cross-boarder deliveries	17	18
Other	651	440

Lawyers

The arbitration board of the legal profession (*Schlichtungsstelle der Rechtsanwaltschaft*) was established on 1 January 2011 to settle disputes between clients and their lawyers, free of charge. The arbitration board is governed by the provisions of section 191f of the Federal Lawyers' Act and the Statute of the Body of the legal profession.[175] The independent mediator must not be a lawyer, and is Dr Renate Jaeger, a former judge of the European Court of Human Rights. The advisory board of arbitration has nine members who support the mediator.

The arbitrator can only make a settlement proposal, not a legaly binding decision, which the parties can accept or reject. If the process is unsuccessful, the parties retain the right to apply to the courts. The procedure can be used when there is a dispute about a suspected error in advice, in conflicts over fees, and for claims for damages, but in every case not above a limit of €15,000. It is a requirement for mediation that both parties are ready for dialogue and the referral criteria for arbitration are met. The arbitrator can decline to handle individual cases, for example where evidence is not available to clarify the facts, or if it is clear that the process has no chance of success.

The procedure[176] specifies that a request for mediation to the dispute resolution service has to be a short written description of the facts and accompanied by the required documentation, which is to include a description of the facts and all relevant correspondence and interviews in chronological order. The procedure is not available if court proceedings are ongoing or have been concluded or settled. The complainant is asked to describe what he or she wants to achieve by the request for mediation, such as repayment of fees or compensation.

Each party bears its own costs and expenses, unless they agree otherwise: no loser pays rule applies. Use of the conciliation board process is free of charge.[177] The board is funded by the legal profession in Germany, each lawyer paying €3 per year. The scheme was set up in 2010, there have been 886 complaints, of which 263 were resolved. A backlog built up since Dr Jaeger could only start her work at the beginning of 2011. It is too early to quote the average duration of the process.

[175] Bundesrechtsanwaltsordnung und Satzung der Schlichtungsstelle der Rechtsanwaltschaft.
[176] www.schlichtungsstelle-der-rechtsanwaltschaft.de/sites/default/files/merkblatt_zum_schlichtungsantrag.pdf.
[177] *Satzung der Schlichtungsstelle*, para 8.

The Failed 'Ombudsman.de' Scheme

Ombudsman.de[178] began as a pilot project in 2004, and was funded for 17 months largely from public sources.[179] After that, until 30 June 2011, it was funded by the *Verbraucher Initiative e.V.*, a Germany-wide consumer association, located in Berlin,[180] and then closed down when they could not afford to finance it any longer. *Ombudsman.de* was a neutral and independent dispute resolution provider, which aimed to resolve disputes arising from online shopping transactions between consumers and retailers. The service was intended to support start-up online companies. It was provided free of charge to both parties. It did not offer legal advice.

Every contracting party to an online shopping transaction was able to make use of *ombudsman.de*. The prerequisites were that the buyer must be a consumer residing in Germany and the retailer was a commercial seller, who had his place of business in the European Union. Both parties had to agree to use this procedure.

The consumer first had to register online.[181] In complaints about a provider of an online shop, the process was an online adaptation of the European Commission's international consumer complaints form. *Ombudsman.de* then checked that the case falls into its responsibility, namely that the dispute was between a consumer and an online-trader. If so, an electronic file was created and the consumer informed by email of the password that allowed access at any time to his or her individual, secure case file. As soon as the information was complete, *ombudsman.de* contacted the provider and tried to solve the dispute by suggesting an agreement between the parties.

If no agreement was reached, *ombudsman.de* offered the parties an arbitration process, in which *ombudsman.de* made either a settlement proposal (*Vergleichsvorschlag*) or an arbitral award (*Schiedsspruch*). If the parties did not accept the decision, then *ombudsman.de* informed the parties that its involvement is terminated. The consumer was able during the process to send comments and documents to *ombudsman.de* via email, with a reference to the specific case.

Contracted lawyers acted as ombudsmen through a special case number online. The ombudsman aimed to contact the trader within 48 hours of the initial complaint documents being completed, and to resolve the issue within 2 weeks. However, it was found that it took much longer to resolve the cases than anticipated. The reason was that most complaints related to new start-up online shops that required a lot of attention and suggestions as to how to comply with the German law and how to change their approach.

Without the scheme being advertised, it attracted about 100 cases per month,[182] of which traders were found to have been at fault in about three-quarters of cases, and consumers in about one-quarter.

At the closure of the scheme, the organizers drew various conclusions.[183] Firstly, the level of workload had been almost unmanageable. Secondly, the scheme did not impose

[178] www.ombudsman.de/ombudsmann.php/cat/1/title/Home.

[179] Funding was the EU 50%, Bund Germany 30% and Verbraucher Initiative 20%.

[180] Elsenstraße 106, 12435 Berlin /Bundesvorsitzender: Dieter Schaper (V.i.S.d.P.), www.verbraucher.org.

[181] At www.ombudsman.de.

[182] There was a large percentage of '*Abo-Fallen*' subscription traps.

[183] Interview with Georg Abel, *Bundesgeschäftsführer* (Federal Director) of Verbraucher Initiative eV on 6 October 2011.

sanctions on traders, since the object was to help them rather than make money. But if they had done so, it would have been possible to have some means of affecting traders' behaviour. Thirdly, the adverse emotional aspect of informing a consumer that they are wrong was not something they liked to hear. Fourthly, the closure of the scheme was seen as a big reversal for consumer politics in Germany. They felt that an ombudsman system that was based on many local ones, as existed in some of the *Länder*,[184] would not be preferable to a single national scheme, as ombudsman.de had been, but the government would have to fund it.

Energy

A conciliation body for energy, *Schlichtungsstelle Energie*,[185] was established in October 2011 as a scheme recognized by the Federal Ministry of Economics and the Federal Ministry of Food, Agriculture and Consumer Protection for the extra-judicial settlement of disputes between energy companies and consumers. It is sponsored jointly by energy associations[186] and the *Verbraucherzentrale Bundesverband e.V*. The conciliation board is intended to be independent, neutral, non-bureaucratic, and free to the consumer. An energy company complained against pays a case-fee as set in a cost regulation.[187] The Ombudsman is Dr Dieter Wolst, a former federal court judge.

Under the Energy Act,[188] utility companies, meter operators and metering services are obliged to deal with complaints from consumers, in relation to concluding a contract or for quality of services provided by the company, within four weeks. If the complaint is not rectified, the company must explain why in writing or electronically. Complaints can be made about the following matters:

- connection to the supply network,
- usage of the connection,
- energy supply,
- measurement of energy.

If a satisfactory agreement is not reached, the conciliation board is the next step, and the conciliation body can only be accessed if the customer can prove that the claim made previously against the energy company was unsuccessfully asserted.[189] The process then begins through filling out an online claim form[190] or sending an email or fax. The energy companies are obliged by law to take part in the concilliation process. Once the Ombudsman

[184] For example those in *Hessen* and *Baden-Württemberg*, see www.online-schlichter.de/de/index.php.

[185] http://www.schlichtungsstelle-energie.de/index.php?id=2.

[186] *Verbände der Energiewirtschaft* .

[187] http://www.schlichtungsstelle-energie.de/fileadmin/Download/Kostenordnung_Schlichtungsstelle_19.09.2011-Gruendung-.pdf.

[188] Since 4 August 2011, Energy Act (EnWG) s 111a and b regulates the right of consumers to approach the arbitraiton board after unsuccessfully dealing with the energy company. The legal relationship between consumers and utilities arises primarily from the contract with the utility contract. Also relevant are the Energy Management Act (Energy Act EnWG), the basic electricity supply regulation (StromGVV), the gas basic service regulation (GasGVV), the low voltage connection Regulation (NAV), the low pressure connection Regulation (NDAV) and the Civil Code (BGB).

[189] Energy Act (EnWG), s 111a and b.

[190] https://secure.e-consult-ag.de/e.consult.6489/webakte/beschwerde_extern.asp.

has decided the admissibility of the claim according to the rules of procedure,[191] the energy company has two weeks to respond to the complaint. The Ombudsman then determines the facts on the basis of the law and issues a non-binding recommendation. Both sides then have four weeks to let the Ombudsman know if they will follow the recommendations or not. The entire complaint process should be finished within three months.

Conclusions

The appearance of private sector alternative dispute resolution schemes for consumer disputes in Germany is comparatively recent. Major reasons why consumer ADR has not emerged as quickly as in some neighbouring states are, first, that the enforcement system for consumer law places a great deal of emphasis on prevention and speedy cessation of infringements backed by the threat of injunctions in the courts, and the fact that the court procedures in Germany for seeking damages are comparatively swift and efficient, and the predictable and low costs regimes have lead to widespread legal expenses insurance. Hence, there has been less need to develop new pathways for ADR for consumer disputes in Germany compared with other countries.

However, some sectors, led by insurers, have started to introduce ombudsmen systems, in order to resolve disputes even more swiftly and cheaply than through the courts, and in order to maintain the client relationship and avoid unnecessary adverse publicity. The Insurance Ombudsman model has been notably successful, and has been copied in the transport and other sectors.

Complaint procedures also exist within various regulatory bodies, but have not been particularly widely used.

The current situation is that consumer ADR is at a relatively early state, but is developing into a confused state of diversity in the types and coverage of ADR bodies. There is considerable variation in the caseload attracted by individual bodies, and some are simply not known about. This diversity in models can confuse consumers, who need a simple ADR structure that is easily comprehensible.

Most ADR schemes in Germany have a regional geographical coverage, while 12 schemes report a national geographical coverage.[192] The sectoral gaps most frequently mentioned by stakeholder organisations are games of chance, scams and pyramid schemes, food services/products, transport, and package travel/tourism. The existence of guilds was an important factor for the development of sector specific ADR schemes.

The European Commission statistics that indicate that there are many consumer ADR bodies in Germany are seriously misleading, since the bodies that have been notified are largely a raft of new bodies that have been created to offer general mediation services, spurred by the high profile that has been given to implementation of the EU Mediation Directive in Germany. A wide debate about the introduction into German civil procedure of a mediation procedure has obscured the reality that mediation-alongside-court-claims is a different animal from consumer ADR.

[191] http://www.schlichtungsstelle-energie.de/fileadmin/Download/Verfahrensordnung.pdf.

[192] DG SANCO, *Study on the use of ADR* (2009).

5

Lithuania

Christopher Hodges

Overview

Lithuania has a national heritage from Soviet times of a centralised state bureaucracy. Citizens and businesses still tend to look to the State to provide solutions, but they do not necessarily trust State institutions, including judges. The adoption of Parliamentary democracy and of EU market legislation is still recent, and although many EU rules have been enacted, the institutions that operate them are both new and, paradoxically, based on a Soviet heritage. This can clearly be seen in relation to the enforcement of consumer protection law.

Although Lithuania has a court system that functions effectively, costs little and attracts a significant volume of cases compared with a population of 3.2 million, it is still too slow (and more expensive) compared with the consumer ADR system. The ADR system is attractive to consumers since it is free. The consumer complaint system is institutionalised in the consumer protection legislation, and integrated within the state enforcement bodies. This arrangement enables the Authorities an opportunity to use complaint data in their market surveillance, and as a basis to respond quickly to developing trends. However, not all Authorities have yet developed the ability to take full advantage of the opportunities, and usage of the ADR system is probably hindered by the fact that decisions are not binding on traders.

Consumer representation in Lithuania is diffused by the existence of several consumer organizations, including the National Consumer Confederation (founded in 2003 as an umbrella association),[1] the Lithuanian Consumer Institute (established in 2000),[2] the Lithuanian Consumer Union,[3] and the Consumer Rights Protection Centre.[4]

Courts

For civil proceedings, Lithuania has a first tier level of around 54 District Courts, a second tier of five Regional Courts, with appeals to a Court of Appeal and the Supreme Court,

[1] vartotojai.eu; vartotojuteises.lt/apie_lnvf/lnvf_ataskaitos/lithuanian_national_consumer_federation.
[2] www.vartotojai.lt/en.
[3] www.lvks.lt.
[4] mereckas@centras.lt.

being a court of cassation.[5] Procedure is governed by the Code of Civil Procedure of the Republic of Lithuania. A party has to pay court charges ('stamp duty'), court expenses related to examination of the case, and the fees of any lawyer hired. The amount of stamp duty is prescribed,[6] and the current sums are shown in Table 5.1.[7]

Table 5.1: Court stamp duty charges in civil disputes[8]

Nature of dispute	Court fees
Property disputes not exceeding ca. LTL 100,000	3 per cent of the amount of the claim, but not less than ca. LTL 50
Property disputes over ca. LTL 100,000 but not exceeding ca. LTL 300,000	ca. LTL 3,000 plus 2 per cent of the amount of the claim exceeding ca. LTL 100,000
Property disputes over ca. LTL 300,000	ca. LTL 7,000 plus 1 per cent of the amount of the claim exceeding ca. LTL 300,000 . The total amount of court fees cannot constitute more than ca. LTL 30,000
In any other disputes, ie non property disputes	ca. LTL 100
Application for a court order	¼ of the amount payable for the lawsuit, but not less than ca. LTL 10
Application for documentary proceedings	½ of the amount payable for the lawsuit, but not less than ca. LTL 20
Non-contentious proceedings	ca. LTL 100
Application for review of default judgment	ca. LTL 50
Appeal against judgments and cassation appeals	Same as payable for primary lawsuit
Application for renewal of court proceedings	ca. LTL 100

A person may be partially or entirely exempted from the obligation to pay court charges, where the court reviews the applicant's personal circumstances,[9] or, *inter alia*, where the claim is for damages caused by personal injuries or death, or property or non-property damages caused by criminal offence.[10]

A person may also be exempt from paying court charges if they are granted legal aid. Primary legal aid covers consultations and general pre-litigation advice, usually provided by municipal officers, although it also can be provided by lawyers or non-profit organisations. Secondary legal aid, which can be provided only by lawyers,[11] covers drafting of legal instruments, defence and representation in the court proceedings. Applicants must qualify under requirements on levels of assets and income, for which there are two levels: those eligible are refunded 100 per cent or 50 per cent of the secondary legal aid costs, depending on whether they qualify at the first or second level respectively.[12] Qualification for

[5] This section is based on information from Dr Rimantas Simaitis, including his Report on Costs and Funding in Lithuania (on file with the author). There is also a system of Administrative Courts, not considered here.

[6] Lithuanian Code of Civil Procedure, Art 80.

[7] R Simaitis, *Bylinejimosi islaidos civiliniame procese* [*Litigation costs in civil procedure*] (Vilnius, Justia, 2007) 92–106. According to the results of a survey, performed in 2005–2006, stamp duty covers only up to 8–9 per cent of the true costs of operation of the courts in Lithuania.

[8] As at 21 December 2010, 1 Lithuanian Litas = 0.29 Euro [1:0.289622]. See: www.lb.lt/exchange/default.asp?lang=e.

[9] Code of Civil Procedure, Art 83(3).

[10] Code of Civil Procedure, Art 83(1).

[11] Law on Legal Aid, Art 17.

[12] Secondary legal aid is administered by specialised regional non-profit organisations, established by the Ministry of Justice of the Republic of Lithuania, and the Bar is responsible for supervision of the qualification of lawyers that provide secondary legal aid.

secondary legal aid excuses a person from liability to pay the stamp duty in civil litigation. Grant of legal aid does not exempt a party from liability for and court expenses related to examination of the case, and the fees of any lawyer: those may be reimbursed, at least in part, by an opponent if the case is won, discussed below.

The court expenses that a party will be required to pay cover the costs of any expert appointed by the court,[13] translator, bailiff, or expenses related to process,[14] enforcement of a judgment.[15] A party will also have to pay the expenses of any witness to attend court.

Lawyers' fees are subject to agreement between client and lawyer,[16] and only regulated in relation to legal aid.[17] Lawyers' fees are usually capped, either for the whole assignment (eg representation of the client in a particular dispute), or for a particular service (eg preparation of a lawsuit). However, an hourly fee rate remains very common. The ability to agree a contingency fee in civil cases was introduced in 1999.[18] The amount of an advocate's fee that depends on the outcome of the case must not contradict the principles governing the practice of advocates: case law has established that 50 percent of the amount awarded is considered to conflict with such principles.

When the court adopts final judgment in a case it is obliged to allocate the parties' liability to reimburse litigation expenses incurred by the court and parties,[19] which include the costs of witnesses, experts, court procedure costs described above.[20] The general rule is that the party in whose favour judgment was made is to be indemnified by the other party, though the latter is not required to pay the stamp duty into the state budget. Where a claim is partly satisfied, the litigation expenses have to be awarded to the plaintiff in proportion to the part of the claims satisfied by the court, and to the defendant in proportion to the part of the claims that were refused by the court. Reimbursement of a lawyer's fees are subject to a tariff of maximum amounts[21] approved by the Minister of Justice together with the Chairman of the Council of the Bar, but subject to consideration by the court of the complexity of the case and time spent on the matter.[22]

There is a small claims procedure for claims up to LTL 5,000 (about € 1450), under which the normal costs rules are applied.[23]

Litigation is frequently used to resolve disputes in Lithuania. In 2010, 201,585 new civil court cases were initiated:[24] data is shown in Table 5.2. It appears that only around 10 per

[13] Code of Civil Procedure, Art 212. Sums to be paid for experts and method of calculation are set out in Resolution No 344 of the Government of the Republic of Lithuania of 6 December 2002. Under Art 90 of the Code of Civil Procedure, a party who files a request to appoint an expert is obliged to pay in advance a deposit to cover the litigation expenses, in an amount established by the court. If both parties require an expertise, they are obliged to pay the deposit in equal parts. If the court on its own initiative calls expertise, the expenses shall be paid from the state budget.

[14] Code of Civil Procedure, Art 88(1).

[15] Code of Civil Procedure, Art 88.

[16] Law on the Bar of the Republic of Lithuania, Art 50.

[17] Particular fees are set forth in the Resolution No 69 of the Government of the Republic of Lithuania of 22 January 2001.

[18] Law on the Bar, Art 50.

[19] Code of Civil Procedure, Art 270(5).

[20] Code of Civil Procedure, Art 93.

[21] set out in the Order No 1R-85 of the Minister of Justice of the Republic of Lithuania of 2 April 2004. Under para 8 of that Order, the maximum remuneration of expenses incurred by the party for legal assistance is capped either in relation to the whole amount or in relation to a maximum hourly rate.

[22] Code of Civil Procedure, Art 98(2).

[23] Code of Civil Procedure, Art 441.

[24] National Courts Administration, *Annual Report on Activities of Lithuanian Courts in 2010*, (2011, National Courts Administration,Vilnius) available at www.teismai.lt.

cent of cases are settled before judgment. More than 90 per cent of all civil disputes are usually determined within 6 months, but complex cases can take longer than a year.[25] Appeal costs are similar to the costs of first instance, and appeals or cassation usually take 6 months. The percentage of cases appealed in 2010 was around 6.43 per cent.

Table 5.2: Litigation rates in Lithuania.[26]

	2001	2002	2003	2004	2005	2006	2007	2008	2009	2010
Cases commenced	118121	127992	127992	152132	148019	145705	156330	185878	236556	201585
Cases solved	117428	125372	125372	149646	148750	145286	153436	180071	229221	205423
Pending cases	No data	No data	9314	17523	17121	17320	18331	21365	35333	31056
Peaceful settlements	No data	No data	No data	No data	801	2441	2650	3467	4601	5246

The Rules of Court Mediation govern court mediation, but this technique is only used in a small number of cases, and where the parties agree. The Council of Judges approved the use of mediation in civil cases in all Lithuanian courts in January 2007. Mediation is conducted in the court by special mediators, who are judges or assistant judges, or persons with the necessary qualification under the Code of Conduct of European Mediators. If the mediation ends with a settlement agreement, the agreement is confirmed by the court and has the power of a court decision.

Arbitration is available but restricted to resolving business-to-business disputes.[27] In 2009 the Vilnius Court of Commercial Arbitration received 18 domestic and 21 international cases, almost all large commercial disputes involving significant sums of money, although 15 per cent were shareholder cases.[28]

There is a debate about the introduction of a class action procedure. Currently, part 45 of Article 49 of the Civil Procedure Code foresees the possibility of seeking to protect the public interest through a group claim, but no group action procedure is provided for. A Concept Paper was presented in 2009 by a working group of the Ministry of Justice. A draft law that would introduce a Class Action procedure was published in January 2012.

In summary, the cost that a consumer would have to pay to bring a low value claim against a trader would be roughly around €163–610 (stamp duty of LTL 50 (ca. €15), court expenses for postal services around LTL10-50 (ca. €3–15) and lawyers' fee of around LTL 500-2000 (ca. €145–580). These figures reflect litigation in one court instance, and would need to be multiplied if the case is appealed. They also exclude calculation of the potential liability for adverse party litigation costs, under the 'loser pays' rule.

[25] National Courts Administration, *Annual Report on Activities of Lithuanian Courts in 2008*, (2009, National Courts Administration,Vilnius) available at www.teismai.lt.

[26] ibid.

[27] Under the Law on Commercial Arbitration, Art 11, disputes arising from sale agreements (as well as disputes arising from constitutional claims, the employment relationship, family law, administrative legal relations, disputes connected with competition, patents, trademarks and service marks, and bankruptcy) may not be submitted to arbitration.

[28] See www.arbitrazas.lt/VCCA_statistics_web1.pdf.

Public Sector Ombudsman

The Seimas Ombudsmen[29] investigate citizens' complaints concerning the abuse of office and bureaucracy of officers of state, government and administration institutions, local government institutions, military institutions and institution ranking as such. The activities of the President of the Republic, members of the Seimas, the Prime Minister, the Government (as a collegial institution), the State Controller and judges of the Constitutional Court and other courts, municipal councils (as collegial institutions), also the legality and validity of procedural decisions of the prosecutors, investigators and officers conducting the inquiry are outside the Seimas Ombudsman's powers of investigation. The Seimas Ombudsmen does not investigate complaints arising from the labour legal relations, complaints that are subject to court investigation, or complaints about the legality and validity of court decisions, judgments and rulings.

Integrated Regulatory and ADR System

Consumer protection policy in Lithuania and its institutional framework is relatively recent.[30] The first Law on Consumer Protection was enacted in 1994, amended in 2001 (establishing a National Consumer Rights Protection Board), and again in 2007,[31] implementing the EU unfair consumer practices legislation and a 2003 National Strategy for Consumer Rights Protection and Lithuanian National Consumer Education Programme. One of the key purposes of that Strategy was to 'aim for establishment of an alternative out-of-court settlement of disputes mechanism in all the areas of Consumer Protection'.

The Law on Consumer Protection of the Republic of Lithuania[32] not establishes only substantive rules on consumer protection but also an institutional system for the protection of consumer rights.[33] In particular, it establishes the State Consumer Rights Protection Authority[34] as a public body, reporting to the Ministry of Justice. The State Consumer Rights Protection Authority is given functions that include ensuring the protection of consumer rights; coordination of the activities of various consumer rights protection institutions; controlling standard terms and conditions of contracts; applying sanctions for breach of consumer law; and provision of consumer ADR.[35]

This Authority has about 65 staff, including 33 lawyers, divided into two internal Commissions: one deals with fines and sanctions, and the other with consumer ADR. It has a number of enforcement powers but does not supervise the market. Thus, a breach of the Unfair Commercial Practices legislation could be raised with a trader by the Authority: if the trader did not change its practice, the Authority could institute a court enforcement procedure, acting in the public interest (and in effect in a collective capacity). Such an

[29] See www.lrski.lt/index.php?l=EN.
[30] See www.ecc.lt.
[31] Law on prohibition of unfair business-to-consumer commercial practices, available at: www3.lrs.lt/pls/inter3/dokpaieska.showdoc_l?p_id=315866.
[32] See www3.lrs.lt/pls/inter3/dokpaieska.showdoc_l?p_id=362796.
[33] Law on Consumer Protection, Art 1.1.
[34] See vvtat.lt.
[35] Law on Consumer Protection, Art 12.

action is classed as a civil action, rather than a criminal procedure. The remedy would be a declaration or injunction, but not compensation. The Authority has power to impose a fine, within statutory maxima and minima set by law for infringements of different provisions, such as advertising, food safety, product safety, unfair commercial practices. Alternatively, an individual consumer could pursue a private enforcement action, and the Authority would provide an expert opinion to the court in the case.

The State Consumer Rights Protection Authority is responsible for coordinating the activities of a number of other sectoral Authorities in relation to consumer protection issues, including:

- Food and Veterinary Authority[36]
- State Non-Food Products Inspectorate under the Ministry of Economy[37]
- National tourism department under the Ministry of Economy[38]
- Civil Aviation Administration[39]
- State Public Health Service under the Ministry of Health[40]
- State Energy Inspectorate under the Ministry of Energy[41]

The Law on Consumer Protection sets out a specific and detailed regime for resolving consumer complaints out of court,[42] which applies in addition to the right to pursue a claim in court.[43] A consumer who presumes that his rights have been infringed by a seller or service supplier must first contact such seller or supplier and make a specific request, to which the trader must, within ten working days, provide a reasoned written reply, substantiated with documents.[44] If the trader fails to satisfy the consumer's request and it relates to unsafe or inadequate quality of goods or services, the latter may then complain to the relevant Service, Inspectorate or Health Service, which must consider and respond to the complaint in a specified manner.[45] A consumer also has a right to file a complaint with the State Consumer Rights Protection Authority or one of the following specialist authorities:[46]

1. the Communications Regulatory Authority,[47] which handles disputes in electronic communication services, post and courier services;[48]
2. the Insurance Supervisory Commission,[49] which handles disputes on insurance;[50]
3. the State Energy Inspectorate of the Ministry of Energy,[51] which handles complaints about consumer protection issues provided in the Law on Energy;[52]

[36] See www.vet.lt.
[37] See ww.vnmpi.lt.
[38] See www.tourism.lt/en.
[39] See www.caa.lt.
[40] See www.vvspt.lt/en.
[41] See www.vei.lt/index.php?id=522.
[42] Law on Consumer Protection, ch 6.
[43] See further, V Mizaras, 'Lithuania – National Report' in J Stuyck et al, *Study on alternative means of consumer redress other than redress through ordinary judicial proceedings* (Catholic University of Leuven, 2007), at http://ec.europa.eu/consumers/redress_cons/collective_redress_en.htm.
[44] Law on Consumer Protection, Art 20.
[45] Law on Consumer Protection, Art 21.
[46] Law on Consumer Protection, Arts 22 and 23.
[47] See rrt.lt/en/home.html.
[48] Law on Electronic Communications, Art 4; Law on Post, Art 3.
[49] See www.dpk.lt/en/.
[50] Law on Insurance of 18 September 2003, Arts 2 and 192 to 207.
[51] See www.vei.lt/index.php?id=522 .
[52] Law on Energy (Arts 18 and 26 para 2). The State Energy Inspectorate is required to operate a preliminary procedure for administration of complaints without judicial proceedings, considers complaints regarding

4. the National Commission for Prices and Energy,[53] which deals with consumer complaints in the areas provided in the Law on Energy;[54]
5. any other bodies established for consumer protection purposes by law.

Prior to January 2012, separate ADR schemes for disputes in the financial service sector existed for banking (within the State Consumer Rights Protection Authority's ADR scheme), insurance (the Insurance Supervisory Commission, noted above), and securities (under the Lithuanian Securities Commission). As of that date, supervision of financial markets, including the responsibility for provision of ADR in the above three schemes) was transferred to the Bank of Lithuania.

The State Consumer Rights Protection Authority therefore operates as a single residual ADR facility, supplementing the similar systems of the specialist sectoral Authorities. It is currently the only ADR institution in Lithuania that is notified to the European Commission. It receives around 12,000 complaints a year, and around 2,300 requests for ADR. The ADR procedure is a conciliation procedure, operated like a small court procedure, and is free of charge to consumers: the consumer ADR system is funded by the State, but parties themselves bear any costs incurred. Examples of how two sectoral Authorities handle complaints are given below.

Procedure

The same procedure is specified in the Law on Consumer Protection for all consumer ADR complaints to any of the designated Authorities. It is described as settling disputes 'in compliance with the adversarial principle and principles of case expedition and transparency' and requiring an Authority to 'disclose the essence of the dispute, examine the available evidence and take measures for conciliating the parties'.[55] The Authorities do not act as representatives of consumers' interests, but as independent decision-makers. The procedure shall be free of charge to consumers,[56] in order to 'give consumers greater confidence in the independence of the ADR provider and the impartiality of the decision taken.'[57]

An application must be in writing, attaching copies of relevant documents and specifying certain particulars, including the names and addresses of the consumer and trader, the rights alleged to have been infringed, the consumer's requests, information on a prior complaint to the trader, and whether any other complaint or legal claim has been made.[58] A consumer association may represent consumers. The Authority must determine whether the complaint is admissible, and then send the documents to the trader, requesting 'within 10 days … written exhaustive explanations and the documents substantiating them'.[59] It may call on experts from other relevant agencies before making a decision in the form of a settlement proposal to the trader. The Authority will normally make a decision using a

damage in relation to energy facilities, equipment and accounting devices, violations in operation, energy quality requirements, energy accounting and payment for the energy consumed, accidents, interruption, suspension or restriction of energy supply and so on.

[53] See www.regula.lt/en/about-us/.
[54] Law on Energy, Art 17.
[55] Law on Consumer Protection, Art 25.3 and 25.4.
[56] Law on Consumer Protection, Art 25.9.
[57] Response to EU ADR Consultation, Ministry of Justice of Lithuania, 2011.
[58] Law on Consumer Protection, Art 23.
[59] Law on Consumer Protection, Art 24.

written procedure, but has discretion to adopt an oral procedure when necessary.[60] Oral hearings are open to the public.

The Authority's decisions are not binding. If the trader and the consumer accept a decision, it becomes a binding contract between the parties. If the Authority receives notification that a trader has not implemented a decision within the time specified for this, the Authority may publicise this fact on its website.[61]

Statistics

Cases take on average 37 working days to complete: far quicker than court procedures. In the period from January 2010 through September 2011, the Authority investigated 2,290 disputes through the ADR procedure. Figures for 2010 alone have not been available. Of these:

- 45 per cent (1020) were settled by the parties before the Authority adopted a decision.
- 7.7 per cent (163) were terminated under one of the reasons provided for in the Law, such as involving no breach of the law, or as being an invalid complaint.
- 48 per cent (1107) involved adoption of a decision by the Authority. Of these, consumers were wholly successful in 72 per cent (797) and partially successful in 16 per cent (180), and traders were successful in 16 per cent (180).

In that period, traders complied with the Authority's decisions in 33 per cent of cases: the 66 per cent of non-compliance included a number of cases caused by bankruptcy of traders. The main sectors in which complaints were received were:

• Consumer goods and services	44%	1017
• Food products, tourism and recreational services	28%	641
• Unfair commercial practice, advertising and construction	15%	347
• Financial services	9%	206
• Energy and utilities	1.5%	34
• Others (sale of mortgages, legal services etc)	2%	45

Communications

The Communications Regulatory Authority is required to ensure that safe and affordable electronic communications and postal services are available to every consumer.[62] It has a shared competence with the State Consumer Rights Protection Authority, and the two agencies collaborate when required: the latter is responsible for the unfair consumer protection legislation. They redirect consumer complaints between them.[63] As a result of the specific competence of each agency, it is possible to end up with two decisions in relation to a single complaint.

The Communications Regulatory Authority has been able to receive complaints online since 2007, and this has become popular with consumers, who upload relevant documents.

[60] Law on Consumer Protection, Art 25.
[61] Law on Consumer Protection, Art 28.
[62] Law on Electronic Communications.
[63] The ADR provisions are at Law on Electronic Communications, Art 36.

This facility enables complaints to be processed speedily. It has never received a complaint from a consumer association.

The Communications Regulatory Authority uses the data that it receives to identify any market problems, whether with companies complained about or other companies or the market generally. It raises issues in regular meetings with companies, and publicises information on their activities (such as where rules on portability are not respected). Companies do not like such adverse publicity, and the Authority finds that they usually respond quickly when issues are raised. That attitude may be affected by the fact that most are multinationals, and have a responsive behaviour pattern. The Lithuanian Authority raises and cross-border issues (but not individual ADR complaints) with its correspondent National Enforcement Bodies in other Member States (lost post arises regularly). It finds that it does not need to resort to the ECC network.

The costs of the Authority are in effect paid by the market, through supervisory operating fees levied on operators. Thus, it is slightly misleading to say that the State funds the ADR system for this sector.

Statistics are published in annual reports, summarised at Table 5.3. In 2010,[64] there were 590 complaints,[65] and the number is increasing. Of these, 70 related to the quality of service, 181 to billing, and 106 to other issues (eg tariffs, conditions of agreements, number portability). Service providers settled 158 during the complaint process (in other words, the supplier conceded), and the Authority issued 32 decisions in favour of consumers and 23 in favour of service providers. The deadline for dealing with complaints is one month, but some take longer as it sometimes takes time for a party to provide all the relevant information: the average time is currently two months.

Table 5.3: Complaint data for communications

	2005	2006	2007	2008	2009	2010
Total	**238**	**281**	**362**	**448**	**1513**	**590**
Regarding quality	46	42	56	74	54	70
Regarding billing	146	178	221	229	318	181
Other issues	46	61	85	145	1141	106

The Authority believes that a potentially far larger number of consumer complaints are settled voluntarily, and are not raised with the Authority, because of the nature of the regulatory system. In this sector, there is little problem over compliance by traders with the decisions of the Authority. This is because the Authority is enabled under the primary legislation to establish secondary legislation, the Rules for the Provision of Electronic Commerce Services. The Authority amends these Rules as necessary, after consultation with the market through regular meetings, so as to clarify conduct on any issues that arise. Hence, if a systemic problem is identified through complaints directed at any single provider, it can be solved for the future in relation to *all* providers and their customers, by means of a Rule change. The Authority has not, therefore, heard of any non-compliance with its recommendations in individual complaints, whether from consumers or from subsequent court cases instituted by either side. Decision on complaints have the status of executive documents, which can be

[64] *Rysiu Reguliavimo Tarnyba*, *Annual Report 2010*, (2011, Communications Regulatory Authority of Lithuania, Vilnius), available at www.rrt.lt/en/reviews-and-reports/rrt-annual-repots.html.

[65] In 2009, there were 1,513 complaints, caused because one communications service provider changed the conditions of the agreement with most of its subscribers.

enforced by a National Regulatory Authority under EU legislation, so are in effect binding. Although the Authority has formal enforcement powers, these are hardly ever used, since issues are resolved through regular discussion with providers, which take place against the background that that Authority has ultimate power to amend the Rules, after consultation. The most effective potential sanction is that the General Activity Conditions that apply to providers' licences to operate include the right for the Authority to impose not only economic sanctions but also impose temporary suspensions of activities. In practice, the Authority finds that it is enough to 'name and shame' companies, thereby keeping the more powerful sanctions as a rarely used but effective threat. It has found that companies have become more sensitive to their reputations as the market has developed.

The Authority maintains internal separation between divisions responsible for ADR and regulation. The legal function assists both. It views the ADR system as an essential regulatory tool, enabling it to respond quickly and consistently to market issues. If consumers were to raise complaints in court, the Authority would lose having access to the information and have greater difficulty in aggregating it to identify trends.

Civil Aviation Administration

The Civil Aviation Administration handles enforcement and complaints as a National Enforcement Body (NEB) under EU legislation,[66] and also handles other air passenger complaints, such as carriers' liability for lost or damaged luggage under the Montreal Convention 1999 or Regulation 889/2006. As an enforcement body, the Civil Aviation Administration's primary objectives are security and safety. Accordingly, its enforcement emphasis is on prevention (providing information to passengers and providers) rather than on sanctions, although sanctions are sometimes imposed. The Code of Administrative Violations of Lithuania prescribes financial penalties for breach if the regulations, although the sanctions are limited to between 1000 LTL and 3000 LTL, so very low.

Most consumer contacts to the Authority are requests for information, rather than complaints.

Recent complaints statistics do not include contacts arising out of two bankruptcies: Star1 Airlines (which led to 760 requests for assistance) and flyLAL – Lithuanian Airlines (LAL). The Civil Aviation Administration usually asks consumers to talk to carriers first, but this can sometimes be difficult, in which case it will contact airlines itself.

Complaint statistics are not published, but are included in reports to the European Commission and the State Consumer Rights Protection Authority. Cross-border complaints are forwarded to NEBs in other Member States. The main types of complaints in recent years are shown at Table 5.4. Delayed boarding is the most frequent issue. The number of complaints upheld or dismissed in 2011 and 2011 is at Table 5.5. The Civil Aviation Administration does not have information on the outcomes of complaints.

[66] Under Regulations 261/2004, 2111/2005 (Chapter III), 1107/2006 and 1008/2002 (Chapter IV).

Table 5.4: Air Transport Passenger Complaints handled by the Lithuanian Civil Aviation Administration

	2005	2006	2007	2008	2009	2010	2011
Total number of complaints	35	89	67	102	62	84	63
Regulation 261/2004	21	62	41	59	40	64	50
1. Delay	10	9	26	15	20	23	23
2. Cancellation of flight	5	46	13	31	17	36	21
3. Denied boarding	6	7	2	13	3	5	6
Delayed, damages or lost baggage (under Montreal Convention)	4	10	11	17	5	3	3
1. Damaged baggage	1	2	1	5	1	1	0
2. Delayed baggage	1	1	3	5	3	2	1
3. Lost baggage	2	7	4	7	1	0	0
Regulation 1008/2008 (prices)[67]	–	–	–	–	–	11	5
Regulation 1107/2006 (reduced mobility)[68]	–	–	–	–	–	0	0
Other complaints	10	17	15	26	17	6	5

Table 5.5: Complaints upheld and dismissed

	2010	2011
Complaints upheld	71	37
Complaints not upheld	13	26

Cross-border Complaints

The ECC-Lithuania office was established in 2005 and has been very active in promotional activities. It has a facebook page, makes regular radio and television appearances (twice a week), uses skype, and has close links with the media and magazines. Eighty per cent of the contacts that it receives are requests for information, and only 20 per cent are complaints. The two most populated areas are e.commerce and air passenger rights. At the end of 2011 it was handling 143 outgoing complaints, mainly over traders in Latvia, Germany and the United Kingdom. Some e.commerce issues relate to non- or partial delivery, but some are criminal scams (such as buying cars online) and can only be referred to the police. In 2011, 34 cases were resolved in the consumer's favour, and 20 were not resolved: the reason for non-resolution is often the non-binding nature of any non-court ADR process. ADR decisions in Latvia are binding, and so the consumer Authority there has greater ability to resolve issues. The EU small claims procedure is sometimes the only option, but it is rarely used by consumers.

[67] Complaints about prices involve agencies as well as carriers.
[68] Complaints about reduced mobility often involve airport operators rather than carriers.

Conclusion

Lithuania has a unified consumer out-of-court complaints resolution system, which is free of charge to consumers. The ADR system is integrated into the regulatory authorities. Complaints may be made to sectoral regulatory Authorities, or to the State Consumer Rights Protection Authority. The State Consumer Rights Protection Authority has a high national profile. However, it considers that there is a lack of consumer information and awareness about ADR.[69] It is concerned that the major flaw in the current system is that decisions are not binding on traders, so compliance rates are lower than they should be. The procedure is adversarial in nature, similar in concept to a judicial procedure.

The architecture of the system, like Sweden, provides full coverage for disputes in any consumer trading sector. Various sectors are covered by specialist arrangements, and the sectors are collated by the 'residual' function of the State Consumer Rights Protection Authority.

Whilst statistics about consumer disputes will inherently be available to the regulatory enforcement authorities, there is not yet full public transparency of data on disputes, sectors and traders. It is, therefore, difficult to evaluate whether the authorities themselves are functioning well as either ADR or enforcement bodies.

[69] 'In Lithuania there are no long established ADR traditions and consumers do not have much knowledge of, or confidence in, ADR bodies.' Response to EU ADR Consultation, State Consumer Rights Protection Authority of Lithuania, 2011.

6

The Netherlands

Franziska Weber and Christopher Hodges

Summary

Alternative Dispute Resolution in the Netherlands is based on a well-established structure and operation of Consumer Complaint Commissions[1] (*Geschillencommissies*). The Commissions operate within a wider structure that contains three elements:

1. Agreement of the Terms and Conditions that will apply within a trade sector. These are negotiated between the relevant trade association and the national consumer association (*Consumentenbond*) and sometimes in cooperation with sectoral consumer associations like *Koninklijke Nederlandse Toeristenbond* ANWB and *Vereniging Eigen Huis* (VEH).
2. Disputes in many sectors are referred to an ADR process overseen by an independent Foundation of Complaint Commissions (*Stichting Geschillencommissies voor Consumentenzaken*), which creates and operates sectoral arbitration Commissions. The process includes direct negotiation between customer and trader, conciliation/mediation, and finally arbitration. The process is notably simple, cheap, effective and widely supported. It has the advantage that it is a national framework, so can maintain both high visibility for consumers and traders, combining sectoral variations within a general model, and a high quality of independence and process delivery.
3. The outputs of the Commissions' decisions are used by traders and their trade associations for self-regulatory purposes in improving their operations. Summaries of important decisions are made publicly available, so as to act as precedents.

The financial services sector has a separate structure, with its own Ombudsman who operates as a first tier, its own Commission as second tier, plus an appeal Commission as third tier.

The first part of this chapter notes the strong national culture of settlement and ADR in the Netherlands, from which the various sectoral *Geschillencommissies* grew and flourished. Then, the structure and operation of the *Geschillencommissies* are examined and illustrated in more detail by the examples of the travel and web-trading sectors respectively. Finally, the slightly different financial sector arrangements are discussed and general conclusions are made.

[1] The word commissie is sometimes translated as commission, committee or board: the first option has been chosen here.

National Culture of Negotiated Settlement

The culture of the Netherlands is strikingly consistent in relation to dispute resolution as between public and private sectors, in adopting a uniformly conflict-avoiding approach to disputes.[2] The Netherlands has a distinct and firmly established culture of resolving disputes out of court as a primary mechanism and as an alternative to the courts.[3] The Dutch have a reputation for tolerance, concern for justice,[4] pragmatism and respect for human rights. National characteristics are hospitality, friendliness, tolerance, fair-mindedness, and an ability to trade and hence negotiate.[5] The development of a culture of achieving pragmatic consensual solutions through settling disputes through direct and facilitated negotiation within less adversarial and confrontational settings and frameworks is consistent with that national culture.[6] Public support for the justice system in the Netherlands has long been extremely high,[7] and remains so, although it appears that there is now a considerable level of discontent with legal institutions, especially in relation to a perceived lack of punitiveness and responsiveness of the justice system on the criminal side.[8]

This national approach is central to the ADR bodies discussed in this chapter. But those ADR systems can be seen in clearer perspective by also considering three other examples, namely the integration of ADR in the normal litigation system, the approach of the National Ombudsman in overseeing disputes involving public sector bodies, and the unique court procedure for settling mass litigation.

Principles of the Civil Court System

A primary principle of Dutch legal doctrine is that although people should have access to justice, litigation should only be available as an *ultimum remedium* after all other options have been exhausted.[9] That policy underpins the principle that litigation should not be free,[10] so litigation costs serve as an incentive to parties only to use litigation after other routes, especially ADR.[11] The concept of fairness (*billijkheid*) also underpins the loser pays rule.[12]

[2] See G Hofstede, *Culture's Consequences: comparing values, behaviors, institutions, and organizations across nations* 2nd ed (Thousand Oaks, CA, Sage Publications, 2011).

[3] See ML Tuil, 'The Netherlands', in C Hodges, S Vogenauer and M Tulibacka, *The Costs and Funding of Civil Litigation. A Comparative Perspective* (Oxford, Hart Publishing, 2010).

[4] Leading illustrations of this international reputation can be seen from the location in The Hague of the United Nations International Criminal Court and Permanent Court of Arbitration, and the Hague Conference on Private International Law.

[5] See S Buckland, *Netherlands. The Essential Guide to Customs N Culture* (London, Kuperard, 2008).

[6] See E Blankenburg, 'Civil Litigation Rates as Indicators for Legal Cultures' in D Nelken, *Comparing Legal Cultures* (Aldershot, Dartmouth, 1997); E Blankenburg, 'Patterns of Legal Culture: The Netherlands Compared to Neighbouring Germany' (1998) 46 (1) *American Journal of Comparative Law* 1; F Bruinsma, 'Judges and Lawyers in the Netherlands—an Overview from 1970 till 2000' in W Felstiner (ed), *Reorganisation and Resistance: Legal Professions Confront a Changing World* (Oxford, Hart Publishing, 2005); F Van Waarden, 'The Societal and Historical Embededness of Dutch Corporatism' in F Van Waarden and G Lembruch (eds), *Renegotiating the Welfare State* (London, Routledge, 2003).

[7] JL Gibson and GA Caldeira, 'The Legal Cultures of Europe' (1996) 30 *Law & Society Review* 55 characterised the Netherlands as one of the most law-abiding countries in Europe. See also E Blankenburg and F Bruinsma, *Dutch Legal Culture* (Deventer, Kluwer Law and Taxation Publishers, 1994), 76.

[8] M Hertogh, 'The Curious Case of Dutch Legal Culture. A Reassessment of Survey Evidence' (2010) 5 *Journal of Comparative Law* 2.

[9] HJ Snijders, CJM Klaassen and GJ Meijer, *Nederlands burgerlijk procesrecht* (Deventer, Kluwer, 2007), 56.

[10] ibid, no 28.

[11] Tuil, 'The Netherlands' (2010).

Mark Tuil has summarized the ways in which the above principles are implemented into rules of professional conduct for lawyers, the rules on civil procedure, and on legal aid:[13]

> ... the rules of conduct for lawyers stipulate that a lawyer should realise that a settlement is often preferable to a litigated outcome.[14] This rule places a duty on lawyers to try to effect a settlement. If a case is still brought before the court, the court will, after the parties have stated their case in their initial briefs, order the parties and their representatives to appear for a meeting (*comparitie* or *mondelinge behandeling*). Such a meeting has multiple purposes. Among those purposes is the exploration of the possibility of a settlement.[15] The judge may facilitate the settlement by giving a preliminary view of the case.[16] Parties are also encouraged to settle their disputes by way of mediation. For this purpose, the Netherlands have a system of court-annexed mediation. The first 2.5 hours of mediation are provided free of charge.[17] Any subsequent hours are billed to the parties, who have to decide how to divide these costs. A mediator will cost approximately €150 per hour.[18] Mediation is also covered by legal aid. Settlement is further facilitated by the possibility of the provisional examination of witnesses or a provisional report by an expert.[19] These measures aim to reduce uncertainty, thereby facilitating a settlement. In some (rare) instances the law obligates parties to negotiate before they are allowed to start their suit.[20]

The government has pursued a specific policy of enhancing ADR to the extent that it and the courts are complementary. The Ministry of Justice sponsored an investigation into the prospects for mediation in court proceedings as long ago as 1996 (Platform ADR). After successful pilot mediation schemes in five courts, reporting in 2003, every court has a mediation facility.[21] The Netherlands has a single national umbrella mediation organization, the *Nederlands Mediation Instituut* (NMI), which was established in 1993 primarily to promote mediation, and has strong links with the Ministry of Justice.

Class Settlements: The WCAM

A notable manifestation of the general approach towards ADR and legal claims is the adoption by the Dutch of a unique and innovative approach towards mass litigation, which is entirely aimed at achieving fair and speedy negotiated settlements, rather than encouraging collective litigation.[22] After complex and lengthy product liability litigation (of

[12] WL Haardt, *De veroordeling in de kosten van het burgerlijk geding* ('s-Gravenhage, Martinus Nijhof, 1945), and EM Wesseling-van Gent, 'Proceskostenveroordeling' in NVv Procesrecht (ed) *De kosten van de procedure* (Deventer, Kluwer, 1993), 2–3.

[13] Tuil (n 3), 405.

[14] Rules of conduct for lawyers 1990 ('Gedragsregels 1990') Rule 3, at www.advocatenorde.nl.

[15] For procedures that start with a summons this objective can be found in Art 87 (Wetboek van Burgerlijke Rechtsvordering) (RV) Dutch Code of Civil Procedure. For procedures that start with a request an explicit rule is absent, however this does not mean to say that the judge is not allowed to try to affect a settlement.

[16] HR 24 September 1999, *NJ* 1999 (*Bleij/Stegeman*).

[17] Policy Resolution '*Stimuleringsbijdrage conflictbemiddeling*' *Stcr* 2009, 63.

[18] According to the website of the Dutch Judiciary www.rechtspraak.nl.

[19] Arts 186 *f* and 202 *f* Rv. See Snijders, Klaassen and Meijer *Nederlands burgerlijk procesrecht,* 247.

[20] The division of co-owned property (Art 3:185 BurgerlijkWetboek (BW) – Dutch Civil Code); see ML Tuil, *Verdelingsbeslagen* (Den Haag, Boom Juridische uitgevers, 2009) 191–93, in collective actions (Art 3:305a BW) and in separation cases concerning children (Art 815 Rv).

[21] J Singer, *The EU Mediation Atlas: Practice and Regulation* (Centre for Effective Dispute resolution, CMS and Lexis/Nexis, 2005).

[22] See WH van Boom, 'Collective Mass Claims in the Netherlands', in M Casper et al (eds), *Auf dem Weg zu einer Europäischen Sammelklage?* (Munich, Sellier, 2009), 171–92; T Arons and WH van Boom, 'Beyond Tulips and Cheese: Exporting Mass Securities Claim Settlements from The Netherlands' (2010) 6 *European Business Law*

individual cases, in the absence of a collective procedure) over cervical cancer in children of mothers who took diethylstilboestrol (DES) during pregnancy, a settlement was negotiated. However, the pharmaceutical company wished to achieve closure involving the settlement being binding on as many individual claims as possible. The Act on the Collective Settlement of Mass Claims (Wet *Collectieve Afwikkeling Massaschade*: WCAM) was passed in 2005 in order to achieve this. Under this procedure, parties to a dispute (whether or not they have commenced litigation claims) can jointly apply to the Amsterdam Court of Appeal for a declaration that the terms of a negotiated settlement are fair and binding on all potential parties in the defined class of claimants unless they individually opt out of the settlement. The WCAM procedure has been criticized by some as omitting a 'front end' mechanism of a procedure to certify a class, or otherwise initiate mass litigation. Instead, it only has a 'back end' procedure of certifying a fair settlement as binding, for those who do not opt out. But that is precisely the point: the cultural and policy objective is to encourage negotiation and settlement, rather than litigation. The WCAM procedure has already proved its worth by attracting a series of large disputes.[23]

The National Ombudsman

The office of the National Ombudsman was created in 1982 and since 1999 is guaranteed in the Dutch Constitution.[24] The Ombudsman investigates complaints brought to him by members of the public and can also launch investigations on his own initiative. The Ombudsman has a staff of around 140 and total expenditure in 2010 of €14.6 million. The Ombudsman is a 'fall-back' provision, only available after the citizen has complained first to the administrative authority itself, including through any appeal procedure, and the matter has not been settled.

The Ombudsman has extensive investigatory powers. Administrative authorities and witnesses are required by law to cooperate with his investigations. The written reports that are produced set out the facts and the reasons for his decision and recommendations. His decisions and recommendations are not legally enforceable, but almost always observed and implemented. Recommendations may relate to resolving an individual case or may be designed to prevent complaints arising in future. The National Ombudsman is required by law to accompany each of his decisions by a statement of the standard of proper conduct that has been breached. Over the years, this has resulted in the development of a list of around 25 standards of proper conduct. They include not just matters such as promptness, adequate information gathering and provision, and proportionality, but also respect for fundamental rights like the right to physical integrity.

The National Ombudsman may adopt a number of approaches in handling complaints, including intervention, mediation, and investigation. He considers that reflection and feedback to public authorities are integral aspects of his work. Feedback is given not just about lessons learned from how individual cases have been handled, but more importantly

Review, 857; F Weber and WH van Boom, 'Dutch Treat: the Dutch Collective Settlement of Mass Damage Act' (WCAM 2005), (2011) 1 *Contratto e impresa / Europa*, 69.

[23] H van Lith, 'The Dutch Collective Settlements Act and Private International Law' (WODC, Ministerie van Justitie, 2010). Following the recent failure of a bank, DSB, its administrator wants to use WCAM as a quicker solution for reaching negotiated solutions than complex bankruptcy procedures. Amendments are being considered to the bankruptcy law in order to facilitate this.

[24] Ch 4, Art 78a.

about the overall systems and whole approach of the public administration towards the public. The current Ombudsman, Professor Brenninkmeijer, has produced a notable series of reflections on the lessons from his work,[25] and wrote in 2010:[26]

> The National Ombudsman does not see the right of complaint and the consequent handling of complaints as ends in themselves. While it is clearly important that individuals, businesses and institutions should be able to express their dissatisfaction with the actions of administrative authorities and that their complaints should be taken seriously, it is better still to prevent such complaints. For that reason, the National Ombudsman needs to exert a more structural influence on the way administrative authorities deal with the public. Proper treatment is not just a question of being 'pleasant' and 'courteous': it lies at the very root of the legitimacy of government action and public compliance. Proper treatment is the concrete expression of procedural fairness. For the people involved, the feeling that government action has been fair is often essential.[27]

Out of that attitude has arisen a campaign to encourage public servants to treat citizens with respect: 'should seek direct personal contact with people presenting complaints and problems, take them seriously, treat them with respect, and deal with them as equals.'[28]

Policy on Consumer ADR

The main policy considerations that are pursued in the Netherlands in relation to business-to-consumer (B2C) ADR are to provide fast, easy and cheap procedures.[29] A consumer is encouraged to use an ADR body where one exists and the trader belongs to it, instead of the courts. This policy has stimulated traders to join what has become an established framework of ADR bodies. Hence, the function of ADR bodies has become comparable to the courts, and the two tracks are viewed as equally valid options for resolving disputes. In practice, the ADR pathway has grown to the extent that it has eclipsed the courts for consumer-to-business claims in most of the sectors where the ADR route exists.

The state's sponsorship of ADR is manifested by the role of the Social and Economic Council (*Sociaal-Economische Raad*, SER) in sponsoring and facilitating the crucial initial stage of formal negotiations between consumer and business representatives to agree standard terms and conditions of trade, which act as the pre-condition to establishment of an ADR system in each sector. The SER, which operates on a public law basis, has its own secretariat, undertakes market studies, and provides an independent chairman (such as a law professor) to chair the negotiations on terms and conditions. Huls has described this approach as the 'standard bearer of the Dutch *polder* model (ie consociational politics).'[30,31]

[25] See the Annual Reports, and AFM Brenninkmeijer, *Apologies in public administration* (National Ombudsman of the Netherlands, 2010).

[26] AFM Brenninkmeijer, *Compliance with recommendations* (National Ombudsman of the Netherlands, 2010), available at www.nationaleombudsman.nl/sites/default/files/2011_gb_artikel_compliance_with_recommendations.pdf.

[27] TR Tyler, *Why Do People Obey the Law? Procedural Justice, Legitimacy and Compliance* (New Haven, Connecticut, Yale University Press, 1990).

[28] AFM Brenninkmeijer, *Compliance with recommendations.*

[29] See A Klapwijk and M ter Voert, *Evaluatie De Geschillencommissie 2009*, available at www.wodc.nl/images/ob278_volledige_tekst_tcm44-237673.pdf.

[30] A Lijphart, *Thinking about Democracy: Power Sharing and Majority Rule in Theory and Practice* (London, Routledge, 2008).

[31] N Huls, 'Consumer Bankruptcy: A Third Way between Autonomy and Paternalism in Private Law' (2010) 3 *Erasmus Law Review* 1, 7, 19.

The government has also encouraged ADR through the Coordination Group on Self-Regulation (CER), which provides information on developments. In the earlier stages of establishment of the ADR system, a decade or so ago, government subsidies were available for those *Geschillencommissies* that were recognized. Currently, the government funds the central administration of the SGC.

Two legal forms of ADR exist in the Netherlands, arbitration (a binding decision) and a binding advice. Arbitration is regulated in detail in similar fashion to many other jurisdictions: the rules are contained in Articles 1020–1076 BW. The *Geschillencommissie* procedure discussed below is based on the 'binding advice technique, which was inserted into the Civil Code (Articles 7:900–906 BW) in 1993. The 'binding advice is a settlement agreement in which a third party rules on a dispute between parties, in relation to which the parties have agreed beforehand on this form of dispute resolution, for example under a specific agreement or by means of the general terms and conditions declared as being applicable to an agreement concluded previously.[32] The parties are, however, not bound by a patently unreasonable decision.[33] Such unreasonableness may pertain to the substance of the decision, or the way in which it was reached. A binding advice may not be directly enforced, but must be first subject to a ruling on compliance obtained from a court.

The Role of the Consumer Authority

Before examining the private sector dispute resolution arrangements in detail, their significance within the Dutch legal and enforcement framework should be seen against the background of the structure of public enforcement of consumer law. There was no structure for public enforcement of consumer law before the creation of the Consumer Authority (*Consumentenautoriteit*) in 2007.[34] There were two reasons to create such an Authority: firstly, the need for a national authority to exist so as to form part of the EU network of national authorities required by Regulation 2006/2004 on consumer protection cooperation in the single market, and secondly, to address issues of non-compliance with regulations in consumer markets, and a lack of knowledge of consumers' rights.[35] When the Consumer Authority was created, it was surprised how many cases were brought to it, which it felt revealed an unmet need.

The Consumer Authority has both public and private law enforcement powers for collective breaches:[36] public law enforcement powers as to clear-cut provisions and private

[32] See Response to the European Commission's Consultation on ADR by the Netherlands Ministry of Justice, 2011, available at ec.europa.eu/consumers/redress_cons/adr_responses/the_netherlands-ministry_of_justice_en.pdf.

[33] Art 7:904 BW.

[34] The Authority falls under the supervision of the Minister of Economic Affairs, Agriculture and Innovation, although it has been granted direct oversight and enforcement powers, thereby providing from independent decision-making.It was announced in March 2011 that the Consumer Authority, the Telecoms Authority and the Competition Authority (NMa) would merge. The Consumer Authority has 42 staff as at 2011, whereas the Competition Authority has 600 staff, including an Economic Bureau.

[35] S Ammerlaan and D Janssen, 'The Dutch Consumer Authority: an introduction' in WH van Boom and MBM Loos (eds), *Collective Enforcement of Consumer Law – Securing Compliance in Europe through Private Group Action and Public Authority Intervention* (Groningen, Europa Law Publishing 2007); MA Heldeweg, 'Supervisory governance. The case of the *Dutch Consumer Authority* (2006) 2 *Utrecht Law Review* 1, 67.

[36] Notably the legislation on unfair commercial practices, services, misleading advertising, E-commerce, consumer purchases, general contract terms, distance selling, timesharing, package travel (all of which is EU-based legislation) and national legislation on doorstep selling and price visibility.

law enforcement powers (via a civil judge) as to provisions that leave room for some discretion. Enforcement of private law is a matter for the private sector, and hence the Consumer Authority does not have power to enforce private law contracts, such as Terms and Conditions, which may promise more than the law requires, and it is not empowered to deal with individual complaints. The Authority does take note of information from all sources on what is happening in the market, so it notes any individual complaints that are brought to its attention. Its resources are slim, with 42 staff as at 2011, but both resource and function are affected by the existence of the extensive private sector arrangements for negotiation Terms and Conditions and resolving complaints, discussed below.

Overall, it can be said that, in the Dutch legal system, consumer protection and enforcement are based on a dual system of civil law and public law. The traditional approach that civil resolution of issues is prioritized has only recently been complemented by public law enforcement. The civil 'pillar' moves from individual action through ADR bodies (*Geschillencommissies*) and consumer associations to collective interests, which are resolved through self-regulation by branch associations.

In relation to public enforcement by the Consumer Authority, 85% of cases are solved by informal means, such as talking or letters.[37] In 2010, the Authority took 5 sanctions decisions, 2 decisions on administrative appeals, 2 other decisions on appeal, 10 judgments on request procedures, and 8 orders combined with incremental penalty payments. Between 2007 and 2010 it closed 310 investigations.

The Consumer Authority is the designated Single Liaison Office for the Netherlands under the CPC network of national authorities. 75% of its cases are national, and 25% are cross-border. But that statistic does not say anything about the importance of particular cases. The Netherlands receives more cross-border cases than any other Member State with the CPC Network (21 new requests for assistance in 2010). It is also number one in dealing with cases quickly: as at end 2010, only 4% of requests were still open. Requests received under the CPC system are individual cases, and can take time to deal with.

The Consumer Authority considers that the ECC-NET system would be improved if it made possible complaints and action about systemic problems. It considers the basis of the network to be good, and there to be effective cooperation between national authorities. The problem with the system lies in its legislative approach: putting the rules into legislation leads to an unnecessarily bureaucratic and legalistic system, and too many discussions about the precise interpretation of terms used. There are many differences between national systems over enforcement powers (criminal or other), enforcement approaches or policies, and the architecture of enforcement bodies. Power is sometimes given to different bodies, such as over airline tickets.

The *Geschillencommissie* Structure

The ADR model is standardized nationally for almost all sectors apart from financial services, and operated by a national body, the Foundation for Consumer Complaint Commissions (*Stichting Geschillencommissie* (SGC)). The Dutch government has financially supported the SGC (see below), and the expansion of the number of Commissions in the 2000s. In

[37] Interview, 23 March 2011.

some sectors, such as electricity, gas, water and taxi, traders are obliged by law to enter into an ADR scheme, although no specific scheme is specified. Notaries will shortly also be required to join an ADR scheme.

The SGC was established in 1970, in order to create and oversee the first Board, and Boards have been created to resolve disputes in different sectors at a steady pace ever since. As at 2011 there are fifty sectoral consumer Commissions, which are listed at Table 6.1, and five business disputes Commissions. The range of sectors covered by Commissions is now very wide, and includes financial services, telecoms, energy and air transport. Legislation in 2012 will provide for a new sectoral Commission on medical claims. The SGC already has two sectoral Commissions for medical disputes, one for Hospitals and one for Nursing, Normal Care and Home Care. A Commission was established on sports and exercise in January 2012.[38] The arrangements are illustrated below in relation to two sectors: those for travel and web trading.

Table 6.1: The 50 Sectoral Complaints Commissions

1.	Air-conditioning	26. Leisure
2.	Aviation	27. Moving firms
3.	Building refinement	28. Newly-built private housing
4.	Bicycles	29. Nursing, Normal care and Home care
5.	Car rentals	30. Opticians
6.	Community aerial systems	31. Paintwork, Glazing and Plasterwork
7.	Crèches	32. Parquet floorings
8.	Dry-cleaning and laundry services	33. Pets and domestic animals
9.	Driving schools	34. Post
10.	Electrical goods	35. Private health care clinics
11.	Electronic communication services	36. Private education institutes
12.	Energy and Water	37. Public Transport
13.	Energy label	38. Rebuilding
14.	(Real-) estate-agency	39. Roofing
15.	Funeral services	40. Selling door-to-door
16.	Gardening	41. Stores for construction supplies/materials
17.	Glass, porcelain and earthenware	42. Sun screens
18.	Grooming industry	43. Taxi transport
19.	Handy men and floor companies	44. Telecommunications
20.	Health Care (eg hospitals)	45. Textiles and shoes
21.	Home furnishing	46. Travel
22.	Home shopping	47. Vehicles
23.	Information service providers	48. Water sports
24.	Installation technicians	49. Care, maintenance and home care[39]
25.	Legal profession	50. Jewellery and clocks[40]

At the end of 2011, two consumer complaints boards stopped: aviation and funeral services as there was no level playing field established. As of April 2012, the complaints boards for the fitness industry and paving companies begin. In July a second complaints board for webshops will open. It is also anticipated to establish a complaints board for notarys and pharmacists in 2012.

[38] Annual report 2011 of ′De Geschillencommissie′, 7.
[39] *Verpleging, Verzorging* and *Thuiszorg*, operating since 1 January 2011.
[40] *Sieraden* and *Uurwerken*, operating since 1 April 2011.

Agreeing Sectoral Terms and Conditions

The usual first step is for trade associations and the consumer association(s) to negotiate and agree the terms and conditions that will apply to members of the trade association in the sector. The *Consumentenbond* is always involved, together with any relevant sectoral consumer association, such as exist for daycare, car drivers, homeowners, bikers, and patients.

The negotiations are undertaken under the auspices of the SER, which makes its facilities available for both sides, thereby providing a neutral environment and also the formal patronage and encouragement of the state for the parties to reach agreement. A law professor with relevant expertise or other legal expert usually chairs the negotiations. Such terms and conditions are based on all applicable law, and never fall below the standards set in the law, but often fill in gaps or more detail that are not covered by legal requirements, thereby sometimes establishing higher standards.[41]

Trade association members who agree terms and conditions under the system are not permitted, under the terms of their trade association membership, to use terms and conditions that are not approved. At the start of 2011 there were 62 sets of agreed terms and conditions. Not all sectors have terms and conditions: healthcare is such an example but they are being introduced there, and awareness is growing of their usefulness in the medical sector.

The process of renegotiation is continuous: all the terms and conditions are revised every three to five years. When entering a renegotiation, the *Consumentenbond* looks at signals from its members and from the Consumer Authority, any other feedback, the published case law from *Geschillencommissie* decisions, and may also undertake site visits. It can insert various provisions aimed at affecting behaviour. For example, if it finds that bills are higher than people expect, a term can be inserted that traders should inform customers of the size of a bill in advance of entering into a contract.

Trade associations consider that the ability of their trader members to operate with terms and conditions approved by the *Consumentenbond*, associated with membership of the *Geschillencommissie* system, contributes significantly to consumer confidence.[42]

Various codes of business practice or conduct are produced by some trade associations, which usually cover advertising issues. They are unilateral statements, and not negotiated with anyone else, such as consumer associations. There is no national scheme for Codes. The codes are not enforceable under private law, and could not form the basis of a compensation claim, which would have to be pursued through the courts, assuming a *Geschillencommissie* route was not available. Codes can form the basis of negotiations on Terms and Conditions between a branch association and consumer association, such as over quality standards. The Advertising Code Commission (RCC) gives non-binding opinions on whether advertisements comply with the advertising law. *Consumentenbond* sometimes comments on such matters.

[41] An example is the *Thuiswinkel* (web traders) conditions, which increased the 7 day withdrawal period required by law to 14 days, in advance of this being required under the forthcoming EU Consumer Rights Directive. *Thuiswinkel* considers that 90% of its terms and conditions merely paraphrase the rules set out in the law.

[42] Interviews with H van Breemen, L Mölenberg and G de Vries Lentsch.

Establishing a Sectoral Commission

The normal situation is for a trade association that has agreed, or intends to agree, general contract terms and conditions for a sector to approach the SGC to establish a Commission. It is not necessary to have terms and conditions as a precondition for the establishment of a sectoral Commission. The existence of the Foundation and the Commission system has operated as an incentive for the creation of terms and conditions in sectors: the output of Commissions' decisions can be used to form the basis of new terms and conditions, as a form of codification. If it decides to do so, the Foundation will draw up a contract with the trade association concerned, which contains details of the Commission jurisdiction and financial support by the association for the SGC to cover the Commission's principal costs. The SGC then sets up the Commission and runs it, in accordance with its normal format, subject to any sector-specific requirements.

The Ministry of Safety and Justice subsidizes the annual costs for the infrastructure with around €750,000, to which some special payments can be added. Business pays for the handling of the cases (caseload) of the system. This means that the annual costs for business depend on the number of cases handled. Over the years, the ministry subsidizes between 15–20% of business between 80–85% of the costs. The total annual costs fluctuate between € 5.5 and 6.5 million, depending on the caseload and 50 trade organizations participating. Other ministries subsidize some of the sectoral Commissions. But the main source of funding comes from annual payments made under the contracts with the various trade associations. This totaled € 3.7 million in 2009.[43]

The trade association pays to the SGC the annual costs for handling the caseload, part of which is paid on account and then subject to adjustment at the end of the year when the total usage of the relevant Commission is known. The year-end adjustment can cause some challenges for those sectors where the claim rate fluctuates significantly between that which was budgeted and which materializes, and which involves either a rebate or an extra bill to be funded.[44] (Individual traders do not pay case fees to the SGC directly with each case, so the associations have to fund the bill and either have a reserve or a means of collecting quickly from members.) The amount of the total sum varies from sector to sector,[45] and depends on factors such as bargaining power, the volume of cases and so on. The financial structure provides an incentive for each branch association to reduce the number of claims in its sector. It is up to each trade association how to distribute the cost amongst its members: roughly half of them raise a general levy amongst their members,[46] and also roughly half impose a cost on individual companies who lose a case. The latter solution can clearly have some effect as a penalty and deterrent to multiple defendants and an incentive to improve their operations.

[43] Between 2005 and 2007 the business sector contribution was about €2.2 million, which decreased immediately after the formation of KiFiD in 2008.

[44] The ANVR finds that the sum initially budgeted can vary against the final account by 50% or 60%.

[45] In 2010, Thuiswinkel's total bill was €30,000, with an average cost of €750 per procedure.

[46] *Thuiswinkel's* members pay an annual membership fee to the association, based on the member's turnover, which includes the cost of the *Geschillencommissie*. The range of annual contributions varies between €150 and €28,000, contributing to Thuiswinkel's annual turnover of €4.5 million. In order to become a full member of *Thuiswinkel*, a firm needs to show 2 years' market history and financial figures. Aspirant members can join until they can show two years' figures, and pay a certification fee of €350 annual contribution of €400. There is a contractual right to charge members separately for the cost of the *Geschillencommissie* but this has never so far been invoked. The association is, in 2011, considering charging a member for the cost of a case where the association considers that the member should have settled it.

Companies that register individually with the SGC, usually because they are not members of a trade association that is registered, pay a fee on registration, subsequent annual fees, and a fee per case. A 2007 survey found that the range of overall costs contributed by individual companies varied from under €100 to over €20,000, as shown in Figure 6.1.[47]

Figure 6.1: Total company costs for *Geschillencommissie* cases in 2007.

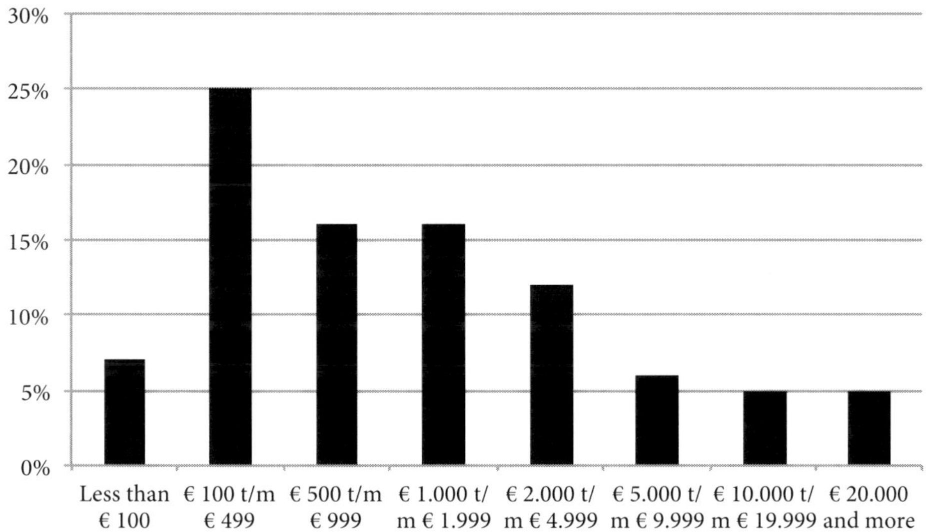

Source: ondernemersenquête.

The Structure of the Foundation and of Dispute Resolution Commissions

The fact that the operation of Commissions comes under an independent oversight body is intended to guarantee that every Commission operates to appropriate standards and impartiality. Every Commission meets the principles that are specified in the Ministry of Justice's Recognition Regulation,[48] which are consistent with the EU's related 1998 Recommendation.[49] The network has its own brand, which is well-recognised. Some separate private sector boards exist, but may not meet the same standards, and the boards that are in the official Commission network are widely recognised and preferred. The system has the confidence of consumers and business. The acceptance of every complaint that is made through the SGC avoids cherry-picking.

A pre-condition to bringing a claim to a Commission is that the trader is registered with the SGC. A trader can register in one of two ways: it can either be a member of the sector organization or it can register independently with the SGC. The possibility of registration by individual traders is designed to raise business standards and provide consumer guarantees,

[47] See Klapwijk and ter Voert, *Evaluatie De Geschillencommissie* (2009), 92. The total sum thus includes costs for travelling, telephone calls, collection of information, contact with lawyers, consumers, and the *Geschillencommissie*.

[48] Stscrt. 1996, 248.

[49] Commission Recommendation (EC) 98/257 on the principles applicable to the bodies responsible for the out-of-court settlement of consumer disputes, [1998] OJ L 115.

since it attracts firms in sectors for which there may be no trade association. Firms therefore apply so as to benefit from the commercial advantage of belonging to a trusted organization.

In accordance with normal arbitration practice, both parties must consent to initiate the procedure. Consumers are left free to choose between going to court and going to the Commission. A standard contract term requiring a consumer to submit a case to a *Geschillencommissie* and thus prohibiting him from bringing the case in an ordinary court is deemed to be unfair.[50] If they choose to go to the Commission, however, in principle they waive their right to a civil procedure. The business' consent is given through its membership of a national organization or its registration with the SGC.[51] A trader may seek to initiate a claim, but if it is to be accepted by a Commission, the consumer must also consent. The government plans to impose a higher personal contribution for citizens who receive legal aid if they decide to start proceedings in court instead of with the *Geschillencommissie*.[52]

The contract between a trade association and the SGC contains a number of key clauses. First, the trade association guarantees that its members will use the general contract Terms and Conditions that have been bilaterally agreed with the consumers' representatives. Secondly, it guarantees that its members consent to consumers taking their complaints to the Commission and that they waive their right to take disputes to a civil court. Thirdly, the association undertakes that if one of its members fails to comply with a Commission decision, it will itself pay the claim.[53] This financial guarantee usually has a ceiling per case of €10,000; for higher amounts, the branch organization will support the consumer in court proceedings, thereby avoiding execution problems for the consumer if the trader is unwilling to pay. Recovery of such costs from the member is a matter between the trade association and the member. Some guarantees used to be unlimited, but the €10,000 ceiling was introduced after the National Bank decided that any firm offering arrangements over that sum per case would be considered to be subject to the onerous regulatory requirements for insurance.

Most claims concern disputes involving contracts, for which compensation is the remedy sought most often. The Commission procedure is not available if a case is already pending in court.[54] This has been true for disputes that involve death, physical injury or illness, but a more nuanced approach has developed and this restriction does not apply to the Boards for Ophthalmic Matters, Hospitals and Nursing, Normal Care and Home Care, and will not apply for the new Boards for medical health care.

The Foundation establishes a list for each sector of individual people who are approved to hear disputes relating to that sector. Each list has three groups: chairmen, who are selected by the Foundation and have expertise in adjudication, usually being a judge or law professor; and individuals nominated respectively by *Consumentenbond* and the business sector, all of whom are required to act in their own personal capacity as experts in the particular field, and not as representatives of any organization or interest. They are all approved by the Council of the SGC, and are responsible to the SGC not to their employers or nominating organizations. As at 2011 the total pool of arbitrators comprises 300 individuals. There were an additional 120 technical experts.

[50] Art 6:236 (n) BW; see MBM Loos and WH van Boom, *Handhaving van het consumentenrecht – Preadviezen Nederlandse Vereniging voor Burgerlijk Recht 2009*, (Deventer, Kluwer, 2010), 90.

[51] J Stuyck, E Terryn, T van Dyck and V Colaert, *Evaluation Report of the Compendium on Consumer Law*, 2006, see national report on the Netherlands, compiled by E Hondius (2006).

[52] See Loos and van Boom, *Handhaving van het consumentenrecht* (2010), 46 referring to *Bijl. Handelingen II* 2008/09, 31 753, nr 1, p 16.

[53] ANVR has a financial guarantee to cover claims against companies that become insolvent, and Thuiswinkel is working towards introducing this, but it is expensive.

[54] Hondius, *Netherlands National Report* (2006).

The key quality required for decision-makers is expertise, whether judicial, technical, or knowledge of the perspective of one or other side in the dispute. This tripartite structure for composition of Commissions is intended to guarantee that all views are represented on the panel, that the penal has appropriate expertise in adjudication and technical issues, and also to guarantee independence and impartiality.[55] The external activities of the members are regulated as to avoid inconsistencies.[56] The SGC asks the trade association when a new arrangement is established what types of disputes can be expected, and chooses arbitrators with appropriate expertise.

Panels of three arbitrators (containing one from each group) chosen at random by the Foundation are booked in advance for hearing days. They will deal with such cases as are ready and next in line for hearing. The panel members are paid a small honorarium, but such posts are attractive to members since they gain good experience. Judges are keen to work closely with the experts on the panels.

The Complaints Boards are supported by independent experts, who are also all approved by the Council of SGC. Where necessary, these experts carry out investigations in order to inform the Board regarding specific technical aspects of a complaint. Examples of Boards for which experts regularly report are those for Automobiles, Installation Technicians and Home Furnishing. Both parties receive a copy of the report of the technical investigation, so they can comment on it in a fully transparent procedure. In a cross-border complaint, the SGC uses its network of national trade associations to contact national associations in the other European state to organize an investigation on the location of the complaint. Similarly, the SGC uses the national European Consumer Centre to support the consumer in arranging any translation that may be necessary.

The Sequenced Approach to Processing Claims

The first stage is always that the consumer is required to contact the trader to try to solve matters between them. The SGC maintains information on its website for each sector which is designed to provide useful information, including Frequently Asked Questions (FAQs) and an index of important previous decisions plus a search engine, so all sides can see standards and decisions that have been previously established.

If direct negotiation is required but fails, the consumer (or the trader) may initiate the complaint to the relevant Commission. A number of trade associations offer the consumer the option of attempting conciliation before cases proceed to the Commission, and the SGC is planning to integrate such activity further into its dispute resolution process. Online mediation is one option being considered, through which the details of every complaint that arises would be entered into the SGC's computer system by, or be available to, the trade association for conciliation purposes.

The procedure is designed to be an efficient logistical process that reaches fair decisions swiftly, as early in the process as possible, and at minimal cost. It operates as a 'quality circle'. It is not intended to be a judicial process. It is administered centrally by the SGC and is fully electronic, ISO certified to an INK quality model. All aspects are designed to facilitate settlement. Although paper complaints are received, almost all are now fully electronic.

[55] See FAQ on the website of the *Geschillencommissie*, www.degeschillencommissie.nl/over-ons/veelgestelde-vragen.

[56] See Klapwijk and ter Voert (n 29), 59.

The consumer completes a standard form, uploads any supporting evidence (which can be done by sending documents to the SGC) and identifies a possible solution. The form must be signed/approved, to signify agreement to the arbitration process being binding. On submission, the complainant is given a unique username and password, and can monitor the progress of the claim online. The SGC reviews submitted forms to ensure that they are complete and the relevant Commission can handle the problem. The digital process drives the workflow through set stages of defence, expert report and hearing.[57] An accepted claim is sent to the supplier by email, again with a user name and password, which has four weeks to submit a response online. The notification to the supplier reminds him of the opportunity to settle, and a significant number contact the consumer during that period and reach settlement.

In many sectors an expert's report is required, such as floor paneling or reconditioned engines.[58] Others, such as disputes on billing by utilities, can be decided on paper evidence. Where required, the SGC will instruct an expert from its panel of 120 to make a field visit and file the report. Some of the experts are trained mediators, and their discussion of a case with the consumer and trader can lead to agreement at that stage.[59]

Although rates vary between sectors, the process facilitates settlement in about 50 cases filed. If necessary, a date for a hearing is then fixed. The hearing is informal, takes around 30 minutes, and is generally open to the public. Both the consumer and the trader are free to attend or not as they wish. If a party is present, he or she may explain their position. The parties can bring witnesses and experts.[60] The Commission can gather information at its own motion, by hearing witnesses and experts, or by initiating an investigation conducted by the commission or an expert. The Commission notifies the parties of its decision in writing.

Legal representation is possible but not necessary. Some consider that the fact that parties do not have to be represented by a lawyer could be to the detriment of weaker consumers.[61] However, the Commissions aim to operate impartially.[62]

Decisions generally turn on applying the sectoral terms and conditions and the general law. The terms and conditions are regularly updated. As with all arbitration procedures, Commissions can decide issues of law where they arise.

Initiating a procedure at the *Geschillencommissie* and obtaining binding advice preludes access to court except for limited appeal options. In general, there is no appeal from Commission decisions. Minor issues like spelling mistakes can be corrected in awards up to 14 days after a decision has been given. Either party may apply to the court within two months for nullification of a Commission decision, but the grounds are limited: the court can annul the decision if the Commission violated fundamental principles of procedural law, such as the right to be heard,[63] or if the decision is unacceptably unfair and unreasonable.[64] Nullification decisions are rare, such as when the knock-on effect of a single Commission

[57] This 'workflow system' was introduced in this form on 1 January 2010: see Annual report 2010 of *De Geschillencommissie*, 9.

[58] Some associations have in-house experts who can assist in resolving complaints at an early stage: the cars association has four.

[59] Three Commissions in particular (*Wonen, Parket en Klussen,* and *Vloerenbedrijven*) have experts that have mediation skills to enable a settlement between the parties.

[60] Hondius, (n 51), 5.

[61] ibid.

[62] WH van Boom and T Jongbloed, personal communications. Professor Jongbloed is a chairman in the travel commission.

[63] Hondius, (n 51), 5.

[64] Art 7:904 BW. AS Rueb, *Compendium van het Burgerlijk Procesrecht* (Deventer, Kluwer, 2009) 328.

decision on other cases is considerable, for example in liability of utility companies for damage caused by power cuts. The rules provide that parties can ask that a member of a panel is replaced when there is doubt about his or her impartiality.[65] Such claims have been brought in the courts of first instance, and lawyers are usually instructed in such cases.[66] Between January 2005 and July 2008 13 cases have come before the courts, of which the 'binding advice' was nullified in 5 cases.[67]

Fees

The party who initiates a complaint has to pay a modest registration fee. The rationale for this is not to be a financing instrument but to ensure that the complainant takes the case seriously. The fee generally ranges between €25 and €125, depending on the sector. An exception is the Commission on *Garantiewoningen* (newly-built private housing) where the fee is €320.[68] The registration fee includes the services of the arbitrators and any expert visit and report. The overall costs for the consumer usually amount to less than €100, and only in one out of 20 cases does the consumer pay more than €500.[69]

The losing party reimburses the registration fee if the claimant wins the case, unless the final decision is similar to a settlement offer made by the defendant at an earlier stage and not accepted by the consumer.[70] Any further costs incurred by a party, such as lawyers' or experts' fees or travelling, telephone calls, photocopies, are not claimable or shifted, so the general principle is of no cost shifting.[71] In very exceptional cases, the losing party can be required to reimburse other costs.

Statistics on Use

The published statistics for 2010 on the number of claims for each sectoral Commission, and outcomes, are shown in Table 6.2 (pp 146–147),[72] which show the following:

- 7,826 claims were initiated (continuing a steady falling trend: 10,483 in 2009, 11,043 in 2008, 11,280 in 2007). The SGC considers that the diminishing trend in cases is caused by its various efforts aimed at encouraging earlier settlement, and increased efficiency due to digitalization, which was introduced in 2008, and its associated earlier exclusion of non-admissible claims.
- 60% of claims were submitted in a digital form, compared to 50% in 2009 and 39% in 2008.[73]

[65] See FAQ on the website of the Geschillencommissie, www.degeschillencommissie.nl/over-ons/veelgestelde-vragen.

[66] See Klapwijk and ter Voert (n 29), 76.

[67] The judgments were accessed at www.rechtspraak.nl.

[68] FAQ on the website of the Geschillencommissie, www.degeschillencommissie.nl/over-ons/veelgestelde-vragen.

[69] These costs entail those for travelling, phone calls, copies, printing and collection of information, see Klapwijk and ter Voert (n 19), 12.

[70] Hondius (n 51), 5.

[71] E Hondius, (2010), 'The innovative nature of consumer law', prepared for the *ius commune* conference in Leuven on 25/26 November 2010, 5.

[72] Due to the introduction of the workflow system in 2010 (see above) there is no full comparability of the 2010 numbers to those of the previous years. See annual report 2010 of *De Geschillencommissie*, 22.

[73] Annual report 2009 of *De Geschillencommissie*, 7.

- 5,799 cases were processed (6,316 in 2009, 6,525 in 2008, 6,112 in 2007).
- 3,046 'binding advices' were given (3,117 in 2009, 3,417 in 2008 and 3,504 in 2007).
- In 2,167 cases, the consumer and the trader settled during the procedure (2,806 in 2009, 2,741 in 2008, 2,650 in 2007).
- In 289 cases, an expert's involvement led to a settlement (393 in 2009, 358 in 2008, 364 in 2007).
- The average claim value and value awarded varies from sector to sector, with being a few hundred Euros (€206 awarded for taxi transport) or a few thousand (the largest average award being €5,980 for housing guarantees).

Duration

The average duration of *Geschillencommissie* cases in 2010 was 4.4 months (4.7 months in 2009).[74] By comparison, although an uncontested small claim might be processed within one week, the duration of small claims cases in court averaged 15 weeks in 2009 (19 weeks in 2008) and averaged 61 weeks for ordinary court proceedings (in both 2008 and 2009).[75]

Enforceability and Self-regulatory Consequences

As a rule, suppliers comply with awards, because they have knowingly committed themselves to the process. But if a trader is unwilling to comply, there are underlying business guarantees by each trade association. The aim is to avoid execution problems for the consumer, as an extra quality aspect of the ADR process of dispute settlement. Such a guarantee entails that a trade association takes over the obligation that the Complaint Board imposes on one of its members, and will pay the award, whenever the member in question does not voluntary comply with the obligation, or submit the binding decision for review to an ordinary court within two months after it was delivered.[76] A firm that is not a member of a trade association provides a similar compliance guarantee arrangement by means of a bank guarantee for each individual dispute, or deposits an amount set by the SGC to serve as a compliance guarantee.

A more important inconvenience is that not all trades and industries are well organized and that enterprises therefore do not take part in the complaints tribunal system.[77] The entry into the market of foreign traders who are probably less prone to seek membership of traditional Dutch trade organisations may also be such an element.[78] Non-registration of a trader with the *Geschillencommissie* was given as the reason for rejection of a case in 8 per cent of the cases in 2008[79] but only 2 per cent of cases in 2009, and 3 per cent in 2010.[80]

[74] Annual report 2010 of *De Geschillencommissie*, 8.

[75] See Rechtspraak Annual Report 2009, 63, table 9a and which can be accessed at www.rechtspraak.nl/Gerechten/RvdR/Publicaties/Jaardocumenten.htm. Note that these numbers include all types of cases, including commercial as well as consumer law cases.

[76] In a rare case in 2011, *Thuiswinkel* paid a consumer and sued its member under to recover the amount under a contractual obligation in its membership agreement. The association also expelled the member.

[77] See also M Y Schaub, 'Handhaving van consumentenrecht', in E Engelhardt, Y Giesen, and CEA Mahé (eds), *Handhaven van en door het Privaatrecht*, (Den Haag, Boom Juridische Uitgevers, 2009) 156 ff.

[78] Hondius (n 51), 1.

[79] See Klapwijk and ter Voert (n 29), 11. Their evaluation ended with the year 2008.

[80] Annual report 2009 of *De Geschillencommissie*, 24; Annual report 2010 of *De Geschillencommissie*, 22.

The SGC copies all awards electronically to the relevant trade association. Many trade associations then use the information for self-regulatory purposes. This enables to use this information in subsequent general contract term negotiations, exert pressure on traders or politics and to use it for marketing purposes. The importance of case-law of the Commission on travel has increased considerably over the years.[81] It is common practice among traders to send each other the judgments to assess their probabilities of winning and losing a case.

The SGC makes a selection of unanimously decided important cases available on its website, together with a search engine, to act as public guidance on decisions. There have been some calls by consumers and academics that all Commissions' decisions should be published, so as to provide full transparency of business practice as well as of the operation of the Commissions, since the selection of decisions is made by the SGC.[82] The SGC resists such calls on the basis that many decisions are identical and would give no added value.

The Consumer Authority can take enforcement action, or exert pressure. An example was a penalty against the branch for kitchen sellers for not applying their terms and conditions when they said they would, for example where they said they would not ask for a fee exceeding 25% of the value of the goods.[83] There is a cooperation protocol between the SGC and ConsuWijzer, a central information point for consumers that also observes consumer problems, administered by the Consumer Authority.[84]

Access: The Public Profile of Boards

The extent to which the existence and work of an individual Commission is well known varies from sector to sector. The Commissions in the utilities and travel sector are well-known. Others can wither. It is not generally known that anyone who takes a taxi he can file a claim with a Commission. Not all taxis are members of the association that subscribes to their sector Commission, and not all those that are members publicise that fact. There is also the cost-benefit issue that applies to any dispute, namely whether it is worth paying €25 for a dispute over a €20 fare.

If the ADR arrangement is mentioned in the general contract terms, such as occurs in the travel sector, it becomes visible and very popular. In the travel sector, about 90 per cent of package travel contracts are concluded on the basis of the standard Terms and Conditions for the sector, and disputes are consequently solved through the sector Commission.

The *Geschillencommissie* initiated a campaign in 2009 to increase the popularity of the boards, particularly targeting sector organisations and traders. They prepared a toolkit for traders to show to consumers that they are members of the ADR Commission.[85] A documentary about the procedure at the Commission was broadcast on television in summer 2010 and on radio.[86]

The system provides an umbrella that professionalises all the individual sectoral schemes, and harmonises the approach of all the trade associations involved. Various motives have

[81] Interview with T Jongbloed, 26 January 2011.

[82] In the travel sector all decisions of the *Geschillencommissie* are made available to ANVR.

[83] See Besluit in zaak 426/Keukenkampioen B.V., 19th November 2009 and Besluit in zaak 427/Keukenconcurrent B.V., 19th November 2009, to be accessed at the homepage of the Geschillencommissie: Besluit in zaak 427/ Keukenconcurrent B.V. www.consumentenautoriteit.nl/besluiten/sanctiebesluiten

[84] forms.consumentenautoriteit.nl/sites/default/files/redactie/Samenwerkingsprotocol%20ConsuWijzer%20 SGC%20SGB.pdf.

[85] See catalogus.degeschillencommissie.nl.

[86] Annual report 2009 of *De Geschillencommissie*, 10.

Table 6.2: General statistics

		Complaints handled in 2010							
Arbitration committee	Number of new complaints in 2009	Overflow problems in 2010	Number of new complaints in 2010	Total number of claims including those brought forward from 2009	Trader not registered	Outside of the Competence of Board	Inadmissible	Others	Still pending
Legal profession	177	68	163	231	2	1	18	25	105
Building refurbishment	30	13	46	59	8	0	1	2	27
Air conditioning	1	0	0	0	0	0	0	0	0
Car rental	9	5	8	13	0	0	1	1	7
Building materials	29	9	14	23	4	0	1	1	6
Community aerial systems	95	16	26	42	5	0	5	4	4
Roofing	3	0	3	3	0	0	0	1	1
Selling door-to-door	1	0	1	1	0	0	0	0	1
DIY companies	23	7	29	36	1	0	0	1	18
Electrical Goods	139	56	100	156	14	0	5	7	51
Electronic communication services	953	157	357	514	16	9	48	30	161
Energy and Water	2493	1284	1334	2618	7	8	162	240	797
Energy label (NEW in 2010)	0	0	0	0	0	0	0	0	0
Housing Guarantee (NEW in 2010)	0	0	211	211	4	2	12	2	105
Pets and domestic animals	2	0	7	7	1	0	0	2	2
Glass, porcelain and earthenware	0	0	1	1	0	1	0	0	0
Gardening	39	27	44	71	4	0	2	2	26
Information service providers	15	5	231	236	2	217	6	2	7
Installation technicians	174	87	126	213	8	2	13	15	78
Crèches	70	14	33	47	1	0	5	5	13
Handy men and floor companies	88	37	87	124	11	1	6	6	50
Aviation	64	44	839	883	5	10	33	65	639
(Real-) estate- agency	232	93	160	253	5	1	15	17	76
Public transport	155	49	79	128	1	1	17	8	37
Opticians	33	14	21	35	0	0	1	1	8
Parquet floorings	59	27	48	75	18	0	2	2	21
Private education institutes	22	12	24	36	0	0	6	2	12
Post	247	56	78	134	0	5	2	12	34
Leisure	268	66	73	139	4	0	13	7	42
Travel	1000	313	772	1085	23	22	54	56	370
Driving schools	11	8	11	19	1	0	1	2	5
Paintwork, Glazing and Plasterwork	30	17	20	37	6	1	2	1	10
Taxi transport	99	23	34	57	3	0	5	4	18
Telecommunications	1499	279	1005	1284	20	87	109	98	421
Textiles and shoes	28	12	20	32	4	0	2	2	12
Dry-cleaning and laundry services	135	42	67	109	13	0	12	18	43
Home shopping	147	53	126	179	14	1	7	6	64
Bicycles	32	20	20	40	2	0	1	3	18
Personal Care (NEW in 2010)	5	2	5	7	2	0	0	0	3
Funeral services	0	0	15	15	0	0	1	3	11
Renovations (NEW in 2010)	0	0	0	0	0	0	0	0	0
Moving firms	26	5	12	17	1	2	1	1	6
Vehicles	569	296	424	720	21	3	21	36	231
Water sports	42	23	30	53	2	0	3	2	18
Newly-built private housing	1379	557	1073	1630	46	3	96	83	421
Private health care clinics	4	0	1	1	0	0	0	0	1
Sunscreens	12	6	11	17	3	0	0	2	5
Health care (eg hospitals)	44	24	37	61	10	1	3	10	16
Total	10483	3826	7826	11652					
Total				11652	292	378	692	787	4001

Awards and Settlements								
Settlements	With expert	Awards in claims made in 2009	Awards in claims made in 2010	Total settlements and judgments	Total settlements and judgments 2009	Average claim value	Average compensation awarded	Arbitration committee
8	0	2	72	82	80	4844	2337	Legal profession
3	0	1	18	22	19	2735	2385	Building refurbishment
0	0	0	0	0	2	-	-	Air conditioning
0	0	0	4	4	3	486	280	Car rental
4	0	1	7	12	15	5913	?	Building materials
19	0	0	5	24	67	200	?	Community aerial systems
1	0	0	0	1	0	-	-	Roofing
0	0	0	0	0	1	?	?	Selling door-to-door
5	4	3	7	19	18	2433	4527	DIY companies
18	0	6	61	85	50	964	292	Electrical Goods
192	0	4	58	254	704	528	471	Electronic communication services
743	0	127	661	1531	913	973	370	Energy and Water
0	0	0	0	0	0	-	-	Energy label (NEW in 2010)
43	23	2	20	88	0	16085	5980	Housing Guarantee (NEW in 2010)
0	0	0	2	2	2	425	425	Pets and domestic animals
0	0	0	0	0	0	-	-	Glass, porcelain and earthenware
5	0	3	32	40	30	5718	2850	Gardening
2	0	0	0	2	0	-	-	Information service providers
15	0	18	82	115	101	2530	1680	Installation technicians
11	0	0	12	23	55	1608	?	Crèches
5	4	6	41	56	55	3171	2374	Handy men and floor companies
83	0	20	48	151	4	1125	915	Aviation
10	0	9	129	148	189	3026	1329	(Real-) estate- agency
16	0	1	48	65	78	285	120	Public transport
2	0	3	23	28	28	960	571	Opticians
0	2	0	30	32	40	5130	1865	Parquet floorings
7	0	0	9	16	8	1282	780	Private education institutes
10	0	6	71	87	145	556	?	Post
10	0	10	63	83	146	1808	739	Leisure
169	0	8	391	568	882	3562	952	Travel
1	0	0	9	10	5	653	583	Driving schools
1	0	5	16	22	14	4272	1873	Paintwork, Glazing and Plasterwork
13	0	0	14	27	46	219	206	Taxi transport
392	0	9	157	558	986	813	?	Telecommunications
1	0	1	11	13	15	892	530	Textiles and shoes
0	0	1	23	24	67	325	309	Dry-cleaning and laundry services
30	0	5	57	92	81	580	420	Home shopping
0	0	1	16	17	11	3824	681	Bicycles
1	0	0	1	2	1	-	-	Personal Care (NEW in 2010)
0	0	0	0	0	0	?	?	Funeral services
0	0	0	0	0	0	-	-	Renovations (NEW in 2010)
1	0	0	5	6	17	1084	?	Moving firms
57	0	7	351	415	374	3285	2269	Vehicles
3	0	0	25	28	30	5027	1062	Water sports
285	256	35	440	1016	1004	3038	2172	Newly-built private housing
0	0	0	0	0	1	?	-	Private health care clinics
0	0	1	7	8	4	1837	?	Sunscreens
1	0	2	20	23	25	2515	1065	Health care (eg hospitals)
2167	289	297	3046	5799	6316			Total
2167	289		3046					***Total***

been asserted for traders to join the scheme. It is primarily regarded as a commercial market tool for traders to set up and then abide by general contract terms in which they authorize the ADR body to settle the disputes. Not to be a member in this sector organization puts a trader in a bad light. Predictably, in those sectors where the level of organisation is low, the self-regulatory system of SER negotiations and the resulting Commission is less satisfactory. Examples in the past were computer shops and child daycare.

Future Developments

Several possible developments are being implemented or proposed that further entrench ADR within the Dutch approach to settlement of disputes.

Firstly, a new Personal Injury Act enables the medical Commission to refer an issue to the court for a decision on law if it will help achieve an amicable settlement. The court's function is essentially to decide a preliminary issue, perhaps on assumed facts. This technique is already widely used. It is difficult to appeal the court's decision. If no settlement occurs and the case ends up back in court, the earlier judgment will stand as preliminary findings unless new factors affect its validity. The advantage is that the subsequent proceedings avoid restarting the whole case afresh.

Secondly, a Bill is being considered in relation to disputes over the price for use of items that are protected under intellectual property law (such as the fee paid by restaurants for playing copyright music, in which there can be disputes about over-pricing). A *Geschillencommissie* will be set up to deal with such disputes, which has the usual advantage of industry expertise in such matters. If either party starts such a dispute in court, the court will be *obliged* to ask the advice of the Commission on any issue within the *Geschillencommissie*'s jurisdiction. The court's jurisdiction is not ousted, since such disputes often involve other legal issues. But this is a striking example of an emerging new relationship between courts and ADR Commissions.[87]

Thirdly, the government plans to impose a higher own contribution by citizens who are awarded legal aid if a *Geschillencommissie* exists but the citizen decides to start court proceedings instead.

Commissions and Collective Redress

The SGC's computerized system and the sectoral Commissions habitually process mass problems. The system can handle test cases more effectively and swiftly than civil courts. One approach is for a series of cases to be allocated for hearing on the same day, thereby providing consistency of adjudication.[88] Mass claims have been experienced in leisure disputes, where the Commission has selected say two individual cases out of 50, determined those as test cases, and then applied the results to the other similar cases. The approach has been developed into a procedure under which individual parties will be notified that their cases are the 'on hold' pending decision by the Complaint Board of a representative selection of similar individual cases. The parties will be notified of the outcome of the representative

[87] It is interesting to note that such an approach may have worked well as a procedure for handling the long-running disputes over unauthorized bank charges in UK that ran between the mid-2000s and 2010.

[88] Interview with T Jongbloed, 26 January 2011.

cases, and invited to settled their cases between them, but if they cannot the Board will decide them. This approach has been particularly used for complaints against airlines, such as over delayed flights. The approach keeps administration expenses down for the majority of cases that are 'on hold', and avoids the need to process large volumes.

There is no possibility for a consumer association to bring a claim, whether in court or in a Commission. The Consumentenbond considers such an option to be undesirable, since it nominates one of the three members of each Board, and has representatives on the executive board of SGC.[89] It can, however, support consumers with advice on how to bring a claim successfully, and it can publish the result if it appears to be a case that many consumers struggle with on their website.

There may be some problems where traders faced with very large liabilities might force issues into court to avoid having to deal with every case individually. For example, the airlines have recently tried to get cases on delay into court, since they argue that the *Geschillencommissie* will be biased if they set a precedent in one case and apply it in all others, since they are supposed to look at every individual case on its facts. In contrast, *Consumentenbond* considers that these issues should be separated. The consumer view is that a *Geschillencommissie* is designed for easy cases involving quick solutions and not much evidence or expertise, with judges who are not so senior; decisions are generally fair, but issues of legal precedent should be dealt with in courts.

Cross-border Capacity

The SGC has an arrangement with the Dutch European Consumer Centre to handle cross-border cases, and this includes a translation facility. Thus, incoming claims can use the *Geschillencommissie* system, apart from airline claims. *Consumentenbond* considers that the ECC-NET seems to be working satisfactorily.

ANVR: Travel Sector

In 2010 membership of the trade association *Algemene Nederlandse Vereniging van Reisondernemingen* (ANVR) 1426 travel agencies, 126 flight agencies and 220 tour operators.[90] Around 90 per cent of all package tours booked in the Netherlands annually are made through ANVR members, covering around 6.5 million people.[91] The members of ANVR can be identified from its website.[92]

In 2010 772 *Geschillencommissie* complaints were made and 391 cases decided.[93] Figures are not available for complaints that are solved at earlier stages. Based on historical trends, around 95 per cent of the claims will be dealt with: 35 per cent settled between the parties before a formal decision, and 60 per cent decided by *Geschillencommissie* decision, of

[89] Interview with B Krijnen, 3 December 2010.

[90] Annual report ANVR 2010, 3.

[91] The terms and conditions, last revised in 2005, are at www.anwb.nl/binaries/pdf/vakantie/service-advies/anvr-reisvoorwaarden-12472.pdf.

[92] See loket.degeschillencommissie.nl/Web/Site/default.aspx?m=commissie&code=rei.

[93] Annual report ANVR 2010.

which around half are in favour of consumers and half in favour of the business. After the *Geschillencommisie* decision, perhaps 10–20 cases have been taken to court during the past 10 years.

Under the terms and conditions, a consumer must complain about a package tour during the trip or within one month of returning, and produce all the evidence.[94] A high number of complaints are successfully settled at that stage, in the light of a 3 month time limit for starting a claim in the *Geschillencommissie Reizen*.[95]

The cost to a consumer of instituting a *Geschillencommissie* cases depends on the costs of the trip: the costs is €50 for travel costs up to € 500; €75 for travel costs from € 500 to € 1,500; and €100 if the trip cost exceeded €1,500.[96]

In 2009, procedures in this particular *Geschillencommissie* took on average 3.8 months In 2009 the largest category of claims related to the quality of accommodation (39 per cent), and the average travel costs were €3,527: in 2010 the largest category was transportation (38 per cent), and the average travel costs were €3,562. The consumer was present in 81 per cent of the 2010 hearings and operators were present in 75% of the cases. Consumers were represented in 13 per cent of cases (almost always by in-house lawyers provided by legal expenses insurers) and traders were represented in only 3 per cent of cases. The cost of any representation has to be borne by the party who obtains it. The average amount of compensation awarded was €952.

ANVR was formed from an amalgamation of three sectoral associations, dealing with tour operators, travel agents and business travel. The tour operators attracted more claims than the other sectors, and used to weight their contributions to the SGC more towards the overhead element with lower costs per case, subject to a penalty element of a higher contribution by a member if its claim level exceeded a set threshold. After amalgamation, the travel agents objected to paying the same level of general contribution towards the system, and argued that the tour operators should pay the larger share, so members currently pay a small level of annual contribution and a higher case fee on a 'user pays' principle. The association has had to raise the case fee considerably in recent years, and staff would prefer to revert to the threshold-penalty approach.

Members who win a *Geschillencommissie* case pay €150 to ANVR and €500 if they lose. The sum used to be the same irrespective of outcome, but the differential incentivises settlement. The €150 rule will be abolished in 2012 as a result of pressure from the members. It occasionally gives financial support to a member over an important case involving a genuine issue of principle. ANVR is considered by some consumers to be a consumer association, but consumers who contact it over complaints are directed first to the member. Members may ask ANVR for advice, but it does not usually intervene in trying to settle disputes. ANVR is looking at extending the mediation function to an early stage of the complaints process.

Members are screened when they join the association but not subsequently–ANVR sees little demand for this in current conditions. The association would intervene with a member if it identifies that something is wrong. It accepts that there is a variation in behaviour

[94] See for exceptions Art 12 ANVR standard contract terms. For non-ANVR travel agencies this period might be shorter. The requirement to contact the travel agent during or soon after the problem is intended to overcome difficulties of proof that arise if where allegations are made some time after an event and cannot be checked.

[95] Interview with Prof. T Jongbloed, 26 January 2011. The 3 month deadline can be extended where the trader does not respond to the initial complaint within one month. That provision was created to react to traders who only responded shortly before the 3 month claim initiation deadline.

[96] Each fee will be increased by € 25 in 2012.

amongst members, and it considers that a degree of variation has to be accepted. The issue is to define what is or is not acceptable in prevailing market circumstances. ANVR can fine members and has kicked some out. It does take active steps to monitor what non-member companies are doing.

ANVR's guarantee (*nakomingsgarantieregeling*) comes into effect if a trader does not comply with the Board decision within 2 months.[97] It has had no problems with the guarantee system. It is very rare that members would refuse to pay a *Geschillencommissie* award. Sometimes a member objects as a matter of principle, but ANVR would kick out non-compliers.

There has been a clear decline over the years in the number of *Geschillencommissie* cases against members, as shown in Table 6.3. ANVR argues that the quality of members' performance has increased, but it accepts that other possible reasons are (as SGC argues) that decisions are now published, and that traders may be more inclined to settle.

Table 6.3: Cases against ANVR members

Year	Number
2000	3,400
2005	2,876
2006	2,378
2007	1,980
2008	1,585
2009	1,299
2010	772
2011 anticipated	1,000

ANVR has confidence in the *Geschillencommissie* system, which it considers to operate well and impartially. It is viewed as being more competent, faster and cheaper than a judge. No complaints have been heard within the sector that any industry-nominated members of the *Geschillencommissie* have been biased in any respect: individuals are experienced and senior industry personnel but sit purely in a personal capacity without any representative function. Experts are almost never required for travel cases.

Traders that are members of the ANVR are also connected to two funds, the catastrophe fund *Calamiteitenfonds* and the *Stichting Garantiefonds Reisgelden* (SGR), an insolvency fund for travel agencies.[98] The latter fund is designed to compensate consumers if their travel agency goes bankrupt before or during their journey. The consumer will also be compensated where he cannot go on the holiday at all and, if the journey has to be interrupted, the costs of repatriation and other losses are covered. The SGR fund is also available for general compensation payments if the consumer has already acquired a 'binding advice' from the *GC* before the company became insolvent. The fund was built up from consumers' contributions since 1999, but the SGR guarantee is now free for consumers, since the fund has sufficient capital. Traders finance its administration. The catastrophe fund is financed by a fee of €2.50 per booking.

[97] Art 17, lid 5, ANVR standard contract terms.

[98] See www.sgr.nl/index.asp; www.anwb.nl/vakantie/zoek-en-boek/service-en-advies,/ANVR--SGR--Calamiteitenfonds.html.

Thuiswinkel: Web Traders

The association of web traders, *Thuiswinkel*, originated as an association for postal order traders, and took over web traders around 2000 from *Consumentenbond*. Membership has grown from 35 firms to 1,200. Its members comprise 30 per cent of web-shops in the Netherlands, and 80 per cent (€5.5 billion turnover) of the national e-commerce market, which has an annual turnover of €9 billion. Its members are both large and small, 80 per cent of which have annual turnover of less than €5 million.[99]

The strategic goal of the association was to address an initial lack of consumer confidence in trading on the web, and this has been achieved. A strong single market new exists. Initially, a wide range of terms and conditions were in use, many of which contained illegal provisions. *Thuiswinkel* has cleaned up practice in relation to matters such as guarantees, pre-payment systems, and exclusions of liability. Members are obliged to use *Thuiswinkel's* terms and conditions. *Thuiswinkel* requires members to be audited by an independent body (ECT *Recht*) both before admission to membership and annually. It checks members' websites, and currently looks at issues such as methods of payment and delivery costs. Members are entitled to use *Thuiswinkel's* logo, which is believed to be widely understood as a mark of quality by the public.

Members operate within a wide range of market sectors, and may belong to other trade associations that are organized by type of product, in addition to *Thuiswinkel*, which is based on a method of distance selling. Members may, therefore, be subject to more than one set of terms and conditions, and more than one *Geschillencommissie*. It accepts other approved terms and conditions without checking them. *Thuiswinkel* agrees arrangements with other trade associations. For example, it is agreed between *Thuiswinkel* and ANVR that travel claims sold on the web that relate to the method of selling should be directed to the *Thuiswinkel Geschillencommissie*, and claims that relate to product service to *Geschillencommissie Reizenh*. If the *Thuiswinkel* member is not a member of ANVR, *Thuiswinkel* has agreed with the *Consumentenbond* that the consumer can rely on ANVR's terms and conditions and use of that *Geschillencommissie* (at *Thuiswinkel's* expense) but without ANVR's guarantee. Consumers have a choice of relying on whichever set of terms and conditions, or *Geschillencommissie*, they wish, and no defensive point will be taken as between different terms and conditions. *Thuiswinkel* sees few conflicts in practice. The SGC will try to direct consumers towards the most appropriate sectoral *Geschillencommissie*, and the trade associations see no problems over this. Consumers have been known to compare the costs of using different *Geschillencommissies*, and to forum shop accordingly.

Thuiswinkel considers that consumer law has evolved to a stage in which the rules are clear and comprehensive, so traders have little scope or excuse for breaking the rules. Accordingly, its approach to compliance and enforcement is 'soft'. It is easier to 'police' the internet shopping sector than some others, since on-line advertisements are transparent so easy to check if traders are complying. *Thuiswinkel* undertakes a yearly audit on compliance, and has a lot of quality standards. If members are not complying, they are given a warning and 2 months to comply. It finds that non-compliance usually results from traders not knowing, or overlooking, what the rules are, and that they can almost always be influenced to comply when they are told what the rules are. *Thuiswinkel* can usually influence the

[99] The picture is affected by the fact that some large players operate from other States, such as Amazon from Germany.

behaviour of its members by pointing to the classic 'big stick' enforcement powers that can be exercised by the Consumer Authority.[100] It quotes a recent fine of €100,000 imposed on a trader by the Consumer Authority for an infringement. That example, even though rare– and precisely because of its rarity–has significant deterrent effect on the majority of traders. *Thuiswinkel* sometimes has to persuade traders to settle and pay up, sometimes because smaller ones are unfamiliar with the law. It does not consider that imposing a fine on its members is a relevant sanction in the current circumstances. Instead, its policy is to rely on the sanction of canceling a firm's membership where it has been shown to have broken the law in a serious fashion. It accepts that things do go wrong, especially where some large members sell as many as 5 million product lines. Common issues include delivery, late delivery, or non-conformity of goods. *Thuiswinkel* believes that consumers accept that things can sometimes go wrong, and that traders are human and can make mistakes, but in such cases consumers want things to be dealt with. Hence, great reliance is placed on addressing problems effectively and quickly.

Against that background, the association is proud of the fact that the number of *Geschillencommissie* cases is very low: 57 judgments in 2010 and 44 in 2009. Of these, consumers and traders each win roughly 50 per cent. *Thuiswinkel* views most *Geschillencommissie* decisions as unsurprising. Members must have a clear complaint system, which must be used as the first line of response, and which resolves the vast majority of issues. The total number of complaints against members in 2010 was around 2,200.[101] *Thuiswinkel* receives some complaints itself, which it directs to traders, but asks a consumer to inform it if the complaint is not dealt with satisfactorily. The association tries to mediate where appropriate, especially by advising members on the legal situation.

Thuiswinkel believes that the quality of the *Geschillencommissie* is high, not less than that offered by the courts and probably better because of the inherent expertise. It sees little evidence that consumers are pressured to 'under-settle' complaints. Where it exerts pressure on members, it would typically say 'Make the consumer an offer he cannot refuse. Even if you're right, it's costing you money to argue'. Settlements can be booked against tax. Given the low value of most claims, the management cost of handling them far outweighs the intrinsic value of a claim, and *Thuiswinkel* believes that this commercial reality tends to result in fair offers and settlements so as to achieve speedy resolution.

Financial Services: KiFiD

The financial services sector has a slightly different structure of dispute resolution to that described above. It has three stages, all administered by the Financial Services Complaints Institute Foundation (*Klachteninstituut Financiële Dienstverlening*: KiFiD). A claim can be pursued in court at any stage, unless the claimant has agreed to binding arbitration. As a pre-condition, a claim must first have been raised with the relevant financial services provider.

[100] A fine can be imposed of up to €74,000 for breach of consumer rights under administrative powers, and of up to €450,000 per case under the fair trading (EU unfair commercial practices) laws.

[101] In March 2011, it received 359 complaints direct, 183 of which were about members and which were solved by members directly, and the rest about non-members.

On reaching KiFiD, the first stage is an Ombudsman process.[102] Cases are managed by a team of case officers,[103] although every decision is made by the Ombudsman personally. The Ombudsman is subject to an obligation to seek a settlement between the parties, and therefore resolves many disputes by conciliating between the customers and the business: some customers are persuaded to drop poor claims and some businesses are persuaded to settle strong claims. If the parties do not agree, the Ombudsman produces a written recommendation. This is not binding on either party, but the compliance by business is effectively 100 per cent. The outcome can be binding if the parties have so agreed in writing beforehand or do so afterwards.[104]

If the consumer does not accept the Ombudsman's decision, the second stage (as an alternative to a court case) is a Commission (*Geschillencommissie*), for which the procedure is the same as other *Geschillencommissies* discussed above. The claim has to be made within 3 months and a claim value of €100 euro is required, with some exceptions. The Rules make it optional for business organizations to accept a decision as binding, but all banks and most intermediaries have agreed to accept all decisions up to €5 million. The consumer also has a choice of whether to accept the result as binding, but if this is accepting this in advance surrenders the right to claim in court. The chairman of the *Geschillencommissie* decides, depending on the kind of claim, whether it will be dealt with by him (or a vice-chairman or a member that fulfills the requirements to be chairman) individually or by a panel (which may consist of 3 or 5 members).[105]

The third stage is an Arbitration Appeal Board, which is available for cases of major significance, meaning a case value of at least €25,000. Exceptions are possible if the importance of the claim justifies this. The appeal must be initiated by the consumer or the trader within 6 weeks of the decision of the *Geschillencommissie*.

KiFiD was established in April 2007 as a merger between the pre-existing sectoral disputes schemes on insurance (which had an ombudsman, whose decisions were not binding and not published), the banks (which used to be in the *Geschillencommissie* system) and securities (which also had a binding arbitration board for consumer claims, established under the Securities Act 1983). The Financial Services Act 2007, which introduced a new supervisory structure,[106] introduced an obligation for all businesses in the sector to join an ADR system for consumer complaints.[107] Rather than use the *Geschillencommissie*, the banks decided to set up their own separate umbrella organization to oversee their ADR system, which would be a twin of the *Stichting Geschillencommissie*.[108] Two large *Geschillencommissie* boards (*Bankzaken and Hypothecaire Financieringen*) therefore transferred across from SGC to KiFiD. The arrangements were further streamlined within KiFiD in 2009–2010 by merging the specialities of ADR in banking, insurance and financial services, so as to provide an integrated approach.

[102] It is a precondition for a case to be considered by the Ombudsman that the internal handling procedure of the trader has first been accessed: see KiFiD rules, Art 13.

[103] The Ombudsman has around 20 staff.

[104] KiFiD rules, Art 25.3.

[105] KiFiD rules, Art 35.

[106] Prudential supervision came under the Dutch Central Bank (*De Nederlandsche Bank* N.V.: DNB), and market behaviour came under the Financial Markets Authority (*Stichting Autoriteit Financiële Markten*: AFM). Both the AFM and the Consumer Authority deal with the law on unfair trade practices.

[107] It is interesting to note that the courts and the *Geschillencommissie* structures are the responsibility of the Ministry of Justice, whereas responsibility for financial services is a matter for the Ministry of Economic Affairs, and this may historically explain the separate development ADR in that sector.

[108] See Klapwijk and ter Voert (n 29), 26.

Approval from the Ministry is required by KiFiD under the Financial Services Act, which is subject to it being run in good order and undertaking to comply with the EU 1998 Recommendation.[109] KiFiD is run by a Board of directors, which in 2011 is shedding its business and ministerial members in order to enhance the appearance of independence from any outside influences.[110] The current Ombudsman is a judge with 25 years' previous judicial experience, and the Chairmen of the Arbitration Committee and the Appeal Board are both leading professors of financial law.

The number of cases in recent years in shown in Tables 6.4–6.9.[111] The total number of cases received in the past three years has fluctuated between roughly six and eight thousand, and is susceptible to variations in claim levels for particular types of claims (such as life insurance or liability insurance). A significant number of complaints received do not fall within the Ombudsman's criteria, the largest category of those being complaints that have not first been referred to the relevant company. The Ombudsman stage results in resolution of roughly ninety or ninety-five per cent of initial complaints, with a few hundred proceeding to the Geschillencommissie, and twenty or so going to the Appeal Committee.

Table 6.4: Cases received by KiFiD

	2010	**%**	**2009**	**2008**
Banking	1586	23	1662	1217
Securities	662	30	1027	602
Mortgages	992	10	1151	770
Life insurance	1465	22	2175	2295
Liability insurance	2014	15	1803	1527
Total	**6719**	**100**	**7818**	**6411**

Table 6.5: Outcome of Financial Services Ombudsman cases in 2010

	Banking	**Securities**	**Mortgages**	**Life insurance**	**Liability insurance**	**Total**	**%**
Handled	**1794**	**930**	**1104**	**1639**	**1971**	**7438**	
Not accepted	**799**	**236**	**459**	**623**	**966**	**3083**	
No internal claims handling	372	99	227	303	493	1494	
No claim	113	21	72	95	120	421	
Unclear claim	79	17	37	62	116	311	
No consumer	66	21	23	11	98	219	
> 3 months	34	33	27	26	31	151	
Bank not registered at KiFiD	59	8	35	19	11	132	
Request for information	21	13	13	54	26	127	
Others	55	24	25	53	71	228	
Accepted	**995**	**694**	**645**	**1016**	**1005**	**4355**	
Ill-founded	404	441	212	310	341	1708	39
Result	258	92	157	321	337	1165	27
Direct	269	92	231	248	254	1094	25
Recommendation	28	54	25	119	4	230	5
'Cessation'; dismissed	36	15	20	18	69	158	4

[109] See ch 1.

[110] See letter of the Minister of Finance to the Chairman of the Second Chamber, 30th June 2011 'Publiekrechtelijke status Ombudsman Kifid'.

[111] KiFiD annual reports, eg available at www.kifid.nl/fileupload/Jaarverslag_2010.pdf.

Table 6.6: Cases received by the Financial Services *Geschillencommissie* in 2010

	2010	**2009**	**2008**
Banking	128	64	73
Securities	158	116	70
Mortgages	101	67	49
Life insurance	107	101	80
Liability insurance	115	95	75
Total	**609**	**443**	**347**

Table 6.7: Outcome of *Geschillencommissie* cases in 2010

Judgments	**249**		52%
Declined		168	
Partially awarded		47	
Awarded		26	
Not admissible		3	
No competence		3	
Interim judgment		1	
Hearing 'applicable'		1	
Procedural irregularity[112]	135		28%
Settled after case filed	79		17%
Withdrawn	13		3%
Total	**476**		

Table 6.8: Outcome of Financial Services *Geschillencommissie* cases in 2010

	Numbers	**%**
Banking	100	21
Securities	96	20
Mortgages	84	21
Life insurance	100	20
Liability insurance	96	18
Total	**476**	**100**

Table 6.9: Financial Services Appeal Committee, 2009 and 2010

Cases received by the Appeal Committee	**2010**	**2009**
	19	9
Cases	**27**	
Withdrawn	5	
Not admissible	7	
Admissible	15	
Outcomes per sector		%
Banking	3	20
Securities	3	20
Mortgages	1	33
Life insurance	5	20
Liability insurance	3	7
Total	**15**	**100**

Kifid's budget has tripled in recent years to round about €9 million accompanying a large rise in claims.[113] The procedure before the Ombudsman is free of charge for the consumer, but a fee of €50 is payable for accessing the *Geschillencommissie*.[114] For traders, the minimum yearly contribution of banks and insurers is €170.[115] For all other members, the lowest contribution is €163. The registration fee amounts to €25.

The Ombudsman and arbitrators make decisions by applying the law. They do not apply any terms and conditions or codes. Hence, an important difference between KiFiD and the SGC system is that terms and conditions are not negotiated in the financial services sector between consumers and business associations, and that requirement is not a trigger for access to the Ombudsman. The Ombudsman treats every claim as if it were a normal civil claim, and ultimately reaches an adjudication in the same way as he would if he were sitting in court (save that the effect of his decision is not binding). Decisions are made on the basis of the law, which is usually contract law and sometimes financial services law, but can sometimes be influenced by regulations made by the AFM. Industry guidelines that may exist will be irrelevant in this context, and indeed, the Ombudsman can decide that industry guidelines are contrary to the law. The Ombudsman's Rules specify that decisions must be 'fair and reasonable'[116] but that standard is has always been interpreted as being the same as that provided for by law. The Dutch courts decided in the 1960s that the Rule of Reason could contradict a contract, for example for reasons of good faith, and that was later codified.[117]

Financial services businesses can produce their own codes of practice: one exists for the insurance sector. Disputes under that code are dealt with by a body established by the insurance trade association, the *Tuchtraad*. (Other similar bodies, collectively known as *Tuchtrecht*, exist for disputes involving medical personnel and notaries.) The *Tuchtraad* consists of at least 5 members and its task is to ensure that when dealing with consumers the affiliated traders maintain the good name, reputation of and trust in the sector.[118] If such a case is brought to the Ombudsman or the *Geschillencommissie*, it is transferred to the *Tuchtraad*. In recent years, the *Tuchtraad Assurantiën* dealt with 1–4 cases per year.[119]

The Ombudsman publishes his decisions that are of wider interest, rather than every decision. This is justified on the basis that decisions are non-binding, many cases result in a conclusion that the Ombudsman cannot help the consumer, and a concern not to diminish the impact of the relatively few decisions that have impact. Decision of the Ombudsman and the Arbitration Board have been seen to affect the behaviour of banks, regulators and trade associations.

[112] eg fees not paid.

[113] Annual report KiFiD 2010, pp. 6, 23. KiFiD is still in the process of setting up (weerstandsvermogen) 1,250,000 euros within the First 5 years of its existence. Twice in 2010 €250,000 were transferred to this reserve (p. 24). The budget for 2011 is to be €8,701,000 (p. 25).

[114] FAQ KiFiD, www.kifid.nl/consumenten/veelgestelde-vragen. If the Ombudsman himself transfers the case to the Geschillencommissie the consumer is free from the fee, see Art 26.2 KiFiD rules, for instance due to procedural complexity. If the Ombudsman has declared the claim 'kennelijk ongegrond' (clearly inadmissible) according to Art 31.2 KiFiD rules the fee is €100.

[115] See cost rules: www.kifid.nl/fileupload/Kostenreglement_2011.pdf.

[116] 'fair en billijk'.

[117] Art 4:2 BW.

[118] See Reglement Tuchtraad Financiele Dienstverlening (assurantiën).

[119] See www.verzekeraars.nl/Over%20het%20Verbond/Zelfregulering%20en%20Klachtenprocedures/Reglement%20en%20uitspraken%20Tuchtraad.aspx.

Consumentenbond have criticized the Ombudsman stage on a number of grounds. One point is that it is an obligatory first stage, and that consumers cannot access the arbitrator so as to get a binding result. *Comsumentenbond* consider that its use should be a matter of choice, with the option of skipping to a binding solution. The other concerns are that there is only a single Ombudsman rather than a panel, and that both the Ombudsman and the arbitrator are within the same organization. These arrangements have been criticised as not ensuring the independence of the arbitrator and the system. Some view the KiFiD system as being set up by banks for their protection.

In response, KiFiD obtained advice from a distinguished judge, Mr van Delden, that the first stage should be voluntary. A key consideration is to maintain the effectiveness of the Ombudsman in handling a sizeable volume of complaints: the annual input of around 4,000 cases is considerably larger than that of any *Geschillencommissie*, and considerations of efficiency and effectiveness arise. KiFiD argues that if all of the claims that it handles went straight to an arbitration committee, the process would be notably slower and more expensive. On the single/triple arbitrator issue, KiFiD believes that requiring an arbitrator panel of three results in two of the members putting forward partisan views and the decision is really made by the single independent chair, so maintaining three members merely adds unnecessary cost and unnecessary window-dressing to give an illusion of balance.

The financial services sector periodically gives rise to mass claims. KiFiD is required to process all claims that it receives, and its experience is that similar claims can build up over time, sometimes creating a 'sleeping mass' that erupts into a major managerial challenge. The two notably examples have been the Legio Lease/Dexia securities case (which erupted before the Ombudsman route existed)[120] and the Woekerpolis case (where the Ombudsman's role in facilitating a solution was criticized by those who were unhappy with his proposed solution).[121] Negotiation has played a part in both of those cases: most of the Legio Lease claims were included in a settlement approved under WCAM. Such cases frequently have wider implications than resolution of individual the disputes to which they give rise, such as issues involving commercial practice and supervisory systems, and sometimes need to be resolved through channels other than those designed for resolution of small disputes. KiFiD's rules provide that if a claim is one of many with a total aggregate of €100,000, the trader can stop the procedure and go to court. The idea behind this is that if there are large implications, large businesses currently prefer a forum in which the wider implications can be authoritatively and exhaustively considered, rather than precedents being set fortuitously by a small number of individual claims that happen to arise at an early stage. There is a feeling that a decision by a senior court is currently a better option than the Ombudsman/arbitration procedures or decisions by lower courts for achieving such an outcome, but that that is not necessarily the best solution.

KiFiD handles all cross-border claims, incoming or outgoing, through the FIN-NET system. It regards FIN-NET as a useful forum for sharing techniques amongst national financial services ADR schemes.

[120] This involved some 400,000 consumers who bought shares with borrowed money, which became loss-making after share process dropped in 2000 and interest tax deductions for consumer credit were halted. After a lengthy period of public anger and litigation in which Dexia Bank sought to enforce its securities, and a negotiated solution was hammered out by a senior respected public figure, Wim Duisenberg, illuminated by the then existing decisions from courts and the Arbitration Board, the settlement was approved under WCAM. Some individuals opted out and pursued individual solutions (often those advised by intermediaries who sought their cuts).

[121] This involved allegations of extortionate life insurance policies, investment funds, and funds combined with mortgages, which were sold with fees amounting to 30 or 40%. After the 2008 financial crash, the final funds were far less than anticipated.

Discussion

Views of Stakeholders

The business community is happy with the *Geschillencommissie* mechanism: it is a 'good working machine' and has solved many cases, keeping them out of court and the press.[122] Businesses fund the system for two reasons: to settle consumer disputes quickly and more cheaply than courts; and to get the feedback that is useful for self-regulatory purposes. Systems do differ somewhat between different sectors, but the umbrella is the same, and has the advantages of reliable quality and a single system that everyone can know about. The *Geschillencommissie* system is voluntary for business, but is widely supported since it offers so many advantages. However, as Government subsidies for the system are decreasing, traders realize that the system is becoming expensive for them. For example, the fees that traders have to pay in the travel sector even where they win a case will be abolished in 2012 because of resistance.

From the consumer perspective, *Consumentenbond* regards the system of negotiating terms and conditions as well balanced. The consumer associations have significant power, led by the involvement of the *Consumentenbond* in all sectoral negotiations. Their position is backed by the power of the media and string enforcement powers available to the Consumer Authority, which together act on the commercial desire of many traders to maintain high reputations within competitive markets. A significant historical factor in the evolution of the system of negotiation of terms and conditions was the introduction in 1992 of a mechanism for the *Consumentenbond* to apply to the court for collective injunctive redress.[123] This powerful weapon was a major factor in bringing business associations to the table, in order to avoid disruptive, uncertain and costly litigation, and associated loss of reputation. Since then, the systems of *ex ante* negotiation and associated dispute resolution mechanism have grown and strengthened. The overall quality of terms and conditions has improved and is continually evolving. The system has spread outwards from a few sectors to cover almost the whole range of consumer-facing commercial activity.

On the other hand, the collective injunctive power is expensive for *Consumentenbond* to use, given the court rules on costs. With the creation in 2007 of the Consumer Authority, the regulatory ability to take action in the common interest, where it is required, has been open to that public agency. Enforcement action by the Authority would be both cheaper and more effective than by the consumer association.

Consumentenbond therefore has a significant regulatory role. However, this is only effective against firms that are members of the *Geschillencommissie* system. The 'bad guys' are rarely in that system, so public enforcement is needed by the Authority. The gap between the 'good guys' and 'bad guys' is widening. Accordingly, *Consumentenbond* is advising its members to be aware of the advantages of trading with members of the *Geschillencommissie* system.

[122] Interview with Hubert van Breemen of VNO-NCW IMKBh on 24 February 2011.

[123] Art 3:305a BW. Whereas injunctive actions could previously name individual traders, the new legislation enabled all members of a particular branch to be sued at once.

Evaluating the ADR System

The official policy on encouraging informal dispute resolution in the Netherlands has produced a thriving ADR system alongside the courts.[124] Each of those two pathways has equal status in resolving disputes. The same criteria of independence, trust, fairness and so on are considered to apply to each pathway.

The *Geschillencommissie* procedure has fewer rules than arbitration. It ends with 'binding advice' that is closer in form to contract than a binding court judgment, but compliance is rarely a problem, given the trade association guarantee arrangements. A Report by Professor Snijders concluded that there was no need to change the *Geschillencommissie* system, since it works.[125] Snijders noted that binding arbitration would be theoretically preferable in sectors where association guarantees do not exist or there are other compliance problems. However, he said that such an approach might create confusion in the minds of consumers and others. Arbitration already takes place at the SGC, namely *Geschillencommissie Garantiewoningen* and *Geschillencommissie Luchtvaart*. Further, the *Geschillencommissie Advocatuur* uses arbitration in all but consumer claims.[126] A problem with the Commission system, but also for enforcement through courts, arises with jurisdiction over foreign traders or any trader that is not registered with the ADR body.[127]

The ADR system offers a number of strong advantages. Firstly, the model is standard across a wide range of business sectors. That consistency promotes visibility of the ADR mechanisms for consumers and businesses. The system is now comprehensive across trade and professional sectors, apart from one major gap, which is doctors. There is a Bill under which doctors and alternative healers will be obliged to join an ADR system, without identifying which system, but it must be one founded jointly by traders *and* a consumer association. Secondly, the national template operates with independent oversight that builds high quality and trust in the dispute resolution system. The range of *Geschillencommissie* is now so wide that, given the high level of trust, consumers tend to expect that a committee will exists for almost every type of dispute that might arise. That consumer expectation in turn places pressure on business sectors to establish a commission for their sector, and to abide by the associated standards of conduct and terms and conditions.

Thirdly, the network is cheap to use. As at December 2010, only 55 staff handle at the SGC the central administration for all 50 of its consumer Commissions and five business Commissions. The ADR Commission procedure is designed to be less costly to access for consumers than the ordinary courts. The Commissions are now focusing on promoting mediation and online solutions, so as to reduce costs further.[128] The low cost and accessibility are thought to encourage some consumers to 'try their luck' in bringing a claim, rather than risking money and time in the courts.

Fourthly, the model is not static, but able to evolve and innovate. As the number of sectors covered has steadily risen over 40 years, the unified GSC structure has not imposed complete uniformity for each sector, but been able to accommodate some variations in

[124] See PMM van der Grinten, 'The Netherlands: Policy Observations' in C Hodges, S Vogenauer and M Tulibacka, *The Costs and Funding of Civil Litigation. A Comparative Perspective* (Oxford, Hart Publishing, 2010).

[125] HJ Snijders, *Arbitrage en/of bindend advies bij de SGC, Een onderzoek in opdracht van de Coördinatiegroep Zelfreguleringsoverleg van de Sociaal-Economische Raad*, CZ/401, 2010; available at www.ser.nl/nl/publicaties/overige/2010-2019/2010/20101015.aspx.

[126] Snijders, *Arbitrage en/of bindend advies bij de SGC* (2010), 7.

[127] Hondius, (n 51), 1.

[128] Annual report 2009 of *De Geschillencommissie*, 6.

procedure or use of experts depending on the requirements of individual types of disputes that arise in sectors.

Fifthly, the ADR arrangements operate as an integral part of a larger system designed to deliver acceptable business practices, through the negotiation of terms and conditions, and post-dispute feedback and self-regulatory controls. The model integrates the different elements of direct negotiation, regulation, ADR and courts into focusing on maintaining standards and providing redress. It encourages public trust in traders and sectors, and assists consumer choice by pointing towards selecting trustworthy traders, who have signed up to observe both approved terms and conditions and the Board procedure and decisions.

The system requires a competitive market. Its effectiveness may be reduced or threatened if there is too small a number of large players, which make the branch organisation too dependent on the income and views of that oligopoly, or where there is a large number of small players, who do not rely on reputation to the same extent as in a more competitive market and who do not seethed the costs of joining the organization and system outweigh the benefits.

Consideration is being given to the establishment of a general *Geschillencommissie* whose jurisdiction would be for traders who are not members of a trade association but who could join on a voluntary basis. Extending the possibilities of business-to-business *Geschillencommisie* is also being considered.

A different approach would be arbitration, so that the decisions would be instantly enforceable at law: some bodies are asking for this, since enforcement can be a problem is some sectors, such as cars, garages, car rental, motor bikes, bicycles, and aeroplanes.

Some Problem Areas

Problems can arise in individual sectors, that relate to the nature of the market or attitude of traders, rather than with the *Geschillencommissie* system as such.

The telecom sector has a poor reputation. It is not organized as an integral sector. Its terms and conditions and *Geschillencommissie* are based on the normal telephone situation, rather than on mobile telephony. There have been difficulties recently in the SMS texting sector, where the members no longer advertise at all on television. The kitchen organization is reported to have found it difficult to kick out large members, since it relies on their income. There are a number not complying in the child daycare sector.

The airlines are reluctant to embrace the terms and conditions system. The *Geschillencommissie* in the airlines sector is based on arbitration, and it deals only with some aspects of their activities, such as denied boarding, which arises under EU-based legislation. The attitude may be based on the historical origin of the Dutch airlines as being state-owned and therefore somewhat resistant to external influences. Airline companies were reluctant to create a sectoral Committee until they were forced to do this as a result of combined pressure from the Minister and the implications of the Denied Boarding Directive.[129] ANVR members have many actions against airlines over commercial or agency issues.

[129] Regulation (EC) No 261/2004 of the European Parliament and of the Council of 11 February 2004 establishing common rules on compensation and assistance to passengers in the event of denied boarding and of cancellation or long delay of flights, OJ L 046, 1–8.

Access to Justice: Courts or ADR?

The consumer has a choice between the *Geschillencommissie* procedure and the special civil court procedure (*kantongerechtsprocedure*). Before 1 July 2011, the subdistrict judge dealt with all cases of a value below € 5,000 and disputes concerning rent and labour contracts (irrespective of the amount).[130] The limit was recently increased to € 25,000 and the judge is now competent in all cases of consumer credit (ie loans up to € 40,000) and all consumer contracts.[131] Both of those procedures usually produce fast results, but the *Geschillencommissie* procedure is cheaper for the cases that it covers. A significant advantage of the *Geschillencommissies*, and a reason for their creation, was in order to provide cheaper and effective solutions than courts, and they certainly provide attractive alternatives.

Judgments in the *kantongerechtsprocedure* in 2010 totaled 661,600 (650,550 in 2009, 561,900 in 2008)[132] and 118,420 in the ordinary civil procedure (111,740 in 2009, 102,010 in 2008).[133] However, since consumer law cases are not registered individually within the figures at civil courts, they are impossible to identify within those total figures. As noted above, in 2010 7,826 claims were initiated in the *Geschillencommissie* system and 6,719 in the financial services system. Hence, general trends are that small claims cases are rising and *Geschillencommissie* claims (excluding the financial services sector, which fluctuates) are falling.

The *Geschillencommissie* costs are clearly attractive when compared with the courts.[134] As noted above, the *Geschillencommissie* costs vary depending on the sector, ranging from €25 to €125 and only rarely over €500. The fee for court cases with no clear monetary value, or where an amount of less than €12,500 is claimed, is €255 for natural persons and €560 for legal entities.[135] The fee for cases where more than €12,500 and less than €100,000 is claimed is €580 for natural persons and €1,165 for legal entities. Cases where more than €100,000 is claimed have a fee of €1,395 for natural persons and €3,490 for legal entities. In addition, there is the cost of bailiffs for service (€72.25), any experts required (€81.23 plus taxes), and lawyers' fees (usually on hourly rates). Parties litigating before a District Court must be represented by an attorney. If a case is lost, there is the risk of liability for opponents' costs in court claims, in a *Geschillencommissie* the risk is limited to reimbursement of the registration fee, but there is no loser pays rule with the small claims procedure (a winning consumer would regard that as a disadvantage).[136]

[130] Hondius (n 51), 1ff.

[131] Evaluatiewet modernisering rechterlijke organisatie, Stb. 2011, 255, Act, of 19th May 2011, www.eerstekamer.nl/behandeling/20110531/publicatie_wet/f=/viqs9moy17pd.pdf.

[132] Annual report Rechtspraak 2010, 54. Statistics from the Central Bureau for Statistics differ: for the small claims procedure 452,400 in 2008 and 519,800 for 2009, and for ordinary civil procedures 31,100 in 2008 and 35,500 in 2009. see statline.cbs.nl/StatWeb/publication/?VW=T&DM=SLNL&PA=70229ned&D1=a&D2=a&HD=090416-1648&HDR=G1&STB=T.

[133] See Rechtspraak 2009, 61. Neither are the results from Raad voor de Rechtspraak, *Rapport commissie Eenvoudige procedure voor eenvoudige zaken – advies* d.d. 23 april 2007 more revealing according to Loos and van Boom (n 50), 27.

[134] Tuil (n 3).

[135] New court fees legislation has been proposed in the Netherlands (*Wet griffierechten burgerlijke zaken*, Stb. 2010, 715), which is intended to increase the court fees in civil matters and also in administrative matters (*Wijziging van de Algemene wet bestuursrecht en de Wet griffierechten burgerlijke zaken in verband met de invoering van kostendekkende griffierechten and Wijziging van de Algemene wet bestuursrecht en de Wet griffierechten burgerlijke zaken in verband met de invoering van kostendekkende griffierechten*). As at January 2012, the proposals had not been introduced in Parliament.

[136] See Loos and van Boom (n 50), 81.

Given the level of irrecoverable costs if the case is won, plus the risk of cost liability if it is lost, there will be a net loss below a certain threshold of claim, and an unattractive recovery-to-cost ratio immediately above that threshold. Some commentators have assumed that a rational consumer would refrain from seeking individual redress through the ADR institutions only if the claim is below €100–200 (depending on the applicable admission fee).[137] In 2009, only 9 per cent of the *Geschillencommissies* dealt with claims of less than €250, there was no claim involving a value of more than €10,000, and the largest segment of claims (24 per cent) were for €1,001 – 2,000.[138]

The legal aid provisions apply to any case with value over € 500.[139] The costs calculations are, of course, affected for those who are eligible for legal aid, which is relatively widely available in the Netherlands.[140] Under current rules a claimant who qualifies financially will only get legal aid for a court claim. It is proposed that there should be legal aid for a *Geschillencommissie* claim, but that the claimant would get less support for bringing a case in court, thereby prioritizing the ADR system.

The costs relationships are, however, set to change as a result of various reforms. Firstly, the government is considering whether the court fee should be set at a level that would recover the real cost, so as to relieve the state from having to subsidise it (kostendekkende griffierechten): that would mean that court fees would rise four-fold.[141] There is also a proposal that a trader who loses would have to pay more costs in defending a court claim where it has not joined a *Geschillencommissie*.

The potential advantage that a court judgment is directly enforceable, whereas a *Geschillencommisie* award is not, has been overcome by the latter being backed by the guarantee of the trade association.

It is important also to consider two structural features that have considerable impact on the choice between the available pathways: firstly, that many decisions on processing disputes in the Netherlands are made by insurers rather than consumers and, secondly, the national situation on who may offer legal advice.

Insurers hold considerable power in deciding choice of claims pathways in the Netherlands. Legal expenses insurance (LEI) covers around 47.8 per cent of households.[142] It is usually the LEI insurers that decide whether a case is sent to court or a Commission. Insured individuals would contact their insurer as first point of call for advice, and insurers in the Netherlands have large in-house legal departments who give advice on claims and any legal aspects that arise. Insurers strongly prefer Commissions because they are cheaper than courts: there is no court fee and no external lawyer's fee, but only a modest Commission filing fee, which is recoverable. Further, around 50% of individuals who attend

[137] MBM Loos, 'Evaluation of the effectiveness and efficiency of collective redress mechanisms in the European Union – country report The Netherlands' (CIVIC Consulting, 2008), available at ec.europa.eu/consumers/redress_cons/collective_redress_en.htm.

[138] Klapwijk and ter Voert (n 29), 43; data from Geschillencommissie on years 2005 – 2008. Note that the financial value is known in 55 % of the cases.

[139] See *Normbedragen Wet op de rechtsbijstand (Wrb) per 1 juli 2011*. ('*Rechtsbijstand op basis van een toevoeging (= gesubsidieerde rechtsbijstand) wordt, als zijnde van onvoldoende belang, niet verleend indien het op geld waardeerbare belang blijft beneden een bedrag van € 500,-*.') www.st-ab.nl/normwrb.htm Certain maximum income limits are valid as well.

[140] See Tuil (n 3), 406.

[141] See Annual report *Rechtspraak* 2010, 6.

[142] ibid, 407. The Dutch Association of Insures (*Verbond van Verzekeraars*) reports that in 2008 at least 2,212,000 households held a BTE policy. *Verzekerd van cijfers 2009* (Verbond van verzekeraars, The Hague, 2009) 94. In addition 1,444,000 BTE policies had been sold that cover motor vehicle related claims.

Commission hearings are accompanied by a lawyer, but it is an in-house lawyer from the insurance company, who has built up considerable experience as repeat players. According to the 2008 evaluation of the *Geschillencommissie* 20% of consumers and small businesses received some kind of legal assistance.[143]

Broadly, consumers use the *Geschillencommissies* for consumer claims, especially where they involve lower amounts, and businesses use the courts or arbitration for their (more expensive) cases, although many businesses sell their claims, to be collected by factoring agencies. Dutch arbitration law does not deal with the recovery of fees or costs. In the absence of agreement on costs between the parties, the arbitrators may decide, and will often adopt a loser pays approach, limited to an amount that they consider reasonable.[144]

It appears that the ADR system provides a forum that enables cases to be brought that would otherwise not be brought in court in view of the expense and inconvenience of the latter.[145] While at first sight it might be assumed that the ADR bodies take cases from courts, it rather appears that many of the cases dealt with by ADR bodies would not have been brought to the ordinary court.[146] Whether more cases are brought in court than in Commissions seems to depend on the sector, and is related to claim value.[147] Consumer cases concerning housing and car contracts are mainly dealt with in the ordinary courts because of their high case value.[148] Research by Verstappen, van Boom, Loos and Rinkers concluded that *Geschillencommissie* disputes were not so much about terms and conditions as other issues.[149]

The total number of claims in both the courts and the *Geschillencommissie* structure appears to be low compared with other jurisdictions. In 2008, the courts of first instance had 522,400 cases that started with a summons (the traditional way of starting a case concerning a normal monetary dispute).[150]

Overall

The *Geschillencommissie* system is an outstanding success, and one of the leading European examples of ADR. The system operates within a distinct national cultures of collaboration and achieving pragmatic solutions. The question for other states is whether such a culture is a pre-requisite for a successful ADR system. If not, and such a culture is independently desirable, would it be a product of a successful ADR system?

[143] See Klapwijk and ter Voert (n 29), 13.

[144] M van Hooijdonk and P Eijsvoogel, *Litigation in the Netherlands. Civil procedure, Arbitration and Administrative Litigation* (The Hague, Wolters Kluwer, 2009), para 3.5.

[145] E Hondius, 'Public and Private Enforcement in Consumer Protection – a Dutch perspective', in F Cafaggi, H-W Micklitz, *New Frontiers of Consumer Protection – The interplay between public and private enforcement* (Antwerp, Oxford, Portland, Intersentia, 2009), 239.

[146] ibid, 235–239.

[147] Interview with T Jongbloed, 26 January 2011.

[148] See Loos and van Boom (n 50), 26.

[149] JMP Verstappen, WH van Boom, MBM Loos and JGJ Rinkes, *Onderzoek naar de rol van algemene voorwaarden in de praktijk van de geschillencommissies SGC*, (Ministry of Economic Affairs, 2007), available at www.rijksoverheid.nl/documenten-en-publicaties/rapporten/2007/07/25/onderzoek-naar-de-rol-van-algemene-voorwaarden-in-de-praktijk-van-de-geschillencommissies-sgc.html.

[150] Based on the figures reported on the website of the Dutch Central Statistic Bureau (*Centraal Bureau voor de Statistiek*) under 'Kerncijfers' on their websitewww.cbs.nl. These figures include small claims.

In any event, a key lesson for other states is how the Netherlands has expanded the use of ADR across so many sectors—it is within sight of providing comprehensive coverage. This has been achieved by having a single basic approach, that is centrally organized, and so provides standardization and control over the performance requirements of independence, quality, low cost and so on, but also permits sectoral variations where necessary. Compliance with the performance requirements is obviously essential for consumer confidence. But it is the visibility of the system as a whole, as produced by its unification, that has enabled the wide proliferation of sectoral Committees, enlisting consumer demand and business support.

Is the particular approach towards negotiating terms and conditions a pre-requisite for a successful ADR system? This would not seem to be the case, since other states have effective ADR systems without this feature. The negotiation stage operates as a gateway to the Committees in the Netherlands, whereas no such gateway exists in most other states. The central question here is whether *ex ante* or *ex post* techniques are preferable for enforcing consumer law, which is beyond the scope of the current enquiry. The Dutch system might result in wide compliance by businesses, since they are involved in the negotiation of their sector's terms and conditions up front, and this should bring both higher understanding and compliance. If so, such a system might cleverly result in what may be a low number of infringements compared to other states' enforcement systems that adopt *ex post* enforcement techniques. That hypothesis will need to be tested further.

7

Poland

Magdalena Tulibacka

Introduction

ADR has seen an unprecedented development in Poland within the past 20 years. This phenomenon is by no means unique in this region of Europe. It can be observed in other post-socialist states of Central and Eastern Europe, such as Slovenia and Hungary,[1] which after 1989 returned to market economy, democracy and rule of law. Their markets are maturing, surrounded by newly reformed laws, regulations, and administrative structures. Their justice systems, both court-administered justice as well as alternative methods of resolving disputes, were overhauled. However, in spite of a true explosion of new forms of alternative dispute resolution and new bodies offering ADR services, ADR in Central and Eastern Europe continues to suffer from quite significant problems. Some of these problems result from the relative novelty of these developments and the on-going process of transformation. Most, however, are quite similar to the problems faced by ADR in other parts of Europe.

This chapter explores ADR mechanisms in Poland and evaluates the problems that remain. It focuses on consumer disputes, and thus ADR bodies dealing solely with commercial ADR, especially commercial arbitration, are not covered. Further, the chapter does not cover criminal and family law ADR. It is solely concerned with civil justice.

The time is indeed ripe for reviewing what Poland has achieved in the area of ADR. By joining the European Union in 2004,[2] Poland also joined its efforts to strengthen civil justice.[3] ADR is seen as a valuable mechanism of accessing justice and therefore it is widely encouraged by EU policymakers. Poland, together with other Member States is actively participating in the process of assessment, revision, and greater popularization of ADR

[1] The website of the European Commission provides data concerning ADR schemes in all Member States, including Central and Eastern European states: ec.europa.eu/consumers/redress_cons/adr_en.htm. This page includes a map with information on ADR bodies notified to the Commission, as well as the 'fiches' on national ADR systems – short notes describing ADR systems in each Member State. It is clear from these documents that the Polish ADR system is the most significant of all the CEE states – both in terms of number of bodies and number of cases considered.

[2] Together with the Czech Republic, Cyprus, Estonia, Latvia, Lithuania, Hungary, Malta, Slovenia and Slovakia, Poland signed the Accession Treaty with the European Union in 2003. The Treaty was published in the Official Journal of the European Communities of 23 September 2003, L 236, Vol. 46.

[3] The EU involvement in civil justice, and in particular civil procedure, is reviewed by: E Storskrubb (2008) 'Civil Procedure and EU Law. A Policy Area Uncovered' (Oxford: OUP); and M Tulibacka (2009) 'Europeanization of Civil Procedure: in Search of a Coherent Approach', 46 *CMLR* 1527–1565. See the following websites for further information on EU activities in the area: http://ec.europa.eu/consumers/redress_cons/adr_en.htm (DG SANCO), and http://ec.europa.eu/justice/policies/civil/dispute/policies_civil_dispute_en.htm (DG FSJ).

mechanisms coordinated by the EU. This is particularly visible in the area of consumer protection. The European Commission's DG SANCO established a database of ADR bodies in EU countries, and four Polish mechanisms have been registered on the database so far.[4] In early 2011, SANCO published the Consultation Document 'On the use of Alternative Dispute Resolution as a means to resolve disputes related to commercial transactions and practices in the European Union'.[5] The Document highlights the dynamic developments in the area, both by the EU and by the Member States, as well as weaknesses and problems. The findings are largely based on the 'Study on the use of Alternative Dispute Resolution in the European Union' of October 2009.[6] The Study found 750 ADR schemes across the EU Member States, of which 24 in Poland.[7]

The key problems identified by the Study were: lack of awareness among consumers and businesses of the existence of ADR schemes, gaps in geographical and sectoral coverage, refusal of businesses to follow non-binding decisions of ADR schemes, or even refusal to altogether engage in proceedings before such schemes. As this chapter will demonstrate, ADR in Poland undeniably suffers from these shortcomings. To some extent they limit its popularity, use, and effectiveness. Thus, Polish ADR is not yet ready to fully embrace the key advantages and aims of ADR: greater access to justice, shifts in the structure and functioning of law and justice, and also improved behavioural standards within society.[8]

The chapter proceeds as follows: first, the main types of ADR which have developed in Poland are set out; second, the ADR bodies and institutions are analysed in detail. Throughout these two parts, emphasis is placed on a number of issues: the internal (also statutory) framework of the ADR methods and bodies, their procedures, costs, and participants, their use and popularity using available statistical information, and any problems which have been detected in practice and in academic writings. The chapter concludes with a short restatement of these problems and some elaboration on their implications.

Forms of ADR in Poland

Within the past 20 years, Polish ADR mechanisms gained policy and judicial recognition, as well as statutory footing. Mediation and arbitration are now firmly established in the Code of Civil Procedure,[9] and the parties to prospective or on-going litigation as well

[4] See fn 1. These bodies are: the Trade Inspection, the Banking Ombudsman, the Arbitration Tribunal of the Financial Supervision Commission, and the Insurance Ombudsman, all examined below.

[5] DG SANCO *Consultation Paper On the use of Alternative Dispute Resolution as a means to resolve disputes related to commercial transactions and practices in the European Union* (Brussels, DG SANCO, 2011). Text of the Consultation Document is available online: http://ec.europa.eu/dgs/health_consumer/dgs_consultations/ca/docs/adr_consultation_paper_18012011_en.pdf.

[6] DG SANCO Study on the use of Alternative Dispute Resolution in the European Union (Berlin, Civic Consulting, 2009).

[7] The Study does not look at the identified mechanisms in detail. With regard to Poland there is also one crucial problem: the Study considers each of the district Consumer Arbitration Tribunals as separate mechanisms. This chapter sees them as branches of the same mechanism. At present, it does not seem justified to make a distinction between them – they are subject to the same legislation, have the same organizational structures and follow the same procedures. As a result, the number of ADR bodies examined here is smaller than 24 identified in the Study.

[8] C Hodges, *The Reform of Class and Representative Actions in European Legal Systems: A New Framework for Collective Redress in Europe* (Oxford, Hart Publishing, 2008).

[9] The Code of Civil Procedure of 17 November 1964, published in Dziennik Ustaw No 43, item 296, later amended. A version updated in 2008 is available on the following website: http://lex.pl/serwis/kodeksy/akty/64.43.296.htm.

as the court are bound to at least consider the use of mediation. Arbitration is used in disputes between businesses as well as in consumer disputes. Ombudsmen, both of a public and private nature, also started appearing, starting with the Civic Rights Ombudsman established by the Act of 15 July 1987.[10] Initiatives to establish new ADR bodies come from public, business and civic initiatives.

Civil law systems such as Poland are good ground for ADR. The position of judges in the mechanics of court proceedings – typical for such largely inquisitorial systems – enables them to effectively entice litigants to engage in alternative dispute resolution, in particular in mediation. The Polish Code of Civil Procedure reiterates this position in the judicial duty to always aim at concluding litigation with an amicable solution. There are also negative costs consequences which can in certain circumstances be imposed on parties who refuse to engage in mediation.[11]

Further, a specific legal-cultural shift that is favourable to growth of ADR can be seen in Poland. Civil justice and indeed civil relations between businesses and individuals are undergoing a specific process of 'privatisation'.[12] The sense of personal empowerment fostered by the new legal and procedural mechanisms gives rise to new ways of approaching law and justice, especially that it is contrasted with the prevalence of public control of the previous socialist period. ADR is undoubtedly an embodiment of this privatisation. It is seen by prominent scholars and members of the judiciary to be a method of resolving disputes that guarantees greater autonomy and flexibility to the parties, and at the same time it is easier for them to access than the formal judicial process.[13]

Mediation

Mediation is a relatively new concept in Polish procedural law. It was first introduced into criminal procedure: the Code of Criminal Procedure was amended in 1997 and 2000 to introduce mediation in criminal and juvenile proceedings. Following this, mediation appeared in public administrative procedure, in 2004. The Code of Civil Procedure was amended in 2005 to include a number of provisions about mediation and its use before and during litigation.[14] The new rules concerning civil mediation followed the Recommendation of the Council of Europe's Committee of Ministers concerning measures to prevent and reduce the excessive workload in the courts.[15] Mediation was designed to be an attractive alternative to litigation: this was achieved by making it a simple, cheaper option.

[10] Amended since. Published in Dziennik Ustaw of 2001, No 14, item 147.

[11] Mentioned below in the part of the chapter concerning mediation [I guess that this foot note will have to be re-maked when the chapters are numbered].

[12] R Morek *Mediacja w Sprawach Cywilnych*' (Mediation in Civil Cases) (Warszawa, Oficyna Wydawnicza Ministerstwa Sprawiedliwości, 2009), 3.

[13] T Ereciński *Kodeks Postępowania Cywilnego. Komentarz. Część Pierwsza. Postępowanie rozpoznawcze (Civil Procedure Code. Commentary. Part One. Trial)*, (Warszawa, 2006), 407.

[14] The amendment of the Code of Civil Procedure of 28 July 2005 (*Dziennik Ustaw* (Journal of Laws) No 172, item 1438. Mediation is regulated by Part II ('First Instance Proceedings'), Chapter 1 (Mediation and Arbitration), sub-chapter 1 ('Mediation') of the Code. For further information on the history and present position of mediation in Poland see: R Morek, *Mediacja w przepisach o postępowaniu cywilnym, karnym, w sprawach nieletnich oraz przed sądami administracyjnymi* (Mediation in civil, criminal, juvenile and administrative procedure), (Edukacja Prawnicza, 2006), No 11, I–II.

[15] Recommendation (CE) R (86) 12 concerning measures to prevent and reduce the excessive workload in the courts [1986].

Civil mediation in Poland takes place outside litigation or during litigation. It can be initiated by parties or by court. In the first case parties can agree on an *ad hoc* basis to mediate a dispute, or mediation can result from a pre-existing mediation agreement. Mediation agreements can take form of independent arrangements, or are part of a larger contract regulating relations between parties. These agreements or clauses can also specify various escalating mechanisms for resolving disputes: starting from negotiations, through mediation and finally arbitration.[16] Article 183.1 of the Code of Civil Procedure provides that all the agreements must specify the subject of mediation (a dispute or a relationship from which it can arise) and appoint a mediator or at least specify the method of his appointment. The agreements need not be in writing.

The second type of mediation takes place during litigation, where the court recommends such course of action for the parties. The court can initiate mediation in such manner until the end of the first day of court proceedings, following which the power to initiate it shifts exclusively onto the parties.[17] If the court does initiate mediation, each party has one week to object, and this will prevent mediation from taking place. Whilst such mediation is not compulsory for litigants, there are negative costs consequences for parties who unjustifiably refuse to engage in mediation to which they previously consented.[18] This regulatory approach to mediation led to a dispute among scholars. Some claim that it limits the parties' autonomy (referred to as 'freedom of disposition') during litigation.[19] Others, however, point out that parties have no obligation to agree to mediation in the first place – thus their freedom of disposition is preserved.[20] There is no doubt, however, that there are incentives to mediate and to settle the case enshrined in the Code of Civil Procedure: for instance if a settlement is reached following mediation, the court repays the claimant 50% of the amount of court fee paid when lodging the case.[21]

Costs of mediation are usually not very significant, but the parties are obliged to pay the mediator's fee.[22] Even legally aided parties are obliged to pay the mediator, unless the latter agrees to forego his remuneration.[23] Normally the parties agree the remuneration, but in court-suggested mediation the Regulation of the Minister of Justice[24] applies. According to

[16] Morek *Mediacja w Sprawach Cywilnych* (Mediation in Civil Cases) (2009), 7, points out that such multi-step dispute resolution clauses are increasingly popular in dealings between commercial partners.

[17] Code of Civil Procedure, Art 1838.

[18] These apply both to situations where the court initiates mediation or when it is done by the parties. The new costs rules were introduced by the same Act (of 28 July 2005) amending the Code of Civil Procedure. The loser pays rule is prevalent in Polish Civil Procedure, but Art 103.2 of the Code introduces and exception from this rule. Court can order a party to pay all costs irrespective of the result of the case if the party behaved improperly (this includes refusing to engage in mediation to which consent was previously given).

[19] Z Miczek, *Mediacja w sprawach cywilnych* (mediation in civil cases) No 6 (Przegląd Prawa Sądowego, 2006), 12, and R Zegadło, 'Mediacja w toku postępowania cywilnego – uwagi na tle projektu Komisji Kodyfikacyjnej Prawa Cywilnego' (mediation during civil procedure – analysis in the light of the draft of the Civil Law Codification Commission), in '*Rozprawy Prawnicze. Księga Pamiątkowa Profesora Maksymiliana Pazdana*' (Legal treatises. In memory of Professor Maksymilian Pazdan), (Zakamycze 2005), 1536.

[20] K Weitz, 'Mediacja w sprawach gospodarczych' (mediation in business disputes), in T Wiśniewski, G Bieniek, E Marszałkowska-Krześ, P Pogonowski, K Weitz (eds) *Postępowanie sądowe w sprawach gospodarczych* (litigation in business disputes), Volume 7 (Warszawa, 2007), 234.

[21] Code of Civil Procedure, Art 104.

[22] As stipulated in a mediation agreement between the parties or in the Regulation of the Minister of Justice of 30 November 2005 on the rates of remuneration and disbursements of mediators in civil proceedings (published in *Dziennik Ustaw* No 239, item 2018). The Regulation only applies to mediation initiated by court.

[23] Legal aid in Poland consists in waiver of court fees and appointment of a lawyer *ex officio.* See M Tulibacka, 'Poland', in C Hodges, S Vogenauer and M Tulibacka (eds.) *The Costs and Funding of Civil Litigation. A Comparative Perspective* (Oxford, Hart Publishing, 2010), 453–466, and 457–459.

[24] ibid. Regulation of the Minister of Justice of 30 November 2005 on the rates of remuneration and disbursements of mediators in civil proceedings.

the Regulation, mediator's remuneration amounts to 1% of the value of the case (if the case concerns pecuniary rights), but not less than 30 PLN and not more than 1000 PLN,[25] or if the value of the case cannot be determined or if the case concerns non-pecuniary rights: 60 PLN for the first meeting in the mediation process, and 25 PLN for each subsequent meeting. These amounts are very low indeed, and they have recently been the subject of an official letter by the Civic Rights Ombudsman to the Minister of Justice. The Ombudsman suggested that one of the reasons for lack of popularity of mediation in Poland are the low amounts paid to mediators. They, according to the Ombudsman, do not attract sufficient quality and quantity of mediation services available to parties willing to mediate.[26]

Outside litigation, the costs of mediation vary. Mediation centres and organisations offer their services at relatively reasonable prices. For instance, *Centrum Mediacji Partners Polska* requires 200 PLN for mediation conducted by 1 – 2 mediators, and an additional 200 PLN for recording the settlement.[27] In cases concerning pecuniary claims, the costs are somewhat higher: 300 PLN for the first mediation session, and 200 PLN for each subsequent session. Business mediation is more costly: in cases worth less than 40,000 PLN the fee is 1000 PLN; in cases worth between 40,000 and 400,000 – it is 1000 PLN + 3 per cent of the amount above 40,000 PLN and in cases worth more than 400,000 – it is 13,000 PLN + 1 per cent of the amount above 400,000 PLN.[28] There are also cost-free mediation centres: such as the Centre for Resolving Disputes at the University of Warsaw Law and Administration School.[29]

Mediators are appointed by the parties, or by the court with the consent of the parties. They are appointed from lists of mediators kept by courts,[30] or parties can use mediators of one of the mediation centres and organisations. Several mediation centres and organisations have been established: including *Centrum Mediacji Partners Polska* mentioned above, *Krajowe Centrum Mediacji*, and *Polskie Stowarzyszenie Mediacji*. Some other non-governmental organisations also offer mediation services or advice, including the abovementioned Centre for Resolving Disputes at the University of Warsaw Law and Administration School.

Mediation should normally last no more than one month, unless both parties agree that it ought to take longer. If a settlement is reached during mediation, the court approves it unless it is contrary to law or to the principles of community life,[31] if it is aimed at evading the law, if it is unclear or inconsistent.[32] The settlement is binding on the parties, and after court approval it has a legal force of an execution title.

Mediation is becoming more and more popular, in particular in commercial disputes, employment disputes, neighbourhood and community disputes, and consumer disputes. The Polish Ministry of Justice noted that in comparison to 2009, in 2010 mediations increased by 36 per cent in civil cases, 65 per cent in commercial cases, and 42 per cent in

[25] At the time of writing this chapter, the conversion rate for the Polish currency (PLN) against the Euro is as follows: 1 PLN = 0.25 Euro.

[26] Gazeta Prawna, 1 June 2011, prawo.gazetaprawna.pl/artykuly/519308,rpo_mediatorzy_zarabiaja_za_malo.html.

[27] www.mediacja.org/info.php/koszty,c8cf12b5386f31b3f9737c9b1ce8f929.html.

[28] www.mediacja.org/info.php/koszty,,e73457406003aae891d4b6f64c43bcfd.html.

[29] www.mediacje.wpia.uw.edu.pl/text.php?cat=70.

[30] The lists of mediators are kept in district courts, and it is the head judge of the district court who decides on including or excluding someone from the list of mediators.

[31] The 'principles of community life' are a general clause with significant prominence in the Polish Civil Code. Their further explanation can be found in: M Tulibacka, *Product Liability Law in Transition. A Central European Perspective,* (London, Ashgate Publishing, 2009), 29, 61, 199.

[32] Code of Civil Procedure, Art 183.14 para 3.

family cases.[33] According to the statistical data collected by the Ministry, numbers of cases referred to mediation by district courts[34] have grown steadily as shown in Table 7.1.[35]

Table 7.1: Cases referred to mediation 2006–2009

Year	Cases referred to mediation by Court	Cases where mediation led to settlement
2006	1053	546
2007	1021	707
2008	1061	760
2009	1349	914

These numbers are not very impressive, considering the number of civil cases brought each year before district courts. For instance, only in the first half of 2010, 143,300 cases were brought.[36] District courts consider cases of higher value and complexity than regional courts, as well as appeals from regional courts, but clearly there is scope for much wider use of mediation. At the same time, it is worth pointing out that in regional courts the numbers are much smaller – normally not reaching half the number of mediations in district courts. This is even more striking when one considers the much higher number of cases brought to regional courts: 3.5 million cases only in the first half of 2010.[37] This may partly be caused by the types of cases that are normally considered by regional courts: over 50 per cent of cases concerning estates registers, and over 25 per cent of cases dealing with injunctions. Of course, it is difficult to ultimately make an assessment of the use of mediation in Poland even based on these numbers. They do not include mediations conducted out of court. However, the widely accepted view is that mediation is not as popular as it should be.

The mediation centres mentioned above continue to promote its value on their websites, and through local events and campaigns. These activities are encouraged and reinforced by a very active role of the Ministry of Justice. The Ministry aims at increasing popularity of mediation by addressing a number of problems pinpointed by legal practitioners and scholars. They continue to bemoan relative lack of use of mediation in Polish civil, criminal and administrative justice. A major problem appears to be insufficient emphasis on mediation by judges, who after all do not have an express duty to inform the parties of the possibility to engage in mediation or to encourage them to mediate. As a consequence, parties often do not consider mediation as a viable and attractive alternative to litigation. One of the reasons for this lack of judicial encouragement is lack of communication between judges and mediators, and unfortunately also lack of trust of the judiciary in qualifications and expertise of mediators. In order to create new communication channels between judiciary and those involved in mediation, the Ministry appointed special 'mediation coordinators' in July 2010. At present there are 91 of them: judges, legal practitioners, professional mediators. Their role is to liaise between mediators and mediation organisations, non-governmental bodies, judges, and the Ministry of Justice: to improve mutual trust and understanding.

[33] Data from the website of the Ministry – note on meeting between the Minister of Justice and mediation coordinators on 3 March 2011: http://ms.gov.pl/pl/informacje/news,3057,masz-prawo-do-mediacji--spotkanie-ministra.html..

[34] The structure of the Polish judicial system in civil cases is as follows: regional courts, district courts, appellate courts, and the Supreme Court.

[35] Data available on the website of the Ministry: http://bip.ms.gov.pl/pl/dzialalnosc/statystyki/statystyki-2010. The data is for civil cases only.

[36] ibid.

[37] ibid.

The coordinators have also been entrusted the role of drafting the code of good practice for mediators.[38]

Other problems with mediation have been highlighted in literature: such as an insufficient number of mediators who are specialists in a specific field.[39] There are postulates to regulate qualifications and requirements of mediators in a more comprehensive manner. Further, some 'white spots', where mediators are scarce and thus the availability of mediation as a viable mechanism is very limited, were identified in certain regions of Poland.[40]

Arbitration

Arbitration is an increasingly popular alternative to litigation in Poland. It has a relatively long history, reflected in a number of Supreme Court judgements concerning the operation of this mechanism as well as the legal force of settlements reached through arbitration.[41] Within the past 20 years it has become an exceptionally popular mechanism for settling disputes, especially among businesses. Its relative simplicity, confidentiality, and the potential for greater expertise of arbitrators (when compared to district or even appeal court judges) are seen as the particular advantages over litigation. The cost of arbitration may however be high, perhaps even higher than the cost of litigation in a comparable case. As an exception to this, Consumer Arbitration Tribunals are free of charge for consumers, and the Consumer Arbitration Tribunal operated by the Chairman of the Electronic Communications Office (UKE)[42] has a 100 PLN charge to lodge the case.

The new provisions of the Code of Civil Procedure introduced in 2005[43] regulate arbitration is some detail. In contrast to mediation, arbitration is to take place of litigation. The jurisdiction of an arbitration tribunal to consider a particular legal dispute is contingent upon an agreement between the two parties (in Poland this agreement is referred to as 'a clause for an arbitration tribunal'—*zapis na sąd polubowny*—a more descriptive manner of referring to an arbitration clause). The existence of such an agreement does not prevent one of the parties from bringing a case to an ordinary court, albeit the other party may object to the jurisdiction of the ordinary court in the case. Following this objection, the court refuses to consider the case, even if the arbitration is to take place outside Poland.[44]

Normally the parties appoint an arbitrator or arbitrators. The Code of Civil Procedure stipulates that current members of the judicial profession cannot be arbitrators. The proceedings before an arbitrator or arbitration tribunal may involve a hearing if one of the parties requests it, or if the agreement between the parties included a clause to this effect. Otherwise the arbitrator or arbitration tribunal may conduct the proceedings based on documents only.

[38] Information from the website of the Ministry of Justice – note on the meeting with the coordinators on 3 March 2011, ms.gov.pl/pl/informacje/news,3057,masz-prawo-do-mediacji--spotkanie-ministra.html.

[39] Morek, (n 12), 8.

[40] Meeting of the Minister of Justice with mediation coordinators, 3 March 2011, http://ms.gov.pl/pl/informacje/news,3057,masz-prawo-do-mediacji--spotkanie-ministra.html.

[41] B Dalka, *Sądownictwo polubowne w PR* (*Arbitration in the Polish Peoples' Republic*), (Warsaw, 1987), 16. A list of the Supreme Court judgments concerning arbitration, with short explanations in Polish, can be found on the following website: http://www.arbiter.org.pl/240,Orzecznictwo-SN.html. The judgments mentioned there stretch over a period of more than 40 years.

[42] Analysed below.

[43] Act of 28 July 2005 added Part Five on arbitration courts (Arts 1154–1217, replacing Part Three (Arts 695–715)) to the Code of Civil Procedure.

[44] Code of Civil Procedure, Art 1165.

The award of the arbitration tribunal (including settlement concluded by the parties approved by the arbitration tribunal) can be referred for review and annulment to an ordinary court.[45] This is not an appeal procedure, but rather a complaint procedure. The court will reject the award or settlement in the following circumstances:

1. If the arbitration tribunal did not have the jurisdiction to consider the case;
2. If the award/settlement is contrary to the fundamental principles of the Polish legal system;
3. If there was no arbitration clause, or if such clause is void, ineffective, or lost legal force according to the law governing it;[46]
4. If one of the parties was not informed of the fact that an arbitrator was appointed, of the fact that the proceedings before an arbitration tribunal commenced, or in any other way was prevented from presenting her case before the tribunal;
5. If the award, or part of it, goes beyond the scope specified in the arbitration clause (in the former case, the court only rejects the part of the award concerning issues which were not covered by the clause), unless the party who participated in the proceedings before the tribunal knew of this fact and did not object to it during the proceedings;
6. If legal requirements, or requirements resulting from the arbitration clause, concerning the members of the arbitration tribunal or the proceedings before the tribunal were not followed;
7. If the award/settlement was a result of a crime, or if its basis was a forged or altered document;
8. If the same case between the same parties was previously decided in a court judgement.[47]

The complaint may be brought by a party within 3 months from the day when the party received a copy of the decision, or from the day when the party has learnt of the reasons for complaint if the reasons are those contained in points 7 and 8 (not later, however, than 5 years since the party received a copy of the decision).[48] In a recent decision, the Supreme Court held that the presence of either one of these conditions is sufficient for nullifying an award. It followed that in most cases the court before which the complaint was brought is constrained by the conditions specified by the complainant. However, two conditions (1 and 2) the court can consider of its own initiative.[49]

There are many arbitration tribunals operating in Poland. The Consumer Arbitration Tribunals functioning within the remit of the Trade Inspection, and the Consumer Arbitration Tribunal of the Chairman of the Electronic Communications Office were already mentioned, and are analysed below. There are arbitration bodies linked with professional associations such as lawyers, doctors, and architects. These are not analysed in this chapter. Other notable examples are: the Arbitration Court of the National Economic Chamber in Warsaw,[50] the Arbitration Tribunal of the Polish Confederation of Private Employers (*Lewiatan*), the Arbitration Tribunal of the Regional Economic Council in Katowice, the International Arbitration Tribunal in Wroclaw, the Arbitration Tribunal of the Cotton

[45] Code of Civil Procedure, Arts 1205–1211.

[46] Art 184 of the Code of Civil Procedure specifies that the court will reject the clause which is illegal, contrary to the principles of community life, or aims to evade the law.

[47] ibid, Art 1206.

[48] ibid, Art 1208.

[49] Supreme Court, decision of 9 September 2010, I CSK 535/09.

[50] This is the largest organization of this kind in Poland, considering between 300 and 500 cases per year.

Chamber in Gdynia, and many others. These bodies deal with commercial arbitration, and thus are not examined in detail here.

There is no doubt that arbitration is a popular ADR mechanism in business disputes. However, in disputes involving consumers it suffers from similar problems to mediation. Although known among many consumers and offered by an ever-growing number of bodies, it is not yet as popular as it could be. In common with mediation, problems relate to lack of awareness of the existence of bodies offering arbitration, as well as lack of general awareness and trust in this ADR mechanism and arbitration bodies. The key issue, as will be seen from the analysis below, appears to be the fact that businesses often do not agree to submit to this method of resolving disputes. Jurisdiction of arbitration tribunals is normally dependent on their consent, and they are not willing to offer it. There are numerous reasons for this attitude, which no doubt include the shape of the Polish justice system in general with its slow and often costly court procedure.[51] Such a court system does not offer sufficient incentives to opt for ADR, especially for those traders whose intention is to discourage the consumer from pursuing the claim.[52] There are also doubts as to independence and objectivity of the bodies conducting arbitration (in particular—the Banking Ombudsman, Trade Inspection, or Arbitration Tribunal of the Financial Supervision Commission analysed below). Considering that their decision would be final for the trader or other professional in question, with the sole remedy of lodging a complaint with a court explored above, this does not always appear an attractive option. This, on the other hand, does not instil confidence in the existing ADR mechanisms in Polish consumers.

Ombudsmen, Evolution of their ADR Functions, and Growth of Civic Society

Ombudsmen have a relatively short history in Poland, but their role in public life, in government administration and constitutional and human rights affairs has already become very significant. The first type of Ombudsmen who appeared are those who do not offer ADR services, although they often have some indirect or informal involvement in ADR proceedings. These are public bodies: Civic Rights Ombudsman, Childrens' Rights Ombudsman, Patients' Rights Ombudsman, and the Regional Consumer Ombudsmen. They are briefly described below.

The Civic Rights Ombudsman (*Rzecznik Praw Obywatelskich*) – was established by the Act of 1987, and is the most renown and respected of all Ombudsmen today. His powers cover a wide range of constitutional, civic and social issues: including civil, criminal and administrative justice. The Ombudsman takes action if human or civic rights are being infringed by a public institution obliged to respect them by the Constitution or another legal provision. In common with the Children's Rights Ombudsman and the Patients' Rights Ombudsman created during 1990's, it is a constitutionally independent public body and performs public functions regulated by statute. As mentioned above, these Ombudsmen do not play traditional ADR functions, and thus are not analysed in detail in this chapter. They

[51] These problems in the Polish civil justice system were explored in M Tulibacka, 'The Ethos of the Woolf Reforms in the Transformations of the Post-socialist Civil Procedure: Case Study of Poland', in D Dwyer (ed), *The Civil Procedure Rules. Ten Years On* (Oxford, OUP, 2010) 395–416. On costs and delays see in particular pp 408–413.

[52] This situation is gradually improving: with reforms to civil procedure, the introduction of a small claims procedure in 2000 and a class action procedure in 2009 (explored in more detail below – in the part of the chapter concerning Ombudsmen and civic society).

investigate complaints, make recommendations and may take part in civil or administrative litigation in support of a particular person or organisation. However, they also increasingly take on complaints from individuals and attempt informal mediation or other ways of resolving the issue. Their public esteem is growing, and thus the success of such efforts is also improving.

The most notable among those new public Ombudsmen are Regional Consumer Ombudsmen. They are local officials whose tasks are regulated by statute.[53] Their role involves taking consumer complaints and referring them to traders. During negotiations or mediations, they make recommendations and suggestions concerning resolving of the dispute in question (albeit with no powers to make binding decisions). When a Regional Consumer Ombudsman refers a complaint to a trader, the latter must respond to the Ombudsman's questions. They can also represent consumers in court proceedings (bring litigation as well as take part in litigation already proceeding) or in mediation or arbitration proceedings before other bodies. Recently, they were entrusted by an additional, potentially even more significant, power: one of bringing class actions in the name of a group of at least 10 people in cases involving consumer protection, product liability, and tort liability.[54]

The Regional Consumer Ombudsmen have established themselves as valuable consumer advice, representation and assistance institutions. They do not have the power to conduct formal ADR proceedings, albeit their involvement in ADR—through direct contact and negotiations with traders in informal or formal proceedings is quite significant. The power to take the consumer's case to court, or before an ADR body if negotiations fail, can be a powerful lever in those negotiations. Just how powerful it can be is illustrated by the effectiveness of the Danish Consumer Ombudsman.[55] Unfortunately, the Regional Consumer Ombudsmen in Poland are not always able to capitalise on the potential of this power. Some are more active than others. There are many reasons for this situation, an important one being that the threat of court proceedings, which in Poland are still wrought with complexity, costs and delays, is not always a serious one. However, this situation is gradually improving—primarily because court proceedings are undergoing reforms. Further, the small claims procedure which has existed in Poland since 2000 is an easier to access, cheaper and less complex option.[56] Its existence is more and more widely known and the procedure is becoming popular among consumers. The new power to bring class actions introduced by the Class Action Act of 17 December 2009 will also strengthen the position of Regional Consumer Ombudsmen. In fact, one such class action has already been brought by an Ombudsman.[57]

Another reason why Consumer Ombudsmen's power to bring cases before courts may not be perceived as a realistic option could be their limited resources and in some cases

[53] Act of 16 February 2007 on the protection of competition and consumers, Art 42.2, published in *Dziennik Ustaw* of 2007, No 50, item 331.

[54] Art 4.2 of the Act on Class Actions of 17 December 2009, published in *Dziennik Ustaw* of 2010, no 7; item 44 p 1 (in force since 1 July 2010).

[55] www.consumerombudsman.dk.

[56] Small claims procedure is regulated in Arts 505.1–505.14 of the Code of Civil Procedure, amended by the Act of 24 May 2000, published in Dziennik Ustaw No 48, item 554. It is available only in cases resulting from contracts, where the amount in dispute is no more than 10,000 PLN, or legal and commercial warranties for products worth no more than 10,000 PLN, as well as residential dwelling lease contracts (with no financial threshold). The procedure is easier to lodge (the claimant fills in an official form available online or in courts), cheaper (court fees are between 100 and 300 PLN depending on the amount in dispute), and less complex as regards evidence and trial.

[57] The action is against BRE bank and concerns mortgages and the calculation of variable interest rate.

also lack of knowledge, expertise and experience which such an initiative would no doubt require. Occasionally, the expertise and knowledge of the Ombudsmen are questioned by consumer organisations and the public bodies that cooperate with them, as well as by consumers themselves.[58] The particular source of criticism is the fact that the Ombudsmen do not have to be lawyers. Indeed, they can be economists or have a degree in any other discipline.[59] They are required to have at least five years' professional experience, but there is no requirement that this experience is related to consumer protection or ADR. They are nominated by the local authorities, and every now and then there are doubts as to their suitability for the position.[60]

Another type of Ombudsmen which appeared in Poland, the most crucial as regards the topic of this chapter, are public (Insurance Ombudsman) or private (created by industry, such as Banking Ombudsman) bodies established specifically for the purpose of settling disputes between consumers and representatives of particular types of industry. The proceedings before them and their involvement in ADR vary, and are analysed below. For the most part, those Ombudsmen offer mediation or arbitration, and sometimes both these methods alternatively, depending on the circumstances.

ADR services offered by Ombudsmen are increasingly popular. Some precise statistical data is provided in the parts of this chapter devoted to the specific Ombudsmen. It is clear that an Ombudsman as an independent third party, possessing the knowledge and expertise required in the respective area can be an effective ADR mechanism, especially when equipped with a large dose of social trust. Unfortunately, here is where weaknesses of some Ombudsmen are most clearly exhibited. The problems with knowledge and expertise of Regional Consumer Ombudsmen were mentioned above. The Banking Ombudsman's independence from the industry it represents is not always trusted.[61] The popularity and use of Ombudsmen would no doubt improve if those concerns were addressed. There is no doubt that the potential of an Ombudsman as an institution is very significant in Poland, and needs to be capitalised on. What is more, Polish consumers increasingly expect Ombudsmen to have wide powers to consider disputes and be able to in some way enforce their decisions. A good example is a new Ombudsman for the Recipients of Fuel and Energy, analysed below. This recently established body operates within the organisational structure of the Office for Energy Regulation. It does not yet possess the powers to formally follow up on complaints or to resolve disputes. The 2010 Report of the Head of the Office for Energy Regulation mentions the increasing number of consumer complaints, with specific requests concerning dispute settlement.[62] The disappointment of the complainants on being informed of the Ombudsman's limited role has been noted, especially in telephone conversations. There are plans to broaden the Ombudsman's powers in the future.[63]

An important phenomenon is also the growth of civic society in Poland—the topic that should not be overlooked in the context of alternative mechanisms for accessing justice. A growing number of civic society associations and groups (often set up with no public funding) with whom the Civic Rights Ombudsman and other Ombudsmen cooperate indicates

[58] I have heard these not very favourable opinions about the preparedness and expertise of the Ombudsmen from the Polish branch of the European Consumer Centres and some representatives of the Consumer Federation.

[59] Act on the protection of competition and consumers, Art 40.2.

[60] Personal interviews with employees of the Polish European Consumer Centre.

[61] Please refer to the part of this chapter devoted to the Banking Ombudsman.

[62] Urzad Regulacji Energetyki, *Annual Report 2010*. The Report can be found on the website of the Office: www.ure.gov.pl/ftp/Biuletyny_URE/2011/2010_03_01-biuletyn_nr1(2).pdf.

[63] ibid, 184–185.

that in this relatively new democracy the level of social and civic awareness has increased. The list of such associations can be found on the Civic Rights Ombudsman's website, and it includes such bodies as: the Association of Civic Advice Bureaux, the Foundation for the Development of Local Democracy, Public Affairs Institute, Foundation for Mutual Assistance '*Barka*', Association for the Promotion of Civic Attitudes, Campaign Against Homophobia, etc.[64] These associations, often in conjunction or with the assistance of an Ombudsman, offer help, including legal assistance in the areas of their concern. Further, the number of consumer associations and organisations dealing with specific aspects of consumer protection is growing as well. They offer a wide range of services to consumers: including advice, information, and other types of assistance. To mention only a few, they are: *Federacja Konsumentów, Stowarzyszenie Konsumentów Polskich*, and the network of Citizens' Advice Offices created in 1996 following the example of the UK's Citizens' Advice Bureaux. According to Article 61 of the Code of Civil Procedure, non-profit consumer organisations and other public interest organisations can bring litigation in the name of a consumer or take part in on-going litigation to support the consumer's case. This power can be extended to most ADR proceedings as well. In common with the Regional Consumer Ombudsmen, those organisations have a potentially significant negotiating tool, albeit with very similar challenges. The problems faced by consumer associations are specifically related to lack of adequate funds and legal support to bring litigation, especially in complex cases.[65] There is unfortunately no reliable statistical data concerning the number of cases that were indeed brought by such organisations, or in which they participated. The Consumers Federation (which is the oldest and the largest consumer organisation in Poland) recorded 2514 cases in which it took part in 2004.[66]

Although it is difficult to assess the impact of those civic organisations precisely, they certainly contribute to the greater awareness of legal remedies, including the availability of ADR mechanisms.

ADR Bodies

A growing number of bodies—also those established by businesses—offer ADR services. As mentioned above, four of these schemes: the Trade Inspection, the Insurance Ombudsman, the Banking Ombudsman, and the Arbitration Tribunal of the Financial Supervision Commission have been officially notified to the European Commission and can be found on the official EU ADR database maintained by the European Commission.[67]

The Trade Inspection and its ADR Services

The Trade Inspection is a public regulatory body with statutory duties in the area of trade and consumer protection. Its powers and organisational structure are set out in the Act

[64] www.brpo.gov.pl/index.php?md=4448&s=1.

[65] I have heard this view from many representatives of Polish (and indeed other Central and Eastern European) consumer organisations.

[66] Data from the website of the Federation: www.ure.gov.pl/ftp/Biuletyny_URE/2011/2010_03_01-biuletyn_nr1(2).pdf.

[67] The database is available on the following website: http://ec.europa.eu/consumers/redress/out_of_court/adrdb_en.htm.

of 15 December 2000 on Trade Inspection.[68] The Head of the Office for the Protection of Competition and Consumers[69] is also the Head of the Trade Inspection. There are regional heads in each district in Poland (16 districts).

The Inspection is primarily intended to control safety and quality of products and services, and its powers are designed accordingly. In addition to those, it also organises the activity of the Consumer Arbitration Tribunals described below, and engages in mediation in consumer cases.[70] According to Article 36 of the Act on Trade Inspection, a district head of the Inspection has the power to conduct mediation proceedings. Mediations are carried out resulting from a consumer's request, or can be initiated by a district head of the Inspection. The authority of the Inspection does not extend upon such areas as health, education, banking, insurance, telecommunications, energy and fuels.

Very often the Inspection becomes involved in disputes between consumers and businesses when the former contact it for advice. The number of such advice requests is growing, and so is the number of mediations. An employee of the Inspection dealing with consumer protection in the Śląsk district also noted that a growing number of such mediations are resolved in favour of consumers.[71] In this region, during 2010, 562 mediation requests were brought by consumers, of which 369 resulted in mediations. 260 of these mediations were resolved favourably for consumers. The national average, regarding the percentage of such favourable results, is 66.4%.[72] Mediations are free of charge for the parties, and often concern very small amounts of money.[73] However, if during mediation an opinion of an expert is sought, the consumer should cover the expert's fee unless the parties agree otherwise.[74]

The success rate for consumers in mediations led by the Inspection and the growing number of mediations may be related to the fact that the Inspection has the power to issue administrative decisions against traders,[75] and there are criminal charges prescribed for the traders who do not follow the decisions.[76] Unfortunately there is no data concerning how many unsuccessful mediations were followed by such administrative steps.

Consumer Arbitration Tribunals

The Tribunals consider disputes between consumers and businesses resulting from contracts of sale of goods or provision of services. They were established in 1991, and

[68] Dziennik Ustaw of 2001, No 4, item 25. Amendments published in Dziennik Ustaw of 2009, No 151, item 1219, and Dziennik Ustaw of 2010, No 182, item 1228.

[69] The Office for the Protection of Competition and Consumers is a government body with wide powers in the area of competition and consumer affairs. Its powers derive from the Act on counteracting monopolistic practices of 24 February 1990, amended in 1996 to change the name of the office to the Office for the Protection of Competition and Consumers. At present the powers of the Office are contained in the Act on the Protection of Competition and Consumers of 15 December 2000.

[70] Act on Trade Inspection describes the powers and responsibilities of Trade Inspection, Art 3.

[71] K Wolwiak – data from interview on the website of the Polish mediation internet portal: www.mediacja.com/index.php/Nie-kupuj-kota-w-worku-akcja-inspekcji-handlowej.html.

[72] Data from the Polish mediation portal: www.mediacja.com/index.php/Spor-o-buty-zalagodzi-mediator.html. The note refers to the Inspection in Lublin, where the percentage of mediations concluded favourably for consumers is 88% (the highest in Poland).

[73] The note quoted above mentions an example of a pair of shoes worth 13 PLN (around €4) being the subject of one such mediation in Gorzów.

[74] The district heads keep lists of such experts.

[75] Act on Trade Inspection, Art 18.

[76] Act on Trade Inspection, Arts 38 and 39.

initially the procedures and structures differed among various regions they were based in. In 2001 the procedures were unified and since then lodging the case with the Tribunals is free of charge.[77] The Tribunals are located in the offices of the Trade Inspection.[78] Although the Trade Inspection offers them administrative and organisational support, the Tribunals maintain their independence in adjudication. Each Tribunal consists of a president and permanent arbitrators. The president is appointed from the list of permanent arbitrators (only those with a law degree) by the district head of the Trade Inspection, after consultation with consumer and business organisations. The arbitrators are appointed in equal numbers by consumer organisations and by business organisations. At least one-third of them must have a law degree.

At present, there are 16 permanent Tribunals and 15 Tribunal offices in Poland.[79] The Tribunals consider cases brought by consumers, businesses, consumer organisations, and Regional Consumer Ombudsmen. The value of the case cannot exceed 10.000 PLN, unless it is brought before the Tribunal in Warsaw, which does not have monetary limits.[80] Both parties must agree for the case to be heard by the Tribunal. The Tribunals do not hear cases which are within the jurisdiction of other ADR mechanisms: energy sector is under the jurisdiction of the Head of the Office for Energy Regulation, the financial sector—the Banking Ombudsman, the Insurance Ombudsman and the Arbitration Tribunal of the Financial Supervision Commission, and the postal and telecommunications services—the Arbitration Tribunal of the Head of the Office of Electronic Communications. The Tribunals also do not hear cases concerning health and social services.

As mentioned above, it is free of charge to lodge a case with the Tribunal, although each of the parties bears the costs of an expert opinion or any other procedural activity, if it was requested by them.[81] The party lodging the case sends a claim document (available online)[82] with the applicable information and evidence to the Tribunal. The Tribunal, after accepting the case, sends a copy of the claim to the defendant. The latter has 7 days for giving consent for the case to be heard by the Tribunal. The defendant's silence cannot be interpreted as consent. If the consent was given, the president of the Tribunal sets the date for a hearing, which cannot be later than 1 month after the defendant's response was received. The parties are also requested to appoint one arbitrator each (one from the group of arbitrators appointed by consumer organisations, and one from those appointed by business organisations). The panel is presided over by the super-arbitrator appointed by the president of the Tribunal. Depending on the position of the parties and whether a settlement is reached, cases can take from between 14 days to 2 months on average to complete.

[77] Following Regulation of the Ministry of Justice of 25 September 2001 on Organization of Permanent Consumer Arbitration Tribunals, published in *Dziennik Ustaw* of 2001, No 113, item 1214.

[78] Art 37 of the Act of 15 December 2000 *on Trade Inspection* and the Regulation of the Minister of Justice of 25 September 2001 *on establishment of the rules of organisation and operation of permanent consumer arbitration tribunals. Dziennik Ustaw (Journal of Laws)* of 2001, No 4, item 25. The Minister's Regulation o*n the establishment of the rules of organisation and operation of permanent consumer arbitration tribunals* (*Dziennik Ustaw (Journal of Laws)* No 113, poz 1214) can be viewed (in Polish) on the website of the Consumers' Federation: www.federacja-konsumentow.org.pl/pagePrint.php?page=37. Before these legislative provisions were introduced, the tribunals were operating on the basis of the provisions of the Code of Civil Procedure.

[79] The 16 permanent offices are placed in each district (in the main city of the district), and the 15 offices are in other cities in larger districts.

[80] Website of the Warsaw Tribunal: spsk.wiih.org.pl/index.php?id=1.

[81] The experts are selected from the lists kept by regional heads of the Trade Inspection.

[82] It is available on the website of the Office for the Protection of Competition and Consumers: www.uokik.gov.pl/stale_polubowne_sady_konsumenckie__informacje.php.

The arbitration proceedings before the Tribunal are open to the public. Indeed, some Tribunals actively encourage members of the public to attend hearings. During the trial, both parties have an opportunity to present their views, and experts' opinions are presented. The fundamental aim is to encourage the parties to settle. If no settlement is reached, the Tribunal makes an award. Both the settlements and the awards are binding on the trader, but the consumer can still bring the case to an ordinary court. For traders, these settlements and decisions have the same force as any other arbitral awards: Tribunals' decisions may be reviewed and annulled by an ordinary civil court following the complaint procedure analysed above, in the part of the chapter concerning arbitration.[83] This is not an appeal procedure.

The proceedings before the Consumer Tribunals are cheaper, quicker, and much more informal than in the ordinary civil courts. They have been commended by the Consumers' Federation for their efficiency and greater suitability for consumer disputes. However, their jurisdiction is conditional upon both parties' consent. The Consumers' Federation pointed out that traders only too often do not agree for the case to be considered by the Tribunal, in hope that the consumers will not bring the matter before an ordinary court.[84] In a recent review of one of the Tribunals (Szczecin), it transpired that 25% of consumers' claims met with such a refusal during the first half of 2010.[85] This is an improvement on the national average of between 33 per cent and 39 per cent observed before 2008.[86] Indeed, in 2010, in 1,065 out of 2,684 cases traders refused to participate.[87]

The speed of the proceedings before the Tribunals is undoubtedly their advantage over normal court proceedings. The average case processing time in Szczecin, in the first half of 2009, was 37 days. The costs of the proceedings tend to be lower than the costs of a comparable case in court. Unfortunately there is no data that would allow one to make meaningful comparisons concerning this issue: mainly because the types of low value cases that reach the Tribunals rarely reach ordinary courts. As mentioned above, lodging the case is free of charge, and the only costs involved are the costs of expert opinions and other activities requested by the parties. Parties can also choose to be represented by lawyers, although this will of course bring further costs. The loser pays principle, which is a leading principle in the Polish civil proceedings,[88] also applies to the Tribunals, albeit it has been modified. First of all, if the consumer loses the case the Tribunal may decide that the costs of the other party are to be paid by the Trade Inspection. This is done if the financial position of the consumer indicates that he would be unable to cover these costs. Further, the costs of legal representation are never covered by the loser pays principle and must be paid by each party respectively.

[83] The complaint procedure was prescribed by the Code of Civil Procedure for arbitration (Arts 1205–1211).

[84] www.federacja-konsumentow.org.pl/pagePrint.php?page=41.

[85] R Wasilewski, 'Spory Konsumenckie a Stałe Polubowne Sądy Konsumenckie', 17.01.2011, http://karieraprawnika.pl/index.php/spory-konsumenckie-a-stale-polubowne-sady-konsumenckie-spsk/menu-id-259.html#_ftnref8.

[86] J Brol, 'Bariery na drodze alternatywnego rozwiązywania sporów w sprawach cywilnych. Sądownictwo polubowne (arbitrażowe)' (*Barriers to alternative dispute resolution in civil cases. Arbitration*) in E Holewińska-Łapińska, *Prawo w działaniu 6. Sprawy cywilne* (*Law in Action 6. Civil cases*), (Warsaw, Oficyna Naukowa, 2008), 74; and E Bagińska, 'Alternative resolution of consumer disputes in Poland', in M Habdas and A Wudarski (eds.), *Festschrift für Stanisława Kalus. Ius est ars boni et aequi*, (Frankfurt am Main, Peter Lang, 2010), 55.

[87] Speech by M Krasnodębska-Tomkiel (Head of the Office for the Protection of Competition and Consumers), Warsaw, 15 March 2011, available at www.uokik.gov.pl/aktualnosci.php?news_id=2502.

[88] See M Tulibacka, 'Poland' in C Hodges, S Vogenauer, M Tulibacka (eds), *The Costs and Funding of Civil Litigation. A Comparative Perspective*, (Oxford, Hart Publishing, 2010), 465–466.

Overall, it should be said that the use of the Tribunals is growing, with the number of cases brought yearly reaching nearly 3000.[89] In 2009, the number of cases was 2,666, and in 2010 it was 2,684.[90] The numbers for Szczecin are at Table 7.2.[91]

Table 7.2: Claims data for Tribunals in Szczecin 1991–2009

1991 - 1994	59 claims
1995	84 claims
2007	130 claims
2008	134 claims
2009	172 claims

The success rate for consumers before the Tribunals is not necessarily high. Again, in Szczecin, in the first half of 2010, there were 121 claims brought, of which 71 were rejected as either baseless or not within the Tribunal's remit. Further 26 claims were decided against the consumer, in 19 a settlement was reached, and in only 6 the consumers won the case.[92] Wasilewski, who researched the cases in detail, points out to a number of interesting phenomena. Over 50 per cent of cases concerned shoes and in most of them consumers' claims were rejected or they lost the case. Further, it appears that in cases involving low value items (such as shoes) consumers tend to lose. Wasilewski suggests that in many of those cases consumers are simply trying to get rid of items they no longer require. In high value cases, consumers tend to win more often. In my own readings of the decisions of the Warsaw Tribunal I noted that claims are considered very carefully in the light of facts and law, albeit there appear to be significant filters on unsubstantiated claims. Cases where consumers' requests were unreasonable, where the evidence was weak, where one of the legal requirements (such as causal link in a case of contractual liability for damage) was not met, the Tribunal proceeded to decide in favour of a trader. However, the Tribunal also did not hesitate to use any *res ipsa loquitur* or other types of presumptions available according to the applicable law in order to assist the consumers.

The Head of the Office for Energy Regulation and the Ombudsman for Fuel and Energy Recipients

The Head of the Office for Energy Regulation has wide-ranging powers in the area of fuels and energy. These powers include settling disputes between fuel and energy suppliers and prospective recipients concerning fuel and energy contracts. In cases where contracts have not yet been concluded, and the parties find it impossible to come to an agreement regarding connection to a commercial network, sales, and other arrangement relating to fuels or energy, the dispute can be referred to the Head of the Office. Also cases of unjustified refusal to supply or refusal to connect to a commercial energy network can be considered

[89] ibid. Brol (2008) 'Bariery na drodze alternatywnego rozwiązywania sporów w sprawach cywilnych. Sądownictwo polubowne (arbitrażowe)', and Bagińska (2010) 'Alternative resolution of consumer disputes in Poland'.

[90] ibid speech by M Krasnodębska-Tomkiel (fn 87).

[91] Source: R Wasilewski, 'Spory Konsumenckie a Stałe Polubowne Sądy Konsumenckie', 17.01.2011, http://karieraprawnika.pl/index.php/spory-konsumenckie-a-stale-polubowne-sady-konsumenckie-spsk/menu-id-259.html#_ftnref8.

[92] ibid.

by the Head of the Office.[93] Nevertheless, the jurisdiction of the Head of the Office does not cover contracts already concluded. These ought to be referred to an ordinary court or another ADR body.

Overall, ADR powers of the Head of the Office are quite limited. They are rather informal powers of negotiation and mediation, with the possibility of issuing an administrative decision if negotiations fail. Such negotiations and mediations are in fact mainly conducted by local departments of the Office for Energy Regulation. They follow complaints from recipients of gas and energy. The 2010 Report of the Office notes that sometimes energy or gas companies continue the conduct that was the subject of the complaint in spite of the negotiations.[94]

The Office also offers the services of the Ombudsman for Recipients of Fuels and Energy. Since 2010 the Ombudsman's office in fact consists of three ombudsmen. The ever-increasing number of cases necessitated this organisational change. The number of complaints referred to the Ombudsman has grown from 108 in 2002 to 3,264 in 2010.[95] The Ombudsman operates in the name of the Head of the Office in order to protect the interests of the recipients of fuels and energy. His powers, however, are quite limited. The Ombudsman offers advice and assistance with complaints from the recipients against energy companies, and can present these complaints to the companies, but is unable to formally conduct mediation and arbitration or make formal decisions. As mentioned above in the part of this chapter exploring the institution of Ombudsman, the 2010 Report of the Office noted that consumers expect the Ombudsman to have powers at least similar to those of Regional Consumer Ombudsmen (in representing consumers before courts and ADR bodies). Frustration of complainants with the limited help the Ombudsman can offer was emphasised and the suggestion was made that the powers ought to be extended. It is to be seen whether the suggestion will be acted upon.

The Office of Electronic Communications and its ADR Services

The Office of Electronic Communications is a government body responsible for postal, telecommunications, spectrum and electromagnetic compatibility sectors. It has wide regulatory powers within these sectors, including setting up schemes to resolve disputes, and consumer protection.

Consumer Arbitration Tribunal of the Office of Electronic Communications

The Tribunal considers pecuniary consumer claims resulting from contracts for telecommunications and postal services.[96] It operates on the basis of legislation dating from 2004.[97] The most common examples of cases involve wrongful billing, problems with internet services, and lost letters or packages. The rules of the Tribunal require that the consumer first exhaust the internal complaint route directly with the service provider.

[93] These powers of the Head of the Office are regulated in Art 8.1 of the Energy Law of 10 April 1997, published in *Dziennik Ustaw* of 2006, No 89, item 625, later amended. The latest version of the Law is at www.ure.gov.pl/portal/pl/25/17/Ustawa_z_dnia_10_kwietnia_1997_r__Prawo_energetyczne.html.

[94] The 2010 Report is available at www.ure.gov.pl/ftp/Biuletyny_URE/2011/2010_03_01-biuletyn_nr1(2).pdf.

[95] The 2010 Report, at p 181.

[96] Complaints of business clients of telecommunications and postal services companies are not within the jurisdiction of the Tribunal.

These complaints are to be addressed within 30 days. After unsatisfactory completion of the complaint procedure, the case can be referred to the Tribunal. The jurisdiction of the Tribunal to consider a case is conditional upon both parties consenting to arbitration. The cost of lodging the case is 100 PLN (around 25 Euro), plus there may be additional costs if a party requests additional procedural activities or an arbitrator who is not a local resident. Cases are considered in session either in Warsaw, or in one of the regional departments of the Office. The arbitration panel consists of 3 persons: a super-arbitrator appointed by the Head of the Office, one arbitrator chosen by the consumer (from the list of arbitrators selected by consumer organizations), and one arbitrator chosen by the service provider (from the list of arbitrators selected by service providers). The decision of the panel is legally binding upon both parties and cannot be appealed against. However, as specified above, in common with other types of arbitration decisions, a complaint can be made to an ordinary civil court to void the decision.

The number of cases brought before the Tribunal continues to increase. In 2008, there were 156 cases brought, of which 23 concerned postal services and the rest – telecommunication services.[98] In 2009, there were 182 cases, of which 18 concerned postal services.[99] In 2010, 206 cases were brought.[100] The effectiveness of this ADR body appears, however, still inadequate. In 2008 no session of the arbitration panel took place, in 2009 only two sessions took place, and in 2010 this number grew to six. It is indeed disappointing in the light of a much larger number of cases initially brought before the Tribunal the cases are not followed through. The Reports of the Tribunal indicate that some are settled before an official session of the arbitration panel. But they also point out that consent of one of the parties upon which the jurisdiction of the Tribunal is contingent is very often refused or withdrawn.[101]

Mediation by the Head of the Office of Electronic Telecommunications

The Head of the Office of Electronic Telecommunications is also empowered to conduct mediation between recipients of telecommunications or postal services and their providers. Only consumer recipients can request mediation as regards telecommunications services, while no such limitation exists for postal services. Similarly with the arbitration process above, there is a requirement that the internal complaint route was exhausted before mediation is commenced. Mediation is conducted in writing and is free of charge.

In the area of telecommunications, the Head of the Office reported over 10,000 mediations between the years 2006 and 2010.[102] In contrast, postal services triggered over 200 mediations between 2006 and 2010.[103] The Head of the Office suggested that the ability of the service provider not to consent to mediation, or at any later point to withdraw such consent, is a deterrent for consumers. This is especially clear in the area of postal services.

[97] Act of 16 July 2004 The Act on Telecommunications Law, published in *Dziennik Ustaw* of 2004, No 171, item 1800.

[98] The 2008 Report of the Office, at www.uke.gov.pl/_gAllery/16/60/16607/Sprawozdanie_UKE_2008.pdf, p 129.

[99] The 2009 Report of the Office, at www.uke.gov.pl/_gAllery/28/64/28648/Sprawozdanie_UKE_2009.pdf, p 192.

[100] The 2010 Report, at www.uke.gov.pl/_gAllery/41/18/41183/Sprawozdanie__UKE_2010.pdf.

[101] ibid, 193.

[102] Information from the Summary of the Activities of the Head of the Office of Telecommunications and Postal Services in the area of telecommunication services for the 2006 – 2011 term: www.uke.gov.pl/_gAllery/40/81/40813/Podsumowanie_kadencji_telekomunuikacja_2006_2011.pdf, 24. The 2010 Report mentions 2600 mediations conducted in 2010 www.uke.gov.pl/_gAllery/41/18/41183/Sprawozdanie__UKE_2010.pdf.

[103] Information from the Summary of the Activities of the Head of the Office of Telecommunications and Postal Services in the area of postal services for the 2006–2011 term, 12: www.uke.gov.pl/_gAllery/40/86/40862/Podsumowanie_kadencji_poczta_2006_2011.pdf, .

Thus, the proposal of new Postal Law includes mandatory mediation for postal service providers in their disputes with consumers. But upon further enquiry about the reasons for such a significant discrepancy in the numbers of mediations in telecommunications and postal services, another explanation is certainly the nature of the services. Whereas telecommunication services (mobile and stationary phones, internet services) are normally provided on a long-term basis and tend to be more costly, postal services are much more often one-offs and tend to be cheaper. One may assume that in disputes involving postal services the consumer would be less likely to persist in attempting to resolve a dispute or obtaining remedy (such as a refund or a price reduction).

To summarise the ADR services offered by the Office of Electronic Communications, while growing in popularity, they are not as effective as one would hope. There are a number of problems with these services: the main one being voluntary jurisdiction of the Arbitration Tribunal, which means that for the time being the majority of cases are not followed through because the service provider does not give consent. Bagińska also points out that in the light of small value of average claims in this area, the payment of 100 PLN could be seen as a deterrent to consumers.[104] This may explain a much greater popularity of mediation, which is free, over arbitration. She also suggests that the fact that consumer organisations or consumer ombudsmen cannot bring claims in the name of consumers is regrettable.[105] Mediation conducted by the Head of the Office appears to be getting more positive outcomes, although it may be assumed that cases which are indeed mediated are not as difficult and contentious as those reaching arbitration.

National Banking Ombudsman[106]

The Ombudsman was established by the Polish Banks Association in 2002[107] to consider disputes between banks and their customers (only consumers: physical persons who conclude a banking agreement with a bank outside the scope of their business activity). The Ombudsman is member of FIN-NET: the financial dispute resolution network of national out-of-court complaint schemes in the European Economic Area (the European Union Member States, Iceland, Liechtenstein and Norway). Members of FIN-NET are bodies responsible for handling disputes between consumers and financial services providers: banks, insurance companies, and investment firms. The network has been established for the purpose of settling cross-border claims concerning financial services.

The disputes which are within the jurisdiction of the Ombudsman pertain to activities of banks, and the maximum value of the claim cannot exceed 8,000 PLN (over €2,000).[108] The rules on the operation and the proceedings before the Ombudsman were established in 2001 and amended in April 2006, and are available online on the Polish Banks Association's

[104] ibid. Bagińska (2010), 61.

[105] ibid, 61.

[106] The Banking Ombudsman is a term used on the website of FIN-NET (the Ombudsman is a member of FIN-NET: http://ec.europa.eu/internal_market/fin-net/index_en.htm). However, the literal translation of the Polish name of the body is 'Consumer Banking Arbitration'.

[107] Following resolutions adopted by the General Assembly of the Polish Banks' Association in May 2001. See K Marczyńska, *Dochodzenie roszczeń przez konsumenta w praktyce orzeczniczej Arbitra Bankowego*, (Pursuing consumer claims in the practice of the Banking Arbitrator), CBKE E-biuletyn 2/2008, (Warzawa, Centrum Banań Problemów Prawnych i Ekonomicznych Komunikacji Elektronicznej, 2008), 3.

[108] This amount does not include interest and additional costs sought by the claimant, apart from the principal sum.

website.[109] They limit their applicability to banks which are members of the Association, albeit other banks may also consent to a complaint against them being considered by the Ombudsman.[110] The Ombudsman is appointed by the Board of the Banking Association for 4 years. He is based in Warsaw, and is supported by the Banking Ombudsman Office. In spite of the fact that arbitration is a term officially referred to in the name of the Ombudsman, the proceedings cannot be classified as arbitration. The rules of the Ombudsman expressly exclude the application of the Code of Civil Procedure's arbitration provisions.[111] The jurisdiction of the Ombudsman, the nature of the proceedings, as well as the legal force of the Ombudsman's decisions, distinguish it from other arbitration bodies. First and foremost, jurisdiction of the Ombudsman is not contingent upon the existence of an arbitration clause between the parties – members of the Association must engage in the procedure.

The proceedings before the Ombudsman are commenced when the consumer sends a written complaint to the Office of Ombudsman. The case will not proceed if the consumer has not exhausted an internal complaint procedure with the bank. Thus, the consumer must attach to his complaint a statement that such an internal procedure was completed, or that the bank failed to respond to the complaint within 30 days. The case will also not proceed if it was already considered, or is being considered by a court or an arbitration tribunal, or if it is within the jurisdiction of an arbitration tribunal.

The fee for lodging the complaint, payable by the consumer, is 20 PLN if the value of the case is lower than 50 PLN, and 50 PLN in higher value cases. This fee is returned to the consumer at the end of the proceedings: in full if the decision of the Ombudsman was favourable to the consumer, and in half if the consumer and the bank settled the case.

The Ombudsman encourages the parties to settle the case, but if they are not willing to settle, the Ombudsman takes a decision (often the decision follows a hearing where representatives of the consumer and the bank are present). The decision is final for the bank, which must execute it within 14 days. The consumer, however, is not bound by the decision and may still bring the case to court. Here is where another crucial difference with arbitration lies. Arbitral awards are binding and, apart from a complaint concerning formal infringements, they cannot be appealed. Until 2008, 5 consumers dissatisfied with the Ombudsman's decisions brought their cases to ordinary courts.[112]

During 2011, 1,066 cases were brought before the Ombudsman, and 1,131 decisions were made, of which 518 rejected the case.[113] In 2010, 1165 cases were brought.[114] This was quite a significant decrease in comparison with the data for 2009 (1,413).[115] The 2010 Report notes that 1,117 decisions were made, in 556 of which the case was rejected.[116] The 2009 Report summarises that 1,284 decisions were made during this time (in comparison to

[109] An English translation of the rules can also be found on the website: www.zbp.pl/site.php?s=MDAwODY5.

[110] According to the website of the Association (www.zbp.pl/site.php?s=MTMxNjU0NDk=), 64 banks are members (website accessed on 6th December 2010). They include Polish banks as well as international banks operating in Poland (such as HSBC, Deutsche Bank, and BNP Paribas).

[111] These provisions were analysed above. Para3 of the rules provides that the proceedings before the Ombudsman are not arbitration proceedings covered by the Code.

[112] Marczyńska, 'Dochodzenie roszczeń' (2008), 4.

[113] 2011 Report: http://www.zbp.pl/photo/NJ747/sprawozdanie%20%20BAK_2011%20FINAL.pdf.

[114] Reported on 2 February 2011 by the Banking Ombudsman Katarzyna Marczyńska for Gazeta Bankowa: wyborcza.biz/biznes/1,100969,9041897,Do_Arbitra_Bankowego_wplynelo_1165_skarg_na_banki.html.

[115] The 2009 Report is available on the following website: www.zbp.pl/photo/konf24-02-2010/INFORMACJA%20BAK%202009%20-%20final.pdf.

[116] 2010 Report: www.zbp.pl/photo/!Struktura/Arbiter%20Bankowy/Dokumenty/Informacja_BAK%202010.pdf.

809 in the previous year, and 707 in 2007), of which 703 consisted in denying to consider or in rejecting the case. It is unclear why so many cases are indeed being rejected by the Ombudsman. In 2011, 151 cases were decided in favour of the consumer, and 422 in favour of the bank. This is a significant increase as regards decisions unfavourable for consumers in comparison with 2009, when 245 cases were decided in favour of a consumer, and 339 cases – in favour of a bank. Katarzyna Marczyńska, the current Banking Ombudsman, notes that within the period of 2002–2006, the percentage of cases won by consumers has been increasing (from 30 to 47 per cent),[117] although at present it seems to be decreasing again. During this period, 3,954 cases were brought. The average value of a claim was 3400 PLN, and the average processing time was 40 days.[118]

The 2002–2006 Report emphasises another very important role of the Ombudsman: one of receiving informal complaints about banks and performing a supervisory function. The report notes that such informal complaints from consumers run in thousands each year, and they are often settled swiftly, albeit not always favourably for the complainants. It is noteworthy that such a privately established mechanism is perceived as having a supervisory function.

Katarzyna Marczyńska noted certain positive changes in the banks' conduct towards consumers (better practices, speedier satisfaction of complaints, more effective and efficient procedures for credit decisions, and a generally more conciliatory attitude to consumer complaints and disputes).[119] She attributed these changes, as well as the overall decrease in the number of certain types of complaints, to the activity of the Ombudsman. She also emphasised the importance of the Code of Good Practice, which was established by the Polish Banks Association in 2006. Consumers increasingly bring claims before the Ombudsman concerning breaches of the Code. The latest decrease in the number of complaints has been attributed by her to the adoption of 2009 Good Practices Recommendation 'Bankassurance' No 1 (in force since 1 November 2009) concerning insurance accompanying various banking products, which the banks have been adhering to since April 2009.[120] Two further recommendations are currently being prepared: concerning mortgage protection insurance, and savings and investments insurance.

This positive view of the activity of the Ombudsman is not, however, shared by all. Indeed, a government institution concerned with finance: the Financial Supervision Commission (*Komisja Nadzoru Finansowego*), sees its position as somewhat problematic. The Commission has been in charge of supervising financial institutions since 2006, and the Act of Supervision of the Financial Market required it to establish an Arbitration Tribunal. The Tribunal is analysed below in this chapter. As far as banking activities are concerned, the Tribunal is a competing ADR body to the Banking Ombudsman. It appears that the Commission is dissatisfied with both these bodies and plans to propose establishment of a body similar to the UK's Financial Services Ombudsman, with mandatory jurisdiction and independent of the banks. Indeed, the problem that the Banking Ombudsman pointed out by the Commission is that questions of the Ombudsman's independence and impartiality may appear.

[117] Marczyńska (n 108), 5–6.
[118] ibid.
[119] wyborcza.biz/biznes/1,100969,9041897,Do_Arbitra_Bankowego_wplynelo_1165_skarg_na_banki.html.
[120] wyborcza.biz/biznes/1,100969,9041897,Do_Arbitra_Bankowego_wplynelo_1165_skarg_na_banki.html.

Arbitration Tribunal of the Polish Banks Association

The Tribunal was established by the Association in 1992. Since then, it considered over 100 cases. It is not, in contrast with the Banking Ombudsman, a body focused on consumer disputes. Rather, it considers any case referred to it (within any area of law, apart from alimony matters) by the parties. The requirement is of course, as in any other type of arbitration body, the existence of an arbitration clause. The Tribunal's seat is in Warsaw, and its president and vice-presidents are nominated by the Association. The Tribunal holds a list of arbitrators (over 30 at the moment) who are specialists in the area of banking, finance and taxation. The arbitrators are obliged to follow the Rules of Ethics of the Polish Banks Association.[121] The Rules concern the qualifications, independence and impartiality, and confidentiality. Their breach may result in removal from the list of arbitrators. The parties can appoint an arbitrator or arbitrators from the list, or can choose a different person. Depending on the agreement between the parties, the proceedings before the Tribunal can include an appeal procedure.[122]

The costs of the proceedings can be quite significant, and depend on the complexity of the case, the number of and the seniority of arbitrators, and whether an appeal is brought against the decision in the first instance. The base costs are specified in the tariff document, and consist of: registration fee, base fee, reimbursement of expenses. Registration fee (which is non-refundable) amounts to 2.000 PLN. The base fee (which is reduced if only one arbitrator considers the case, and increased if five arbitrators consider the case) depends on the amount in dispute (Table 7.3).

Table 7.3: Fees for the Arbitration Tribunal of the Polish Banks Association

AMOUNT IN DISPUTE (in PLN)	BASE FEE (in PLN)
Less than 10.000	2,000
10.000 – 50.000	2,000 + 7% of the amount over 10,000
50.000 – 100.000	4,800 + 5% of the amount over 50,000
100.000 – 1.000.000	7,300 + 4% of the amount over 100,000
1.000.000 – 10.000.000	43,400 + 0.8% of the amount over 1,000,000
Over 10.000.000	115,300 + 0.5% of the amount over 10,000,000

Arbitration Tribunal of the Financial Supervision Commission

The Financial Supervision Commission (*Komisja Nadzoru Finansowego*) has been in charge of supervising financial institutions[123] since 2006, and the Act of Supervision of the Financial Market[124] required it to establish the Arbitration Tribunal. The Tribunal has been in operation since 31 March 2008. It considers disputes between all participants in the financial markets, and in particular between financial institutions and their customers. Similarly with the Banking Ombudsman, the Tribunal is member of the FIN-NET network.[125] It has also been registered with the Commission's ADR database.[126]

[121] The Rules of Ethics, established on 31 March 2010, are available on the following website: www.zbp.pl/photo/!Struktura/Sad%20Polubowny/zasady%20etyki%20arbitra_310310.pdf.

[122] The new Rules of the Tribunal, applicable since 22 April 2010, are available on the website of the Association: www.zbp.pl/photo/!Struktura/Sad%20Polubowny/Regulamin_SP_220410.pdf.

[123] These are banks, insurance companies, investment companies, brokers and investment funds.

[124] Act of 21 July 2006, published in *Dziennik Ustaw* No 157, item 1119, later amended.

[125] ec.europa.eu/internal_market/fin-net/index_en.htm.

The cases considered by the Tribunal must have a minimum value of 500 PLN, although disputes concerning non-pecuniary rights may also be considered. Further, disputes worth less than 500 PLN can be accepted by the Tribunal if the claimant is a consumer.[127]

The Tribunal offers two types of proceedings: mediation and arbitration. Both the mediators and the arbitrators who are involved in the Tribunal's proceedings follow the 'Principles of Ethics of Mediators and Arbitrators of the Arbitration Tribunal of the Financial Supervision Commission'.[128] These require them to be impartial and independent, honest, efficient, acting with best care and skill and according to the rules of law. Mediators are nominated by the Head of the Tribunal. Arbitrators are appointed by the General Assembly of Arbitrators of the Tribunal (they can at the same time be employees of the Financial Supervision Commission).

Mediation

Mediation is conducted between two consenting parties by a mediator chosen by them from the list kept by the Tribunal. The parties can withdraw their consent at any stage. Mediators are academics or professionals working in the area of finance. If the parties cannot agree on the appointment of a mediator, the Head of the Tribunal appoints one. The costs of mediation are 250 PLN for each of the parties. 70% of this amount is returned to the parties if they settle the case. There could be additional costs if the parties request an expert opinion or any other additional procedural step – in such cases they need to bear the costs of these. Mediation before the Tribunal is usually concluded during the first session. The settlement is binding upon both parties, and if it is confirmed by a court it has the legal force equal to a court decision.

Arbitration

Arbitration before the Tribunal is always preceded by mediation. It is also contingent on consent by both parties. If the value of the case is lower than 50,000 PLN, the parties appoint one arbitrator; if it is higher – each party appoints one arbitrator, and they choose a super-arbitrator. In especially complex cases the Head of the Tribunal can decide that a panel of five arbitrators should take part in the arbitration.

The costs of arbitration are: for cases where the recipient of financial products or services is the claimant, 250 PLN; and for other cases the amount depends on the value of the case and is established as shown in Table 7.4.

Table 7.4: Fees for the Arbitration Tribunal of the Financial Supervision Commission

Cases worth less than 25,000 PLN	3.5% of the value (at least 250 PLN)
Cases worth less than 250,000 PLN	875 PLN + 3% of the amount exceeding 25,000 PLN
Cases worth more than 250,000 PLN	7,625 PLN + 2.5% of the amount exceeding 250,000 PLN (not more than 100,000PLN)

[126] This is an EU-wide database, updated regularly and published on the DG SANCO's website. The Polish ADR bodies are at http://ec.europa.eu/consumers/redress_cons/ecc_poland_en.htm.

[127] See the Rules of the Tribunal at www.knf.gov.pl/Images/Regulamin%20Sadu%20Polubownego_tcm75-9718.pdf.

[128] Available at www.knf.gov.pl/Images/Zasady_etyki_arbitrow_i_mediatorow_Sadu_Polubownego_przy%20 KNF_tcm75-7304.pdf.

Similarly with mediation, other costs may be involved: such as costs of expert opinions. The arbitration can be done in writing or can involve a session with the parties and arbitrators present. The arbitrators' decisions are binding on both parties and cannot be appealed. Only a complaint prescribed in Articles 1205–1211 of the Code of Civil Procedure (mentioned above in the part analysing arbitration) is possible.

The Tribunal's jurisdiction is voluntary, and so far the uptake has not been notable. The numbers shown in the Report for the period between 1 April 2009 and 31 March 2010 are indeed unimpressive.[129] During this period, 133 claims were brought. 68 of them requested arbitration, and 65 mediation. The claims were brought mainly by recipients of financial products and services (consumers and businesses). However, in only 7 cases the defendant institution consented to mediation or arbitration requested by the other party. In additional 9 cases the Tribunal was informed that the parties settled the case. Between 1 April 2010 and 31 March 2011 the numbers were even smaller: 93 claims brought (30 concerning arbitration and 63 mediation), and in only 3 the defendant institutions consented. In additional 6 settlements were reached, and a small number of cases were withdrawn (4).[130] The Tribunal is a relatively new institution, and it is still too early for assessing this mechanism. It is, however, instructive that Łukasz Szymański, a representative of the Financial Supervision Commission, spoke of ineffectiveness of such mechanisms being a consequence of their voluntary jurisdiction.[131] Szymański was negative about the prospects of the Tribunal, but he was equally unimpressed with the activity of the Banking Ombudsman who, albeit possessing mandatory jurisdiction, according to him does not necessarily guarantee independent consideration of consumer claims. He proposed establishment of a body similar to the UK's Financial Ombudsman Service. The proposal is being considered by the Office for the Protection of Competition and Consumers. The Ombudsman would be financed largely by the banking industry, and its jurisdiction would be mandatory for banks in cases worth less than 10,000 PLN. Both consumers and banks would be able to appeal its decisions in a court.[132]

The Tribunal is currently undergoing reforms, which are mostly aimed at improving its efficiency and its reputation among recipients and those who offer financial services. There is to be a requirement that the arbitration proceedings before the Tribunal ought not take more than 3 months. New requirements concerning arbitrators: their qualifications and conduct while processing cases will be introduced.[133]

Arbitration Tribunal of the Insurance Ombudsman

The Insurance Ombudsman[134] was established in 1995 by the amendment of the Insurance Law of 1990.[135] At present, its powers and organisation are governed by the Act of 22 May

[129] The Report for the period of 1 April 2009 to 31 March 2010 is available at www.knf.gov.pl/Images/sprawozdanie_SP_2009_tcm75-23145.pdf.

[130] Report for the period of 1 April 2010 to 31 March 2011, at www.knf.gov.pl/Images/sprawozdanie_SP_2010_tcm75-26447.pdf.

[131] Statement at a Conference concerning ADR in the area of finance, March 2011. Quoted on the banking industry website: banki.onet.pl/2259776,wiadomosci.html.

[132] http://banki.onet.pl/2259776,wiadomosci.html.

[133] The Report (1 April 2010 – 31 March 2011), at www.knf.gov.pl/Images/sprawozdanie_SP_2010_tcm75-26447.pdf.

[134] The Polish title, *Rzecznik Ubezpieczonych*, means literally: Ombudsman for the Insured. This chapter adopts the shorter: Insurance Ombudsman.

[135] The amended Act was published in *Dziennik Ustaw* of 1996, No 11, item 62.

2003.[136] The Ombudsman is required to submit an annual report of its activities to the Prime Minister.[137] Its functions are primarily of a supervisory nature, and within the scope of these functions the Ombudsman receives complaints from the insured, the insurers, the insurance brokers, and members of pension schemes. The Ombudsman may also bring representative claims before ordinary courts in the name of consumers in cases concerning unfair commercial practices.[138]

Since 2004, the Ombudsman has also been in charge of establishing and running the Arbitration Tribunal. The Tribunal operates on the basis of the Rules of Procedure of 5 April 2004. It considers disputes between:

- the insured and the insurers,
- the recipients of payments from the Insurance Guarantee Fund and the Fund,
- the recipients of payments from the Polish Office of Traffic Insurance and the Office,
- the members of pension funds or their families and these funds,
- the members of employees' pension funds or their families and these funds,
- the insured or the insurers and insurance agents or brokers.

Normally, only monetary claims of at least 1,000 PLN can be brought. In exceptional circumstances, smaller claims can be accepted if one of the parties requests it and the other party consents. Further, cases that do not qualify for arbitration may with the consent of the parties be considered in mediation, which is also conducted by the Tribunal. Both arbitration and mediation are conducted by arbitrators who are appointed by the Ombudsman. At present, there are 26 arbitrators. The Rules require that at least half of them have a law degree. They also need to have professional knowledge and experience in the area of commercial and social insurance. Trade organisations, the Office for the Protection of Competition and Consumers, consumer associations, and academics can suggest candidates. Candidates cannot be employees of the office of the Insurance Ombudsman, insurance companies or pension funds.

The arbitration and mediation proceedings before the Tribunal are analysed below.

Arbitration

The claimant brings the case before the Tribunal using a written form which is available online.[139] After confirming its jurisdiction to consider the case, the Tribunal also confirms whether the other party consents to the case being considered in arbitration. Such consent could have been given before the case was brought (arbitration agreement or arbitration clause between the parties). The claimant must pay the registration fee of 15 PLN only if the consent was not given in advance. Interestingly, in such cases the registration fee will not be reimbursed if the other party refuses consent. The amount of 15 PLN is relatively insignificant, and thus it does not appear to be a deterrent to bringing claims.[140] If the consent is obtained and the case is set to proceed, the claimant is requested to nominate an

[136] The Act on Insurance and Pension Funds Supervision and on Insurance Ombudsman was published in *Dziennik Ustaw* of 2003, No 124, item 1153.

[137] The Reports are published on the Ombudsman's website: www.rzu.gov.pl/publikacje/sprawozdania.

[138] The Act of 23 August 2007 on unfair commercial practices amended the Act of 22 May 2003 on Insurance and Pension Funds Supervision and on Insurance Ombudsman and gave the Ombudsman the power to bring action concerning unfair commercial practices before court in the name of consumers, and to take part in such litigation already brought.

[139] The form is published at www.rzu.gov.pl/files/184__55__Wniosek.pdf.

[140] Bagińska (2010), at p 57, is of the same opinion.

arbitrator and to pay the arbitration fee. The panel of three arbitrators is used more often (each party nominates one arbitrator from the list on the Ombudsman's website, and the super-arbitrator is nominated by joint consent). However, in cases worth less than 5,000 PLN (unless they are complex or there is another good reason) one arbitrator (nominated by joint consent of the parties) is sufficient. The arbitration fee is either a percentage of the amount in dispute or a lump sum. The rates are published on the website of the Ombudsman (Table 7.5).[141]

Table 7.5: Fees for the Arbitration Tribunal of the Insurance Ombudsman

Case value	Arbitration fee
1,000 – 5,000 PLN	5% (not less than 100 PLN)
5,001 – 10,000 PLN	4.5% (not less than 350 PLN)
10,001 – 20,000 PLN	450 PLN for 10,000 PLN + 4% of the rest
20,001 – 50,000 PLN	800 PLN for 20,000 PLN + 3.5% of the rest
50,001 – 100,000 PLN	1,750 PLN for 50,000 PLN + 3% of the rest
More than 100,000 PLN	3,000 PLN for 100,000 PLN + 2.5% of the rest
More than 300,000 PLN	Established *ad hoc*

In cases where the value cannot be determined, there is a fee of minimum 100 PLN if one arbitrator is involved and minimum 350 PLN if three arbitrators are involved. In addition to the arbitration fee, the claimant or the party who suggested additional procedural activities (such as expert evidence or medical examination) must pay their cost.

Normal costs rules apply in arbitration conducted by the Tribunal.[142] The usual loser pays principle is used, and the costs are normally awarded to the winner in the decision finalising the proceedings. In exceptional circumstances, partial or no costs can be awarded. If the parties reached settlement, costs are divided between them.

Settlements or arbitration awards are binding on both parties.

Mediation

As an alternative to arbitration, especially in cases that are worth less than 1,000 PLN and thus do not normally fall within the Tribunal's jurisdiction, the parties can agree to mediation. It is conducted by an mediator appointed by the parties from the Ombudsman's list of the Tribunal's mediators. The party brining the case must pay the same registration fee as is due in the case of arbitration. The mediation fee payable constitutes 75 per cent of the arbitration fee explained above and it is normally paid by both parties in equal amounts.

Mediation is usually conducted on the basis of written documents, and it ought to be concluded during the first seating. If it takes longer, the case can be referred to arbitration. Settlements reached before the mediator and approved by him have the same legal force as the arbitral awards given by the Tribunal.

The Tribunal certainly has the potential to become an effective alternative to court proceedings. Its services are relatively inexpensive, and the proceedings are less complex

[141] www.rzu.gov.pl/sad-polubowny/Taryfa_oplat_Sadu_Polubownego_przy_Rzeczniku_Ubezpieczonych__182.

[142] For these rules see elaboration on costs assessment and allocation in M Tulibacka, 'Poland' in C Hodges, S Vogenauer, M Tulibacka (eds), *The Costs and Funding of Civil Litigation. A Comparative Perspective*, (Oxford and Portland, Oregon: Hart Publishing, 2010), pp 405–406.

and lengthy. However, so far its record has been quite poor. Since its creation until October 2010, 253 cases were brought before the Tribunal. The majority concerned traffic insurance (this tendency corresponds with complaints brought to the Insurance Ombudsman).[143] Only in 14 cases the other party (insurance company) agreed to arbitration. The percentage of cases that are indeed pursued before the Tribunal is so low indeed that some authors refer to the 'boycott' of this body by the insurers.[144] The key arguments put forward by the insurers concern independence and impartiality of the Tribunal and the independence and expertise of the arbitrators. Because the Tribunal is linked, operationally and financially, to the Ombudsman whose main task is to protect those on the receiving end of the insurance and pension products, insurers question whether it is sufficiently prepared to also understand the needs of the insurance industry.[145] There are also doubts whether the arbitrators, appointed by the Ombudsman, are capable of independently and impartially considering the position of both parties, and whether their expertise in the area of insurance and pensions is adequate.[146] Interestingly, however, in spite of the possibility for the industry associations to nominate candidates, the industry has not so far participated in nominating any arbitrators.[147] Perhaps dialogue between the Ombudsman and the insurance industry was neglected initially—thus the lack of trust. Those concerns are recognised by the Ombudsman's office, and the Ombudsman took some steps towards constructive dialogue and cooperation with insurers. Meetings with some major players in the industry took place in 2008, although not all of the insurers attended. The Ombudsman was attempting to convince the insurers that their participation in arbitration and mediation by the Tribunal enhances their reputation among the insured. The participants considered the possibility of creating mandatory jurisdiction for the Tribunal in certain types of cases. These ideas have not led to any results so far, albeit one hopes that they signify important changes in the area and the dialogue will continue.

In the light of these problems, the Ombudsman continues to promote the activities of the Tribunal among businesses and consumers. On the consumer side, there is still some work to be done as regards accessibility of the Tribunal. The costs of the proceedings can constitute an obstacle to bringing a case, especially that the loser pays rule may increase the costs exposure even further.

Polish Centre for Mediation

The Centre has been established in 2000 as a continuation of a Group on Introducing Mediation in Poland. It is a non-governmental, not-for-profit organisation the members of which are volunteers (at present there are 1000 members—mostly mediators, but also organisations supporting mediation). Its focus is on enabling those people who are interested in using mediation in civil, family, labour, commercial and criminal cases, to contact mediators, as well as on training mediators and popularising mediation. The Centre drew up the Code of Conduct for Mediators in 2001.[148] Its members who are mediators must respect

[143] E Kiziewicz, 'Sąd Polubowny przy Rzeczniku Ubezpieczonych' (*Arbitration Tribunal of the Ombudsman of the Insured*), *Monitor Ubezpieczeniowy* (2010).

[144] Bagińska (2010), 58.

[145] Kiziewicz, 'Sąd Polubowny przy Rzeczniku Ubezpieczonych' (2010).

[146] ibid.

[147] ibid.

[148] The Code is available on the website of the Centre: http://mediator.org.pl/images/dokumenty/kodeks%20 2006.pdf.

the Code. The Centre operates through 46 local offices. So far, the Centre has conducted over 9000 mediations across Poland.[149] The explanatory note to the Code of Conduct for Mediators mentioned that in 70 per cent of cases the parties managed to reach a settlement.

Mediation Centre 'Partners Polska'

The Centre is affiliated and supported by the Foundation 'Partners Polska'. The Foundation supports organisations working in the area of democratic transformations in Poland. Similarly with the Polish Centre for Mediation, this Centre also offers mediation in various areas: including consumer, neighbourhood, labour and family disputes.[150] The costs of mediation offered by the Centre have been mentioned above: in the part of the chapter describing mediation in general.[151]

Summary and Assessment of Lingering Problems

The popularity of ADR mechanisms is growing in Poland. In a recent survey of lawyers by IPSOS, 68 per cent were of the opinion that ADR was faster than ordinary judicial proceedings, and over 50 per cent—that it was more effective.[152] The most common forms of ADR are arbitration and mediation. While arbitration has been used for some time, mediation is a new mechanism. The use of arbitration increased significantly, especially in business cases but also in consumer disputes in many areas. Various arbitration bodies dealing with business disputes are reporting growth in case numbers.[153] Also Consumer Arbitration Tribunals are used more often. As far as mediation is concerned, Poland does not have significant experience but its use and the awareness of it among legal professionals, judges, as well as consumers, has improved markedly.[154]

While the legal and organizational infrastructure creates favourable conditions for the use of ADR in Poland, many problems still remain. Is ADR in Poland efficient and effective? Does it constitute a viable alternative to court-administered justice? Does it enhance a culture of law abidance and the rule of law? The answers to these questions are not easy to give. They involve issues that go beyond the scope of this chapter. Poland's position is very complex. Some of the reasons for this situation are systemic, and are inherently linked to the shape of the Polish justice system. Others are concerned with the lingering

[149] See website of the Centre, above.

[150] See the website of the Centre for more details: www.mediacja.org/info.php/o,nas,acf7f74b41b8537ff6acb85fbe5de1ce.html.

[151] 200 PLN for mediation conducted by 1 to 2 mediators, and an additional 200 PLN for recording the settlement. In cases concerning pecuniary claims, the costs are higher: 300 PLN for the first mediation session, and 200 PLN for each subsequent session. Business mediation is more costly. The website of the Centre sets out the costs in detail: www.mediacja.org/info.php/koszty,acf7f74b41b8537ff6acb85fbe5de1ce.html.

[152] Data published in *Gazeta Prawna* on 29 June 2010: prawo.gazetaprawna.pl/artykuly/432491,arbitraz_i_mediacja_staja_sie_coraz_bardziej_popularne.html.

[153] The Arbitration Tribunal of the National Commercial Chamber reported that only in the first 9 months of 2010 360 cases were brought (this is 100 more than in the entire 2008): prawo.gazetaprawna.pl/artykuly/461751,przedsiebiorcy_czesciej_korzystaja_z_arbitrazu.html.

[154] Interview with Dr R Morek of the Dispute Settlement Centre by the Law Faculty of the University of Warsaw, in Gazeta Prawna of 29 June 2010, prawo.gazetaprawna.pl/artykuly/432491,arbitraz_i_mediacja_staja_sie_coraz_bardziej_popularne.html.

state of transition from socialism and some cultural factors peculiar to Poland. There are issues concerning the increasing but still relatively weak position of regulators. There is the improving and yet overloaded civil justice system. There is the interestingly complex legal culture that, on the one hand, does not entail trust in judges and authority and, on the other hand, does not often see the possibility of obtaining justice outside the courts. The author of this chapter wrote about these factors elsewhere.[155]

What is most instructive in the context of this chapter are the problems common to EU states, and even to jurisdictions beyond the EU. Poland has had some useful experiences in this area, and it is important to point them out here, following from the analysis of ADR mechanisms conducted throughout this chapter.

The problems identified across Europe by the 'Study on the use of Alternative Dispute Resolution in the European Union' of October 2009:[156] lack of awareness of ADR mechanism, gaps in coverage, and refusal to engage in ADR procedure or to recognise decisions of ADR bodies, are no doubt prevalent in Poland. Many of those weaknesses are a result of the still to some extent proceeding transformation from socialism to democracy and market economy and are gradually disappearing. However, the Polish ADR experience so far has already demonstrated how such problems may be effectively targeted.

A growing number of civic society associations, and in particular consumer associations, working together with government actors (such as the Ministry of Justice), are able to increase awareness and indeed the reputation of ADR bodies. Coherent and well thought through regulatory requirements concerning quality of ADR, encouraging or even leading of dialogue between various actors involved in ADR, and comprehensive advertising campaigns, all done by the Ministry, have been shown to achieve this aim. The awakening of civic awareness and the belief in benefits of ADR can also contribute to closing in the gaps in coverage—another problem identified throughout Europe. Poland can indeed serve as an example of how such gaps can be identified and limited in a relatively short period of time: new mechanisms in the areas of finance, banking, telecommunications and media appeared recently and are already quite active. Some were the result of a regulatory intervention, others: business initiatives. There still remain some gaps, the most pressing of which seem to be the areas of health and social services.

As far as the latter problem: one of failure to agree to engage in ADR is concerned, here also one may draw useful suggestions from the Polish experiences. It is crucial that both sides of disputes trust the knowledge, expertise and independence of the ADR body. A number of ADR bodies in Poland, specifically the Banking Ombudsman, the Regional Consumer Ombudsmen and the Arbitration Tribunal of the Insurance Ombudsman, struggle with the lack of trust. Their attempts to improve the situation by emphasising quality of adjudication and their independence, also through dialogue with the parties concerned, appear to have already achieved some level of success. Further, it is also clear that ADR bodies which are capable of escalating the dispute or at least escalating the position of the parties through bringing cases to courts or making administrative decisions are more effective in compelling the parties to get involved in ADR. They are also much more effective in achieving settlements between the parties. The Regional Consumer Ombudsmen, albeit they have yet to fully capitalise on their powers to bring cases to court, are a good example of how this combination of powers can be utilised. The most effective

[155] See Tulibacka, 'The Ethos of the Woolf Reforms in the Transformations of Post-Socialist Civil Procedures: Case Study of Poland' (2009), 395–413.

[156] DG SANCO *Study on the use of Alternative Dispute Resolution* (2009).

manner in which such blunt refusals to engage in ADR can be tackled, however, seems to be mandatory jurisdiction of the ADR bodies – at least as far as businesses are concerned. While this solution may often appear radical, especially in relation to ADR which is still largely associated with voluntary activities, its effects are clear: especially in the operation of the Banking Ombudsman.

Poland, similarly with the rest of Europe, has great potential as regards creation of an efficient civil justice system including effective alternatives to court-administered justice. Such a system, however, requires a comprehensive approach involving the regulatory environment, the court system, ADR bodies, and civic society.

Evaluation

The architecture of consumer ADR in Poland is developing and not yet clear. In brief, there is scope for clarifying the national architecture and techniques.

The most notable aspect of the system, which is distinctive to post-socialist countries, is the role of public regulatory authorities in ADR. Thus, the regional offices of the Trade Inspection have power to conduct mediation, and the regional Consumer Arbitration Tribunals are located within the Trade Inspection's structure. This structure provides inherently complete coverage of all types of consumer disputes with all traders, and a clear national network that is accessible locally.

A second feature is that sectoral ADR bodies have developed for some major sectors, notably banking, insurance, energy and electronic communications: that feature is not surprising given the size of the Polish market.

However, the third feature introduces some confusion for consumers and businesses in accessing ADR. This is that there is no consistency between the modes of operation of different ADR systems: some use arbitration models only, some mediation, and some both. The position is somewhat confused by the fact that it is not clear whether schemes may be intended for resolution of business-to-business or consumer-to-business disputes, or both. Although some sectoral bodies can be called Ombudsmen (in energy and banking sectors) they operate differently: the Energy Ombudsman can only provide advice (and not mediate or arbitrate) whereas the Banking Ombudsman can mediate and arbitrate. Many of the ADR bodies use arbitration involving panels of three arbitrators, so they offer balanced decision-making functions, but do not adopt the more streamlined single-ombudsman models found in some other Member States. It is interesting that enforcement officials, like those of the Trade Inspection and the Head of the Office of Electronic Communications, have power to mediate in consumer disputes.

8

Slovenia

Aleš Galič and Christopher Hodges

Slovenia became a Republic on 25 June 1991. It is a small country in EU terms, with two million inhabitants, covering 20,256 square kilometres. Mediation options exist in some sectors, such as for banks and insurance. Implementation of EU legislation has introduced the idea of ADR into sectors such as telecommunications and payment services, but so far arrangements are limited. Experiments in introducing ADR into the court system date back to the late 1990s and there have been recent new approaches but results are uncertain, and cases take up to two years if not settled earlier, and involve cost and a loser pays risk.

Mediation in Business Sectors

The primary business organizations are the Chamber of Commerce, the Employers organisation, the Chamber of Enterprise (which covers smaller businesses and trades), the banks association and the insurers association. Some sectors established mediation schemes in the early 2000s. A mediation scheme for banks (*Poravnalni svet*: The conciliation council) has existed for some time in Slovenia, established by the sectoral trade organisation (Association of Slovenian Banks: *Združenje bank Slovenije*).[1] Up to 2012, if no consensual settlement was reached by mediation, a reasoned decision could be issued that is not binding for both parties. Extracts of these decisions are published on the website. The rules have been amended in 2012 and now no longer provide that the Conciliation Council is authorized to issue a non-binding decision where no consensual resolution of a dispute is reached. There is no experience yet with the new rules. Proceedings are predominantly written and no oral hearing takes place. The practical importance of the scheme is limited, as demonstrated by the fact that in 2011 26 cases were submitted to the Conciliation Council. In 2 of these cases, a settlement was reached, in 13 cases it was established that the complaint of the consumer is ill-founded, and in 10 cases the complaint was found to be at least partially well-founded.

The Law on payment services and systems[2] (which transposed, inter alia the EU Directive 2007/64/EC of 13 November 2007 on payment services in the internal market) also provides for the obligation of the providers to adopt out-of-court mechanisms for resolution of consumer disputes (Article 218). The provision aims at fulfilling the obligation from Article 80 of the Payment Services Directive and is framed in similar fashion. Thus,

[1] www.zbs-giz.si/zdruzenje-bank.asp?StructureId=371 (In Slovenian language only).

[2] Official gazette, No 58/2009.

it does not establish an ADR scheme but rather only requires the providers to do so—either individually or in cooperation with other providers. Providers may therefore jointly establish an ADR scheme.

In the insurance sector, the trade association (The Slovenian Insurance Association: *Slovensko zavarovalno združenje*) established a mediation scheme (The Mediation Centre attached to the Slovenian Insurance Association) in 2003.[3] The procedure is voluntary for the consumer (the scheme is open to all parties to insurance contracts, not only consumers) and free of charge. The scheme is voluntary for insurance companies as well, whereby the members of the trade association have declared that they will be bound 'whenever possible' to participate in an out-of-court dispute resolution procedure if the other party to the dispute initiates the mediation proceeding. In practice, however, the number of cases where insurance companies give consent for mediation in this scheme has drastically decreased in recent years. Although the Scheme is run by the sectoral trade association, insurance companies are much more willing to consent to the court-annexed mediation (see below). Since the number of cases where insurance companies give consent to the mediation in the established scheme is in reality very low, it is questionable whether the scheme effectively fulfills the obligation imposed by the Insurance Act.[4] The Act determines that insurance companies must establish an ADR mechanism for consumer disputes.[5] Furthermore it is questionable whether mediation that is merely a settlement facilitation procedure can be at all in line with the statutory requirement. The latter foresees that there should exist an ADR body that *decides* the dispute.[6] The wording that the ADR body should 'decide' the dispute would imply that a procedure should result in a reasoned (although possibly non-binding) decision.

The Law on electronic communications,[7] which transposed the EU Universal Services Directive, provides for the establishment of the Agency for postal and electronic telecommunications of the Republic of Slovenia, which is an independent regulatory body. The Agency can conduct administrative proceedings and issue administrative decisions (decrees), which are subject to judicial review in an Administrative court. The law also provides that the Agency can conduct conciliation proceedings, aimed at reaching a consensual settlement between parties in dispute.[8] Proceedings must be in accordance with the principles of impartiality, equality, equity and confidentiality.[9] The mechanism is open to all parties, not only for consumer disputes. It is entirely unclear from the text of the law what the relation is between this procedure and matters in which the Agency conducts administrative proceedings.[10] It seems that the Agency can conduct conciliation proceedings in all disputes between parties, concerning rights deriving from that law, thus including disputes for which otherwise a regular civil court of law would have jurisdiction.[11] The law provides that where such a conciliation does not result in a consensual settlement, the Agency has jurisdiction to decide a dispute with a decision,[12] unless one of the parties

[3] www.zav-zdruzenje.si/resevanje_sporov.asp.
[4] *Zakon o zavarovalništvu*, Official Gazette No. 99/2010 (Consolidated version).
[5] ibid, Art 333.a, para 1
[6] ibid, Art 333.a(2), para 2.
[7] Official Gazette 13/2007, consolidated version.
[8] ibid, Art 63.
[9] ibid, Art 63, para 3.
[10] ibid, Art 119.
[11] ibid, Art 129.
[12] ibid.

has already brought the case to the regular court. The system is rather unclear and there is no experience in practice yet. However, one can have very serious doubts, whether parties will 'play with open cards' in a conciliation procedure when they are aware that the 'conciliator' is the regulatory body, which—if conciliation fails—may decide the matter with the authority of an administrative decision. The fact that the regulatory body has a wide range of administrative and repressive powers does not make a possible comparison with the MED-ARB[13] technique well founded. The system as a whole leaves an impression that the legislator just wanted to adopt a purely formal transposition of the obligation from Article 34 of the Universal Services Directive, without paying much attention to whether the ADR system provided for would be at all effective in practice.

General Consumer Arrangements

A Consumer Protection Office existed for some years within the Ministry of the Economy but was abolished in September 2011 when the new Consumer Protection Act came into force, and its functions are taken over by the Ministry. This change was partly to save money and partly because it was felt that the Office had not been sufficiently effective. There has been debate over whether there should be an independent Consumer Agency, and whether the Consumer and Competition protection functions should be combined.

Consumers who experience problems with goods or services can contact their sellers. There is no mechanism under which trade associations might assist in responding to complaints and there are no ombudsmen for consumer-to-business disputes. The general view is that contacting the Consumer Protection Office has been ineffective.

The Consumers Association has a 20 year history and around 6,000 members. The Consumers Association hosts the ECC-Net office for Slovenia, which has four full-time staff, including a lawyer and a case handler. ECC Slovenia is funded in equal parts by the European Union and by the Slovenian Ministry of the Economy.

Consumers do contact the Consumers Association (such contacts are a major source of new members for the Association) and do contact EEC Slovenia, although its jurisdiction is only for cross-border claims: the two organisations cross-refer cases regularly, facilitated by being in the same building. The annual membership fee of the Consumers Association is €40, which buys free legal advice, a monthly magazine, and a mediation facility. In comparison, advice from a lawyer costs €100 per hour.

Statistics for EEC Slovenia in 2010 are in Table 8.1.

[13] A procedure when 'third party neutral' starts to participate in the dispute as a mediator, but if mediation fails, the same person continues to act as an arbitrator— thus with full authority to decide the case in a binding matter.

Table 8.1: Statistics for EEC Slovenia in 2010

	2010	2009
Cases received	837	754
– Requests for information	573	524
– Consumer complaints	264	230
Countries most frequently dealt with		
– Germany	43%	?
– Great Britain	15%	?
– Italy	9%	?
– Spain	9%	?
Types of cases		
– online shopping	63%	?
– in-store shopping	26%	?
– air passenger rights	15%	?
– other	13%	?
Cases successfully resolved	42%	?

The Consumer Protection Office presented a draft Alternative Resolution of Consumer Disputes Act as long ago as 2008. After some public debate, work on this draft law came to a temporary halt in the Ministry of Economy, seemingly for lack of sources in the state budget for financing the establishment of the proposed public ADR scheme. However, the draft law received critical responses from the business sector (which fears that the proposed scheme would result in further financial burdens for the economy) as well as from consumer organisations (which find it too 'trader friendly'). The fate of this draft therefore remains uncertain.

The draft act, provides for the establishment of a special public body for resolution of consumer disputes (*Razsodišče za potrošniške spore:* The Consumer Disputes Tribunal) and provides for a certain combination of a non-binding evaluation and a voluntary binding arbitration. It is foreseen that the Tribunal would, upon the request of the consumer, conduct two main types of procedures, depending on whether the trader had accepted its binding jurisdiction. In the latter case, the Tribunal can resolve a dispute with a binding decision (with effects of *res iudicata* and enforceability). Otherwise it can only render a non-binding, however written and reasoned decision (recommendation). Concerning non-binding recommendations, it is expected that they would offer guidance to both parties as an authority of argument but, if not respected, the claimant still needs to pursue the case in court or (where the evaluation is not favourable to the claimant) is not prevented from pursuing the case in court.

The Tribunal can also conduct mediation proceedings and in general, assist parties to reach settlements, provided that certain guarantees are fulfilled. A consumer cannot enter a jurisdiction agreement (which would exclude access to court) before the materialization of a dispute. This restriction is imposed because, at the time when the consumer enters into a contractual relationship, he or she usually does not pay due attention to stipulations concerning dispute settlement included in pre-formulated or general contract terms. Due consideration is given to principles of independence, effectiveness, representation and the adversarial principle (right to be heard) in relation to the course of proceedings and the organization of the Tribunal and its membership.

Certain types of consumer disputes are excluded from the jurisdiction of the Tribunal, as they are not suitable for an accelerated and simplified dispute resolution scheme, due to the complexity of the subject matter or high value of dispute. Emphasis is given to the request that, prior to seeking redress in an out of court scheme, the consumer should exhaust internal complaints mechanisms of the trader, and, on the other side, the trader is obliged to give appropriate response to the consumer's complaint and attempt to reach an amicable solution.

Decisions or extracts from decisions are to be made public, both in order to assure public scrutiny of the Tribunal's activities and public awareness of consumer rights as well as to put an additional pressure upon a trader voluntarily to fulfil the decision of the Tribunal. A system is established involving a limited right to have a decision of the Tribunal reviewed by a regular court of law where the Tribunal's decisions are binding, similar to procedures for setting aside arbitration awards.

The procedure of the Tribunal is framed in such a manner that it should enable lay parties to effectively participate without legal representation, there is a fee of €20 for procedures (reimbursable in case of at least partially successful complaint) and the system also strives to keep other costs of the proceedings low. Legal representation is possible, but not reimbursable. The proposed scheme is open for individual disputes only and not for the protection of collective interests.

The ECC Slovenia office has found it a challenge to promote ADR. It organised a conference on ADR in 2008, where the aforementioned draft act was critically assessed. The EEC office believes that if an effective national consumer ADR system could be created, this would assist both consumers and business, not only resolving disputes that go unresolved at present (the courts being too slow or expensive) but also raising business standards to levels that would be internationally competitive. Since Slovenian consumers experience levels of service provided by traders in other EU states, they increasingly expect higher standards from domestic suppliers, including better levels of responsiveness than can be provided.

The experience of the Protector of Human Rights, and also the courts, shows that if an independent dispute resolution body has no effective power, business (or government) will not pay attention to its pronouncements, and consumers will not seek to use it. The EEC-Slovenia office, for example, can undertake extensive publicity through media appearances and organising meetings, and seek to affect public opinion in general and in relation to specific traders, but coercive powers can only be exercised where cases are referred to the courts or a governmental Inspectorate.

Courts and ADR

Pilot-programmes on voluntary mediation were initiated by certain Slovenian courts as long ago as the late-1990s, and proved to be quite successful.[14] Following this experience, the Civil Procedure Act was amended in 2002 in order, for the first time, to take account of court-annexed and other mediation schemes.[15] It provided that the court is empowered to stay civil proceedings for up to three months if parties voluntarily agree to try an ADR procedure, whether out of court or court-annexed. In order to reach an in-court settlement,

[14] A Galič, 'Alternative dispute resolution in Slovenia', 6 *ADR Bulletin* 4, Art 3, available at: epublications.bond.edu.au/adr/vol6/iss4/3.

[15] A Galič, 'Slovenia' *Civil Procedure – Suppl. 49* (Wolters Kluwer, 2008).

but also to examine whether an ADR approach might be appropriate, the court can call a settlement conference (*poravnalni narok*) as a special stage in the civil procedure, following follows receipt of a reply to an action and prior to the trial.[16] A settlement conference is conducted by the judge who remains responsible for the procedure at the first instance court, who, in accordance with case management principles, tries to bring about a consensual resolution of the dispute with the parties.

The court may omit the settlement conference if:

1. the parties have already (unsuccessfully) carried out a procedure of out-of-court ADR (eg, mediation, early neutral evaluation). Mere unsuccessful negotiations between the parties without participation by a third party-neutral do not meet this requirement. The court may omit the calling of a settlement conference also,
2. if, giving consideration to the assertions contained in the action and the reply to the action and to the nature of the dispute, it decides that there is no possibility for a settlement (the latter also applies if there is a dispute concerning the rights of which the parties cannot freely dispose – in such case a settlement is not allowed – Article 3/3, CPA). However a statement of parties in the claim and the defence plea that the settlement is not possible, even if given by both parties, does not per se mean that the court shall refrain from ordering a settlement conference. The experience shows that even in such cases of initial refusal, a settlement can often be reached.3 Furthermore, the court may do the same, if
3. it evaluates that a settlement does not represent a suitable means to resolve a dispute (eg, essential actual inequality between the parties, violent disputes, precedents or pattern cases that dictate a decision on merits, an action in which the legal and factual situation is clear, evidently ill-founded claims etc.).[17]

In practice, settlement conferences do not play as important a role as it was expected. Court-annexed mediation programmes are successful (see below), but the court makes the proposal to the parties and (where they consent) refers them to mediation in an early stage of the proceedings before the settlement conference (usually the defendant is invited to give consent to the mediation upon service of the claim; if the consent is given, the court then invites the claimant to do the same). Thus, by the time a settlement conference is called, the parties have usually already been through an (unsuccessful) mediation or refused to participate in one. On the other hand, and in line with traditional role of the judge in an Austrian-based type of civil procedure, a civil judge in Slovenia undertakes an active role in assisting parties to reach settlement during the whole trial, not only in the settlement conference. The judge often openly discusses the case with parties and gives his preliminary evaluations, which, if done in appropriate manner, is not considered to be incompatible with the request of impartiality.

Mediation was further recognised by the Mediation in Civil and Commercial Matters Act 2008, which encourages the use of mediation as a voluntary procedure.[18] In 2009, Slovenia introduced the Alternative Legal Dispute Resolution Act, which provided that all Slovenian courts of first instance must offer mediation to parties from June 2010 and that by mid-2012 all higher courts must also offer mediation or another ADR method.[19] In this regard the Act relied heavily on the experience of court-annexed mediation programmes which existed in many Slovenian courts before enactment of this obligation. The Act introduced a

[16] Civil Procedure Act, Arts 305a–305c.
[17] ibid,102.
[18] Mediation in Civil and Commercial Matters Act (*Zakon o mediaciji v civilnih in gospodarskih zadevah*), Art 1.
[19] Alternative Legal Dispute Resolution Act 2009 (*Zakon o alternativnem reševanju sodnih sporov*), Art 4.

quasi-compulsory procedure with an opt-out. While the court can make an order requiring the parties to mediate,[20] any party can object. There is, however, the potential for an adverse outcome for the objecting party as the court can order a party it considers has unreasonably objected to mediation to pay all or part of the other party's costs.[21] The programmes are administered by the court; in larger courts, separate ADR offices were established for that purpose. The court provides a roster of mediators and establishes criteria for inclusion on the roster, adopts rules regarding assigning neutrals to the case and guidelines for conducting the ADR sessions.[22] Mediation sessions are held in the court. When the programmes were first introduced, most mediators were judges (who of course cannot mediate cases that are assigned to them for adjudication), but over time attorneys and retired judges were included on the roster.[23] In practice, mediation is offered to parties automatically very early in the proceedings and the invitation letter is a general one, not tailored for a case. Consent of both parties for the mediation procedure is reached in about 30 per cent of cases and about 50 per cent of mediations are successful, resulting in a settlement. Pursuant to the Act, mediators are reimbursed for their services from the state budget. In civil cases (including small-claims) the first three hours of mediation are free of charge for the parties.

Mediation has existed longest in district courts, which are courts of first instance that deal with relatively higher value disputes (today: over €20,000). Overall, mediation in civil cases is most successful in disputes concerning claims for non-contractual damages, claims from insurance contracts (including consumer contracts) and property cases. In county courts, which deal also with small-claim procedures, programmes of court-annexed mediation have been introduced only recently. Mediation is offered also in the small claims procedure, but with limited success. There are no special rules concerning mediation in small claims, which would make it even more expeditious and less formal (eg 'on the spot mediator') than in normal cases.

The downside of court-annexed mediation is that the existence and successful conduct of mediation in courts, which is almost free of charge for the parties, makes it more difficult for private ADR providers to establish their activities on a market oriented basis. Furthermore, the danger exists that the existence of court-annexed mediation schemes might result in a decreased interest in self-regulation and promotion of autonomous ADR mechanisms in important sectors of the economy. The decreasing workload of the Mediation Centre at the Slovenian Insurance Association, established by their own association, where even traders now prefer the court-annexed mediation over the scheme, shows that this concern might not be entirely without value. However, the expectation that the court-annexed ADR programmes could at least partially take over the role of genuine out-of-court ADR mechanisms, even those which are purely consensus-oriented (such as mediation), is foremost limited by the restriction that court-annexed programmes are only offered to the litigants after they have already started litigation in the court (and paid the required court fee).

Nevertheless, it can be expected that the positive experience of court-annexed mediation in Slovenia can benefit the further development of out-of-court resolution of consumer disputes. As the value, goals and position of the ADR in the justice system have been widely

[20] ibid, Art 19(1) and (2).

[21] ibid, Art 19(4) and (5).

[22] N Betetto, 'Court-based Mediation and its Place in Slovenia', in A Uzelac and CH Van Rhee (eds), *Public and Private Justice*, (Antwerpen, Intersentia, 2007), 211–223, 212.

[23] See G Ristin, 'New Legislation on Alternative Dispute Resolution in the Republic of Slovenia', 18 *Croatian Arbitration Yearbook*, (2011), 143–149.

promoted and accepted in Slovenia, both in the predominant part of the legal community as well as society in general, this forms a solid ground for the promotion of different ADR mechanisms for consumer disputes as well.

In regard to out-of court settlement of consumer disputes, the new Slovenian Arbitration Act[24], adopted in 2008 is also worth mentioning. The Act is based upon and closely follows the UNCITRAL Model Law on International Commercial Arbitration. The Act is aimed at resolving business-to-business disputes but is not restricted to such disputes and neither is it restricted to international cases. Arbitration pursuant to this Act can be used for deciding consumer disputes as well. Indeed, the Act includes a separate chapter for consumer cases and provides for certain safeguards to the benefit of the consumer which depart from the general rules of commercial arbitration (such as concerning language of proceedings, seat of arbitration, venue of hearings and scope of judicial review; Articles 44–47 of the Arbitration Act). The most important provision, however, is the restriction that the consumer may not enter an arbitration agreement (for binding arbitration) and thus waive his right of access to court prior to the materialization of the dispute. This is in line with the EU Commission Recommendation 98/257/EC.

Small Claims Procedure in Regular Courts

In cross border disputes, claimants in a Slovenian court may directly avail themselves of the European Small Claims Regulation.[25] The European small claims procedure is thus available in Slovenia, but it has practically never been used so far. Small claims proceedings are, therefore, conducted pursuant to the Slovenian Civil Procedure Act (CPA), which includes a separate chapter on small claims. The CPA, including its chapter on the small claims procedure (which is applicable if the amount in controversy does not exceed €2,000), has been extensively amended in 2008.

Regrettably, the legislator did not find much inspiration in the aforementioned EU Small Claims Regulation and did not use the opportunity to extend (at least some) positive innovations from the European small claims procedure to domestic cases as well. In general, the small claims procedure under the CPA does not significantly differ from the procedure for regular cases. It is, therefore, dubious whether it can facilitate access to justice in low value disputes and achieve the outcome that the costs and loss of time incurred by litigation shall not be disproportionate to the value of the claim. For example, proceedings are commenced with a regular and fully reasoned statement of claim, whereby the use of standard forms is neither required nor facilitated.

Unlike in Articles 15–17 of the Brussels I Regulation in regard to international jurisdiction, there are no special rules on territorial jurisdiction in the CPA, favourable for consumers, which would enable the consumer to bring an action in the place of his or her domicile. The consumer is thus required to bring an action to the court in the place of the defendant's (the trader's) domicile or the place of the trader's subsidiary or agent if the dispute arises out of its operation. Neither are there any restrictions for the possibility of entering jurisdiction agreements (in favour of the court in the place of the trader's domicile)

[24] Official Gazette No 48/2008.
[25] Regulation No 861/2007.

in consumer cases. Parties are strictly prevented from asserting new facts and evidence in the oral phase of proceedings (trial). New facts and evidence can only be adduced in the claim, the defence plea[26] and in one further written submission each.[27] True, on one hand, this system contributes to acceleration and concentration of proceedings.

On the other hand, however, since no new facts and evidence can be adduced in the trial, in which the adversarial principle is strictly adhered to and no facts and evidence can be considered and taken *ex officio*, a judge cannot really play a more active role by stimulating (with hints, questions and observations) a legally non-represented party (eg a consumer) to supplement his or her insufficient factual assertions and evidence offered in written pleadings.[28] Thus, a party's failure to state all relevant facts in the written stage of proceedings (perhaps because he or she was unaware of the legal relevance of certain facts) cannot be rectified during the discussion of the case in open court at a later stage. An active role by the judge would be necessary in cases where parties do not have the benefit of legal advice, such as is often the case in consumer disputes. The impossibility of conducting such an active role makes legal representation, although not required by the law, rather necessary in order to effectively pursue the case.

In regard to costs, the principle of 'loser pays' applies in Slovenian civil procedure. This covers the right to recovery of opponent's (necessarily occurred) attorney fees up to the limit calculated pursuant to the state lawyers' tariff. There are no exemptions from this rule for small claims. The cost risk for a weaker party (eg a consumer) in a small claims procedure is thus rather high. Not only is he or she encouraged to seek legal representation (as the court, as explained above, cannot really play an active role in proceedings), but must be aware of the risk of needing to reimburse the opponent's (eg the trader's) cost of legal representation in case of losing the case. As long as the attorney fees are calculated in accordance with the state's lawyers' tariff,[29] the court has no authority to refuse to award costs that are disproportionate to the claim. It is, however, true that reimbursable attorney fees under the state tariff are rather low for small claims (the calculation is based on the amount in controversy, not according to eg hours spent). In a typical case with a value of €1,000, the reimbursable fee would (for procedure in two instances) amount to about €200[30] Court fees, calculated in accordance to the Court Fees Act[31] would also amount to about € 200.[32] Poor litigants can seek free legal

[26] CPA, Art 451.

[27] CPA, Art 452.

[28] An active role of the decision making body is viewed as an element of the principle of effectiveness. See both the Commission Recommendation (EC) 98/257 on the principles applicable to the bodies responsible for the out-of-court settlement of consumer disputes [1998] OJ L 115, and the Commission (EC) 'Proposal for a Directive of the European Parliament and of the Council on alternative dispute resolution for consumer disputes and amending Regulation (EC) No 2006/2004 and Directive 2009/22/EC (Directive on consumer ADR)', COM (2011) 793/2, final, 29 November 2011, 4.

[29] *Zakon o odvetniški tarifi*, Official Gazette No. 67/2008. However, the system is expected to be significantly changed in the near future.

[30] Naturally, the calculation presented here does not mean that a lawyer can claim only such a fee from his client. A different agreement between the lawyer and the party is possible. The state lawyers' tariff is however applicable when it comes to a question of reimbursement of costs from the opponent. In fact, it will be practically very difficult for a party to find a lawyer who is willing to accept the case for such a low fee. In practice this often means that the party will remain legally not represented in a small claims dispute or she will need to be aware that her legal costs will not be reimbursed to a full extent to what she has paid.

[31] *Zakon o sodnih taksah* (ZST-1), Official Gazette No. 37/2008.

[32] This brings the overall cost risk in a typical small claims dispute with a value of €1,000 to an amount of about € 800, which includes the party's own and her opponent's costs. In a regular dispute for a value of €10,000 a rough estimation to the cost risk would amount to about € 800 court fees (for the first instance and appellate court's procedure) and about €1,200 attorney fees pursuant to the state lawyers' tariff. Taking into account the need to

aid pursuant to the law but it must be noted that even if a full free legal aid is granted in only covers that party's costs (her court fees and reimbursement of her lawyer's fees). If, however, the party loses the case, she remains fully and personally responsible for reimbursement of her opponent's costs (court and attorney fees).

On a more positive side, in the small claims procedure, a court may omit the oral hearing if it establishes that only law, and not the facts, are in dispute. An oral hearing can also be omitted if the court opines that the disputed facts can be established on the basis of written evidence, but only if neither of the parties has requested an oral hearing to take place. The court may not refuse such a request.[33] Evidence taking is simplified[34] in order to reduce costs and speed up the litigation, but the adversarial principle must be respected. An appeal against the judgment rendered in a small claims procedure is restricted to violations of the substantive law and to grave procedural errors, but is still always available (in case of an appeal the judgment is only enforceable after the case is decided on the appellate level). In this regard it must be noted that the possibility to appeal against the first instance court's decisions comes as a matter of a constitutional guarantee[35] and the legislator is thus not able to entirely exclude an appeal in any kind of court proceedings.

The statistics of county courts, which decide—*inter alia*—small claims disputes, do not show separate figures for small claims procedures (see Table 8.2). In any case, the duration of proceedings and existing back-logs differ greatly among particular courts. In general, however, a party cannot count on getting an enforceable decision (in a procedure involving two instances) in less than a year and a half. Mediation is offered in county courts and thus in small claims procedures as well. There are no separate statistics in that respect either.

Table 8.2: Statistics for civil litigation cases in all county courts in Slovenia

Unsolved cases as at 1.1.2010	15,202
New cases in 2010	3,864
Solved cases in 2010	4,296
Unsolved cases as at 31.12.2010	14,770

In general, Slovenia is still hampered by excessive duration of court proceedings in civil cases and by backlogs in (some) courts, although the situation has improved considerably in recent years. A typical case is, however, not finally decided until two years after the filing of the claims.

Evaluation

Mediation has a comparatively lengthy history in Slovenia within the court system, although independent 'consumer ADR' systems are relatively undeveloped. Data on the effectiveness of current arrangements are scarce, but it does not seem that, for small consumer claims,

reimburse the opponent's fees in case of losing the case, the overall cost risk is about €4,000 where both parties are legally represented.

[33] CPA, Art 454.

[34] CPA, Art 9.

[35] Art 25 of the Constitution of the Republic of Slovenia.

sectoral ADR bodies have yet been established on a basis that would attract sufficient support or custom, or that the problems of cost and duration have been overcome in the court system and associated mediation techniques.

The size of the national market means that it would not be feasible to construct a large number of sectoral ombudsmen, such as in the Netherlands or the United Kingdom.[36] A possible solution may be to create a single dispute resolution facility (perhaps a single ombudsman covering both public and private sectors), and to outsource some sectoral disputes (such as in telecoms or energy) to specialist providers located outside Slovenia.

[36] The available resources mean that the solutions that apply in relation to public and private sector functions differ from larger countries. This is illustrated by the fact that it was the EEC Slovenia office that in 2010 produced a leaflet and handbook on hazardous chemicals, an educational video on chemical safety, and a brochure on the European Small Claims procedure: these materials are produced in the United Kingdom by the Health and Safety Executive (agency) and the Courts Service of the Ministry of Justice, possibly with duplicating materials also being produced by trade associations or other bodies. See EEC Slovenia *Annual Report 2010*.

9

Spain

Iris Benöhr and Franziska Weber

Introduction

Alternative Dispute Resolution (ADR) in Spain consists of three major out-of court models – arbitration, conciliation and mediation. The most important out-of-court scheme is the comprehensive and unique arbitration system for consumer disputes,[1] which functions at national and regional level. Another peculiarity of the Spanish ADR systems is that the schemes are mainly public and free for both consumers and companies.

This chapter describes existing dispute mechanisms for consumers in Spain, focusing in particular on out-of-court schemes. Section 1 provides a general overview of the judicial system for civil litigation and highlights key regulations on consumer protection. Section 2 then outlines the existing consumer ADR options available, ie arbitration, mediation and conciliation at national and local levels. Section 3 finally indicates key consumer ADR schemes in specific sectors, including financial services and transport.

The Legal Framework and Consumer Claims within the Court System

The Spanish state is organised into a central government and 17 autonomous communities, which are divided into provinces and local authorities.[2] Based on national unity, with guarantees of autonomy for the regions,[3] the Spanish constitution determines the respective competences of the state and the communities.[4] The autonomous regions and local authorities have a range of powers to administer local affairs,[5] including dispute resolution and consumer protection services.[6]

[1] *Real Decreto* 231/2008, *por el que se regula el Sistema Arbitral de Consumo* and *Ley* 60/2003 *de Arbitraje.*

[2] L Carreras del Rincón, 'Spain', in Alexander Layton and Hugh Mercer (eds) *European Civil Practice*, vol 2 (London, Sweet & Maxwell, 2004), 500.

[3] Spanish Constitution 1978, Art 2.

[4] Carreras del Rincón, (2004), 500.

[5] *Ley* 7/1985 *Reguladora de las Bases del Régimen Local*

[6] Spanish Constitution 1978, Arts 140–142.

Importantly, Article 51 of the Spanish constitution includes a section on consumer protection. It establishes obligations on public authorities to guarantee the defence of consumers, to protect their health and safety and economic interests through effective procedures, and the promotion of education and information through consumer organisations.

The Ministry of Health, Social Policy and Equality (*Ministerio de Sanidad, Politica Social e Igualdad*) is the national body of public administration that is responsible for the promotion and support of consumer protection laws.[7]

The national authorities have competence over the administration of justice.[8] Civil procedure is mainly determined by the Spanish code of civil procedure (*Ley de Enjuiciamiento Civil,* (LEC))[9] adopted in 2001. The LEC does not provide for a particular procedure for consumer claims within the court system, so that general procedural rules apply.

The LEC distinguishes two types of proceedings, depending on the amount or type of claims involved. *Juicio verbal* proceedings are applicable for small claims not exceeding €6,000 (Articles 250.2 LEC), and *juicio ordinario* proceedings apply to claims over €6,000 (Articles 249.2 LEC).[10] While the *juicio ordinario* generally deals with more complex cases the *juicio verbal* is simpler and conceived to deal rapidly with small cases. In both types of proceedings the claimants must first submit their allegations in written form; however in the *juicio verbal* procedure this can be less detailed.[11] At the next stage, the defendant in an *ordinario* proceeding is allowed to present a written defence, whereas the *verbal* proceeding is oral and the defendant will only have to appear at the hearing.[12]

The latter type of procedure is usually more relevant for consumers, given that their claims often concern smaller amounts and will be explained in greater detail below. In the *juicio verbal* the party who does not accept the decision of the Court of First Instance is entitled to reiterate the case in the Court of Second Instance. Evidence is put forward and taken orally during the hearing in a concentrated manner, concluding with submissions by the parties.[13]

A judgment can be appealed within five days of its notification. The application for an appeal is then forwarded to the other parties who must respond within ten days.[14] Once these pleadings have been submitted, the proceedings will be transferred to a higher court, with the parties being summoned to appear before it.[15]

Particular rules apply for small claims regarding a value below €2,000,[16] which state that legal representation is not required in such cases.[17] Another specific feature of these small claims is that an application may be submitted by means of an optional standardised form.[18] These rules have been in existence since March 2011; before this they only applied for cases valued below €900. The new provisions were adopted to facilitate the application of

[7] www.consumo-inc.es/GuiaCons/leyes/RDL_1_2007.htm.
[8] Spanish Constitution 1978, Arts 117–127, and Art 149; *Ley Organica* 6/1985 *del Poder Judicial.*
[9] *Ley* 1/2000, *de Enjuiciamiento Civil.*
[10] *Ley* 13/2009 of 3 November 2009 has changed the amount of claims from € 3,000 to € 6,000.
[11] Carreras del Rincón (n 2), 513.
[12] ibid.
[13] ec.europa.eu/civiljustice/simplif_accelerat_procedures/simplif_accelerat_procedures_spa_en_claim.htm#1
[14] ibid.
[15] ibid.
[16] *Ley* 4/2011 that changed the LEC in 2011.
[17] See LEC, Art 23 (2.1).
[18] This standardized form is provided by the Court of First Instance, ec.europa.eu/civiljustice/simplif_accelerat_procedures/simplif_accelerat_procedures_spa_en_claim.htm#1.

Regulation (EC) 861/2007 of 11 July 2007, establishing a European small claims procedure in the Spanish system.[19]

Finally, Article 19 LEC states that the parties have the right to withdraw from a case or submit it for arbitration. If the parties reach a settlement, they have to appear together before the court to receive the court's approval to terminate the case.

Two types of judicial conciliation procedures exist in civil justice cases: conciliation before the formal procedure has started and conciliation during the court procedure.

Before the formal procedure has started, the Court of First Instance or the Judge of Peace can attempt to conciliate the parties under the Spanish Conciliation Act (Articles 460–480 *Ley de Enjuicimiento Civil de 1881).*[20] The conciliation procedure is initiated by the judge, who contacts the parties after the claim is brought. The plaintiff will then present the claim and the defendant will counter with the necessary documents to support the arguments. Both parties are given the possibility to respond to the other party's argument.[21] If the parties do not reach an understanding directly, the judge will try to reconcile them.[22] If this remains unsuccessful, the regular court procedure will be applicable.[23]

Once the procedure has started and the parties appear before the court, the judges will check if the dispute remains unresolved between them. If the parties have reached an agreement or are willing to conciliate or require the court to approve an agreement the court will examine the formal conditions and approve the agreement (Articles 415 LEC). The approved agreement can then be enforced by the courts. Depending on the case, the court can also ask the parties to attempt conciliation (Article 428.2 LEC 1/2000). If the parties do not reach an agreement or are not willing to conciliate, the hearing will continue as planned.

Furthermore, both collective consumer actions for damages and injunction procedures[24] can be brought before the court in Spain.

According to Article 6 and 11 LEC affected consumers as well as the consumers associations complying with national or regional legislation have a procedural standing to defend consumer rights in courts. Public bodies such as the National Consumer Institute, entities in autonomous communities dealing with consumer protection and entities from other European Member States are also allowed to file cases.[25]

Consumer associations are only permitted to bring a collective consumer claim if they comply with the provisions of Royal Decree Law 1/2007, which define and regulate consumer associations.[26] This means in particular that they must be non profit organisations included in a State Register of Consumers and Users. For instance, the Spanish Organisation

[19] See *Ley* 4/2011, *de 24 de marzo, de modificación de la Ley* 1/2000, *de 7 de enero, de Enjuiciamiento Civil, para facilitar la aplicación en España de los procesos europeos monitorio y de escasa cuantía.*

[20] These provisions remained even in force after the adoption of the LEC, see: noticias.juridicas.com/base_datos/Privado/lec.l2t1.html; see also *Ley* 13/2009, *de 3 de noviembre, de reforma de la legislación procesal para la implantación de la nueva Oficina judicial.*

[21] Leuven Study, *National Report on Spain*, 15 November 2006, 5.

[22] ibid.

[23] ibid.

[24] Directive 98/27/EC on injunctions for the protection of consumers' interest [1998].

[25] Organisations that are established for the protection of collective and diffuse interests of consumer and are included in a list published in the Official Journal.

[26] See Leuven Study, *National Report on Spain*, 2006; see also JA Fontanilla Parra, 'Legitimación de las asociaciones de consumidores y usuarios para litigar en interés de sus asociados y derecho de asistencia jurídica gratuita', *Diario La Ley* 5740, 1448–1463.

of Consumers and Users (OCU) is a major consumer association that is allowed to bring collective consumer claims.[27]

Representative collective claims can be brought in respect to a large range of consumer rights, such as unfair contract terms and breach of e-commerce regulations.

The LEC does not provide for a particular procedure for collective actions, so that the ordinary proceeding usually applies, ie *juicio ordinario* and *juicio verbal*.[28] However, LEC provides specific rules that only apply to collective action. This will not be further explained, as the focus of this chapter lies on out-of-court redress mechanisms.[29]

Overview of the ADR System in Spain

Apart from the judicial procedures various ADR mechanisms exist in Spain, including a general arbitration system for consumers and a number of specialized schemes. While the most characteristic ADR model is the system of arbitration for consumer disputes, mediation and conciliation schemes are also available throughout the country.[30]

Arbitration for Consumer-related Disputes

With the adoption of the Spanish Consumer Protection Act 1984 *(Ley* 26/1984*)* the government was obliged to set up an arbitration system specifically conceived for consumer disputes.[31] As a result, first experiences with consumer arbitration procedures were gathered in 1986 when the system started as a pilot project. In 1993 the *Real Decreto* 636/93[32] established a basic legal framework for a consumer arbitration system (*Sistema Arbitral de Consumo*). Since 2007, the current basis for the Spanish consumer arbitration system is provided in Articles 57 and 58 of the *Real Decreto Ley* 1/2007,[33] adopted with the aim of merging several Acts. This regulation, changed substantive and procedural laws concerning consumer protection.

Real Decreto Ley 1/2007 provides for an extrajudicial arbitration system for the resolution of disputes between consumers and businesses that is voluntary for the parties. This informal resolution procedure is of a general nature and can apply to most types of consumer-related disputes. However, the arbitration board is not competent to deal with disputes where a final judicial decision already exists or that requires the intervention of the public prosecutor. In particular, consumer arbitration is not permitted in cases of intoxication, injury, death or upon reasonable suspicion of a crime.[34]

[27] See BEUC The European Consumer's Organization, *Country Survey of Collective Redress Mechanisms: where does collective redress for individual damages exist?* July 2010, groupaction4consumers.eu/docs/Country%20survey_Traffic%20Lights.pdf, consulted 15 February 2012.

[28] F Gomez and M Gili, *Evaluation of the effectiveness and efficiency of collective redress mechanisms in the European Union – country report Spain* (2008, Civic Consulting).

[29] More information can be found in JC Garnica Martin, 'Las acciones de grupo en la LEC 1/2000 (I)', *Diario La Ley* 5391, 1–7; see also F Gomez and M Gili, *Evaluation* (2008).

[30] For disputes between the government and citizens specific Ombudsmen (*defensores del pueblo)* provide ADR services in the different regions and there is also a central Ombudsman at the State level.

[31] *Ley* 26/1984, *regarding consumer protection,* Art 31.

[32] Today this regulation was replaced by the *Real Decreto* 1/2007 (Arts 57 and 58) and the *Real Decreto* 231/2008 specifically regulates the consumer arbitration system.

[33] *Real Decreto Ley* 1/2007.

[34] *Real Decreto Ley* 1/2007 Art 57 (1).

Under the current framework access to arbitration is organised on a regional basis, while a National Arbitration Board is responsible for supervision. The Spanish National Consumer Institute (*Instituto Nacional del Consumo* (INC)) is responsible for the implementation, development and dissemination of the consumer arbitration system.[35] It is part of the arbitration department of the Spanish Ministry of Health, Social Policy and Equality.[36] Furthermore, the National Consumer Arbitration Board (*Junta Arbitral Nacional*) is attached to the INC. This Board contains a Committee on Consumer Arbitration Boards (*Comisión de las Juntas Arbitrales de Consumo*), which establishes uniform criteria in the arbitration system and decides on appeals against decisions of the presidents of the Consumer Arbitration Boards.[37]

The regional governments are responsible for the enforcement of consumer law in their territory. Accordingly, arbitration boards exist at municipal, provincial and regional levels.[38] INC provides legal and technical help and supports the regional arbitration boards (*juntas*) with funding. The regional arbitration boards, in turn, periodically report back to INC.

The arbitration board (*Junta Arbitral*) plays a key role in the administration of the procedure and designation of an arbitration body (*órgano arbitral*). It is this arbitration body that will assess the case and issue the award. There are at present 71 arbitration boards in Spain ranging from municipal to provincial, regional and national authorities.[39]

The *Real Decreto* 231/2008 that was enacted in 2008 defines the functions, composition and competencies of consumer arbitration boards.[40] Depending on the case, the arbitration body can be composed of a single person or three accredited arbitrators.[41] The body is designated respectively by the public administration, a consumer association and a business organisation to ensure a fair representation of interests.[42] If arbitrators violate basic principles of independence, impartiality and confidentiality they may lose their accreditation or be withdrawn.[43]

The use of the arbitration system is voluntary for the parties. The *Real Decreto* is flexible with the formalities required for the arbitral agreement to be valid.[44] The Spanish consumer arbitration system represents an important exception to the rule of the invalidity of consumer arbitration clauses agreed before a dispute has arisen.[45] According to the law, companies can officially adhere to the Spanish arbitration system by making a 'public offer' (*ofertas de adhesión*). In such a case, the arbitration agreement will be concluded between the parties by the consumer's submission of a complaint and request for arbitration. A list of the adhering traders can be found online, since the INC administers a public register of companies participating in the scheme.[46]

[35] www.consumo-inc.es/Arbitraje/home.htm.

[36] *Subdirección General de Calidad del Consumo, Subdirección General de Normativa y Arbitraje and Centro de Investigación y Control de la Calidad* (CICC).

[37] *Real Decreto* 231/2008 *por el que se regula el sistema arbitral de consumo*, Arts 9–11.

[38] ibid, Art 2(2).

[39] www.consumo-inc.es/Arbitraje/juntas.htm.

[40] For the Spanish consumer arbitration system, see F De la Rosa and G Orozco Pardo (eds), *Mediación y arbitraje de consumo, una perspectiva española, europea y comparada* (Valencia, Tirant lo Blanch, 2010).

[41] *Real Decreto* 231/2008, Arts 19–20.

[42] *Real Decreto Ley* 1/2007, Art 57(3).

[43] *Real Decreto* 231/2008, Arts 22–23.

[44] An agreement can be done in writing, by any electronic means or other legally authorized means. See *Real Decreto Ley* 1/2007, Art 58(1).

[45] See *Real Decreto Ley* 1/2007, Art 57.4, stating that an arbitration agreement concluded with a consumer other than a consumer arbitration agreement can only be entered into once the dispute has arisen.

[46] INC, *Memoria 2010* (Madrid, Instituto Nacional del Consumo, 2010), 14. There are currently about 100,000 companies registered although some might have disappeared during the financial crisis.

In some sectors, special good practice codes exist that promote the participation of companies in the arbitration system. For instance, in the the e-commerce business the traders that participate in the code *confianza online*, also agree to adhere to an arbitration procedure.[47]

Procedure

Real Decreto 231/2008 regulates in detail the arbitration procedure, from filing complaints to the final binding decision.[48] As a first step, an arbitration request form has to be filled in by a consumer, his lawyer or a consumer association.[49] It is not possible for traders to file cases at the boards. Selecting the most suitable arbitration board usually correlates to the consumer's place of residence.[50] The arbitration procedure is flexible and can be purely written or partly oral depending on the nature of the case. It can also be conducted via electronic means[51] and allows collective claims, if required.[52]

The arbitration board will first assess if the dispute can be resolved through consumer arbitration. If the company officially adheres to the arbitration system, the procedure can start right away. If this is not the case, first an acceptance request has to be sent to the company, which will be given 15 days to accept the competence of the arbitration board for the particular case.[53] Importantly, companies can adhere to the board just for a certain type of case, or part of their business. Likewise, they can register with some regional, provincial, or municipal boards whilst not registering with others.

In the second step a mediator will be appointed by the arbitration board who will try to settle the dispute.[54] This is excluded if one of the parties opposes this step or it has been established that mediation has already been unsuccessful. Mediators must be impartial, independent and have to respect the confidentiality requirements. The mediation will be carried out by someone else than the arbitrator. The recommendations by the mediator are consensus-orientated and voluntary, unlike the decision by the arbitrator that imposes a binding solution upon the parties. The mediation procedure has to be finalised within a month.

If the mediation attempt is not successful the arbitration board will nominate the arbitration body and the actual arbitration begins. Cases are dealt with by a single arbitrator if both parties agree, the dispute is simple and straightforward, and the amount in dispute is less than €300.[55] The arbiter is usually appointed by the public administration.

For all other cases three arbitrators will be designated: one by the public administration (who will act as the president) and the two others by each party (one from the consumer side, one from the company side). Under certain circumstances, for instance when it comes to doubts as to the arbitrator's impartiality, parties can agree on a different president.[56] Parties can insist on a procedure involving three arbitrators instead of a single arbitrator.

[47] See www.consumo-inc.es/Arbitraje/distintivo.jsp. For annual report 2010, see www.confianzaonline.es/confianzaonline/MEMORIA_CONFIANZA_ONLINE_2010.pdf.

[48] *Real Decreto* 231/2008, Arts 33–50.

[49] For the details of the procedure see Art 33 of the *Real Decreto* 231/2008.

[50] ibid, Art 8.

[51] ibid, Arts 51–55. The online procedure is often applied in arbitration cases.

[52] See more in J Paredes Pérez, 'La nueva Regulación del Sistema Arbitral de Consumo', in *Arbitraje Revista de arbitraje commercial y de inversiones* 1, 189–190; see also *Real Decreto* 231/2008, Arts 56–62.

[53] See *Real Decreto* 231/2008, Art 37.

[54] ibid, Art 38. The mediation services offered in Spain vary significantly throughout the country.

[55] ibid, Art 19. Prior to 2008 the decision was always to be taken by a board of three, but due to budget cuts this single arbitrator system was established.

[56] ibid, Art 20 (2).

By default all procedures and decisions are based on equity rather than law (more than 90 per cent of cases).[57] Parties can, however, unanimously opt for a procedure in law. If the procedure takes place on the basis of equity only one board member needs to have a legal degree; in case of a procedure based on law all need to be fully qualified lawyers.

There is no limit regarding the amount of money that can be claimed. The use of the arbitration mechanism is free of charge for both consumers and businesses. However, costs incurred regarding evidence have to be borne by the party submitting the evidence. Parties can submit additional evidence or alter the claim at any time before the end of the hearing.[58]

An ADR procedure will usually not take longer than six months and ends with an award that has the same value as a court judgment. This means that the award is enforceable through the courts if the trader does not comply with the arbitration decision.[59]

The compliance rate is very high; approximately only 1 per cent of traders do not comply with the awards. However, these numbers are shaped by the fact that traders with no intention to comply will not accept arbitration procedures in the first place.[60]

As with a court judgment, the parties can appeal against an arbitration decision in the courts within two months. In addition, an appeal can be brought against decisions to admit or reject requests for arbitration of consumer disputes by the *Junta Arbitral de Consumo*.[61] Those cases are reviewed by a special committee, called *Comisión de las Juntas Arbitrales de Consumo* or by the President of a *Junta Arbitral territorial.*

Despite a harmonised law procedure the arbitration boards are to a large extent independently organized and work in different ways.[62] The '*Juntas*' receive all cases of consumer complaints even though some of the boards are specialised. This specialisation is, however, not apparent to the consumer from the outside with the exception of some special *Juntas* for tourism or transport.[63]

For collective actions a unified arbitration procedure exists.[64] If a larger number of similar cases occur the *Junta* that has to be put in charge is that located where most of the victims reside. If they are widespread, the *Junta Nacional* will be responsible. So far, there has only been one case, and the trader did not accept the arbitration request for this case. In a collective arbitration case the claimants have to join the procedures from the beginning.[65]

[57] ibid, Art 33. See also, *Sistema Arbitral de Consumo, Annual Report 2007* (Madrid, Sistema Arbitral de Consumo, 2007), 23. In 2007 out of 18,653 awards, 93.8% were decided in a procedure based on equity and thus 6.2% in a procedure based on law.

[58] See Arts 43–45.

[59] This procedure might conflict with the principle of self-representation in courts, which sets a limit of €2,000. In a court case up to €2,000 consumers do not need a legal representative; if, however, the claims value of the ADR award is higher they would need representation when enforcing the award through the court. This appears to be very costly for cases involving a claim value of more than €2,000 and might dilute incentives to follow this procedure. Some courts construe this to mean that ADR cases will never need to involve legal representation and thus despite a higher value than €2,000 no legal representation is needed when enforcing the award through the courts.

[60] Interview with OCU's officials, 16 November 2011.

[61] See *Real Decreto* 231/2008, Art 36.

[62] Note that only some of them have their own homepage: Example: Cataluña, www.consum.cat/index_es.html; An overview of the existing boards and addresses can be found at: www.consumo-inc.es/Arbitraje/juntas.htm.

[63] The special *juntas de transporte* have been created in all autonomous regions. Their key legal bases are: *Ley* 16/1987, *de Ordenación de los Transportes Terrestres*, Art 37 and 38, modified by the *Ley* 29/2003; the *Reglamento* of this Law, approved by the *Real Decreto* 1211/1990, Arts 6–12; *Orden de 30 de marzo de 2001 por la que se establecen normas para la realización por las Juntas Arbitrales del Transporte de funciones de depósito y enajenación de mercancías*. *Juntas de turismo* also exist in various autonomous regions.

[64] *Real Decreto* 231/2008, Arts 56–62.

[65] In contrast, in a collective court case the parties are allowed to join the case at a later stage of the procedure.

Financing and Data

The ADR system in Spain is financed by the government, and is free to both consumers and traders. The Spanish National Institute of Consumer Affairs grants €900,000 of funding to the system.[66] The main share of the funding comes from the municipalities or the regions in which each board is situated and no comprehensive data is available on this.

The vast majority of complaints occur in the telecommunications sector, of which many companies are registered with the arbitration board.[67] Companies in the financial sector do not generally register with the boards, and insurance or airplane companies are very reluctant to register with the boards.

Due to the diffuse nature of the system the overall costs are not known, but on average a procedure costs above €400.[68]

The last public annual report dates back to 2007 in which 61,759 applications were filed. The number of personnel varies depending on the specific board.

More recent data suggests that the average value of an award in 2010 throughout the country was €366. In 2010 92,355 applications for arbitration were received by the system overall, which confirms the rising trend since 2007.

20,302 of the cases were resolved at the mediation phase. Awards were made in 33,849 cases, of which 22,216 were in favour of the consumer, 9,568 against the consumer and 2,065 resolved by conciliation. In 16,573 complaints, the arbitration procedure could not be started because of non-acceptance by the trader, for which most occurred in relation to mobile phones (1,439) and fixed phones (1,211).

The most complained-about sector was telecommunications, with 68.24 per cent (63,029) of all applications comprising 38,284 applications filed over mobile phones (38,284 in which traders adhered, 2,322 about non-adhering traders of which 1,439 were rejected by the traders), fixed phones (13,674 adhering and 1,193 non-adhering traders, of which 1,211 of the latter were rejected) and internet providers (6,159 adhering and 1,397 non-adhering traders, of which 773 of the latter were rejected).

In more than 50 per cent of cases the applications were brought directly by consumers, 38.74 per cent by consumers associations, and 5.93 per cent by public bodies. Only 4,912 of the total number of applications were directed to companies that were not registered with the ADR system.

In 2010 in total 33,849 awards were pronounced out of which 65.68 per cent totally or partially in favour of the consumer. The remaining cases were decided against the consumers or still settled in a mediation procedure.

[66] *Instituto Nacional del Consumo, Annual report 2010* (Madrid, Instituto Nacional del Consumo, 2010), 14; see also www.consumo-inc.es/Arbitraje/docs/resolucionConvocatoria2010.pdf.

[67] In addition a customer contact point exists, called *Oficina de Atención al Usuario de Telecomunicaciones* (OAUT) within the SETSI, which resolves telecommunication-related disputes and provides information. Consumers can contact this body if a company does not adhere to the ADR system or if the end user is a company, which tries to solve the dispute within 6 months and the outcome can only be challenged through the administrative courts. See *Real Decreto* 1554/2004 that develops the basic institutional structure of the Ministry of Industry, Tourism and Trade, Art 8.3. See *Ley* 32/2003, Art 38.

[68] Interview with ICN's officials, 15 November 2011, Madrid.

Mediation and Conciliation

Mediation and conciliation procedures are also available to resolve consumer disputes out-of-court, but are given less attention in the Spanish civil justice system. As explained above conciliation can occur within or outside a court procedure and mediation can take place in the context of an arbitration procedure.[69] Nevertheless, a comprehensive national framework regulating consumer mediation is missing, as the autonomous regions often adopt their specific provisions. The legal framework regarding mediation is however, currently changing due to the impact of the EU Directive on mediation in civil and commercial matters adopted in 2008. Spanish legislation implementing this measure has already been approved by government but is not yet in force.[70]

Consumer associations or chambers of commerce play a key role in the mediation and conciliation procedures. They often offer mediation and conciliation services in the autonomous regions without distinguishing clearly between both types of ADR.[71] In Spain 11 major consumer associations exist.[72] Some of these associations receive funding from the Spanish National Institute of Consumer Affairs, which is part of the Ministry of Health, Social Policy and Equality.[73] Others are financed via membership fees and projects such as OCU (a major consumer organisation), FACUA—a regional consumer association with headquarters in Sevilla—or AUC, a specialized consumer association for the communications sector.[74]

For example, the Spanish consumer organization OCU only offers a mediation service to its members, who pay membership fees. OCU's mediation procedures have doubled over the last years.[75] While there were 4,321 procedures in 2008 and 5,239 in 2009; a large number of 8113 procedures were managed in 2010. A mediation procedure on average takes 1.5 months. In 2010, 52 per cent of the cases were solved in a satisfactory manner, in 17 per cent no response was given and the remaining 31 per cent did not result in a dispute resolution.

[69] *Royal Decree* 231/2008, Art 38.

[70] European Directive (EC) 2008/52 on certain aspects of mediation in civil and commercial matters, [2008] OJ L 136/3.

[71] See conclusions of a recent study on mediation for Cataluña: www.llibreblancmediacio.com/phpfiles/public/WBDownloadCounter.php (the rest of the study is only available in Spanish).

[72] For more information on the associations see ec.europa.eu/consumers/overview/country_profile/ES_web_country_profile.pdf.

[73] In 2010 the total amount was €3,641,140.00, for a more detailed description of which amounts went to which association see: *Instituto Nacional del Consumo, Annual report* (2010), 14.

[74] There are only two specialized consumer associations operating in the country: AUC and *Asociacion de Usuarios de Bancos Cajas y Seguros* an association in the banking sector (www.adicae.net).

[75] OCU meeting 16 November 2011.

Figure 9.1: The mediation process managed by OCU

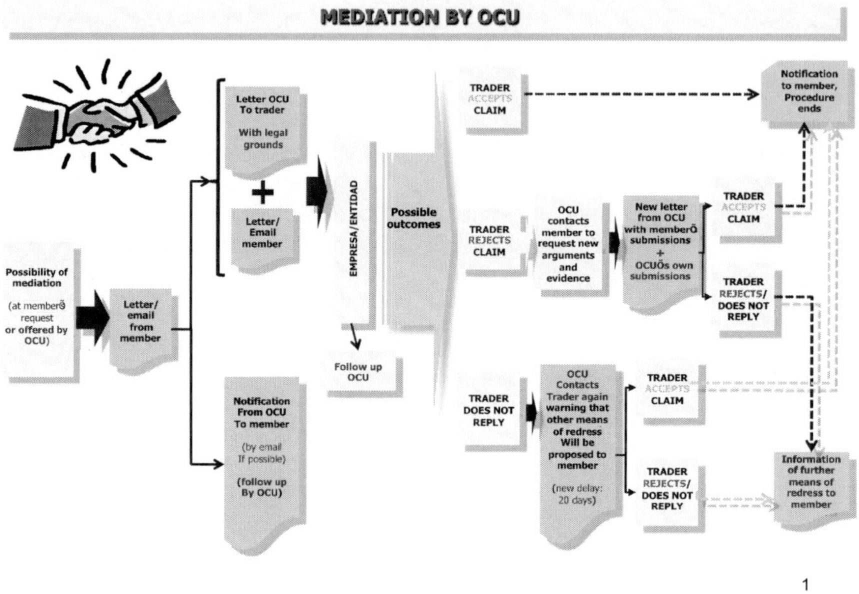

Consumer associations in Spain often also educate and inform consumers, including issues on ADR. In addition, information centres have been established for consumers at local and higher governmental level.[76] These centres are consumer service points provided by the government, which sometimes also offer mediation.[77]

No legal concept of conciliation exists in Spain.[78] In the broad sense, conciliation covers any form of agreement to solve a conflict.[79] In the narrower sense it covers situations in which two parties appear before a third party in order to avoid litigation. Extra-judicial conciliation takes place before a body established by law or by custom and is also called preventive or pre-procedural dispute resolution. Where there is a successful conciliation, it is guided by the ordinary means of interpreting general contract law. Mediation and conciliation are similar as they both aim at eliminating the dispute and take place before non-judicial bodies. The outcome has the same value as a private agreement between parties. However, an important difference is that mediation necessarily requires the existence of a mediation procedure while conciliation does not.[80]

[76] OMIC (*Oficinas Municipales de Informacion del Consumidor*), see: aplicaciones.consumo-inc.es/cidoc/Consultas/dirMapas.aspx?tabla=omic for an overview of all OMIC.

[77] In addition, in various sectors customer services centers have been established some of which employ company internal Ombudsmen, meeting of the authors with Alicia Menéndez González, Director of the Arbitration Department at the Spanish National Institute on Consumer Affairs and Secretary of the National Arbitration Board (Jefe del Área de Arbitraje del Instituto Nacional de Consumo y Secretaria de la Junta Arbitral Nacional).

[78] M Blanco Carrasco, *Mediación y Consumidores* (Madrid, ICN, 2005) 45.

[79] Judicial conciliation is explained above in this chapter.

[80] While the conciliator has usually a more passive role, the mediator is active.

ADR in Specific Sectors

The Complaints Services for Financial Services Disputes

In the financial sector three specialised institutions are competent to resolve consumer-related disputes out-of-court. These schemes provide alternative dispute resolution for consumers to the arbitration and court system. Depending on the kind of claim the following institutions are responsible for resolving a financial services dispute: the Spanish Central Bank (*Banco de España*), the Directorate General of Insurance and Pension Funds (*Dirección General de Seguros y Fondos de Pensiones*),[81] and the Investors Office of the National Stock Exchange Commission (*Comisión Nacional del Mercado de Valores* (CNMV)).[82]

While the three authorities, providing complaints services are independent from each other, they act as a singly entry point for claims. This means they are obliged to assess their competence for a claim and forward it to the appropriate authorities in case they are not directly competent for a specific case.[83]

All three financial institutions follow similar procedures and requirements in their ADR schemes, which are free of charge for both parties. The ADR schemes have been influenced by a number of Spanish regulations that required the state to provide out-of-court procedures for consumers in financial services from 2002 onwards.[84] The Spanish Act 44/2002 introduced a measure to reform the financial system and in particular provided rules to strengthen the protection of financial services users.[85] In addition, Order ECO/734/2004 provided detailed provisions about the departments, consumer help services, and defenders of consumers in financial entities.

The Claims Service of the Spanish Central Bank

The Claims Service of the Spanish Central Bank (*Servicio de Reclamaciones del Banco de España*, hereafter the 'Bank') aims to resolve disputes by users of financial institutions supervised by the Bank. This Service is independent and operates on the principle of transparency, efficiency, legality, freedom, representation and the adversarial principle.[86]

Established in 1987, it was based on and influenced by the Spanish Ministerial Order (1987) concerning codes of practice of credit entities and the Ministerial Order (1989) about codes of practice, providing information to consumers, and publicity of credit entities.[87]

The Claims Service provides dispute resolution support and advice to financial services users. On the one hand, it assesses claims related to breaches of the transparency and consumer law or best financial practices by a financial institution.[88] On the other hand, it

[81] see www.dgsfp.meh.es/reclamaciones/index.asp.

[82] www.cnmv.es/PortalInversor/section.aspx?hid=20.

[83] www.bde.es/webbde/en/secciones/servicio/reclama/reclama.html.

[84] *Ley* 44/2002 *Medidas de Reforma del Sistema Financiero*; *Real Decreto* 303/2004 by which the rules for the commissioners that defend users of financial services are approved; *Real Decreto* 1/2007 which contains the General Law for the Defense of Consumers and other complementary laws; and the *Ley* 22/2007 about telemarketing of financial services.

[85] *Ley* 44/2002 *Medidas de Reforma del Sistema Financiero.*

[86] ibid.

[87] The Claims Service was also influence by the Circular letter 8/1990 of 7 September concerning transparency while conducting operations and consumer protection.

[88] www.bde.es/webbde/en/secciones/servicio/reclama/reclama.html.

deals with enquiries about applicable legislation on matters of transparency and customer protection.[89]

Approximately 30 employees work for the Claims Service, which is divided into three sections: the General Secretariat; the Report Unit; and the Advice Unit, containing a call centre.[90]

Consumers or organisations of financial services users representing consumer or group interests have the standing to file a case with the Claims Service. The claimants can be Spanish or foreign, but must be correctly identified and authorized as users of banking services.[91]

A complaint may be lodged at the Claims Service against a large range of financial services institutions, including:

- Credit institutions authorised to operate in Spain, which includes banks, savings banks, the Official Credit Institute (ICO), the Spanish Confederation of Savings Banks (CECA), credit co-operatives and specialised credit institutions.
- Valuation companies.
- Currency exchange establishments authorised to sell foreign banknotes and travellers' cheques or to make international transfers.
- Payment institutions.[92]

Before lodging a claim, the claimant should have tried to resolve the issue directly with the Customer Care Department or Customer's Ombudsman of the financial institution in question.

By law, all institutions supervised by the Bank are obliged to have a Customer Care Department or optionally a Customer's Ombudsman.[93] After formal verification of the established in house schemes, the Bank publishes a list with the names and contact details of all the Customer Care Departments and Customer's Ombudsmen that are available to claimants in Spain.[94]

If the consumer contacts the customer services section of the financial institution in writing they have to acknowledge receipt of the claim and provide a written reply with the reasons for their decision. The claimant can then file the case with the Bank's Claims Service, by proving that the request has been rejected or that two months have passed since it was filed and it remains unresolved.[95]

A claim may be refused by the Banks' Claims Service among others, if the claim relates to issues within the jurisdiction of administrative, arbitration or judicial bodies. Furthermore, a claim cannot be admitted if it repeats previous claims or if the time limit within which a claim may be made or action taken has elapsed. Importantly, as to the kind of complaints,

[89] The Claims Services Advice Unit has an assistance and consultation function, serving as an informal reference point providing information and opinions regarding financial services matters, see: www.bde.es/webbde/en/secciones/servicio/reclama/reclama.html.

[90] Interview with officials of the Spanish Central Bank, 16 November 2011, Madrid.

[91] If a financial institution belongs to another European Union country claims may be introduced through FIN-NET, a European network solving cross-border financial disputes, see the description of FIN-NET in the EU chapter of this book.

[92] www.bde.es/webbde/en/secciones/servicio/reclama/gen_contra.html.

[93] Spanish law: Orden ECO/734/2004, de 11 de marzo.

[94] In the case of credit institutions, electronic money institutions and payment entities, the Bank also publishes their regulations, see www.bde.es/webbde/en/secciones/servicio/attcliente/attcliente.html.

[95] www.bde.es/webbde/en/secciones/servicio/reclama/gen_cuando.html.

the Claims Service of the Bank is not empowered to evaluate damages nor may it issue decisions about amounts awarded as compensation.[96]

A claim against a financial service entity may be filed in two ways: either online or by using an official form provided by the Bank. The claim may be presented directly to the General Registry of the Bank or to any of its branch offices, or sent by post to the Claims Service.[97]

Once the claim is admitted, the financial institution has 15 working days to submit its allegations. The arguments are then assessed by the Bank. Interestingly, the Bank can assess a case only on the basis of the law, not on principles of equity.[98]

The procedure may be terminated early if the financial institution recognises the claimant's allegations or if the claimant voluntarily withdraws the claim. If this is not the case, the Claims Service issues a reasoned report for the parties. This report is of a voluntary nature and is thus not an administrative ruling that can be appealed.

If the report is unfavorable for the defendant, the financial services entity has to inform the Claims Service whether it is willing to accept the decision and then comply with it accordingly.[99] Where the financial entity decides not to comply with the Bank's report, the Claims Service cannot impose a sanction, but may inform the supervisory department of the Bank of any legal violations. As a result, the supervisory department may then start an investigation and impose administrative sanctions if deemed necessary. However, this scenario does not happen very often.

The Spanish court and the Bank sometimes mutually influence each other in their decision-making process. The court may consult reports made by the Bank, whereas the Claims Service has been inspired by the courts' case law when taking decisions on cases. In specific cases the courts may require the Bank to provide an expert opinion on a technical question. Conversely, the Bank can refer a case to the court regarding questions on evidence and for specific unresolved legal questions.[100]

The Bank aims to improve transparency on market practices in the financial sector in order to promote consumer information and protection. It publishes a detailed annual report on the amount of complaints and compliance rate by the financial institutions to boost best practice.

In 2010 the Claims Service received 14,760 new complaints, compared to 13,640 in 2009. Since 2001 there has been a continuous increase in complaints, with a particularly high increase in 2009 and 2010. During 2010, 84.1 per cent of claims were submitted by individuals, 15.3 per cent by companies and 0.6 per cent by others, including public institutions.[101]

In 2010 the Claims Service also received 3,368 requests for advice through their virtual platform and 29,529 information requests by telephone.[102]

The average duration of a complaint procedure is between four and six months from the date of submission.

[96] www.bde.es/webbde/en/secciones/servicio/reclama/gen_supuestos.html.
[97] www.bde.es/webbde/en/secciones/servicio/reclama/gen_como.html.
[98] Interview by the authors with officials of Central Bank's Claim Service, 16 November 2011, Madrid.
[99] www.bde.es/webbde/en/secciones/servicio/reclama/gen_como_tra.html.
[100] Interview by the authors with officials of Central Bank's Claim Service, 16 November 2011, Madrid.
[101] Data from the Bank's Annual Report 2010, *Memoria del Servicio de Reclamaciones Banco de Espana* 2010.
[102] Data from the Bank's Annual Report 2010, *Memoria del Servicio de Reclamaciones Banco de Espana* 2010.

Complaints Service of the Directorate General of Insurance and Pension Funds

The Spanish Directorate General of Insurance and Pension Funds (*Dirección General de Seguros y Fondos de Pensiones*: IPF)[103] manages financial services-related complaints and provides legal advice to consumers. This out-of-court disputes service was established after the adoption of Spanish Law 44/2002 regarding measures to reform the financial system in 2002.

The complaints service of the IPF consists of approximately 35 employees that provide consultations and assess complaints free of charge. These complaints must relate to insurance contracts and pension plans issued by insurance entities, companies specializing in pension funds' management, and insurance mediators.[104]

A case can in particular be revised to highlight irregularities in the financial services provided by corporate entities. Those irregularities could be caused by delays or any other type of behavior, with the exception of a request for repayment or restitution. Furthermore, complaints can be submitted when actions or omissions by financial organizations have caused damage to financial users' interests or rights. This damage can be due to lack of compliance with contracts, transparency regulations and consumer protection or good practices.

Individuals or organizations that are entitled to make a complaint and ask for consultations include:

- Insurance takers
- Beneficiaries
- Damaged third parties or their representatives
- Participants and beneficiaries of pension plans
- Associations and organizations which represent legitimate collective interests of users of financial services.[105]

The complaints procedure contains the following steps. First, the complaint is submitted to the Directorate General of the IPF (either on paper or digitally). For a claim to be admitted, the claimants must prove that he unsuccessfully attempted to solve the problem directly with the financial services company. This means that at least two months must have passed with no response or the claim must have been dismissed by the financial services provider. The IPF will then contact the parties within ten working days. A copy of the complaint is sent to the financial service provider so that it can provide an answer within 15 working days. Once the answer from the relevant organisation is received, it will be sent to the claimant for comments within 15 working days.

The case will finally be concluded with a reasoned decision by the IPF, based on the law rather than equity. In its recommendation, the IPF will state if the financial service organisation has breached the regulations on insurance and pension plans or violated the principles of good practices and financial customs. However, the IPF never evaluates the economic damages that a company might have caused.[106]

[103] www.dgsfp.meh.es/reclamaciones/index.asp.

[104] See www.dgsfp.meh.es/reclamaciones/index.asp.

[105] Besides, the Information Offices and Services for Consumers and Users are also authorized to present consultations, see www.dgsfp.meh.es/reclamaciones/index.asp.

[106] See www.dgsfp.meh.es/reclamaciones/index.asp.

Since this recommendation is not an administrative act; it is not binding and can be followed by the parties on a voluntary basis. Therefore, no appeal is possible against such a decision. The parties will be informed of the decision by the IPF within ten working days, starting from the date of issuance. The entire procedure has to be terminated within four months of the date of submission of the claim.

Besides the dispute resolution services, the IPF also provides advice and information to financial services users regarding their rights. However, consultations over the interpretation of laws or regulations cannot be put forward. In such a case a formal claim has to be submitted.

The Annual Report of the IPF[107] shows that in 2010 a total of 9,574 requests and complaints applications were resolved. This means that there has been an increase in complaints compared to the previous year. From this total number of applications, 5,702 were admitted as complaints, from which 2,231 were decided in favour of the financial services institution, whereas 1,882 of the cases were decided in favour of the claimants. The remaining cases were terminated in other forms.

Investors Department of the *National Stock Exchange Commission*

The National Stock Exchange Commission *(Comisión Nacional del Mercado de Valores* (CNMV)) is the agency in charge of supervising and inspecting the actors in the Spanish Stock Markets. It was created by the Spanish Securities Market Law, which instituted in-depth reforms of this segment of the Spanish financial system.[108] Law 37/1998 updated the aforementioned Law and established a regulatory framework that is in line with the requirements of the European Union.[109]

The CNMV aims to ensure the transparency of the Spanish market and the correct formation of prices to protect investors.[110] The Investor Assistance Office (*Oficina de Atención al Inversor*)[111] provides a public ADR scheme free of charge that is established by law and is part of the legal department of CNMV. It offers both claims management services and practical advice to investors and is permitted to handle investors' complaints filed in relation with the activities it supervises.[112]

In order to be admitted by the Investor Assistance Office a complaint should firstly be submitted directly to the client service or ombudsman of the financial institution to which they refer. The financial intermediaries are obliged to inform the public about the existence and function of these services. If the claimant does not receive a reply within two months of the filing of a complaint or if the case is not resolved, they can bring a complaint to the CNMV.[113] The average duration of the ADR procedure is four months.

The Investor Assistance Office issues a non binding recommendation, which cannot include any economic evaluations regarding damages to the users of financial services.

Given that procedure of the CNMV is similar to the ADR scheme provided by the Bank outlined above, it will not be described further here.[114]

[107] www.dgsfp.meh.es/sector/documentos/Informes%202010/Informe%20Servicio%20Reclamaciones%202010.pdf.

[108] www.cnmv.es/portal/quees/Funciones/Funciones.aspx?lang=en.

[109] ibid.

[110] ibid.

[111] www.cnmv.es/PortalInversor/section.aspx?hid=20.

[112] CNMV, *Annual Report 2010* (2010, CNMV, Madrid) 177, www.cnmv.es/portal/Publicaciones/Informes.aspx.

[113] ibid.

[114] ibid.

The data from the Annual Report of the CNMV shows a gradual increase of complaints. Between 2008 and 2009 the complaints have doubled, which is also due to the financial crises. In 2010 2,296 complaints were filed by the CNMV and 1,774 were resolved.[115]

Table 9.1: Processed complaints by type of resolution

	2008		2009		2010		
	Number	% of total	Number	% of total	Number	% of total	% change 10/09
Resolved	722	80	823	72	1,774	85	116
Report favourable to claimant	226	25	292	25	807	39	176
Report unfavourable to claimant	365	41	255	22	534	26	111
Report without decision	10	1	57	5	154	7	170
Resolved by mutual agreement	112	13	198	17	241	12	63
Complaint withdrawn	9	1	21	2	32	2	52
Unresolved	177	20	314	28	313	15	0
Competence of other authorities	41	5	86	8	128	6	49
Not accepted	136	15	228	20	185	9	-19
Total complaints handled	899	100	1,137	100	2,087	100	84
Pro memoria							
Total filed	1,058		2,154		2,296		7

Source: CNMV.

Transport Arbitration Boards

Specialised arbitration boards (*juntas de transporte*) exist within the transport sector which are independent of the general consumer arbitration system.[116] Every autonomous region in Spain has one transport arbitration board,[117] whereas the coordination of the arbitration system is ensured by the *Departamento de Prensa de la Consejería de Transportes e Infraestructuras*.[118]

The competence of the boards covers road transportations, railways, buses, cars, taxis, metros, trains, trams, and funiculars—whether urban, interurban or international. Arbitration boards decide on both disputes between consumers and traders and disputes between traders. Transport cases can involve a large range of actors such as operators, loaders and users of land transport (eg passengers, car rental and goods). The transport arbitration board is also entitled to handle the storage, valuation and auctioning of goods that are not paid for by the recipient and store-rejected goods. However, it cannot decide on disputes regarding air transport, for which claims should be brought to the general arbitration system.[119]

[115] ibid.

[116] The key legal acts are: *Ley 16/1987, de 30 de julio, de Ordenación de los Transportes Terrestres, Arts 37–38, (BOE del 31 de julio), modificada por la Ley 29/2003, de 8 de octubre; El Reglamento de esta Ley, aprobado por Real Decreto 1211/1990, de 28 de septiembre, Arts 6–12, (BOE del 8 de octubre); Orden de 30 de marzo de 2001 por la que se establecen normas para la realización por las Juntas Arbitrales del Transporte de funciones de depósito y enajenación de mercancías (BOE del 14 de abril).*

[117] Interview with officials of ICN, 15 November 2011, Madrid.

[118] In turn, the *Consejero de Transportes e Infraestructuras* is responsible for the development and monitoring of the government's transport policy. *Ley* 1/1983, Art 41.

[119] www.madrid.org/cs/Satellite?c=CM_InfPractica_FA&cid=1109168011158&idConsejeria=1109266187248&idListConsj=1109265444710&language=es&pagename=ComunidadMadrid%2FEstructura&sm=1109265843983.

The territorial competence of the board is based on the place of origin or destination of the transport. Jurisdication can be based on the place where the contract has been concluded, or at the arbitration board's location that both parties voluntarily accept.

Generally, the boards intervene in cases involving up to €6,000, but they can also act when the case exceeds that level if the parties agree.[120] The procedure starts with a written complaint, which can be submitted online and is similar to the general arbitration procedure.[121] The parties will then receive an invitation to a hearing, for which no legal representation is required. In the hearing the parties make their allegations and adduce the evidence. The board will pronounce its award within a maximum of six months from the day following the hearing. The legal value of the award is, as in the ordinary consumer arbitration, final and binding and enforceable on almost equal terms to a judicial decision.

In 2010 2,175 arbitration requests were made and 925 awards were issued,[122] which are published online.[123] Generally, the transport arbitration board seems to work effectively, and has been evaluated positively by the consumer organisations.[124]

The Energy Customer Ombudsman

In the energy sector no specialised consumer arbitration boards exist.[125] Consequently, consumers can usually choose between two key ADR options to solve disputes: the general public arbitration scheme or a private scheme.

The public consumer arbitration boards are available for all types of consumer related disputes and have been described before.[126] They can resolve disputes when both parties agree to the procedure and the arbiter's decisions are binding. However, the companies in the energy sector are generally reluctant to adhere to these arbitration boards,[127] so that they are of little practical use in this area.[128] While new European legislation requires Member States to establish a single contact point for consumer complaints in the energy sector, this has not yet been set up in Spain.[129]

Alternatively, a private ADR scheme is provided by ENDESA (*Empresa Nacional de Electricidad, S.A.),* the largest electric utility company in Spain.[130] Complaints can be

[120] www.fomento.es/mfom/lang_castellano/direcciones_generales/transporte_por_carretera/servicios_transportista/juntas_arbitrales/.

[121] The arbitration procedure is set out in *Ley* 16/1987, de 30 de julio, de Ordenación de los Transportes Terrestres y por el *Real Decreto* 1211/1990, *por el que se aprueba el Reglamento de desarrollo de dicha Ley*. See also among others *Ley* 36/1988 on arbitration, and *Real Decreto* 42/1991 that establishes the *Juntas Arbitrales del Transporte de Madrid*.

[122] E-mail communication with Ignacio Pérez Pérez (Jefe de Servicio de Juntas Arbitrales), 15 November 2011.

[123] www.madrid.org/lauj/run/j/BusquedaLaudos.icm.

[124] The major Spanish consumer association OCU reported that they receive few complaints about transport, which indicates that the arbitration system is working satisfactorily. Interview with officials of OCU, 16 November 2011, Madrid.

[125] The public regulator at state level is the National Energy Commission (*Comisión Nacional de Energía* – CNE). For consumers a CNE customer contact point was established, where they can obtain information and are forwarded to the competent body to solve their disputes. See www.cne.es/cne/contenido.jsp?id_nodo=375&&&keyword=&auditoria=F.

[126] See this chapter p 214.

[127] See conversation with OCU's officials, 12 December 2011; interview by the authors to ICN's officials, 15 November 2011, Madrid. ENDESA, for instance, adheres to the Board in Cataluña.

[128] According to the CCU, arbitration in the energy sector is non-existent.CCU annual report 2010, 126.

[129] ibid, 126.

[130] http://www.endesa.com/en/aboutEndesa/ourStrategy/Paginas/Home.aspx.

submitted to ENDESA's 'Customer Ombudsman', established since 2002.[131] This Ombudsman resolves complaints from ENDESA's customers who have previously contacted the client services department and are not satisfied with its response or have not received an answer within two months.[132] However, the Ombudsman cannot act if a consumer has previously opted for any other dispute resolution route to solve the case (eg judicial).

The Ombudsman is designated by the Board of Directors of the Company and has a duty to provide feedback and recommendations to the Board with proposals for improving the quality of the customer services. Yet, the Ombudsman is independent from the company's management and has his/her own budget and team.[133] In the assessment of a case the Ombudsman is required to remain impartial and has to respect principles of independence and fairness.[134]

After receiving a complaint, the Ombudsman starts a mediation procedure. He/she analyses all the documentation received and may organise a meeting between the customer and representatives from the company, in order to reach a mediation agreement.[135] If no amicable solution is found the Ombudsman issues a written resolution, which is binding on the company but voluntary for the customer.[136] ENDESA has agreed to automatically accept resolutions issued by the Customer Ombudsman and must comply with the decision within a 30 day period starting the day after the customer expressly accepts the agreement.

The dispute resolution procedure takes on average two months and is free of charge for the customer.

ENDESA is the only energy company in Spain with an Ombudsman and is a member of the European Energy Ombudsman Group (EEOG), which is an independent non-profit organization made up of the Ombudsmen of the main energy companies in the European Union.[137] The EEOG aims at ensuring consumer protection and at promoting mediation between companies and consumers, fostering good practice in customer services.[138]

Every year the Costumer Ombudsman presents a Memorandum detailing his recommendations to ENDESA's CEO and Board of Directors and to the relevant bodies representing clients.

In 2010 the Costumer Ombudsman's office received a total of 2,104 complaints, of which 1,182 fell within the Ombudsman's direct remit. The complaints in 2010 were concerned with billing (36 per cent), the quality of supply (21 per cent), contracts (14 per cent), meter readings (13 per cent) and the collection of payments and others (8 per cent). 89 per cent of the complaints were resolved satisfactorily, with 80 per cent resolved by mediation between the customer and the company, 18 per cent resolved via a resolution by the Ombudsman and the remaining 2 per cent resolved by other means.[139]

The Customer Satisfaction Index for the ENDESA Ombudsman generally displays a high score, averaging 8.1 out of 10 across various categories in 2010. As a private scheme it has the advantage of having direct access to information from within the company.[140] However,

[131] See ENDESA, *Annual Report 2010 Activities* (2011, ENDESA).

[132] http://www.energyombudsmen.com/spain.html.

[133] http://www.defensordelcliente.endesa.es/defcl/quien_es.jsf.

[134] www.defensordelcliente.endesa.es/defcl/index.jsf.

[135] http://www.energyombudsmen.com/documentsmembres/ENDESA_Spain.pdf.

[136] Customers remain free to bring the case to the court or to the public arbitration system: see http://www.energyombudsmen.com/documentsmembres/ENDESA_Spain.pdf.

[137] See for a list of participants, www.energyombudsmen.com.

[138] http://www.defensordelcliente.endesa.es/defcl/datosArticulos.jsf.

[139] ENDESA, *Sustainability report 2010* (ENDESA, 2011), 60; see also *Annual report* (ENDESA, 2011), 69.

[140] Information from ENDESA, October 2011.

the fact that it is an internal unit of the company is unavoidably a matter of concern from the point of view of impartiality. The scheme is limited in scope to ENDESA's clients.

Conclusions

Spain contains a distinct alternative dispute resolution system at national and local level, which consists of three general out-of-court models – arbitration, mediation and conciliation. Arbitration is the main out-of-court redress model established for consumer related disputes, which is applicable to all sectors with a few exceptions. Specialised ADR schemes exist in areas such as electronic trade, financial services and transport.

The arbitration system is well developed and effectively functions in general in many areas of consumer law. The large number of cases in which decisions were formulated in favour of consumers suggests that the ADR system is in fact consumer friendly.[141] However, the adherence to the arbitration system is voluntary and does not work when the parties do not agree to the procedures. Traders can adhere to the system *ex ante* for all cases or only some issues or accept arbitration on an *ad hoc* basis. This might lead to confusion, as companies do not always make their partial adherence to the arbitration system sufficiently clear when they advertise it to consumers. Furthermore, past experience has shown large differences of effectiveness depending on the specific sector. While in sectors such as telecommunications the arbitration system deals with many cases and seems to work effectively, in others such as the air transport, energy or insurance arbitration remains underdeveloped. The reason is often that companies in these sectors remain reluctant to agree to resolve their disputes via arbitration.

Therefore, other alternative dispute resolution mechanisms remain important in Spain – such as small claims procedures, mediation and conciliation – to provide consumers with inexpensive and easy redress. Consumers are in general reluctant to file cases with the court because of the complicated formal procedure.[142]

Mediation and conciliation procedures play a significant role in resolving consumer disputes out of court. These schemes are often offered by consumer associations or chambers of commerce that help to resolve disputes before arbitration or court procedures are initiated. However, at present a comprehensive legal framework regulating in particular consumer mediation is missing.

In-house dispute resolution services also sometimes exist in specific companies or consumer sectors, which are provided by costumer services or company ombudsmen. These might offer valuable support to resolve problems informally between traders and consumers, but sometimes raise concern regarding impartiality. In particular sectors, such as the energy sector, they provide de facto the only available option to resolve disputes out of court.

Finally, another aspect of the Spanish consumer law enforcement landscape is that public authorities often have sanctioning powers. Their existence and the threat of a sanction can put pressure on traders to settle consumer disputes out-of-court. Here the effectiveness

[141] The numbers have to be read with caution since only in very clear cases might consumers be encouraged to go to the ADR board.

[142] ec.europa.eu/consumers/consumer_empowerment/docs/report_eurobarometer_342_en.pdf.

again depends on the sector. While in the telecommunications the system seems to works well, in the energy sector the different public authorities in the independent regions work in a rather uncoordinated fashion and produce sometimes contradictory results.

10

Sweden

FRANZISKA WEBER, CHRISTOPHER HODGES AND NAOMI CREUTZFELDT-BANDA

Introduction

Swedish consumer policy is based on providing consumers with access to advice both before and, where necessary, after transactions, to enable consumers to make the right choices. Most municipalities have local consumer advisers, and four complaints bureaux exist, covering banking and financial services, insurance, telecommunications and electricity. The standard path for resolving disputes is for consumers to be directed first to talk directly with traders, then to contact local or sectoral consumer advisers before referring any unresolved complaint to ADR.

The ADR system is comprehensive, developed, and widely used; the courts have almost no function for C2B disputes. A range of ADR Boards exist for specific types of injuries or sectors. The National Board for Consumer Disputes (ARN) is the comprehensive catch-all option, which is a public authority that functions like a court, well-known and widely used. Almost all of the ADR bodies are free to users. The ARN is funded by the state. It has thirteen specialist chambers. It takes 5 to 6 months to deliver a recommendation in a case, which is not binding but is highly likely to be observed by the parties. ARN decisions are published and a consumer magazine uses the data to publish the names of traders who do not comply with ARN decisions, which is given wide publicity and provides a strong incentive for business compliance. Consumers may still go to court, but rarely do so:[1] the objective would usually be to sue after obtaining an ADR decision in the limited number of instances where a trader has not implemented one.

The Policy of Prioritising Consumer Advice

Successive governments have emphasized the importance of providing local consumer advice in documents on consumer policy,[2] on the basis that many consumer issues relate to having adequate information and pre- and post-sale advice. The first points of access are local Consumer Advice Centres (*konsumentvägledare*),[3] which exist in 266 of the 290

[1] A Bakardjieva-Engelbrekt, *Sweden National Report*, (2006), 1, available at http://ec.europa.eu/consumers/redress_cons/collective_redress_en.htm.

[2] See Prop. 2000/01:135; Ds 2004:51; cf. Prop. 2005/06:1.

[3] www.konsumentverket.se/sv/Personlig-Radgivning. The local consumer advisors have their own organization, *Konsumentvägledarnas Förening*. The number of municipalities with consumer advisers was 235 out of 288 in 1994, and 254 out of 290 in 2004.

municipalities (*kommuner*) in Sweden, and employ expert staff, many on a part-time basis. Municipalities are required by law to have finance and debt advisers, although employing consumer advisers is voluntary. Some municipalities have recently chosen to 'buy' consumer advice services from other municipalities. The consumer experts have good knowledge of local traders and markets, and good links with many traders, which can be used to support consumers so as to sort out issues that arise. The local Advice Centres always start by advising consumers to discuss problems with traders direct. If necessary, the Advice Centre may use its position and links with traders to mediate informally.

The Swedish Consumer Agency (*Konsumentverket*) is the central point for consumer issues and advice. It works closely with the ECC-SE office, *Konsument Europa* (see below), the ECC being a unit within the Consumer Agency. Information on consumer law and rights is provided on various official websites, notably by the Consumer Agency,[4] Konsument Europa[5] and by advice bureaux and trade associations. In recognition of the fact that the requirements of consumer and regulatory law can be complex, and a challenge for businesses (especially SMEs) as well as consumers to understand, the ARN is launching in 2012 part of its website aimed specifically at businesses to explain legal requirements. The objective is to increase compliance and prevent disputes arising.

The four major business sectors maintain their own national advice Bureaux, which provide free advice on problems and also to the local Consumer Advice Centres. The sectors are insurance,[6] banking and financial services,[7] electricity supply[8] and telecoms.[9] The Bureaux are governed collaboratively by government and the trade associations concerned, although the sector formally owns them and pays all the costs. They all have websites giving information and refer consumers who have a problem with their supplier to first contact the company. The Bureaux can provide the consumer with guidance and information how to deal with the problem, such as information about relevant legislation and how it is applied by companies. The Bureaux offer conciliation between consumers and companies but do not offer other ADR functions themselves, but would refer consumers who have not resolved their problems with companies to refer consumers initially to the in-house Consumer Ombudsmen that exist within many large companies.

If a dispute is not resolved by these informal means, the advisers would always promote sectoral ADR schemes, where they exist, or refer consumers to the ARN, the National Board for Consumer Disputes, since it has comprehensive jurisdiction for any type of

[4] www.konsumentverket.se.

[5] ibid.

[6] *Konsumenternas försäkringsbyrå*, see http://www.konsumentverket.se/kopa/Konsumentbyraerna/Konsumenternas-forsakringsbyra. This Bureau may attempt to conciliate disputes between policyholders and their insurance companies, free of charge. Its principals are the Swedish Consumer Agency, the Financial Supervisory Authority and the Swedish Insurance Federation.

[7] *Konsumenternas bank- och finansbyrå*, see http://bankforsakring.konsumenternas.se. This Bureau is financed by the Swedish Bankers Association, the Swedish Mutual Fund Association and the Swedish Association of Securities Dealers; the Bureau's Board of Directors also includes representatives of the Swedish Financial Supervisory Agency and the Swedish Consumer Agency.

[8] *Konsumenternas elrådgivningsbyrå*. www.konsumenternas.se. This Bureau's principals are the three authorities Swedish Consumer Agency, Swedish Energy Agency and the Energy Markets Inspectorate together with the electricity industry organization Svensk Energi (Swedenergy).

[9] *Telekområdgivarna, see www.telekomradgivarna.se.* This Bureau is owned by the Swedish IT and Telecom Industry Association and is financed by the telecom, TV and Internet operators who have chosen to support the agency. Its Board also includes representatives of the National Post and Telecom Agency and the Swedish Consumer Agency. The authorities and industry representatives have an equal number of votes on the Board, and one of the state authorities has the casting vote if this is necessary to facilitate a decision on the bureau's operations.

consumer dispute. The sectoral Boards comprise independent members who represent all those interested: most of the members are lawyers. They function well, and therefore such disputes are rarely brought to the ARN. Sectors that contain smaller businesses are less likely to have sectoral dispute resolution schemes, so the comprehensive coverage afforded by the ARN is an advantage.

Private Sector ADR

There is a large number of private consumer redress schemes organized by individual companies, by business associations in certain sectors of industry and trade, or working across industry sectors. In 2006, there were at least 45 such schemes, varying from in-house company ombudsmen, consultative and advisory boards, dispute settlement boards, and ethical boards.[10] There is a wide variation in the number of cases attracted by sectoral boards: some attract few claims.[11] Johansson commented that in addition to resolving disputes, sectoral boards: 'also inform on the legal practice of the [ARN] and of the Swedish courts. They effectively work as, figuratively speaking, a filter for the dispute settlement bodies and thus contribute to lessen the workload of the courts and the [ARN].'[12]

Three examples are given below of sectoral structures, which illustrate different configurations of prioritising advice from an expert Bureau, in-house ombudsmen, and specific ADR bodies, and their relationships with the ARN. Another example of a sectoral ADR is that of the trade association for real estate agents.[13]

Financial Services

Banks and the Swedish Consumers' Banking & Finance Bureau[14] provide advice to retail customers and others on any finance issue. The Bureau is particularly active, and provides advice on products, standard terms and prices. It has around eight employees, who are mostly lawyers. It operates a phone advice line every weekday morning, and accepts questions by email or letter. In 2010 the Bureau received approximately 6,000 contacts.

This sector relies primarily on in-house complaint schemes, and does not have its own ADR body. Guidelines of the Swedish financial supervisory authority (*Finansinspektionen*, FI) require the institutions under its supervision to establish satisfactory consumer complaint management, including an in-house Consumer Ombudsman.[15] Consumers who wish to raise issues are first directed to the bank's Customer Relations Department, which

[10] A Bakardjieva-Engelbrekt, *Sweden National Report*, (2006), 3.

[11] Bakardjieva-Engelbrekt (n 1), 4. Note that in 2002 the cases settled by Boards for plumbers were 3, driving schools 25, undertakers 4, coin traders 0, hotel and restaurants 15–20, and heating pumps 40.

[12] T Johansson, 'Alternative dispute resolution in Sweden – The National Board for Consumer Complaints at a glance' (ARN, 2009), paper on file with the authors.

[13] The Real Estate Market Board (*Fastighetsmarknadens reklamationsnämndt*: FRN) handles disputes between eg a buyer/seller and a real estate agent/agency, also between buyers and sellers. Where a consumer succeeds in the case brought here, the trader's liability insurer has agreed to pay the compensation awarded. If the trader then raises the dispute in court, it will not be allowed to be indemnified under the legal expenses insurance included in its liability insurance.

[14] http://bankforsakring.konsumenternas.se/Sidfot/Om-oss/In-English.

[15] The latest guidelines are dated 29 November 2002 (FFFS 2002:23).

is headed by the internal Ombudsman. In a large bank, that Department might comprise about 10 people. Statistics are not published but the banks believe that many issues are solved at that stage, against the background that unsatisfied consumers may always bring a claim in the ARN—provided the claim is worth over SEK 2,000.

The FI and the Swedish Banking Association recommend that consumers turn to ARN if the consumers are dissatisfied with a company's response. The financial sector is fully supportive of the ARN, and has a high rate of compliance with ARN's recommendations (94 per cent in 2011: the remaining 6 per cent are believed to be smaller companies that are not members of the trade association). It is very rare that a customer would bring a court case: this occurs sometimes for customers with high net worth who complain about losses on securities.

It is notable that the number of financial complaints that reach the ARN is noticeably small (480 in 2010, 427 in 2011) and consumers succeeded in being awarded compensation in only 18 per cent of cases in 2011.[16] A survey of Swedish consumers' confidence in traders rates banking highly, second only to healthcare.[17]

Insurance

Extensive information and advice is provided to consumers by the Swedish Consumers Insurance Bureau (KFB). It has twelve employees, and receives 13,000 inquiries a year, 80 per cent of which relate to insurance claims and 20 per cent other questions, such as requesting pre-contract advice. The KFB is active in the market, trying to reach customers and provide authoritative information and advice. It will advise on competing contract terms and price issues. When it receives details about a dispute, the KFB will attempt to conciliate a settlement.

Some of the insurance companies have in-house committees that review disputes with a view to reaching settlement with the claimant.[18] Most also have Customer Ombudsmen,[19] some of whom are located in companies separately from Customer Relations Departments or in-house complaints settlement boards,[20] and some of whom are not. The Ombudsmen have often previously occupied senior positions within a company before being appointed as Ombudsmen. Although they are usually appointed from company staff, their function is to adopt a pro-consumer advocacy stance from within, and they are viewed as acting independently and voicing strong opinions about how the company should treat consumers so as to be fair.

[16] www.arn.se/Om-oss/Statistik.

[17] Svenskt Kvalitetsindex, available at www.kvalitetsindex.se/images/stories/Results/2010/press_ekonomin_11.pdf.

[18] An FI guideline requires companies to have complaints officers, who tend to have separate regulatory functions.

[19] *Kundombudsmannen Folksam. Kundsombudsmannen och kundpanelen (If); Kundombudsmannen (Länsförsäkringar I Stockholm).*

[20] eg *Försäkringsnämnden (Trygghansa).* The company If, has operated an interesting two-tier complaint scheme involving Customer Ombudsman and Customer Panel. Complaints could be made to one of five *Kundombudsmäh*, who were under the supervision of the Board of Directors of the company but organizationally independent from the company's operative activity. A review of their decisions could be requested from a *Kundpanelen*, comprised of eight members, of which six were ordinary. If customers without experience in insurance matters, and the other two were a lawyer and a representative of the company who also administers the files. *Kundpanelen* can also deal with certain issues without prior handling by *Kundombudsmannen*, for instance complaints concerning the company's marketing.

If disputes are not resolved by companies, there are two statutory and five voluntary other ADR entities that may decide any case that has been rejected by an insurance company that has agreed that such cases may be so considered. All are free to consumers. All of these Boards are owned by the Swedish Insurance Association, but are operated independently and free to make their own decisions, each under an independent Chair, who is a senior current or former judge. The Boards issue non-binding recommendations, almost all of which (in practice 100 per cent) are followed by the insurance company members. Cases are considered in writing, by five people: the Chair, two members representing customer interests and two insurance experts. Expert external medical experts may also be asked to contribute. Together, the Boards handle a total of around 1,800 cases a year.

The Swedish Insurance ADR is not notified to the European Commission because it is fully financed by the industry. However, it is widely regarded (including by officials) as operating rapidly, independently, impartially and objectively,[21] and to fill an important gap given the limited competence of ARN in disputes involving medical expertise.[22] This is partly because of the high standing of the chairs (respected judges) and of the involvement of consumer representatives. Their details are as follows.

The Road Traffic Injuries Commission

The Road Traffic Injuries Commission (*Trafikskadenämnden*) and the Patient Injuries Commission are established by law and hence mandatory for all insurance companies. The Road Traffic Injuries Commission was created in 1936 in order to bring consistency to awards of compensation.[23] Under the Traffic Insurance Decree,[24] all insurance companies that provide traffic insurance must 'maintain and pay for' a road traffic injuries commission. The regulations require that the Commission's task is to work for 'fair and uniform' compensation,[25] that the Chairman is appointed by the Government, and that its regulations must be approved by the government. The Commission comprises 68 people, in three groups: six deputy Chairmen and their substitutes (all judges) appointed by the Financial Supervisory Authority; thirteen representatives of insurance companies and substitutes, appointed by the Financial Supervisory Authority on the recommendation of the Swedish Association of Traffic Insurance; 13 lay representatives and substitutes, appointed by the Financial Supervisory Authority on the recommendation of the labour market's organizations. Every case is decided by a panel of six, comprising two from each of the above three groups. The secretariat has 20 employees, 17 of whom are lawyers, who present cases to the meetings of the Commission and write up the recommendations.

An injured person has a choice of going to court or to the Commission. The Commission must hear certain cases, before the victim and insurance company reach agreement, if the case is not heard in court:

[21] Bakardjieva-Engelbrekt (n 1), 4.

[22] L Heuman, *Reklamationsnämnder och försäkringsnämnder*, (Stockholm, Norstedt & Söner Förlag, 1980); 14 *Konsumentpolitik i en ny tid* (SOU 1994:14), 119.

[23] A similar scheme exists in Finland.

[24] *Trafikförsäkringsförordningen.*

[25] Traffic Injuries Commission Regulations, s 1.

(a) where there is medical disability of 10 per cent or more; or annual loss of income of approx. SEK 22,000 (the sum being connected to the Swedish consumer price index); loss of support; or retrial (on certain conditions).[26]

(b) where the victim asks for the Commission's recommendation.[27]

The Commission issues about 5,000 recommendations a year. It also annually publishes compensation tables, which are used by courts and the Lawyers Association, and recommendations on special matters. It applies tort law, and therefore the principle of full compensation for relevant losses. The Commission applies decisions of the Supreme Court. Any court may require the Commission to issue a recommendation on a compensation issue.[28] The Commission takes three to five months to process claims.

Decisions are not binding, but are accepted in 99 per cent of cases. Companies are required to inform the Commission if they do not follow a decision, but it is not known how many do not tell the Commission this.

The Patient Insurance

Sweden created a distinctive system for investigating and compensating medical accidents in 1975,[29] which was copied with some variations by other Nordic States.[30] Compensation is paid where an injury[31] was avoidable.[32] Unavoidable personal injuries caused by pharmaceuticals are compensated by a similar scheme funded by the pharmaceutical manufacturers.[33]

The Patient Insurance system provides 'no blame' compensation, and the National Board of Health and Welfare deals separately with aspects of professional standards and discipline.[34] Policy-makers believe that this system has created a basis for increased confidence and openness between medical staff and patients. This is illustrated by the fact that 60 to 80 per cent of cases reported to Patient Insurance, the physician, nurse or social worker involved helped the patient report the matter—rather than trying to cover it up or not accept that it happened.

[26] ibid, s 3.

[27] ibid, s 4.

[28] ibid, s 2.

[29] A voluntary scheme was introduced in 1975, which covered 99% of claims, and was extended by law to full coverage in under the Patient Injury Act (1996:799). See www.patientforsakring.se/Articl;es-in-English.html. See generally U Hellbacher, C Espersson and H Johansson, *Patient Injury Compensation for Healthcare-Related Injuries* (Visby, 2007).

[30] Finland 1987; Norway provisional rules in 1988, law in 2003; Denmark 1992; and Iceland in 2001.

[31] Both physical and mental injuries are compensated, as is defined economic and non-economic losses, and death expenses.

[32] Compensation is paid if the injury is caused by medical treatment, and could have been avoided either by a different performance of the chosen procedure or by adopting some other procedure that, according to a retrospective medical assessment by an experienced specialist, would have satusfied the need for treatment in a less risky way. The rarity or severity of the injury are irrelevant.

[33] www.lakemedelsforsakringen.se/default.aspx?id=16720. See C Hodges, 'Nordic Compensation Schemes for Drug Injuries' (2006) *J Consumer Policy* 29, 143–175; J Dute, MG Faure and H Koziol (eds), *Tort and Insurance Law: No-fault compensation in the Health Care Sector* vol 8 (New York, Springer, 2004). The drug scheme was introduced in 1978.

[34] Until 2011, this was the Health and Medical Care Liability Board. In 2010 it received 4,500 complaints, and issued 400 reprimands.

Most healthcare in Sweden (perhaps 95 per cent) is public, funded by county councils. Patients pay only SEK 100 a day to public providers for any kind of treatment, from a minor procedure to a triple heart bypass. Every healthcare provider (ie clinic, not individual) is required to purchase patient insurance. The insurance companies are affiliated to the Patient Insurance Association. If such insurance is not held, the Patient Insurance Association will itself investigate and compensate the injury, thereby guaranteeing cover, and reclaim sums paid from the caregiver. Councils pay insurance premiums of SEK 135 per inhabitant.

Independent Patient Advisory Committees exist in every region that help patients who run into problems by offering information and advice: they receive 25,000 contacts a year.[35] Patients usually register a claim with a social worker in each clinic, who sends notifications to the relevant insurance company. A claim adjuster (usually a lawyer or nurse) appointed by the insurer will investigate the facts from the records, usually obtaining an opinion from a relevant medical expert, who is a member of a panel of around 90 specialists. The patient merely has to say that he or she has an injury: unlike a legal claim, it is not necessary to make any allegation of causation or fault, nor to provide evidence. A claim to the Patient Insurance is completely free to the patient. The cost of Patient Insurance is around €900 per claim, compared with an estimated €22,000 per court case.

If the patient is unsatisfied with the insurance company's response, he or she may refer the claim to the Patient Claims Panel operated by the Patient Insurance Association (or to court). The Panel consists of a chairperson and six other members. The Chairman must be, or must have served as, a regular judge. Three of the other members represent the interests of the patients, one must be a medical expert, one must be familiar with the personal injury settlement process of the insurers, and one must have special knowledge of health care activities. The Panel's opinion differs from that of the insurer in about 10 per cent of cases. The questions considered by the Panel are predominantly highly technical, and are resolved by applying combined medico-legal expertise. Some grey areas arise, in which case the Panel tends to err on the side of a patient.

Around 12,000 claims are made a year, of which around 6,000 patients are compensated. The Panel receives around 1,100 claims, of which 110 are awarded compensation: the courts receive around 10 cases a year of which perhaps two succeed. The Patient Insurance system resolves 50 per cent of claims within 6 months, and 80 per cent within 12 months. The types of claims are shown in Table 10.1. The most expensive claims are those involving brain-damaged infants: of 100,000 babies born each year, around 30 claims are made for birth-related brain injuries, of which 12 cases are compensated as avoidable, and the total compensation comprises 20 per cent of that awarded in the 6,000 total annual cases.

Table 10.1: Types of patient insurance claims: average 1997–2001

Specialty	**Percentage of claims**	**Percentage of costs**
Orthopaedic surgery	21	23
General surgery	15	13
Obstatrics & gynaecology	8	25
District care	9	7
Dental clinics	11	2

[35] From 2010, the Patient Safety Act requires hospitals to inform patients of the system. The intention has been to make the system more well-known and open: a similar change in Denmark, where notifications can be made anonymously, resulted in a dramatic increase in claims.

A major reason why the Patient Insurance system is economic is that its awards are subsidiary to benefits paid by the national welfare system. Thus, the general welfare system provides 80 per cent of salary during sick leave and 64 percent of salary if early retirement occurs because of illness for income up to €32,000 a year. The Patient Insurance only pays amounts over those levels, on the basis of the damages that would be awarded in court under the Tort Liability Act. The cost is €7 per claim per inhabitant per year, with administration costs taking 20 per cent of the total.

Voluntary Insurance Boards

There are five ADR Boards that are established voluntarily by the insurance sector. These are:

- The Board for Insurance of Persons (PFN). This deals with disputes involving terms and conditions and claims adjustments for life assurance, accident insurance and sickness insurance, provided the dispute involves a medical assessment. Only the consumer can start the procedure, and must apply in writing. The insurance company is required to provide a written response, which is sent to the consumer for comment. There are around 850 cases a year, and the Board recommends a change in the company's decision in about 5 per cent of cases.
- The Board for Bodily Injury Liability Insurance (APN). This reviews cases of serious bodily injuries. Under its rules, it is compulsory for ascribing companies to consult the APN (unless the claimant has a legal representative who agrees with the insurance company that the process is unnecessary) before making a decision, whenever a case involves medical disability of 10 per cent or more, a specified yearly loss of income (SEK 22,000 in 2012), compensation for loss of financial support, re-evaluations of agreed cases where facts have changed, or if the claimant so requests on any other issue. The APN also provides opinions to courts, the ARN or authorities where requested to do so. It handles around 200 cases a year, and recommends a change in about 20 per cent of insurance companies' decisions.
- The Board for Legal Protection Issues (FNR). This issues recommendations on disputes involving (a) the extent of a legal and traffic insurance policy and the right to claim for damages under such policies, and (b) the suitability of a legal representative chosen by a customer when the insurance company objects to the representative. The claimant has to apply in writing. Around 60 cases a year are handled, and the Board recommends a change in about 20 per cent of cases.
- The Insurance Appeal procedure concerning an attorney's suitability (POL).
- The Attorney Cost Board (OKN).

Disputes that are not resolved at the above stages may be dealt with by the ARN. However, the existence of the advice and insurance ADR bodies means that many cases do not reach the ARN (which handled 849 insurance cases in 2012).

Telecoms

As with other sectors, customer complaints may be directed at companies, who have in-house Customer Relations Departments (only one provider has an in-house Ombudsman).

The Authority (PTS) can receive complaints, and takes note of their content in relation to provider and market behaviour, but cannot advise or resolve them. Instead, an impartial sectoral advice Bureau, called Telecom Advisors, was created in 2006, to provide advice and conciliation.[36] There were various reasons for this. Firstly, the authorities perceived there to be low standards of service by providers. Secondly, the ARN was excluded from accepting complaints from small businesses, which had many problems similar to consumers (especially around aggressive marketing) but were not able to rely on the extensive consumer rights and could not afford to go to court. Thirdly, providers themselves were dissatisfied with the fact that consumers who were frustrated by their inability to have problems resolved tended to go to the media, which created bad publicity for the industry even if they had acted correctly. Fourthly, the ARN has the ability to process telecom complaints, but over a threshold of SEK 1,000, and many customers have problems below that limit: many are young, and the financial impact on them can be significant. Fifthly, the ARN procedure is mainly written, and some telecom complaints needed oral evidence.

Telecom Advisors is owned by the Swedish IT and Telecom Industry Association, and its Board also includes representatives of the National Post and Telecom Agency and the Swedish Consumer Agency. In contrast to the Bureaux for other sectors, Telecom Advisors is funded by (currently eleven) operators under bilateral agreements, so it spends a lot of time negotiating and collecting fees, and not all of the smaller providers fund it.

Telecom Advisors' website gets around 100,000 hits a year. The number of complaints it received from 2001 to 2011 is shown in Figure 10.1. Telecom Advisors adopts a policy of positive conciliation, by telling both sides which one they expect to win or lose a case when looking at it as an impartial organisation. An increase in complaints in 2010 was caused by accepting cases relating to television.

Figure 10.1: Contacts received by Telecom Advisors 2007–2011 (cases per year)

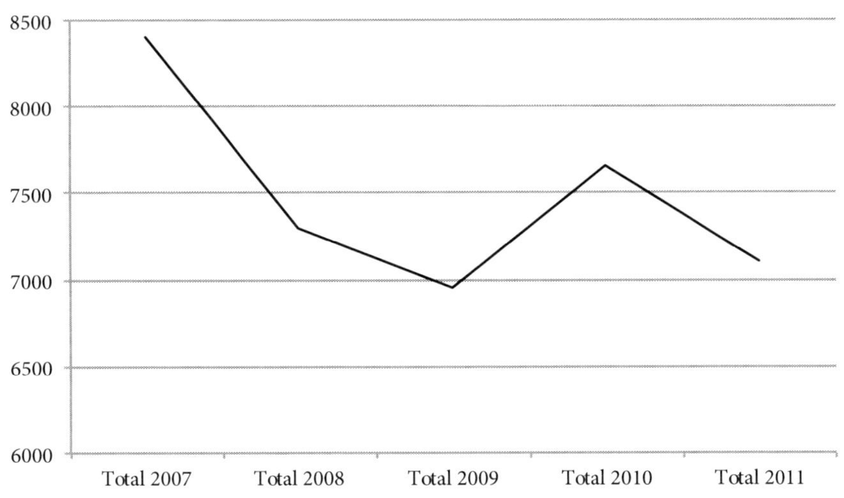

[36] It comprises 8 employees (a CEO, 6 lawyers and 1 communicator). See telekomradgivarna.se and Facebook.

In comparison, the number of complaints received by the Authority has fallen considerably since 2000, as shown in Figure 10.2. In 2011, roughly 700 complaints related to mobile telephony, 350 to mobile, 300 to internet and 80 to other services.

Figure 10.2: Contacts received by Telecom Advisers 2005–2011

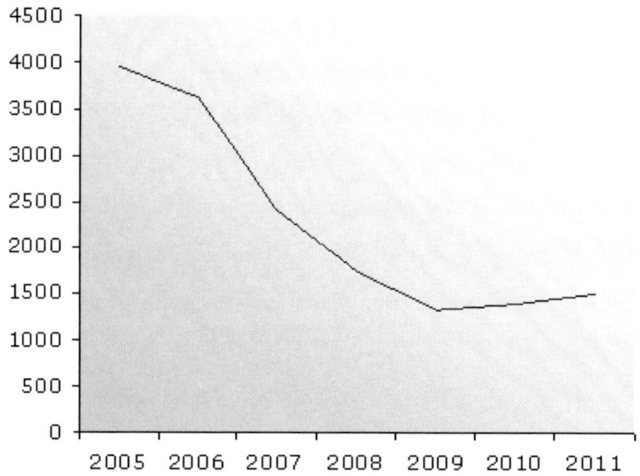

Telecom Advisors has a strong role in providing feedback. It publishes the general common statistics on complaints and their subject matter, and provides providers' individual statistics to them (but is not permitted to inform PTS or others of the individual statistics).

Telecom Advisors arranges regular meetings with operators, organisations and authorities, individually and together, to discuss trends and issues, and to find constructive solutions to consumer problems that occur on a larger scale. Providers currently find that Customer Relations is one of their largest costs: there is therefore some interest in improving performance on both service levels and complaint handling. The Swedish Quality Index does not rank telecom providers particularly highly (around 67 per cent in 2011), although they have increased slightly since 2005.[37]

Telecom Advisors considers that is has achieved a number of useful outcomes in market practice. One change has been over marketing of broadband speeds, which used to be one of the most complained about issues (together with complaint handling). Advertised speeds were maximum speeds, and not only was that not made clear, speeds delivered were often some way below. After Telecom Advisors raised this issue, providers changed to advertising minimum speeds, and have found that they are now making money out of providing good levels of service.

Other changes have been introduction of a code of conduct on information when new contracts are agreed; agreement on information when number portability fails; a 30 per cent decrease in consumer debts relating to mobile telephony after a joint project with The Swedish Enforcement Authority and the operators. PTS has noted that there has also been a decrease since 2000 in aggressive call centres, especially those of small new operators trying to win market share. This is attributed partly to the activity of Telecom Advisors and partly because a problem in modem hijacking reduced.

[37] http://www.epsi-uk.org:80.

There has also been a fall in the number of telecoms cases dealt with by ARN. Providers have found that since Telecom Advisors became able to handle complaints, they win more cases in the ARN, because issues are raised earlier with providers through the Telecom Advisors route, so can be dealt with more promptly, and by the time some consumers complain, the providers have changed their practices.

The National Board for Consumer Disputes

Structure

The Swedish National Board for Consumer Disputes (*Allmänna reklamationsnämnden*: ARN)[38] is the body at the apex of the national approach to settlement of consumer-to-business dispute.[39] ARN was established in 1968 as a quasi-adjudicatory body, although the idea originated in the 1950s. It was originally attached to the Swedish Consumer Agency but since 1981 has functioned as an independent public authority, financed from the state budget. Issues over breaches of consumer protection law, such as unfair commercial practices or advertising rules, are referred to the Consumer Agency. Its legal mandate from 2008 is established in Regulation 2007:1041.[40]

ARN's principal task is to settle disputes between consumers and traders or businesses arising out of goods, services or other utilities provided to the consumer. It also has a number of other important tasks: to provide opinions on consumer disputes at the request of courts; to support the municipal consumer counselling service in its handling of disputes by providing education and information; and to inform consumers and businesses about the Board's case-law. The information function has been seen as increasingly important, and in 2011 the ARN made a number of changes to its website, discussed below. Since the ARN is a national body established by statute, it can handle a complaint against any trader in Sweden.[41]

The Board consists of the Chairman (who is also the administrative head of the agency), the Vice-Chairman (both of whom are appointed by the government, having been judges), around 20 Chairmen of the thirteen divisions (who are all qualified judges or senior lawyers, appointed by the government)[42] and more than 200 individual members, the number of which is determined by the government.[43] The members are nominated by the Consumer Agency (representing consumer interests), and consumer, labour, industry and other interest organizations specified by the government, but are appointed by the Chairman of the Board for a limited time.[44]

[38] http://www.arn.se. A small but significant change was made in the ARN's name in 2011: 'Complaints' was changed to 'Disputes'.

[39] See T Johansson, 'Alternative dispute resolution in Sweden – The National Board for Consumer Complaints at a glance' (ARN, 2009), paper on file with the authors.

[40] Förordning (2007:1041) *med instruktion för Allmänna reklamationsnämnden.*

[41] Thus, in contrast to the Netherlands, the trader does not need to be a member of a trade association that has made an agreement to abide by decisions of a particular ADR body.

[42] Instruction, s 11.

[43] Typically they have a popular lawyer on board, see Lindblom (n 59).

[44] Instruction, ss 31, 32. The Chair therefore has a veto.

Attached to the Board is a Consultative Council, which consists of representatives of consumers, industry and of local government (municipalities) appointed by the government. The Council assists the Chairman in decisions on important matters of policy and direction of the Board's activity.[45] The composition thus serves a balanced participation of the consumer and the business side.

There is an Administrative Secretariat, and disputes are handled by case officers in the Legal Secretariat. The Board employs around 35 people, of whom 22 are lawyers, but also has at its disposal a number of part-time lawyers working on specific disputes and other members.

ARN has thirteen different departments, as shown in Table 10.2.

Table 10.2. ARN's Departments

Department	Scope
General	Goods and services that do not belong to any other department, eg leisure equipment, sporting goods, timepieces, optics, removal assignments.
Banking	Services carried out by banks, financial institutions, brokerages, etc.
Housing	Goods and services concerning housing and electricity, eg carpentry, paintwork, construction or refurbishment of houses, plumbing and heating.
Boating	Leisure craft, sailboats, motorboats, repair services and boating accessories.
Electronics	TV, radio, mobile phones and other electrical domestic appliances and home electronics.
Estate Agents	Estate agents services.
Furniture	Furniture.
Insurance	Insurance policies, eg rights to compensation or level of compensation.
Motor vehicle	New and used cars, motorcycles, tyres, accessories and repairs.
Travel	Travel, scheduled and chartered flights, railway, coach or boat services, package tours, eg delays, cancellations and lost luggage, cabin or cottage rental etc.
Shoe	Shoes and boots.
Textiles	Clothes and household textiles.
Cleaning services	Services provided by laundries.

The ARN is financed exclusively from public funds provided by the government. Its budget in 2010 was SEK 28 million (around €3,017,000). There is no fee for submitting a complaint to the Board, and no charges are allocated to any defendant company. There is no 'loser pays' rule. In Norway and Denmark, the similar organisations are funded by business, although consumers also pay a small fee in Denmark.

Since ARN handles around 10,000 claims a year, its pro rata cost per case is roughly €300, that figure needs to be seen in the context of its function in providing a 'shadow of ADR' below which a greater number of disputes are solved through other ADR routes or negotiated at earlier stages.[46]

[45] Instruction, s 9.

[46] Sweden has a population of 9.1 million.

Procedure

A consumer must first try to solve the issue with the trader bilaterally. The ARN does not provide advice on individual cases. A complaint at the ARN has to be lodged no later than six months after the trader has turned down a consumer complaint.[47]

A claim must normally[48] exceed the following value thresholds, applicable to the various departments:[49]

- 500 SEK: matters that fall under the Shoe, Textiles (clothes or household textiles) or General Departments;
- 1000 SEK: matters that fall under the Electronics, Motor Vehicles, Travel, Textiles (furniture), or Cleaning Service Departments
- 2000 SEK: matters that fall under the Banking, Housing, Boating or Insurance Departments.

Certain types of disputes are excluded by the Board:

- disputes between private persons or between business operators;
- disputes concerning health care or medical care services: the Medical and Drug Compensation Schemes handle such matters;
- disputes concerning legal services: complaints must be made to the Bar;
- disputes concerning the purchase of property and houses/flats;
- rental disputes and disputes with tenant-owners' societies: special courts handle such matters;
- disputes that have been submitted to court for trial;
- disputes concerning art and antiquities, to the extent that the dispute deals with the goods' artistic value or collector value;
- disputes where the business operator has entered bankruptcy.

The Board can also reject matters that cannot sufficiently be investigated or that are otherwise not appropriate to the Board's procedure, such as matters that require submission of verbal evidence, or large or complicated cases that require a comprehensive investigation. Claims of 'insignificant value' cannot be handled.[50] It is not possible to obtain an ARN recommendation if one has already been issued in the same matter.[51]

The Board normally only deals with contracts concluded in Sweden, so a complaint against a foreign trader cannot normally be dealt with. It will accept cases where it thinks that a foreign company will respect it, especially if there is a representative office in Sweden, or the company is established in a neighbouring Nordic state. If a trader cannot be traced the Board has to dismiss the case.[52]

The ARN procedure is purely written. The consumer does not need a representative. Officially, the Board only accepts petitions and communications in Swedish, but it will accept English if the trader understands English. The consumer files a written complaint

[47] Instruction, s 5.

[48] The Board can grant leave for handling the complaint although the redress sought does not exceed the applicable level if it is of interest in principle or there are special reasons for such a deviation.

[49] At 4 February 2012 the exchange rate was 1 SEK: 0.11 EURO.

[50] Bakardjieva-Engelbrekt (n 1), 2.

[51] AH Persson, 'Evaluation of the effectiveness and efficiency of collective redress mechanisms in the European Union – country report Sweden' (2008), 10.

[52] There is no legal possibility to transfer a case to a district court. Overall the board dismisses many cases.

with the Board, seeking a legal remedy (such as damages, to have a contract rescinded, repair or replacement of faulty goods, or reduction of the price).

The complaint is allocated to one of the case administrators in the relevant sectoral department. If the complaint is in due and proper form, the Board will send it to the defendant, providing him or her with the opportunity to file an answer to the claim. If the complaint is deemed not to be sufficiently clear, the plaintiff will first be requested to supplement it, before the complaint is dismissed. The defendant's answer is communicated to the plaintiff. The plaintiff will be given the opportunity to provide a reply. In principle, both sides see all evidence, and can submit comments: most do. From 2011, parties are able to file cases online using ARN's website, and to use it to view all subsequent materials: they are allocated case numbers and passwords. Otherwise the papers are sent by post with a letter informing a party what to do next. Within a few months of the introduction of this system, 50 per cent of cases were filed this way. ARN considers this to be is a considerable innovation, enabling cases to be processed more quickly.

Parties have to prove their statements, producing adequate evidence on burden of proof rules as used in court: the Board itself does not collect any evidence. The types of evidence involved are usually limited to simple documents, such as a receipt of purchase or pictures. If a case can only be decided with external expertise, the party who needs to rely on the expertise has to produce this, at their own cost, as for court proceedings. This cost can be refunded at the end by the loser. In some sectors, it can be difficult to identify suitable experts: lists can be consulted at local Chambers of Commerce, consumer advisers, or ARN's website

The merits of a dispute are decided upon at a meeting of the sectoral department, at which the parties may not be present, nor are witnesses called. A complaint can be adjudicated on in either of two ways: at a session of the Board, or at the Secretariat (without a session). In the first situation, the meeting of the Board is chaired either by the President or the Vice-President or by one of the Chairmen of the Departments, and with four sector representatives (two from an organization representing consumer interests and two representing a business organization). All members act impartially. The representatives have the advantage of bringing sectoral expert knowledge. A quorum is four people, provided one is present from each side, but any member can call for a full Board to sit on a case. The participation of representatives nominated by both business and consumer organisations is considered to increase the legitimacy of the operations of the Board.

A large number of cases are dealt with at every session, which usually lasts three hours. Each case is presented to the Board by a case administrator of the Secretariat or by an external legal officer. The Board has at its disposal the documentary evidence (eg contracts, photographs) presented by the parties and sometimes also exhibits (physical evidence). Any member of the Board may express a dissenting opinion, but the vast majority of decisions are unanimous. After the session the legal officer drafts a proposal for a decision and sends it to the chairperson for approval or amendments. When the chairperson has signed the decision it is distributed to the parties to the dispute by the Secretariat and becomes public.

Straightforward cases, such as those where precedents exist, or where the defendant has not presented an answer to the plaintiff's complaint, are delegated to the secretariat: about 5,000 of the 10,000 cases are solved by the secretariat. The trader cannot, therefore, block the proceedings by not providing an answer. Such cases will be tried by the President, or Vice-President, or another officer of the Board who has been granted such authority.

The Board is not competent to embark actively on mediation or conciliation in an individual dispute. If a trader has made an offer to the consumer to settle the dispute in an amicable way, a local Consumer Adviser would be able to advise. A case administrator at the ARN would be allowed, if asked, to give an opinion as to whether the consumer should accept or reject the offer, but the decision would rest with the consumer. The ARN has rejected a reform proposal for an official mandate to mediate between parties, and also the introduction of an oral hearing in the preparation phase.

In deciding a case, the Board applies the law, namely legislation, general legal principles, and legal precedents, such as the Consumer Sale of Goods Act, Consumer Services Act, Act on Civil Aviation, Maritime Code and Package Tour Act. Where no legislation or precedent exists, such as with coach services, the Board seeks to follow law in analogous fields. The Board's written judgments refer to Supreme Court cases and preparatory works. The recommendation is generally about a page long, and never longer than 10 pages.

From July 2009, cases that are of significance for the application of the law (such as complicated or new law, or where there are few precedents), or cases of major interest (such as involving issues that arise frequently), can be heard by an enlarged Board (3 judge Chairs, chairman and 4 members). On some occasions, plenary sessions of all members have been held, to decide extremely important issues of law or to produce uniform application of the law.

The Board's decisions are mere recommendations, and thus not legally binding upon either of the parties. They are in principle not subject to appeal.[53] However, under certain narrowly defined circumstances there is a possibility for the Board to review a decision.[54] A request for reconsideration must be filed within two months from the date of the disputed decision. A party may resort to the district court. An advantage of the court procedure is that it can hear witnesses, who might prove favourable to the case.

Cases normally involve straightforward subject-matter. The Board's recommendations are limited to issues of contractual liability,[55] so the most typical remedy is compensation for damages for breach of contract.[56] However, the Board's recommendations can include more flexible instructions on how disputes should be resolved, for example a price reduction (if the issue related to promised quality, such as if a breach of the travel contract has occurred),[57] or conduct remedies (such as an obligation to perform, change or terminate contractual agreements, or that the business operator shall repair the defect on a product).

Compliance and Publication

ARN publishes an annual report, summarising its activities and giving overall statistics. It also updates its website every three months, showing general statistics of cases handled and outcomes, and compliance with decisions. The motor vehicle trade association has produced two books of compilations of decisions by the ARN, which are widely used.

[53] Instruction, s 29.

[54] (i) if the party makes it credible that he or she has had valid reasons for not having submitted a statement in the matter; (ii) if the party refers to evidence and circumstances that have not earlier been referred to, that could lead to a substantially different outcome and the party proves it probable that this could not have been done earlier; (iii) the decision is manifestly wrong due to a mistake or omission on the art of the Board. The request for review shall be made in writing within two months after a decision on a dispute. See Bakardjieva-Engelbrekt (n 1).

[55] Persson, *Evaluation of the Effectiveness and Efficiency of Collective Redress Mechanisms in the European Union* (2008), 11.

[56] 'From the practice of ARN it follows that the Board does not issue decisions on claims for corporal damages and for 'non-material' damages.'

[57] Interview with L Nordling, Chair, formerly Director, of the ARN.

There are strong legal requirement over privacy of personal information in Sweden, and as a result names of companies (and certainly of consumers) are not given. Details of the more interesting cases are given, with names anonymised. These can be referred to as precedents by courts, and by consumers and businesses as examples of how to resolve everyday cases. However, under freedom of information law, the ARN will, if asked, give out the names of those involved in any individual identified case, and the media frequently make use of this route, although they rarely themselves publish the company's name.

ARN's 2011 IT system records the details of every claim and supporting documents, status of case, outcome, and whether the business complied. The Authorities can access ARN's IT system and therefore extract all 'market behaviour' information that they wish.

The rate of compliance by traders with ARN's decisions was 75 per cent in both 2008 and 2009, and 71 per cent in 2010. The compliance rate varies between sectors: that for package travel cases being said to be 100 per cent. There is no mechanism for enforceability other than commencing a separate court action, but many trade associations have undertaken to follow the Board's decisions.[58] There is high media cover of consumer affairs in Sweden, and companies contesting the decisions of the Board will in many cases be reported on by the media. The level of compliance is considered to be high by ARN, and attributed to the fact that the names of traders who do not comply with the Board's decision can be published on a 'black list'[59] in a consumer magazine,[60] which is cited widely in the media. Appearing on such a list is not thought to be good for business, and the perceived high level of compliance has, in turn, increased consumers' faith in the ARN system. ARN would like to be allowed to publish names itself. Attention is being given to highlighting companies that have good service records, through white lists.

Statistics

National cases

In 2010 it took on average 197 days to conclude cases where the Board held a meeting, and 155 days when settled by the Secretariat. In 2010, 2,119 of the 9,335 cases were dismissed (23 per cent), 93 per cent of which were dismissed because the parties settled before the ARN award, and the remaining 7 per cent were withdrawn.[61]

In general, it is believed that far more consumer law cases are decided at the ARN than in the courts,[62] but it is not possible to verify this from court statistics.

The number of cases received by ARN for the years 2008 to 2011, broken down into sectoral boards, is shown in Table 10.3.[63] The number of cases for some types, such as banking, estate agents and insurance, are low because many such cases are dealt with in-house or by sectoral dispute resolution boards.

[58] See also PH Lindblom, 'ADR – The Opiate of the Legal System? Perspectives on Alternative Dispute Resolution Generally and in Sweden' (2008) *European Review of Private Law* 1, 63–93, 81.

[59] www.radron.se/Svarta-listan.

[60] *Råd & Rön*. The magazine contacts a trader before publishing its name, and that procedure itself can result in a trader accepting an ARN recommendation to pay. An example of such 'naming and shaming' concerned Ryanair in 2008, see http://www.thelocal.se/10154/20080228.

[61] ARN annual report for 2010.

[62] Lindblom, *ADR – The Opiate of the Legal System?* (2008), 81; confirmed in authors' interview with P Hammarskiold.

[63] See www.arn.se/Om-oss/Statistik.

Table 10.3: Cases received by ARN 2008–2011

Division	**2008**	**2009**	**2010**	**2011**
General	1,072	1,119	988	1,071
Banking, financial services	398	629	480	427
Housing	1,426	2,035	1,345	1,312
Boating	102	89	72	61
Electronics	1,981	1,974	1,565	1,446
Estate agents services	114	96	78	94
Insurance services	779	796	849	793
Motor vehicles	1,657	1,575	1,520	1,702
Furniture	349	361	317	341
Travel	1,507	1,558	1,679	1,668
Footwear	141	124	139	128
Textiles	195	209	183	193
Cleaning services	137	117	120	106
Total	**9,858**	**10,682**	**9,335**	**9,342**

Thirty-five to forty per cent of ARN's decisions are in favour of consumers, and 55–60 per cent in favour of businesses. This rate illustrates the fact that many disputes are dealt with at earlier stages, before being referred to ARN: the system is designed to make clear to businesses where they should settle cases, and ARN finds that the majority of the cases that are referred to it are ones where consumers are wrong to pursue them.

The reasons why ARN rejected cases in 2010, were: incomplete documentation (32 per cent); exceeded time limitation of 6 months (22 per cent); below minimum value threshold (19 per cent); lack of competence (13 per cent); and absence of a conflict (10 per cent).

Cross-border cases

The number of cross-border cases handled by ARN between 2006 and 2010 is at Table 10.4. The percentage of cross-border cases is usually under four per cent, but rose in 2010 because of the Icelandic volcanic ash problem.

Table 10.4: Total number of cross-border cases handled by ARN 2006–2010

	2006	**2007**	**2008**	**2009**	**2010**
National Total	**8,694**	**9,096**	**9,858**	**10,682**	**9,335**
Complainant from other country	75	88	94	140	176
Trader from other country	183	269	289	285	489
Total cross-border	**258**	**357**	**383**	**425**	**665**
Total cross-border in percentage	2.97%	3.92%	3.89%	3.98%	7.12%

The outcome of cross-border decisions in 2008–2010 is at Table 10.5. Significantly more cases are resolved in favour of consumers in relation to foreign traders (outgoing) than foreign consumers (incoming).

Table 10.5: Type of decisions in cross-border disputes 2008–2010

Decision	**2008**		**2009**		**2010**	
	Foreign cons	**Foreign trader**	**Foreign cons**	**Foreign trader**	**Foreign cons**	**Foreign trader**
Dismissed	40	62	40	58	40	48
In favour of consumer	16	102	21	103	70	232
Rejected	24	80	59	62	33	69
Solved without decision	14	38	15	49	23	82
Other	0	7	5	13	10	58
Total:	**94**	**289**	**140**	**285**	**176**	**489**

The compliance rate for cross-border disputes is at Table 10.6: the rate is again higher for incoming than outgoing cases.

Table 10.6: Compliance rates 2008–2010

Decision	**2008**		**2009**		**2010**	
	Foreign cons	**Foreign trader**	**Foreign cons**	**Foreign trader**	**Foreign cons**	**Foreign trader**
Follow up	15	100	24	108	58	218
Correction	13	64	21	76	37	94
Compliance in percentage	**87%**	**64%**	**88%**	**70%**	**64%**	**43%**

Courts

Starting an action in the courts always remains a separate option, but this pathway would rarely be used in preference to an ADR option.[64] Swedish people tend to avoid courts. There is a clear cost advantage for ADR over the courts. Even though the cost of court fees for typical consumer cases (small claims) is limited, there is a loser pays risk. In contrast, the ARN system involves no cost and no cost risk. Instead, the courts might be used after an ADR procedure where the trader does not follow the recommendation of the ADR body. The decisions of the numerous private ADR schemes can be confirmed in a court order.[65] It follows from the reliance on in-house and external ADR bodies that the national expenditure on the ARN, and especially on the court system, is kept low.

The legal system has the normal distinction between public and private law, with the former being dealt with in administrative courts, and the latter in 48 district courts (*tingsrätt*) and appealed to one of six courts of appeal (*hovrätt*; but labour cases go to *Arbetsdomstolen*, which is highly regarded[66]) and then the Supreme Court (*Högsta domstolen*).[67]

[64] It has not been possible to identify consumer claims from within the general court statistics.
[65] Lindblom (n 59), 81.
[66] PH Lindblom, 'National Report: Group Litigation in Sweden' (2007) at http://globalclassactions.stanford.edu.
[67] A Layton and H Mercer, *European Civil Practice* (Thomson, Sweet & Maxwell, 2nd edn, 2004).

The Swedish small claims procedure was not specifically designed for consumer disputes—unlike the cross-border European Small Claims Procedure. The former applies where the value of the claim does not exceed SEK 21,400 (c€2,300).[68] A simplified procedure for any small claim under a financial limit was introduced in 1974,[69] and revised in 1988.[70] It seems that the procedure has mainly been used by traders to collect their debts from consumers.[71] A consumer would have to pay the court fee of €50 to start a small claim.

The loser pays rule applies in courts, in relation to costs that were reasonably incurred, but not for court costs in small claims.[72] Loser pays still applies in small claims to lawyers' fees but the only recoverable costs are:

(a) one hour of legal counselling (at a fee fixed by the state);
(b) the application fee (SEK 450);
(c) travel expenses for appearance at one court session;
(d) witness testimony; and
(e) translation of documents.

There appear to have been *no* cross-border cases through the EU Small Claims Procedure, in or out of Sweden. Konsument Europa surveyed the courts in 2010 to see if they used the EU Small Claims procedure and found that it was unknown as well as unused.[73]

Professor Lindblom asserted in 1988 that Sweden did not have a wide tradition of mediation within or outside of the court.[74] A major reason for this may have been limited demand for mediation *within* court proceedings because of the widely used ADR system. The Swedish Code of Procedure now requires the court, if it is not considered inappropriate, considering the nature of the dispute and other circumstances, to encourage the parties to reach a settlement.[75] If the parties agree, the court can instruct them to appear in a mediation session before a mediator appointed by the court. In practice the courts consult with the parties before issuing a mediation order. The extent to which judges will order mediation varies.[76] The approach appears to have been widely used for some types of claims,[77] but rarely used for consumer disputes, perhaps because of the general absence of cases in courts that might be suitable for mediation, given the wide reliance on ADR, and the fact that the mediator has to be paid by the parties. If an agreement is reached, parties may have it confirmed in court by a judgment. The current provision on this type of mediation is very soft but it is currently being considered whether some form of obligatory pre-trial mediation can be feasible.[78] Amendments to several interacting codes concerning ADR came into force August 1, 2011.[79]

[68] This is calculated as half of the base amount according to the National Insurance Act, in 2012 being SEK 42,800.

[69] Lag 1974:8 om rättegång i tvistemål om mindre värden.

[70] A revision of the Code of Judicial Procedure (Prop. 1986/87:89).

[71] PH Lindblom, 'Procedure', in S Strömholm (ed), *Introduction to Swedish Law* (Stockholm: Norstedts, 1988), 105–145, 130; E Hällströmer, *Konsumenttvister om mindre värden – en omöjlighet? Uppsala 2004, examensarbete*, available at www.alumn.uu.se/jurist/index.php?option=com_docman&task=doc_download&gid=25&Itemid=48.

[72] Swedish Code of Judicial Procedure (*Rättegångsbalken*), ch 18, section 8a. English translation available at www.sweden.gov.se/sb/d/3926/a/27778.

[73] Information from J Girzl: the findings are published in the ECC-Net report about EU Small Claims Procedure, spring 2012.

[74] Lindblom (n 59), 82. An area in which this works is the tenant landlord relationship. Here it is sometimes mandatory before a trial can be initiated.

[75] Ch 42, s 17 para 2.

[76] The mediator can act more freely than a judge and take into consideration matters that are not strictly legal. The mediator is also allowed to express an opinion both as to matters of fact and law.

[77] T Johansson, 'Alternative dispute resolution in Sweden – The National Board for Consumer Complaints at a glance' (ARN, 2009), paper on file with the authors.

[78] Lindblom (n 59), p 83. This is the case in Finland and Norway.

[79] See preparatory works (prop. 2010/11:128).

Further aspects of procedure are summarised by the Swedish government as follows:[80]

> The Swedish Code of Judicial Procedure states that when the court has issued a summons in a civil case, oral or written preparatory proceedings must take place. One of the aims of the preparatory proceedings is to clarify whether there are prospects for conciliation. If conciliation is permitted in the case, the court must endeavour to ensure that the parties are reconciled where appropriate, having regard to the nature of the case and other circumstances. It is therefore the court which, if it deems it appropriate, takes the initiative for conciliation talks between the parties. The presiding judge in the case chairs the conciliation talks. The conciliation procedure is not required to take any specific form, nor is it mandatory. The parties can therefore declare that they are not interested in holding conciliation talks without suffering any repercussions. If the conciliation talks do not lead to a settlement between the parties, the judicial proceedings continue as normal. The judge who takes part in conciliation must ensure that he or she is impartial throughout the procedure. Like judicial proceedings in general, the conciliation procedure is free of charge. However, an application fee must be paid when the case is brought to court (currently around EUR 50).
>
> If, having regard to the nature of the case, it is more appropriate for special mediation to take place, the court can appoint a special mediator to chair the conciliation talks. The mediator is then not the judge in charge of the case, but an outsider. The parties are usually consulted before the court orders mediation. The costs for the specially appointed mediator are borne by the parties.

Parties may choose to refer any dispute to mediation outside the court system. There is a National Mediation Office, whose mediation work is governed by statute. 'The National Mediation Office provides mediators for disputes between employers and employees over negotiations on wages and general terms of employment or for disputes where a company refuses to sign a collective agreement with a professional organisation.'[81] The National Mediation Office can also appoint mediators at the request of the parties, or even in the absence of such a request, for example if one of the parties has given notice of a conflict and the National Mediation Office[82] considers that mediators can bring about a successful resolution of the dispute. The procedure is free of charge.

The Stockholm Chamber of Commerce provides mediators where both parties agree to refer disputes. The parties are jointly and severally liable for all costs and, unless otherwise agreed, bear the mediation costs in equal shares.

The Consumer Agency

The Swedish Consumer Agency[83] is a state agency whose task is to safeguard consumer interests, including safety of goods and services, company advertising and contract conditions, domestic finances and consumer-related disabled and environmental issues. Its consumer policy objectives are determined by the government and Parliament. It has a staff of about 120 people. The Agency trains the municipalities' consumer advisers as well as budget and debt advisers.

The Consumer Agency is headed by a Director General who is also Consumer Ombudsman (*Konsumentombudsmannen*, KO). The reason why there are two functions

[80] http://ec.europa.eu/civiljustice/adr/adr_swe_en.htm.
[81] ec.europa.eu/civiljustice/adr/adr_swe_en.htm.
[82] www.medlingsinstitutet.se.
[83] www.konsumentverket.se/otherlanguages/English/About-the-Swedish-Consumer-Agency.

and titles is historical: the KO used to be separate from the Consumer Agency, and the functions were joined in 1976. The KO's core function is to represent consumer interests in relations with businesses and represent consumers in individual cases and marketing issues. The KO can take a case to the ARN, the civil courts, or the Market Court. When the KO threatens to start a case, the company usually quickly settles it, in order to avoid attracting adverse publicity. The KO has also been given the 'group action' power, discussed below.

Since 2007, the KO can participate in a court case commenced by an individual consumer,[84] although it only does so in two or three cases a year where general consumer issues are raised. It does not answer individual questions or intervene in individual disputes, but refers consumers to advisers in the local municipalities' Advice Centres. However, the ECC unit, Konsument Europa, co-located with the Consumer Agency, does actively involve itself in seeking solutions to individual cases in cross-border disputes.

Group Claims

Nordic states have a distinctive model for handling mass individual cases, with some variations between the Nordic states themselves. In Sweden, the Group Proceedings Act of 2002[85] provides that Group proceedings can be instituted by (i) an individual member of the group, which can be a natural person or a legal entity (a private group action), (ii) an association of consumers or wage-earners (an organizational group action) and (iii) a designated public authority (a public group action).[86] For consumer disputes the Government has designated the KO as the appropriate public authority. The KO may institute a group action either in court or in the ARN.[87] A consumer or wage-earner organization may also bring a group case in the ARN.

According to an inquiry by the Government,[88] 10 private group actions were commenced up to October 2007, but in reality the figure is much higher (probably 40-50 cases), since most cases have either been settled or withdrawn before coming to court.[89] There are clear reasons for consumers to avoid instituting private group actions and instead to rely on a public group action brought by the KO, notably costs, user-friendliness, and ability to rely on inherent powers of status and enforcement. Starting a group case in a normal court is unattractive, since the procedure requires all consumers to opt-in, and that becomes a slow, cumbersome and costly process. One court class action has been brought involving

[84] SF 2006: 1021. Before 2007, this was piloted for financial services cases, and extended in 2007 for all consumer cases.

[85] *Lag* (2002: 599) *om grupprättegång, GrL.*

[86] Before a special form of out-of-court group action before the ARN was introduced to Swedish law: *Förordning* (1997:9) *om försöksverksamhet med grupptalan vid Allmänna reklamationsnämnden.*

[87] A recent example is *KO vs Kraftkommision*. The energy distribution company *Kraftkommission* (now Stävrullen Finans AB) had agreed to distribute electricity to their customers at a fixed price. When the company later cancelled the distribution, the customers where referred to another distributor that demanded a higher price for the distribution. The consumers (and KO) claimed that Kraftkommission was obligated to remunerate the consumers for the added cost. On 4 November 2011, the court of appeal ruled in favour of KO and the 2,300 energy consumers (*Hovrätten för Övre Norrland* (T 154-10)). The case has been appealed to the Supreme Court.

[88] DS 2008:74. Some are described at PH Lindblom, 'National Report: Group Litigation in Sweden' (2007) and PH Lindblom, 'Global Class Action – National Report: Group Litigation in Sweden, update paper' (2008), both at http://globalclassactions.stanford.edu.

[89] Information from P Hammarskiold.

an energy company, and the appeals have taken seven years. There have as yet been no group proceedings initiated by consumer or wage-earners' organizations,[90] perhaps because consumer associations do not play a strong role in Sweden.[91]

In contrast, a two-stage process applies where the KO brings a case in the ARN, thereby avoiding the requirements for giving notice and opt-in procedure that apply for a group action in court. In the first stage, the KO can seek a generic[92] decision on breach of consumer law,[93] and individual consumers can subsequently bring individual claims based on that generic decision. In practice, it may not be necessary for individual consumers to launch formal claims after such a generic decision, since they may be able to opt-in informally.[94] It is open to the Board to recommend, although this is a spontaneous option not stated formally under a power in the law, that a trader should compensate all consumers who are in a similar situation and who have not complained to the board personally.[95] Problems may, of course, arise in cases where consumers are unknown to the trader.

Where the ARN has received several private individual complaints against the same business operator, it may ask the KO if he wants to bring a group action so that a group of consumers can be covered by a single decision. It is reported that the availability to settle rises 'dramatically' after the KO becomes involved.[96]

Cross-border Claims

The Swedish European Consumer Centre (*Konsument Europa*: ECC-SE),[97] the Swedish member of the ECC-Net, is a unit within the Swedish Consumer Agency, co-financed equally by the Agency and the European Commission. There was a significant 39 per cent rise in complaints in 2010 due to the Icelandic volcanic ash issue.

The ECC-SE office firstly seeks to put a consumer in touch with the trader's office to discuss a complaint directly. If that does not resolve the issue, ECC-SE will share the case with the ECC office where the trader is situated and the latter will contact the trader to try to resolve the issues as an intermediary. ECC-SE has good contacts with many Swedish companies, which facilitates case handling, and has access to the ARN database. This informal mediation approach often assists in resolving problems. It has found that having the EU internet claims form and facilities has greatly facilitated resolution of issues.

[90] PH Lindblom, 'Group Litigation in Scandinavia,' *ERA Forum* 10 (2009) 7–35, p 26.

[91] ibid.

[92] This does not involve an opt-in or opt-out procedure, since a generic issue of breach of law is decided, which has a generic effect, similar to opt-out. An advantage of the ARN may be that the ARN will have greater flexibility and acceptance in its standardized calculations of damages. However, a potential disadvantage is that a trader is not bound by the ARN's decision. See the *Kraftkommission* case discussed at PH Lindblom, 'Global Class Action – National report: Group Litigation in Sweden, update paper' (2008), p 11, at http://globalclassactions.stanford.edu.

[93] The KO had brought 19 such group claims in the ARN up to the end of 2010.

[94] An example of a case brought by the KO was where the ARN awarded a reduction in price to all passengers on a summer bus trip to Spain, where the bus company had promised modern buses but the air conditioning was defective. See http://www.konsumentverket.se/mallar/en/artikel.asp?lngCategoryId=665.

[95] K Viitanen, 'Enforcement of consumers' collective interests by regulatory agencies in the Nordic countries', in WH Van Boom and M Loos (eds), *Collective Enforcement of Consumer Law Securing Compliance in Europe through Private Group Action and Public Authority Intervention*, (Groningen: European Law Publishing, 2007), 83–103, 98.

[96] Persson (n 52), 11.

[97] www.konsumenteuropa.se.

ECC case handlers are themselves members of ARN's boards, unless they have a conflict in an individual case. Twenty per cent of contacts received by ECC-SE are national, so are referred to the local Consumer Advisers and then, if not successful, to the ARN or a relevant ADR scheme (including the UNCITRAL ODR pilot scheme). This shows the high profile of ECC-SE within Sweden. It finds that in order to deal successfully with claims against foreign companies, it is necessary to have experienced case handlers, and to be quick in responding. The sense of community amongst the leading national ECC-Net offices is notably strong and collaborative. A response by a public authority is frequently best, in case the trader disappears quickly.

Evaluation

Sweden could be described as an ADR state. The ADR system has worked well for some decades, and is far more preferred and used by consumers than the courts, which are kept as a long-stop for enforcing the few ADR decisions that are not observed by businesses. The use of ADR for consumer disputes is culturally entrenched, and operates within a stable structure.

The architecture of the system is in one sense simple, in that there is at the apex of the system a single national ADR body that acts as a generic ADR body for any kind of dispute. The ARN has competence to try a wide range of disputes and thus operates as a 'one stop shop', although most personal injury cases are dealt with separately. This comprehensive coverage is a clear advantage, as is the fact that the ARN is funded fully by the state, and imposes no cost or cost risk on either consumers or business.

The architecture is in another sense more complex and less transparent, since an unregulated number of private ADR bodies may exist in individual sectors. However, such ADR bodies operate to high standards, and have an incentive to do so because of the existence of the ARN as a residual competitor and the Swedish culture of resolving problems without resort to the courts.

The availability of preliminary advice steps, with ADR and/or the ARN being available as a last step, produces the effect that most disputes are solved at the preliminary stages, which reduces the case load on ARN itself, and makes reliance on the courts particularly low, thereby minimising public expenditure on the court system. Although the ARN is funded by the state, the various private ADR bodies are funded by business sectors.

The fact that such emphasis is placed on the availability of expert and user-friendly advice for consumers is a distinctive feature. This is intended to reduce the number of problems that occur, as well as resolve those that do occur swiftly. The Advice Centres and sectoral Bureaux seem particularly effective in achieving these aims. Not all sectors publish complaint figures, but the general impression is that the number of consumer disputes that occur may be comparatively low, and that they are resolved quickly. Such a situation has obvious advantages in relation to cost-effectiveness of expenditure.

ADR in general, and the ARN in particular, is evaluated within Sweden in a very positive way, particularly because of its low-cost procedure combined with a high rate of compliance. An advantage of the ARN structure is that centralization in one single public body can attract a lot of attention. Competences are accumulated and 'transparency and uniformity of the decisions of the Board' is said to be ensured. The consumer can complain without a representative at the ARN and cases are dealt with quickly. This guarantees low costs for the consumer.

The ADR bodies function like a court and, when viewed from the perspective of some ADR systems in other Member States that were established more recently, may appear slightly old-fashioned and formal. The real problem is the duration of ADR processes, which is constrained by the architecture and procedure, such as relying on decision-making at meetings of panels of three or more people. Although the typical durations of 5 to 6 months are relatively short, some ombudsmen in other countries can now function more quickly. The ARN does not include a mediation function, and the boards make decisions in accordance with legal rules and procedures. Coverage might be wider if it had the possibility of collecting evidence. The board can only be activated if the trader is located in Sweden and if its location is known.

All decisions of the ADR bodies are non-binding recommendations. However, the maintenance of a right by either party to go on to court mitigates to some extent concerns over the lack of enforceability of decisions. ARN is proud of its 75 per cent compliance rate by companies, which should be viewed against the fact that many decisions are settled before they get to the ARN. However, that compliance rate is lower than the rate achieved by the (not fully comprehensive) Netherlands system, although figures for particular sectors in Sweden are virtually 100 per cent. The system might be tightened if the ARN's decisions were binding, or if there was a fast-track enforcement procedure in court, or the public regulatory authorities could be given some oversight enforcement function.

Advice Centres, Bureaux, Ombudsmen, Boards and the ARN in Sweden exist not only as an alternative to courts in the administration of justice, but as the main pathway.[98] Indeed, the courts play a very limited long-stop role in C2B disputes, even to the extent that their procedures need not be designed for such cases. However, the relationship between the ARN and the courts has evolved towards some cooperative integration, rather than competition. The ARN and several Bureaux and Boards are asked by courts to give an advisory opinion in consumer disputes at the request of a court of law. This recognises the ADR bodies' deep and disinterested expertise.

It is unlikely that the courts could manage all the disputes that arise if the Boards did not exist. The culture of using Boards may be a factor in explaining why mediation has been slow to be used for consumer disputes at least, whether in courts in Sweden or in the ARN system, the latter having so far rejected introduction of a mediation role in every case.

Some of the ADR systems provide effective feedback on behavior and standards in the market and on individual companies. Having feedback has proved to be particularly effective in some sectors, a notable example being telecoms. Some improvements could, however, be made in the feedback loop and in transparency of such information.

[98] B Lindell, 'Alternative Dispute Resolution and the Administration of Justice – Basic Principles,' (2007) *Scandinavian Studies in Law* 51, 311, 340.

11

The United Kingdom

NAOMI CREUTZFELDT-BANDA, CHRISTOPHER HODGES AND IRIS BENÖHR

Introduction

Consumer ADR is highly developed in the UK, operating on a sectoral basis without unification or a single model, but with a number of different models. The crucial national issues are the variability in the visibility of sectoral ADR systems, and some gaps in sectoral coverage.

Ombudsmen have spread from sector to sector since the 1960s, often being designed as an integral part of a new regulatory structure, operating alongside public regulators of privatised or opened markets. In some sectors, an ombudsman operates under a statutory mandate: decisions by the Financial Ombudsman Service, the Pensions Ombudsman, and the Legal Services Ombudsman bind all traders operating in the sector. The services are usually paid by levies on traders.

The UK also has a strong national policy and culture of self-regulation, complementing a robust cadre of public regulatory authorities, which has provided a platform for a separate universe of consumer ADR to grow since the 1990s. That universe comprises private sector ombudsmen services, overseen by public authorities, with a high level of transparency both of the performance of the ombudsman and of regulated businesses. In some sectors there is a statutory obligation for traders in a sector to belong to a private ADR scheme, without specifying which scheme. Other sectors have voluntary ADR systems, with some Code-based systems qualifying for official approval. Under some Code schemes, trade associations have provided effective conciliation services, coupled with outsourced arbitration where relevant (sometimes fees are charged).

The public sectoral regulators usually oversee both public and private ADR systems, providing both scrutiny of the operation of the ADR provider and also using the published outcomes of ADR decisions as a means of regulatory control over the sector and individual operators. Several ADR providers and/or regulators publish complaints data on complaints that they receive: the combination of data received by regulators and by ADR providers can be powerful information for the market (consumers and competitors) and provide pressure to raise standards.

Courts have been expensive for all claims for many years, and legal aid, which was once extensive, has been drastically cut. Since 1999, ADR, in the shape of mediation, has been systemically integrated into civil procedure, where it has had a profound effect on claims brought in courts. Mediation has also spread widely into specialist types of claims, from disputes by citizens against government to family and employment disputes. Introducing informality and mediation into the Small Claims procedure has had some success but has been outperformed by Consumer ADR systems.

Courts and Mediation

It has been widely understood for many years that the English and Welsh common law system of courts and lawyers paid primarily on hourly rates has led to costs that are often disproportionate in low value cases, and hence individuals cannot afford to bring or defend such claims.[1] Compared with a European civil law civil procedure system, the primary causes[2] of such high costs in England and Wales are the need for parties to fund their lawyers on the basis of hourly rate for work done, the rules on pleading of cases, the requirements for parties to produce wide documentary and expert evidence, the unpredictability of work done by either side and the amount of time that the court will take, and the absence until recently of any ability to control costs on the basis of proportionality to the sum in dispute.

Since the 1950s, the solution to these problems that the state put in place in order to maintain access to justice for citizens was state funding of legal services through the legal aid scheme. However, the continuing inability to address rising costs on the side of supply of legal services, and the fact that the decisions on grant of legal aid were made by lawyers (a classic problem of capture by suppliers), meant that successive governments restricted the availability of the supply of legal aid, and it has long since not been possible for individuals rationally to be able to fund consumer claims. From 1995 to 2010, a private regulated mechanism was permitted for funding of litigation by lawyers, who were incentivised by the availability of success fees (Conditional Fee Agreements: CFAs) and the clients' risk of liability for adverse costs if the case was lost was able to be covered by after-the-event insurance. However, various problems arose with the CFA system, such as distortions of balance between claimants and defendants, and excessive cost in the system, and it was not successful for some types of small claim. Although legal expenses insurance grew significantly since the 1970s, many people did not realise that they had such cover. Instead, two mechanisms were encouraged to overcome this access to justice gap: the small claims procedure and the introduction of mediation.

One response to the growing costs problem was a simplified 'small claims arbitration', introduced in the county courts as long ago as 1973 for claims of up to £100. The 1999 Civil Procedure Rules replaced the small claims arbitration system by introducing a new Small Claims Track, involving mediation, which applies to most straightforward claims with a financial value of up to £5,000, or £1,000 for personal injury claims and claims by tenants against their landlords in relation to disrepair of a property.

The fees for commencing claims are based on a tariff depending on the amount claimed.[3] For example, the fee for an amount up to £300 is £30, and over £500 but not over £1,000 is £65. Cost shifting applies for cases allocated to the multi-track and fast track, but for the small claims track only in respect of court fees and disbursements, not lawyers' fees.

The number of civil cases in county courts has fallen significantly since 2006, in 2010 standing at 1,617,000 non-family cases, typically relating to debt, repossession of property, personal injury and insolvency, of which 79,925 were allocated to the small claims track.[4] Of

[1] See J Peysner, 'England and Wales' in C Hodges, S Vogenauer and M Tulibacka (eds), *The Costs and Funding of Civil Litigation* (Hart Publishing, Oxford, 2010).

[2] Sixteen causes of high costs were listed at R Jackson, *Review of Civil Litigation Costs: Final Report* (London, The Stationery Office , 2010), ch 4, para 3.1.

[3] hmctscourtfinder.justice.gov.uk/courtfinder/forms/ex50_e.pdf.

[4] Annual Judicial Statistics http://www.justice.gov.uk/.

those, many seem to be settled or undefended, since only 291,000 defences were filed, with only 42,786 small claims hearings and 17,517 trials of fast and multi-track cases. On average, small claims hearings occurred 31 weeks after the claim was lodged, and trials at 50 weeks.

By the mid-1990s, high, unpredictable and disproportionate costs for both low and high value litigation, had led to a costs crisis[5] and resulted in the fundamental reform of the civil procedure system,[6] along lines devised by Lord Woolf.[7] The new procedure included mediation as a fundamentally important goal of civil procedure. Pre-action contact between parties was strongly encouraged by pre-action protocols, which should result in negotiations and settlement in many instances,[8] and the entire focus of civil procedure was shifted from adversarial trial towards facilitating settlement, encouraging 'the use of ADR at case management conferences and pre-trial reviews'.[9] Mediation was not made compulsory, but was strongly encouraged, ultimately by introducing a power for the court to impose cost sanctions on parties who had not made reasonable attempts to resolve issues, before and during the process.[10]

Mediation fever spread through the legal and judicial professions: pilot mediation schemes were trialled in different courts and for different types of claims,[11] such as small claims, county courts, and higher specialist courts. In 2003, the Civil Mediation Council was established by institutions, mediators and the government to encourage use of mediation in civil cases and to address issues of standards. In 2005, that Council introduced an accreditation scheme for mediation organisations. Also in 2005 a National Mediation Helpline was established to provide a central resource of mediators available on a rota system. Since 2007, dedicated mediation advisers have been embedded in most county courts to handle small claims cases.[12] However, it appears that many of the calls to the National Mediation Helpline (around 10,500 by 2009) were requests for advice, and few ended as mediations (under 5 per cent around 2008), and that court referrals to mediation do not show any evidence of a steady increase in the use of mediation since 1999.[13]

The Woolf Reforms led to a clear overall reduction in the average time from the issue of proceedings to trial in the Queen's Bench Division of the English High Court.[14] Parties were

[5] A Zuckerman, *Civil Justice in Crisis: Comparative Perspectives of Civil Procedure* (Oxford, Oxford University Press, 1999).

[6] Civil Procedure Rules 1999.

[7] See Lord Woolf, *Access to Justice: Interim Report* (London, HMSO, 1995); Lord Woolf, *Access to Justice: Interim Report to the Lord Chancellor on the Civil Justice System in England and Wales: Final Report* (London, HMSO, 2006).

[8] Practice Direction—Protocols (London, HM Court Service, 2008).

[9] Lord Woolf, *Final Report to the Lord Chancellor on the Civil Justice System in England and Wales*, (London, HMSO, 1996).

[10] CPR, r 44.5(3).

[11] See H Genn, *Central London County Court Mediation Scheme: Evaluation Report* (London, Lord Chancellor's Department, 1998); H Genn, *Twisting Arms: Court Referred and Court Linked Mediation under Judicial Pressure* (London, Ministry of Justice, 2007); S Prince and S Belcher, *An Evaluation of Guildford County Courts* (London, Department for Constitutional Affairs, 2006); L Webley, P Abrams and S Bacquet, *Evaluation of the Birmingham Court-Based Civil (Non-Family) Mediation Scheme* (London, Department for Constitutional Affairs, 2006).

[12] Based on a comparison of three approaches in different courts, the winning scheme being reported in M Doyle, *Evaluation of the Small Claims Mediation Service at Manchester County Court* (London, Department for Constitutional Affairs, 2006).

[13] See S Prince, 'ADR after the CPR: Have ADR Initiatives now assured mediation and integral role in the Civil Justice System in England and Wales?' in D Dwyer, *The Civil Procedure Rules Ten Years On* (Oxford, Oxford University Press, 2009).

[14] In 1999, the average time to trial was 174 weeks, and it had dropped to 97 weeks in 2004: *Judicial Statistics*, Ministry of Justice, 1999 to 2004.

better prepared before commencing litigation, and possibly therefore able to settle cases more quickly, but at the expense of 'front-loaded' preparatory cost. By 2009, the perception that cases remained too expensive again reached crisis point,[15] and prompted a further fundamental Costs Review by Lord Justice Jackson.[16]

Added impetus came from the negotiations leading up to the 2008 EU Mediation Directive,[17] although in England and Wales implementation of the Directive in 2011 had limited impact, because mediation was by then so well established within the court system.

In January 2010, Lord Justice Jackson's extensive Review of Civil Litigation Costs concluded that ADR is 'under-used, its potential benefits are not as widely known as they should be' and recommended the promotion and embedment of a better understanding of mediation in civil procedure by introducing a programme to educate litigants. Jackson's review only considered the role of the courts as a pathway for dispute resolution, and was a wasted opportunity in that it almost completely[18] omitted any consideration of the considerable landscape of ombudsmen that had arisen for both public and private claims. He considered that the prescription for restoring access to justice lay in ensuring an adequate supply of privatised funding for lawyers and the introduction of more extensive controls by courts on costs, so as to ensure proportionality. On the funding side, he favoured the extension of contingency fees ('damages-based agreements') and third party funding, in place of the unsuccessful CFA experiment. He stated that the goal was that all lower value cases would be subject to fixed costs,[19] but this would take time to introduce. As a first step, all costs for personal injuries claims in the fast track should be fixed, and there should be an upper limit of £12,000 (12.5 per cent higher for London) on pre-trial costs for any non-personal injury fast track case.[20] Many of the Jackson reforms have been implemented in the Legal Aid, Sentencing and Punishment of Offenders Act 2012, and others in Court rules. Among the proposals is that the small claims limit be raised to £15,000, and all small claims should be referred to mediation.[21]

Experience was noted from the United States of America, where the 1990 Civil Justice Reform Act required every district court to introduce local rules requiring the litigants in all civil cases, unless exempted by local rules,[22] to consider the use of ADR at an appropriate stage.[23] Local rules making mediation mandatory for certain types of claim have been introduced in various States, including California, Florida, Texas, Oregon and New York.[24]

[15] Jackson's Final Report referred to a survey of 128 cases dealt with by district judges, in which the total costs paid to claimants were on average 203 per cent of the damages paid in CFA cases, but on average 55 per cent in non-CFA cases. Other surveys produced similar differentials, the evidence overall showing that claimant costs ranged between 158 and 203 percent in CFA cases and between 47 and 55 per cent in non-CFA cases. The implicit conclusion was clearly that the disparity between the two types was unacceptably large.

[16] R Jackson, *Review of Civil Litigation Costs: Preliminary Report* (London, The Stationery Office, 2009); R Jackson, *Review of Civil Litigation Costs: Final Report* (London, The Stationery Office, 2010), at. See C Hodges, 'England and Wales: Summary of the Jackson Costs Review' in C Hodges, S Vogenauer and M Tulibacka (eds), *The Costs and Funding of Civil Litigation* (Oxford, Hart Publishing, 2010).

[17] Council Directive 2008/52 on certain aspects of mediation in civil and commercial matters [2008] OJ L136/3

[18] The exception was a suggestion that housing disrepair claims might be better dealt with under an ombudsman system: Jackson, *Final Report*, ch 15, para 6.17.

[19] This did not say so, but the idea was copied from the German system.

[20] Jackson, *Final Report* (2009), ch 15.

[21] *Solving disputes in the county courts: creating a simpler, quicker and more proportionate system*, Consultation Paper CP6/2011(London, Ministry of Justice, 2011), www.justice.gov.uk/docs/solving-disputes-county-courts.pdf.

[22] Alternative Dispute Resolution Act 1998, s 652(b).

[23] ibid, s 651(a).

[24] JR Coben, SR Cole, CA McEwen, N Hardin Rogers, PN Thompson, *Mediation: Law, Policy and Practice*, (Westlaw, 2010).

Despite the advantages of the small claims procedure, and some degree of use, the statistics do not appear to show it to have been a notable success as a solution to consumer claims. Simply adopting a mediation technique within a court setting was never going to be a structural solution to claims of modest value. Instead, consumer ombudsmen have appeared during the 2000s, spreading from sector to sector, to the extent that ombudsmen and code-based ADR schemes have now increasingly—and silently, without many people noticing—provided a solution to large numbers of consumer-to-business disputes that had otherwise fallen out of the court system, or any other pathway. Court small claims timescales of 31 weeks have been undercut by ombudsmens' and private ADR providers' faster performance, and perhaps more importantly by the latters' high user-friendliness.

The Wide Culture of ADR

A policy of encouraging the resolution of disputes outside the courts can be identified in many situations and sectors, but has emerged in an uncoordinated fashion. First, many types of disputes are handled by 50 public sector tribunals rather than in the courts. Administrative tribunals have been reconstructed into a highly judicialised system by the Tribunals Courts and Enforcement Act 2007. Around 75 per cent of claims made to employment tribunals are resolved without a hearing, many through the involvement of ACAS.[25] Use of mediation has been promoted for employment disputes,[26] and the government proposed in 2011 to promote the wide use of early dispute resolution, requiring all potential employment claims to be lodged with ACAS, which would offer parties a voluntary conciliation service, before being lodged with an employment tribunal.[27]

Secondly, public sector ombudsmen (notably The Parliamentary and Health Service Ombudsman,[28] and The Local Government Ombudsman[29]) handle complaints of maladministration brought by individuals against public authorities.[30] This pathway has various advantages compared with judicial review.[31] Strong government encouragement for resolution of disputes between citizens and public sector bodies by extending the use of

[25] Advisory, Conciliation and Arbitration Service. See *Success at Work. Resolving disputes in the workplace. A Consultation* (London, DTI, 2007), www.acas.org.uk/index.aspx?articleid=1461.

[26] M Gibbons, *Better Dispute resolution. A review of employment dispute resolution in Great Britain* (London, DTI, 2007).

[27] The government also proposed to extend mediation, and introduce a non-judicial paper-only determination of low value straightforward employment claims, akin to an ombudsman function. *Resolving Workplace Disputes: Government response to consultation* (London, Department for Business Innovation & Skills, HM Courts & Tribunals Service, 2011). Employment claims are usually heard in an employment tribunal rather than a court.

[28] The Parliamentary Ombudsman for Administration (Parliamentary Ombudsman) was first appointed under the Parliamentary Commissioner Act 1967. During the next ten years other public sector ombudsmen were appointed, so that by the end of the 1970s there were parliamentary, health and local government ombudsmen services in each country of the British Isles. The Health Service Commissioner was created under the Health Service Commissioners Act 1993.

[29] Established under the Local Government Act 1974.

[30] See T Buck, R Kirkham and B Thompson, *The Ombudsman Enterprise and Administrative Justice* (London, Ashgate, 2010).

[31] Judges are restricted to identifying *unlawful* procedures, whereas Ombudsmen, committees, and auditors can recommend *better* procedures: T Endicott, *Administrative Law* (Oxford University Press, 2009). See also M Adler (ed), *Administrative Justice in Context* (Oxford, Hart Publishing, 2010).

public sector ombudsmen and other ADR routes has been stated since 2010.[32] Some public sector bodies use private sector ADR providers, such as Ofsted,[33] the Charity Commission, the Tenant Services Authority,[34] the Land Registry, the Audit Commission and the Youth Justice Agency (Northern Ireland).[35]

Thirdly, there are many private sector ombudsmen. The first such scheme, the Insurance Ombudsman Bureau, was established in 1981 and was followed by many others, especially in financial services.[36] In 2001 a number of voluntary and statute-backed schemes (banking, building societies, insurance and investment) were brought together to form a statutory Financial Ombudsman Service (see below).

Realisation that discussion rather than adversarialism was far more appropriate for assisting people who found themselves in disputes about family or child matters has led to mediation being increasingly used in such areas.[37]

All social housing providers are required by law to belong to the Housing Ombudsman Service (HOS), which decides complaints after landlords' internal complaint procedures and is free to tenants.[38] This is mandatory for all providers registered with the Tenant Services Authority, such as landlords, managing agents, and developers, and also non-social housing providers that have joined it voluntarily. The Ombudsman's decision is based on what is 'fair in all the circumstances of the case', may order the landlord to do something to put things right, to pay compensation or take a particular action. The HOS remit does not include local authority housing: council tenants must complain to the Local Government Ombudsman.

Models of Consumer ADR

In May 2010 the OFT published a summary guide to consumer dispute resolution systems,[39] which identified 95 discrete schemes across 35 sectors.[40] More schemes related to consumer services than goods (87 to 17), and more than half of the schemes offered conciliation/mediation, many as a first stage of a two or three stage process. Just under half

[32] *Common Sense, Common Safety. A report by Lord Young of Graffham to the Prime Minister following a Whitehall-wide review of the operation of health and safety laws and the growth of the compensation culture*, (London, HM Government, 2010), available at www.number10.gov.uk/wp-content/uploads/402906_CommonSense_acc.pdf; *Open Public Services. White Paper* (London, HM Government, July 2011) www.cabinetoffice.gov.uk/sites/default/files/resources/open-public-services-white-paper.pdf; *Public Services Ombudsmen* Law Commission No 329 July 2011 www.justice.gov.uk/lawcommission/docs/lc329_ombudsmen.pdf.

[33] Office for Standards in Education, Children's Services and Skills, see www.ofsted.gov.uk.

[34] Complaints about how these three agencies themselves handled complaints may be referred to CEDR Solve, for which see below.

[35] Complaints about the latter three agencies may be made to an Independent Complaints Reviewer, Jodie Berg.

[36] See A Samuel, 'Consumer Financial Services in Britain: New Approaches to Dispute Resolution and Avoidance' (2002) *European Business Organization Law Review* 3, 649–694.

[37] Since the Family Law Act 1996.

[38] Established under the Housing Act 1996, amended by the Housing & Regeneration Act 2008.

[39] *Mapping UK consumer redress. A summary guide to dispute resolution systems*, (London, Office of Fair Trading, 2010), OFT, available at: www.oft.gov.uk/shared_oft/general_policy/OFT1267.pdf.

[40] The sectors where consumer ADR does not currently exist were identified by the OFT as food and drink; DIY materials/cleaning products; clothing and footwear; toiletries and beauty services; jewellery, silverware and clocks; tobacco; nursery goods; sports and hobby equipment; toys and games; CDs, DVDs and computer games; and photography: Office of Fair Trading *Mapping UK consumer redress* (2010).

provided arbitration as an option. The distribution is shown in Table 11.1. There has been considerable change since a 2004 study found that coverage of consumer ADR was limited and *ad hoc*, although the continued absence of a coherent national structure means that the position 'depends either on the type of problem faced or where the problem arises'.[41]

Table 11.1: Summary typology of Consumer ADR Schemes in UK

	Consumer Goods	**Services**	**Goods and Services**	**Total**
Adjudication	1	16	2	19
Arbitration	3	35	5	43
Conciliation/Mediation	5	41	7	53
Ombudsmen	0	14	1	15
Unspecified	1	3	0	4
Total	10	109	15	134

Individual ADR systems are often overseen by sectoral regulators. Some of the major sectors, regulatory authorities, and providers of consumer ADR services are shown in Table 11.2.

Table 11.2: Major sectors, regulatory authorities and consumer ADR providers

Sector	**Regulatory Authority**	**Sectoral Consumer ADR Providers**
Financial services	Financial Services Authority (FSA): this is likely to be replaced by two new regulators: the Prudential Regulatory Authority and the Financial Conduct Authority[42]	Financial Ombudsman Service and Finance and Leasing Association Code Scheme
Pensions	The Pensions Regulator	Pensions Ombudsman
Communications	OFCOM[43]	Ombudsman Services: Communications,[44] and CISAS[45]
Postal services	OFCOM	POSTRS[46]
Electricity and gas	OFGEM[47]	Ombudsman Services: Energy[48]
Safety and economic issues for railways	ORR[49]	none[50]
Water and sewerage	OFWAT[51]	The Consumer Council for Water[52]
Higher education	none	Private bodies,[53] and Office of the Independent Adjudicator[54]
General consumer trading	OFT (proposed CMA, see text)	Many private sector schemes[55]
Legal services	Legal Services Board	Legal Ombudsman

[41] *Seeking resolution: the availability and usage of consumer to business alternative dispute resolution in the United Kingdom* (London, Department for Trade and Industry and National Consumer Council, 2004).

[42] *A new approach to financial regulation: the blueprint for reform* (London, HM Treasury, 2011) www.hm-treasury.gov.uk/d/consult_finreg__new_approach_blueprint.pdf; *The Financial Conduct Authority: Approach to Regulation* (Financial Services Authority, June 2011) available at www.fsa.gov.uk/pubs/events/fca_approach.pdf. See also *Independent Commission on Banking: Final Report Recommendations* (London, Independent Commission on Banking, September 2011), available at bankingcommission.s3.amazonaws.com/wp-content/uploads/2010/07/ICB-Final-Report.pdf, and *The Government response to the Independent Commission on Banking*, Cm 8252 (London, HM Treasury, 2011), available at cdn.hm-treasury.gov.uk/govt_response_to_icb_191211.pdf.

It will be seen that various different models exist. In financial services and pensions services there are statutory ombudsmen, but this does not exclude the existence of some private ADR bodies. The Legal Ombudsman is a service established by a statutory body, although its architecture is not specified in legislation. In communications, postal services and energy, private ADR schemes are approved by the sectoral regulators: in communications there are *two* competing schemes, but there is only a single approved scheme in the other two sectors. In water and sewerage the complaint body, which may unusually mount an investigation, is a non-departmental public body that is primarily responsible for consumer representation: that arrangement may soon be reformed. ADR is set to expand for various types of disputes within higher education.[56] In the general consumer trading sector, not covered by any specific sectoral arrangements, many private ADR schemes exist, some of which have been officially certified. In the 2011 consultation, the government proposed that redress schemes could be set up by business for consumers in the water, rail, coach, bus and tram sectors to mirror those in the energy and postal services sectors, if the relevant Departments and Devolved Administrations[57] so decide.[58]

[43] See www.ofcom.org.uk. Ofcom was created in 2004 by merging five authorities: The Broadcasting Standards Commission, the Radio Communications Agency (covering spectrum management), the Independent Television Commission, Oftel (telecoms regulation) and the Radio Authority. On 1 October 2011, responsibility for the regulation of the UK's postal services moved from Postcomm to Ofcom: see stakeholders.ofcom.org.uk/post. Complaints about Ofcom may be made to its internal independent adjudicator.

[44] See section below.

[45] Provided by CEDR Disputes Group: see below.

[46] Provided by CEDR Disputes Group: see below.

[47] See www.ofgem.gov.uk.

[48] See below.

[49] Office of Rail Regulation, see www.rail-reg.gov.uk.

[50] Complaints should be made to individual train companies, and assistance can be given by Consumer Focus or other bodies. See *A short guide to how rail passenger complaints are handled in the rail industry* (ORR) www.rail-reg.gov.uk/upload/doc/comp-rlpasscmplnt_hndlng.DOC. However, the 2011 White Paper signified that an ADR scheme is likely to be introduced.

[51] The Water Services Regulation Authority, see www.ofwat.gov.uk.

[52] See www.ccwater.org.uk. The Consumer Council for Water (CCWater) is a statutory organisation representing consumers in water and sewerage, whose functions include handling and investigating complaints, established in 2005 under the Water Act 2003, replacing earlier WaterVoice committees. Providers are required to have a complaints procedure, which must be approved by Ofwat: Water Industry Act 1991 (as amended) ss 86A(1) and 116A(1). If providers do not resolve complaints themselves, CCWater has a duty to investigate. Many issues are resolved by companies themselves, and after CCWater's intervention. Where a service failure remains unresolved, or if it considers the company should do more, CCWater undertakes a formal investigation. In 2009/20 companies received nearly 200,000 written complaints from customers, of which 15,389 were referred to CCWater and CCWater received separately 22,802 enquiries including 7,479 Consumer Support site contacts. In 2009/20 CCWater initiated 635 complaint investigations. See *Review of Ofwat and consumer representation in the water sector* (London, Department for Environment, Food and Rural Affairs and Welsh Government, 2011), 95.

[53] Including the Improving Dispute resolution Advisory Service for Further and Higher education (IDRAS), the Equalities Mediation Service, and the Oxcheps Higher Education Mediation Service.

[54] See www.oiahe.org.uk and *Pathway 3 Consultation. Towards early resolution and more effective complaints handling* (London, Office of the Independent Adjudicator, 2011).

[55] See below.

[56] *Higher Education. Putting Students at the Heart of the System* (London, Department for Business Education & Skills, 2011), at bis.gov.uk/assets/biscore/higher-education/docs/h/11-944-higher-education-students-at-heart-of-system.pdf.

[57] Scotland, Wales and Northern Ireland.

[58] *Empowering and Protecting Consumers. Consultation on institutional changes for provision of consumer information, advice, education, advocacy and enforcement* (London Department for Business Enterprise and Skills, 2011), at www.bis.gov.uk/Consultations/empowering-and-protecting-consumers; http://www.bis.gov.uk/assets/biscore/consumer-issues/docs/e/11-970-empowering-protecting-consumers-consultation-on-institutional-changes.pdf.

Thus, for C2B disputes, three broad models exist, which can be summarised as:

1. Statutory sectoral Ombudsmen systems, whose decisions are by law binding on all traders in the sector but not consumers. Primary examples are the Financial Ombudsman Service, and Legal Ombudsman.
2. Private Ombudsmen systems, which typically end in decisions that are binding on the trader, irrespective of whether it agrees to be bound. Some of these systems are created under (usually EU-based) legislation, which requires there to be an ADR system without specifying how it should operate. The arrangements that have developed usually involve private sector ombudsman providers, whose decisions are accepted as binding by traders.
3. ADR built into sectoral business Codes of Conduct operated by trade associations, which include dispute resolution systems. The model often involves a first mediation stage operated either by a trade association or a body that is legally separate from a trade association but close to it. There is usually a second stage that delivers recommendations, which are accepted as binding by trade association members, made by ADR providers or committees that are more independent of the trade association. Criteria have been established by the OFT for Codes of Conduct that are deemed to be worthy of official approval under the Consumer Code Approval Scheme (CCAS, discussed below).

Examples of these three models are set out below from different sectors. Irrespective of the model, they almost all involve arrangements that are based on applying first a mediation technique, and if the dispute is not resolved, a second stage in which an independent person has the ability to issue a recommendation that is binding or voluntarily accepted by traders, but not binding on consumers unless the result is accepted.

ADR within Consumer Regulation

It is not possible to understand the architecture of consumer ADR in Britain without clarifying its integral relationship as part of the regulatory structure. The United Kingdom has maintained a strong system for regulation of markets and enforcement consumer protection law since at least the 1960s, overseen by government departments, under which are a number of public authorities, and often matrices of self-regulatory and/or ombudsmen or other dispute resolution arrangements. There is a large number of public regulatory authorities, working vertically and horizontally, whose activities might have particular assistance in delivery of compensation to consumers. Consumer protection has been the primary responsibility at national level of the Office of Fair Trading (OFT),[59] shared with sectoral regulators, and at local level of Trading Standards Services (TSS) operated by local councils.

ADR developed spontaneously in a number of sectors but has increasingly become subject to legislative regimes, usually as part of the imposition of a new regulatory regime within a sector. Thus, in financial services a number of ADR schemes were merged by statute in 2001 into the Financial Ombudsman Service (FOS) when the Financial Services

[59] Established under the Fair Trading Act 1973.

Authority (FSA) was created; the Pension Ombudsman (1993), the telecoms ADR regime (2003), and the Legal Ombudsman (2007) were all designed as integral parts of regulatory regimes. The Energy Ombudsman was created in 2007 to follow a similar model, upgrading the previous voluntary scheme. ADR schemes in general (non-vertically regulated) sectors have been encouraged to adopt an official model, under the OFT's CCAS.

The Consumers, Estate Agents and Redress Act 2007 required relevant businesses to establish new statutory redress schemes for gas, electricity, postal services and estate agents, to investigate and resolve complaints. The Act provided for these statutory arrangements for redress to be overseen by powers for the relevant sectoral regulators to set standards of complaint handling for businesses in each sector,[60] and approve ADR providers.

The making of policy on markets, regulation and complaints has been supported by data and research. Consumer Direct, the government-funded telephone and online service offering information and advice on consumer issues, received over 1.6 million contacts and recorded 1,171,794 cases in 2008–09.[61] Four of the Top 10 Consumer Direct complaints for 2009 were the subject of complaint for more than 10 per cent of consumers under a 2009 Consumer Conditions Survey.[62] There were just over 5,400 complaints to Consumer Direct in 2009 related to personal banking and in excess of 14,000 related to insurance.[63] The 2009 Survey found that the following markets received complaints on average from one in five consumers: renting a property or management services from a private landlord, gas/electricity, internet service providers, and TV service providers. ADR schemes are available in the first three of these markets but TV service providers are not regulated and there are no ADR mechanisms for this market.

OFT consumer detriment research assessed consumer complaints behaviour to measure the overall value of detriment in the economy.[64] The report found that smaller value problems are much more commonly experienced but the consumer is more likely to complain or take action in relation to high detriment problems. When taking action most consumers choose to complain direct to the company providing the goods/service rather than any other organisation. Consumers who complained only reported complaining through Consumer Direct in three per cent of cases.[65] Consumers were more likely than average to complain to Consumer Direct in relation to home maintenance and improvements, furniture and second hand cars and less likely than average to complain about postal services, domestic fuel, personal banking, insurance and internet facilities.[66] Overall, consumers are more likely to complain about insurance and personal banking problems than any other category. These categories are also those with the highest average financial detriment levels. They do not, however, feature in Consumer Direct's Top 10.[67]

The government's 2009 Consumer White Paper introduced significant reforms in the consumer sector,[68] in order to enhance aspects of scrutiny, representation and assistance

[60] The Consumer, Estate Agents and Redress Act 2007, s 43.

[61] OFT (n 39).

[62] *Report on the 2009 Consumer Conditions Survey. Market research survey conducted for Consumer Focus* (London, ipsosMORI, 2009), available at www.consumerfocus.org.uk/assets/1/files/2009/12/Consumer-Conditions-Survey-2009.pdf.

[63] OFT (n 39), para 3.28.

[64] *Consumer detriment: Assessing the frequency and impact of consumer problems with goods and services*, OFT992 (London, Office of Fair Trading, April 2008).

[65] OFT (n 39), para 3.25.

[66] ibid, para 3.26.

[67] ibid, para 3.27.

[68] *Modern Markets: Confident Consumers, The Government's Consumer White Paper* (London, Department of Trade and Industry, 1999).

for consumers. First, a national first point of contact was established for consumers, called Consumer Direct, which refers consumers to high quality specialist advice and redress services.[69] Secondly, seven pre-existing consumer bodies were amalgamated into a single body, Consumer Focus,[70] so as to enhance the regulatory effect of the consumer 'voice' in a competitive marketplace.[71] Thirdly, significant effort was put into consumer education, particularly access to information on rights, responsibilities and options on redress.[72]

In 2011, the subsequent government announced plans so rationalise the landscape further. First, the 'front line' of advice and support for consumers should be an enhanced Citizens Advice service, deconstructing Consumer Focus and related bodies.[73] Secondly, the 'front line' of enforcement should remain local level TSS and the OFT would lose its consumer protection role, national issues being coordinated by a new Trading Standards Policy Board.[74] Thirdly, consumer ADR arrangements are to be extended to new sectors but, as a result of the proposed merger of the OFT and the Competition Commission to create The Competition and Markets Authority,[75] the OFT's approval process for consumer ADR schemes, the Code Approval Scheme (CCAS) is to be scrapped.[76]

The United Kingdom has a lengthy history of encouraging self-regulatory, or co-regulatory, systems in preference to formal regulation.[77] Self-regulatory structures, which exist in a wide range of manifestations,[78] are usually based on codes of practice, which contain both 'alternative' dispute resolution procedures and sanctioning processes.[79] Self-regulatory systems can be designed to minimise self-interest bias (known in regulatory theory as 'capture' of a system by those who should be subject to its controls)[80] by harnessing

[69] www.consumerdirect.gov.uk.

[70] *Strengthen and Streamline Consumer Advocacy: Consultation on consumer representation and redress* (Department of Trade and Industry, (2006). This estimated that expenditure of £29.9 million on the seven bodies could be reduced by £18.0 million. An earlier example of such advocacy was a report that identified wide variations in accessibility, standards and performance of dispute resolution mechanisms: *Seeking Resolution* (London, National Consumer Council, 2004).

[71] AO Hirschmann, *Exit, Voice and Loyalty: Responses to Decline on Firms, Organizations, and States* (Cambridge MA, Harvard University Press, 1970).

[72] *Consumer education: A strategy and framework*, (London, Office of Fair Trading, 2004).

[73] The bodies folded into Citizens Advice would be Consumer Focus, Consumer Council for water, Passenger Focus, the Legal Services Consumer Panel, the Communications Consumer Panel, the Aviation Consumer Advocacy Panel, Which?, and others in financial services and health. Department for Business Enterprise, *Empowering and Protecting Consumers* (2011).

[74] *Empowering and Protecting Consumers. Consultation on institutional changes for provision of consumer information, advice, education, advocacy and enforcement* (London, Department for Business Enterprise and Skills, 2011). Further, the Local Better Regulation Office would be transferred to the Department for Business, as the Better Regulation Delivery Organisation (BRDO).

[75] *A Competition Regime for Growth: A Consultation on Options for Reform* (London, Department for Business Inovation and Skills, 2011), at www.bis.gov.uk/Consultations/competition-regime-for-growth?cat=open.

[76] The CCAS is discussed below at p 312.

[77] OECD, European Commission and UK Better Regulation Task Force published a sequence of reports pressing the advantages of self-regulation from 1999: see *Commission Communication on 'A Strategic Review of Better Regulation in the EU'* COM (2006) 689, 14.11.2006; *The economics of self-regulation in solving consumer quality issues* OFT 1059 (London, Office of Fair Trading, 2009), available at www.oft.gov.uk/shared_oft/economic_research/oft1059.pdf; and *Better business practice. How to make self-regulation work for consumers and business*, PD 54/P/00 (London, National Consumer Council, January 2001).

[78] *Business leadership in consumer protection. A discussion document on self regulation and industry-led compliance*, OFT1058 (London, Office of Fair Trading, 2010), available at www.oft.gov.uk/shared_oft/reports/consumer-policy/oft1058.pdf.

[79] The European Commission also adopted 'new ideas' for incorporating self-regulatory codes within a legislative framework in its 2001 Green Paper on EU consumer protection. Commission (EC) 'Green Paper on EU consumer protection', COM(2001) 531, final, 2 October 2001, available at: ec.europa.eu/consumers/cons_int/safe_shop/fair_bus_pract/green_pap_comm/fair_comm_greenpap_en.pdf.

[80] AI Ogus, *Regulation: Legal Form and Economic Theory* (Oxford, Oxford UP, 1994).

a series of forces, notably maximising transparency of the performance of markets and companies.[81] This is done by:

(a) affecting the market reputation of those businesses that rely for commercial success on maintaining high reputations,[82] especially in competitive markets and heavily branded companies;[83]
(b) a tiered regulatory structure in which code sponsors (usually trade associations) oversee enforcement of codes on their members, but are themselves subject to scrutiny or formal supervision by a public regulatory body, which operates with sufficiently strong enforcement powers, and is itself subject to governmental and public, Parliamentary scrutiny and accountability.[84]

The operation and performance of all tiers are subject to public transparency, through ensuring that the structure, rules, operation, personnel and decisions taken by the private sector body are fully available for external scrutiny by the population, the media, the regulator, and the legislature. This can be achieved through making regular reports, and having all information on the website. The objective is to ensure that the key consumer requirements are met: having adequate information on price, quality and terms of trade, to enable full and fair purchasing choices to be made, and to ensure democratic accountability through transparent governance systems that involve adequate external personnel. This structure also means that the scope and cost of the formal regulatory structure can be contained.

One approach is for an official model to be created by the government or the regulator of the parameters of how the business' self-regulatory system will be designed or will operate. An example of this is the OFT's CCAS, which establishes benchmarks for approved redress schemes, including a template and requirements that provide for oversight and governance aspects in both horizontal and vertical dimensions. Reflexive law theory suggests that the oversight of the self-regulatory body should be procedural, on the basis of controlling systems and transparency rather than intervening in individual outcomes.[85]

A further feature is for supervisory functions over the code, and decisions on disputes, which are taken at trade association level, should be outsourced to independent committees, somewhat akin to a 'separation of powers' approach under constitutional theory. Thus, both the substance of business codes, and decisions on their interpretation and enforcement, are often dealt with by decision-making and sanction-imposing committees that are administered by the trade association but whose members are independent of the business sector. Thus, the separate committee will have a chair and majority of the members are independent of the sector (professors of law, consumer representatives, other outsiders).

[81] I Bartle and P Vass, *Self-regulation and the regulatory state – a survey of policy and practice*, Research Report 17 (Bath, Centre for the Study of Regulated Industries, University of Bath, 2005) available at www.bath.ac.uk/management/cri/pubpdf/Research_Reports/17_Bartle_Vass.pdf.

[82] Research found that reputation and the influence of consumers was the most important driver of business compliance or non-compliance. *Consumer Law and Business Practice. Drivers of Compliance and Non-compliance* (London, Office of Fair Trading, 2010), available at www.oft.gov.uk/shared_oft/reports/Evaluating-OFTs-work/OFT1225.pdf.

[83] See *The Anderson Review of Government Guidance on Regulation. Business Perspectives of Government Guidance. Research Study Conducted for Department for Business, Enterprise and Regulatory Reform. Final Report* (London, Ipsos MORI, 2008), available at www.berr.gov.uk/files/file49883.pdf.

[84] The Australian ACCC even has power to impose a Code.

[85] J Black, 'Constitutionalising Self-regulation', 59 *Mod L Rev* 24–55 (1996); I Bartle and P Vass, *Self-regulation and the regulatory state – a survey of policy and practice* (2005).

An international review in 2010 focused on four aspects of transparency: disclosure of complaints data, disclosure of firms entering an enforcement process, the transparency of regulators' governance procedures, and disclosure of complaints data about financial promotions.[86] These factors parallel the approach adopted by the OFT's CCAS and similar requirements of OFCOM and other regulators.

A 2010 research report on the CCAS found that evidence of how codes signalled quality, measured by surveying customer satisfaction levels across three different codes, was variable.[87] Three codes were studied, each at different stages of development. The satisfaction rates of customers in the carpet sector, for which the Carpet Foundation Code had been approved in 2007, was higher for customers of those firms who were members than were not members (respectively 64 and 47 per cent). There was a similar but less marked favourable variance for customers in the assisted-mobility products market, for which the British Healthcare Trades Association had only achieved OFT code approval after the research was undertaken (68 and 60 per cent for members and non-members respectively). But for customers of motor vehicle service and repair garages, for which the relevant Motor Industry Service and Repair Code[88] only completed stage one of the OFT approval process during the research, the reverse was true, with 24 per cent of clients of non-applicant garages strongly agreeing that their purchase provided value for money, compared with nine per cent for applicant garages.

A survey conducted by Ipsos Mori in late 2006 for Ernst & Young asked 1,925 consumers about their experience of complaint handling, focussing mainly on complaints about financial services.[89] This survey included a question about consumers' satisfaction with the way their complaint was handled for a number of different industries. The results are shown in Figure 11.1.

[86] J Leston, *Transparency as a regulatory tool. An international literature review* (London, The Financial Services Consumer Panel, 2010), available at www.fs-cp.org.uk/publications/pdf/fscp_transparency.pdf.

[87] *Consumer Codes Approval Scheme: Evaluating Consumer Experiences: Report by IFF Research*, OFT1247 (London, Office of Fair Trading, 2010), available at www.oft.gov.uk/shared_oft/reports/Evaluating-OFTs-work/oft1247.pdf.

[88] The Service and Repair Code received full OFT approval in November 2011.

[89] n 62 above.

Figure 11.1: Level of satisfaction with how a complaint was handled.

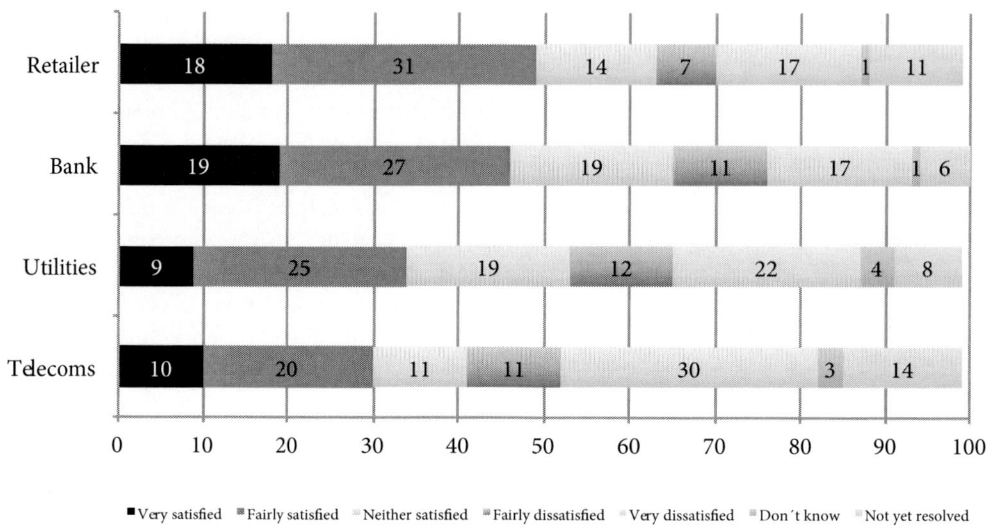

Private Sector ADR Bodies

The growth of ADR has occurred in parallel with the development of professional and commercial organisations providing mediation services.[90] The existence of a body of 'ADR professionals', with their enthusiasm and commercial motivation to seek extended roles for 'ADR', has provided the basis for the rapid growth of the ombudsman service industry. Such consumer ADR services have grown out of the pre-existing community of legal practitioners experienced in higher value commercial and international disputes based in the City of London, who sought to extend their work into any further form of ADR. The development of ADR in London took inspiration from earlier developments in the United States of America.[91]

The Chartered Institute of Arbitrators (CIArb)[92] established its first trade association scheme in the late 1960s for ABTA, to handle the disputes that arose out of the collapse of a number of travel companies. This was the first attempt to structure such a non-court approach, although a model based on arbitration alone was not successful. Over succeeding decades, business attitudes towards consumers changed radically, and techniques based on adjudication and mediation grew in effectiveness and popularity. In 2007 CIArb established a subsidiary IDRS Limited to provide third tier external dispute resolution services, as

[90] The authors are grateful to Tim Hardy and Frances Thomas of CMS Cameron McKenna LLP for information on the following paragraphs.

[91] The concept of a 'multi-door courthouse' was coined by Professor Frank Sander in 1976 at the Roscoe Pound Conference in Minneapolis. Institutional milestones in the spread of ADR were the establishment in 1979 of The Centre for Public Resources by General Counsel of leading corporations, the 1979 Judicial Arbitration and Mediation Services (JAMS), and the 1996 International Center for Dispute Resolution (ICDR) of the American Arbitration Association.

[92] CIArb was established in 1915 to provide supervision of arbitrators in response to an increase in demand for arbitration in the Great War to resolve construction and munitions disputes under public contracts. www.ciarb.org.

part of a pyramid of dispute resolution resting on a first tier of company in-house direct negotiation, and a second tier of mediation/conciliation by a code sponsor or IDRS.

In 1991 a conference of ombudsmen from both the public and private sectors was held, at which it was agreed to set up an association for ombudsmen, their staff, and other organisations and individuals, such as voluntary bodies and academics interested in the work of ombudsmen. The Association came into being in 1993 as the United Kingdom Ombudsman Association and became the British and Irish Ombudsman Association (BIOA)[93] when membership was extended to include ombudsmen from the Republic of Ireland in 1994. Its members comprise both public and private ombuds providers. It published principles of good governance in 2009.[94]

The City Disputes Panel (CDP)[95] was established by the Chartered Institute of Arbitrators in 1994, primarily to develop ADR solutions for mass claim redress mechanisms. It provides a specialist approach and experience,[96] particularly for financial services. A panel was recently formed for claims involving high net worth investors, which combines judicial wisdom and experts in the field.

Various providers of mediators emerged, bringing mediation into business practice and into the judicial system in England and Wales, creating a professional approach in commercial mediation in the UK and internationally, and lobbying for ADR as a cheaper and more effective means of conflict prevention and resolution. ADR Group was founded in 1989. The Centre for Effective Dispute Resolution (CEDR) was launched in 1990, attached to the commercial world of the City of London.[97] The Civil Mediation Council was established in 2003 to provide a forum for mediators and to promote mediation.[98] The Ministry of Justice launched the Civil Mediation Online Directory in October 2011, which lists CMC accredited civil mediation providers by county.[99]

The two major private sector providers of consumer ADR services are the CEDR Disputes Group and Ombudsman Services, the range of whose services are outlined below.

CEDR Disputes Group

The CEDR Disputes Group provides all forms of commercial and consumer ADR services, notably conciliation, mediation, arbitration, adjudication and neutral evaluation. The Group comprises CEDR Solve, which primarily provides commercial services, and IDRS

[93] www.bioa.org.uk.

[94] www.bioa.org.uk/docs/BIOAGovernanceGuideOct09.pdf.

[95] www.citydisputespanel.org.

[96] An example of a bespoke ADR solution is an industrial illness scheme, created for a specific company that had purchased an industrial site and later found that it was contaminated. The company did not wish to spend years in litigation, so a scheme was designed that dealt with several hundred claims over 3 years. The company accepted liability, and the issue was to determine harm/detriment in individual cases. The panel comprised an epidemiologist, a cancer specialist and a retired judge. Individual cases were decided on their particular facts, some in favour of both sides. See case study on CDP website www.citydisputespanel.org/media/downloads/cdp_18131276914b16998d5187a.pdf.

[97] It was launched with the support of The Confederation of British Industry (CBI) and leading law firms, businesses and public sector bodies. CEDR Solve is the largest independent alternative dispute resolution body in Europe, assisting with the resolution of disputes and deadlocked negotiations of all types and sizes around the world and has access to over 5,000 mediators and neutrals worldwide. Its expertise has been called on by over 40,000 individuals and organisations across the globe. See: http://www.cedr.com/solve.

[98] www.civilmediation.org. It was created by a senior judge, Sir Henry Brooke, to mirror the statutory Civil Justice Council.

[99] ibid.

Ltd, acquired from the Chartered Institute of Arbitrators in November 2011, and which covers a range of consumer schemes. The CEDR organisation also provides consultancy and training services, including the internationally recognised Mediator Skills Training and Accreditation programme.[100] In 2011 CEDR established offices in Dublin and Hong Kong.

The CEDR Disputes Group provides more than fifty consumer ADR schemes, ranging from disputes involving funerals,[101] to coal mining subsidence,[102] and including The Communications & Internet Services Adjudication Scheme (CISAS), The Postal Redress Service (POSTRS), The ABTA Arbitration Scheme, my|deposits for tenancy deposit disputes,[103] The National House-Building Council (NHBC)[104] scheme for disputes arising under the guarantee to rectify defects in newly built houses, and The Consumer Code for Home Builders' Adjudication Scheme, subscribed to by a number of major building companies and the NHBC under the Consumer Code for the House Building Industry.[105]

CEDR Disputes Group operates a generic 'catch all' scheme for consumer disputes, called the Independent Consumer Redress Service (ICRS),[106] aimed at one-off consumers and small businesses. This grew out of the existence of various sectoral schemes that were created but experienced very low levels of complaints, that did not justify the cost of the sponsors' annual fees, so they were rationalised into a generic scheme in which CEDR Disputes Group itself sets the rules and complaints may be referred to the scheme as required.

CEDR Disputes Group operates three core models in consumer dispute resolution: adjudication, arbitration, and conciliation. The adjudication model, such as for CISAS, is the most widely used, and aims to end in a fair and reasonable outcome whilst employing a simple 'documents only' process that delivers low cost, fast and proportionate resolution of small claims. All CISAS adjudicators are trained in consumer law and qualified in applying adjudication skills (training is a mixture of academic and skills modules). Settlement is usually embedded in the adjudication process, by allowing a two week period for a company respondent to settle spontaneously, and incentivised since CEDR Disputes Group will charge a reduced fee if the company settles. Around 40 per cent of cases resolve at that stage. The adjudicator's written and reasoned decision is sent to both parties and is not binding unless

[100] CEDR also provides the Independent Complaints Adjudication Service for Ofsted (the Office for Standards in Education, Children's Services and Skills, which inspects and regulates services that care for children and young people, and those providing education and skills for learners of all ages), founded in 1990: www.ofstedadjudicationservice.co.uk.

[101] Clients who feel they have not received the service desired may, under the Code of Practice of the National Association of Funeral Directors first try to resolve matters with the supplier, and may then contact the Funeral Arbitration Scheme at 618 Warwick Road, Solihull, West Midlands B91 1AA, which provides independent conciliation and arbitration through IDRS.

[102] Claims for subsidence damage are made to the Coal Authority in respect of coal mining subsidence damage under the framework of the Coal Mining Subsidence Act 1991: coal.decc.gov.uk/en/coal/cms/services/claims/claims.aspx.

[103] See section below.

[104] www.nhbc.co.uk.

[105] www.consumercodeforhomebuilders.com/dispute_resolution_service.html. The homebuyer lodges all the evidence, plus a case registration fee of £100 plus VAT. If the builder resolves the complaint without a formal adjudication ('early settlement') the builder pays a reduced case fee of £100 plus VAT, but if it files a statement of evidence, the fee is £300 plus VAT. The adjudicator may make an award up to a maximum of £15,000 inclusive of VAT, to include a discretionary award for inconvenience, up to a maximum of £250. The adjudicator's decision can be accepted or rejected by the home buyer, without appeal, save the option of instituting a court case.

[106] www.idrs.ltd.uk/?p=36&parent=33&lang=e. The members as at 2011 were Albion Insurance, British Holiday & Home Parks Association, Chartered Institute of Architectural Technologists, Flights of Fancy, National Society of Allied and Independent Funeral Directors, National Caravan Council.

the consumer accepts it, at which point it is immediately binding on the company.[107] If the consumer does not accept the decision, he or she has the option of instituting a case in court.

In regulated industry sectors such as communications and postal services, CEDR Disputes Group monitors compliance with decisions by companies. On average, 60 per cent of adjudicated cases are decided in favour of the consumer. Overall, the model typically achieves about 80 per cent of acceptances by claimants, the difference of 20 per cent being that claimants accept adverse decisions after they have seen the written reasons for the decision, so accept the decision even if they lose. Compliance with decisions is high in the regulated industries, many of whose Codes contain sanctions for breach, and this would cover non-compliance. Compliance protocols are written into contracts between CEDR Disputes Group and companies, with expulsion from the relevant service as the ultimate sanction. An exception is the postal services industry where statute prevents expulsion from the redress service. As an alternative, CEDR Disputes Group could take a company to court to enforce compliance, based again on contractual provisions of membership, but it has not needed to take such action to date. CEDR Disputes Group provides feedback on firms' performance. A website page of case studies was introduced in 2007, and the range of published data is being extended in 2012.

The conciliation model was introduced in 2007. Conciliation typically has an 80 per cent success rate. The time allowed for negotiation is 3–4 hours: the period is deliberately longer than for other types of dispute, so as to allow for emotional aspects to be effectively aired. If agreement is reached, it is recorded in writing by the conciliator (who is a CEDR Accredited Mediator and may be legally trained) and sent to the parties to be signed by them. If no agreement is reached, the conciliator either proposes a solution or identifies further points for the parties to think about and makes a recommendation. Around 90 per cent of such recommendations are accepted.

Ombudsman Services

Ombudsman Services (OS)[108] is a private company limited by guarantee, established to be an Ombudsman for the communications industry (as OTELO) in 2003, that provides independent dispute resolution services in four sectors (communications, energy, property and copyright licensing) in each of which its formal role differs.[109] On 6 April 2011, OS reorganised the four sectoral schemes into a single unified structure, so that the four schemes operate as a 'family' of brands aligned under a single corporate umbrella. It has a core set of terms and conditions, with appropriate variations for each sector. This approach supports OS's policy of being more consumer focused, improving accessibility and saving costs. The four schemes are:

- Communications scheme[110]
- Energy scheme[111]

[107] A variation in the model applies in tenancy disputes. The Housing Act 2004 provides that tenancy deposit protection decisions are binding as soon as they are issued, and the courts have upheld that position. www.legislation.gov.uk/ukpga/2004/34/contents.

[108] www.ombudsman-services.org.

[109] OS is appointed (by Ofcom) for telecoms, has a mandatory role under legislation for energy, and a contractual role for property and copyright licensing.

[110] www.otelo.org.uk. See p 296 below.

[111] www.energy-ombudsman.org.uk. See p 307 below.

- Property scheme[112]
- Copyright licensing.[113]

OS comprises a Board and a separate Member Board for each sectoral service. It has 7 ombudsmen and 160 staff, divided into an Enquiry Department, which deals with incoming consumer requests, and an Investigations Department, which looks at the complaints in more depth.[114]

OS states that its vision is:

- to provide excellent, independent complaint resolution for consumers and participating companies;
- to make recommendations for improvements or changes to companies procedures within the sectors; and
- to promote the benefits of independent complaint handling to other industries and their customers.

OS aims to make it as easy as possible for consumers to contact it to register a complaint. It deals with complaints via online complaints forms on its website, by telephone, textphone, post and email. OS operates a contact centre that can receive complaints from the consumer and provide him or her with advice. OS can supply information to consumers in most languages and formats and also arrange for a translation service if this is required.

The OS has jurisdiction to accept a complaint when a complaint has been made to a company that is a member of an OS scheme and it has not been resolved within eight weeks, or the company has issued a 'deadlock letter' within the eight week period. Where a third party has written permission from a consumer, the third party may use the services of the OS.

The complaints system essentially operates as a pyramid, which people join at the bottom, enabling individuals to obtain answers quickly without the system becoming too top heavy. It is intended to be simple, so as speed up the process, and proportionate, to deal with cases in an appropriate way. There are four stages: complaint, report, representations and decision. The first stage is a triage system. If the resolution appears to be straightforward OS will work with the consumer and the company to find an appropriate settlement that is acceptable to both. An initial phone conversation by the OS case manager may solve a complaint straight away. Around 35–40 per cent of cases are resolved at this stage.

If a complaint is more complicated, OS will investigate the case, starting by asking the company to supply all relevant information. OS will look at all the facts and produce a written report which gives its view of the complaint and recommend what action, if any, should be taken. OS used to produce a 5 page report on a complaint, but since January 2011 this has been cut down to a much shorter letter, based on a template. This takes less time, is clearer for the complainant, more personal, keeps the cost and the time to a minimum, and has been welcomed by consumers and businesses. Investigators can order site visits, but it

[112] www.os-property.org. See p 86 below.

[113] www.prsformusic-ombudsman.org The Performing Right Society (PRS) deals with copyright licensing, and this scheme is available for disputes arising out of its decisions. From 2009 it was required to have an ADR scheme, which OS provides under contract. In 2010 the scheme was broadened to include musicians. The scope is pan-European.

[114] All the Enquiry Department staff are based at the Warrington headquarters. The Investigation Department staff tend to work on a regime of 5 days at home and 5 days in the office. There are teams that lead on the four sectors, but staff do not work exclusively in one sector. All staff are trained in both inquiries and investigations, which increases flexibility, independence and capacity. The policy of independence is applied to mean that neither organisation nor staff take sides, but make disinterested decisions based on the facts.

is not the norm. OS would employ an expert to deal with a specific issue if needed, but also has some in-house expertise. OS considers it to be important that an expert should not be the one to make a decision on a case, which is the responsibility of the ombudsman.

Disputes that remain unresolved are escalated through Decisions by Investigation Officers,[115] Recommendations by Senior Investigation Officers, and ultimately to one of the Ombudsmen. Only around 10 per cent of complaints now proceed to final determination by an Ombudsman. It is an OFT requirement that an ombudsman should be able to order a hearing in a case. Hearings are at the ombudsman's discretion, but are rare in OS' practice. There has only been one hearing, which was in the property sector.

When making decisions OS will use its experience of complaints handling to reach a fair conclusion and may also make recommendations about how a participating company can improve its procedures. Where OS find that the company has not acted correctly, OS will recommend what it should do to put things right. This may include:

- Some practical action
- An apology or explanation
- A financial award (there are limits to any financial award we can make)
- OS may also recommend that the company makes changes to its procedures so that the same problem is less likely to happen again.

OS works to set time limits so it is important that they know as soon as possible whether a consumer accepts or declines a recommendation. OS provides the same report to the consumer and the company. If the consumer or the company feels that there was a significant error in the facts, or there is important new evidence that would affect the proposed resolution, the parties may inform OS about this in writing. OS will then review the case and make a decision.

If the consumer and the company then agree, OS will write and confirm the decision. If at this stage the consumer or the company is still unhappy with the resolution, they can write and tell OS why, and the ombudsman will consider the complaint and make the final decision. OS work to set time limits and aim to resolve complaints as quickly as possible. It is important that OS know as soon as possible whether a consumer and company accepts or declines a recommendation or decision.

A consumer has 28 days to accept a final decision. If a consumer accepts the final decision, the company must put in place any remedy that OS have asked for. OS final decisions are legally enforceable. The implementation of decisions has not been found to be a problem. In the property Scheme, the Royal Institute of Chartered Surveyors (RICS) guarantees that its members will action OS decisions: there has been one disciplinary action by RICS against a member firm. If a consumer rejects the final decision, he or she loses the right to any resolution that OS has offered and retains the right to take the complaint elsewhere, such as to court. With most complaints, both parties will agree with the decision and that concludes the process. OS then make sure that the company carries out what they have asked it to do.

OS is entirely funded from the private sector, and is free to consumers. Funding is a combination of a subscription fee and a case fee.[116] The balance between the two fees has

[115] In 2010 around 45% of Provisional Conclusions were challenged by one or both parties, which lead to a demand for Final Decisions: *Independent Review of the Energy Ombudsman, Report commissioned by Ofgem* (Risby, Sohnassociates, 2010), 30.

[116] For the Property Scheme, RICS pays the subscription fee and decides how it is distributed amongst its members. Individuals pay the case fees. Up to now RICS has paid part of the case fee for everybody.

sometimes proved to be difficult to strike, for example because volatility in the number of complaints can upset budgets. A 50/50 balance between the two fees is currently operated, thus with a measure of 'polluter pays'. The fee structure varies between schemes and individual members. Big firms pay a large subscription fee up front and smaller case fees. The big firms therefore fund the fixed infrastructure costs through subscriptions, since it is in their interests for the scheme to exist. Small firms tend to pay a small subscription fee but a big case fee (partly because they have few cases).

OS' annual turnover was £5,739,894 in the year to 31 March 2010 and £6,385,718 in the year to 31 March 2011.[117] The allocation of costs between sectors is shown in Table 11.3.

Table 11.3: Allocation of Ombudsman Service costs between service sectors

Expenditure	2009–2010 (£'000)
Communications	2,210
Energy – major suppliers	2,120
Energy – Networks	50
Energy – Small suppliers	19
Surveyors Ombudsman Service	19
Reserves	120

The OS's Annual Report records major cases and trends. The aggregation of individual decisions creates a body of 'case law', and the ability to feed back decisions in such a way as to be able to be apply pressure for change through regulatory or public mechanisms on companies' behaviour is currently a problem with the ombudsman scheme. OS is currently setting up a system that analyses the data more closely, and feeds them back to the organizations. In 2011 it changed from publishing one in ten decisions on cases (but all decisions involving property, and all decisions by an Ombudsman) to publishing a case of the month that highlights a particular issue from one of the sectors, on the basis that this would be a more useful and effective approach to achieving impact for traders.

Financial Services

Regulatory Powers

The policy for resolving customer disputes with financial services providers is that the parties should first try to resolve their differences direct, so a regulatory obligation is imposed on providers to operate complaint handling systems. That primary stage is supported, as a secondary stage, by the existence of a statutory Financial Ombudsman Service (FOS),[118] and at least two private sector ADR systems, run by the Finance and Leasing Association and the CEDR Disputes group. The FOS exists as an alternative to the courts, and functions

[117] Annual Report 2011, Ombudsman Services Limited, at www.ombudsman-services.org/useful-downloads-os.html.

[118] The Personal Insurance Arbitration Service and the Mortgage Code were established and run by the Chartered Institute of Arbitrators, later under IDRS Ltd, but later, along with FIMBRA (covering financial advisers), transferred to the FOS when it assumed statutory jurisdiction in 2001.

in close cooperation with the public regulatory authorities, the Financial Services Authority (FSA)[119] and the OFT (which is responsible for consumer credit licensing). Part of the function of the FOS is to balance the bargaining powers of consumers against companies.[120] The 2008 financial crisis placed renewed focus on financial consumer protection and on strengthening consumers' confidence in the financial sector,[121] and as a result the regulatory system is to be significantly reformed.[122]

The FSA can include redress within its enforcement activities, as part of an extensive range of disciplinary, criminal and civil powers under the Financial Services and Markets Act 2000 (FSMA).[123] These include power to take assets and distribute them (restitution order),[124] although this is not generally used. The FSA can turn on or off the ability for customers to have a right to damages for breaches of the rules made by the FSA. The purpose of this is to prevent inconsistent decisions between the FSA on regulatory issues and the courts in a damages case.[125]

Redress is included in a significant number of agreed arrangements,[126] especially cases involving small losses to individuals, such as mortgage and payment protection insurance (PPI).[127] If a company settles a case, and agrees liability and a penalty, the FSA can then agree a redress scheme. Such agreements can be encouraged by FSA's power to reduce the penalty, and reductions up to 30 per cent might be made.[128]

Since 2010 the FSA has been able to use powers in the revised section 404 of the FSMA 2000 that enable it to set up redress schemes under which firms can be required to review their 'back book' proactively and pay redress according to criteria set by the FSA.[129] These criteria also 'bind' the FOS in the sense that, if it receives a complaint that is within the scope of a redress scheme, it must determine that complaint not on its 'fair and reasonable' basis (see below) but on the basis of what the outcome would have been had the firm applied the FSA's redress criteria correctly.

[119] Its four objectives under the Financial Services and Markets Act 2000 (www.opsi.gov.uk/acts/acts2000/ukpga_20000008_en_1) are: maintaining market confidence; promoting public understanding of the financial system; providing the appropriate degree of protection of consumers; and fighting financial crime. It has a wide range of rule-making, investigatory and enforcement powers and is funded by the financial services industry: www.fsa.gov.uk/pages/About/What/index.shtml. Complaints against the FSA itself may be referred to its Office of the Complaints Commissioner.

[120] I MacNeil, 'The Future for Financial Regulation: The Financial Services and Markets Bill' (1999) 62 *Mod L Rev* 725.

[121] www.fsa.gov.uk/pages/Library/Communication/Speeches/2010/0624_sn.shtml.

[122] See *A new approach to financial regulation: securing stability, protecting consumers,* Cm.8268 (London, HM Treasury, January 2012), available at www.hm-treasury.gov.uk/d/fin_fs_bill_policy_document_jan2012.pdf.

[123] See www.legislation.gov.uk/ukpga/2000/8/contents.

[124] FSMA, s 382–384.

[125] FSMA, s 150.

[126] See aggregate complaints statistics by the FSA (2006–2009): www.fsa.gov.uk/pubs/other/complaints_data09.pdf; see also the enforcement statistics at www.fsa.gov.uk/pubs/annual/ar08_09/enforcement_report.pdf.

[127] See www.fsa.gov.uk/pages/Library/Corporate/Annual/ar09_10.shtml.

[128] See the FSA Enforcement Information Guide: www.fsa.gov.uk/pages/doing/regulated/law/pdf/enf_procedure.pdf.

[129] S Orton and K Edwards, 'Consumer Redress in the Financial Services Sector' (2010) 7 *Journal of International Banking and Financial Law* 403.

Complaint Handling Rules of the FSA

The FSA's role includes setting and overseeing the rules about how firms handle complaints.[130] Principle 6 of the FSA's Principles for Businesses requires firms to treat customers fairly.[131] The obligations placed on firms' complaint handling include standards for:

- having an accessible process for handling complaints;
- assessing complaints promptly and fairly;
- identifying and putting right the underlying causes of complaints; and
- considering other affected consumers who have not yet complained.

Chapter 1 of the Dispute Resolution: Complaints (DISP) sourcebook sets out the minimum standards for firms' complaint handling. In 2007 these rules were updated,[132] with the aim of making them more effective, by removing some of the prescriptive detail and focusing on the following key outcomes:

- dealing with complaints fairly and promptly;
- informing complainants appropriately of their rights; and
- seeking to minimise the number of complainants who turn to the ombudsman service because they have not received a substantive response from the firm.

These rules were further updated in 2011 by, among other things, introducing requirements for firms to:

- identify a senior individual responsible for complaints handling; and
- take account of ombudsman decisions and guidance, and carry out root cause analysis in the light of ombudsman findings.[133]

The Financial Ombudsman Service

The FOS was established in 2001 under the FSMA 2000[134] as an independent body to resolve disputes between consumers and financial firms quickly and with minimum formality. It is free to consumers and its recommendations are binding on providers. In addition to the regulatory function noted above, the FOS assists in application of the law and rules. Although the FOS is not a regulator it can influence the regulatory process in an indirect way through cooperation with the FSA. The FOS was intended to form an integral part of a new regulatory scheme that created a single sectoral regulator (the FSA) in place of previous multi-sectoral regulators and more self-regulatory approaches.[135] One of the advantages

[130] AC Fawcett, 'Examining the Objectives of Financial Regulation. Will the New Regime Succeed? A Practitioner's View' in E Ferran and CAE Goodhart (ed) *Regulating Financial Services and Markets in the 21 Century*, (Oxford, Hart Publishing, 2001) 37.

[131] See FOS/FSA/OFT, *Consumer Complaints (Emerging Risks and Mass Claims)*, 10/1 Discussion Paper, (London, FOS/FSA/OFT, 2010) 9.

[132] ibid.

[133] See FSA/FOS, *Consumer complaints: the ombudsman award limit and changes to complaints-handling rules*, 10/21consultation paper, (London, FSA/FOS, 2011).

[134] See R James and P Morris, 'The new Financial Ombudsman Service in the United Kingdom: Has the Second Generation Got it Right?' in C Rickett and T Telfer (eds), *International Perspectives on Consumers' Access to Justice* (Cambridge: Cambridge University Press, 2003) 167.

[135] FSMA ss 226, 226A and 227, as amended by the Consumer Credit Act 2006. See HM Treasury, *Financial Services and Markets Bill: A Consultation Document. Part One. Overview of Financial Regulatory Reform* (London, HM Treasury,1998) 8.

of the new system was to create a single point of contact for consumers' enquiries and complaints and clearer lines of accountability.[136]

The FOS cannot give personal advice about financial matters or debt problems. However, it plays an important role in sharing knowledge and experience, helping consumers and businesses settle problems themselves, and helping to eliminate the causes of complaints.

The technique of using an ombudsman for disputes with private-sector bodies was first introduced with the Insurance Ombudsman Scheme of 1981. It was based on two principles that still apply: decisions would be based on what was 'fair and reasonable' and companies would be bound by decisions while consumers were free to take their cases to court if they wished. The second aspect was important in order to encourage consumers to use the ombudsman scheme. An ombudsman scheme for financial services disputes was intended to overcome the clear reluctance of consumers to take disputes to court[137] and barriers such as lack of familiarity about the law, the cost of litigation and lack of legal expertise in comparison to a bank.[138] The Banking Ombudsman started operating in 1986 when companies joined a scheme under the Building Societies Act 1986. The Financial Services Act 1986 (operational 1988) for investments led to other schemes, such as the PIA Ombudsman, established by the Personal Investment Authority, and the Investment Ombudsman, established by the Investment Management Regulation Organisation. All existing financial services schemes were merged into the FOS on 1 December 2001, with rationalisation of differences in eligibility criteria and time limits.[139] The approach was influenced by an increasing interest in the UK in ADR mechanisms, including arbitration, early neutral evaluation, expert determination, mediation and conciliation,[140] which were promoted as an alternative to courts, including the small claims procedure.[141]

The FOS deals with complaints about most financial products and services, the way firms make their business decisions, and investment performance evaluations. Products and services include banking, insurance, mortgages, pensions, savings and investments, credit and store cards, loans and credit, hire purchase and pawn broking, money transfer, financial advice, stocks, shares, unit trusts and bonds (exceptions include occupational pension schemes).

The FOS has three statutory jurisdictions:[142]

- *compulsory jurisdiction*: this applies compulsorily to around 21,000 financial services firms (such as banks and building societies) authorised by the FSA, and includes consumer complaints about acts or omissions by these firms in relation to certain of their pension activities. In practice, this jurisdiction covers 98 per cent of the complaints to the FOS.
- *consumer credit jurisdiction*: this applies compulsorily since April 2007 to around 100,000 businesses with standard licences issued by the OFT under the Consumer Credit Act 1974 (as amended), and covers consumer complaints about these businesses' consumer credit activities. However, if the licensee is also authorised by the FSA, its

[136] A Georgosouli, 'The FSA Regulatory Policy of Rule-Use: A Move Towards More Effective Regulation?' (London, WP University of London – Centre for Commercial Law Studies, 2006) 2.

[137] *Banking Services and the Consumer, A Report by the National Consumer Council*, (London, NCC, 1983), 106.

[138] I Ramsay, *Consumer Protection, Text and Materials* (London, Weidenfeld and Nicolson, 1989) 140.

[139] H Davies, 'Reforming Financial Regulation: Progress and Priorities' in E Ferran and CAE Goodhart, *Regulating Financial Services and Markets in the 21st Century* (Oxford, Hart Publishing, 2001).

[140] E Ferran, *Dispute Resolution Mechanisms in the UK Financial Sector*, (Cambridge, Cambridge UP, 2002) 12.

[141] R James, *Private Ombudsmen and Public Law* (Aldershot, Dartmouth Publishing, 1997) 3.

[142] www.dwp.gov.uk/docs/sub-financialombudsmanservice.pdf.

consumer credit complaints are covered instead by the compulsory jurisdiction. The FOS's jurisdiction does not apply to holders of group consumer credit licences, such as some solicitors or accountants.

- *voluntary jurisdiction*: this applies voluntarily to financial businesses and activities that have chosen to opt in to the service provided by the ombudsman, including National Savings & Investments, some cross-border business originating elsewhere in the EEA directed at UK consumers and PayPal.[143]

The Financial Ombudsman Service Procedure

Consumers first have to complain to the financial service companies[144] in order to give them a chance to evaluate the problem.[145] If the complaint handling by the firm is not satisfactory or no solution is found within eight weeks the complaint can be referred to the FOS.[146] The consumer must do this within six months of the firm's final response letter.

The FOS can be accessed by website, email, letter or phone. An adjudicator is assigned to each case. The adjudicator will contact both parties and attempt to mediate a solution. If the case is not settled, the adjudicator will make a finding. Either party may then appeal against this finding to one of around 90 ombudsmen for a fresh review and final determination.

The requirement noted above that the FOS is to base decisions on what is 'fair and reasonable' on a case by case basis gives it an extensive scope of discretion. This has been criticised by firms since the FOS can, at least in theory, depart from the legal requirements and lead to confusion. The FSA Handbook, however, requires the Ombudsman, in considering what is fair and reasonable, to take into account relevant law and regulations, regulators' rules and codes of practice.[147] In practice, most cases revolve around factual situations only, for example where a customer alleges that she or he was not given a specific piece of information (eg 'she/he didn't tell me this was excluded from my policy'), and the firm asserts the converse. Many cases are also of low value, and the 'fair and reasonable' test is intended to avoid the disproportionate cost of a full judicial-style inquiry, in order to facilitate access to justice and an equalisation of power between firms and consumers. The FOS has power to dismiss a case if it would be better dealt with in court, for instance, if there is an important question of law.

The Ombudsman can award up to £150,000.[148] Historically, some complainants have limited the amount of their complaints to the FOS to that figure, and may either forgo a court claim, or not accept a favourable decision by the FOS but quote it in a subsequent court claim, thereby increasing their negotiating position. The FOS considers that a high

[143] On relocating from the UK to Luxembourg, PayPal opted to continue to accept the FOS jurisdiction to resolve disputes.

[144] www.financial-ombudsman.org.uk/consumer/complaints.htm#1; H Davies, 'Reforming Financial Regulation' in E Ferran and CAE Goodhart (eds) *Regulating Financial Markets in the Twenty First Century* (Oxford, Hart Publishing, 2001), 20; E Ferran and CAE Goodhart 'Regulating Financial Markets in the Twenty First Century: An Overview' in CAE Goodhart and E Ferran (eds) *Regulating Financial Market and Services in the Twenty First Century* (Oxford, Hart Publishing, 2001), 5.

[145] See the webpage of the Financial Ombudsman Service: www.financial-ombudsman.org.uk/consumer/complaints.htm#1. As noted above, the FSA regulates the procedures that firms must put in place in relation to their complaints procedures, including provision for fair compensation for upheld complaints: See FOS/FSA/OFT, Consumer Complaints (2010), 9.

[146] In 2010–11 the business had not issued a final response in 40% of cases referred to the FOS: *Annual Review*.

[147] DISP 3.5.4R.

[148] This was increased from £100,000 in 2011.

net worth investor is adopting this tactic, and it tends to dismiss such cases on the ground that they are more suitable for a court.

If a consumer does not agree with the decision by FOS he or she can file a civil legal action in court.[149] In Scotland, most small claims are started in the Sheriff Court. In practice, courts often agree with the FOS. If a consumer accepts an ombudsman's decision, it is binding on both them and the business. If a consumer rejects an Ombudsman decision, neither party is bound.

Transparency and Feedback

In addition to resolving individual complaints, an essential objective of the FOS is to inform firms how to improve handling of their complaints. In order to achieve this, a major tactic is to use transparency to harness market forces. The FOS believes that transparency is a major motivator of good behaviour in increasing compliance by companies and facilitating complaints handling.[150]

Various approaches are adopted in order to enhance transparency. Firstly, under FSA rules, individual financial services firms are required to publish their own complaints data.[151] This requires firms to publish information on how they handle complaints, to help people see how firms are performing in this important area and to drive up complaints handling standards across the industry.[152] Firms that receive 500 or more complaints in a six month period have to publish the following information twice a year:

- How many complaints they have opened and closed;
- The percentage closed within eight weeks; and
- The percentage of complaints upheld.

Firms need to present this information by five product areas: banking, home finance, general insurance and pure protection, life and pensions, and investments.

Secondly, the FSA uses this information to publish a consolidated list of complaints data covering all affected firms twice a year. It publishes the aggregate complaint figures on its website showing how many complaints regulated firms have received and how they have dealt with them.[153] This data covers:

- the volume of complaints firms have received, by product type and cause of the complaint, eg delays and misleading advice; and
- how firms have handled complaints, including the speed of complaints-handling and the proportion of complaints that have been upheld by firms.

The most recent data published covered the period from 2006 to the first half of 2011 and indicated that the overall number of complaints has increased by 32.6 per cent over this period. The speed of firms' complaints handling and the proportion of complaints upheld

[149] FSMA, s 228.

[150] See FOS policy statement on its strategic approach to transparency published in July 2008, which sets out a transparency agenda, designed to provide a range of information about complaint-handling: www.financial-ombudsman.org.uk/publications/policy-statements/transparency.html.

[151] PS10/1: *Publication of complaints data including feedback to CP09/12*, January 2010.

[152] See the FSA's websites: www.fsa.gov.uk/pubs/policy/ps10_01.pdf and www.fsa.gov.uk/pages/Library/Other_publications/complaint_handling/index.shtml.

[153] See the FSA website at: www.fsa.gov.uk/pages/Library/Communication/PR/2009/116.shtml.

by firms remained fairly stable over the period—during the period, around 13 per cent of complaints took longer than eight weeks to resolve and around 40 per cent of complaints were decided in customers' favour.

The FSA carried out a review of complaint handling by the major banks in 2009/10 that found that although examples of good practice existed, most banks had poor standards of complaint handling.[154]

Thirdly, the FOS also publishes businesses complaints data on its website in order to help people to see how individual firms handled their customer complaints.[155] The complaints data is published every six months, showing the number and outcome of the cases the FOS has received, highlighting new cases received by the ombudsman which therefore show the number of consumers dissatisfied with the financial business's response to their complaint. It also shows the percentage of resolved cases where the ombudsman service made a change in favour of the consumer.[156]

Complaints tend to relate to firms' behaviour, to specific products, or to a firm's complaint handling system. Problems with all of these aspects can be highlighted through having transparent mechanisms. External commentators, such as *Which?* and the financial press report them, and their comments have an impact on firms' reputations ('naming and shaming') and hence the ability to bring about internally led modifications in behaviour or systems.

Finally, the FOS publishes enforcement case studies in its 'Ombudsman News', which explain how cases have been handled and how many cases have been upheld. Over 1000 cases have now been published, which highlight issues, such as if a company has not trained its staff adequately.[157]

Mass Cases

The statutory remit of FOS is to deal with individual cases, not mass issues. Thus, it lacks specific collective redress mechanisms, such as the equivalent of a court's Group Litigation Order. However, the FOS inherently identifies market trends and issues that arise in similar cases. It has, therefore, developed a number of procedures that can deal effectively with such aggregate issues. The principal tools are:

1. Lead case process

The FOS identifies if a common principle exists in a group of cases. This is usually only the case involving claims against an individual provider, in view of the fact that contractual terms vary between different providers. If a common principle exists, the FOS can group cases and identify an individual 'clean case' for each group (ie one in which the common issue arises without other complications). The other group cases would be put on hold until the resolution of the lead case. The FOS writes to individuals to inform them what is going on. After the lead case has been decided, the FOS could 'lean on' the provider, who would

[154] *Review of complaint handling in banking groups* (FSA, 2010).

[155] See the complaints data at: http://www.ombudsman-complaints-data.org.uk/ (accessed 29 November 2010).

[156] These figures cover financial businesses *only* where FOS received at least 30 new cases *and* resolved at least 30 cases in this six-month period from 1 January to 30 June 2010. Complaints relating to these businesses made up around 90% of the total number of cases handled by the ombudsman service in this period.

[157] See www.financial-ombudsman.org.uk/publications/ombudsman-news/90/90.htm.

usually settle the rest of the group cases. If the consumer lost the lead case, FOS would send an anonymised copy of the decision to all group consumers, and say that if they think that the circumstances in their case are different, they should inform FOS. It has been found that only around 10 per cent of people tend to revert in those circumstances, usually on the basis that they disagree with the lead case finding on principle rather than that they claim that their cases are different.

The risk with this procedure is that a party will come up with a new argument that the FOS has not considered during resolution of the lead case. This has not so far happened—it is also an inherent risk in any court decision—but the FOS has addressed the point through the 'Wider Implications Process' (see below).

2. Test case procedure

If one or more cases concern purely a point of law, and the provider agrees to pay the consumer's costs, a case can be referred to the High Court for determination. This avoids the risk that a determination by the FOS will be taken to judicial review. The procedure has not yet been used, although the House of Lords decision in Equitable Life was a similar procedure, on referral from the former PIA Ombudsman. The case on interest rates for unauthorised bank overdrafts reached court by a different route, by agreement between the OFT and the banks.[158]

3. Wider Implications Process

This process arose from the 2-year review of the Financial Services and Markets Act 2000, and was designed to enable regulatory solutions to be determined by FSA or OFT where systemic problems had been identified from FOS's caseload. It applied where there were significant new implications for consumers in general, or for the industry, or even for one business. Most issues were identified by the FSA or the FOS. The procedure required a decision by the FOS and the relevant regulator to agree whether the issue had a wider implication and whether the procedure should apply.[159] However, the FSA did not always have adequate powers to intervene.

The Wider Implications Process was replaced in 2011 by new procedures for liaison between FSA, OFT and FOS, including a Co-ordination Committee made up of senior staff from the three organisations. The stated purpose of this committee is to help to identify emerging issues that could lead to widespread consumer detriment, and to co-ordinate each organisation's separate response to these.

Cost and source of finance

The Ombudsman service is free of charge for consumers. The budget of the FOS is calculated on the basis of workload forecasts. For the financial year 2009/2010 the FOS operated on a budget of £92 million and the total number of staff averaged 1,015 (in 2010/2011 £115.7 million and 1,300 staff).[160] Actual income for 2009–2010 was £98.4 million, expenditure

[158] *Office of Fair Trading (Respondents) v Abbey National plc & Others (Appellants)* [2009] UKSC 6.

[159] See more at: www.wider-implications.info.

[160] *Annual Review.* Financial year 2009/2010 (FOS, 2010) and *Annual Review.* Financial year 2010/2011 (FOS, 2011).

was £92.4 million, with a unit cost (ie cost per case) of £555 (respectively in 2010/11, £98.3 million, £105.9 million and £639).

The FOS is funded by an annual levy paid by the businesses it covers and by case fees that it charges businesses for settling disputes. About 80 per cent of the budget comes from these fees: a defendant currently pays £500 per case. In the financial years 2009/2010 and 2010/2011 the FOS did not charge businesses case fees for the first three disputes involving them. Businesses were charged case fees only for the fourth (and any subsequent) dispute during the year. The result is that only 5.5 per cent of firms ever pay this fee. The other 20 per cent of the budget comes from a levy on all firms, based on the justification that the existence of the FOS and its ability to deal with and defuse many enquiries underpins public confidence in the industry. The rates paid are aligned to the volume of work undertaken per sector each year: number of accounts held by banks, and volume of investment income for insurance. Financial details at Table 11.4.

Table 11.4: FOS budget figures

	actual **year ended 31 March 2011** £ million	*budget* **year ended 31 March 2011** £ million	*actual* **year ended 31 March 2010** £ million	*actual* **year ended 31 March 2009** £ million	*actual* **year ended 31 March 2008** £ million
Income					
annual levy	20.9	19.5	20.6	19.3	19.6
case fees	77.1	94	77.6	46.1	35.5
other income	0.3	0.2	0.2	0.4	0.4
total income	**98.3**	**113.7**	**98.4**	**65.8**	**55.5**
Expenditure					
staff-related costs	88.8	99.7	78.3	47.8	41.2
other costs	15.0	13.9	12.3	8.7	10.0
financing charges	0.0	0.2	0.0	0.1	0.2
depreciation	2.1	1.9	1.8	1.4	1.7
total expenditure	**105.9**	**115.7**	**92.4**	**58.0**	**53.1**
surplus/(deficit)	(7.6)	(2.0)	6.0	7.8	(0.5)

Statistics

In 2010/2011 FOS received 1,012,371 initial enquiries and complaints from consumers (a 17 per cent annual increase), averaging over 4,000 each working day. Only around 1 in 5 of the initial enquiries, 206,121 cases, turned into a formal dispute requiring the involvement of adjudicators and ombudsmen (an annual increase of 26 per cent).[161] The average number of cases resolved every week by each adjudicator in 2010 was 4.1. The number of cases requiring the direct involvement of an ombudsman in issuing a final decision was 17,465. Ombudsmen were more likely to be involved in pensions and investments, reflecting the complexity of these disputes and the larger amount of money involved. In 2010–11, 61 per cent of cases involved insurance (including PPI), 31.5 per cent banking and credit, and 7.5

[161] FOS Annual Review 2010/2011.

per cent investments and pensions. The FOS resolved disputes in 49 languages. Seventy-eight per cent of adults in UK said they were aware of the FOS.

Fifty-one per cent of the total number of cases related to just four of the UK's largest financial services groups, while 3,592 businesses accounted for only 5 per cent of the caseload (in 2009/10, 2,259 businesses had one complaint each). In 2009–10, 164,899 cases were resolved, resulting in compensation for consumers in 51 per cent of complaints. Apart from PPI cases, which were delayed because of legal action by the banks, almost half of disputes were resolved within three months, and three-quarters within six months.

The volume of cases received by the FOS can be subject to sudden surges, related to particular issues that arise.[162] This can present a major managerial challenge for firms and the FOS, and can lead to a fall in the quality of complaint handling. Behaviours by companies can sometimes be driven by market issues that might lead to keeping complaints unresolved, such as firms' need for cash in 2009–10. In 2009/10 and 2010/11 PPI cases increased by 58 and 113 per cent respectively. In 2010/11, insurance disputes increased by 38 per cent and complaints about banking and credit rose by 30 per cent, but the number of investment complaints stayed the same, motor insurance disputes decreased by 13 per cent, and pension complaints fell by 27 per cent.

In its first ten years of operation, up to 2010/11, the FOS received a total of 1,172,719 cases, of which 26 per cent were about the sale of mortgage endowments, 17 per cent about the sale of payment protection insurance and 4 per cent about unauthorised current account overdraft charges. Recent complaints data is shown in Table 11.5.

Table 11.5: Complaints types 2007–2010[163]

Type of complaint	**2010**		**2009**		**2008**		**2007**	
	%	No of cases	%	No of cases	%	No of cases	%	No of cases
banking and credit	44%	71,700	43%	55,038	66.5%	69,238	21%	20,099
insurance	42%	69,034	39.5%	50,168	22%	27,286	17%	15,730
investments and pensions	14%	22,278	17.5%	22,265*	10.5%	12,787	13%	12,429
mortgage endowments	*mortgage endowment complaints included with investments and pensions		*mortgage endowment complaints included with investments and pensions		11%	13,778	49%	46,134
new cases in total	**163,012**		**127,471**		**123,089**		**94,392**	

[162] Examples in recent years include investors in Equitable Life, bank charges for unauthorised overdrafts, split capital investment trusts, tax exempt special savings accounts and payment protection insurance. Issues have often been driven by consumer champions, such as leading consumer advocates or claims management companies, who may be seeking fees through furthering issues, as drove a general increase in consumer credit cases.

[163] FOS Annual Review 2010/2011 p 32.

Finance & Leasing Association

The Finance & Leasing Association (FLA) is the leading trade association for the consumer credit, motor finance and asset finance sectors, and the largest organisation of its type in Europe.[164] Its ninety members are banks, subsidiaries of banks and building societies, the finance arms of leading retailers and manufacturing companies, and a range of independent firms, which collectively provide facilities that account for a third of the UK's unsecured lending and half of all car purchases. Options include finance leasing, operating leasing, hire purchase, conditional sale, personal contract purchase plans, personal lease plans, secured and unsecured personal loans, credit cards and store card facilities.

The FLA operates two codes; the Lending Code, for B2C transactions, first introduced in 1992;[165] and the Business Finance Code, for B2B finance.[166] This analysis is primarily concerned with the Lending Code, which specifies FLA's complaints procedures and requires members to make it known to customers at the time of taking out a loan and subsequently. The FLA considered applying for approval of its Codes under the OFT's code approval scheme,[167] but decided against this because it regarded the approval procedure as too lengthy.

The FLA Code scheme pre-existed the establishment of the FOS's consumer credit jurisdiction in 2007, following which consumer credit complaints had to be handled in accordance with the FSA's complaint-handling rules in DISP 1 (see above), under which firms are allowed 8 weeks to resolve consumer complaints, at the end of which they must send the complainant a final response letter which signposts them to the FOS if they remain dissatisfied. The members of the FLA are able to refer customers to an outsourced ADR facility operated by the FLA, with a view to reducing the number of complaints later referred on to FOS, for reasons of maintaining customer relationships and avoiding the £500 FOS case fee. FLA believes that it deals with roughly 30 per cent of its members' cases that would otherwise be decided by the FOS. The FOS refers to FLA cases that are outside the jurisdiction of the FOS: the number of such referrals was 39 complaints in 2009 and 64 in 2008.

The jurisdiction of the FOS to decide cases on the basis of what is 'fair and reasonable' is mirrored in the FLA Lending Code's first 'Key commitment' to 'act fairly, reasonably and responsibly in all our dealings with you'. Individual complaints by personal or business customers about a full member of the FLA may be made to FLA, provided the complaint has not been subject to court proceedings. FLA can be contacted by phone[168] or through its website.[169] Complaints are handled by the Compliance Team, and are dealt with in three escalating stages: direct negotiation, conciliation, and arbitration.

The Compliance Team first encourages customers to contact their lenders and try to sort out problems direct. The Compliance Team frequently acts as a conciliator between the two sides. Team members are able to use their expertise in explaining legal arrangements to consumers who might find them difficult to understand. This information

[164] www.fla.org.uk The FLA was formed in 1992 from the merger of the Equipment Leasing Association and the Finance Houses Association.

[165] See www.fla.org.uk/consumer.

[166] www.fla.org.uk/business/The_Business_Finance_Code.

[167] See section below.

[168] 020 7836 6511.

[169] www.fla.org.uk/consumers/complaints-process.

function is particularly useful for educating customers, and the provision of a channel of communication is useful for both sides. Equally, the Team can use its authority to persuade members to behave appropriately in responding to complaints.

Where the consumer does not accept the decision reached through the Conciliation Scheme, and the type of complaint is not eligible for consideration by the FOS, it may be referred to binding arbitration. The arbitration service is provided by IDRS in its standard form.[170] Two cases were dealt with in this arbitration scheme in 2009. The low number is partly due to the success of the Conciliation Scheme.

The above procedures are capable of handling multiple similar cases. All cases are considered individually on their merits, whilst general approaches can be applied. Examples of mass situations have involved administration charges and Payment Protection Insurance (PPI).

Consumers pay nothing to use the FLA's conciliation or arbitration services. The FLA member pays a £25 registration fee per case, and the FLA pays the remainder of IDRS' £500 fee. The arbitration agreement includes the usual power for the arbitrator to award costs against the losing party, but this power has not been exercised in any of the cases in recent years. The arbitration agreement contains the standard provision on the award being binding, so a consumer who signs the arbitration agreement waives the right to take the case to the court or the FOS, unless in a judicial review.

In addition to providing a conciliation service, the FLA Compliance Team monitors the number and type of complaints and reports them to the relevant Group. This information is important in identifying potential industry-wide problems and emerging trends relating both to compliance with the Code and the operation of the conciliation scheme. The Group may also decide that further guidance might be needed to address a particular problem. Where a significant breach of a Code has occurred, which the member company has failed or refused to remedy to the satisfaction of the Group, or where it is considered that the actions of the company have resulted or may result in serious consumer detriment or significant reputational damage to the code, the Group will refer the matter to the FLA Disciplinary Panel. The Disciplinary Panel comprises two members of the FLA Board and three independent members,[171] and is able to impose a hierarchy of sanctions.

In 2010, the total number of consumer complaints received by the FLA from members of the public was 1,726. Of these, 1,084 were referred to FLA members for investigation, of which 1,071 (99 per cent) were resolved.[172] In the other 642 cases, the complainant chose not to pursue the complaint further, or the complaint was resolved without the need for FLA conciliation, or was referred to the FOS. This represents a decrease both in the number of complaints received by the FLA and in those referred to the FLA membership for further investigation.[173] In 2010, 63 per cent of complaints came direct from consumers, and the majority (623) related to PPI cases.

[170] www.cedr.com/about_us. For more details on IDRS, part of the CEDR Disputes Group, see p 267 above.

[171] The chair is Professor Geraint Howells, a professor of law at Manchester University, who is a barrister and Member of the Board of the International Association of Consumer Law.

[172] Of the total, there were 623 complaints about payment protection insurance (PPI) policies (57%).

[173] Source: FLA *Complaint statistics, 2010, Lending Code Group Annual Report for 2011* (FLA, 2011).

Pensions

Problems relating to pensions can be resolved or assisted by a number of possible mechanisms, which differ for different types of pensions. The advisory, investigatory and dispute resolution functions of the Pensions Advisory Service and the statutory Pensions Ombudsman are outlined below: they can be regarded as a sequence of escalating stages. The CEDR Disputes Group (see above) also provides a Pensions Mediation Service with the National Association of Pension Funds.[174]

The Pensions Advisory Service

The Pension Advisory Service (TPAS) was established in 1983 as the Occupational Pensions Advisory Service (OPAS) as a charity. From 1990 it became a voluntary organization and has been in receipt of government funding. Its name changed from OPAS to The Pensions Advisory Service. The TPAS is now a company limited by guarantee and is independent of both the Government and the pensions industry. It provides free information, advice and guidance on the whole spectrum of pensions, including state, company, personal and stakeholder schemes.[175] While TPAS deals with complaints about how company (occupational) and personal pension schemes are run it does not deal with how they are performing.[176] Disputes about the selling or marketing of pensions are dealt with by the Financial Ombudsman Service.

TPAS can be approached after a complaint could not be resolved directly with the pension scheme administrator or manager and any of the following apply:

- the consumer is paying contributions,
- the consumer has a deferred pension from previous employment,
- the consumer is already receiving a pension,
- the consumer is the dependant of any of the above.

The Pensions Ombudsman

The Pensions Ombudsman deals with complaints about the *administration* of private pensions and pension schemes.[177] The office was created under the Pension Schemes Act 1993.[178] The Pensions Ombudsman is appointed by the Secretary of State for the Department of Work and Pensions (DWP), who may remove him at any time.[179] The office is funded by grant-in-aid from the DWP, which is recovered from a general levy on pension schemes that covers the Pensions Regulator (TPR), TPAS and the Pensions Ombudsman, and is

[174] www.cedr.com/?location=/library/releases/20060207_70.htm.

[175] It was established as OPAS, a charity providing free advice and a free mediation service. It comprises experienced advisers from the pensions world, mainly volunteers but with some technical resource.

[176] www.pensionsadvisoryservice.org.uk.

[177] Problems with State pensions have to be raised with the Pension Service, which is part of the Department for Work and Pensions: see www.thepensionservice.gov.uk.

[178] It was considered that a series of tribunals for pensions disputes should be created, but this was rejected and the office of the Pensions Ombudsman was created instead. The office was inspired by the role of ACAS in relation to Employment Tribunals.

[179] Pension Schemes Act 1993, s 145(3).

invoiced and collected by TPR.[180] The Pensions Ombudsman and the Deputy Ombudsman currently have 35 staff.

Jurisdiction and functions

The architecture of the Pensions Ombudsman is unique. The Pensions Ombudsman has two distinct statutory functions. In addition to having the authority to decide disputes of fact or law relating to pensions, and to issue binding decisions akin to a judge or arbitrator, he also acts akin to a public sector ombudsman in relation to both public and private pensions in determining complaints about *maladministration* of pensions.

The functions of the Pensions Ombudsman are established in section 146 of the Pension Schemes Act 1993:

> (1) The Pensions Ombudsman may investigate and determine any complaint made to him in writing by or on behalf of an authorised complainant who alleges that he has sustained injustice in consequence of maladministration in connection with any act or omission of the trustees or managers of an occupational pension scheme or personal pension scheme.
> (2) The Pensions Ombudsman may also investigate and determine any dispute of fact or law which arises in relation to such a scheme between—
> (a) the trustees or managers of the scheme, and
> (b) an authorised complainant,
> and which is referred to him in writing by or on behalf of the authorised complainant.
> ...
> (7) The persons who, for the purposes of this Part are 'authorised complainants' in relation to a scheme are—
> (a) a member of the scheme,
> (b) the widow or widower, or any surviving dependant, of a deceased member of the scheme;
> (c) where the complaint or dispute relates to the question—
> i. whether a person who claims to be such a person as is mentioned in paragraph (a) or (b) is such a person, or
> ii. whether a person who claims to be entitled to become a member of the scheme is so entitled,
> the person so claiming.

The Pensions Ombudsman also acts as the Pension Protection Fund Ombudsman (PPFO), and considers applications related to decisions made by the Board of the Pension Protection Fund (PPF)[181] under their internal procedures and appeals against decisions made by the Scheme Manager under the internal review procedure of the Financial Assistance Scheme.[182]

Many bodies covered by the Pensions Ombudsman are unregulated, although some bodies are regulated by either the FSA or the Pensions Regulator (TPR).[183] There are both

[180] In 2009/2010 the grant-in-aid was £2,930,000, and net expenditure was £2,864,625: see Annual Report & Accounts 2009/10, available at http://www.pensions-ombudsman.org.uk/Publications/docs/AnnualReport2009-10.pdf. A second levy supports the Pensions Protection Fund.

[181] The role of the Pension Protection Fund (PPF) is to give compensation to members of eligible pension schemes, when there are not enough assets in the pension scheme to cover the PPF level of compensation. www.pensionprotectionfund.org.uk/Pages/homepage.aspx.

[182] The Financial Assistance Scheme offers assistance to some people who have lost out on their pension because they were a member of an under-funded defined benefit pension scheme that started winding up between 1 January 1997 and 5 April 2005. www.pensionprotectionfund.org.uk/FAS/Pages/FAS.aspx.

[183] This contrasts with the position for general financial services firms that come under the jurisdiction of the FSA and FOS.

overlaps and gaps between the jurisdictions of FOS and the Pensions Ombudsman. The FOS, under its compulsory jurisdiction, deals with consumer complaints about the regulated pension activities of firms authorised by the FSA. These activities potentially concern the sale or administration of personal pension schemes and related investments, and in some circumstances investments of occupational schemes. Conversely, the Pensions Ombudsman deals with complaints and disputes concerning the management of both personal and occupational pensions against the body responsible for management (including employers) regardless of whether the body is subject to regulation—by either FSA or TPR.

The most significant overlap is that FOS and the Pensions Ombudsman can both deal with complaints from individual consumers about the management of personal pensions by a provider firm. In an attempt to make matters simpler for consumers, a memorandum of understanding has been agreed between the two bodies.[184] This states, in broad terms, that the Pensions Ombudsman deals with complaints predominantly about management of personal and occupational schemes and FOS deals with complaints predominantly about sales or marketing.

The memorandum of understanding has not provided a complete solution, as it removes neither the lack of clarity for consumers seeking redress nor the confusion amongst firms. Although the majority of complaints come initially to the right ombudsman, many do not. Each regulator requires signposting of complaints, but the requirements are not themselves consistent with the memorandum of understanding. The system thus relies on the wrongly signposted ombudsman transferring the case to the other. This does not imply unsatisfactory performance on the part of the signposting firms, as interpretation of the jurisdictional boundaries is complex.

The most significant gap relates to complaints about advice on transfers within and between occupational pension schemes. This gap exists because FOS cannot deal with such complaints because the activity is not an FSA-regulated activity. However, Pensions Ombudsman cannot deal with them because they relate to advice about a scheme.

Procedure

The statutory rules[185] of procedure encourage a sequencing of direct negotiation, and conciliated settlement, against the backdrop of powers to make binding decisions. Thus, before approaching the Pensions Ombudsman an individual should:

- try to resolve the complaint with the pension scheme administrator or pension scheme manager: many schemes have a formal Internal Dispute resolution (IDR) procedure;
- if the above fails, usually then contact the Pensions Advisory Service[186] who may be able to help resolve the complaint, before making a complaint to the Pensions Ombudsman.

A person who complains to the Pensions Ombudsman has to fill in the application form, which can be done on the website.[187] This sets out what the complaint is, who the complainant thinks is at fault, and what he or she thinks should be done to put things right. Documents

[184] www.financial-ombudsman.org.uk/publications/pdf/ memoran.dum-of-understanding.pdf.

[185] The Personal and Occupational Pension Schemes (Pensions Ombudsman) (Procedure) Rules 1995, SI 1995/1053, as amended by the Personal and Occupational Pension Schemes (Pensions Ombudsman) (Procedure) Amendment Rules 1996, SI 1996/2638.

[186] www.pensions-ombudsman.org.uk/Complaints/How_we_deal_with_complaints/index.aspx.

[187] www.pensions-ombudsman.org.uk.

not already held by TPAS are requested: they will usually be shown to the people who are being complained about. All cases are screened to determine that the matter falls within the Pensions Ombudsman's mandate and rules. A complaint has to be made within three years of the problem arising. The Ombudsman then has discretion about how to take the matter forward, such as by asking one or other side for comments or more information, or writing to one or both parties with the investigator's preliminary view of the complaint.

The procedures of the Pensions Ombudsman are also designed and sequenced to achieve tiered resolution of cases.[188] First, the office may attempt to mediate a dispute informally (for example by phone) on receiving a new complaint.[189] Secondly, the investigator dealing with the matter may inform one or both parties of his or her preliminary view of the matter. Prior to 2009, such letters would only be written where it was thought that a company was not going to succeed in its case, but since then views can be expressed on general likely outcomes. Both sides have an opportunity to comment on a preliminary view before a final decision is taken.

Cases are then passed to the Ombudsman or Deputy Ombudsman. He or she can then write to the parties saying whether or not he or she agrees with the investigator's initial view, and that may produce settlement. If the view is not accepted by the party being complained about, any further information sent by that party will be considered before the Ombudsman issues a final and binding decision, which says whether or not the complaint is upheld and, if so, what should be done to put matters right.

A complainant can nominate someone to help, including a solicitor. Around 24 per cent of claimants are represented by someone else, whether legally qualified or not. In general, the costs of any external advice or representation by either party are not recoverable from the other party, but could be ordered to be payable in rare circumstances.

The Pensions Ombudsman may refer any question of law arising for determination in connection with a complaint or dispute to the High Court or, in Scotland, the Court of Session.[190]

The rules of procedure, made by the Secretary of State, have an adversarial model, but are in practice not often referred to, since principles of natural justice are instead applied. The Ombudsman has power to require production of documents (which is used occasionally, but the threat of use is usually sufficient in cases where a party is failing to respond) and has power to require individuals to give evidence. Oral hearings can be held, and this tends to occur when the honesty of a party is in issue, if there are large sums involved, or if there is a conflict of evidence that cannot be decided on paper.

A decision in favour of an applicant will usually include instructions on how the other party should put things right. Orders may include such matters as:

- putting a pension into payment;
- reconsidering a decision, for example concerning ill health and early retirement;
- delaying transfers;
- determining that a trustee is personally responsible and should make good the fund.

A determination by the Ombudsman is binding on all parties and has the status of a County Court judgment. If it is necessary to enforce a decision, the complainant has to

[188] The sequenced procedures noted here have developed over time: when the office was started in 1991 every case went straight to the Ombudsman personally.

[189] This stage is referred to in the official statistics as 'resolved/withdrawn'.

[190] Pension Schemes Act 1993, s 150(7).

institute enforcement proceedings in the County Court. That can present problems in practice. However, only a handful of awards are not complied with every year: the Pensions Ombudsman is aware of this since the Court procedure requires him to provide a certified copy of his award.

Decisions of the Pensions Ombudsman can be appealed to the High Court.[191] A limited number of Pensions Ombudsman decisions have been appealed. A notable one involved upholding the Pensions Ombudsman's decision to order the Department of Transport to repay a large sum that ended in a settlement of £355.8 million.[192]

The Pensions Ombudsman has appeared as a party in appeals to the High Court from his jurisdiction, which is an unusual situation. However, the current Pensions Ombudsman only does this in rare situations involving cases that concern his powers or jurisdiction, rather than cases involving the merits of a dispute.

Cost

The complaints process involving the Pensions Ombudsman is free to applicants. There is no adverse costs risk, so the procedure has obvious attractions as compared with a court case. There are two reasons for the absence of a costs rule. Firstly, most pensions cases are not appropriate for a cost shifting rule since it would penalise pensioners. Secondly, it is quite often difficult to say who has won or lost. There has been discussion over whether it is necessary to impose a registration fee so as to discourage frivolous complaints, but this has not to date been thought appropriate. There are now very few pensions litigation cases that involve an individual against trustees: there are many cases involving employers and trustees.

The Pension Ombudsman is funded by grant-in-aid paid by the Department for Work and Pensions (DWP), which is mainly recovered from the general levy on pension schemes. In 2010/11 the office received £2,810,000 grant-in-aid, incurred net expenditure of £2,678,353 and had net assets at 31 March 2011 of £75,913.[193]

Statistics

In 2009/2010,[194] the Pension Ombudsman accepted 950 complaints for investigation (43 of which concerned the same issue and could be dealt with as one). The three highest areas of complaint were ill-health pensions, misleading information and transfers. It took an average of 9.6 weeks for the Ombudsman's office to deal with initial enquiries and decide whether to accept a complaint for investigation. The average time taken to complete investigations was 10.9 months.

Of the 889 investigations closed during 2009/2010, only 231 needed to be formally determined by the Ombudsman or his Deputy. Of the remainder, 187 cases were discontinued, withdrawn or resolved informally, 152 investigations closed after a decision of the investigator using the informal procedures, and 319 cases were determined by the Ombudsman under the informal procedures following the investigator's initial decision.

There were 4 appeals of Ombudsman determinations over the course of the year, with 6 other appeals remaining to be heard as at 31 March 2010. The Ombudsman observes that

[191] Pension Schemes Act 1993, s 151(4).

[192] See in *re National Bus Superannuation Scheme* [1999] 48 *PBLR*.

[193] Annual Report and Account 2010/2011 of the Pension Ombudsman.

[194] www.pensions-ombudsman.org.uk/Publications/docs/AnnualReport2009-10.pdf.

notice for 4 applications for judicial review had been received 'most unusually and for no obvious reason'.

The Ombudsman also undertakes the role of Pension Protection Fund Ombudsman. In 2009/2010, 45 applications for review of PPF decisions were received, 38 of which were accepted for investigation, 18 cases were concluded (almost exclusively relating to the calculation of the risk-based portion of the PPF levy) and in each case the decision of the PPF was upheld. As at 31 March 2010, one notice of appeal of a PPF Ombudsman determination had been received.

The Legal Ombudsman

Following the introduction of statutory regulation of the legal profession under the Legal Services Act 2007,[195] an Office for Legal Complaints (OLC) was created,[196] with a duty to administer an ombudsman service for England and Wales. The OLC must have regard to best practice of those who administer ombudsmen schemes,[197] and appoint a Chief Ombudsman and, with the Chief Ombudsman's consent, assistant ombudsmen.[198] The service is known as the Legal Ombudsman.[199] The new scheme began on 6 October 2010, to provide a single gateway for consumers of legal services to channel their complaints while at the same time driving systemic improvement by feeding back to the profession information and methods to improve. The Legal Services Consumer Panel stated in 2012: 'The Legal Ombudsman is a very important partner organisation for the Legal Services Consumer Panel. It forms a vital part of the consumer protection machinery through its twin functions of providing a dispute resolution service and using intelligence from complaints to help raise standards.'[200]

The scheme rules, which set out the framework for how the Legal Ombudsman resolves complaints about legal services, are approved by the Legal Services Board and the Lord Chancellor, as required by the Legal Services Act.[201] The first step is for a client to tell the lawyer, and allow up to eight weeks to resolve the complaint. If the consumer is not happy with the lawyers' final response, they have up to 6 months to bring the compliant to the Ombudsman. The complaint should also be brought to the Ombudsman no later than 12 months from when the problem first occurred, or from when the consumer should reasonably have become aware of the problem. An ombudsman may fix (and may extend) a time limit for any stage of the investigation, consideration and determination of a complaint. If any party fails to comply with such a time limit, the ombudsman may proceed

[195] The Legal Services Board was established as oversight regulator (Legal Services Act 2007, Part 2 and Schedule 1) of ten Approved Regulators (including the bar, solicitors, and others), together with a Legal Services Consumer Panel (s8 of the Act).

[196] Legal Service Act 2007, s114 and Schedule 15.

[197] Legal Service Act 2007, s116(3).

[198] Legal Services Act 2007, s122.

[199] www.legalombudsman.org.uk.

[200] *Consultation response: Legal Ombudsman: Strategy 2012–2015, Business Plan 2012–2013* (Legal Services Consumer Panel, January 2012), available at www.legalservicesconsumerpanel.org.uk/publications/consultation_responses/documents/2012-01-09_LEO_strategy2012businessplan2012.pdf.

[201] www.legalombudsman.org.uk/downloads/documents/publications/OLC_Scheme%20rules_v1_201104-1_FINAL.pdf.

with the investigation, consideration and determination; draw inferences from the failure; where the failure is by the complainant, dismiss the complaint; or where the failure is by the authorised person, include compensation for any inconvenience caused to the complainant in any award.

The service is free to consumers. The Ombudsman service is open to all members of the public and to very small businesses, charities, clubs and trusts. An ombudsman will determine a complaint by reference to what is, in his/her opinion, fair and reasonable in all the circumstances of the case. In determining what is fair and reasonable, the ombudsman will take into account (but is not bound by): what decision a court might make; the relevant Approved Regulator's rules of conduct at the time of the act/omission; and what the ombudsman considers to have been good practice at the time of the act/omission.

If the Legal Ombudsman agrees that the lawyer's service has been unsatisfactory, he can ask them to:

- apologise to the consumer,
- give back any documents needed by the consumer,
- do more work for the consumer if this can put right what went wrong,
- refund or reduce the legal fees, or
- pay compensation if the consumer has lost out or been badly treated anything up to £30,000.

Once accepted, an Ombudsman's decision is final. A binding and final determination can be enforced through the High Court or a county court by the complainant. A binding and final determination can also be enforced through the High Court or a county court by an Ombudsman, if the complainant agrees; and the Ombudsman considers it appropriate in all the circumstances. A court which makes an enforcement order must tell the Legal Ombudsman, and then an Ombudsman will tell the relevant Approved Regulator; may require that Approved Regulator to tell the Ombudsman what action it will take; and may report any failure by that Approved Regulator to the Legal Services Board. The Legal Ombudsman may publish a report of its investigation, consideration and determination of a complaint. The report will not name (or otherwise identify) the complainant, unless the complainant agrees.

A complaint is potentially chargeable to the lawyer unless the case is dismissed or discontinued. No case fee is payable for the first two potentially chargeable complaints closed during the Legal Ombudsman's financial year relating to a business/partnership that is responsible for any act/omission of any employee/partner; or any individual authorised person for whom no business/partnership is responsible. The case fee is £400 for all chargeable complaints. The remaining costs of running the Legal Ombudsman are covered by a levy on Approved Regulators by the Legal Services Board.

In the first six months of operation,[202] 38,155 people contacted the Legal Ombudsman by phone, email and letter. Of these, 3,768 complaints were accepted for investigation. A total of 1,450 cases was resolved, of which 55 per cent were resolved within three months of a consumer's first contact, 76 per cent within four months and 92 per cent within five months. Failure to advise and failure to follow instructions were the most common categories of complaint. The annual budget in 2011 was £19.9 million.

[202] *Annual report 2011.*

Telecoms

This section considers general complaints to the regulator, complaints about broadcasting issues and Premium Rate Services, and complaint handling and dispute resolution requirements on providers.

Complaints to the Regulator

Complaints about a service provider made to the regulatory body, OFCOM, will be processed under published procedures in relation to various types of issues such as:

- considering complaints and carrying out investigations relating to breaches of licence conditions;[203]
- handling complaints about unfair treatment or infringements of privacy during the making or showing of programmes and advertising ('fairness and privacy complaints'—see below);[204]
- imposing sanctions for non-payment of licence fees;[205]
- consideration and determination of statutory sanctions.[206]

The number of contacts and complaints that OFCOM received between 2007/8 and 2009/10 is shown in Table 11.6, for the main types. By far the highest number of complaints each year related to telecommunications issues, although the trend has been downward. In 2009/10, 127,300 contacts were initiated by telephone and 67,200 from internet forms, emails, letters and faxes. Until 2011, OFCOM have felt obliged to look at every single complaint that is received, but this policy is now under review, in order to save money: a general discretion may be sufficient, which would allow OFCOM to focus on major issues.

Table 11.6: Total number of complaints to Ofcom 2007/8 to 2009/10

	2009/10	2008/9	2007/8
Telecommunications	105,400	140,000	152,000
Spectrum issues and licensing	62,500	49,800	57,600
General enquiries	2,200	3,200	5,000
Broadcasting	24,400	29,100	22,000
Total	194,500	222,100	236,600

OFCOM has powers to enforce breaches of the statutory requirements by imposition of penalties and taking enforcement action in court, but the primary means of control is through use of setting 'General Conditions' in licences that apply to all communications providers

[203] *Procedures for the handling of broadcasting standards or other licence-related cases* (Ofcom, 2009) available at stakeholders.ofcom.org.uk/broadcasting/guidance/complaints-sanctions/standards.

[204] *Procedures for the handling of fairness & privacy complaints* (London, Ofcom, 2009) available at stakeholders.ofcom.org.uk/broadcasting/guidance/complaints-sanctions/fairness.

[205] *Procedures for the consideration of statutory sanctions in cases of non-payment of license fees* (London, Ofcom, 2009), at stakeholders.ofcom.org.uk/binaries/broadcast/guidance/complaints-sanctions/complaints_sanctions.pdf.

[206] *Procedures for the consideration of statutory sanctions in broadcasting or other licence-related cases* (London, Ofcom, 2009) available at stakeholders.ofcom.org.uk/broadcasting/guidance/complaints-sanctions/procedures-statutory-sanctions.

who provide an electronic communications network and/or electronic communications service in the United Kingdom.[207] The sanction of being able to revoke a licence in response to non-compliance with a General Condition, or to impose more detailed conditions, is a powerful weapon.[208]

Complaints under the Broadcasting Code

Complaints may be made to OFCOM under the Broadcasting Code[209] where a person has been offended or unfairly treated, including unwarranted infringement of privacy of people appearing in (or in connection with the obtaining of material included in) programmes.[210] OFCOM must consider and, where appropriate, adjudicate on fairness and privacy complaints.[211] There is no charge for making a complaint to OFCOM: OFCOM bears its own cost of the investigation and enforcement.

OFCOM has a team of around 20 people working on maintenance and operation of the Broadcasting Code, plus six additional people who deal with low-level complaints. 90 per cent of complaints are received through the website. A complaint is reviewed through internal procedures, and then an investigation may be held. The process is changing to be more streamlined. In the initial phase nearly 30 per cent of complaints get filtered out. 80-90 per cent of complaints do not raise issues under the Broadcasting Code: in such cases the complainant will always be sent a letter to that effect. However, OFCOM records all complaints, not least because they usually relate to the 10 major channels.

OFCOM divides cases into 'straightforward' cases, those in which OFCOM does not need to contact the broadcaster to deal with the complaint, and 'complex' cases, those which require investigation with the broadcaster. In 2009–10, 99.2 per cent of straightforward cases were closed within 30 working days (target 80 per cent), and 72.1 per cent of complex cases were closed within 60 working days.[212]

Ten per cent of the complaints lead to a serious investigation. OFCOM first writes to the broadcaster for comments, and then makes its decision. For TV and radio complaints the investigation team requires recordings. The findings are reported in a 'bulletin' that appears fortnightly on OFCOM's website. It contains complaints, compliance issues and high-profile complaints. Some 'not upholds' are still important to establishing standards of conduct, since they relate to relevant issues. The totality of complaints represents a tool for

[207] Communications Act 2003, ss 45–51. Power to impose sanctions for breaches of license conditions or other enforceable requirements are set out in the Communications Act 2003, the Competition Act 1998, the Enterprise Act 2002, the Broadcasting Act 1990, the Broadcasting Act 1996, EU Regulations and the Wireless Telegraphy Act 2006, depending upon the type of license which has been granted to the relevant broadcaster.

[208] Communications Act 2003, ss 94–104.

[209] stakeholders.ofcom.org.uk/broadcasting/broadcast-codes/broadcast-code. See guidance at stakeholders.ofcom.org.uk/broadcasting/guidance/programme-guidance/bguidance The Broadcasting Code is updated regularly. The code was reviewed in 2009: *Broadcasting code review, Statement on the Ofcom Broadcasting Code*, (Ofcom, 2009), available at stakeholders.ofcom.org.uk/binaries/consultations/bcode09/summary/main.pdf; procedures were reviewed in 2010 and streamlined: *Review of procedures for handling broadcasting complaints, investigations and sanctions*, stakeholders.ofcom.org.uk/consultations/broadcast-complaints-review; it was them changed in 2011.

[210] See *Procedures for handling of Fairness and Privacy complaints*, at stakeholders.ofcom.org.uk/binaries/broadcast/guidance/fairness.pdf. The Code requirements are Communications Act 2003, ss 319, 326 and Broadcasting Act 1996 (as amended) s 107.

[211] 1996 Act, s 110.

[212] Annual Report 2009–10.

measuring what the public think and feel about particular issues and 'generally accepted standards', since these shift over time.

Some investigations into complaints are more complex. Some cases raise issues of 'impartiality', which is required by section 5 of the Broadcasting Code. News programmes need to give equal exposure to all. Non-news items can give rise to rights on freedom of expression under ECHR, and this can be difficult on issues on which there is controversy, so it is necessary to look at issues widely. Other cases raise issues of fairness and privacy, on which the Broadcasting Act sets out much detail.

A complainant can request a review of a decision by OFCOM. This gets dealt with afresh by a different OFCOM executive, and does sometimes result in a different view. OFCOM will consider whether to refer a matter to the Broadcast Committee. From 2011, a draft decision will be shown to the provider, although not to the complainant, so as to provide some opportunity and pressure for the broadcaster to respond spontaneously in resolving the issue. It is always open to a broadcaster to seek judicial review of OFCOM's process or a decision, but this occurs very rarely.[213]

The number of complaints closed under the Broadcasting Code for three recent years is shown at Table 11.7. The vast majority of complaints concerned programme standards.

Table 11.7: Number of complaints closed under the Broadcasting code[214]

2009/10	28,281 complaints, of which 28,072 were complaints about programme standards (including issues relating to political advertising and the scheduling of television advertising), and 209 were complaints about alleged unfairness and/or unwarranted infringements of privacy.
2008/9	27,549 complaints
2007/8	64,742 complaints (including 194 over 44,500 complaints about 'Celebrity Big Brother' 2007)

In 2009/10, of the 10,679 closed cases (28,072 complaints) relating to programme standards:

- 152 cases were found to be in breach either of the Broadcasting Code, other OFCOM codes or of licence conditions. Of these, six cases were subject to statutory sanctions (involving six separate broadcasters);
- 13 cases were resolved; and
- 10,514 cases were not in breach or out of remit.

Premium Rate Services and PhonepayPlus

Premium rate services (PRS) offer some form of content, product, facility or service that is charged to a consumer's bill for electronic communications services.[215] OFCOM has the power to approve a code for PRS that meets the legal requirements set out in section 121 of the

[213] An example was a judicial review taken by Jon Gaunt/Talksport in 2008, which upheld OFCOM; www.guardian.co.uk/media/2008/nov/18/utv-commercialradio; media.ofcom.org.uk/2010/07/13/high-court-backs-ofcoms-judgment-in-jon-gaunt-case.

[214] The following data is taken from OFCOM Annual Reports and relates to complaints considered under the Broadcasting Code and closed in that reporting year.

[215] PRS are defined in s 120(7) of the Communications Act 2003. They may be accessed by way of a conventional voice call, but may also be accessed in other ways, such as SMS, PC, mobile phone downloads or interactive

Communications Act. OFCOM has approved the PhonepayPlus[216] (formerly ICSTIS) Code of Practice for these purposes.[217] The most recent version is the PhonepayPlus Code (12th Edition), dated 2011.[218] In relation to those PRS that fall within the definition of 'Controlled PRS', compliance with the Code is *mandatory* and OFCOM retains backstop powers under the PRS Condition, which it may set.[219] From 2011, all Controlled PRS providers are subject to the PRS Condition, which enables OFCOM to require such providers to comply with enforcement directions made by PhonepayPlus.[220] Insofar as a particular PRS is not caught within the definition of Controlled PRS, the PhonepayPlus Code of Practice applies to it, but compliance is *voluntary*.

PhonepayPlus adjudicates complaints that are referred to it by consumers, members of the public, industry, and through its monitoring of services. Complaints are recorded and analysed, grouped with similar complaints relating to the same service, and are then investigated by a specialist team. Adjudication is undertaken by an independent tribunal. Tribunals meet fortnightly, and are drawn from a larger panel (the Code Compliance Panel), which is chaired by a qualified barrister or solicitor having not less than 15 years' relevant experience. Members of the Code Compliance Panel are appointed by the Board of PhonepayPlus in consultation with the Chairman of the Panel, who is also appointed by the Board. Tribunals are made up of three people, and comprise a legally qualified Chair, and either two lay members or a lay member and a member of the PhonepayPlus board who has no industry relationships.

PhonepayPlus currently operates three procedures for dealing with apparent breaches of the Code. The Informal Procedure is used where the incident in question has caused little consumer harm and the service provider has an acceptable history of complying with the Code. In this instance, there is no formal investigation if the service provider acknowledges the breach and agrees to take remedial action. At the other end of the spectrum, the Emergency Procedure is used where the apparent breach has caused serious consumer harm which requires immediate remedy. In this instance, PhonepayPlus undertakes an immediate investigation of the service and presents its early findings to the Code Compliance Panel with a view to securing their agreement to the service being immediately removed from operation, pending formal adjudication within a subsequent 10 working day period.

In all other cases, PhonepayPlus operates the Standard Procedure. This involves the service provider being supplied with all the necessary information giving rise to the apparent

digital TV. Common forms of PRS include TV voting lines, competitions, adult entertainment, chat lines, business information services, mobile phone ringtones, game downloads, horoscopes, and directory enquiry services.

[216] www.phonepayplus.org.uk. PhonePayPlus was formerly an agent of Ofcom, functioning like the ASA. It is non-profit making and consists of eight non-executive part-time Board members (with one Chair and one Executive Board member), supported by a full time Executive. Board members are required to make and keep up-to-date declarations of any conflict of interest. See Governance Statement at www.phonepayplus.org.uk/~/media/Files/PhonepayPlus/Corporate/GovernanceStatement.pdf.

[217] The relationship between OFCOM and PhonepayPlus is set out in a Framework Agreement, which is available at stakeholders.ofcom.org.uk/consultations/phonepayplus.

[218] *Approval of the PhonepayPlus Code of Practice (12th Edition) A statement and notification approving the PhonepayPlus Code of Practice for regulating Premium Rate Services under section 121 of the Communications Act 2003* (London, OFCOM, 2011), at stakeholders.ofcom.org.uk/binaries/consultations/ppp/statement/statement.pdf.

[219] Communications Act 2003, ss 120–124.

[220] *Modifying who is subject to the Premium Rate Services Condition Statement on amending the PRS Condition to mirror the remit of PhonepayPlus under its new Code of Practice* (OFCOM, 2011), at stakeholders.ofcom.org.uk/binaries/consultations/prs-2011/statement/statement.pdf.

breach of the Code, which has been received or acquired by PhonepayPlus. The service provider is given the opportunity to respond in detail to this information, and following such response, a report is prepared by PhonepayPlus for submission to a Tribunal. A service provider may request, or a Tribunal may invite, oral representations from service providers prior to an adjudication.

PhonepayPlus also operates a procedure that enables the information, or content, provider to respond to allegations of breach of the Code in place of the service provider, upon satisfaction of certain conditions and on receipt of appropriate assurances and undertakings.

PhonepayPlus has a Sanctions Guide[221] that sets out criteria for imposition of sanctions, the power to order a party to make refunds to complainants where there has been a serious breach and/or intent to mislead or defraud,[222] the power to impose bars on the service provider, and to fine. There is an Independent Appeals Body.

Code of Practice for Complaint Handling and Dispute Resolution

Background and research

OFCOM is required to set general conditions governing:

(a) the handling of complaints made to public communications providers by any of their domestic and small business customers;
(b) the resolution of disputes between such providers and any of their domestic and small business customers;
(c) the provision of remedies and redress in respect of matters that form the subject-matter of such complaints or disputes.[223]

OFCOM must also secure so far as they consider appropriate that the dispute resolution procedures are 'easy to use, transparent and effective', and free of charge for customers to use.[224] OFCOM shall approve a code submitted 'if and only if, in their opinion, it makes all such provision as they consider necessary in relation to the matters dealt with in the code for the protection of [customers].'[225]

The task of approving over 300 individual codes would have imposed too great a burden on OFCOM, so a self-regulatory system was adopted. Until 2011, OFCOM exercised the above duties through two regulatory obligations on communications providers regarding the handling of consumer complaints:

1. providers must have a Complaints Code of Practice that is approved by OFCOM and with which they must comply;[226] and
2. providers must belong to an OFCOM-approved Alternative Dispute Resolution (ADR) scheme and adhere to the final decisions made by that scheme.[227]

[221] www.phonepayplus.org.uk/~/media/Files/PhonepayPlus/Policy%20_Industry%20support/Sanctions_Guide_20080408.ashx.

[222] The Guide states that the Tribunal will take into account when imposing a sanction whether the party in breach has already begun to issue refunds or intends to issue refunds: p 6.

[223] Communications Act 2003, s 52.

[224] Communications Act 2003, s 52. This implements the Universal Services Directive 2002/22/EC arts 20(1) and 34(1), as amended by Directive 2009/136/EC.

[225] Communications Act 2003, s 53(1).

[226] General Condition 14.4.

[227] General Condition 14.7.

The ADR schemes are independent bodies that can examine complaints that have not been resolved within eight weeks, at no cost to consumers. Two such ADR schemes were approved by OFCOM: the Office of the Telecommunications Ombudsman (OTELO, since 2011 renamed Ombudsman Services: Communications) and the Communications and Internet Services Adjudication Scheme (CISAS). Providers could be a member of either scheme.

There is no legal requirement for internet service providers to belong to a dispute resolution scheme, but the vast majority (over 95 per cent of the Broadband market) belong to the Internet Service Providers' Association (ISPA). ISPA's Code provides that members will attempt to resolve complaints within ten working days of receipt, after which the customer can complete an ISPA complaint form, which ISPA takes up with the member, who has five working days to respond, after which a second complaint may be made and will be referred to CISAS unless resolved within two months.[228]

The approach was reviewed extensively from 2008, based on market research[229] and consultation,[230] and revised in 2011. The 2008 review concluded:[231]

> 3.3 ADR is a well established and important mechanism for giving a consumer access to justice where recourse to the court system by the consumer may be impossible or impractical due to cost and resource restraints. It is an important way to redress the power imbalance in disputes between consumers and [Communications Providers (CPs)] – who normally have greater resources, knowledge and control over the products and services which are in dispute.
> 3.4 We think that the current regulatory regime for ADR is successful in many ways. However, we think that there are ways in which it is appropriate to improve it.

The principal issues identified were:

- the period before consumers have a right to go to ADR was set at twelve weeks, and this was thought to be too long, and reduced to eight weeks;[232]
- the level of awareness amongst consumers of the right to go to ADR was too low, so providers were required to notify their consumers about ADR (5 days after a complaint is lodged and subsequently when the consumer has the right to go to ADR); and
- the ease of access to the ADR Schemes, including the level of support provided to consumers by the ADR Schemes themselves.

The 2011 regime set minimum standards for complaints handling by establishing a single OFCOM-approved Complaints Code of Practice, instead of CPs having to submit their individual codes to OFCOM for approval. It also facilitated OFCOM monitoring by requiring CPs to keep appropriate records of their contact with consumers; and set the criteria for its review of the approval of ADR schemes.

Research conducted between July and August 2007 indicated that 15 per cent of adults were aware of at least one of the two ADR schemes. Awareness was higher for OTELO (13

[228] See www.ispa.org.uk/complaints.

[229] By Futuresight in 2006, at stakeholders.ofcom.org.uk/consultations/alt_dis_res/futuresight and by Synovate in 2009, at stakeholders.ofcom.org.uk/binaries/consultations/complaints_procedures/annexes/annex8.pdf.

[230] Available at: stakeholders.ofcom.org.uk/binaries/consultations/complaints_procedures/summary/adr_condoc.pdf.

[231] *Review of Alternative Dispute Resolution and Complaints Handling Procedures,* 10 July2008, at stakeholders.ofcom.org.uk/binaries/consultations/alt_dis_res/summary/condoc.pdf.

[232] The original 12 weeks timeframe (now reduced to 8 weeks) came from the companies' quarterly billing cycle. The energy regulator made this change before telecoms.

per cent) than CISAS (7 per cent). However, the vast majority of consumers had not heard of either of the ADR Schemes (83 per cent). Market research showed that awareness of ADR was considerably lower in the telecommunications sector than in most comparable industries, as demonstrated in Figure 11.2.[233]

Figure 11.2: Awareness of official dispute resolution bodies

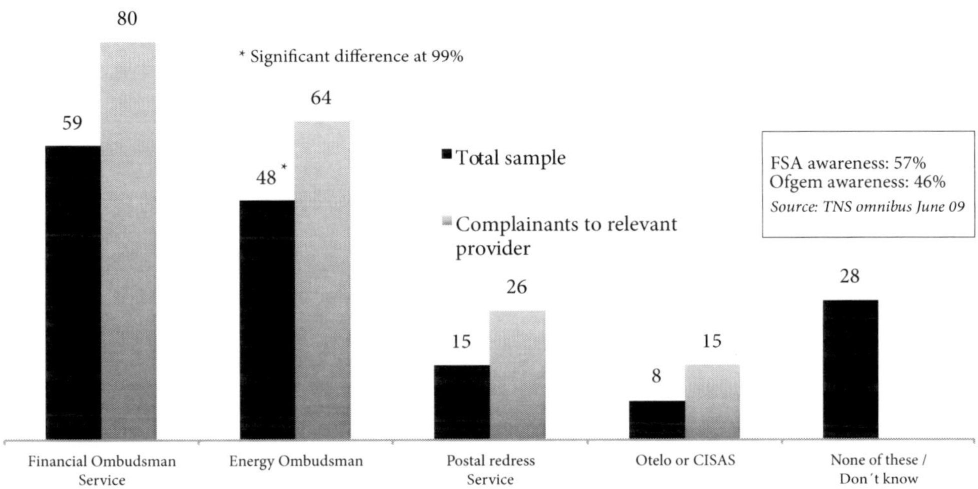

Those consumers who were aware of at least one of the ADR Schemes were asked how they had found out about it. Results highlighted a range of sources most notably the media—magazines/newspapers (22 per cent) and TV/Radio/Advertising (20 per cent). Friends and family (15 per cent) and the internet (12 per cent) were the next most mentioned sources of information. Notably, relatively few (5 per cent) mentioned their phone bill as their source of information. This suggested that an approach which relied merely on requiring CPs to include details of ADR Schemes on the back of their bill, as Otelo did, would not be particularly effective in raising awareness.

Further evidence showed that a significant proportion of consumers had a very poor experience when pursuing a complaint with their provider:[234]

- 23 per cent of the population had made a complaint[235] to a mobile, broadband, or landline provider in the preceding year, with 30 per cent of these complaints being unresolved 12 weeks later, representing around 3 million consumer complaints each year;
- the majority of consumers who could not resolve their complaint promptly had considerable difficulty getting their provider to recognise they were trying to make a complaint and in finding out information about the complaints process;

[233] The sample sizes do not allow for a comparison of awareness levels across the industries amongst those complainants that could potentially take their complaint to their respective ADR schemes.

[234] *A Review of Consumer Complaints Procedures. Statement*. 22 July 2010, at stakeholders.ofcom.org.uk/consultations/complaints_procedures/statement.

[235] A 'complaint' was defined as 'an expression of dissatisfaction made to a service provider related to its products or services, or the complaints-handling process itself, where a response or resolution is expected.'

- those consumers who were unable to resolve their complaint within 12 weeks were much more likely to suffer financially or through stress;
- ADR significantly improved outcomes for consumers, but awareness of ADR in the telecommunications sector was considerably lower than comparable schemes in other sectors, undermined its effectiveness as a remedy of last-resort;[236] and
- OFCOM continued to receive nearly 1,000 complaints a month from consumers who were unhappy with their provider's complaints handling process.

Research showed that dispute resolution services improved the outcome for those consumers who would otherwise fail to pursue complaints out of frustration with their provider's response or lack of response. For example, of those complaints about mobile providers that were not resolved within 12 weeks, 91 per cent of complaints were subsequently resolved when taken to a dispute resolution service, compared with 51 per cent of complaints where the consumer did not go to a dispute resolution service.

OFCOM proposed key criteria for approval of an ADR Scheme, as shown in Table 11.8.[237]

Table 11.8: OFCOM's key criteria for an ADR scheme

Criteria	Description
Accessible	Consumers to be able to access an ADR Scheme free of charge. Procedures must be easy to use and understand, including for disabled and vulnerable consumers.
Independent	The ADR Scheme to be impartial and independent of both the consumer and the CP.
Fair	Decisions to be based on principles of fairness, taking into account relevant principles of law and equity.
Efficient	The ADR Schemes to operate efficiently. They must deal with complaints in a timely manner and use their resources in a responsible and efficient manner.
Transparent	The ADR Schemes to be transparent about the rules which govern the use of their services and about the decisions which they make.
Effective	The ADR Schemes to have procedures in place, which are followed, to monitor the implementation of its decisions and compliance with rules. They must make sure that decisions are implemented by CPs.
Accountable	The ADR Schemes to provide detailed and transparent reporting on their operation to us and the public. OFCOM anticipated that 'it will be appropriate to review the current KPIs which the ADR Schemes are required to provide to us to ensure that they remain relevant and useful and to make them comparable where possible'.

The Synovate market research demonstrated that ADR improved the prospect of a resolution for complaints that had not been resolved within 12 weeks. For example, as shown in figure 8 below, 91 per cent of mobile complaints that went to ADR were completely or partially resolved, compared with 51 per cent of mobile complaints that were not resolved within 12 weeks (labelled as 'eligible ADR non-users').

[236] Only 8 % of consumers were aware that they could take unresolved complaints to ADR, less than half that in a number of other sectors with similar schemes): 23% of respondents to a survey had made a complaint in the telecommunications in the preceding year, compared with 4% in post, 12% in energy, and 6% in financial services.

[237] 2008 Review.

Figure 11.3: The outcome of consumer complaints

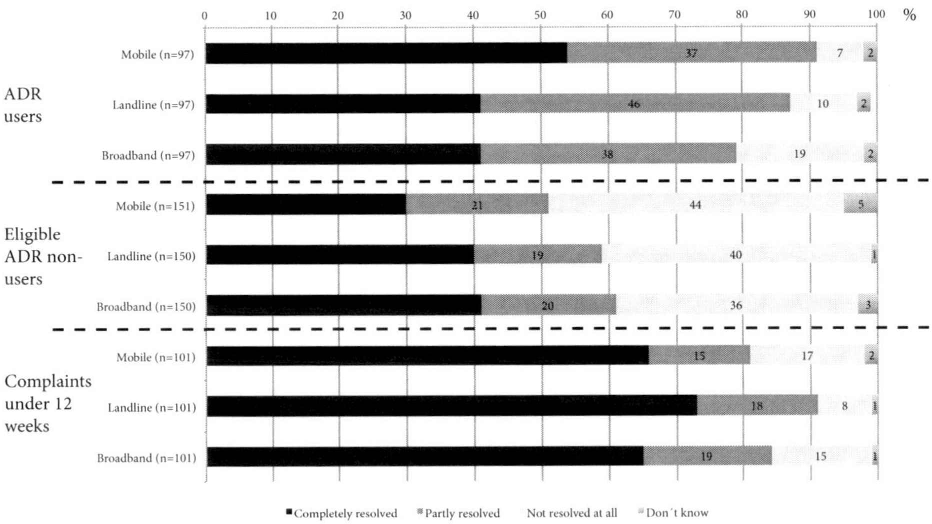

However, OFCOM noted that the evidence set out in its consultation suggested that there was not a clear link between awareness of ADR and use of ADR. For example it said that although awareness of the Energy Ombudsman was much higher than that of the respective telecommunications ADR schemes (48 per cent and 8 per cent respectively), both the energy and telecommunications sectors had a similar proportion of long standing complaints going to ADR (10 per cent of energy complaints lasting 8 weeks go to ADR, while 12 per cent of telecommunications complaints that lasted 12 weeks go to ADR).

The Code on Complaints Handling

The 2011 OFCOM Approved Code of Practice for Complaints Handling in relation to complaints made by residential and small business customers (see Figure 11.9)[238] establishes a number of requirements, including:[239]

- Relevant text about ADR is to be included on paper bills provided to domestic customers (providing the name of the relevant ADR scheme, noting that the ADR scheme offers a dispute resolution service that is independent of the CP, noting that the scheme cannot be accessed unless eight weeks have passed since the consumer first complained to the CP, and stating that ADR can be utilised by the consumer at no cost);
- CPs must ensure consumers whose complaint has not been resolved within eight weeks of first being made to a front-line agent receive written notification about their right to go to ADR;
- CPs must ensure front-line staff are fully informed of the right of consumers to use ADR; and

[238] The Code of Practice came into force on 22 January 2011. The new requirements to improve awareness of dispute resolution services came into force on 22 July 2011.

[239] See clause 4 of OFCOM code.

- On request from a complainant, CPs must issue a deadlock letter referring a matter to ADR unless the subject-matter of the complaint is outside the jurisdiction of the ADR scheme, the complaint is vexatious, or the CP has genuine and reasonable grounds for considering the matter will be resolved in a timely manner and subsequently takes active steps to do so.

Initially, the customer (consumer or small business) takes the complaint to the telecoms provider. If the provider is unable to resolve the complaint within 3 months, or if the provider tells the customer that the complaint cannot be resolved ('deadlock'), the customer may take the complaint to an ADR scheme. The role of the ADR scheme is to investigate complaints fairly and decide what actions should be taken to resolve the complaint.

The aim is to make it easier for consumers to exercise their right to take unresolved complaints to a free independent resolution service. The Code of Practice will provide consistency in standards and will give OFCOM powers to take enforcement action against those providers who do not treat complainants fairly. The Code requires providers to ensure the fair and timely resolution of complaints, and have procedures that are transparent and accessible so that consumers can easily find out how to make a complaint.

Figure 11.4: The OFCOM Approved Code of Practice for Complaints Handling[240]

This Ofcom Approved Code of Practice for Complaints Handling (the 'Ofcom Code') sets out the minimum standards that Ofcom has set for Communications Providers (CPs) in the handling of Complaints made by Domestic and Small Business Customers (as those terms are defined in General Condition 14.7) about the provision of Public Electronic Communications Services (as defined in the General Conditions of Entitlement). A list of further definitions can be found on the page following the specific obligations. Explanatory guidance can be found on the Ofcom website.
A CP must have complaints handling procedures that:

1) Are **transparent**:
   a) A CP must have in place a written code for handling complaints ('Customer Complaints Code') made by their Domestic and Small Business Customers. A CP must comply with its Customer Complaints Code in relation to each Complaint it receives.
   b) The Customer Complaints Code must be concise, easy to understand and only contain relevant information about complaints handling procedures.
   c) The Customer Complaints Code must be kept up to date and as a minimum include information about: i) the process for making a Complaint;
      ii) the steps the CP will take to investigate with a view to resolving a Complaint;
      iii) the timeframes in which the CP will endeavour to resolve the Complaint, including when the CP is likely to notify the Complainant about the progress or resolution of a Complaint;
      iv) the contact details for making a Complaint to the CP, including providing details about the low-cost points of contact required in clause 2(c) below; and
      v) the contact details for the CP's Alternative Dispute Resolution scheme, with details on when a Complainant will be able to access the service (with reference to the requirements on a CP in both clause 4(c) and 4(d) below).
2) Are **accessible**:
   a) The Customer Complaints Code must be well publicised and readily available, including:
      i) being easily accessible on a webpage, with either:
         1. a weblink to the Customer Complaints Code being clearly visible on a CP's primary webpage for existing customers (ie '1 click' access); or

[240] stakeholders.ofcom.org.uk/binaries/consultations/complaints_procedures/statement/statement.pdf.

2. a weblink to the Customer Complaints Code being clearly visible on a 'how to complain' or 'contact us' page, which is directly accessible from a primary webpage for existing customers (ie '2 click' access).

ii) ensuring the relevant terms and conditions for a product and/or service refer to the existence of the Customer Complaints Code and should signpost consumers to how they can access a copy; and

iii) being provided free of charge to Complainants upon reasonable request in hard copy or other format as agreed with the Complainant.

b) Complaints handling procedures must be sufficiently accessible to enable consumers with disabilities to lodge and progress a Complaint.

c) The means by which a CP accepts Complaints should not unduly deter consumers from making a complaint. A CP must have in place at least two of the following three low-cost options for consumers to lodge a Complaint: i) a 'free to call' number or a phone number charged at the equivalent of a geographic call rate;

ii) a UK postal address; or

iii) an email address or internet web page form.

3) Are **effective**:

a) A CP must ensure the fair and timely resolution of Complaints.

b) There must be clearly established timeframes and a clear and reasonable escalation process for dealing with Complaints.

4) [Facilitate appropriate **access to Alternative Dispute Resolution**:

a) A CP must ensure front-line staff are fully informed of the right of consumers to use Alternative Dispute Resolution.

b) Every paper bill provided to domestic customers must include, in a reasonably prominent manner, relevant text regarding the right of consumers to take unresolved complaints to Alternative Dispute Resolution. Such text will:

i) provide the name of the Alternative Dispute Resolution scheme;

ii) make reference to the fact that the scheme offers dispute resolution, which is independent of the CP;

iii) make reference to the fact that the scheme can only be accessed eight weeks after a Complaint was first made to the CP; and

iv) make reference to the fact that consumers can utilise the scheme at no cost to themselves.

c) A CP must promptly issue a written Deadlock Letter when requested by a Complainant, unless:

i) the CP has genuine and reasonable grounds for considering that the Complaint will be resolved in a timely manner and subsequently takes active steps to do so; or

ii) it is reasonable to consider the Complaint to be vexatious; or

iii) the subject-matter of the Complaint is outside the jurisdiction of the CP's Alternative Dispute Resolution scheme.

d) A CP must ensure Complainants receive prompt Written Notification of their right to go to Alternative Dispute Resolution eight weeks after the Complaint is first brought to the attention of the CP, unless:

i) it is reasonable to consider the Complaint has been resolved; or

ii) it is reasonable to consider the Complaint to be vexatious: or

iii) the subject-matter of the Complaint is outside the jurisdiction of the CP's Alternative Dispute Resolution scheme.]

5) Retain appropriate **records** of contact with Complainants: a) A CP must retain written records collected through the complaints handling process for a period of at least six months including, as a minimum, written correspondence and notes on its customer record management systems.

Definitions for the Ofcom Code The following definitions should be used for interpreting this Code of Practice: '**Alternative Dispute Resolution**' means any dispute procedures approved by Ofcom under section 54 of the Communications Act 2003. **'Complaint**' means:

a) an expression of dissatisfaction made by a customer to a Communications Provider related to either:
i) the Communications Provider's provision of Public Electronic Communications Services to that customer; or
ii) the complaint-handling process itself; and b) where a response or resolution is explicitly or implicitly expected.

'**Complainant**' means a Domestic or Small Business Customer who makes a Complaint to a Communications Provider. '**Deadlock Letter**' means a letter or email from a Communications Provider to a Complainant agreeing that the Complaint can be referred to the relevant Alternative Dispute Resolution scheme. **'Written Notification'** means a written notification sent to a Complainant that:
a) is in plain English;
b) is solely about the relevant Complaint;
c) informs the Complainant of the availability of dispute resolution, which is independent of the CP;
d) provides the name and appropriate contact details for the relevant Alternative Dispute Resolution scheme; and
e) informs the Complainant that they can utilise the scheme at no cost to themselves.

OFCOM stated in 2011 that there are a number of benefits of a regulatory regime that promotes effective access to ADR:[241]

- Giving consumers access to justice where recourse to the court system may be impossible or impracticable due to cost and resource constraints, as well as reducing the 'system costs' that would occur if a high volume of relatively low monetary value disputes were instead required to be resolved by the legal system;
- Reducing the power imbalance between consumers and CPs, who normally have greater resources, knowledge and control over the products and services in dispute;
- Improving the outcome for those consumers who would otherwise fail to pursue complaints out of frustration with their CP's response or lack or response;
- Empowering consumers to pursue their rights more effectively with their own CP, with the knowledge that they have an alternative option for redress if the complaint becomes intractable; and
- Providing additional incentives for CPs to improve their complaints handling procedures and to resolve complaints quickly and effectively.

Feedback

Data on complaints made to the government's Consumer Direct line ranks telecoms as the most complained about sector in the UK. New entrants to a market may concentrate most on obtaining market share and less on retaining customers. However, the telecom market has changed since 2009, and there is now a reduced emphasis on 'churn', and more on retaining the customer base. Thus, companies attend more closely to customer satisfaction. There has also been consolidation in the market, and may be more.

Therefore, in order to increase transparency, OFCOM has published performance data. In April 2011, OFCOM published for the first time the data on the consumer complaints that it received in relation to telecom providers in the period October 2010 to February 2011, as the

[241] *The use of Alternative Dispute Resolution as a means to resolve disputes related to commercial transactions and practices in the European Union* (London, OFCOM, 2011).

first of a series of quarterly publications.[242] It believed that the average of about 450 telecoms complaints received a day from consumers were likely to be made where a consumer was unable to resolve an issue with their provider to their satisfaction. By considering evidence from the dispute system and its own consumer contact centre, OFCOM is able to address systemic issues, recognize a trend, deal with it and reduce the detriment.

The approach to consumers and to seeking feedback varies significantly between companies. Some consumers who ring call centres of mobile phone companies receive a text message shortly afterwards asking them to rank the performance of the person who dealt with them; the responses can be used not only in monitoring complaint handling but also the remuneration or employment of individual handlers.

Companies differ in how they record complaints data. They are not required to make their internal complaints data transparent. This was a major issue in the 2010 consultation. The energy system has required logging every complaint, but it was thought to be too expensive in telecoms. Escalations are logged if people ask to speak to a manager. OFCOM can compel disclosure of the data by enforcement action.

ADR schemes: CISAS and OS:C

As noted above, the two ADR providers in the sector are CISAS[243] and OS:C.[244] Some 206 providers use the former (now run by CEDR Disputes Group) and around 250 companies use OS:C. The former has 70 per cent of internet service providers, the latter 95 per cent of fixed line providers, with mobile services split roughly equally. Although competition between private sector providers is theoretically beneficial, it is only communications providers who are able to choose between them, not consumers.

There is a slight difference between the modes of operation of the two schemes. CISAS was originally modelled on arbitration, and OS:C invested strongly in mediation and in identifying cases that would respond to mediation, but since 2011 both provide conciliation stages. Attending a mediation hearing might cause significant inconvenience to a consumer or small trader. Dealing with matters by documentary means, especially on the internet, or by telephone, can be much more user-friendly.

In the ombudsman process, a case handler makes a précis of each side's case, which is sent to the other side and used as the basis of any final report and decision, whereas in the CISAS process all documents of either side are sent to the other party and then to the adjudicator. No comparative evaluation has been done on the advantages and disadvantages of either approach, or whether there may be any difference in relevance for different types or sizes of case. It is difficult to choose between these two models since either might be swifter or more appropriate in particular circumstances.

The two schemes coordinate, so if a member of one does not comply with a ruling, that scheme's operator will inform the other, and the other will not accept the company into membership until they have complied with all required conditions. The regulator can also

[242] stakeholders.ofcom.org.uk/market-data-research/telecoms-research/complaints/oct-2010-feb-2011.

[243] www.cisas.org.uk. CISAS was established in 2003, and is administered by IDRS Ltd. It was created following discussions between the Chartered Institute of Arbitrators, Orange, NTL, Telewest, The Internet Service Providers' Association and others who wanted their ADR provision to continue to be provided by the CIArb rather than through an ombudsman model.

[244] www.otelo.org.uk.

apply its authority to achieve compliance, since the operator may be in breach of Ofcom's General Conditions.

In 2010, OS:C had roughly 100,000 contacts a year (in 2009/10 averaging 392 a day, and 412 in 2009/10[245]) and 8,000 adjudications; CISAS had almost 5,000 contacts and 2,000 adjudications. In recent years, the number of contacts to OS:C have been fairly stable (Table 11.9) but those to CISAS have risen and fallen (Figure 11.4).

Table 11.9: Contacts received by OS:C 2007/08–2010/11

Year	Contacts
2007/08	105,600
2008/09	101,882
2009/10	102,025
2010/11	103,702

Figure 11.5: CISAS enquiries and valid applications 2005–2010

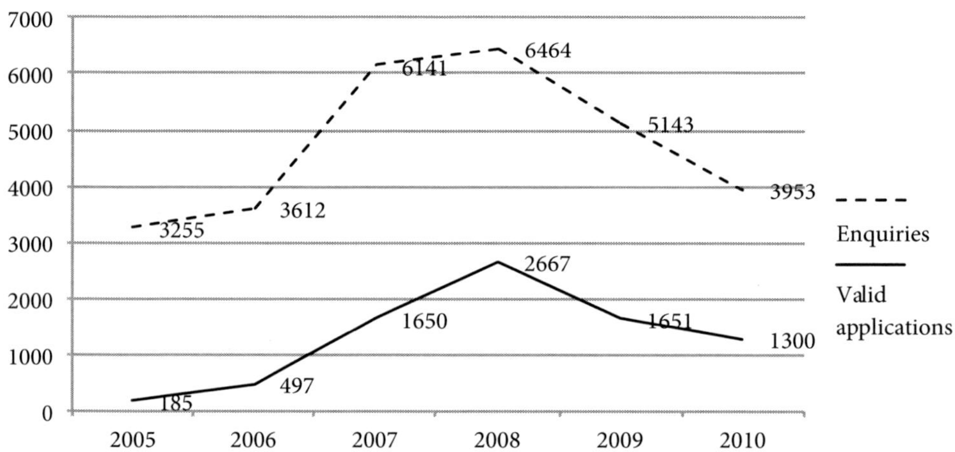

The main reason for rejection of complaints to both schemes has been the same every year, namely that consumers apply too early and do not give the company a chance to deal with their complaint in line with its published complaints procedures (Table 11.10). However, OS:C's main reason for accepting a complaint is that companies do not deal with complaints within the 8 week deadline (Table 11.11).

Table 11.10 Number of complaints 2009–2010

	OS:S 2009–2010	CISAS 2010
General enquiries	70,435	3,953
Complaints outside terms of reference	42,383	1,072
Valid applications	7,012	1,300
Cases concluded	6,801	1,327

[245] Complaints received in 2010–11 were 68% by telephone (43% new calls / 57% follow-up calls) and 32 per cent in writing (40% letter, 60% email and under 1% fax).

Table 11.11: Reasons for OS:C accepting a complaint 2009–2010

	OS:C 2009–2010	OS:C 2010–2011
Greater than eight weeks (12 weeks before September 2009)	76%	84%
Deadlock letter	23%	13%
Ombudsman's discretion	1%	3%

The breakdown of contacts to OS:C for 2009–2010 is shown in Table 11.12.[246] If a complaint form is issued, consumers usually return it and it becomes an investigated case (of the 13,165 complaint forms issued in 2010–2011, 10,789 (82 per cent) were returned), though a small percentage are withdrawn by the consumer or are subsequently discovered to be premature or outside of the ombudsman's jurisdiction. However, in many instances there is a delay of several weeks between the date the form is issued and the date it is returned.

Table 11.12: OS:C Complaint Data 2009–10 and 2010–11

	Total Calls	**Total Written**	**Forms Issued**	**Forms Returned**	**Informally resolved cases**	**Number of awards**	**Average value of financial awards**
2009–2010	70,435	27,500	10,747	8,936	1,467	7,038	£99.47
2010–2011	63,244	30,523	13,165	10,789	2,229	7,175	N/A

The range of financial awards is shown in Table 11.13. The average amount claimed in OS:C cases in 2009–10 was £587, an increase of £72 over 2009 (£515). The lowest average claim value of £461 was in 2006. The total amount awarded as compensation by adjudicators in 2010 was £146,882, representing an average award of £198 (an increase of £25 on 2009). Thus consumers received on average about 34 per cent of their claim in 2010 (also in 2009).

In 2010–2011, 68 per cent of OS:C final decisions issued contained a financial award and the majority of them (81 per cent) also contained a non-financial award. In 17 per cent of cases a non-financial award only was made. A non-financial award may include an apology, an explanation, a service or some practical action to be provided by the member company.

Table 11.13: Ranges of awards made by OS:C 2009–10 and 2010–11

Amount awarded	**Number of awards 2009–2010**	**Number of awards 2010–2011**
£ 1–50	2,619	3,282
£ 51– 100	1,216	1,744
£ 101– 200	626	914
£ 201– 300	204	225
£ 301– 400	73	89
£ 401– 500	61	44
£ 501– 1,000	67	44
£ 1,001– 2,000	13	21
£ 2,001– 3,000	6	6
£ 3,001– 4,000	2	1
£ 4,001– 5,000	6	1

[246] Otelo performance report 2010, www.ombudsman-services.org/downloads/Otelo_performance_report_Oct_2010.pdf.

The classification used by the two bodies for the nature of complaints is different (Table 11.14) and makes it difficult to compare the performance of communications companies and the nature of their problems: it would be better if a standard classification were used.

Table 11.14: Nature of complaints to OS:C and CISAS

	OS:C 2009/10	OS:C 2010–2011	CISAS 2010
Customer service	51%	55%	2.2%
Disputed charges	22%	20%	39%
Service	15%	17%	–
Billing	8%	6%	17.5%
Equipment	2%	1%	–
Security	1%	1%	–
ISP Service	–	–	21%
Terms and conditions	–	–	11.6%
Loss of service	–	–	3.6%
Disconnection/reconnection	–	–	2.8%

Key Performance Indicators (KPIs) are agreed by the ADR bodies with OFCOM on an annual basis. Performance figures are provided monthly to OFCOM, and published on the ADRs' website. The KPIs and performances in 2010 are shown in Table 11.15.[247] In comparing these, it should be noted that the types of cases dealt with may differ.

Table 11.15: Performance against OS:C Key Performance Indicators

	OS:C 2009–2010 target	OS:C 2009–2010 actual	OS:C 2010–2011 actual	CISAS 2010 target	CISAS 2010 actual
Calls answered in less than two minutes[248]	more than 80%	90.4%	85%	95%	100%
Written correspondence responded to in less than 10 working days	100%	99.2%	59%		
Written correspondence responded to in less than 5 working days				90%	95%
Provisional conclusions issued within six weeks	more than 90%	46.3%	81%	88%	85%
Provisional conclusions issued after more than eight weeks	less than 1%	33.3%	4%	10%	5%
Unit cost as an indication of improved efficiency: 100% of total cost divided by the number of valid applications		N/A	N/A		£300.90[249]

[247] OS:C annual report 2010/11, available at: www.ombudsman-services.org/attachments/download/369/Communications%202011%20AR.pdf. Annual Report 2010 CISAS, http://www.cisas.org.uk/media/text/CISAS-Annual-Report-2010.pdf.

[248] The 2 minutes includes an allowance for the caller to listen to a pre-recorded information message, which for CISAS lasts 1 minute 41 seconds and gives options to the caller on whether to record a message, request

Energy

Consumers may complain to their suppliers, then to the independent ombudsman, or to Consumer Focus,[250] the regulator, or may start a claim in court. Various codes established by the trade association, the Energy Retail Association, are also relevant for disputes and can be referred to the ombudsman.[251]

Establishment of the Energy Ombudsman

In 2005, OFGEM determined that a *voluntary* redress scheme should be introduced by the six largest energy supply companies[252] to resolve outstanding billing disputes relating to retail energy supply. This followed an investigation by OFGEM into energy suppliers' billing practices, and a 'super-complaint' in relation to such practices by Consumer Focus. Consequently, in July 2006, energy suppliers who were members of ERA introduced an alternative dispute resolution scheme. The scheme was operated by the Energy Supply Ombudsman (part of The Ombudsman Service Limited). Initially, the Energy Supply Ombudsman's remit was limited to complaints relating to customer switching between the constituent ERA member companies, however, the remit was later expanded to include complaints relating to energy selling.

The Consumers, Estate Agents and Redress Act 2007 introduced, among other things, a requirement that energy supply companies and energy network businesses should belong to a redress scheme that is approved by the GEMA.[253] In addition, a new duty was placed on GEMA to establish binding complaint handling standards for energy suppliers. Accordingly, in October 2008 the voluntary scheme established by the energy companies was replaced by a statutory redress scheme. After a robust selection procedure, OFGEM decided to approve a single redress scheme in the energy sector and appointed OS to provide this function.[254] The name of the scheme was changed from the Energy Supply Ombudsman to the Energy Ombudsman (EO). The terms of reference for the EO were broadened to include complaints from micro-business as well as those from domestic consumers.

information or speak to a CISAS staff member. After the message or on selection by the customer, the average time for CISAS staff to answer any call is 10 seconds.

[249] The figure for 2010 was an increase of 9% over 2009, driven by two factors. Firstly, in 2010 the number of cases concluded under the lower cost 'Early Settlement Procedure' rather than being referred to an adjudicator reduced from 58% to 46%. Secondly, the total number of valid cases received dropped by 21%, increasing the effective fixed cost per case.

[250] The functions of the consumer body Energywatch (the Gas and Electricity Consumer Council) were taken over by Consumer Focus (the National Consumer Council) under the Consumers, Estate Agents and Redress Act 2007, ss 13, 30. In October 2010, the Government announced the abolishment of Consumer Focus and the transfer of some functions to the Citizens Advice, Citizens Advice Scotland and the General Consumer Council in Northern Ireland. It is expected that this transfer will occur in Spring 2013.

[251] Such as the 2002 Code of Practice for Face-to-Face Marketing of Energy Supply, and the 2005 Code of Practice for Accurate Bills.

[252] British Gas, EDF Energy, E-ON, npower, Scottish Power and Scottish and Southern Energy.

[253] Consumers, Estate Agents and Redress Act 2007, ss 42–52; The Gas and Electricity Regulated Providers (Redress Scheme) Order 2008, SI 2008/2268, available at www.legislation.gov.uk/uksi/2008/2268/contents/made.

[254] OFGEM Decision report 26/08, 14th March 2008.http://webarchive.nationalarchives.gov.uk/20080806055225/http://www.ofgem.gov.uk/MARKETS/RETMKTS/COMPL/CONSREP/Documents1/Redress%20Schemes%20Decision.pdf.

Thus, the scheme of the legislation in energy is that the Minister has a duty, but delegates to the regulator, who delegates to OS. Hence, since OS is acting on behalf of the minister in energy, it is subject to judicial review. The statutory scheme initially covered business suppliers to households, and was expanded from 1 October 2008 to include all complaints by networks, domestic and micro-businesses.

OS was reviewed for OFGEM in 2010.[255] The independent review found that the model delivered fair and independent redress, had appropriate governance, was accessible and well organised, with well trained personnel. No evidence or belief was found that there was bias in the views, behaviours or actions of the Ombudsman or Investigation Officers. The major subject of criticism related to matching resource to fluctuating complaint levels: various recommendations were made, most of which have been implemented.

The role of the Ombudsman is widening. The scheme is currently looking at including feed-in tariffs and social aspects. Complaints against commercial decisions are now being accepted, so OS is operating in a manner that is closer to a public sector ombudsman, by taking all the circumstances of a customer's requirements and complaint into account. This extension in scope is interesting and it is unclear where it will end. OFGEM recently delegated determinations on connection charges to the OS.

The 2010 review of OS' energy function found that only 6.5 per cent of nearly 90,000 contacts and attempted contacts fell within the Energy Ombudsman's terms of reference.[256] A significant proportion of OS' costs were therefore being spent on handling enquiries for which it could make no impact. A major issue for the complaints handling process as a whole, therefore, is how to capture complaints at the most appropriate stage (ie by companies before outside authorities are involved) or how to reduce the total volume of complaints overall. The former issue would seem to be one of providing information to consumers and ensuring that companies seek and deal effectively with complaints. The latter issue is one of seeking to reduce the total volume of complaints, by providers performing at a higher level of service.

Market research indicates that the general public is becoming more aware of the Energy Ombudsman.[257]

The Energy Ombudsman Scheme

All regulated energy providers holding a licence to domestic and/or micro business customers are required to be members of the EO service.[258] The EO has Memoranda of Understandings (MoUs) in place with a number of bodies, including consumer representative organisations such as Consumer Focus, and the regulatory body GEMA/OFGEM, to cross-direct any complaints that fall within the remit of each other.

The services provided by EO members that fall within the scope of the EO's powers include:

- the metering and billing of customers for the supply of energy;
- problems relating to the transfer of customers between energy suppliers;

[255] Sohn associates, *Independent Review of the Energy Ombudsman*,(2010).
[256] ibid.
[257] *Customer satisfaction report commissioned by the Energy Ombudsman*, July 2009.
[258] The CEAR Act amended the relevant sections of the Gas Act 1986 and the Electricity Act 1989.

- complaints about an energy supplier's sales activity, including sales of products and services and the provision of regulated products and services by holders of a gas transportation licence or electricity distribution licence;
- physical issues and problems relating to the supply of energy to a home such as power cuts.

All EO service members are subject to the jurisdiction of the EO in relation to complaints regarding such services. The EO does not deal with complaints about energy companies that are not members of its service; pre-September 2007 complaints; complaints about physical supply problems to homes before April 2008; problems being dealt with by the courts or other complaints processes, or where the EO considers that the problem should be dealt with by the courts of other complaints procedures; cases considered malicious or unjustified; and issues relating to commercial decisions by member companies relating to whether or not to provide a product or service, and the related terms (ie reduction in energy tariffs).

The EO has an absolute discretion to decide whether a complaint is within the Ombudsman's jurisdiction, as prescribed by its Terms of Reference, and has the power to refuse a complaint if it is considered that the complainant does not have a reasonable prospect of success, recovery or redress.

The first step in the complaints process is to contact the energy company, to give them a chance to sort out the problem. The consumer can do this by phone, email or letter, following the energy company's published complaints procedure. After eight weeks of making the complaint to the energy company, the complainant can pass the complaint on to the EO. This has to be done within nine months from the date the problem was first brought to the company.

The ombudsman will also consider a complaint for investigation if a participating company has issued a deadlock letter, before the end of the eight week period, stating that it cannot do any more for the complainant. A deadlock letter can be issued if:

- there is no new information to be gained on the complaint;
- the complaint escalation processes have been followed;
- no agreement can be reached within the company's complaint procedures; and
- having more time will not improve this position.

The complainant has six months from the date of the letter to pass the complaint to the EO. The EO can accept a complaint if the complaint was brought to the gas or electricity company within 12 months of first knowing about it. The ombudsman may also accept a complaint for investigation at the ombudsman's discretion, for example if a complaint is just outside the required timeframes, but the complainant would have had no opportunity to raise the complaint any sooner.

If the EO decides it has the power to deal with the complaint, it sends the complainant a filled-in form to check, sign and return with copies of all the supporting documents. By signing the complaint form, the complainant gives the energy company the permission to release information relevant to the complaint.

The overall objective of the EO, as with communications, is to seek to achieve a mutually acceptable settlement of a complaint wherever practical and appropriate. However, where such a mutually acceptable settlement is not forthcoming or is withdrawn, the EO may conduct a formal investigation of the complaint.

Following a formal investigation the EO will inform the complainant and the participating company concerned in writing of the Investigation Report and its suggested remedies, and will invite comments within a specified period. If this is accepted by both the energy company and the complainant as a settlement of the dispute, then it will become the final decision.

Following an investigation, the EO may decide to do the following:

- If it considers that the participating company is offering a fair and reasonable settlement, or alternatively if the EO considers that no settlement is required, the EO may terminate its consideration of the complaint.
- Where the complainant and the participating company accept the Investigation Report, then that will become the final decision.
- If the complainant or the participating company do not accept the Investigation report then a Final Decision will be issued. The Final Decision will be made after considering any submissions and representations made in relation to the Investigation report and the suggested remedies.

Where the EO issues a Final Decision that concludes that a participating company has not acted fairly or reasonably, the Ombudsman is required to set out its reasons in writing and may impose any of the following remedies requiring the participating company to: (i) apologise or provide an explanation to the complainant; (ii) compensate the complainant to an amount not exceeding £5,000; (iii) take other practical action to the direct benefit of the complainant; or (iv) provide any combination of the above remedies. By signing a 'deed poll', the final decision of the EO is binding on the participating company, but not the complainant/ customer. In addition to these remedies the EO may also make a (non-binding) recommendation to the participating company concerned about changing its policies or procedures, including the provision of services.

The complainant has 28 days to decide to accept the decision of the Ombudsman. After the 28 day period, the complainant looses the right to the solution offered by the Ombudsman.

Statistics

At the start of 2012 the EO had 113 participating companies.[259] The complaint statistics are shown in Table 11.16.

Table 11.16: Energy Ombudsman complaints 2008/09 to 2010/2011

	2008/09	2009/10	2010/11
Contacts received	77,604	78,528	54,794[260]
Contacts were about companies that were not members of the Energy Ombudsman	729	N/A	N/A
Complaint forms issued	6,163	7,192	6,727
Signed complaint forms received	5,077 [80%]	6,419 [89%]	5,812 [86%]

[259] Energy Ombudsman annual report 2010/11, available at: www.ombudsman-services.org/attachments/download/333/2010%20annual%20reportEnergy.pdf.

During 2010/11, 24 per cent of new contacts related to complaints that could be considered by Ombudsman Services: Energy: see table 11.17. The majority of new contacts (72 per cent) related to complaints that could not be accepted by the service at that time. Complaints about participating companies accounted for 93 per cent of new contacts, but almost three quarters of these could not be accepted. Most commonly this is because the complainant has contacted the Energy Ombudsman too early in the complaints process and has not allowed the company adequate opportunity to resolve the complaint. About four per cent were general enquiries or literature requests. Complaints usually include more than one issue, and customer service is an element of most. It is common to have a delay of several weeks from the date the complaint form is issued to the date it is returned and received.

Table 11.17: Reasons for accepting a complaint 2010–2011

Unresolved in 8 weeks	66%
Final response from the company (Deadlock letter)	25%
Ombudsman Decision	9%

In 2010–2011, 60 per cent of resolved complaints included a financial award (with an average of £137), and of these 96 per cent also included a non-financial award, such as an apology, an explanation, a service, or some practical action to be performed by the company. The reasons for complaints are at Table 11.18.

Table 11.18: Reasons for the complaint 2010–2011

Billing dispute	88%
Transfer	8%
Sales	4%

Feedback

The EO is required to bring to the attention of OFGEM any trends or issues that are arising across the industry. This includes any problems or patterns of behaviour that relate to an individual energy provider.

The number of complaints about the six large energy companies made to Consumer Direct, Consumer Focus and the Energy Ombudsman is compiled by Consumer Focus and published every three months.[261] The different types of complaints are weighted to reflect the seriousness of the complaint.

[260] This represented an average 214 contacts a day.

[261] See energyapps.consumerfocus.org.uk/performance.

General Consumer Trading Sectors: Resolution of Disputes under Codes of Business Practice

The OFT Consumer Code Approval Scheme

The approach to codes of practice, described above,[262] has developed since at least the 1980s. Some trade association schemes succeeded from an early stage in resolving significant numbers of consumer claims.[263] Initially, the OFT assessed the detailed wording of individual codes, but found this to be resource intensive. From 1991, it endorsed codes that met a series of 'best practice' criteria.[264] White Papers in 1999[265] and 2001[266] proposed new regimes for codes of practice. A strong consumer brand was intended to be established for codes that were endorsed by the OFT. The new approach introduced a two-stage approach which aimed to encourage trade associations to re-assess their existing codes of practice or introduce new codes of practice that address consumer detriment within their sectors. The first stage (establishing core criteria) could be delivered within OFT's existing powers, and the second stage (an approval power) was mandated under the Enterprise Act 2002. The core criteria for the new OFT CCAS were published in July 2001[267] and core criteria and guidance notes were issued in 2008.

Overview of the Scheme

Under the CCAS,[268] the OFT publishes criteria that it regards as best practice for a business code of practice. If a sectoral code satisfies the criteria, through a specified evaluation process, that code gain formal approval by the OFT. Individual businesses operating to that code qualify to use and display the OFT approved code logo. The assumption is that businesses will see commercial advantage in marketing their business as having OFT code approval, and that consumers will see advantages in choosing traders who are members of an OFT approved scheme. The OFT's function is to monitor codes of conduct operated by the private sector and oversee their general development, without day-to-day involvement in how they are run. The scheme is intended to raise standards of business practice and provide a signpost to consumers so that they can identify businesses that will provide them with excellent service and protection over and above the law.[269]

[262] pp 261 ff.

[263] Between 1983 and 1989, the ABTA scheme conciliated 42,253 cases, of which 1,764 were referred to arbitration with 1,362 claims being upheld and 340 claims rejected in arbitration; equivalent figures for the National Association of Retail Furnishers were 3.063, 3, 1 and 2: R Thomas. 'Alternative Dispute Resolution – Consumer Disputes' (1988) 7 *Civil Justice Quarterly,* 206–219.

[264] New guidelines were established: www.oft.gov.uk/shared_oft/reports/consumer_protection/oft183.pdf. G Howells and S Weatherill, *Consumer protection law*, 2nd ed (London, Ashgate, 2005) 72–77 and 580–585.

[265] Department of Trade and Industry, *Consumer White Paper* (1999). The main critique of the previous scheme had been that it took too long to get through the approval process. There were also problems of signposting for consumers, since there were too many different badges and logos of different codes: this was too confusing for consumers.

[266] *The OFTs new approach to consumer codes of practice, A consultation paper*, (2001), available at www.oft.gov.uk/shared_oft/Approvedcodesofpractice/oft331.pdf (accessed on 27 July 2010).

[267] Available at: www.oft.gov.uk/shared_oft/Approvedcodesofpractice/oft344.pdf (accessed 8 June 2010). An earlier version was *Consumer Codes Approval Scheme: Core Criteria and Guidance* (London, OFT, 2004).

[268] *Consumer Codes Approval Scheme: Core Criteria and guidance 2008*, available at: www.oft.gov.uk/shared_oft/Approvedcodesofpractice/oft390.pdf (accessed on 1 November 2010).

[269] OFT Report: *Consumer Codes Approval Scheme – update of core criteria OFT's response to the consultation* (London, OFT, 2006), available at: www.oft.gov.uk/shared_oft/Approvedcodesofpractice/oft855.pdf.

Responsibility for drafting codes rests with the code sponsors (usually trade associations) who have the necessary expertise in their sectors.[270] The core criteria set out the standards the OFT expects a code sponsor and its members to achieve in order to be approved by the OFT.[271] Codes developed by sponsors will only be approved if the OFT believes that they will be effective in protecting and promoting consumer interests, and which offer consumers benefits beyond the protection afforded by law. The core criteria are summarised at Figure 11.6, they can be summarised as:

- a commitment to provide customers with adequate information about goods and services,
- the use of clear and fair contracts,
- the protection of deposits or prepayments,
- low cost, independent dispute resolution if a complaint is not dealt with satisfactorily.[272]

The application process for OFT approval a consumer code has two stages. Code sponsors complete Stage One by making a promise that their code meets the core criteria in principle. They can then move on to Stage Two where they have to demonstrate with evidence that their codes are compliant in practice and that consumer disputes are properly resolved. This process usually takes at least 6 months. It includes auditing, consumer satisfaction surveys and a final review of the code by the OFT. The approval process is intentionally diligent and the benefit is that the scheme is now connected to outside support for the scheme, the consumer advisory bodies, who are regarded as 'critical friends'. Sponsors provide an annual report to the OFT on the operation of their codes. There is a fundamental code-review every three years where the code sponsors must consult with other bodies that are committed to the scheme, such as Which?, Age Concern , Consumer Focus and Trading Standards.

Figure 11.6: Overview of the core CCAS criteria:[273]

1. Organizational criteria
  a. Code sponsors should have a significant influence on the sector.
  b. Codes shall include a provision that compliance with the code is mandatory. Code sponsors must be able to demonstrate that members are prepared to observe the code's provisions.
  c. Code sponsors shall have adequate resources and funding to ensure the objectives of the code are not compromised.

2. Preparation of the code criteria
  a. Code sponsors shall be able to demonstrate that organizations representing consumers, enforcement bodies and advisory services have been adequately consulted throughout the preparation of the code.
  b. Code sponsors shall be able to demonstrate that organizations representing consumers, enforcement bodies and advisory services have been adequately consulted throughout the operation and monitoring of the code.

[270] Sponsors of an approved code can be any body that can influence and raise standards within its sector. See the Enterprise Act 2002: www.oft.gov.uk/about-the-oft/legal-powers/legal/enterprise-act/#.

[271] *Consumer Codes Approval Scheme. Core Criteria and Guidance* OFT 390 (Office of Fair Trading, 2008), available at www.oft.gov.uk/shared_oft/Approvedcodesofpractice/oft390.pdf.

[272] www.oft.gov.uk.

[273] OFT *Consumer Codes Approval Scheme* core criteria and guidance 2008 available at: www.oft.gov.uk/shared_oft/Approvedcodesofpractice/oft390.pdf.

3. Content of the code criteria

a. The code shall include measures directed at the removal or erasing of consumer concerns and undesirable trade practices arising within the particular sector.
b. The code shall require that code members ensure that their relevant staff know about and meet the terms of the code as well as their legal responsibilities. Appropriate training is to be provided.
c. The code shall address clear and truthful marketing and advertising as appropriate to the sector.
d. The code shall address clear and accessible pre-contractual information as appropriate to the sector.
e. The code shall address high-pressure selling as appropriate to the sector.
f. The code shall address clear terms and conditions of supply and fair contracts as appropriate to the sector.
g. The code shall address delivery and completion dates as appropriate to the sector.
h. The code shall address cancellation rights as appropriate to the sector.
i. The code shall address guarantees and warranties as appropriate to the sector.
j. The code shall address protection of deposit or prepayments as appropriate to the sector.
k. The code shall address customer service provisions as appropriate to the sector.
l. The code shall address the additional effort/help to be provided to vulnerable consumers as appropriate to the sector.

4. Complaints handling criteria

a. the code shall include a requirement that code members shall have in place speedy, responsive, accessible and used friendly procedures for dealing with consumer complaints. A specific reasonable time limit for responding to complaints shall be prescribed.
b. The code shall include a requirement that code members will offer the same level of co-operation with local consumer advisers or any other intermediary acting on behalf of a consumer when making a complaint as they would to the complaint.
c. The code shall include procedures for dealing with complaints including the availability of conciliation services directed at arranging a decision acceptable to both parties.
d. The code shall include the availability of a low-cost, speedy, responsive, accessible and user-friendly independent redress scheme to act as an alternative to seeking court action in the first instance.

The scheme shall be binding in respect of code members who shall not be able to refuse to allow a complaint to go before the scheme if a customer so chooses.
The code member shall be bound to accept a decision made under the scheme. Any such scheme shall be able to take into account possible breaches of the code where relevant to the complaint.

5. Monitoring criteria

a. The code sponsor shall develop performance indicators, eg mystery shopping exercises and independent compliance audits, to measure the effectiveness of the code.
b. The code sponsor shall implement the performance indicators and make available the results of their monitoring procedures and satisfaction surveys to demonstrate the effectiveness of the code.
c. The code sponsor shall provide a written report annually to the OFT on the operation of the code to include:
   - Changes to the code agreed with the OFT and implemented
   - Numbers and types of complaints including information on outcomes from the conciliation process and the independent redress scheme
   - Results from monitoring, satisfaction surveys and the disciplinary process

   It would be preferable if the report were compiled by an independent person or body with powers to recommend actions.

d. The code sponsor shall provide copies of the annual reports to the OFT.
e. The code sponsor shall regularly review the code and update its provisions in the light of changing circumstances and expectations.
f. Consumer satisfaction shall be regularly assessed.

6. Enforcement criteria

a. code sponsors shall establish a procedure for handling on-compliance by members with the code. The procedure shall include independent disciplinary procedure and reasonable timescales for action.
b. The code sponsor shall also set out a range of sanctions, e.g .warning letters, fines, terminations of membership, for dealing with non-compliance.

7. Publicity criteria

a. codes sponsors and members shall ensure that theur customers are aware of the code.
b. Code members are to make clear, eg in advertising, point of sale, their adherence to a code of practice.
c. Copies of codes shall be available without charge to customers, to members, to local consumer advisers and to others with a legitimate interest.
d. Copies of any code related publicity generated by the code sponsor shall be provided to the OFT in advance of publication.
e. Code sponsors and members shall publicise the fact that OFT has approved the code by using the CCAS logo in the prescribed manner.
f. Code sponsors shall comply with the terms of the standard copyright licence, disseminate the terms to their members and monitor their members' use of CCAS logo. Appropriate action shall be taken by the code sponsors against a member for non-compliance with the copyright licence.

Stage Two was introduced in 2005, and extended the duration of the process. The CCAS was criticised for taking too long for codes to gain approval, but the OFT defended its position on the basis that to lower the criteria or cut corners in proof of compliance would undermine the standards of consumer protection.

In 2011, the government proposed, as a cost-cutting measure, that the OFT would cease to exist and the proposed new Competition and Markets Authority would not continue operation of the CCAS. It explored alternative options for future accreditation of Consumer Code Approvals, including roles for BSI, Trading Standards, and private and/or third sector organisations.[274] At the time of writing, it appears that the most likely way forward will involve a Trading Standards body taking over control of the system.

Existing codes

As at 2011, 10 sponsors have achieved OFT approval for their codes, with dates of approval:

1. Motor Codes Ltd (New Car Code), 2004;[275]
2. Vehicle Builders and Repairers Association Ltd, 2004;[276]

[274] *Empowering and Protecting Consumers. Consultation on institutional changes for provision of consumer information, advice, education, advocacy and enforcement* (London, Department for Business Enterprise and Skills, 2011), at www.bis.gov.uk/Consultations/empowering-and-protecting-consumers; www.bis.gov.uk/assets/biscore/consumer-issues/docs/e/11-970-empowering-protecting-consumers-consultation-on-institutional-changes.pdf.

[275] www.motorcodes.co.uk. The trade association SMMT comprises all volume car makers, and the majority of smaller manufacturers, totalling 99.7% of the 2.5 million new car market. Several codes exist in relation to different services for cars, such as those of the Retail Motor Industry Federation (RMIF) and the Vehicle Builders Repairs Association.

[276] www.vbra.co.uk.

3. Direct Selling Association, 2004;[277]
4. The Property Ombudsman Ltd (sales), 2005;[278]
5. The Carpet Foundation, 2007;[279]
6. Bosch Car Service, 2006[280]
7. British Association of Removers, 2008;[281]
8. Debt Managers Standards Association, 2008;[282]
9. British Healthcare Trades Association, 2009;[283]
10. Institute of Professional Will Writers, 2010;[284]
11. Motor Codes Ltd (Service and Repair), 2011.[285]

The following code sponsors have successfully completed stage one and are working towards OFT approval of their codes of practice (as of October 2010):

- Motor Codes Ltd (Vehicle Warranty Products),
- Renewable Energy Association,
- SafeBuy.

Statistics

The cost to the consumer for accessing the ADR procedure under the approved codes, and the fees charged for businesses, are shown in Table 11.19.

[277] www.dsa.org.uk. Membership accounts for over 70 per cent of direct sales to the home.

[278] www.tpos.co.uk. The Estate Agents Company Limited represents around 40% of estate agency offices in the UK.

[279] www.carpetfoundation.com. This is the trade association for carpet manufacturers and retailers, with 1,090 independent retailers, whose sales make up over half of the independent sector, and a further 11 carpet manufacturers.

[280] www.bosch.co.uk/content/language2/html/715_5770.htm. Bosch Car Service is a 400-strong network of garages.

[281] www.bar.co.uk/Default.aspx. The British Association of Removers is a trade association for professional removal and storage businesses representing over 650 members in the UK, ranging from small family businesses to multinational companies.

[282] http://www.demsa.co.uk. DEMSA currently has four members, who between them deal with around 38 per cent of all fee-paying debt management cases handled in the UK.

[283] aaa.bhta.net. BHTA's membership consists of over 400 companies who provide a variety of products including first aid medical equipment, mobility access and stair lifts, prosthetics, rehabilitation products and visual impairment products. Many of the healthcare products of this sector are personal in nature, and are often sold to consumers in the home.

[284] www.ipw.org.uk. The IPW is a trade body for suppliers of will writing services, assistance in estate planning and related legal services. It currently has 190 full members, representing an estimated 20% of independent will writing businesses in the UK.

[285] http://www.motorcodes.co.uk/; The code of practice is run by Motor Codes and has 6,500 franchised dealers and independent garages as members.

Table 11.19: Cost to the consumer and fees for businesses of accessing ADR for the OFT approved codes[286]

Code sponsor	**Cost of ADR to the consumer**	**Cost of ADR to the member business**
Codes that have completed Stage 2 approval		
Robert Bosch Ltd (Bosch)	Free	£350
Vehicle Builders and Repairers Association (VBRA)	Conciliation by the code sponsor is free. There is a fee payable if the complaint is taken to arbitration: Claim up to £1000 is £42.35 net Between £1001–£5000 is £62.92 net. Over £5000 is £83.49 net.	*No information held*
Motor Codes Ltd (New Car Code)	Conciliation by the code sponsor is free. The consumer and member business share the cost of arbitration, £500 plus VAT per case, on a sliding scale dependent upon the amount of money claimed. For the consumer: Claim up to £1000 is £60 +VAT Between £1,001 and £5000 is £100 + VAT Between £5,001 and £10,000 is £200	The consumer and member business share the cost of arbitration, £500 + VAT per case, on a sliding scale dependent upon the amount of money claimed. For member businesses: Claim up to £1000 is £440 + VAT Between £1,001 and £5000 is £400 +VAT Between £5,001 and £10,000 is £300+VAT
Direct Selling Association (DSA)	Free adjudication	*No information held*
Carpet Foundation	Conciliation by the code sponsor is free. Arbitration is £55 net (refundable if shown not to be at fault)	£55 + VAT
British Association of Removers (BAR)	Conciliation by the code sponsor is free. The arbitration fee is dependent on claim amount. Claim up to £5000 is £100. Claims over £5000 are possible but may incur further one-off costs	£100
Debt Managers Standards Association (DEMSA)	Free	N/A
British Healthcare Trades Association (BHTA)	Free	*No information held*
The Property Ombudsman (TPO)	Free	£120 + VAT
Institute of Professional Willwriters (IPW)	Arbitration cost is £75.	£450 + VAT (correct as at 2008)

[286] Annual reports provided by code sponsors vary in period covered, so do not fall neatly into calendar years. The cost to the consumer of using the ADR/independent redress service if activated data from OFT under the FOIA December 2010.

Codes that have completed Stage 1		
Code sponsor	**Cost of ADR to the consumer** *(Please note that there may be further negotiations on the code/ ADR before OFT approval of the code.)*	**Cost of ADR to the member business**
Renewable Energy Association	N/A	Both the consumer and member business pays an initial fee equivalent to the County Court Fee (this fee is refunded to the consumer if the independent arbitrator finds in his or her favour, or recommends it. Any further costs will be explained to both sides and divided between the consumer and member business, as the independent arbitrator may decide.
SafeBuy	Mediation by code sponsor is free. Arbitration costs to the consumer is £25 plus VAT	£250 plus VAT
Motor Codes Ltd (car service and repair)	Conciliation by the code sponsor is free. The consumer and subscriber share the cost of arbitration, £500 + VAT per case, on a sliding scale dependent upon the amount of money claimed. For the consumer: Claim up to £1000 is £60 +VAT Between £1,001 and £5000 is £100 + VAT Between £5,001 and £10,000 is £200	The consumer and member business share the cost of arbitration, £500 + VAT per case, on a sliding scale dependent upon the amount of money claimed. For member businesses: Claim up to £1000 is £440 + VAT Between £1,001 and £5000 is £400 +VAT Between £5,001 and £10,000 is £300+VAT
Motor Codes Ltd (vehicle warranty products)	Conciliation by the code sponsor is free. The consumer and subscriber share the cost of arbitration, £500 + VAT per case, on a sliding scale dependent upon the amount of money claimed. For the consumer: Claim up to £1000 is £60 +VAT Between £1,001 and £5000 is £100 + VAT Between £5,001 and £10,000 is £200	The consumer and member business share the cost of arbitration, £500 + VAT per case, on a sliding scale dependent upon the amount of money claimed. For member businesses: Claim up to £1000 is £440 + VAT Between £1,001 and £5000 is £400 +VAT Between £5,001 and £10,000 is £300+VAT

The administration cost of the code and their ADR systems for code sponsors and individual businesses are not known, but include both one-off initial costs and on-going running costs. The OFT criteria state that 'Code sponsors shall have adequate resources and funding to ensure the objectives of the code are not compromised'.[287] It requires a written statement from the code sponsor to confirm adequate resource and funding. A 2006 evaluation found that the costs to businesses of implementing and maintaining an OFT approved code were not substantial (little more than the costs of adhering to pre-existing codes), and were estimated at between £142 and £252 per business per annum.[288] The review also found that costs to code sponsors varied substantially, dependant on whether satisfactory processes were already in place (such as to meet the requirement for comprehensive monitoring of members), and ranged from 'minimal' costs, to £50,000 per annum. It was suggested that such costs were a factor in determining the uptake of the scheme. OFT's budget for 2010/11 estimated its total staff cost for the CCAS at £0.8m.

The volume of cases dealt with under CCAS ADR schemes that were dealt with through conciliation and/or an ADR mechanism, based on annual reports from sponsors, are shown in Table 11.20.

Table 11.20: code sponsor complaint information

Code sponsor	**2009**			**2010**		
	Complaints	Conciliation	ADR	Complaints	Conciliation	ADR
VBRA	12		0	21[289]		0
Motor Codes (New Cars)	3,692 contacts	430	13			
DSA	45		4			
TPO	3,194		456	3,157		646
CF	9		3	10		1
Bosch		37	0			
BAR	360	360	22			
DEMSA		7	0	44		0 via DEMSA (68 direct to FOS, of which 12 were upheld and 56 rejected by Ombudsman)
BHTA	20	20	0	22	10	0
IPW	3	3	0	5	5	0
Renewable Energy Assurance Ltd						
Motor Codes (Car service and repair)						
TOTAL	**7,323**	**866**	**498**	**3,244**	**10**	**647**

[287] *Consumer Codes Approval Scheme: Core Criteria and Guidance* [2008], CCAS criterion 1c.

[288] *Review of the impact of business of the Consumer Codes Approval Scheme* (OFT, 2006) oft.gov.uk/shared_oft/Approvedcodesofpractice/oft870.pdf.

[289] http://www.vbra.co.uk/downloads/OFT%20Code%20Report%202011.pdf.

The annual reports to the OFT do not reveal details or percentages of outcomes of cases.

As examples of how the dispute resolution aspects of codes operate, further details are given below of two code schemes, that for Motor Codes and that for Travel Agents.

Motor Codes

Overview

The motor vehicle sector currently has several motor codes. Three codes, dealing respectively with new cars, with service and repair, and with vehicle warranty products, are run by a dedicated company, Motor Codes Limited, which is a wholly-owned subsidiary of The Society of Motor Manufacturers and Traders (SMMT).[290] A CCAS approved code for member garages is run by Robert Bosch, and is linked to garages selling Bosch products. A Good Garage Scheme is backed by Fortis Oil, tied to sale of Fortis products by approved garages but with no dispute resolution component.

Background

The motor vehicle trade associations were amongst the first to develop codes when they became relevant from the 1970s. The Motor Industry Code of Practice operated from 1976 to 2004. That code covered everything from new car advertising through to the sale of petrol across three trade associations, the SMMT, RMIF[291] and the SMTA.[292] The establishment of CCAS induced manufacturers to produce their New Car Code of Practice so that it could gain OFT recognition. That Code was achieved CCAS Stage 1 approval in June 2004, Stage 2 approval in September 2004, and was officially launched in December 2004.

Alongside those developments, an industry initiative to produce a series of modernised codes was the result of a threat in 2005 by the National Consumer Council[293] to institute a competition law super-complaint[294] against the car sector over service and repair issues. The claim was that multiple small amounts of consumer detriment amounted to some £4 billion, and it was suggested that the industry should put its house in order.[295] Subsequent discussions between the government, the OFT and SMMT led to an industry-wide initiative to create a conciliation scheme within new car codes (the government asked SMMT to draw up a Service and Repair Code), and to obtain CCAS approval for them.

Dealer groups that were members of RMIF operated under a Repair Code prior to 2009, but the manufacturing and dealership groupings within the industry all wished to operate

[290] SMMT is the lead trade association that promotes the interests of the UK automotive industry to UK and EU governments. It was registered as a company on 16 July 1902, and today is of the largest and most influential trade associations, representing over 500 automotive companies. See www.smmt.co.uk.

[291] The Retail Motor Industry Federation, which represents retail motor traders and providers of motor services to businesses. It has around 8,000 members, including around 5,500 franchised garages in the United Kingdom, the majority being single businesses. In addition, there are some 15,000 to 17,000 independent garages that are involved in service and repair.

[292] Scottish Motor Trade Association www.smta.co.uk.

[293] Now part of Consumer Focus.

[294] Under the Enterprise Act 2002, s 11.

[295] S Brooker, *At A Crossroads* (Bertrams, 2005).

under a unified approach, so in 2009 the SMMT launched a rebranded New Car Code and Vehicle Warranty Products Code (formerly the SMMT Mechanical Breakdown Insurance Schemes) and expanded the latter to cover all insured and non-insurance products in addition to extended warranty products and insurance warranty products.

Since CCAS codes should be independent of trade associations, SMMT, RMIF and SMTA created a separate entity to operate the codes and be responsible for the self-regulation of the motor industry, Motor Codes Limited (MCL). MCL is an independent subsidiary of SMMT and has its own brand.[296] The trade associations are not involved in operation of the codes by MCL. MCL's aim is to raise standards and increase consumer protection for motorists. MCL has a Board comprising executive and non-executive directors. It has nine employees and produces statistics on a regular basis, as required by OFT, as part of MCL's oversight function as code sponsor. MCL has a Committee for each Code, which works with SMMT's relevant committees to review issues and improve industry practice. Thus, the New Card Code Committee works with SMMT's Customer Service Committee, and MCL's Vehicle Warranty Products Committee works with SMMT's Vehicle Warranty Products Committee. Decisions on oversight of the Codes and on sanctioning are taken by the Independent Compliance Assessment Panel (see below).

The Service and Repair Code was the first code to be launched by MCL in August 2008. The Motor Industry Code of Practice for Vehicle Warranty Products achieved Stage 1 approval in May 2009, and Stage 2 and full OFT Code approval in 2011. The sector found that obtaining Stage 1 approval of the CCAS was very difficult and took some time.

Some thirteen attempts have been made by various entities at producing a Service and Repair Code: they have been unsuccessful broadly because they were too costly for small garages and membership never reached critical mass. An attempt was made in 2010 to launch a code for the 30,000 independent garages by the RMIF, but this was not taken forward.[297] MCL's approach has been to get manufacturers to pay for the garages in their franchised networks, but each individual garage still has to agree the terms and conditions to join with MCL, and this involves multiple individual negotiations. The MCL Service and Repair Code was launched in 2009 with 5,500 members, and numbers have since reached 6,000, including 700 independents. The government wishes to see equal numbers of independent and franchised members, so as to ensure a competitive market.

As discussions on codes have developed since the 1990s, there has been a sea change in the attitude of industry towards the benefits of maintaining reputation and the advantages of codes in assisting this. This can be seen in the approaches towards compliance and sanctions, discussed below.

Before the codes were in place, OFT claimed that millions of pounds were lost by consumers, since there was a large number of complaints that were then recorded by Consumers Direct and Trading Standards Departments. OFT challenged SMMT to reduce what they saw to be a high level of complaints. Consumers Direct have logged any contact and counted it as a complaint. However, when complaints were re-routed to MCL, which was able to analyse complaint data in greater detail, and to differentiate between types of contact, it became clear that the clear majority of contacts that had been recorded as

[296] www.motorcodes.co.uk.

[297] RMIF has operated a National Conciliation Service since 1990, which can refer unresolved cases to independent arbitration, drawing on a pool of four independent arbitrators, who are all Fellows of the Chartered Institute of Arbitrators, supported by a pool of nine technical experts (who act free of charge), for which both parties pay a modest cost, not exceeding £262.

'complaints' were in fact merely requests for information or advice, and not substantive complaints at all. Since 2004, MCL has consistently found that the ratio of contacts that seek advice compared with those that make a complaint is 10:1.

One consequence of this recognition has been to highlight the importance of providing consumer advice and information. Consumers Direct now directs all calls that it receives to MCL. MCL has focused its main activity on its Customer Advice Line, which is its first contact and means of assistance for consumers. A second consequence is recognition that the number of complaints previously alleged was a misrepresentation of the true figures and that the level of quality provided by the industry is far higher than was alleged. This has changed the external perception of the industry with government, regulators and customers, as well as internally.

Membership figures for each Code as at 2010 are shown in Table 11.21. All the major vehicle manufacturers, franchise dealers and major quick fit chains subscribe to the codes, since they see the advantages for their reputations and businesses.

Table 11.21: Code membership statistics 2010

	New Car Code	Service and Repair Code	Vehicle Warranty Products
	Vehicle manufacturers	Garages	Warranty administrators
Current subscribers	40	6,500	7
Market coverage	99%	25%	60%
OFT CCAS approval stage	OFT approved code	OFT stage 1 approval[298]	OFT stage 1 approval

The current challenge is to persuade enough small garages to subscribe to the S&R code. Small businesses see the length of time, effort and cost to gain accreditation as off-putting barriers. It is important for consumer protection that coverage should be widespread, but consumer choice is currently limited in this respect. Gaining accreditation is a slow process. Under the S&R code, there is a £75 initial subscription fee, and a compliance check by the RAC, which visits a garage every 24 months. There is a tension here between ensuring that the level of consumer protection and performance is sufficiently high, and not compromised, and between setting the entry requirements at a level that smaller traders find too high. At present, the policy is not to compromise on standards, such as demonstrating a consistent commitment to monitor. MCL has introduced a number of incentives for traders to subscribe, such as a weekly newsletter to garages, running competitions under which consumers nominate 'best garage'.[299]

[298] OFT approved code since November 2011.

[299] Golden garage consumer survey, available at: http://www.motorcodes.co.uk/press-releases/14-million-uk-motorists-feel-ripped-off-by-their-garage.html; information about the golden garage scheme: http://www.goldengarages.co.uk.

The Three Codes

Motor Industry Code of Practice for New Cars

The Motor Industry Code of Practice for New Cars[300] was the first code of practice in any industry to gain 'full approval' from the OFT in 2004. In April 2009 Motor Codes took over responsibility for running the Code from the SMMT. Over 98.9 per cent of all new cars registered in the UK are covered by the Code. The code commits car manufacturers to providing high levels of customer satisfaction as a core element of their business. The Code states:

> [Subscribers] confirm their promises made by vehicle manufacturers in the provision of new cars and the cover provided by the manufacturer's warranty. The code sets out standards that subscribers will comply with regarding:
> - Advertising
> - Availability of Replacement Parts
> - New Car Sales
> - Complaints Handling
> - Car Manufacturer's Warranties
>
> Subscribers are obliged to accept the Code in its entirety and ensure that their staff are aware of their legal responsibilities as well as their responsibilities under this Code.
> A consumer who feels dissatisfied with a subscriber's performance under any item covered by this Code is able to submit a grievance to the Conciliation and Advisory Service. The principles set out in this Code are not intended to interpret, qualify or supplement the law, and are not intended to be applied to non-consumer sales.
> This Code has been developed by the motor industry to provide a self regulatory regime by which vehicle manufacturers can demonstrate their intention to operate as responsible businesses and have in place a cost-effective and speedy dispute resolution service that consumers can readily access in the event of a disagreement.

Motor Industry Code of Practice for Service and Repair

The Motor Industry Code of Practice for Service and Repair[301] was the launched to the public in August 2008. The launch marked a major development in consumer protection in the automotive sector. With the support of the industry, government, Consumer Focus and Trading Standards, the Code completed full CCAS approval in 2011 and is now active in more than 6,000 garages across the country.

Motor Industry Code of Practice for Vehicle Warranty Products[302]

The Motor Industry Code of Practice for Vehicle Warranty Products was officially launched on 14 July 2009. The Code sets the standards that Vehicle Warranty Product Administrators must comply with regarding the sale and administration of vehicle warranty products. Over 50% of all vehicle warranty products are covered by this Code.

[300] *Motor Industry Code of Practice: New Cars*, 2008. Available at: http://www.motorcodes.co.uk/images/stories/documents/new_car_code.pdf.

[301] *Motor Industry Code of Practice: Service and Repair, 2008*. Available at: www.motorcodes.co.uk/images/stories/documents/code_document_web.pdf.

[302] *Motor Industry Code of Practice: Vehicle Warranty Products*, 2009. Available at: www.motorcodes.co.uk/images/stories/documents/vehicle_warranty_products_code_[web].pdf.

The subscribers to a code agree to:

- Take effective and immediate action to achieve a just settlement to a consumer complaint.
- Have in place an easily identifiable and accessible written complaints procedure.
- Provide every assistance to their dealers in handling and resolving complaints
- Co-operate with local consumer advisors or intermediaries where necessary.
- Give every assistance to the Code Advisory and Conciliation Service.

The Dispute Resolution Procedures

Initial complaint

The first stage is always to encourage dialogue between the consumer and the relevant company. The New Car Code states:

> A consumer or intermediary who has a complaint about a subscriber should, in the first instance, refer the matter verbally to the subscriber's dealer network. In the event that a complaint remains unresolved at both dealer and manufacturer level, it is the subscriber's obligation to make clear to the consumer their right to refer the complaint to the Code Advisory and Conciliation Service. …
> A consumer or intermediary who has a complaint about the quality of the vehicle or parts supplied should, in the first instance, refer the matter to the selling dealer.
> The complaint, preferably in writing, should be addressed to a senior executive, director, or the proprietor of the selling dealer.
> If the complaint relates to new car warranty and the dealer is unable to resolve the matter, a consumer should take the complaint directly to the customer relations department of the manufacturer. The claims procedure and the manufacturer's (subscriber's) contact details can be found in the new car warranty document.
> Any letters will receive a reply from the subscriber within 10 working days of receipt.[303]

The leading car manufacturers operate in-house Consumer Service Departments, which keep in contact with their customers with the aim of keeping them for life. This provides direct care, and is a means of resolving any problems directly. Some disputes or individuals, however, benefit from being dealt with at a distance, so a court might be appropriate, or in a middle way through a code. The key question in any dispute is: 'what does the customer want? Does the individual want a remedy, or is he simply expressing anger, frustration or unrealistic desires?'

Consumer Advice Line and Conciliation

Where direct contact between customer and company is not proving fruitful, MCL will attempt to assist through its Motor Codes Advisory and Conciliation Service. This provides a free consumer advice line to assist consumers with motoring advice and help with disputes consumers may have with a subscriber of one of the three codes of practice. If an issue can be fixed with a phone call, MCL will contact the garage at that stage and suggest that the garage takes the initiative to fix the dispute without further ado. MCL finds that it is able to resolve the vast majority of issues at this stage by offering an independent channel of

[303] Motor Industry Code of Practice New Cars 2008, available at: www.motorcodes.co.uk/images/stories/documents/new_car_code.pdf.

communication, informed by experience, and by offering an objective view to both sides. It leans on companies to be more responsive, and equally tries to inform rational attitudes on both sides. Hence, warranty claims on clutches outside the six month warranty period would not be supported.

However in certain complex cases it is not always possible to resolve a dispute quickly, as it can take some time to gather all the information necessary to reach a decision and a satisfactory outcome. The Code Advisory and Conciliation Service will advise both subscriber and consumer on a remedy as appropriate.

If the consumer enquiry raised is a potential breach of a code, MCL's Conciliation Service will try to resolve the concern by investigating the potential breach and aim to review and resolve any dispute with as little disruption to the consumer as possible. MCL will collate all the documents, and then send a pack to the garage, and request its full written response within 10 working days. MCL will assess the response. Consumers will be kept informed of the progress and outcome of their conciliation case. If MCL is satisfied, it will tell both sides.

Arbitration

If a case remains unresolved or there is a difference of opinion that cannot be satisfactorily addressed through conciliation, the case can be referred to independent arbitration. If a consumer wishes to instigate an arbitration, the company may not object. The arbitration service is provided by IDRS Ltd.[304] The parties will be required to sign an application for arbitration and pay the arbitration fee, which is split between them (see below). If the consumer loses, the manufacturer has the right to reclaim the cost from the consumer.

The Code Advisory and Conciliation Service will submit the case file to IDRS. The case file includes all documents submitted by the consumer and subscriber. The Arbitrator has the power to direct any party to provide any additional document or information considered relevant. As the arbitration service is designed to be low cost to allow it to be accessible, any hearing will normally rely on documents only. None of the parties to the dispute may be present or be represented by another person, unless the Arbitrator decides to conduct an oral arbitration, in which case parties may attend to present their evidence. Legal representation may only be employed if the Arbitrator so directs.

IDRS' arbitrators apply the law, the Code and their common sense in deciding cases. Arbitrators issue a thorough, reasoned decision. The decision of the Arbitrator is legally binding upon both parties and concludes the complaint.[305] There are only limited circumstances where a case already considered under the terms of the Arbitration Act can then proceed to court. The award of the Arbitrator will be published in writing to all parties involved in the dispute and is enforceable in the Courts by any party.

Instead of opting for arbitration by IDRS, it is open to a consumer to start court proceedings, or use any available alternative dispute resolution facility. MCL can accelerate a case through its conciliation process where both sides wish to proceed to arbitration. This occurred when Land Rover wanted to have the decision of an arbitrator in what it saw as a test case so that it could apply it to a number of similar cases.

MCL has found that the number of consumers who wish to jump straight to the arbitration option is increasing. However, MCL is trying to educate members and consumers about

[304] Part of the CEDR Disputes Group, see p 267 above.

[305] The authors were consistently informed by trade personnel interviewed that businesses trust the consistency of decisions from the arbitration scheme more than they do those of the courts.

the service they provide, so as to avoid this. Trading Standards have a good working relationship with MCL, and usually redirect the consumers back to MCL.

MCL's experience has been that where customers choose to involve a solicitor or Trading Standards, they have very high expectations of what their rights are, or something has gone drastically wrong. Most consumers seek legal advice from solicitors, Trading Standards or citizens advice because a 'bloke in the pub' tells them they are entitled to a new car or compensation. MCL would like to see more solicitors advising consumers of the various Code and ADR options, and see courts either refusing to accept cases that have not tried an ADR approach or imposing cost penalties for not doing so.

The issues that arise under the New Car Code and Service and Repair Code relate principally to warranty issues. It is almost inconceivable that issues of law would arise. The law on supply of consumer goods and services is clear and well settled.

The number of cases dealt with under the schemes are shown in Table 11.22. The number of cases involved at both conciliation and arbitration stages has been fairly constant in these years. The conciliation stage resolves around 95 per cent of disputes, and under 15 cases go on to arbitration every year.

Table 11.22: Complaint Statistics

Total	**2005 Total**	**2006 Total**	**2007 Total**	**2008 Total**	**2009 Total**	**2010 Total**	**2011 Total**
Contacts	4189	4315	3871	4038	7482	8494	8997
Conciliation	395	353	350	527	478	293	417
Fast track[306]	N/A	N/A	N/A	N/A	N/A	274	255
Arbitration	9	5	10	16	20	10	17

Transparency and Oversight

There are various vertical and external means aimed at making operation of the system transparent, monitored and accountable. The OFT's CCAS scheme requires a Code to be subject to an independent compliance assessment panel. MCL's Independent Compliance Assessment Panel (ICAP)[307] monitors the operation of the Code and subscriber compliance. The membership of ICAP comprises individuals from the motor industry, consumer lobby, advisory services, Members of Parliament and the broader business world. From 2011 its Chair is a senior Trading Standards official. The report from each meeting, including details of all monitoring and sanctions imposed, is circulated to all members of ICAP and is available on the website. Each report will also form the core of evidence supplied to the OFT for its monitoring purposes. The quarterly reports also form the basis of the Motor Codes Annual Report.[308]

The outcomes of all IDRS arbitration cases are assessed to determine whether any Code compliance issues have been raised and if any amendments to the Code are required to address any specific issues raised by the case. ICAP will also review cases of persistent or serious breaches of the Code by subscribers.

[306] Fast Track process before conciliation is a new approach whereby consumers can avoid the longer full conciliation process, through one telephone call from Motor Codes to the Code subscriber to resolve the consumer's concerns. If Fast Track doesn't resolve the concerns the case can then move to conciliation. If the consumer remains dissatisfied after conciliation the consumer can request the case be progressed to independent, legally binding arbitration.

[307] http://www.motorcodes.co.uk/about-motor-codes/icap.html.

[308] *Independent Compliance Assessment Panel February 2011 Report.*

The motor industry believes that in placing authority placed in an independent ICAP reflects the serious nature with which it views non-compliance. The industry now feels that it is under constant scrutiny and reassessment of issues raised and the performance of the code system. ICAP issues regular reports on all code operations. ICAP will also review cases of persistent or serious breaches of the Code by subscribers, and impose sanctions. Consumer Focus also constantly monitors the codes. ICAP has the authority to instigate an independent investigation, with which the subscriber is required to assist fully.

Depending on the outcome of any investigation, the Panel can impose a varied selection of sanctions upon a subscriber. The sanctions policy adopted by ICAP has been that of a stepped response dependent on the seriousness of the offence. Sanctions include education and training, undergoing monitoring, put warning about a trader on MCL's website, marking the trader on the website as 'EXPELLED' from the Code regime and stating the reason for the expulsion,[309] and imposing financial penalties. If a financial penalty is imposed on a subscriber, the penalty sum is donated to the motor industry charity BEN. A trader that has been sanctioned may redeem itself, such as after inspection. The imposition of sanctions attracts the attention of the local and motoring press, which picks up and publicises the sanction and affects the local market. MCL also has support from 'What Car?' magazine and the 'Honest John' column in the Daily Telegraph newspaper.

The process and outcome of any disciplinary action and of any customer complaint are kept separate. However, where a number of similar conciliation cases occur regarding the same subscriber, a disciplinary action could be instituted.

There is little evidence of any challenge to the motor codes schemes on the basis of lack of independence of effectiveness in operation. The major challenges facing the code scheme are limited awareness by consumers and gaining comprehensive coverage of industry subscribers for the S&R code. Increased attempts are likely to make Citizens Advice Bureaux and Law Centres aware of the existence of codes, and their advantages.

Costs

The costs for consumers and companies under the arbitration scheme are shown in Table 11.19. The full administration cost of the system is not published. The subscription and annual costs for company members of the codes are shown in Table 11.23.

Table 11.23: Code subscription costs

	New car code		**Service and repair code**
Annual fee for vehicle manufacturers	£1,250 plus VAT	Garage annual subscription fee	£75 plus VAT
Fee per conciliation case opened invoiced quarterly	£75 plus VAT	Fee per conciliation case	£75 plus VAT
		Annual garage inspection by the RAC	£175 plus VAT

309 This sanction has been used once, for a single garage.

Travel Disputes: The ABTA Code and Schemes

Background

The Travel Association (formerly The Association of British Travel Agents, but still known by its familiar acronym ABTA) was established in 1950 by 22 leading travel companies. The ABTA brand is widely recognised by consumers.[310] In 2010 its members comprise over 5,000 travel agencies outlets and more than 900 tour operators, ranging from small, specialist tour operators and independent travel agencies through to publicly-listed companies, with business models including call centres, internet booking services, and high street shops. Members account for around 90 per cent of package holidays sold in the UK.

One of its founding objectives was to create a Code of Conduct that would be recognised by the public as a guarantee of a high standard of service by members. The Code of Conduct, which ABTA members are required to follow as a condition of membership,[311] includes requirements for dispute resolution processes.

It is also a condition of ABTA membership for an agent to provide ABTA with security in the form of a bond or other applicable security for this purpose. If the agent's business should fail financially, this bond or security will help to ensure that their customers can continue with their travel arrangements or are reimbursed the cost of their travel arrangements. ABTA will also ask the agent to make a contribution to the Travel Agents' Bond Replacement Scheme (TABRS), a low-cost alternative to bonding. In exceptional circumstances, ABTA may also ask the agent to contribute to the Retail Fund.

ABTA has no bonding requirements for principals, but ensures that members acting as a principal provide financial protection for their customers' travel arrangements in accordance with the law.[312] The agent can bond their non-licensable packages or single-element business with ABTA. If the agent decides to bond with ABTA, then they are asked to make a contribution to the Shortfall Insurance scheme.

The ABTA Code of Conduct was approved by the OFT under its Consumer Code Approval Service (CCAS) on 29 September 2005. However, ABTA voluntarily withdrew its code from the CCAS on 1 September 2006 after it decided to change its financial protection arrangements in a way that OFT concluded did not comply with the CCAS requirements.[313]

The withdrawal from the CCAS arose after the OFT considered that ABTA should provide financial protection for customers of any member business if it were to fail financially. However, ABTA did not consider that members should protect consumers' deposits and prepayments irrespective of the motives or reasons for customers' losses. ABTA held to its position that it was not appropriate for it to insure members and consumers against every eventuality, including organised crime or fraud by members or their employees. ABTA's position remains that as a privately run protection scheme it should cover genuine business failure, as most other payment protection schemes do. The extent of the commercial risk to

[310] An Ipsos MORI survey in 2008 found that 74% of consumers recognised the ABTA brand: *Business leadership in consumer protection. A discussion document on self regulation and industry-led compliance,* OFT1058 (London, Office of Fair Trading, 2010), available at www.oft.gov.uk/shared_oft/reports/consumer-policy/oft1058.pdf.

[311] The current ABTA Code of Conduct was adopted on 20 January 2009: www.abta.com/filegrab/?ref=84&f=codeofconduct270410.pdf.

[312] www.abta.com/join/member_introduction/financial_protection.

[313] OFT: ABTA withdraws from OFT Consumer Codes Approval Scheme, 31 August 2006. Available at: www.oft.gov.uk/news-and-updates/press/2006/127-06.

ABTA if it were to cover 'gold-plating' would simply be too great. It considers that consumers have a large amount of information available to them. ABTA assesses each member company's risk under its strict financial security requirements, but cannot guarantee that it is always told about every risk and every aspect of the member's business. ABTA's financial ability to provide such unlimited insurance is limited by the fact that its bondholders would not accept too great a commercial risk, nor could the second tier captive in Guernsey. ABTA accepts that it is fair for traders to accept some risks, and consumers to accept some. Separate insurances are available for consumers and they can also receive protection by paying with credit cards and by VISA Debit Card. The OFT disagreed on the above issues, so ABTA seceded from CCAS in 2006. Nevertheless, in all other respects ABTA's Code and the manner in which it is operated is recognised as being of benchmark status.

ABTA monitors all complaints to see if members have breached the Code, and if so can launch a Code Investigation, for which there is a dedicated in-house team. If a breach is found, the consumer is informed of the outcome. This procedure is intended to enable ABTA to exert self-regulatory pressure over its members. ABTA considers that its leadership has educated members in raising standards. The process of gaining OFT approval was influential in pressuring industry to improve its processes and standards further. ABTA has the ability to impose a fixed financial penalty on a member (set at £400 in 2010) and can refer serious matters to the Code of Conduct Committee (see below). The penalties imposed are listed monthly on ABTA's website.

Two standing committees manage matters relating to ABTA's membership rules. The Membership Committee oversees the Accounts rules, and the Code of Conduct committee oversees the Code. Both committees are made up of members of ABTA, and their responsibilities include considering breaches of the rules, and ensuring that both sets of rules remain relevant, proportionate, and fair. Independent consumer representatives and Trading Standards officials sit on the Code of Conduct Committee, which reviews the content of the Code and decides disciplinary cases. In 2008 ABTA's Board structure was changed to include both elected and appointed members, and two non-executives from outside the travel industry. ABTA's Secretariat, operating from the company's offices in London, comprises some 60 members of staff, who work to provide members with services, to represent their interests, and to administer the membership systems and Codes. The Code of Conduct Committee may impose a range of sanctions on members: accepting an undertaking by a member, issuing a reprimand, imposing a fine, or terminating membership. Fines have no financial limit, and vary in size depending on the seriousness of the offence and the member's previous record of conduct.[314]

Before the Code was introduced, there was a steady stream of cases that were brought through the county courts: the court route has almost dried up now (perhaps to fewer than one per cent of claims), although solicitors can still use the court route rather than the code route.[315] When cases go to court, the anecdotal but widely-held industry view has consistently been that some judges make unpredictable and very curious decisions, ignorant of the Code or of commercial realities. Judges have little experience or analysis of travel and holidays other than a generic media-influenced aura of criticism so it's arbitration presents more certainty for businesses and consumers.

[314] In the early 1990s, a fine of £100,000 was imposed in relation to a collection of offences; a fine of that magnitude is unusual.

[315] Industry stories circulate about solicitors objecting to companies seeking to contact their customers with settlement offers after the solicitors had not passed on offers to their clients.

The industry views the Code as performing an essential commercial and social function of enabling companies to placate unhappy customers swiftly, and also in managing customers' expectations. The number of complaints dealt with under the Code procedure (including through direct contact between customers and companies) has clearly increased overall since say the 1970s. Companies that trade on the basis of their reputations seek to maintain them, and to avoid dissatisfied customers from failing to buy again. In achieving customer satisfaction, industry practice adopts two approaches. First, swift response to complaints and speedy resolution is critical. It is essential to have the right front line people to handle complaints. They must act fast, know what they are advising about, be efficient, and have sufficient authority to settle a case themselves without referring to a manager. The call centres have to be well resourced and well staffed. Telephone mediations are thought to be useful but rarely settle things: views tend merely to be further entrenched, whereas the consumer wants someone to make a decision.

Companies are sometimes inundated by complaints, usually because they are insufficiently resourced to handle them, such as after a merger, when it takes time to achieve operational merger of complaint handling functions. ABTA can, and does, make help available to members in such situations, so as to maintain the sector's standards in complaint handling. A good example of where companies ran into problems was when flights were suddenly grounded in 2010 as a result of the Icelandic volcanic ash: companies did not have enough people to deal with the volume of claims that arose.

Procedures

The Code: direct then assisted negotiation by ABTA

The stages in the process that customers are expected to follow, backed by time limits under the Code for members to react, are as follows:

- Customers should first send their complaint directly to the ABTA member. The company is required to send a full response within 28 days. The Code of Conduct specifies that ABTA can impose a £400 fixed penalty fine on a member for failing to respond to a complaint within the timescales set out in the Code of Conduct. ABTA's policy is to encourage a customer to make a reasonable attempt to resolve the complaint with the company, and members must reply to each contact within 28 days.
- If attempts at direct discussion have failed to result in agreement, ABTA's Consumer Affairs Team will attempt to assist in resolving the dispute. Customers are encouraged to send their complaint to ABTA online (with travel documentation if the holiday has already taken place) by clicking on 'Register a complaint' on the ABTA website.

An individual complaint reference is given when each complaint is lodged with ABTA. If an amicable settlement cannot be reached with the help of the Consumer Affairs Team, the consumer will then have to decide whether to take formal action, and if so choose between a court claim, the CEDR Solve Arbitration Scheme, or the separate scheme for personal injury cases (see below). The arbitration rules require participants to try to settle issues through direct negotiation first. ABTA's complaints procedure and website signposts meet this requirement.

The ABTA arbitration scheme

The arbitration scheme is administered by CEDR Solve[316] for ABTA.[317] The following are the key elements of the arbitration process.

- Arbitration is used for claims for general compensation arising from breach of contract and/or negligence by or on behalf of any person named in the booking form or other contractual documents. If such a general compensation claim includes an element of minor illness or personal injury then this can also be considered by the arbitrator, although for this specific element the arbitrator cannot award more than £1,500 per person. The scheme does not cover disputes concerning serious personal injury etc, which may be dealt with under the separate scheme for Personal Injury and Illness Mediation, below.
- The application can be made by post, online, or a combination. The online complaint form provides a step-by-step guide to effective complaining, helping consumers to understand the nature of their claim and how compensation is assessed by judges and arbitrators. ABTA has found that this process tends to concentrate the minds of companies on what is being complained about and encourages them to settle.
- ABTA must receive copies of the documentation within eighteen months of the date on which the problem arose, or of the date of return from holiday, whichever is the later.[318] Within the 18 month period, arbitration is compulsory if the consumer chooses, so the ABTA company cannot object to the process. After eighteen months it can still be used if the company consents.
- ABTA then issues a pre-arbitration process notice, which the customer must complete, setting out the basis of the claim, and attaching evidence, and return it to ABTA within 14 days.[319] A request can be made for a compensatory payment to be made in cash or vouchers (to be used against a future booking). After the pre-arbitration form was introduced, it was found that the numbers proceeding to arbitration fell since the need to fill in the form focuses claimants' minds on what they are requesting and helps to resolve the majority of claims. ABTA had been considering introducing a pilot conciliation stage, but decided to drop this because of the success of the pre-arbitration notice.
- ABTA then forwards the materials to the member for its defence. The member then has the opportunity to resolve the issue prior to more formal procedures or submit its evidence and defence, which ABTA sends on to CEDR Solve.
- The consumer has to pay a fee on registering an arbitration claim, as shown in Table 11.19 above, but from 2011 this is not due until the consumer's comments to the defence are requested by CEDR Solve, so if he settles prior to the defence being submitted he have not been penalised.
- The claim will be dealt with 'on the basis of the documents, including any photographic evidence'. There is no hearing. Accordingly, the format is not suited for some matters, for example, serious illness or injury claims.
- The arbitrator's award is issued in writing and gives a summary of the facts, the conclusions, and their reasons for reaching them. The arbitrator's decision is legally binding on both parties and is enforceable directly through the courts.

[316] www.cedr.com/solve/schemes.

[317] www.abta.com/consumer-services/travel_problems/arbitration.

[318] The period was 9 months for many years, then extended to 12 months in May 2010, and to 18 months in July 2011, in order to attract more cases through the scheme, rather than the courts.

- The arbitrator will normally order the loser to pay the winner's costs.
- Any party can ask for a review of the arbitrator's decision, on paying a non-reimbursable £350 review fee, although there are limited grounds on which this can be challenged. An application to CEDR Solve must be made within 14 days of the date of the award being dispatched. It must be accompanied by a copy of the arbitrator's award together with a statement setting out the reasons why the award is one that no reasonable arbitrator should have reached on the basis of the documents presented.

The fees are fixed at a similar level to the fees payable in the courts' Small Claims Track, and at a level intended to discourage frivolous cases being lodged. Both consumers and members have lodged cases for appeal. Arbitrations are usually concluded within seven weeks of commencement.

Personal Injury and Illness Mediation

ABTA initially operated a separate scheme for personal injury claims, but it was never used because lawyers invariably brought a claim in court. The court rules say that non-court alternatives should be used first,[320] but most courts are unaware of the ABTA scheme and do not enforce that rule. The original personal injury scheme was replaced in 2008 with a generic mediation scheme operated by IDRS, and was in turn replaced in 2011 by an enhanced scheme from CEDR Solve. This scheme can also be used by members and their employees for employee personal injury issues.

The Scheme applies to personal injury, serious illness, nervous shock, death or the consequences of any of these. The following are the main elements of the process:

- Mediation does not apply to disputes where one or other of the parties has already initiated legal action, unless it has been suspended or discontinued by agreement.
- Mediation takes the form of a meeting attended by the decision-maker for each of the parties. Costs of representation are the responsibility of the parties, unless agreed otherwise in any settlement agreement.
- The rules governing the mediation process will be set out by the mediator in advance of the mediation day. It will take place at a venue to be arranged and agreed by all parties and at their cost.
- If the dispute is resolved during mediation, the mediator will record in writing the agreement reached by the parties. The signed agreement will be a binding contract and, as such, can be enforced by the Court.

The cost of the mediator are set on a case-by-case basis by CEDR Solve. It has been found difficult to set fixed fees for personal injury claims, partly because injuries can change during the course of the mediation. CEDR Solve aims to appoint a mediator within 5 working days. The mediator, who would only take the case if he or she is available to deal with it expeditiously, would then contact the parties to arrange a suitable time to deal with the case. The mediator should keep the parties informed of progress. It is difficult to generalise over how long a case would take.

[319] Before July 2011, the form had to be forwarded by the customer to the travel company, but it was thought that returning the form to ABTA would encourage greater adherence to the scheme.

[320] CPR, r 44.5(3).

Outcomes

The number of complaints received by ABTA, and the number of arbitrations initiated, since 2000 is shown in Figure 11.8. The number of claims in the arbitration scheme has fallen during this period. In 2010, 12,702 case files were opened, of which 1,216 were sent a Pre-Arbitration Notice, of which 591 requested further details of the Arbitration Scheme, of which 255 progressed to an award being issued (2 per cent of cases opened). An additional 19,169 telephone enquiries were received.

The overwhelming majority of complaints (perhaps 90 per cent) are settled in the mediation stage. The existence of three stages (direct negotiation, mediation, then arbitration) might be criticised as presenting a succession of barriers for consumers. However, a different perspective is that it acts as a filter through which simple disputes can be settled with lesser formality and cost. The referral of a case to arbitration frequently itself produces settlements. Taking this step requires consumers to focus on the merits of their claims and to be realistic about what it is they are seeking. Conversely, the cost of defending a case through the formal process of either arbitration or the courts has the effect of frequently encouraging companies to make a settlement offer so as to avoid the costs of the process. A number of companies resent making offers of a few hundred pounds at that stage to compensate what they regard as valueless claims, and argue that it is ultimately all customers who are paying the costs of business customer complaint departments and defence costs. However, a different viewpoint is that the process acts as a regulatory control on business behaviour.

Figure 11.7: ABTA Complaint Statistics 2000/01–2008/09[321]

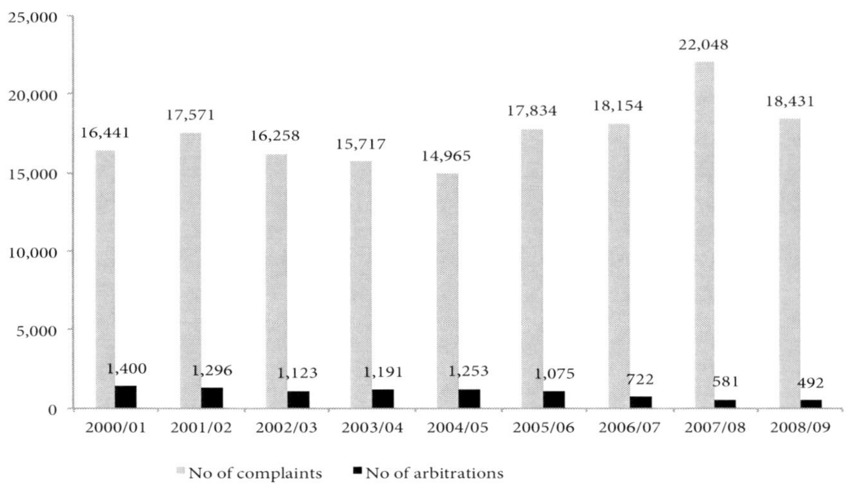

[321] The arbitration figures here do not tally exactly with those in ABTA's annual reports since the figures relate to the financial year (1st July to 30th June) and there is a time lag in the arbitrations that start during that period, so that such arbitrations might not have been worked their way through the system by the time that the annual reports are produced.

As at 2010, the average amount claimed through arbitration was £1,750, compared with a ceiling on awards of £25,000. The average award was £630. For this level of claim, the fee paid by the consumer was £62 (prior to 1 May 2010) and £90 (post 1 May 2010), and the company pays £265(prior to 1 May 2010) £350 (post 1 May 2010).

There is an imbalance of expectation on the outcomes between some consumers and businesses. Research undertaken by ABTA around 2009 shows that consumers claimed a full refund of their holiday cost in about 24 per cent of claims. 76 per cent of consumers who complain are successful in getting a solution through the Scheme – although not always the solution that they were asking for, whereas in 17 per cent of all claims, consumers are awarded no compensation at all. The existence of the fee, and differential between consumer and company fees, gives rise to a cost risk: there is a cap on the total cost liability of the consumer which equates to their original arbitration fee (which will not be refunded if the customer loses the claim) plus having to pay the same amount again as a contribution towards the company's costs.[322]

The Code operates within a relatively stable legal environment of customer rights and trader obligations,[323] so the need to clarify the law arises very rarely and most cases turn on facts and the extent of any compensation that should or might be paid.

ABTA sees no need for any extra collective procedure, since multiple similar individual claims can be processed through existing channels. It is rare for large numbers of similar claims to arise: numbers delayed by airlines or suffering health problems with hotels, for example, are generally modest, but can sometimes mount up to hundreds but not thousands. The system may be challenged by multiple cases, but can cope with them. A member occasionally asks or agrees that similar claims by all family members should be dealt with in a single arbitration, since this is more convenient for all and saves costs.

Customer complaints provide essential feedback for tour operators and travel agents on whether standards are being met by their own suppliers, such as airlines and hotels. When claims are received, UK operators notify their suppliers, and generally have contractual rights to negotiate and settle claims bilaterally with customers. In larger claims, however, suppliers' insurers may become involved.

Aggregated statistics are published monthly on claims but not outcomes in individual cases. ABTA used to publish anonymised case examples, which was found to be useful for members initially but less so as experience with the Code grew. In 2010 website publication of statistical data was introduced, which is being extended in 2012. Media reports, such as by *Holiday Which?* give wider dissemination to potential purchasers.[324]

Estate Agents

The property sector has statutory regulation that is 'diverse and incomplete. … It is a patchwork of laws that have built up over decades in a piecemeal fashion that lacks a logical

[322] Until 2011, ABTA used to maintain a budget from which to refund members' fees where the consumer won compensation but failed to beat any offer previously made by the member (reflecting the CPR Part 36 process in the courts).

[323] Notably The Package Travel, Package Holidays and Package Tours Regulations 1992 (SI 1992 No 3288), as amended, implementing Directive 90/314/EEC on Package Travel and Holiday Tours.

[324] See www.holidaytravelwatch.net.

consistency, a reflection of the historic development of legislation which initially focused on physical standards and rent levels rather than consumer rights.'[325] Partly because of this, the concept of the ombudsman has grown into being widely accepted as an approach to dealing with complaints across all aspects of public and many private services including the legal and financial sectors.[326]

Schemes have been introduced in the housing market for deposits, accreditation of estate agents, and landlords. From 2007 it is compulsory for landlords and letting agents to belong to a scheme for resolving tenancy deposit disputes.[327] Three approved schemes exist: the Deposit Protection Service,[328] my|deposits,[329] and the Tenancy Deposit Scheme.[330] Each scheme offers an independent adjudication for disputes about tenancy deposits at the end of a tenancy, which is free to tenants.

Statutory regulation required those engaging in estate agency work for residential property to join an approved estate agents redress scheme by October 2008.[331] The OFT website provides the criteria that the members have to satisfy in order to be able to sign up to the scheme,[332] see Figure 11.6. The OFT is designated as the approval authority, and has approved two schemes:[333]

- The Property Ombudsman.[334] By the end of 2010,[335] TPO had a total membership of 8,008 firms covering 13,756 offices, with 11,321 of them handling property sales

[325] *Government review of regulation and redress in the UK housing market: Final Report to the Department for Communities and Local Government (CLG) and the Department for Business, Enterprise and Regulatory Reform* (London, BERR, 2009), available at: www.bis.gov.uk/files/file49743.pdf.

[326] ibid.

[327] The Consumers, Estate Agents and Redress Act 2007, (CEAR).

[328] www.depositprotection.com/default.aspx?bhjs=1&fla=1. This holds deposits during the tenancy, and the ADR element is funded by the interest, which results in no case fees for landlords or letting agents. Both landlord and tenant have to agree to use the scheme, as the adjudicator's decision is binding.

[329] www.mydeposits.co.uk. This scheme is run by Tenancy Deposit Solutions Limited, a company jointly owned by the National Landlords Association and HFIS plc trading as Hamilton Fraser Insurance (the Scheme Administrator. If there is a dispute about the return of the deposit at the end of the tenancy, and the tenant chooses to use the arbitration scheme, the disputed amount is lodged with my|deposits while the dispute is resolved by an independent adjudicator appointed through IDRS. If the landlord refuses to lodge the disputed deposit with the scheme, then the tenant cannot use the free ADR scheme, and will have to go to court. However, the scheme guarantees to pay any amount ordered by the court, and will take responsibility for recovering this amount from the landlord.

[330] www.thedisputeservice.co.uk. This is run by The Dispute Service (TDS), and builds on a voluntary scheme established in 2003 to provide dispute resolution and complaints handling for letting agents. Decisions are overseen by the scheme's own Independent Complaints Examiner, who has a team of adjudicators to deal with disputes. If there is a dispute about the deposit, the landlord or agent has ten working days to try to resolve it. If this is not possible, then the tenant, the landlord or the agent can refer the dispute to the TDS. The landlord or the agent will transfer the deposit to TDS, and TDS will take responsibility for paying it out, as decided by the ICE. If the deposit is not transferred, then the TDS will pay the tenant whatever is decided, and pursue the landlord or agent for the money.

[331] The Estate Agents (Redress Scheme) Order 2008, No. 1712, available at: www.statutelaw.gov.uk/content.aspx?LegType=All+Legislation&title=estate+agents+redress+scheme&searchEnacted=0&extentMatchOnly=0&confersPower=0&blanketAmendment=0&sortAlpha=0&TYPE=QS&PageNumber=1&NavFrom=0&parentActiveTextDocId=3493912&ActiveTextDocId=3493912&filesize=4489. This was made under The Estate Agents Act 1979, as amended by The Consumers, Estate Agents and Redress Act 2007.

[332] oft.gov.uk/OFTwork/estate-agents/EARS.

[333] A concern remains that people are paying twice in view of belonging as both individuals and as firms, and to the Estate Agents and RICS schemes.

[334] www.tpos.co.uk. This was established in 1998 as the Ombudsman for Estate Agents, and changed its name in 2009 to The Property Ombudsman (TPO). The Scheme is open to all those firms of estate agents with a principal, director or partner who is a member of the National Association of Estate Agents (NAEA) or Royal Institution of Chartered Surveyors (RICS); to all corporate estate agents (defined as those who are subsidiaries of a bank,

and 7,851 dealing with lettings. There were a total of 1,316 general enquiries, 11,794 complaint enquiries against all agents, of which 1,338 cases were opened. The total amount of cases closed in lettings and sales was 1083. The total value of awards for lettings £145,900.92 and sales £81,571.60. The financial award, if issued, is published in the anonymous summaries of all cases on the TPO website.

- Ombudsman Services: Property (OS:P).[336] It has about 7500 members.[337] The OS:P received over 5,843 contacts during 2010–2011, 74 per cent by phone and 26 per cent by letter.[338] It issued 465 complaint forms, 428 of which were returned, and resolved 260 cases. The origin of such complaints was: 29% non-company complaint; 37% members outside the OS:P terms of reference; 16% general enquiries; 16% member complaints inside the terms of reference; 1% non-member enquiry; 1% member enquiry. The subject matter of complaints is shown in Table 11.24. The average award over the year was £900.

Both schemes are free for consumers to use, but subject to a maximum award of £25,000 (including VAT).

Table 11.24: Subject matter of complaints to OS:P in 2010–2011

Valuations/surveyors	59%
Property management	23%
Residential sales	9%
Professional advice	4%
Auction	1%
Other	4%

building society or insurance company, or are themselves quoted on the Stock Exchange) and to other estate agents who are sponsored and seconded by existing member agents. From June 2006, the OEA extended its services to Lettings and Property Management agents. Many estate agents have in addition agreed to follow the CCAS-approved TPO Code of Practice for Residential Estate Agents. Lettings and property management agents who join the TPO also subscribe to the Code of Practice for Letting Agents.

[335] TPO annual report 2010 available at: www.tpos.co.uk/downloads/reports/TPO_Annual_Report_2010.pdf.

[336] www.surveyors-ombudsman.org.uk. This scheme started as a Scottish pilot scheme for chartered surveyors, registered with the Royal Institution of Chartered Surveyors (RICS) to deal with complaints about RICS members, and was later extended across the UK: being subject to the determinations of the ombudsman is a requirement of membership of the RICS. Non-RICS members, and also *firms*, can join voluntarily, so it has extended to letting agents, estate agents, and management agents. The scope of the ADR scheme is global since RICS has members across the world, especially across Europe. RICS funds the administration of the scheme, and firms that receive cases pay a fee to the Ombudsman of £176.25 per case, so that OS:P costs nothing for firms whose complaints are not converted into actual cases that require formal decisions by the Ombudsman. CCAS approval was obtained in 2008: *How the Surveyors Ombudsman Service demonstrates that it meets the OFT's criteria for approval of estate agents redress schemes* OFT1075 (London, OFT, 2010). Available at: www.oft.gov.uk/shared_oft/estateagents/oft1075.pdf.

[337] The list of members is at www.os-property.org/pages/26members.php.

[338] *Ombudsman Service Property, Annual report 2010*, available at: www.os-property.org/downloads/2010_annual_report_property.pdf.

Figure 11.8: Summary of OFT's criteria for approval of the schemes[339]

1. The Ombudsman must be independent.
2. The scheme must be adequately staffed and funded and be able to demonstrate its ability to attract and retain a sufficient number of potential members to ensure it is viable.
3. The scheme must be easily accessible to all those entitled to use it.
4. Members of the scheme should be required under the terms of the scheme to have an effective internal complaints procedure set out in writing which should include:
   - full contact details
   - any information the complainant must provide – this must be reasonable and not require excessive detail or form-filling
   - reasonable timescales for dealing with the complaint, including a timescale for resolution, and
   - details of the approved redress scheme and how the complainant can access it.
5. The Ombudsman must proceed fairly and in accordance with the principles of natural justice.
6. Complainants must be informed that the decision will not be legally binding on them, and that they will have the power to either accept or reject that decision, but that it will be binding on the estate agent if accepted by the complainant. They must also be kept informed of what their alterative or additional actions could be at each stage of the procedure.
7. The scheme must make provisions for dealing with all types of complaints from actual and potential buyers and sellers of residential property against those engaged in estate agency work in the UK. The scheme's complaints handling procedures must include reasonable timescales for dealing with the complaint, including a timescale for a decision to be made.
8. The scheme's operation and its procedures must be transparent.
9. There must be a free exchange of information between all parties relating to a complaint.
10. There must be a range of awards which take into account the level and type of detriment caused.
11. The scheme shall ensure that decisions are implemented and that procedures are in place to deal with non-compliance with the ombudsman's decision and/or the scheme's rules.
12. Appropriate information on complaints dealt with by the redress scheme must be routinely provided to:
    - Other OFT approved estate agents redress schemes.
    - Other consumer redress schemes.
    - The OFT or any other person/organisation exercising regulatory functions in relation to the activities of persons engaging in estate agency work.
13. Membership requirements to join the scheme must be fair and ensure that all those who are required to sign up to a redress scheme can do so.
14. The scheme's effectiveness must be monitored on a regular basis.
15. The scheme operator must publicise the scheme to consumers and to existing and potential members.
16. There must be independent procedures in place to consider and resolve complaints by consumer or member business about the service provided by the ombudsman.

[339] *OFT approval of estate agents redress schemes Criteria – final* (London, OFT, April 2008), available at: http://www.oft.gov.uk/shared_oft/business_leaflets/general/oft919.pdf.

Evaluation

The UK has a lengthy history of ADR in general, including consumer ADR. ADR has appeared in many public and private disputes, but has been allowed to grow organically, and now exists in a highly confused state such that it is difficult to say that a national architecture of ADR exists. Nevertheless, ADR is now so widespread—although ironically the existence and extent of ADR systems are little known—that it would take only small further steps for consumer ADR to be made fully comprehensive in coverage, and for ADR in general to be far more widely known. The different examples of Sweden and the Netherlands show what can be achieved if the populace thinks 'ADR' instead of 'courts', and if the consumer landscape could be simplified so as to have higher visibility and hence become better known.

On one view, the current picture is confused by the existence of differing types of public and private ADR systems, such as statutory regimes and ADR bodies or—a British speciality—code-based private sector ADR systems closely integrated with self-regulatory systems involving trade associations and separate specialist ADR providers. It might be wondered whether the price of creating higher visibility for consumer ADR would be the need to standardise all ADR bodies. However, existing practice shows that it would not, in fact, be necessary for all consumer ADR bodies (or systems) to be statutory or private, as long as every ADR system delivers a high quality of performance and outputs, and can be recognised as operating within an integrated national system.

Indeed, in relation to the practice of ADR, the UK demonstrates a number of leading examples of best practice across Europe. The FOS has achieved very high visibility, attracting so many contacts that it has to confront human resource challenges. It handles more consumer contacts and complaints than any other consumer ADR system across Europe. Many other consumer ADR bodies achieve notably swift processing of complaints. There is evidence of competition in relation to processes and duration of processing between ADR providers, especially the two main private sector bodies, apparently without issues of quality or mistrust by consumers who experience these services.

The UK places some emphasis on providing information and advice to consumers, both before entering into transactions (so as to avoid problems arising later) and once a problem has arisen (but there is less official emphasis on the latter aspect). This policy can also be seen in other jurisdictions, but in UK it is not as advanced as in say Sweden. However, the position may improve after the current government implements proposals to simplify the consumer landscape, by rationalising a diverse range of bodies into a 'first line' of consumer advice focused on a network of Citizens Advice Bureaux and by rationalising consumer enforcement as between local Trading Standards Services and the OFT (with the latter in a somewhat reduced role).

The involvement of regulators in controlling and encouraging improvements in complaints handling by companies, and hence in private ADR schemes, is clear. Improvements in telecoms took place as a direct result of the oversight and intervention of Ofcom, improvements in general consumer ADR occurred as a result of the OFT's CCAS, and in energy as a result of the requirements of OFGEM. In all those cases, legislative frameworks and support were necessary to empower the regulators, but the task of making detailed specifications was omitted from legislation and delegated to regulators.

12

Best Practice in Customer Care in the UK

CHRISTOPHER HODGES

Introduction

There is widespread agreement that the first tier in resolving issues between consumers and traders is for them to communicate directly. This is a formal rule in almost every consumer ADR system examined in this book. The expectation is that direct contact will resolve the vast majority of problems, many of which will, at that stage, be queries rather than disputes. An initial contact may turn into a dispute if it is handled badly. A rule requiring direct contact as first stage, and banning referral to a third party within a reasonable timescale unless there is good reason for the involvement of the third party, incentivises economic efficiency in dispute resolution by avoiding the costs and time of third party involvement and three-way communications. It also incentivises traders to have good customer relations facilities.

Clearly, if traders are to respond well to customer feedback—good or bad—they will need to have in place effective and responsive systems. There will no doubt be very considerable variation amongst customer care systems, depending on national characteristics, the state of a particular market, the extent of corporate resources, the need to maintain reputation, and other factors. This chapter examines some examples of current best practice in direct B2C customer care systems, taken from visits to three large traders located in the United Kingdom. It is not claimed that these three are representative of any others, but the findings are useful as a snapshot of corporate attitudes and systems.

An International Standard dated 2004 specifies how companies should approach the process of complaints handling.[1] It sets out a number of general principles (visibility, accessibility, responsiveness, objectivity, freedom from charge to customers, confidentiality, a customer-focused approach, accountability, and continual improvement), followed by sections on the complaints-handling framework, planning and design, operation, maintenance and improvement of systems. It also includes a specimen complaint form. One of the most important requirements is that 'Every reasonable effort should be made to investigate all the relevant circumstances and information surrounding a complaint. The level of investigation should be commensurate with the seriousness, frequency of occurrence and severity of the complaint.'[2]

Directive 2006/123 on services requires that Member States shall 'take the general measures necessary to ensure that providers respond to the complaints referred to in

[1] *Quality management—Customer satisfaction—Guidelines for complaints handling in organizations*, ISO 10002:2004.

[2] ibid, para 7.6.

the first subparagraph in the shortest possible time and make their best efforts to find a satisfactory solution.'[3] Member States shall also ensure that, at the recipient's request, providers of services shall supply information that includes:

> where a provider is subject to a code of conduct, or member of a trade association or professional body which provides for recourse to a non-judicial means of dispute settlement, information in this respect. The provider shall specify how to access detailed information on the characteristics of, and conditions for, the use of non-judicial means of dispute settlement.[4]

Since the 1960s, there has been a transformation in the attitudes of major businesses in competitive markets towards their customers. This change has, of course, run in parallel with the rise of 'consumerism' and the implementation of extensive consumer legal rights. Marks & Spencer was the first company to offer its customers a comprehensive 'money back without obligation' returns policy. An important aim of the UK approach towards redress mechanisms, as established in a sequence of papers by successive governments,[5] is to make it easier for business and consumers to resolve complaints between themselves. The stated policy was strongly consistent with 'responsive regulation' and the 'Hampton principles':[6]

> For most consumer complaints the least costly solution for both parties is direct resolution of a complaint or claim. ... A common incentive for businesses is the need to keep customers happy and in most markets this will act as a deterrent against behaviour which causes consumers major problems. Most consumer problems are dealt with bilaterally and retailers often compete in terms of the ease with which they are willing to accept returns and correct faults. Building a reputation for high levels of service is seen as a key variable in brand building and growing profitable companies.[7]

It was said that where brand reputation plays little role, settlement by traders may depend on the ease of access by consumers to advice on remedies and use of 'small claims' courts and any mechanism for alternative dispute resolution (ADR) which is available to consumers.

In its 2010 'Statement of consumer protection enforcement principles'[8] the OFT asserted:

> most businesses aim to treat their customers fairly and comply with consumer protection law' and that OFT aims to enable and encourage them to do so, and to take enforcement action only where there is no better route to securing compliance.

Effective meta use of complaint data requires standardisation in data recording. In order to facilitate this, in 2010 the Commission issued its harmonised methodology for classifying and reporting consumer complaints and enquiries, which encouraged Member States to

[3] Directive 2006/123/EC of the European Parliament and of the Council on services in the internal market (OJ No L 376, 27.12.2006, p 36, Art 27.1. Services that are excluded from this measure are finaicial services, electronic communications, transport, temporary work agencies, healthcare services, audiovisual services, gambling services, social services, private security services, notaries ands bailiffs.This is implemented in the UK by the Provision of Services Regulations 2009/2009, which impose on suppliers duties to (a) respond to complaints from recipients of the services as quickly as possible, and (b) make their best efforts to find a satisfactory solution to complaints from such recipients. Para (b) does not apply to complaints that are vexatious.

[4] ibid, Art 22.3(e).

[5] Notably, Consumer White Paper, *A Better Deal for Consumers. Delivering Real Help Now and Change for the Future,* 2009, Cm 2669, available at http://www.bis.gov.uk/files/file52072.pdf.

[6] P Hampton, *Reducing administrative burdens: effective inspection and enforcement* (HM Treasury, 2005).

[7] *Comparative Report on Consumer Policy Regimes*, (Department of Trade and Industry, 2003).

[8] *Statement of consumer protection enforcement principles* (Office of Fair Trading, 2010), OFT1221 available at http://www.oft.gov.uk/shared_oft/reports/consumer_protection/OFT1221. See also *OFT Prioritisation Principles*, (Office of Fair Trading, 2008), OFT953; *Criminal Enforcement of the Consumer Protection from Unfair Trading Regulations 2008*, (Office of Fair Trading, 2010) OFT1273, 2010.

collect and register such data so as to develop a better understanding of market outcomes.[9] The Commission noted that data on consumer complaints was a key indicator for market monitoring and the development of outcome oriented policies in general. It said that such data can be used to develop better regulation, to target enforcement and to design information campaigns. Accordingly it produced a harmonised methodology for classifying and reporting consumer complaints, so that the data could be compared.[10]

Examples are set out below of the internal complaint handling systems of three leading companies: Boots is primarily a health and beauty care retailer, with some internal manufacturing capability as well as extensive external manufacturing suppliers; BT is a large telecommunications provider; and Procter & Gamble is a major multi-national consumer product manufacturer. Hence, these examples offer contrasting products and services, from different sectors.

The findings from the interviews strongly support the policy objectives of the importance of maintaining high brand reputation and consumer trust for major brands in general consumer trading, as commercial imperatives. The strength of the focus on customer care is striking. It recognises that problems will occur and customers be hurt and unsatisfied, but seeks to minimise and reverse customer dissatisfaction. That attitude may surprise some, and it is undoubtedly not a universal approach, but the finding is striking. Academic theory notes the importance of the surrounding culture in achieving compliance with regulatory standards,[11] and these findings illustrate what best practice can achieve.

Boots

Boots is a United Kingdom-based leading international pharmacy-led health and beauty group delivering a range of products and services to retail customers.[12] It is one of the businesses of Alliance Boots Limited, whose revenue for the year ended 31 March 2010 was £22.5 billion. It has around 50,000 product lines, over 115,000 employees, and dispensed over 245 million medicines and related items annually through 2,600 stores and 600 opticians (3,250 stores worldwide). It serves 9 million customers every week (second only to the Post Office in the United Kingdom), and 100,000 online each week through Boots.com.

This company's approach to 'complaint handling' (which is a term it does not use) has made recourse to legal processes by customers, and to standards set by the substantive law, irrelevant.

[9] *Commission Recommendation of 12.5.2010 on the use of a harmonised methodology for classifying and reporting consumer complaints and enquiries*, COM(2010) 3021, available at http://ec.europa.eu/consumers/strategy/docs/consumer-complaint-recommendation_en.pdf (accessed 2 August 2010).

[10] *Commission Staff Working Document on the results of the public consultation and the introduction of a harmonised methodology for classifying and reporting consumer complaints and enquiries Accompanying document to the Commission Recommendation on the use of a harmonised methodology for classifying and reporting consumer complaints and enquiries*, SEC(2010) 572, available at http://ec.europa.eu/consumers/strategy/docs/consumer-complaint-swd_en.pdf.

[11] F Haines, *Corporate Regulation. Beyond 'Punish or Persuade'* (Oxford: Clarendon Press, 1997).

[12] See http://www.boots-uk.com/About_Boots.aspx.

The Customer Care Approach

Boots' vision is to be the world's best pharmacy-led health and beauty retailer. In order to achieve that status, it aims to be 'number one' in customer care. 'In everything we do, we will make the customer want to like us, including when things go wrong. We want to make it easy for people to interact with us'. This policy is reflected in the company's language: it refers to problems to be solved rather than complaints.

The key is that everybody in the company is empowered to put things right if something goes wrong. Such empowerment applies whenever a customer touches the company: in a shop, online, by phone, or in a comment in social media. Every employee should feel involved in customer care. Matters should only be referred to others if absolutely necessary, for example if the customer wants this.

The aim is to deliver 'legendary customer care' – to deliver the best service.[13] It is to provide a level of involvement with, and understanding of, the customers' points of view that are closer than a traditional arm's length trading relationship. It also involves acceptance that, although the production and selling processes are intended to make things go well, some things will go wrong in an enterprise of this size. Where that occurs, the company will do what it can to put things right. The approach to customer care is inextricably linked with the company's policy on Corporate Social Responsibility,[14] both of which reflect how the company aims to behave.

The aim is to behave at a standard that is considerably in excess of legal requirements, which are viewed as a basic consumer protection minimum. Accordingly, the company's refund and exchange policies go much further than those specified in the sale of goods or unfair commercial practices legislation. In such circumstances, the attitude is: 'If it was your mum or grandma, what would you do?'

An illustration of this occurs with the development service for photographs. In the event that any customer's photographs are spoiled or lost, the legal liability is to refund the cost of the film and provide a new film. Boots would respond to the situation in which the customer found himself or herself. If wedding photos were involved, Boots would arrange for repeat pictures to be taken.

Similarly, many consumer products involve electricity and many of Boots' products are medicines. It is unavoidable that such products may be associated with safety issues.

Companies that operate a high quality Customer care approach consider that compliance issues arise only infrequently.

Being involved in the retailing function inevitably produces the result that a business tends to be more customer-focused than some manufacturers are, since the latter are at least one remove from daily interaction with human customers. Where a major retailer adopts a Customer Care approach, however, the system inherently produces pressure on manufacturers to look at things from the costumers' point of view, since the retailer will be the customer's advocate in this process and be able to use commercial and legal pressures.

[13] The company's internal web lists stories of exceptional dedicated care, such as a manager staying in the store all night so as to enable it to open on the following day in difficult weather conditions, and an employee driving an elderly man home in the employee's car with his medicine in atrocious weather when public transport failed. It also states 'Our customers trust us with their health and wellbeing and they expect us to provide safe, high quality products and services. .. The CARE approach is **not** about apportioning blame where things have gone wrong. It's a process that allows us to put things right for customers now, learn from the past and ensure that similar situations don't happen again in the future.'

[14] See http://www.boots-uk.com/Corporate_Social_Responsibility.aspx.

An example is over recalls of products, in which Boots has found that it wants to go further than some manufacturers.

In earlier times, major companies had a central complaint function, with written procedures, which grew over time. The focus on product recall and integrated pre- and post-marketing safety systems was given increased emphasis during the early 1990s when the EU General Consumer Product Safety legislation was introduced.[15] Around the mid-1990s, the complaint handling function at leading companies was expanded to embrace any customer care issue. Having details of customers through the loyalty card scheme enables Boots to write immediately to 80 per cent of the 14 million active loyalty card members if any safety issue arises.

An historical model of handling any liability issues was to refer claimants to external insurers. That process would result in a financial settlement, but little customer satisfaction with the outcome, process or attitude. The model still exists, but is anathema to companies driven by modern standards of customer care. Boots handle all issues in-house, so as to provide the desired content and style of response.

Perhaps surprisingly, Boots has no written customer care policy statement. Instead, everyone in the company who inter-relates with customers is empowered to respond immediately and effectively to any customer concerns. The company feels that having a written policy may be too rigid. It thinks that a policy is something that can be hidden behind, and interpreted in a legalistic fashion. Instead, Boots have an approach that allows instant responsiveness, flexibility, empowerment and discretion. 'It is designed to get people to contact us.'

A determination to set the highest standards is driven by competition. It incentivises a value-led approach to business. It seeks to trade profitably on brand value and reputation, through which consumers have confidence and faith in major brands. Cheaper suppliers might not have the same approaches or systems. Indeed, less consumer oriented, 'pound shops' cannot afford sophisticated customer care model. In contrast, the market is well aware that Ryanair operates on a cost-cutting basis and does not offer refunds beyond the legal requirements and may not respond to complaints: the low cost of its services take such policies into account. The behaviour of other sellers does not cause the industry leaders a particular problem, but may do for consumers.

The culture aims to delight customers. Accordingly, the company is constantly striving to drive up its measures of Customer Care. Shop employees are incentivised by being awarded bonuses on their individual scores. This process is linked to the Institute of Care Management. The market leaders in customer care include John Lewis and Tesco.

What the Customer Sees

The objective is to make it easy for customers to contact the company, and to enable them to choose whichever channel he or she chooses for contacting the company, and for the company to be able to respond accordingly, consistently and effectively to satisfy the individual customer. The slogans are 'accessibility' and 'customer choice and satisfaction'.

Customers can talk to any person in any store, not just the one from which they purchased a product. Contact details are on the back of every till receipt.[16] Most brands have a contact

[15] Directive 1992/95/EEC and 2001/95/EC.

[16] The till receipt also states: 'Please keep this receipt .... and we'll happily give you an exchange, giftcard or refund if you change your mind. Without a receipt, we'll give you an exchange. There are some exceptions and we'll always make these clear. For the safety of our customers we can't accept returned medicines, cosmetics or food, unless faulty. This does not affect your statutory rights.'

phone number on the product. Boots also have the Advantage Card loyalty scheme, with customer benefits. The company's website at Boots.com[17] has a facility saying 'Contact us' which leads to 'Email us', 'Write to us' and 'Phone us', all with the Customer Care team details.

As a result of this high level of visibility and positively attracting customer feedback and contact, Boots finds that many customers prefer to contact them rather than others, such as well-known product brands. Thus, people who are unhappy over the quality of a bar of chocolate could contact the chocolate manufacturer, but many choose to contact Boots. Similarly, customers write to Boots rather than to the Financial Ombudsman Service in relation to issues with some insurance products.

Making a complaint or contact to Boots should cost the customer nothing. The outcome of the process should be that no further action, whether through the courts or any other channel, is unnecessary. Boots has no time limit on when a complaint may be made: the statutory limitation periods are ignored. Some other retailers have recently introduced limitations.

Organizational Aspects

The complaint process is illustrated in Figure 12.1. Boots has a Central Customer Care Team in the company's headquarters at Nottingham, comprising 250 people,[18] which handles all phone and email contacts from customers. It works with, and is supported by, all the company's other functions, notably technologists and the legal department. Thus, any technical issue would involve analysis and advice from the technical staff, and any legal issue (such as threats to involve the legal system, lawyers, regulators (Trading Standards), or the media) would involve liaison with in-house legal assistance.

The Central Customer Care Team handles all direct customer contacts, including maintaining the loyalty card, and initiates action on all customer insights, namely:

- Analysing central customer contact data
- Communication of key customer issues to the business
- Proposing product/service change & monitoring the effect
- Consultancy – products, services, initiatives, development & implementation
- Public Recalls
- Risk assessment
- Stakeholder management
- Customer/Store Communication.

The 250 Customer Care Advisers are considered to have trained expertise. They aim to ensure consistency of response, and only members of that central team respond to complaints. The care process has been recognised by the Department for Business, Innovation and Skills in being published as an example of best practice.[19]

[17] http://www.boots.com/en/Help/Contact-Us.

[18] Cadburys have 30 people.

[19] Examples of good practice by Early Learning Centre, NEC (UK) Ltd and Lego were given in *Consumer Product recall. A Good Practice Guide* (Department of Trade and Industry, Confederation of British Industry and British Retail Consortium, 199) available at http://webarchive.nationalarchives.gov.uk/tna/+/http://www.dti.gov.uk/ccp/topics1/pdf1/consumer.pdf. See also Sambrook Research International, *Product Recall Research* (Department of Trade and Industry, 2000) available at http://webarchive.nationalarchives.gov.uk/+/http://www.berr.gov.uk/files/file21808.pdf.

One advantage of a centralised customer care function is that data are captured that inform the business about all issues with the quality, safety and effectiveness of goods, services and procedures. All the data is reviewed by management, particularly with the aim of identifying any pattern of similar issues, so that action can be taken such as a risk assessment[20] or a 'Red Alert'.[21] The review process is 'owned' by the Customer Care Team, which represents the customer internally. All product recalls that have occurred have been instituted through internal generation of data, rather than being externally generated from Trading Standards or other sources. By the time that most contacts are made, the company is already dealing with a problem. The company holds regular business briefings to review all aspects of the care process and data generated, on products, services, organization and procedures. The company sends daily and instant electronic customer care communications to all its stores.

Two examples illustrate the approach. If a number of complaints are seen of breakages of glass jars containing face cream, the answer may be that jars packed at the bottom of a pallet have been broken because the packaging was inadequate or hen a pallet was dropped. Appropriate changes are then introduced.

Isolated reports were received of glass in sandwiches. This was a curious occurrence. The glass was analysed and found to be from ceiling lights. The matter was investigated with the particular sandwich supplier, and evidence was found that the night shift had been playing football and had shattered a light fitting, which had showered the production line and the items had not been binned as should have happened. The shift members were sacked.

The system is designed to be highly responsive to customers. It is not designed to be suspicious or defensive, although there are certain means, within the law, of identifying habitual and fraudulent claims. The cost of responding generously to possibly unjustified complaints is thought to be minimal, and certainly not worth jeopardising the advantages of the positively focused approach.

A contact will be escalated to a business advisor if the customer or the handler needs more information, or if the customer insists on talking to a more senior person, or if the issue involves personal injury. There are 14 such senior staff, who therefore handle the 'more tricky stuff'.

Boots aims to respond to all contacts within 48 hours. On receiving a contact, Boots liaises with the supplier, which may be internal (Boots manufactures some products itself) or external. The response to the customer is that Boots will write to the supplier and expect to see the supplier respond to the customer, copied to Boots, within 14 days. All major retailers (such as Marks & Spencer and Waitrose and other supermarkets) have a supply manual that sets out the terms and conditions of business between retailer and suppliers. These manuals specify responsiveness to any issues that arise, and how things will be handled. Boots retains control of making decisions on all customer complaints, rather than hand things over to the manufacturer or insurers for either party. Boots charges suppliers for the time of its in-house handling where the manufacturer has been in breach of contract.

[20] Company policy is that a risk assessment meeting shall be held 'within 24 hours of discovering a potentially serious problem that could have a major impact on the safety of our customers or the integrity of our brand. The attendees will rapidly agree a course of action to minimise the risk to customers and the brand, and put steps in place to avoid a recurrence.' All relevant departments are to be involved: see Figure 12.2.

[21] A Red Alert is a process that facilitates rapid response to incidents or issues that have the potential for high risk to customer safety and/or brand integrity.

For personal injuries, Boots will retain control of the issue and work with the supplier to a resolution, rather than be unilateral. Personal injury issues are handled by a dedicated team in Boots' legal department, whether relating to customers or employees. External insurance with the National Pharmacy Association is held for claims arising out of dispensing errors. Such injuries are rare but some can be serious. Appropriate reports are referred for professional and regulatory control to the Boots Superintendent Pharmacist and the regulator, the General Pharmaceutical Council.

Issues taken up by external media, notably the television programme *Watchdog* or the *Daily Mail* have almost no internal effect on how the company operates. The company views such media channels as aiming to provide stories or entertainment, rather than substance. No such external stimuli have identified or affected the course of the company's actions. Boots has used *Watchdog* itself twice in order to communicate the recall of a product. If a consumer threatens to 'report' the company, the response is 'We are happy for you to go to *Watchdog* or Trading Standards, and we will assist them'. The company notes a difference in consumer attitudes in different companies: there is more of a claims culture in Ireland ('What are you going to give me?') than in the United Kingdom.

If a customer chooses to involve a lawyer, which only a tiny percentage (perhaps two or three a week) do, the company's response is to respond by asking the customer to get in touch direct.

The Customer Care Team will write to every customer to inform them of any action taken as a result of their contact. For example, feedback will be given of any redesign of a product, accompanied by a free sample: this is intended to generate a 'wow' factor and to make the customer feel involved in the enterprise.

The company also asks customers how the contact process was for them: 'Did we exceed your expectations?' As at late 2010, 77 per cent say that Boots more than exceeded expectations. The industry produces an externally-researched Net Promoter Score,[22] which gives a ratio of customers who were unhappy at the end of the contact process (dissenters) against those who were happy (advocates). Boots' score is 62 per cent; British Airways in below zero, British Gas has recently moved from 4 to 5 per cent.

The existing procedures are capable of handling any mass problem. There is no need for any new collective procedure. The management process is shown at Figure 12.2.

Statistics

The Customer Care Team receives 53,000 contacts a week. 3.5 per cent of those are complaints, of which a 'tiny' percentage are classified as serious. Statistics are not kept on issues that are resolved at store level. The Team gives 26,000 customer responses a week.

Over 90 per cent of contacts are resolved by the person who answers the phone call. An independent company offers Right First Time accreditation[23] and surveys customers, asking 'Was your complaint resolved at the point of contact?' Boots was the first company in that scheme to reach an 80 per cent positive answer.

[22] See http://www.netpromoter.com/np/index.jsp.

[23] See http://www.rightfirsttime.org/?gclid=CI-inIex86UCFc0e4Qodwwsupw.

Relationship with Regulatory Authorities

The company has agreed a Primary Authority relationship with its local Trading Standards Department, so any contact by customers to any Trading Standards officers around the country have to be routed through the Nottingham Department. Boots is in regular contact with its Principal Authority, and pro-actively informs it of any significant issues, so that the Authority is in a position to inform or respond to other Authorities. The relationship is positive and professional: there is no sense of 'capture' but of a professional arm's-length relationship If the authorities decide to prosecute, they will do so, although they have not done so since 2000. Perhaps one individual complaint a year comes to the company from Trading Standards, usually because the complaint has expectations that are higher than normal. Since prosecuting authorities need to satisfy a public interest test before instituting a prosecution, almost any issue is likely to fail that test as long as a company is already taking appropriate action to rectify a problem once it has been identified and it did not arise as a result of system failure.

Figure 12.1: The complaint journey process

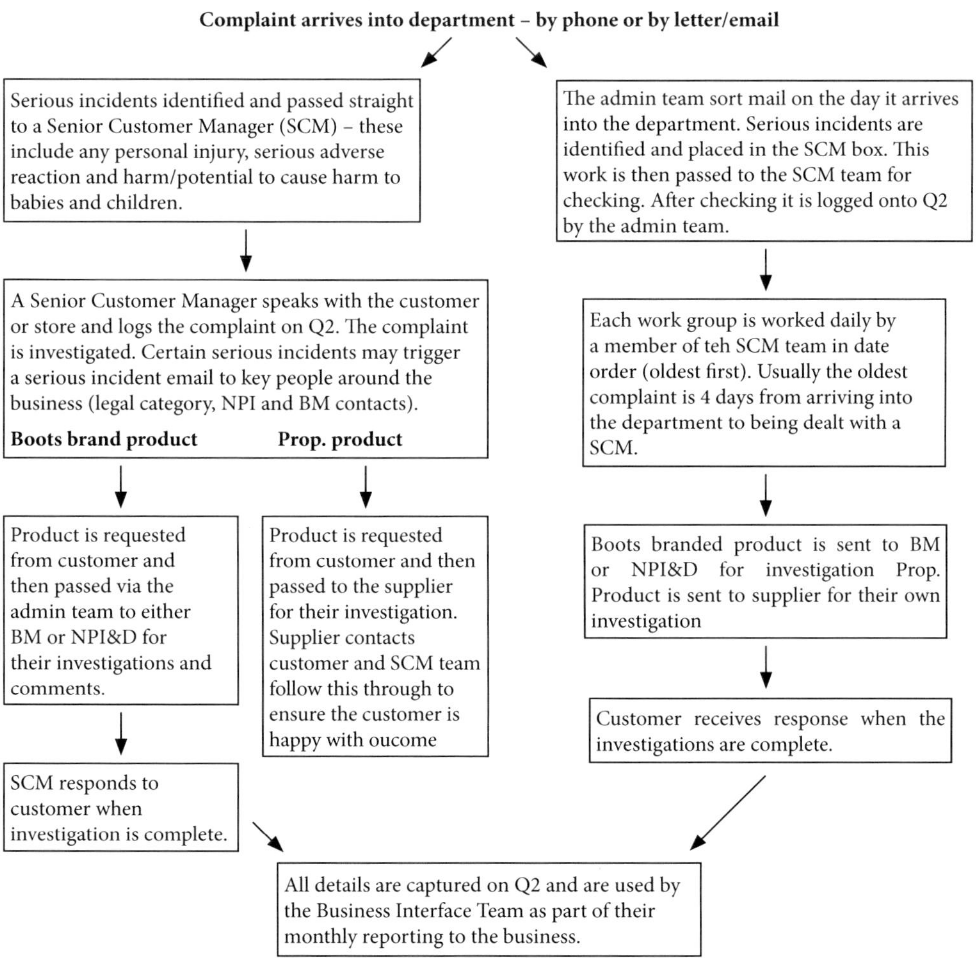

Figure 12.2: Boots Retail Issue management process

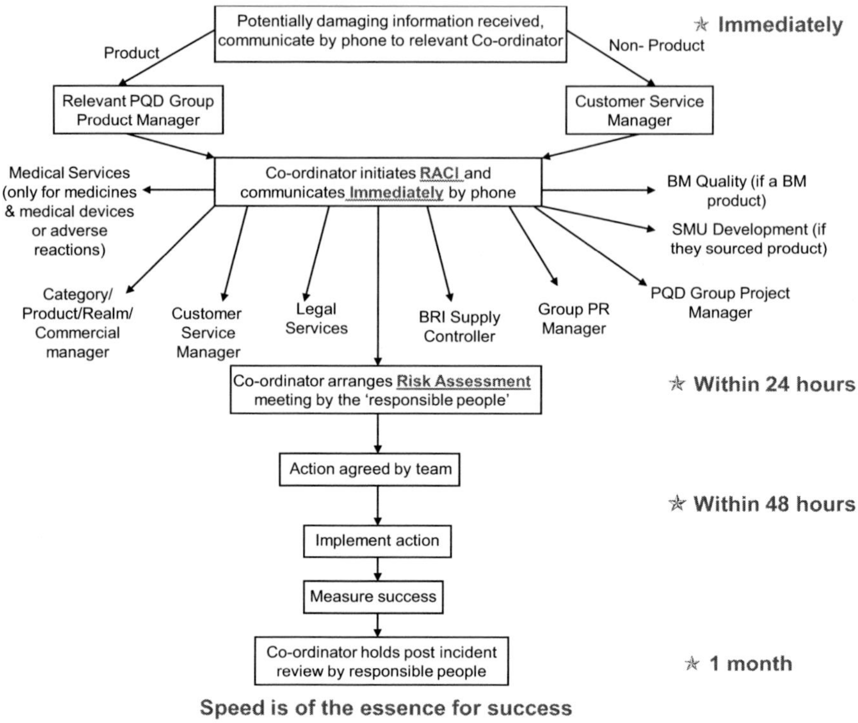

British Telecom

BT's Customer Services Department has the lead on complaints. Complaint handling comprises a funnel, with claims entering at the top and being filtered as they progress, and are settled. BT has a series of different teams to handle special issues. If a complaint ultimately cannot be resolved using the company's internal resources, and takes the external route involving Ombudsman Services, it is passed over to the 'Specialist Dispute Resolution' Team. BT's view is that although use of an external ombudsman function is new territory, it is a good thing. Commercial disputes go along a separate, legal track.

The consumer can reach BT through many channels: call/ write/email/twitter/blog/ facebook. BT uses social media as a pro-active way to reach out to customers and deal with their concerns as soon as they are identified. The key to this external involvement is that it all comes down to being a brand issue.

When a consumer calls into the voice channel, every adviser is expected to be able to deal with the caller (empowerment) and to log the complaint. BT's call centre advisers aim to identify the customer's *need* without the customer necessarily having to express that he/she is 'complaining'. Here, the challenge is to deal with situations where the standard operating model does not fit with the specific customer's needs. If the caller is not satisfied with the advice provided then the complaint is escalated up to the next line manager. If the complaint goes through two line managers, the team then look at the complaint operationally and take it to the Complaints Review Service. Some complaints go around the side, for example complaints directly made to directors or high-level complaints.

The company feels that its essential challenge is to identify who needs what help. BT has several thousand advisers in the UK and India, trained in specific products (billing, faults, initial orders, etc). BT uses algorithms to spot where a customer is in trouble, or shows signs of distress. The advisers are trained to question and find out what the cause of an issue is. BT receives hundreds of thousands of contacts every week 'at the top of the funnel': the biggest challenge is to ensure that the right response is made so customers get the right help. Each consumer has a personal log-in the system, into which the adviser logs each contact with the customer. BT tries to make sure that operators log exactly what was said to a customer, in order to record that issues were resolved, since sometimes customers come back and it is unclear whether complaints are new or repeats of the same issue.

There is a specialist service desk that deals with chronically sick and disabled people: some receive a call on the day the bill arrives to check if they have any issues or need help. This service is viewed as worthwhile, since the cost for managing customers who need individual attention if they make complaints within the general funnel system would be too high.

If the consumer is not happy after 8 weeks and there has been no deadlock-letter, then the consumer can go to the Ombudsman. When the 'customer journey' reaches stalemate within the 8 week period, and BT is not able to advise or negotiate any further with a customer, it issues a 'deadlock letter', which sets out the final position on a matter. The deadlock letter is a fairly comprehensive letter, reviewing what steps have been taken, giving an overview of the position reached, repeating any offer made, and stating that the Ombudsman may be able to help the consumer take the issue further. The Ombudsman deals with service issues. He cannot deal with issues regarding pricing and commercial policy; content, like vision; complaints about infrastructure such as the position of 'poles and holes'; and commercial decisions like broadband speeds. It is up to the customer to take the complaint further, and only about 30 per cent go on to consult the Ombudsman after receiving a deadlock letter. The Ombudsman system is a good way of drawing a line under an unreasonable customer.

If a matter is taken to the Ombudsman, it is referred internally (electronically) within BT to the Special Disputes Resolution Team. If the Ombudsman accepts a complaint then the Special Dispute Resolution Team produces a case file for the Ombudsman, within 10 days. This contains the case file (screen-dumps) of the complaint with a brief summary and recommendation. The Ombudsman can call for any information he wishes to see. He has the power to hold an oral hearing but this is hardly ever done.

BT finds that most consumers accept the Ombudsman's decision. The mediation stage introduced in 2010 by the Ombudsman (called 'Mutually Acceptable Settlement') proved to be quite effective: the objective was to resolve 40 per cent of Ombudsman complaints this way.

Only about 200 cases are started by consumers against BT in court per year. Many start if the consumer consults a solicitor, but BT does not feel that this gains the consumer and particular advantage. Very few do so after they have been through the Ombudsman process, and the claimants loose most of them: judges tend to side with the Ombudsman. BT tries to mediate such cases.

BT operates a feedback review from complaints and Ombudsman decisions. It samples its data for what went wrong. The company target in 2009 was to reduce complaints by 50 per cent. The 2011 focus is on insight, to identify the underlying issues of the complaints. This was driven by failure, customer expectations, and performance/service. BT takes a close look at the cases that go to the Ombudsman, and undertakes an in-depth analysis of representative cases. BT works together with the Ombudsman Services to be able to forecast the volume of complaints, for example before new products are put on the market. BT does not see any cross-border issues.

Procter & Gamble

Procter & Gamble is the world's top maker of household products, household care, beauty and grooming, and health and well-being. The firm also makes pet food. The company's products are subject to several specific regulatory regimes, such as medicinal products, cosmetics, general consumer products, electrical and low voltage items, batteries, and toys (supplied with promotions).[24]

Its Consumer Relations team in Newcastle handles all consumer relations issues for the United Kingdom and Ireland. The team comprises:

- A Contact Centre Manager
- Team Leads, who look after the consumer relation advisors (people management) and handle escalations
- Senior advisors, who handle consumer calls and work on more complex cases (eg health effects, damages etc)
- Consumer relations advisors, who handle consumer contacts (phone, e-mail, letter), fully trained in product knowledge and processes.

The mission statement for consumer relations has been consistent for decades. The company does not have a written customer care policy, but adopts a general approach towards seeking to delight its customers. It has a Global Consumer Relations division, which adopts a consistent approach across the company's global operations. The company's Consumer Care goals are to:

> increase consumer loyalty to P&G and its brands by building strong relationships with those who contact us, representing their needs within the company, using these consumer insights top increase our ability to delight consumers with improved products and services.

The company and its personnel see a clear commercial imperative in adopting an approach that seeks to delight customers, given the desire to be the best in its chosen competitive markets. The above Consumer Care mission is integrally linked with the company's core values.[25]

[24] See C Hodges, *European Regulation of Consumer Product Safety* (Oxford University Press, 2005).

[25] These include leadership, ownership, integrity, passion for winning, and trust. Integrity is defined as 'We always try to do the right thing. We are honest and straightforward with each other. We operate within the letter and spirit of the law. We uphold the values and principles of P&G in every action and decision. We are data-based and intellectually honest in advocating proposals, including recognizing risks.'

Complaints Handling

The company has a standardised approach towards handling each consumer contact, which varies only depending on the nature of the product and requirements of local regulation.

Complaints are received via phone, e-mail or letter. Telephone services are available from 9 am until 5 pm every weekday, whereas a 24 hour service is provided to respond to email, since email users tend to expect fast responses. The company is increasingly using social media sites for promoting brands, and these are monitored for customer issues and responded to. The company is always looking for further ways in which to get customers to contact it.

Some contacts may come via retailers, especially large supermarkets. Procter & Gamble's policy is always to seek to contact the consumer direct, even if the retailer has already formally closed an issue. Some retailers have a policy of not wanting brand manufacturers to contact consumers, in which case Procter & Gamble cannot establish direct contact. It considers that it is in the best interests of the customer to have a direct line of contact with or from the manufacturer. In any event, all details of every case received are logged, since they may provide relevant product information.

Contacts are handled by the team of consumer relations advisors, who:

- listen to the consumer to fully understand what the complaint relates to.
- utilise handling guidelines to provide the best advice/guidance.
- use this opportunity to further educate the consumer where relevant.
- will personally close out the majority of complaints based on internal guidelines/policies.
- have the opportunity to escalate the case to a Senior Advisor and/or a Team Lead if deemed relevant/necessary.

The objective is to deal with all issues consistently and quickly, in a way that is positive and constructive. The company wants the customer to feel happy at the end of the process. The essence of the process is one of constant listening, so as to identify issues. Advisers respond in accordance with the company's internal Guidelines, which contain all relevant information on products, both before and after use, and provide them with a full briefing, and with its Codes on uniform reporting. The way that individual advisers handle contacts, and the feedback from customers, are monitored internally. Advisors are trained to accommodate individual customers' requests and personality types. Advisers mark consumers who reveal unusual insights or emotion, since these may be particularly revealing. Some consumers wish to talk to a more senior adviser, so will be passed on, but every adviser has authority to close any issue.

The standard response by advisers is to reimburse the cost of the product by sending the customer a voucher that can be exchanged with a retailer. Advisers have some discretion on how to respond to particular facts in individual cases, within defined limits set out in the Guidelines. Higher approval is needed before limits can be exceeded, and internal controls monitor responses. The company's policy is to treat everyone in a fair, consistent and balanced way, and it believes that this principle will not allow it to respond to similar situations in different ways, such as in responding to threats with excessive generosity.

Certain issues will trigger particular responses or internal processes. Issues are escalated as necessary. Information will be shared as necessary with other parts of the company that deal with such functions as Research & Development, Quality Assurance, Manufacturing,

External Relations, Legal, Regulatory, Knowledge and Advocacy (especially for new brands). Safety issues, for example, will be tracked every day. Specific regulatory or legal reporting requirements are covered in the Guidelines. If a consumer claims that products have caused damage after use, there will be further investigation. This will particularly apply if the consumer claims to have had a health effect as a result of using P&G products.

At present, from a P&G perspective, the majority of health effects concern the use of hair colourants, with some individuals claiming they have had a personal sensitivity to the product. Once personal sensitivities are identified, a user should not use a product with the relevant ingredient. In very rare cases, anaphylactic shock may result. A dedicated team deals with health issues, and can refer individuals to a dermatologist for sensitivity testing and advice. Razors, especially if they are misused by banging the blade, can cause cuts, although injuries are rarely serious enough for customers to go to their doctors. The company requests photographic evidence of all personal injuries.

All contact details are logged. Consumers are rarely confrontational in their contacts with the company. Very few consumers involve solicitors. When they say that they wish to do so, the company's response is to state that that is their choice and if they do so, the case will be passed to the Legal Department. Until a solicitor becomes involved, the company will continues to work with the consumer to try to resolve the issue. The involvement of solicitors, or threat to do so, does not affect the outcome of complaints.

The company employs means of identifying repeat complaints. It will err on the side of generosity in responding to repeat contacts, since consumers may genuinely be returning for further care or advice. In the rare instances where company personnel perceive the contacts are not genuine, they will escalate to higher-level management who will coordinate with their Legal Department for guidance/advice. If a consumer states that he or she plans to go to Trading Standards, the advisor will state that P&G will cooperate fully with Trading Standards. Contact with any Trading Standards Office is routed through the company's Legal Department, which has a good working relationship with the Principal Authority at Surrey County Council.

Statistics

The company has various measures and targets in place to check the level of service it is providing. These measures include the following:

- Timeliness of response – percentage of calls answered, percentage of emails answered within specified timeline.
- Quality of response – internal quality monitoring is carried out on calls and emails to continuously coach advisors to provide excellent customer care.
- Quality of response – requesting feedback from consumers who have called or e-mailed, via a Consumer Satisfaction survey.

The profile of contacts differs depending on the type of product. The percentage of contacts that the company's Newcastle team received for consumer contacts the UK in calendar 2010 were categorised as follows:

- Availability of product – 17%
- Complaints – 51%
- Inquiry – 29%
- Testimonials – 3%

Around a third of contacts are requests for advice or information. Roughly half of the contacts are classed as complaints, but on closer examination the causes of a compliant may be inappropriate use of the product by the consumer or some reason other than a cause attributable to the company. Use of hair colorants is one of the major issues: users may fail to follow the instructions to do a strand test, or may fail to do a key sensitivity test for personal sensitivities, before applying the product to the entirety of their hair. It is very rare that products have been contaminated, and extremely rare that they are not in accordance with specification.

The company benchmarks the level of customer satisfaction with how calls are handled (always in the 80 or 90 per cent satisfaction rate) and intent to repurchase (always over 70 per cent). Repurchasing intent can be affected by the company's ability to identify which retailers may hold stock of an item, which can be difficult to do.

Certain longer-term trends have been noted. Over recent decades, the number of contacts over personal sensitivities appears to have increased, and this is attributed to heightened cultural awareness of sensitivities in some countries (rates differ between countries) over sensitivities, rather than changes in safety controls.

Advisers have also noted a change in language used by callers, with increased use of the word 'compensation' and more demanding adversarial language during the past decade. In contrast, the company's policy is that compensation is not paid since legal liability is an irrelevant issue, but it responds by making gestures of goodwill.

Procter & Gamble is a large company, with significant resources and sophisticated structures, which enable it to deal with complaints as it wishes, and to escalate issues. It invests considerable time and effort in its advisers, providing training, refresher training, and monitoring performance quality, processes and policies.

13

Cross-border Consumer ADR

Christopher Hodges, Naomi Creutzfeldt-Banda and Iris Benöhr

This chapter examines some of the existing mechanisms that provide for handling disputes made by consumers in one Member State against a trader in another Member State. The important EU-level institutional arrangements under ECC-NET and FIN-NET have been noted in Chapter 1 so are not mentioned further here. A number of pan-EU CADR schemes are being established, of which we note here two created by business, the European Car Rental Conciliation Service (ECRCS) and the Direct Selling Association (SELDIA)'s ombudsman scheme, and one network created by national ombudsmen for energy. At global level we then note the long-established online dispute resolution (ODR) systems for domain names and developments on ODR led by UNCITRAL. The European Commission's 2011 proposals for ODR have been noted in Chapter 1 above.

European Car Rental Conciliation Service

The European Car Rental Conciliation Service (ECRCS)[1] is a conciliation service aimed at assisting all EU citizens[2] who have an unresolved dispute against a rental company relating to a cross-border car rental. It was established on 1 July 2010 with the involvement of Leaseurope,[3] the European trade association,[4] after it was noted at the 2009 EU consumer summit that there was an increasing number of unresolved complaints being reported to ECC Net. A number of national schemes existed prior to the launch of this pan-European scheme, but there were variations between them in terms of design and effective performance. Having surveyed the practical options, the four major European rental companies decided to establish the scheme to gain sufficient volume and momentum. It is now subscribed to by Hertz, Avis, Alamo, Europcar, Budget, National car rental and Sixt, which together cover an estimated 80 per cent of all 55 million car rental transactions taking place in Europe. Other rental companies that provide cross border rental transactions are eligible to subscribe to the ECRCS.

Companies subscribing to the scheme agree to adhere to a Code of Best Practice,[5] which includes standards on advertising, customer information, vehicle condition, pre- and

[1] www.leaseurope.org/index.php.

[2] The service is open to any consumers with EU residence.

[3] A European association was established in 1972 as ECATRA, which subsequently merged with Leaseurope. ECATRA, formerly the association for rental companies, was integrated into Leaseurope in 2006.

[4] Alamo, Avis, Budget, Europcar, Sixt and Hertz.

[5] www.leaseurope.org/uploads/Code%20of%20Best%20Practice.pdf.

post-rental inspections and billing. BVRLA was selected to operate the ECRCS, since that association had successfully operated a national ADR scheme for 20 years, handled by IDRS.[6] ECRCS and the British national scheme are operated separately, but are based on similar principles of offering an alternative dispute resolution which aims to offer restorative justice. The scheme is funded by an annual subscription paid by all of the subscribing rental companies: the amounts are not published.

The complainant must contact the company first. Only when he/she is not happy with the outcome then there are two options to proceed, either the rental company makes the EU citizen aware of the ECRCS within their final outcome letter, or the consumer can approach ECRCS directly. The subscribing rental company refers the full complaint file to ECRCS. ECRCS reviews the case file and identifies if there are any breaches of the Code of Best Practice. The EU citizen and rental company are informed of the decision within 30 days: up to February 2012 the average duration has been between 10–15 days. ECRCS launched a website in 2012 to make the complaint process simpler and more accessible. If any money is owed to the EU citizen this should be refunded within 10 working days. The decision is binding on the subscribing company but is not binding on the consumer and there is no cost to the consumer to use the system.

The service investigates potential breaches of the agreed Code of Best Practice, which sets out the standards it expects from the vehicle rental industry. The conciliation service is unable to investigate any matters which are criminal in nature, involve personal injury, or fall outside the scope of the Code of Best Practice.

Statistics are published in the annual report. The initial results are:

- The ECRCS received a total of 123 complaints in 2011. The volume of complaints increased in the second half of the year suggesting increasing awareness of the service.
- The number of complainants lodging their complaint directly with the service rather than it being referred by the rental company has also increased.
- The average time taken to resolve a case was 11.83 days.
- The largest number of complaints related to charges. Complaints included charges for winter tyres, and toll fees.
- 64 per cent of cases investigated were not upheld.
- The majority of cross border complaints related to rentals taking place in Spain, Italy, Germany and France (respectively 23, 21, 18 and 26 per cents).
- 64 per cent of all complainants reside in the UK.
- Spanish customers raised 19 per cent of complaints.
- These statistics mirror those provided by the European Consumer Centre.

SELDIA: The European Direct Selling Association

Direct selling is a method of marketing and retailing goods and services directly to the consumers, in their homes or in any other location away from permanent retail premises. It is usually conducted in a face-to-face manner, either where products are demonstrated to an individual or to a group (party plan), or where a catalogue is left with the consumer

[6] BVRLA, established in 1967, is the UK trade body. See ch 11 for further details about IDRS.

and where the direct seller calls later to collect orders.[7] In 2010, the total EU sales of direct selling companies were €11.5 billion, the largest markets being Germany, Italy, France, UK and Poland.[8] From May 2011, the EU trade association Seldia[9] revised its Code of Conduct,[10] linked to the sector's World Code of Ethics of the world direct selling association (WFDSA).[11] Every company that is a member of a Direct Selling Association (DSA) must adhere to the Code of Ethics and should have a Code Compliance officer.

A consumer who has a complaint against a direct selling company that is a member of a DSA in respect of any business practice believed to be unethical, illegal or a possible violation of the Code of Conduct should first try to resolve the matter directly with the company, particularly with the Code Compliance officer. A complaint should be in writing, and should include the following basic information:

- The date and details of the incident;
- The parties involved;
- If possible, identify the Code violation you believe has occurred;
- Efforts you have made to resolve the matter;
- List the amount and cost of product, if relevant, include invoices or other supporting documents;
- Any responses the other parties have made to resolve the matter;
- The current status of the complaint;
- How you would like to see the complaint resolved or remedied.

After that stage, if the consumer is not satisfied, he/she can complain to the independent Code Administrators of national DSAs, which will accept consumer complaints by phone or (e)mail. National DSAs have found that a great number of complaints can be handled by the associations, notably where the consumer cannot trace the direct selling company, the consumer is not aware of his rights, such as on the cooling off period. Where the DSA is not able to solve the issue immediately, it will pass the complaint on to the national code administrator. There are no time limits for national DSAs, but this may be reviewed.

Complaints may be made to the European Code Administrator[12] where complaints at national DSA are not effective in the following four instances:

1. Complaints from parties (consumers, direct sellers, direct selling companies, consumer bodies etc) from one of the EEA countries without a DSA in membership of Seldia involving a direct selling company in membership of Seldia or of a DSA in membership of Seldia
2. On complaints from parties related to cross-border transactions and involving a direct selling company in membership of Seldia or of a DSA in membership of Seldia from one of the EEA countries

[7] Direct selling is suited to the sale and distribution of almost every category of consumer goods that can be found in traditional retail locations and in department stores, especially cosmetic and personal care products, household items and wellness, and is also cost effective for services such as telecoms, gas and electricity supplies.

[8] Sales respectively of €2.8 billion, €2.4 billion, €1.8 billion, €1.3 billion and €0.5 billion. See www.seldia.eu/sites/default/files/pdf-documents/annual_report-2010-2011_1.pdf.

[9] www.seldia.eu. Members of Seldia represent directly and indirectly around 80% of the EU direct selling market.

[10] European Code of Conduct towards consumers and direct sellers; available at: www.seldia.eu/~wwwseldi/sites/default/files/uploads/content-pdf/seldia_codeofconduct.pdf. A list of code administrators can be found at: www.seldia.eu/~wwwseldi/sites/default/files/uploads/content-pdf/ethics_commitee.pdf.

[11] See www.wfdsa.org.

[12] The European Code Administrator is the Ethics Committee of Seldia, at 2011 comprising: Professor Jules Stuyck of Leuven University (Chairman), with Anders Berglund (Swedish DSA), Juan Turró (Spanish DSA), Philippe Dailey (French DSA) and Maurits Bruggink (Seldia).

3. Decide on complaints from DSAs in membership of Seldia in one of the EEA countries involving a direct selling company in membership of Seldia and;
4. Complaints from DSAs in membership of Seldia from one of the EEA countries involving direct selling companies in membership of WFDSA, WFDSA CEO Council or of DSAs outside membership of Seldia with the aim of mediation together with such direct selling companies, WFDSA and the DSA in question.

The national DSA's and national code administrators do not like the idea of a European code administrator as a sort of 'appeal administrator'. The national DSAs therefore try and help consumers at national level, and will only turn to the European code administrator in the above circumstances. Seldia also operates a B2B code, under which a national DSA may alert the European ombudsman about bad practice of a company that has generated a number of similar complaints. For example, if a company has confusing order forms that lead to several consumer complaints, the national DSA will ask the European code administrator to pick up the case.

European Energy Ombudsman Group

European Energy Ombudsman Group (EEOG)[13] is an independent, non-profit Europe-wide professional association made up of ombudsmen and mediators from European energy companies. The principal aim is to promote mediation between companies and consumers within the energy sector as a means to solve disputes and complaints. In the context of the EU's Third Energy Package,[14] the Commission set up in November 2010 a Working Group to identify best practices in ADR in the energy sector,[15] which reported in 2011.[16] Members of EEOG organize meetings, exchange information and work together to increase awareness and acceptance of mediation and its practice in the energy industry. EEOG members also participate to reflections and works coming from the European Commission. EEOG does not handle complaints submitted directly by consumers.

ODR

Any dispute resolution system, including courts,[17] may adopt information and communications technology (ICT), and this will usually assist in speeding up the process. ODR has emerged as an ADR technique that is completely online, and is frequently now

[13] www.energyombudsmen.com.

[14] Directive (EC) 2009/72 concerning common rules for the internal market in electricity and repealing Directive 2003/54/EC [2009] OJ L211/55, and Directive (EC) 2009/73 concerning common rules for the internal market in natural gas and repealing Directive 2003/55/EC [2009] OJ L211/94.

[15] Commission Staff Working Paper 'An energy policy for consumers', SEC(2010)1407.

[16] Working Group Report on Alternative Dispute Resolution in the Energy Sector. Report prepared for the 4th Citizens' Energy Forum – October 2011, available at http://ec.europa.eu/consumers/citizen/my_rights/docs/energy_adr_report_en.pdf.

[17] For example the Online Money Claim of the courts in England and Wales, the online Small Claims Procedure in Ireland, and the eCourt initiative in Australia; see Cortés, above, ch 1.

referred to as a separate technique and dispute resolution world.[18] Like ADR, ODR has capitalised on situations in which traditional dispute resolution techniques were inefficient or unavailable.[19] The adoption of ICT into dispute resolution is continuing to grow.

The driver for the expansion of ODR is commerce.[20] In the United States the value of e-commerce was at best $33 billion in 1999 and is projected to rise to $279 billion by 2015.[21] The global volume is projected to be $1.4 trillion by 2015, of which 34 per cent will be in the EU.[22] The sheer volume of disputes that arise with e-commerce, and the cost of resolution, in addition to legal challenges such as applicable law and enforcement, have led to the development of solution-oriented (as opposed to blame-oriented) approaches to conflict resolution.[23]

The first ODR schemes appear to have been created in U.S.A. in the mid-1990s, such as a voluntary online arbitration procedure Virtual Magistrate founded by the National Center for Automated Information Research at Villanova University, Philadelphia, U.S.A. in 1995, but turned out to be unsuccessful.[24] In 1996 there emerged the Online Ombudsman Office, which offered mediation services for all internet disputes,[25] and CyberTribunal, which was replaced in 1999 by eResolution.[26] As of 2006, at least 149 ODR services had been launched worldwide, although many had closed down.[27]

Paypal.com has a dispute resolution centre that facilitates communications between buyers and sellers that use its payment services.[28] Cortés quoted Paypal as having found that, after the launch of this centre, buyers' claims decreased by 50 per cent, and seller losses caused by chargebacks fell by 20 per cent.[29] The dispute resolution service adopted escalation techniques, starting in effect with conciliation through assisted communication, before a formal complaint, If the buyer makes a complaint within 45 days after the payment, Paypal will retain the funds in escrow until the matter is resolved, where the product purchased did not arrive, or the product delivered was significantly different from that ordered.

EBay's ODR platform handles over 60 million e-commerce disputes annually,[30] primarily relating to the following types:

1. The buyer did not receive the items within the estimated delivery date, or
2. The item received was wrong, damaged, or different from the seller's description. For example:

[18] For recent legal studies see J Hörnle, *Cross-Border Dispute Resolution* (Cambridge, Cambridge University Press, 2009) and P Cortés, *Online Dispute Resolution for Consumers in the European Union* (Abingdon and New York, Routledge, 2010).

[19] Cortés, *Online Dispute Resolution* (2010) 9.

[20] L Del Luca, C Rule and Z Loebl, *Facilitating Expansion of Cross-Border E-Commerce—Developing a Global Online Dispute Resolution System (Lessons Derived from Existing ODR Systems - Work of the United Nations Commission on International Trade Law)* The Pennsylvania State University Legal Studies Research Paper No 25-2011 (State College, Pensilvania State University, 2011), available at http://ssrn.com/abstract=1970613.

[21] K Saleh, *How Big is E-Commerce Industry. THE INVESP BLOG*, available at www.invesp.com/blog.

[22] ibid.

[23] Del Luca, *Facilitating Expansion of Cross-Border E-Commerce* (2011).

[24] United Nations Conference on Trade and Development, 'Online Dispute Resolution: E-Commerce and Beyond' in *E-Commerce Development Report* (2003) 203.

[25] http://www.ombuds.org/center/ombuds.html.

[26] Cortés (n 18), 55.

[27] M Conley Tyler, 'Evaluating Recent Developments in Online Dispute Resolution', Presentation on 22 March to the Fourth International Forum on ODR, Cairo.

[28] Buyer and Seller Protection Policies at www.paypal.com.

[29] Cortés, (n 18), 60.

[30] Del Luca (n 20).

(a) Buyer received a completely different item.
(b) The condition of the item is not as described.
(c) The item is missing parts or components.
(d) The item is defective during the first use.
(e) The item is a different version or edition displayed in the listing.
(f) The item was described as authentic but is not.
(g) The item is missing major parts or features, and this was not described in the listing.
(h) The item was damaged during shipment.
(i) The buyer received the incorrect amount of items.[31]

Automated negotiation can be carried out on an ODR platform without the intervention of a third party. Cortés found that current systems usually involve a 'blind bidding' negotiation process, and it was attractive for insurance compensation and commercial claims.[32] The principal provider was CyberSettle, which handled over 200,000 disputes between 1998 and 2010 in the United States, but failed to take off in the U.K. because of the then inability of lawyers to be paid out of the claimant's proceeds. SquareTrade handled disputes between sellers and buyers on eBay until 2008. Its software matched solutions to problems, and an online mediator was also available for asynchronous e-mail and web communications.[33] Trustmarks, such as Trusted Shops[34] and Euro-label,[35] have been a technique that has developed in ODR, along with customer feedback systems such as 'rate this transaction' and the ability to comment on a trader's level of service and responsiveness to complaints.

ODR for Domain Names

An example of a private ADR scheme that operates on an international basis, and incorporates ODR as an integral operational feature is the Uniform Domain Name Dispute Resolution Policy (UDRP) of the Internet Corporation for Assigned Names and Numbers (ICANN) on the recommendation of the World Intellectual Property Organization (WIPO).[36] The UDRP came into effect in 1999. The speed, low cost, international application and transparency of the UDRP have attracted considerable use in resolving trademark disputes, and especially domain name disputes. By 2011 there had been around 22,000 UDRP cases.

The UDRP administrative procedure only covers disputes cconcerning an alleged abusive registration of a domain name. This means that disputes need to meet the following criteria:

1. The domain name registered by the domain name registrant is identical or confusingly similar to a trademark or service mark in which the complainant (the person or entity bringing the complaint) has rights; and
2. The domain name registrant has no rights or legitimate interests in respect of the domain name in question; and

[31] See *Unpaid Item Policy*, EBAY, INC. available at http://pages.ebay.com/help/policies/unpaid-item.html.
[32] Cortés (n 18), 64.
[33] ibid, 66.
[34] www.trustedshops.com.
[35] www.euro-label.com.
[36] The following summary is taken from N Smith and E Wilbers, 'The UDRP: Design Elements of an Effective ADR Mechanism' (2004) 15 *American Review of International Arbitration* 215; from information kindly supplied by Erik Wilbers, the Director of the WIPO Arbitration and Mediation Centre, Geneva, and details on arbiter.wipo.int.

3. The domain name has been registered and is being used in bad faith.[37]

The scheme relies on several key aspects. Firstly, practice in relation to the registration of domain names is uniform around the world. There are currently around 100 million domain names registered, and the number is set to expand considerably in 2012. However, a domain name will be registrable without a check of existing trademark rights. Nevertheless, action can be taken contractually under the UDRP, which applies universally. The ICANN-imposed registration agreement imposes a contractual condition on all domain name applicants to be bound by the UDRP, and on registrars to apply decisions taken under the UDRP. Hence, breach of the UDRP can be invoked against all domain name holders at any time, regardless of their identity or location, and decisions will be immediately implemented. Thus, the problems of choosing, dealing with, and enforcing under different legal systems are avoided.

The UDRP Procedure

A complainant who asserts breach of trademark rights may lodge a complaint to an ICANN-accredited UDRP dispute resolution provider, of which there are currently four: the WIPO Arbitration and Mediation Centre, the National Arbitration Forum (NAF),[38] the Asian Domain Name Dispute Resolution Centre (ADNRC),[39] and the Czech Arbitration Court (CAC).[40]

In the WIPO procedure, the complainant has to choose whether to have the dispute resolved by a single arbitrator or a Panel of three.[41] On inception of a procedure, the complainant pays the fee, which is subject to two variables: the number on the Panel and the number of domain names involved. For cases with up to 5 domain names (which involves 95 per cent of cases, the average number being one and a half) the fee for a single arbitrator is U.S.$1,500, and for a Panel of three is U.S.$ 4,000.[42] The fees have stayed the same since the inception of the scheme. WIPO does not seek to make a profit from this service, which it offers for policy reasons to support the sector.

The dispute resolution provider then contacts the registrar of the domain name to confirm the identity of the domain name holder (the respondent) and to lock the domain name so that it cannot be changed during the proceedings. The dispute resolution provider will then send the complaint to the respondent, using all means of communication and all available addresses. After 20 days, during which the respondent may file a response, the dispute resolution provider forwards the file to an administrative Panel of one or three legal experts for decision. Panels are selected from external, independent trademark lawyers based around the world. The Centre maintains a list of around 400 such Panelists from 50 countries, whose details are published. If a complainant requests a panel of three, he may nominate one member and the respondent may nominate another.

Once a Panel has been appointed, it has 14 calendar days to submit its decision. If the Panel finds that the complainant has established its case under the requirements of the

[37] UDRP Policy Rule para 4(a), see www.wipo.int/amc/en/domains/guide/index.html#a1.
[38] Based in Minneapolis, Minnesota, see domains.adrforum.com.
[39] Offices in Beijing and Hong Kong, see adndrc.org/adndrc/index.html.
[40] See www.adr.eu.
[41] UDRP Rules, para 3(b)(iv).
[42] Schedule of Fees at arbiter.wipo.int/domains/fees/index.html.

UDRP, it will issue a decision ordering the transfer of the domain name. The claimant must establish the following:[43]

1. The domain name is identical or confusingly similar to a trademark or service mark in which the complainant has rights; and
2. The domain name holder has no rights or legitimate interests in respect of the domain name; and
3. The domain name has been registered and is being used in bad faith.

The complainant must choose between requesting the transfer or the cancellation of the disputed domain name. The Panel is confined to accepting or rejecting such request.

The decision is forwarded to the registrar, who will implement it unless the decision is challenged in court within 10 days. According to paragraph 4(k) of the UDRP Policy Rule, the mandatory administrative proceeding requirement shall not prevent either the respondent or the complainant from submitting the dispute to a court for independent resolution. It is possible for a party to start a lawsuit in court before an administrative proceeding is commenced. A party can also commence a lawsuit after the administrative proceeding is concluded if it is not satisfied with the outcome.[44]

The Center posts all Panel decisions on its website shortly after they have been notified to parties.[45] In order to assist Panels and the public, a Legal Index of decisions is available.[46]

Design Aspects

The UDRP was designed to encourage its use and to avoid legal challenge. Several features are noteworthy. Firstly, parties retain the option of litigating in a competent court: the arbitration jurisdiction is not stated to be exclusive. Secondly, the UDRP procedure does not permit a damages claim. Parties use courts if they wish to pursue compensation,[47] but the delays and costs that can be inherent in a compensation claim are avoided by the UDRP procedure.

Thirdly, the complainant pays the only fee required by the procedure. A party may retain lawyers or other experts if it wishes, but no extra costs are required, and costs are not shifted. The fee is payable in a single lump sum at the start.

Fourthly, the language of the proceeding is normally the language of the registration agreement used by the respondent to register the domain name.[48] This rule optimises the chance of properly notifying the respondent of a case and should minimise the cost of defence. The parties can agree to apply a different language. The Centre has conducted proceedings in 19 languages involving parties from over 150 countries in 1212.[49] About 40 per cent of complains come from the United States,[50] and the overwhelming majority of cases were in English.

[43] UDRP Rules, para 4(a). Examples of bad faith are an indication that the respondent acquired the domain name primarily for the purpose of riding on the goodwill of a trademark holder to attract internet users to the respondent's website for financial gain, or circumstances indicating that the respondent acquired the domain name to sell to a trademark holder for profit: ibid, paras 4(b)(iv) and 4(b)(i).

[44] www.wipo.int/amc/en/domains/guide/index.html#a1.

[45] See arbiter.wipo.int/domains/decisions.

[46] arbiter.wipo.int/cgi-bin/domains/search/legalindex.

[47] The Centre believes that parties litigate in only 0.2% of its cases.

[48] UDRP Rules, para 11(a).

[49] www.wipo.int/amc/en/domains/statistics/countries_a-z.jsp.

[50] www.wipo.int/amc/en/domains/statistics/countries.jsp?party=C.

Fifthly, the procedure is kept simple. No legal representation is required. Model forms of complaint and defence are available online.[51] The short time limits, limitation on remedies, and built-in enforcement are noted above. There is a single round of pleadings, although the Panel has discretion to conduct proceedings as it sees fit. Pleadings are limited to 5,000 words. All communications are online: the Center offers an online system, the WIPO Electronic Case Facility (WIPO ECAF), which provides a secure electronic docket into which case files and procedural orders can be uploaded. It has proved to be particularly useful in massive patent arbitrations, where lawyers and Panels are geographically dispersed.

Overall, this system has the effect of protecting both registrars and squatters from the serious penalties that could be imposed by courts, whilst speedily policing the global system through enforcement of holders' rights.

Studies have criticised WIPO and NAF for deciding disputes more often in favour of trade mark interests,[52] and been met with strong rebuttal.[53] Scholars have also criticised the system.[54]

A dispute resolution service provider is usually required to publish all decisions in full on the Internet.[55]

Statistics

The total number of cases from 1999 to 2011 are shown in Table 13.1 and the outcomes in Table 13.2.[56]

Table 13.1: Total number of WIPO cases 1999-2011

Year	1999	2000	2001	2002	2003	2004	2005	2006	2007	2008	2009	2010	2011
No.	1	1857	1557	1207	1100	1176	1456	1824	2156	2329	2107	2696	2764

Table 13.2: Outcomes of WIPO cases 1999-2011

	1999	2000	2001	2002	2003	2004	2005	2006	2007	2008	2009	2010	2011	Total
Terminated	0	357	292	236	215	278	384	486	581	618	514	551	597	5107
Transfer	1	1182	983	792	753	770	926	1125	1326	1437	1331	1876	1741	14243
Transfer, cancellation in part	0	1	0	1	1	1	3	1	0	3	2	3	1	17
Transfer, cancellation in part with dissenting opinion	0	0	0	0	0	0	0	0	0	0	0	0	0	0
Transfer with dissenting opinion	0	7	10	6	3	2	2	5	3	5	3	5	1	52
Transfer, denied in part	0	7	6	5	5	5	7	8	6	8	7	3	5	72
Transfer, denied in part with dissenting opinion	0	0	0	0	0	0	0	1	0	1	0	0	1	3

[51] See arbiter.wipo.int/domains/gtld/udrp/index.html.

[52] M Mueller, *A New Profile of Domain Name Trademark Disputes under ICANN's UDRP* (Syracuse University School of Information Studies, 2002); M Geist, 'Fair.com? An Examination of the Allegations of Systematic Unfairness in the ICANN UDRP' (2002) 27 *Brooklyn Journal of International Law*, 903.

[53] International Trade Mark Association (2002).

[54] J Hörnle, *Cross-Border Dispute Resolution* (Cambridge, Cambridge University Press, 2009), 186 ff; see also Cortés (n 18).

[55] Except where an Administrative Panel decides otherwise in exceptional circumstances: see para 16(b) of the Rules.

[56] WIPO web page 2012, at wipo.int/amc/en/domains/statistics/cases.jsp.

Transfer with concurring opinion	0	1	0	0	0	0	0	0	0	0	0	0	0	1
Transfer with dissenting and concurring opinion	0	0	0	0	0	0	0	0	0	0	0	0	0	0
Cancellation	0	7	12	11	8	9	7	11	25	32	44	48	26	240
Terminated by panel	0	0	0	0	0	0	0	0	0	0	1	1	9	11
Cancellation with dissenting opinion	0	0	0	0	0	0	0	0	0	0	0	0	0	0
Cancellation, denied in part	0	0	0	0	0	0	1	0	0	0	0	0	0	1
Cancellation, denied in part with dissenting opinion	0	0	0	0	0	0	0	0	0	0	0	0	0	0
Cancellation, transfer in part	0	0	0	0	0	0	1	0	0	0	0	0	1	2
Cancellation, transfer in part with dissenting opinion	0	0	0	0	0	0	0	0	0	0	0	0	0	0
Cancellation with concurring opinion	0	0	0	0	0	0	0	0	0	0	0	0	0	0
Complaint denied	0	261	245	148	110	108	143	183	211	218	197	203	207	2234
Complaint denied, cancellation in part	0	0	0	0	0	0	0	0	0	0	0	0	0	0
Complaint denied, cancellation in part with dissenting opinion	0	0	0	0	0	0	0	0	0	0	0	0	0	0
Complaint denied with dissenting opinion	0	12	3	4	2	3	0	4	3	6	8	4	5	54
Complaint denied, transfer in part	0	4	6	3	3	0	1	0	1	1	0	0	2	21
Complaint denied, transfer in part with dissenting opinion	0	0	0	1	0	0	1	0	0	0	0	0	0	2
Complaint denied with concurring opinion	0	0	0	0	0	0	0	0	0	0	0	1	0	1
Complaint denied with dissenting and concurring opinion	0	0	0	0	0	0	0	0	0	0	0	1	3	4

EU ODR

As noted in chapter 1 above, the EU has taken steps over a number of years to promote e-commerce and e-dispute resolution. Examples include, the Directive on the Protection of Consumers in Respect of Distance Contracts,[57] and the 1999 Consumer Complaint Form[58] now available in 11 languages.[59] The Electronic Consumer Dispute Resolution (ECODIR) was funded by the European Commission at the Universities of Dublin and Namur,[60] but suffered from lack of awareness and the withdrawal of funding, and was sold to the National Arbitration Forum.[61] It adopted a tiered approach, starting with negotiation, then mediation, and finally recommendation. It can operate in English and French. In the area of domain name disputes for .eu domains, ADR/ODR is regulated by Regulation (EC) No. 874/2004[62] which has been inspired by the UDRP Rules discussed above. There has been

[57] Directive (EC) 1997/7 on the protection of consumers in respect of distance contracts [1997] OJ L144/19.

[58] Commission (EC) 'Communication by the European Commission on the out-of-court settlement of consumer disputes', SEC(1998)576, final, 30 March 1998. It contains a European consumer complaint form.

[59] At ec.europa.eu/consumers/redress/compl/cons_compl/acce_just03_en.pdf.

[60] www.ecodir.org.

[61] See G Kaufmnn-Kohler and T Schultz, *Online Dispute Resolution: Challenges for Contemporary Justice* (The Hague: Kluwer Law International, 2004), 346.

[62] As amended by Regulation (EC) No. 1654/2005, Regulation (EC) No 1255/2007 and Regulation (EC) No 560/2009.

only one designated ODR provider for all .eu-related disputes, the Czech Arbitration Court, which has been providing ODR services in 21 EU languages since 2006.[63]

The OECD has encouraged in-house dispute settlements, customer satisfaction systems, and call centres, before resort to external ADR,[64] as has the Global Business Dialogue on E-Commerce[65] and Consumers International.[66]

The EU considers that 'the development of electronic commerce and online services offers enormous potential for economic, social and societal change'[67] and set a target for building trust in the Digital Single Market by 2015 since it is far too low,[68] and has enormous potential to generate growth. One of the key objectives of this strategy is to facilitate the settlement of online disputes. A 2009 survey found that reasons for lack of confidence in e-commerce were difficulty of resolving after-sales problems (88 per cent) and the problem of initiating legal action in the courts (83 per cent).[69]

The European Commission adopted a new action plan to double the share of e-commerce in the EU by 2015 on 11 January 2012.[70] Consisting of 16 initiatives, it aimed at fostering a more dynamic digital single market with better cross-border access to online products, improved internet security and more consumer protection. E-commerce currently accounts for just 3.4 per cent of retail sales, with an estimated value of €11.7 billion. If this figure were to be increased to 15 per cent, the value could be as high as €204 billion. To this end, the Commission considered that improving consumer confidence, transparency and payment and delivery methods are vital.

Consistent with this policy, the Commission's 2011 proposals included the establishment of an EU ODR platform for consumer disputes, as outlined in Chapter 1.

UNCITRAL

These developments run in parallel with the development by UNCITRAL of model procedural rules for cross-border ODR of low value high volume disputes related to both B2C and B2B e-commerce transactions.[71] In addition to, and in close association with, the preparation of UNCITRAL ODR rules, a number of ODR experts take the view that the creation of a cross-border system for providing redress in low value, high volume e-commerce transaction disputes requires certain pieces of digital infrastructure that do not currently exist.

[63] See www.adr.eu.

[64] *E-commerce Guidelines* (Paris, OECD,1999) and *Recommendation on Consumer Dispute Resolution and Redress* (Paris, OECD, 2007) 8.

[65] Global Business Dialogue on e-commerce, New York Recommendations (2003), 56.

[66] Consumers International, *Disputes in Cyberspace 2001: Update on Online Dispute Resolution for Consumers in Cross-Border Disputes*, (Consumers International Office for Developed and Transition Economies, 2001).

[67] 'Stimulating growth and employment: an action plan for doubling the volume of e-commerce in Europe by 2015', European Commission Press Release IP/12/10.

[68] In 2007 consumer spending constituted 58 per cent of the gross domestic product of the EU, yet only 29 per cent of EU small and medium sized enterprises are involved in cross-border transactions, although 48 per cent of them would be prepared to sell to consumers in other member States online, *per* M Kuneva, 'Consumer Strategy 2007–2013', Press Conference, Brussels, 13 March 2007.

[69] Flash Barometer, 14 November 2009, 39–40.

[70] Commission (EC) 'Communication: A coherent framework for building trust in the Digital Single Market for e-commerce and online services' COM(2011) 942, final, 11 January 2012.

[71] www.uncitral.org/uncitral/commission/working_groups/3Online_Dispute_Resolution.html.

Such a cross-border resolution system will only be possible if there is a complimentary system enabling the various resolution end-points (eg government agencies, buyers and sellers, online dispute resolution service providers, entities involved in enforcing judgments etc.) to exchange information in real time in multiple languages. This information may include new dispute filings, messages between disputants, and proposed solutions, resolution status, and agreement adherence. This information exchange system will not provide case adjudication or enforcement of outcomes; it will only enable data about disputes to be shared around the globe in multiple languages in an efficient and seamless manner.[72]

This backbone cross-border ODR infrastructure, called ODR Exchange, will in principle consist of a common ODR communication standard called ECRI (E-Commerce Resolution Interchange) and a technology-neutral ODR technical protocol. ODR Exchange has launched its cross-border pilot in January 2012 with participants from Europe, America and Asia.[73]

The UNCITRAL Working Group considers that ODR providers are systems accessible online, operated by private businesses. It has developed draft Principles applicable to ODR providers and neutrals, which are:

1. Maintaining a roster of competent neutrals;
2. Independence;
3. Disclosure of terms of service and confidentiality;
4. Establishing identity of the parties;
5. System reliability and security;
6. Record and publication of decisions;
7. Sensitivity to language and culture;
8. Fees and costs;
9. Enforcement.

The Working Group is aiming to develop a multi-stakeholder model with stakeholders including public agencies (policy makers, legislators and regulators), consumers, online businesses, payment channels, and ODR providers. The model envisages a three-stage approach:

1. In the first phase, the parties would negotiate with each other;
2. In the second phase a neutral would be appointed for the purpose of facilitating a solution; and
3. In the third phase to resolve the very few cases not resolved by use of the first two phases, a neutral (possibly the same neutral used in the second phase) would arbitrate the dispute.

[72] United Nations Commission on International Trade Law Working Group III (Online Dispute Resolution), Twenty-third session, New York, 23–27 May 2011.

[73] See www.odrexchange.com.

14

Empirical Findings

Naomi Creutzfeldt-Banda

This chapter highlights some of the data findings from the national studies in previous chapters.[1] It is not, however, a complete statistical analysis of every scheme discussed in this book. Depending on the structure of the national CADR architecture and method of claim-data-collection, it is easier to access data for some schemes and more complicated or impossible for others. It is evident that the disclosure and transparency (or lack thereof) of data presentation in annual reports varies significantly. Moreover, there is a huge variety in the approach of claim-data-collection which makes it very difficult to understand, compare and draw general conclusions. If there was a basic harmonized approach to claim registering, it would increase efficiency, save time, enable an exchange between schemes and could encourage appropriate reactions by industry to consumer trends.

The incidence of claims by country[2] is presented as a collection of detailed complaint information. *Bar charts* represent the total number of contacts per scheme, divided into the proportion that was classed as a complaint and the proportion of contacts redirected and/or inquiries. It is clear that throughout the countries and across sectors, most contacts are not complaints but information requests or do not fall into the contacted scheme's terms of reference. *Data tables* below the bar charts display, as far as possible, information on the number of complaints that are accepted by a scheme and resolved/redirected.

Then, data is presented for telecoms and financial services sectors, as far as it is available. Those two sectors are important because they attract the majority of contacts.

Following this, thresholds and limits, case fees for consumers, levels of loss and detriment, the cost of major CADR schemes, the cost per inquiry and the average duration are presented. Finally, a brief overview of EU consumer complaint data is provided.

Readers should note an issue over comparability of some of the following figures. First, there are significant demographic variations between the countries for which data has been collected. Those variables could theoretically be reconciled through per capita analysis of the claims data. However, this has not been undertaken because the results would not necessarily be conclusive, due to the fact that there are also notable variations in data collection methodology and presentation employed by the relevant CADR providers. In certain cases, the number of claims accepted and the number of claims redirected do not add up to the figure provided for total contacts per CADR scheme in any given year. This is due to irregular or unreported data, and deployment of variable methodology by the relevant organizations in calculating the number of claims for each year. For example, some schemes add the number of unresolved claims brought forward from the previous year to

[1] 2010 statistics were collected from annual reports and interviews.

[2] France, Germany, Lithuania, the Netherlands, Poland, Slovenia, Spain, Sweden and the United Kingdom.

the current annual report without specifying that as a result the total figure given for that year is a composite of new contacts and pre-existing unresolved claims. Some contacts may not get logged at all. Further, the timeframe of the annual reports can vary according to the financial year of the individual CADR providers. These variables in methodological approach by the CADRs preclude comprehensive statistical comparison. Therefore, there is no claim for entire accuracy of the figures below, and detailed conclusive comparison between schemes is not possible. However, the data allows a best attempt to highlight trends and give the reader a better understanding of the variations between the schemes.

Incidence of Claims

The Commission's 2009 study found that incidence of ADR cases was increasing across the EU with 410,000 cases recorded in 2006, 473,000 in 2007 and 530,000 during 2008.[3] It also found the median compliance rate by businesses was 99 per cent for those schemes that had data, ranging from 100 per cent for schemes with binding decisions to 90 per cent where decisions were non-binding.

In relation to cross-border ADR cases, 40 per cent of EU consumers bought goods and services over the internet in 2010,[4] and the ECC Network recorded 23,987 information requests, 17,310 'simple' complaints and 11,821 'normal' complaints and disputes.[5]

The following main points emerge. Firstly, there is a considerably wide range in the incidence of claims directed at CADR schemes between different states, from the one million contacts received by the UK FOS, to far smaller numbers in many other countries, whether generally or for financial services complaints. Secondly, it is almost impossible to state any accurate data on this, since only a minority of CADR schemes have full national coverage (the data indicate that there is one ARN claim for every 938 people in Sweden).

Thirdly, there is a consistent difference between the number of contacts received by a CADR scheme and the number of claims that are accepted for processing. The latter are often far lower than the former—sometimes dramatically so. This raises issues over whether consumers do not allow enough time in contacting traders before contacting a CADR scheme, whether CADR schemes have rules or jurisdictions that are sufficiently wide or restrictive, whether there are gaps in coverage in adjacent schemes that encourage consumers to try contacting an existing scheme, whether sufficient information is available about the remit and rules of CADR schemes, and whether the cost of dealing with many requests for information is too high or whether the function is useful but could be located elsewhere.

Data on ECC-Net and FIN-Net are given in chapter 1. A summary of further EU complaints data is at the end of this chapter.

[3] *Study on the use of Alternative Dispute Resolution in the European Union* (Civic Consulting, 2009), at http://ec.europa.eu/consumers/redress_cons/adr_study.pdf.

[4] Consumer Conditions Scoreboard. Consumes at home in the single market. 5th edn—March 2011.

[5] ibid.

By Country

A. France

Figure 14.1: Total number of contacts per sector divided into proportions of redirected contacts and those categorized as complaints

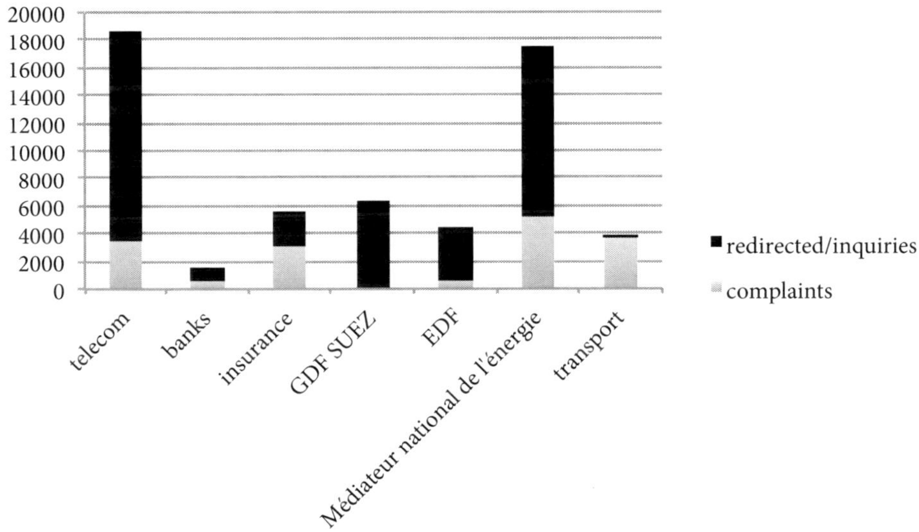

Telecoms: Mediateur des communications electroniques[6]/*Banks*: l'Autorité des marchés financiers[7]/ *Insurance*: Fédération Française des Sociétés d'Assurance[8]/*Energy*: GDF SUEZ[9] / Médiateur national de l'énergie[10]/*Transport*: SNCF[11]

[6] www.mediateur-telecom.fr/home; annual report 2010: www.mediateur-telecom.fr/ressources/media/files/Rapport_Mediateur_2010.pdf.

[7] www.amf-france.org/; annual report 2010: http://www.amf-france.org/affiche.asp?id=10086.

[8] www.ffsa.fr/; annual report 2010: www.ffsa.fr/sites/jcms/p1_460033/rapport-annuel-ffsa-2010-/ffsa-annual-report-2010?cc=fp_8800.

[9] Mediator's report 2010: www.gdfsuez.com/document/?f=files/fr/16rm1-44.pdf .

[10] http://www.energie-mediateur.fr/; annual report 2010: www.energie-mediateur.fr/fileadmin/user_upload/RapportMNE_2010_UK.pdf .

[11] www.sncf.com/fr_FR/flash/#/CH0001/BR0998/; annual report 2010: www.clubdesmediateurs.fr/sites/clubdesmediateurs.fr/files/upload/document/pdf/Mediation_der.pdf .

Table 14.1: Details of complaints by scheme

	Telecoms *Mediateur des communications electroniques*	**Banks** *l'Autorité des marchés financiers*	**Insurance** *Fédération Française des Sociétés d'Assurance*	**Energy** *GDF SUEZ*	**Energy** *Médiateur national de l'énergie*	**Travel** *SNCF*
Total Number of contacts	18,672	1,561	5,316	6,351	17,467	3,731
Redirected	15,118	1,041 inquiries	2,593	6,246	12,227	773 Not within competence 556 resolved meanwhile by after-sales services
Complaints	3,554	520	3,056	105	5,240	3,671
Resolved	3,554 opinions given	520	Formal advice by mediator: 391 Opinions: 274	105	3,563	2,342

B. Germany

Figure 14.2: Total number of contacts per sector divided into proportions of redirected contacts and those categorized as complaints

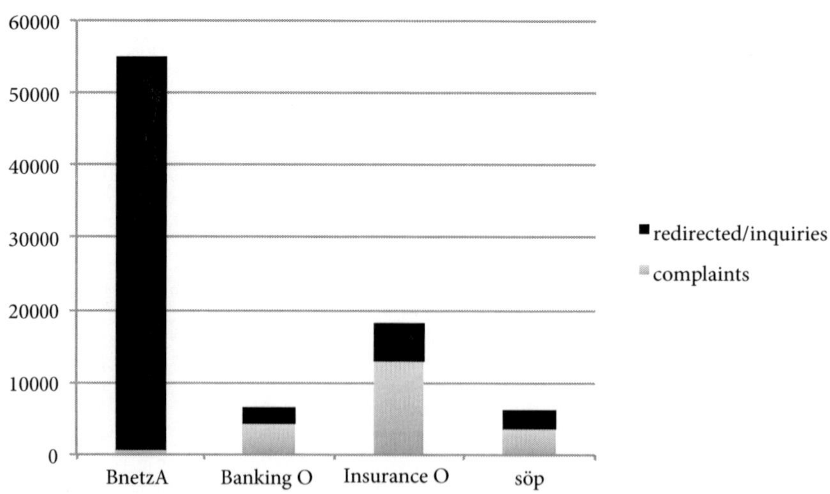

Telecoms: BnetzA[12] /*Banks*: Ombudsman Bundesverband deutscher Banken[13]/*Insurance*: Ombudsman für Versicherungen[14]/*Travel:* söp[15]

Table 14.2: Details of complaints per scheme

	Telecoms *BnetzA*	**Banks** *Ombudsman Bundesverband deutscher Banken*	**Insurance** *Ombudsman für Versicherungen*	**Travel** *Söp*
Total Number of contacts	BnetzA: 69,886 of which: Telekom: 54,880[16]	6,494	18,357	6,200
Redirected	(174[17])	1,036 not admissible 1,234 not pursued by customer	5,636	124
Complaints	Conciliation Telekom: 703	4,224	12,721	3,628
Resolved	679 9% withdrawn cases 46% rejected not complying with the TKG	1,716 resolved in favor of customer, 1,048 resolved in favor of bank, 178 agreement proposed	18,609	1,611 of which: 1,508 train 98 plane

C. Lithuania

The State Consumer Rights Protection Authority[18] receives around 12,000 complaints a year, and around 2,300 requests for ADR. It takes an average of 37 working days to complete a claim. In January 2010 through September 2011, the Authority investigated 2,290 disputes through the ADR procedure. Figures for 2010 alone have not been available. Of these:

- 45 per cent (1020) were settled by the parties before the Authority adopted a decision.
- 7.7 per cent (163) were terminated under one of the reasons provided for in the Law, such as involving no breach of the law, or as being an invalid complaint.
- 48 per cent (1107) involved adoption of a decision by the Authority. Of these, consumers were wholly successful in 72 per cent (797) and partially successful in 16 per cent (180), and traders were successful in 16 per cent (180).

In that period, traders complied with the Authority's decisions in 33 per cent of cases: the 66 per cent of non-compliance included a number of cases caused by bankruptcy of traders. The process is free of charge to the consumer.

[12] www.bundesnetzagentur.de/cln_1912/DE/Home/home_node.html; annual report 2010: www.bundesnetzagentur.de/SharedDocs/Downloads/DE/BNetzA/Presse/Berichte/2011/Jahresbericht2010pdf.pdf?__blob=publicationFile.

[13] www.bankenverband.de/themen/geldinfos-finanzen/schlichtungsstelle/index_html; Annual report 2010: https://www.bankenverband.de/publikationen/ods/ombudsmann-taetigkeitsbericht-2010/ombudsmann-taetigkeitsbericht-2010/download.

[14] www.versicherungsombudsmann.de/home.html; annual report 2010: www.versicherungsombudsmann.de/Ressourcen/PDF/Jahresbericht-2010.pdf.

[15] https://soep-online.de/; annual report 2009/2010 https://soep-online.de/assets/files/Service/20110225_soep-Jahresbericht-2010.pdf .

[16] 98.7% of telecom claims were redirected.

[17] Of the 703 cases accepted, 174 were redirected. It is not clear if these 174 are included in the overall amount of redirected contacts.

[18] See vvtat.lt.

D. The Netherlands

Figure 14.3: *De Geschillencommissie* number of contacts per year showing the proportions of initiated and processed claims

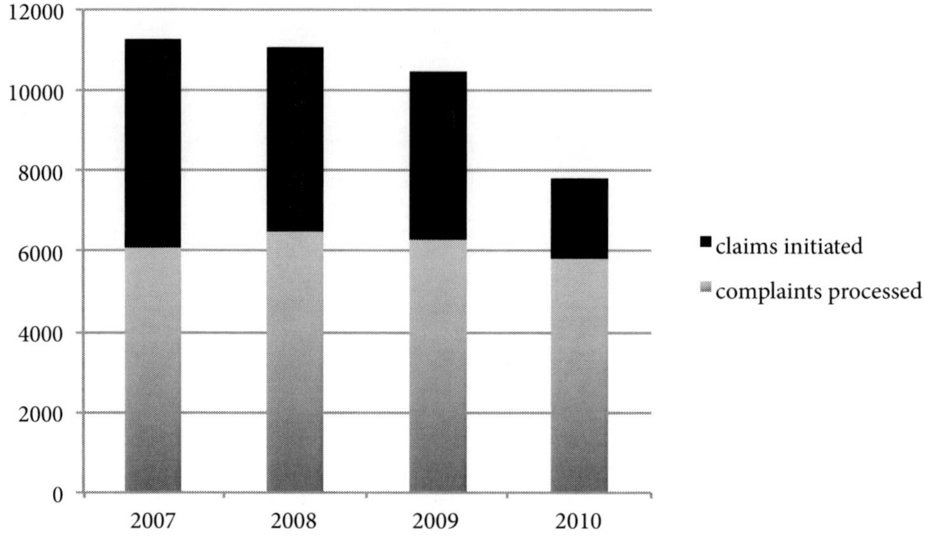

E. Poland

Table 14.3: Total number of contacts (if available) by sector showing accepted and resolved cases

	Telecoms (*Head of the Office of Electronic Telecommunications (OET), Consumer Arbitration Tribunal of OET*	**Banking** (*Banking Ombudsman)*	**Energy** *(Head of the Office for Energy Regulation and Ombudsman for Fuel and Energy Recipients)*	**Consumer Arbitration Tribunals** (*general consumer issues apart from those covered elsewhere, health and social services)*	**Trade Inspection** (*consumer affairs)*
Total No of Contacts	No data	1,165	No data	No data	No data
Cases accepted	2,600 mediations by Head of OET 206 cases before Ombudsman	561 (of 1117 decisions, 556 consisted in rejecting the case)	3,264	2,684	No data
Resolved	No data on Head of OET; 6 arbitrations by Ombudsman	561	3,045	1,599 (in the remaining cases – traders refuse to take part)	No data

F. Slovenia

Figure 14.4: ECC NET Slovenia proportion of complaints and request for information

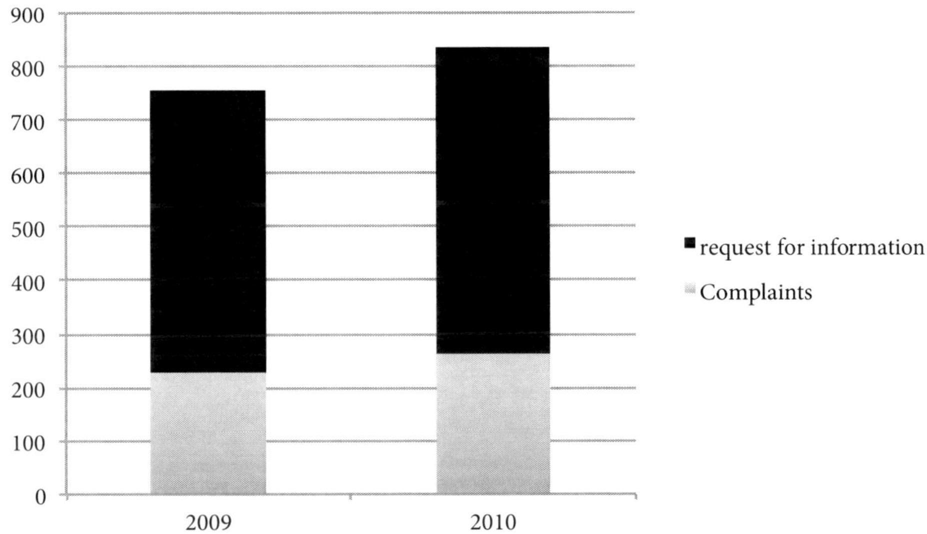

G. Spain

Spain has various ADR schemes, Figure 14.5 shows data for the general arbitration system for consumers and Figure 14.6 and Table 14.4 highlight some specific sectors.

Figure 14.5: Spanish arbitration system for consumer disputes *Sistema Arbitral de Consumo* proportion of complaints and redirected contacts

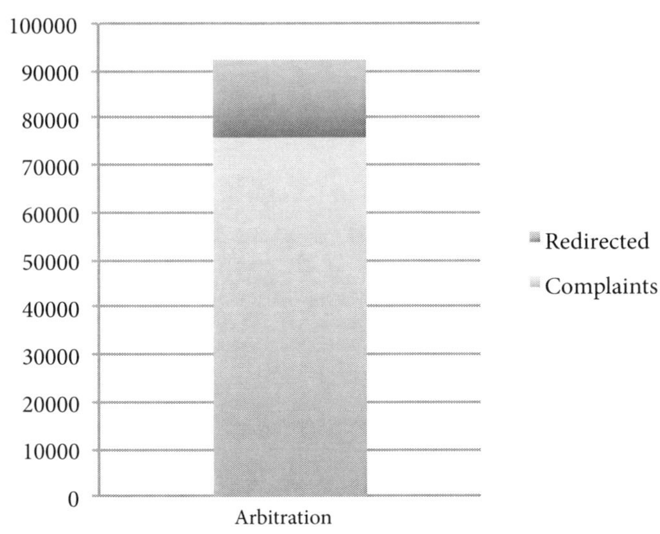

Figure 14.6: Total number of contacts per sector divided into proportion of redirected contacts and those categorized as complaints

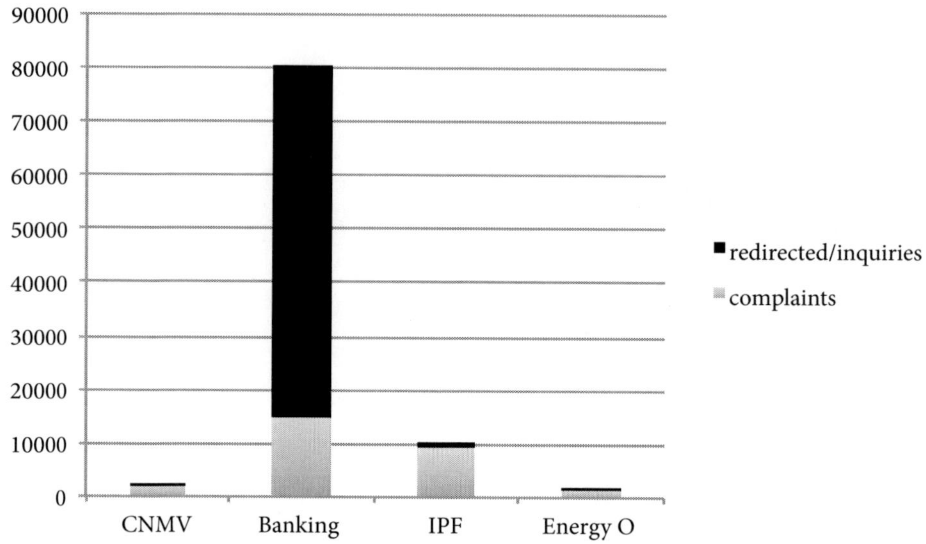

Investment: The *Comisión Nacional del Mercado de Valores* (CNMV)[19] /*Banking:* Servicio de Reclamaciones Banco de Espana[20]/*Insurance/ Pensions:* Directorate General of Insurance and Pension Funds[21] (Servicio de Reclamaciones de la Dirección General de Seguros y Fondos de Pensiones)/ *Energy: Energy Ombudsman*[22]

Table 14.4: Details of categorized complaints:

	Investment The *Comisión Nacional del Mercado de Valores (CNMV)*	**Banking** *Servicio de Reclamaciones Banco de Espana*	**Insurance and pensions** *Servicio de Reclamaciones de la Dirección General de Seguros y Fondos de Pensiones (IPF)*	**Energy** *Energy Ombudsman ENDESA*
Total Number of contacts	2,296	47,657 (Plus 3,368 requests for advice, 29,529 information inquiries by phone)	10,225	2,104
Redirected	313	32,897	3,529 rejected	922

[19] www.cnmv.es/PortalInversor/section.aspx?hid=20; Annual Report of the CNMV 2010, pp. 177, www.cnmv.es/portal/Publicaciones/Informes.aspx.

[20] Memoria del Servicio de Reclamaciones Banco de Espana 2010 www.bde.es/webbde/es/. annual report: www.bde.es/webbde/es/secciones/informes/Publicaciones_an/Informe_anual/anoactual/.

[21] Servicio de Reclamaciones de la Dirección General de Seguros y Fondos de Pensiones, see: www.dgsfp.meh.es/reclamaciones/index.asp.

Annual report 2010: www.dgsfp.meh.es/sector/documentos/Informes%202010/Informe%20Servicio%20Reclamaciones%202010.pdf .

[22] www.defensordelcliente.endesa.es/defcl/index.jsf.

Cases accepted	2,087	14,760 new complaints 84.1 % of claims were submitted by individuals, 15.3% by companies and 0.6% by others, including public institutions	9,231 (5,702 were admitted complaints, of which 2,231 in favour financial services institution, 1,882 in favour of claimants remaining cases were terminated in other forms)	1,182
Resolved	1,774	No data	5,702	89% satisfactory resolved, of which 80% resolved by mediation and 18% via resolution by Ombudsman 2% other means

H. Sweden

The data here are from the national body, the National Board for Consumer Complaints, *Allmänna reklamationsnämnden*,[23] rather than sectoral boards.

Figure 14.7: ARN proportion of complaints dealt with and those dismissed

[23] www.arn.se/.

I. The United Kingdom

Figure 14.8: Total number of contacts per sector showing proportions of redirected/ inquiries and complaints

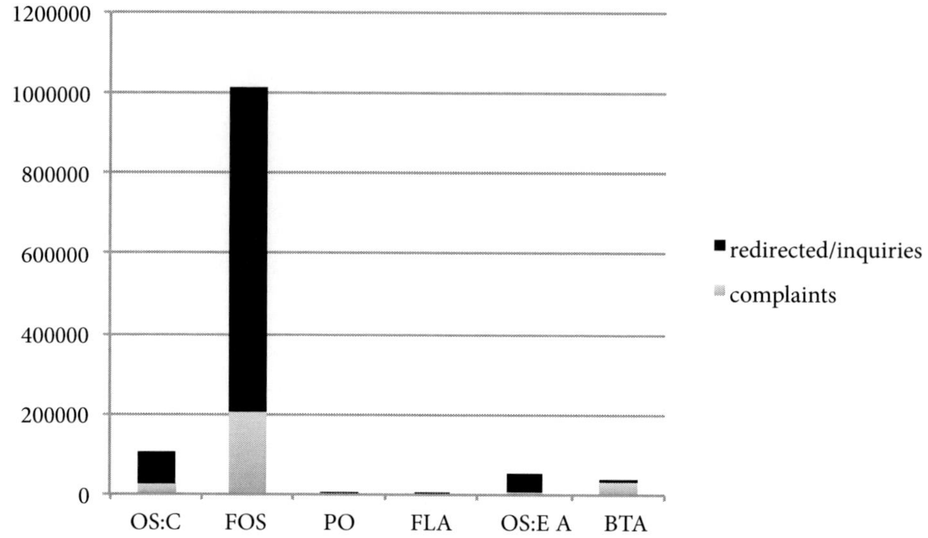

Telecoms: Ombudsman Services: Communications[24] /*Banks/ Insurance*: FOS[25] / *Pensions Ombudsman/ FLA*[26]/*Energy:* Ombudsman Services: Energy[27] /*Travel*: ABTA[28]

Table 14.5: Details of categorized complaints:

	Telecoms *Ombudsman Services: Communications*	**Pensions** *Pensions Ombudsman*	**Banks/ Insurance** *FOS*	**FLA**	**Energy** *Ombudsman Services: Energy*	**Travel** *ABTA*
Total Number of contacts	103,702	3947 (3632 new written enquires and 315 from previous year)	1,012,371	1,726	54,794	31,858 (12,689 case files + 19,169 telephone inquiries)
Redirected	66,369	2,520	806,250	642	48,067	No data

[24] www.ombudsman-services.org/communications.html; annual report 2011, published in July: www.ombudsman-services.org/attachments/download/369/Communications /annual report 2010: www.ombudsman-services.org/attachments/download/337/2010%20annual%20report%20Otelo.pdf.

[25] http://financial-ombudsman.org.uk/ ; annual review 2010/2011: http://financial-ombudsman.org.uk/publications/ar11/index.html.

[26] www.fla.org.uk/home.

[27] www.ombudsman-services.org/energy.html ; Annual report 2010/11: http://www.ombudsman-services.org/attachments/download/367/Energy%202011%20AR.pdf.

[28] www.abta.com/home; annual review 2010: www.abta.com/filegrab/?ref=444&f=2010annual-review.pdf.

Complaints	25,925	1427 (950 new inquiries 477 from previous year)	206,121	1,084 referred to FLA members for investigation	88% billing 8% transfer 4% sales 5% other 6,727 complaint forms issued 5,812 returned	12,504 complaints and 363 arbitrations
Resolved	71% Formally resolved complaints 29% Informally resolved complaints	889 231 formally determined 187 cases were discontinued, withdrawn or resolved informally 152 investigations closed after a decision of the investigator using the informal procedures, 319 cases were determined by the Ombudsman under the informal procedures following the investigator's initial decision.	164,899 cases were resolved of which: 147,434 Resolved by mediation 17,465 Resolved by Ombudsman formal decisions	642 cases, either the complainant chose not to pursue the complaint further or the complaint was resolved without the need for FLA conciliation	5,812 majority of returned complaint forms are accepted and the case is resolved 84% formally 16% informally.	255 progressed to an award being issued 1,216 were sent a Pre Arbitration Notice 591 have requested further details of the Arbitration Scheme

By Sector

It is apparent in this study that the two sectors with notable claims data are telecoms and financial services. Part A presents the telecoms sector showing the total number of contacts in 2010 across countries. Part B has two figures; the first chart shows the total number of contact by country, and in view of the very high number of contacts to UK FOS the next chart shows the same figures excluding the FOS, for a clearer comparison between countries. A table with the number of contacts is below the figure.

A. Telecoms

Figure 14.9: Total contacts in 2010

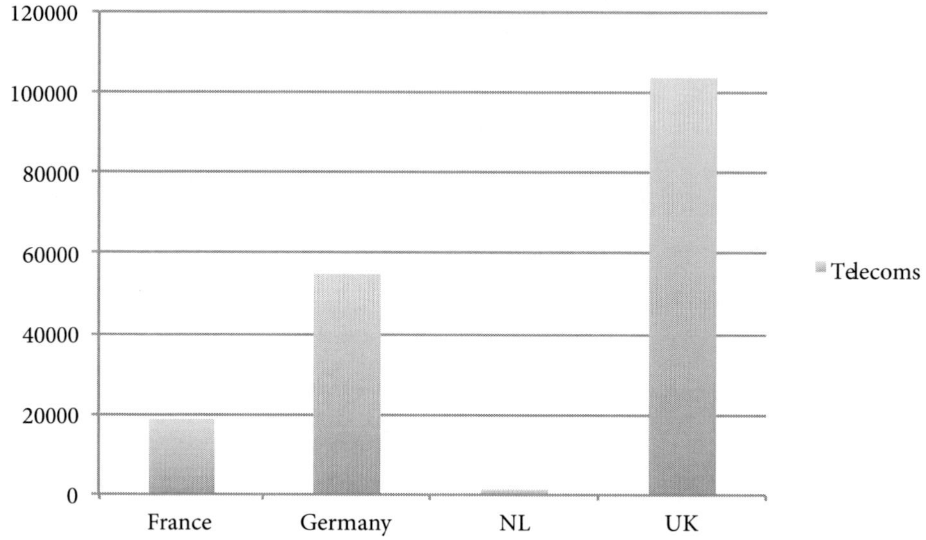

Table 14.6: Total number of contacts telecoms by country

France	18,672
Germany	54,880
the Netherlands	1,284
United Kingdom	103,702

B. Financial Services

Figure 14.10: Total contacts in 2010

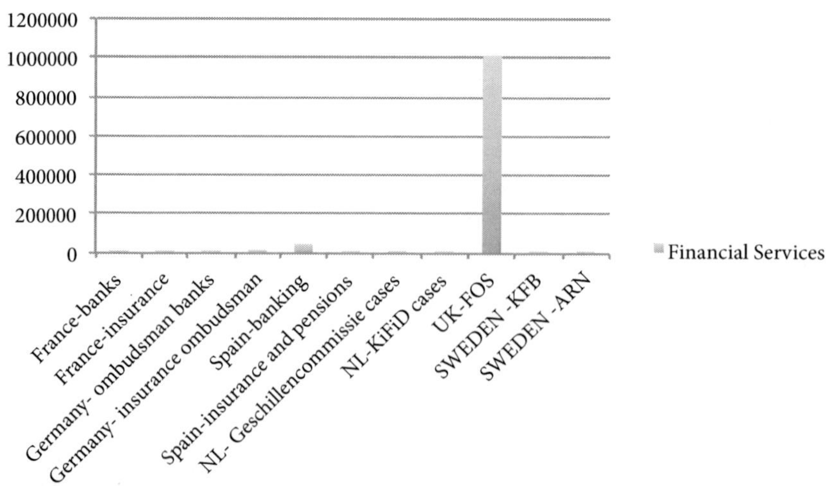

Table 14.7: Total number of contacts financial services by country

France	Banks	1,561
	Insurance	5,649
Germany	Ombudsman banks	6,494
	Ombudsman insurance	18,357
Spain	Bank	47,657
	Insurance / pensions	10,225
The Netherlands	Geschillencommissie cases	609
	KiFiD cases	6,719
United Kingdom	FOS	1,012,371
Sweden	KFB	13,000
	ARN	480

Figure 14.11: Total number of contacts without FOS

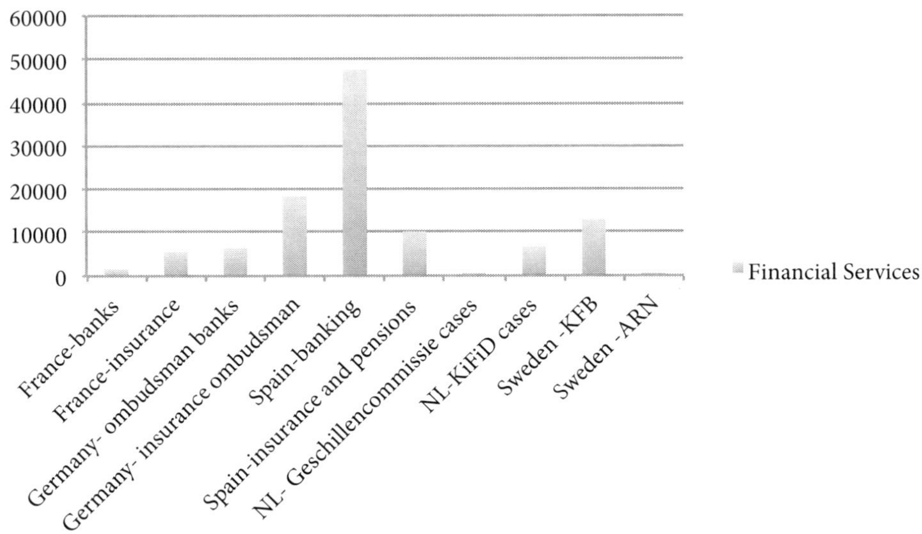

Thresholds and Limits

Many CADR schemes are subject to high and/or low financial thresholds, or time limits for making claims. Financial limits can often be found in financial services sectors, both to limit exposure from what might be large individual claims and to ensure that large cases are deflected to the courts, since they may be more complex and involve points of legal principle. Examples that we have found are as follows.

- In Germany, the Insurance Ombudsman can make a legally-binding decision up to €10,000, and a non-binding recommendation up to €100,000. The transport ombudsman (Söp) has an upper claim value limit of €30,000. The Ombudsman of Private Commercial Banks can make a binding decision on claims valued up to €5,000, and a non-binding recommendation above that sum. The Legal Arbitration Board can make a recommendation only in claims worth up to €15,000.

- In financial services cases in KiFiD in the Netherlands, the second Geschillencommissie stage (after the Ombudsman first stage) has a minimum claim value of €100 and a time limit of three months, and the third Arbitration Appeal Board stage has a threshold case value of at least €25,000. At the second stage, all banks and most intermediaries have agreed to accept all decisions up to €5 million.
- The value of a case before the Polish Tribunals of the Trade Inspection cannot exceed 10.000 PLN, unless it is brought before the Tribunal in Warsaw, which does not have monetary limits on the value of claims under its jurisdiction. The jurisdiction of the National Banking Ombudsman cannot exceed 8,000 PLN (around €2,000). A claim must exceed 1,000 PLN to be brought before the Arbitration Tribunal of the Insurance Ombudsman.
- Different types of claims brought to the Swedish ARN must exceed certain thresholds: 500 SEK for shoes, textiles or general types; 1000 SEK for electronics, motor vehicles, travel, textiles (furniture), or cleaning services; and 2000 SEK for banking, housing, boating or insurance. There is a series of types of claims that are excluded.[29]
- In UK, the Financial Ombudsman Service cannot award compensation over £150,000.

It would follow that if there were to be an obligation on Member States to provide full coverage for all C2B disputes, this could not be satisfied unless there was either some leeway to justify the seemingly quite widespread existing variations in coverage provided by thresholds and other limitations, or their complete removal.

Case Fees for Consumers

As shown in Table 14.8, the vast majority of CADR schemes are free to consumers. This is a general principle in France, Spain and Sweden, and applies in almost all of the schemes in Germany[30] and the UK (save for those post-conciliation arbitration stages of many private schemes, for which a charge is imposed).[31] An exception applies in the Netherlands, where consumers pay a registration fee to SGC that varies depending on the sectoral Board, and generally ranges between €25 and €125.

The principle of no cost to consumers has not been established in Poland. The Polish Consumer Arbitration Tribunals are free of charge for consumers, although the Consumer Arbitration Tribunal operated by the Chairman of the Electronic Communications Office has a 100 PLN charge to lodge a case. The cost of lodging a case in the Consumer Arbitration Tribunal of the Office of Electronic Communications is 100 PLN, and may involve further costs. The fee for lodging a complaint with the National Banking Ombudsman is 20 PLN if the value of the case is lower than 50 PLN, and 50 PLN in higher value cases. Fees for lodging cases with the Arbitration Tribunal of the Polish Banks Association are far higher, on a tariff basis, which for a claim over 10 million PLN will be 115,300 PLN plus 0.5 per cent of the amount of the claim over 10 million PLN. Costs are also high in the Arbitration Tribunal of the Insurance Ombudsman.

[29] See p 241 above.

[30] An exception is the BnetzA, there is a small fee of a minimum of €25 and increases with the value of the sum in dispute.

[31] See pp 312 ff above.

Table 14.8: Overview of cost to consumer by country and scheme

France	*Telecoms: free*	*Insurance: no data*	*Banks: no data*	*National Energy mediator: free*	*Energy GDF/ SUEZ: free*	*Travel: free*
Germany	*Telecoms: cost*	*Insurance: free*	*Banks: free*			*Travel: free*
Poland	*Telecoms: cost*	*Consumer arbitration tribunals: No cost of lodging the case*[32]	*Banking: cost*	*Trade inspection consumer*: free	*Energy: free*	
Spain		*Insurance /pensions: free*	*Banking: free*	*Investment: free*	*Energy: free*	
UK	*Telecoms: free*	*Pensions: free*	*Banks/ Insurance: free*	*FLA: free*	*Energy: free*	*Travel: cost for arbitration*

Levels of Loss and Detriment

Consumer disputes typically involve very small sums, but this varies from sector to sector. Data reported above in this book for 2010 includes:

- In France, the FFSA *médiateur* reports handling many cases valued at around €100 and some as low as €5. The average award of the national energy *médiateur* was €373, the average amount in dispute in the cases of the médiateur of EDF was €1,120 (with 23 per cent of cases over €2,000).
- In Germany, 86 per cent of claims made to the Insurance Ombudsman involved claims under €5,000, and over 90 per cent were under €10,000. A normal claim made to the transport ombudsman (Söp) is between €10 and €200.
- In the Netherlands, the average claim value for Geschillencommissie cases varies between sectors, from €206 for taxis and an average of €5,980 for housing guarantees. In 2009, 9 per cent of the *Geschillencommissie* claims were less than €250, there was no claim involving a value of more than €10,000, and the largest segment of claims (24 per cent) were for €1,001–2,000.
- The average value of an award in the arbitration system in Spain was €366.
- The average amount claimed in cases before the UK's Ombudsman Service: Communications was £587 and the average award was £198.

The Leuven Report concluded that small claims procedures would only be used by European consumers if the amount involved exceeds around €500.[33] However, it is clear from the data in our study that many existing CADR claims are under that level. Discussions in Brussels have considered whether a lower threshold might be introduced that would exclude very small claims. The evidence, however, is that many C2B claims involve very low sums, and CADR schemes can process them at relatively proportionate cost, if an inherent purpose of a scheme is to collect aggregated data on generic market effects and act as a means of raising standards in a sector.

[32] Costs of experts and lawyers are covered by parties, with loser pays principle applicable.

[33] J Stuyck, E Terryn, V Colaert, T Van Dyck, N Peretz, N Hoekx and P Tereszkiewicz, *Study on Alternative Means of Consumer Redress other than Redress through Ordinary Judicial Proceedings* (Catholic University of Leuven, January 17, 2007) published April 2007.

The Cost of Major CADR Schemes

Total costs are not always published by schemes. Summarised below are some data for selected major schemes: the residual Swedish scheme, the two Dutch systems, and large individual sectoral schemes from Germany, France and the UK.

Sweden

The national CADR body, the ARN, which is fully funded by the state, had a 2010 budget of just over €3 million, and received 10,000 claims covering all sectors (but others were made to some sectoral boards).

The Patient Insurance scheme, which covers residual expenses not covered by social security arising out of personal injury claims, which are usually more expensive to process, costs around €900 per claim, and receives 12,000 claims a year of which about half receive compensation.

The Netherlands

Across 50 sectoral Boards (excluding financial services), 7,826 claims were initiated in 2010, 5,799 of which were processed. The operational cost of the administrative coordinating organisation, *De Geschillencommissie Stichting*, was only €5.5 million.[34] The Ministry of Safety and Justice subsidizes the annual costs for the infrastructure. Business pays for the handling of the cases (caseload) of the system. This means that the annual costs for business depend on the number of cases handled. Over the years, the ministry subsidizes between 15 to 20% of business between 80–85% of the costs.

The financial CADR system (KiFiD) had a budget of €9 million in 2010 and received 6,719 cases. Traders' minimum yearly contribution was €170 for banks and insurers[35] and the lowest contribution for other members was €163. The registration fee per case was €25 for traders and €50 for consumers.[36]

Germany

In 2010 the Insurance Ombudsman received 18,357 claims, 12,720 of which were admitted. The Insurance Ombudsman cost €3.2 million to run, for a staff of 45, had an income of €3,6 m which means a profit of €0,04 m.[37]

[34] The total annual costs fluctuate between € 5.5 and 6.5 million, depending on the caseload and 50 trade organizations participating.

[35] See cost rules: www.kifid.nl/fileupload/Kostenreglement_2011.pdf.

[36] FAQ KiFiD, www.kifid.nl/consumenten/veelgestelde-vragen. If the Ombudsman himself transfers the case to the Geschillencommissie the consumer is free from the fee, see Art 26.2 KiFiD rules, for instance due to procedural complexity. But if the Ombudsman has declared the claim 'kennelijk ongegrond' (clearly inadmissible) according to Art 31.2 KiFiD rules the fee is €100.

[37] Annual report 2010, www.versicherungsombudsmann.de/ressourcen/PDF/jahresberichte-2010.pdf.

The principal transport scheme (Söp) is funded by members' annual fees (€1,000 for a single company but groups of companies like *Deutsche Bahn* pay a maximum of €5,000) and a case fee (€25 for unjustified claims and €150, €200, €300, €400, €600 or €800 per case, depending on the time and expenditure involved). The scheme is too new for the level of claims to have stabilized. The cost per case in 2010 was between €25 and €350. Since 2012 a new fee structure has been implemented as the case handling efficiency increased and this enables Söp to lower the cost per case by 20 per cent.

France

The national Energy *Médiateur* had a budget of €6.6 million for 40 staff in 2011. In 2010 he received 17,467 complaints. 68 per cent of cases that fall within the ombudsman's remit have been resolved or a recommendation was issued.

The *Médiateur* des communications electroniques had a budget of 1.3m€ and 12 employees.

The *Médiateur SNCF* has no defined budget: he requests funding from the President of SNCF, who then grants necessary funds. A budget of €120,000 was allocated to set up the online scheme in 2011.

UK

The largest CADR system in Europe, the Financial Ombudsman Service, received 1,012,371 initial inquiries and complaints in 2009/10, which yielded 206,121 formal disputes, of which 17,465 required the involvement of an ombudsman. The annual budget for 2009/2010 was £92 million for a staff averaging 1,015 people. Actual income was £98.4 million, 20 per cent of which was funded by a charge levied on financial institutions (adjusted every year to reflect the volume of work undertaken per sector each year: the number of accounts held by banks, and volume of investment income for insurance), and 80 per cent from case fees. A defendant currently pays £500 per case, but no case fees were charged to businesses for their first three disputes, which resulted in only 5.5 per cent of firms paying case fees. The FOS had a unit cost (ie cost per case) of £555.

The Pensions Ombudsman, fully funded by the government, received £2,810,000 in 2010/11 and accepted 950 complaints for investigation. The subject-matter is often complex, and average duration of investigations is 10.9 months.

The Legal Ombudsman had a budget of £9.9 million in 2011, obtained from a levy on all firms regulated and a case fee of £400, which was not payable for the first two potentially chargeable complaints in a year. He received 38,155 contacts and accepted 3,768 cases for investigation.

The UK private Ombudsman Services had a turnover of £5,739,894 in the year to 31 March 2010 and £6,385,718 in the year to 31 March 2011.[39] The allocation of costs between sectors is shown in Table 14.9.

[39] Annual Report 2011, Ombudsman Services Limited, at www.ombudsman-services.org/useful-downloads-os.html.

Table 14.9: Allocation of Ombudsman Service costs between service sectors

Expenditure	2009–2010 (£'000)	Number of contacts received	Cases opened
Communications	2,210	102,025[40]	8,936
Energy	2,189	78,528	7,192
Property	19	5,843	428

The private travel sector arbitration scheme operated by ABTA involved 12,702 requests in 2010, a further 19,169 telephone inquiries, and 255 awards. The average award was £630, for which the consumer paid a fee of £90 and the trader £350. The total administrative cost of the scheme is unknown, since the administration is largely assumed by the trade association.

The cost of sectoral conciliation-plus-arbitration schemes established in various sectors varies: a 2006 review of OFT-approved schemes found that the cost to members ranged from 'minimal' sums to £50,000 pa. The costs of the Motor Codes' were, for manufacturers, an annual subscription to the new car scheme of £1,250 and case conciliation fee of £75, and for garages a subscription to the service and repair code of £75, annual garage inspection fee of £175 and case conciliation fee of £75 (all sums plus VAT).

WIPO

The cost of a single arbitrator involving up to 5 domain names is U.S.$1,500, and for a panel of three arbitrators is U.S.$4,000.

Cost per Inquiry

In comparing processing costs of different schemes, it must be remembered that the annual budget is expended in responding to initial inquiries and a smaller number of formal investigations. Figures are not available that would accurately enable the cost of those two functions to be differentiated. The cost of responding to many inquiries might be modest, but the volume received might be large—and in some countries is clearly relatively limited, for reasons discussed above. It is striking that the number of disputes referred to the Swedish ARN and the Netherlands system are so low.

In contrast, the cost per case of handling formal disputes might be higher than that of responding to individual inquiries, but much might depend on the nature of the case. The UK Pensions Ombudsman has a high cost per case (roughly £3,000) but his cases are clearly more complex than many simple consumer disputes, as indicated by the longer average duration.

The above figures indicate that some recent ombudsman-style CADR systems are capable of processing cases for under £400 each, and sometimes lower than that. The cost per case in

[40] The regulator, OFCOM, also received 194,500 complaints in 2009/10.

Sweden was €300 and the Netherlands perhaps €900, but it must be remembered that these are very general figures, averaged across many different types of cases. Comprehensive cost data is not available from Spain, but the average cost per case is over €400, and the average value of awards was €366 in 2010.

The costs of CADR schemes are lower, or at least compare favourably, with the cost of court procedures in almost all countries, even small claims procedures.

All the major schemes raise funds by charging an annual fee to traders that are members or imposed by law, and a separate case fee. In some cases, the case fee is not charged for the first or second case. The reason for this is to encourage traders to resolve cases themselves before they become complaints, and to recognize that some cases have poor merits for which individual traders should not be penalised. Some case fees can rise as the number of claims received rises. Similarly, the UK's ABTA scheme incentivises both sides to resolve their case between them by deferring the fee until after the consumer is sent the company's comments on the cases, shortly before the arbitrator sees the papers.

In some CADR schemes, the cost paid by traders covers more than a dispute handling facility. Firstly, it may cover the administration of a self-regulatory Code of Practice, which has extra value for traders and involves advice to them from the trade association (and might be an insurance against the imposition of more costly regulation). Secondly, the system may provide information and advice services to actual or potential customers that would otherwise have to be funded separately.

Duration

The average duration reported for of the CADR processes are shown in Table 14.10. It is precisely because the sums involved are small that there is a need to design a process that involves proportionate cost, and does not merely try to adapt previously existing formalistic processes (like the introduction of mediation into court procedures).

Table 14.10: Average duration per case in months by country and scheme

France	*Telecoms:* 3	*Insurance:* 3–6	*Banks:* 6		*GDF/SUEZ:* 2 *National Energy mediator:* 6	*Travel:* 2–4
Germany	*Telecoms:* 4	*Insurance:* 4.1	*Banks:* *no data*			*Travel:* 3
Poland	*Telecoms:* *no data*	*Consumer arbitration tribunals:* 0.5–2	*Banking:* 1.1	*Trade inspection consumer: no data*	*Energy: no data*	
Spain		*Insurance /pensions:* 4	*Banking:* 4–6	*Investment: no data*	*Energy:* 2	
UK	*Telecoms:* 6 *or less*	*Pensions:* 10.9	*Banks/Insurance:* 2.2	*FLA:* 2	*Energy:* 3	*Travel:* 2–2.5

EU Consumer Complaint Data

Types of Disputes: Lessons for Prioritisation of ADR

The EU collects data on which types of disputes arise more frequently than others. The 2011 Consumer Markets Scoreboard reported that one tenth of EU consumers had experienced one or more problems with a large range of surveyed markets for which they considered they had a legitimate reason to complain.[41] In 2011, one in five consumers who experienced a problem had not complained to the company, a complaint body, friends or family. The sectors that experienced the largest number of problems in 2011 (with very similar rankings to 2010) were, in descending order, internet, TV, mobile phone, trains, second hand cars, real estate services, house and garden, current bank accounts, vehicle upkeep and repair services, fixed telephone services, investments, pensions and securities. Consumers were most satisfied with 'books, magazines and newspapers', 'personal care services', and 'glasses and lenses', and least satisfied with 'investments, pensions and securities', 'mortgages', 'real estate services' and especially 'train services'.

The gap between problems and complaints, indicating that businesses in these sectors should look at improving their services and complaint accessibility, was widest in train services, legal and accountancy services, tram, local bus and metro services, airline services, and second hand cars.[42]

The Commission collates consumer complaint data reported by national authorities. However, it is difficult to draw conclusions over which countries are the ones in which consumers make the most and least complaints: comparability of such data is problematic because of the demographic variations between states, and because some countries (such as Germany and Poland) include inquiries as well as complaints. The raw 2010 data indicated that there were 2.4 million consumer complaints in Germany, 835,591 in the UK, 655,771 in Poland, 396,797 in Spain, 123,951 in Sweden, 114,279 in France, 80,058 in Belgium, 64,063 in the Netherlands, 22,954 in Lithuania, and 15,830 in Slovenia.[43]

Responses to Problems

Important data was collected in February to April 2010 in relation to consumers' preferences about their reactions to encountering problems.[44] More than one in five (21 per cent) of respondents from 56,471 interviews across the EU had encountered a problem with a good, a service, a retailer or a provider in the previous 12 months, for which they had a legitimate cause to complain. The average estimated value of the losses was €375, and median €18. More than three-quarters took some form of action in response (77 per cent) while 22 per cent took no action. Those who took action were most likely to have made a complaint to

[41] Commission Staff Working Paper. The Consumer Markets Scoreboard. Making markets work for consumers. Sixth edition—October 2011, SEC(2011) 1271, 21.10.2011, para 2.4. See also Eurobarometer, Consumer attitudes towards cross-border trade and consumer protection. Analytical report, 2011, at http://ec.europa.eu/consumers/strategy/docs/consumer_eurobarometer_2011_en.pdf.

[42] ibid, para 2.5.

[43] Commission Staff Working Paper. The Consumer Markets Scoreboard. Making markets work for consumers. Sixth edition—October 2011, SEC(2011) 1271, 21.10.2011, p 25.

[44] Special Eurobarometer 342. Consumer empowerment (European Commission, 2011), at http://ec.europa.eu/consumers/consumer_empowerment/docs/report_eurobarometer_342_en.pdf.

the retailer or provider (65 per cent), with far fewer complaining to a public authority (16 per cent), the manufacturer (13 per cent), utilizing an ADR body (5 per cent) or court (2 per cent).

The most frequently cited reason for *not* making a complaint was that the individual had already received a satisfactory response from the retailer/provider (44 per cent). The major reasons for not making a court claim were that the individual had already received a satisfactory response from the retailer/provider (40 per cent), the sum involved was too small (26 per cent), it would have taken too much effort (16 per cent), it would have been too expensive (13 per cent) or too long (12 per cent). The level of financial loss that would have caused people to go to court was given by the majority (53 per cent) as between €101 and €2,500. In comparison, the Commission's 2004 Eurobarometer found that only 18 per cent of EU citizens were prepared to go to court for amounts higher than €500 and another 18 per cent for amounts higher than €1,000.[45]

In the 2010 survey, the threshold for using an ADR body was given by 38 per cent as around €200, and €101 by 15 per cent. A different survey, carried out in September 2010, found that 52 per cent of EU consumers who had made a complaint were satisfied or very satisfied with the way it was dealt with by the trader.[46]

In a 2010 study of retailers,[47] only nine per cent had used ADR mechanisms to settle disputes within the previous two years, and 44 per cent were unaware of the existence of such mechanisms. Only six per cent said they were members of an ADR body. A slim majority (54 per cent) said they would prefer to use an ADR mechanism to resolve issues.

The 78 per cent of respondents who had *not* encountered a problem in the February to April 2010 study were asked what they would have done if they had, and 71 per cent responded that they would have made a complaint while 22 per cent felt they would not. The countries where most respondents felt they would have complained were Sweden (91 per cent), Luxembourg (87 per cent), the Netherlands, Germany and Cyprus (84 per cent).

The 2006 survey found that an average of 42 per cent of Europeans considered it easy to assert their claims against suppliers through some alternative means of dispute resolution such as arbitration, mediation or conciliation.[48] However, the Commission noted that a substantially higher percentage of consumers in northern member states, Cyprus and Greece, as compared to consumers in Spain, Portugal and most new member states including those in Central Europe, believed that resolving disputes through an arbitration, mediation or conciliation body as well as through court is easy.[49] With regard to alternative dispute resolution, only around 30 per cent of consumers in the latter group of countries considered it to be easy, against over 60 per cent of consumers in the former group.[50]

A 2008 UK survey found that although 34 per cent reported experiencing one or more problems with goods or services in the previous year, amounting to an estimated 26.5 million problems within the UK and estimated consumer detriment of £6.6 billion,

[45] Special Eurobarometer, *European Union citizens and access to justice*, October 2004, at http://ec.europa.eu/consumers/redress/reports_studies/execsum_11-04_en.pdf.

[46] Eurobarometer, Consumer attitudes towards cross-border trade and consumer protection. Analytical report, 2011, at http://ec.europa.eu/consumers/strategy/docs/consumer_eurobarometer_2011_en.pdf.

[47] Eurobarometer, Retailers' attitudes towards cross-border trade and consumer protection. Analytical report, 2011, at http://ec.europa.eu/consumers/strategy/docs/retailers_eurobarometer_2011_en.pdf.

[48] Eurobarometer Special Report 252 'Consumer Protection in the Internal Market', European Commission, 2006, QB28.1.

[49] The survey found that the majority of Slovaks (66%), Czechs (57%), Slovenes (57%), Portuguese (53%), Poles (52%) and Hungarians (50%) find it harder to resolve disputes with suppliers through an arbitration, mediation or conciliation body.

[50] See Commission Staff Working Document, First Consumer Markets Scoreboard, COM(2008) 87, para. 3.2.

55 per cent of these resulted in consumer detriment below £5, only 4 per cent involved detriment over £1,000, and no less than 64 per cent complained or took action (70 per cent where detriment was over £5), of whom most (28 per cent) contacted the public authority's Trading Standards enforcement services or the national Consumer Direct service.[51]

[51] *Consumer detriment: Assessing the frequency and impact of consumer problems with goods and services*, (Office of Fair Trading, 2008), OFT992.

15

Findings and Conclusions

CHRISTOPHER HODGES, IRIS BENÖHR, NAOMI CREUTZFELDT-BANDA

Findings on the State of CADR in the EU

The Unique Concept of CADR

CADR systems must be distinguished from what has hitherto been described as ADR. ADR is a *technique*, such as mediation or early neutral evaluation, which may be adopted in any given dispute, but particularly in a dispute that exists within, or in the context of, the court system. Thus, ADR has hitherto been *alternative* because it is alternative to the courts. But ADR, as it is generally known, occurs within the architectural context, or shadow, of dispute resolution through the courts. There is now often a formal link between court procedure and ADR, in that many national civil procedure rules now encourage or require ADR to be attempted for a claim that is proceeding in court, or before a claim is commenced in court.

In contrast, this book shows that CADR exists as its own distinct dispute resolution pathway, within its own architectural structure that is independent of the courts. To some extent CADR takes place within 'the shadow of the courts' and is an alternative pathway to resolve disputes to that of courts, since consumers might choose to raise disputes in the courts or CADR processes. But in reality CADR occupies its own world, and has its own 'stand alone' architecture and validity that is entirely unique and does not relate to the courts. CADR provides a complete, integral dispute resolution structure and pathway that does not particularly depend on the ability to fall back on a court procedure in order to resolve C2B disputes. The stage has now been reached where CADR and courts are alternatives to each other, on a theoretically equal footing, and in which the 'extra-court alternative' is not an adjunct but an equally valid means of dispute resolution, subject to its own structures and rules.

The Extent of CADR

CADR is far more widespread than is widely thought. Every Member State has a system of state courts. But until recently CADR systems did not exist. The first systematic CADR models were created from the 1960s, for example in Nordic States and the Netherlands. CADR systems have grown steadily since then. Recent studies have suggested that there are 750 CADR systems across the EU,[1] and in the United Kingdom 130 ADR systems of any type[2] or 95 CADR systems.[3]

[1] J Stuyck et al, *Study on alternative means of consumer redress other than redress through ordinary judicial proceedings* (Catholic University of Leuven, January 17, 2007), published April 2007; *Study on the use of Alternative Dispute Resolution in the European Union*, (Brussels, Civic Consulting, 2009).

This book has not attempted to verify the number of CADR schemes that exist, but has confirmed that there are indeed many individual schemes. The numbers previously claimed may, however, be inaccurate. The large number claimed for, for example, Germany (247) appears to be a significant over-calculation in that many schemes that have registered as ADR schemes are in fact mediation or arbitration schemes that are primarily designed to operate alongside, and in conjunction with, the court system, and are not designed to be CADR schemes. Indeed, they are frequently rather small in scope, sometimes one or a small number of individual mediators/arbitrators, and would not be designed for or expected to handle many, if any, C2B disputes. On the other hand, we have found some national CADR schemes of reasonable size that are not registered with the European Commission, such as several sectoral schemes in Sweden.

CADR is growing in both the numbers of consumers who use existing systems, and in the number of business sectors that offer a dispute resolution option. There has been a significant increase in CADR schemes during the past five years. However, as a dispute resolution technique, CADR has considerable further potential.

Coverage

There is a difference between *coverage* and the *binding effect* of decisions. The coverage issue relates to the width of a given scheme, and the extent to which all existing schemes together leave gaps in their collective individual jurisdictions so that certain types of complaints cannot be directed to any particular CADR scheme. The 'binding effect' issue arises because it does not follow from the fact that a CADR scheme exists, that traders will comply with its outcomes. We now consider the coverage issue: binding effect and compliance are dealt with below.

Some Member States have not yet developed more than embryonic CADR systems whereas others have developed far more extensive coverage of market sectors. Such development seems at least partly a question of timing (when an CADR system was introduced, and over what period it has evolved), as well as of the State's historical background. It is reasonable to assume that CADR will develop further in every State, in both sectoral coverage and sophistication of operating model, given further time. But if such development is left to spontaneous forces, it may be slow. The Netherlands has taken 40 years since 1970 to reach its current sophisticated state. The pace of development of CADR, and the volume of usage and functional utility, can clearly be increased if external pressures are applied.

Broadly, the Nordic, Spanish and Central and Eastern European (CEE) states have systems that have full coverage of all types of disputes. They are all (broadly) state-funded. The structural difference is that the Nordic bodies are separate from the enforcement agencies, whereas the CEE CADR functions tend to be located within the enforcement agencies, as a historical hangover from Soviet systems. However, in our view, it would be preferable for CADR systems to be independent of regulatory bodies.

[2] M Tulibacka, *Civil Justice in England and Wales – Beyond Courts. Mapping out Non-judicial Civil Justice Mechanisms* (Centre for Socio-Legal Studies, 2009) available at *www.csls.ox.ac.uk/CivilJusticeSystems.php.* Note that the Civic Study above identified 43 schemes in the UK, whereas Tulibacka and the OFT found far higher numbers.

[3] *Mapping UK consumer redress. A summary guide to dispute resolution systems*, (Office of Fair Trading, 2010).

In contrast, CADR schemes have grown piece-meal, on a sector-by-sector basis, in the Netherlands, UK, Germany and France. Many sectors are now covered in the Netherlands and the UK, the difference between those two countries being that the Netherlands broadly has a single, unified system for all CADR bodies apart from the separate structure for financial services, whereas in the UK there is no unifying structure and the sectoral systems are a somewhat confusing mixture of models. Those two countries have more sectors covered by sectoral CADR bodies than in Germany (a major reason for this is the comparative efficiency of the German court system and people's reliance on it until comparatively recently) and in France (where CADR has been concentrated until recently on schemes at *Département* level, which seem to have failed since their funding has dried up and on in-house systems).

Knowledge of CADR

Knowledge of the existence of courts must be taken to be universal. Knowledge of the existence of ADR—where the alternative pathway is alternative to the courts, and often closely linked in structural terms with court litigation systems—has increased considerably in recent years, partly because of the wide adoption of mediation and related techniques by lawyers and courts, and partly through the increased profile that mediation has received through the passing and implementation of the EU Mediation Directive. Indeed, ADR is probably now well familiar as a name, even if not always in practice, to lawyers, judges and most European academics who specialise in either EU law or civil procedure.

In some states, consumers use the courts for their claims. We note above that in Germany and similar states, the efficiency and comparatively low cost of courts, taken with the availability of cheap insurance and predictable costs, is a reason for this, together with cultural preferences. Cultural approaches towards direct negotiation and settlement clearly apply in the Nordic states and the Netherlands. The Central and Eastern European states tend to mistrust officials, courts and judges, but paradoxically also look towards state institutions to provide solutions.

In contrast, knowledge of CADR systems—that is, systems that resolve B2C disputes without involving the courts but through a different, separate architecture—appears to be low amongst consumers, as reported in chapter 14.[4]

The existence of CADR is not generally well known in many Member States, even in those where knowledge and use of ADR is extensive. One reason is that CADR structures often exist within particular sectors, such as telecoms, energy or utilities. Such mechanisms are well known to the businesses and (few) lawyers who work in each specific sector. But the existence of a wide range of CADR only becomes known to consumers generally and then to lawyers and judges where the number of sectors covered has grown to a sufficient number, and especially where the sectoral schemes are either similar in operation or are linked together as part of a formal or informal general system. Clear examples of where a national umbrella of CADR bodies has developed now exist in the Netherlands and the Nordic States. In short, CADR exists in vertical structures in many Member States, and not horizontal structures.

[4] Special Eurobarometer No 342, Consumer empowerment, April 2011, http://ec.europa.eu/consumers/consumer_empowerment/docs/report_eurobarometer_342_en.pdf.

The split of disputes between courts and CADR systems, or any other pathways, clearly differs from country to country. It also appears to be changing, towards CADR systems and away from courts. Although there are currently strong attempts to introduce or re-invigorate mediation and similar techniques into court procedures, notably as a result of the EU Mediation Directive, such procedures remain to overcome the user-friendliness, cost and duration barriers for small C2B claims. It is unclear whether the number of C2B court claims has fallen in most states, but this has occurred in England and Wales (to 80,000 small claims in 2010). In contrast, numbers of CADR inquiries and claims have been rising significantly in many states.

In some countries, one may suspect that CADR systems have not yet achieved sufficient visibility, effectiveness or efficiency to attract the level of consumer disputes that exist. But in some countries, the low number can more confidently be attributed to efficient prevention (through advice) and weeding out (through in-company and sectoral mediation arrangements).

The National Context of CADR Schemes

It is important to understand the influence that national culture and the pre-existing national architecture of the legal system (especially courts and regulatory bodies) have had on the development of the different models of CADR in different countries. CADR has so far been primarily a national phenomenon, not an international or EU one. The impact of the EU on national CADR systems in the past decade has been very limited. The various EU measures, notably the 1998 and 2001 Recommendations and the existence and development of ECC-Net bodies, have so far not had significant impact on the architecture of national CADR systems, nor on the operation of national CADR schemes.

Principal examples of the impact of national context are as follows. Firstly, efficient and low cost courts in Germany were thought to provide effective dispute resolution for consumer claims—as for many other types of claims—until relatively recently. Blankenburg found some decades ago that CADR had flourished in the Netherlands, but not in neighbouring Germany, because the German court system was less costly than the Dutch and lawyers had kept a monopoly on legal advice in Germany, whereas insurance companies, trade unions and many other civil society bodies were able to develop their own solutions to legal problems in the Netherlands.[5] German reliance on clear rights, and the importance of everyone doing what they say they will do, also affects reliance on courts as the fora to restore social equilibrium. The introduction of mediation as a dispute resolution tool has only occurred in Germany in the late 2000s with implementation of the Mediation Directive, and almost all of the extensive discussion about mediation there has been about how mediation fits into the context of court proceedings. The spread of consumer ombudsmen is clearly more recent and slower than in some other Member States, but it is gathering momentum.

The Dutch consensual approach, and their unique system of agreeing terms and conditions, produced the Geschillencommissie system. In large part, this 'back end' dispute resolution system grew out of the more important 'front end' of the unique system that emerged for regulation of business' consumer trading activities. A key driver for this

[5] See recently E Blankenburg, 'Patterns of Legal Culture: The Netherlands compared to Neighbouring Germany', in *The American Journal of Comparative Law*, (1998) vol 46, 1 at 26; see ch 4 above.

approach was the Dutch 'polder' model, whereby parties compromise their individual objectives so as to create a way forward in which all parties get something, and the total good created is beneficial for all: that approach is widely applied to many situations in the Netherlands.

The Nordic States' consensual approach to problems produced the court-like separate arbitration boards. Similarly, Nordic states developed no fault injury compensation schemes that fitted their national cultures of social solidarity.[6] The dispute resolution Board approach in Sweden has a single national level apex (the ARN), under which sectoral Boards, and in-house schemes, are incentivised and can operate as a holistic system. The ARN provides both a last-resort appeal-like function sitting above the other ADR systems, and also a long-stop function that fills any gaps. In view of these features, it does not attract a particularly high volume of cases, but it provides a 'shadow of the law' function within which cases may be resolved 'below' ARN. Significantly, the ARN is funded by the state. Further, the ARN functions in close contact with the regulatory authority, the Swedish Consumer Agency, and with the ECC-SE office.

The Nordic States have also continued to innovate by enabling regulators with powers to order restitution of compensation, as an adjunct to their traditional enforcement powers.[7] This restitution approach has proved to be extremely successful, since it provides an incentive for traders to take the initiative in resolving all issues arising out of an infringement at the same time. Collective solutions can therefore be negotiated that provide speedier compensation, at lower transactional cost, than any court or ADR procedure. Sweden's Group Proceedings Act 2002 is an example of this procedure, and similar systems exist in Finland, Norway and Denmark.[8] The Danish model is interesting because only the Consumer Ombudsman has a collective redress power that is opt-out (since an opt-out approach makes some sense where the collective mechanism is intended to have a regulatory function) whereas all private claimants operate on an opt-in model (which makes sense for individual private claims). In Finland, the collective compensation mechanism is restricted to the Consumer Ombudsman, and not available to private parties.[9]

The growth of *médiateurs* in France within institutions of the state and within companies is consistent with the integrated institutional architecture of the French state and economic structure.[10] Equally, the development of private CADR schemes in the UK is part of national emphasis on self-regulatory structures and pragmatism.

The perception of expensive courts and lawyers in some jurisdictions has clearly spurred the development of lower cost alternative pathways for any and all types of disputes. Leading examples are the United Kingdom, the Netherlands, Spain, and perhaps the Nordic States. In England and Wales, mediation grew for family cases, ombudsmen were increasingly used for citizen-state disputes, and so on. CADR systems were attractive for C2B complaints.

[6] J Dute, MG Faure and H Koziol *(eds), No-Fault Compensation in the Health Care Sector* (Vienna/New York: Springer, 2004); C Hodges, 'Nordic Compensation Schemes for Drug Injuries' *J Consumer Policy* (2006) 29:143–175.

[7] K Viitanen, 'Enforcement of Consumers' Collective Interests by Regulatory Agencies in the Nordic Countries' in W van Boom and M Loos, *Collective Enforcement of Consumer Law: Securing Compliance in Europe through Private Group Action and Public Authority Intervention* (Europa Law Publishing, 2007).

[8] C Hodges, *The Reform of Class and Representative Actions in European Legal Systems: A New Framework for Collective Redress in Europe* (Hart Publishing, 2008).

[9] Class Actions Act 2006. See comments of the Consumer Ombudsman at www.kuluttajavirasto.fi.

[10] For a stimulating comparative analysis of the architectures and cultures of law in Germany, France and the United Kingdom, see H-W Micklitz, 'Social Justice and Access Justice in Private Law', EUI Working Papers Law 2011/02, available at ssrn.com/abstract=1824225.

But a more important factor in the adoption of CADR in the UK, and in EU legislation, was the introduction of modern regulatory systems on a sector-by-sector basis. Such systems were designed to be overseen by public regulatory bodies, working with a dispute resolution system as an integral component. In part, the CADR component was intended to have a regulatory function, since it would be able to capture information about the behaviour of the market and of individual traders. Another rationale was that the imposition of a regulatory system and its higher standards of behaviour on traders would produce an increased number of disputes. Higher costs would be imposed on traders by both the increased regulatory requirements and by the need to respond to the complaints. Hence, systems that could solve customer complaints speedily and at low cost would be welcome. In that context, CADR systems offered a more attractive solution than courts.

In Central and Eastern European States such as Poland and Lithuania, the legacy of Soviet times is that citizens tend to look to the state to provide structural solutions to problems, so CADR systems have evolved that are housed within state regulatory authorities. Thus, a central role in CADR is played by the Trade Inspection in Poland, and by the State Consumer Rights Protection Authority in Lithuania.

The insight that ADR forms part of differing national architecture and differing approaches is of fundamental importance when considering to what extent any form of harmonization or cross-border coordination may be possible. It cannot be assumed that a technique that has arisen in a particular context, because it fits that context, will be able to operate in a different context. In short, it would be foolish to specify at this point in time that a particular CADR model or technique should apply in every EU Member State for every type of dispute. Not enough is yet known about the extent to which national or sectoral contexts differ, and hence what might be the parameters and preconditions for particular ADR techniques, and whether they would work if transplanted to different systems.

It follows that three political decisions are appropriate at the current time. Firstly, decisions on dispute resolution at national level should seek to examine best practice from other jurisdictions, and see to what extent national systems could be amended so as to incorporate new or innovative techniques. Such an approach would provide benchmarking of best practice, removing obsolete techniques and adopting better ones, and may provide a measure of alignment between national systems. The European Commission could facilitate that process by encouraging and specifying best practice. Secondly, cross-border disputes, especially those in new sectors such as internet trading, could adopt new dispute resolution systems based on best practice. Thirdly, it is possible to define common criteria for CADR systems—or any dispute resolution system. Hence, effort should be put into agreeing such criteria, considering how they relate to standards of best practice and to the current status of CADR systems, and making any appropriate reforms in existing schemes. These issues are examined further below.

The Historical Development of CADR Models and Techniques

The national consumer CADR systems can be viewed in a historical context as representing evolving ideas of what extra-court ADR should be. The procedures that are applied in national CADR systems have clearly been influenced by different ideas depending on when the national CADR model was created.

Courts were, and remain, the paradigm context within which justice is sought and dispensed within civil societies. Court procedures are subject to well-established norms of due process, such as no-one being a judge in their own cause, full opportunity for parties to be heard.[11] The precedent of courts influenced the procedures adopted in the major private sector break-away from state structures when arbitration systems were introduced. The major change in moving courts to arbitration was in the number of decision-makers: what was usually (but not always) a single state judge was typically replaced in arbitration by a panel of three arbitrators, one appointed by each party and one neutral chair.

Accordingly, it is not surprising that CADR models that were created around the 1970s were heavily influenced by the architecture, culture and procedure of state courts. The Boards in Nordic States and the Netherlands all have operational structures and procedures that look like courts or arbitration tribunals—as, by definition, does the Spanish arbitration system. Panels of three decision-makers always have the function of representing consumers and business 'sides'. Thus, in the Netherlands, which established their sectoral boards from the 1970s onwards, decisions are made by a panel of three 'arbitrators' of whom, based on standard arbitration practice, one comes from a consumer list, a second from a business list, and the third, the chair, from a neutral list of lawyers. Procedures involve a stage of submission of written complaints and evidence, followed by gathering of any expertise, and then a decision stage.

In CEE States, where state authority can be exercised by officials within state regulatory authorities as much as by state officials in courts, it is not surprising to see the former making decisions on disputes, perhaps with less 'due process' requirements than would typically operate in Western European States.

CADR systems that have been established more recently, especially in the United Kingdom and in cross-border systems during the 2000s, the procedure is far more streamlined, and might even dispense with a number of steps that are regarded as essential in courts if 'due process' requirements are to be complied with. Thus there might be no 'hearings' at which both parties present their cases, hear the opponents' case, and have an opportunity to respond. In recent systems, both parties might simply present their case and evidence in simple format, often online, to a single neutral person, perhaps collated by a case handler. Such a system assumes, firstly, that the parties have already exchanged the relevant evidence in the initial required stage of direct contact between them, and have debated the arguments, and secondly, that the facts are usually sufficiently straightforward for there to be no need for any further evidence or elaboration by the parties. The neutral party will simply be in a position to take a clear view of the merits of the dispute by considering the evidence presented.

Three issues therefore arise for consideration below: to what extent should due process requirements apply to CADR systems, should certain models of CADR be considered to be best contemporary practice, and should some models be streamlined further?

Market Regulation, Reducing Cost and Maintaining Business Reputation as Drivers of CADR

It has been identified above that CADR systems have either been imposed by law on traders, or they have established them voluntarily. Why have these events occurred? Three broad

[11] DJ Galligan, *Due Process and Fair Procedures: A Study of Administrative Procedures* (Oxford: Clarendon Press, 1996); European Convention on Human Rights, Art 6; *Procedural Fairness: Transparency Issues in Civil and Administrative Enforcement Proceedings* (Paris: OECD, 2010).

drivers are examined here, which arise from the evidence of this study. Firstly, there is a clear link between the creation of CADR systems as part of the regulatory landscape, to control commercial behaviour in regulated markets. Secondly, businesses and governments increasingly see cost saving advantages in CADR systems when compared with courts. Thirdly, some businesses perceive that CADR systems will assist in maximising commercial advantages, retaining customer loyalty and maintaining brand reputation. These three factors are sometimes inter-linked, and their cumulative effect can be strong.

CADR occurred in some sectors as part of the imposition by the authorities of new regulatory systems. Some governments privatised major service sectors, and this was also frequently interlinked with simultaneous moves to create the EU internal market. These objectives led to statutory imposition of requirements for CADR as part of market regulation, transparency and competition. Legislation frequently either created a sectoral ombudsman, whose decisions are binding on *all* traders in the sector, or required all traders to have *an* ADR system, leaving the choice of system to the traders or the sector. The latter approach left the choice of architecture of ADR to the market and, as noted above, has led to some diversity of models.

Otherwise, where CADR has not been imposed by law, the origination and growth of ADR almost always occurred because *traders* wished to provide cheaper and quicker solutions, in order to support the commercial reputation of sectors. In some instances, CADR was imposed by law, especially in sectors such as energy and telecoms where governments privatised markets and/or were concerned at an absence of full competition in a sector. CADR systems never originated because *consumers* wanted quicker and cheaper disputes resolution system to the courts, even though the benefits to consumers would have been, and are, considerable. To this extent, business support for CADR is crucial: systems are not established, or paid for, or not marketed, or decisions observed, in this voluntary system, without active business support. Further, where CADR schemes are financed by businesses, usually on a sectoral basis, rather than by public funds, the commercial scrutiny provides pressure both for efficiency and for innovation, to keep costs low.

In competitive markets, many sectors have radically changed their attitude to CADR systems. Although this view is far from universal, there is strong evidence that long-standing opposition to responding constructively to consumer complaints has given way to enthusiastic support for a responsive approach, and for a CADR system, in order to achieve the advantages of maintaining market reputation and hence market share and commercial success. This change can even be called a 'flip effect'. The realisation is that CADR systems can defuse consumer problems, at lower cost and more cheaply than courts, thereby saving money. They also identify market trends.

A principal benefit of CADR for both businesses and consumers is in overcoming the problem that the courts in many States have been too expensive (and hence delivered a service that was disproportionate in value, especially in terms of cost) and too slow, and so little used by consumers. The 2009 Oxford study on litigation costs and funding in 36 jurisdictions found that high litigation costs and difficulties over obtaining funding for bringing claims through the court system had led to the growth of pathways for resolving disputes outside courts.[12] Users want dispute resolution systems that are accessible, cheap, swift, responsive, and easy to use. Courts often do not satisfy these consumer requirements.

[12] C Hodges, S Vogenauer & M Tulibacka, *The Costs and Funding of Civil Litigation: A Comparative Approach* (Oxford: Hart Publishing, 2010).

This situation has come about as a result of both over-pricing by lawyers, and a failure of courts. Lawyers do not earn money by referring consumers to CADR systems, but many lawyers may not be aware that CADR pathways exist. Even the Small Claims systems are not that user-friendly. As the data in this study shows, the cost of using Small Claims systems is often low but there is sometimes a loser pays risk. CADR systems, in contrast, have been designed to be no more expensive than courts—and often lower cost or no cost. Small Claims procedures have been designed to reduce procedural complexity and to use effective and cheap techniques such as mediation. But above all they remain not user-friendly.

It might be expected that since many legislators have referred so often to gaps in access to justice, which they wish to fill, they would have pursued CADR as a means of filling a gap in bringing small C2B claims. However, it is clear that CADR has not been pursued for that reason. One reason for this is that CADR comes under the governmental responsibility of ministries of business, rather than ministries of justice. CADR systems are not only not administered by the latter, they may even be largely invisible to them. Although an empirical evaluation of the EU Small Claims Procedure is premature,[13] small claims systems nationally generally represent a failure of planning by those ministries of justice that did not provide a proper service or alternative to the courts for C2B disputes. The CADR alternative has largely been business-driven and driven by business and finance ministries that have imposed ombudsmen under regulatory systems, such as for telecoms, banks and other sectors, or have encouraged innovation by business sectors in adopting voluntary CADR systems. Within long-standing political and academic debates over failures in access to justice, consumer redress has been an area in which a major solution has arisen Cinderella-like from an unexpected quarter, driven by regulation and by business, not by the justice system or civil procedure.

In short, effective ADR systems have clearly provided major new avenues of access to justice for consumer-to-business disputes. Such avenues have often provided pathways to justice that were in practice not available through courts, for reasons of cost and complexity.

Why has CADR become topical in the political arena in the early 2010s? Three major reasons are suggested. Firstly, the development of regulation of markets and of consumer protection legislation has matured to a stage when dispute resolution and behaviour control are the next issues on the agenda. Secondly, the European Commission has given strong impetus to CADR as an alternative to adopting court-based class actions in an ongoing debate over the best responses are to issues of collective redress.[14] Thirdly, in seeking an appropriate pathway for resolution of C2B disputes, the need by governments to cut public expenditure programmes as a result of the current financial crisis has forced cuts on court and judicial budgets, thereby raising the issue of whether other, and privately funded, means of dispute resolution might be available and could be encouraged and expanded. The Council of Europe's Commission for the efficiency of justice (CEPEJ), established in 2002, demonstrates the level of shared concern about the need to reduce the cost of accessing justice in national systems.[15]

[13] XE Kramer, 'Small Claim, Simple Recovery? The European Small Claims Procedure and Its Implementation in the Member States' *ERA Forum: Journal of European Law*, vol 1, (2011) 119–134.

[14] See CJS Hodges, *The Reform of Class and Representative Actions in European Legal Systems: A New Framework for Collective Redress in Europe* (Oxford, Hart Publishing, 2008); CJS Hodges 'Collective Redress in Europe: The New Model' (2010) *Civil Justice Quarterly* 370.

[15] See *European judicial systems – Edition 2010 (data 2008) Efficiency and quality of justice* (Council of Europe, 2010), at http://book.coe.int/EN/ficheouvrage.php?PAGEID=36&lang=EN&produit_aliasid=2341.

Indeed, introducing a compulsory stage of mediation into an efficient civil procedure system may positively add to costs and duration of cases with not particular advantage for the parties. If a cheap 'mediation' option is too cheap, some providers may prefer to delay addressing complaints and direct them towards mediation, since this would reduce the size of their internal Complaints Handling resources. Adjudication requires consumers to be more articulate in putting their case. There is clearly a trend towards making it compulsory for traders to refer customer disputes to CADR systems and to abide by outcomes, whether compulsorily or mandatorily.

Italian law made pre-trial mediation mandatory in telecoms disputes involving the universal service obligations[16] (USOs) established in EU law.[17] The *Alassini*[18] case serves as an example of the need to re-examine the EU principles of effective judicial protection and national procedural autonomy.

CADR in the Context of DR

It is important to see CADR within the context of all forms of DR (dispute resolution). The main dispute resolution models can be characterised in a number of ways, one of which is:[19]

1. Direct negotiation between complainant and respondent.
2. Involvement of independent assistance, whether by mediation, arbitration or adjudication services.
3. Restitution or compensation brought about by public regulatory authorities, as part of their enforcement functions. An authority might have express powers to seek a court order for payment of compensation (or itself order compensation), or compensation might be paid by a trader voluntarily (in the shadow of an enforcement threat) or as part of a plea-bargain as a result of a negotiation with the authorities. This interesting and developing area is beyond the scope of this book.[20]
4. Civil litigation in the state courts.

In relation to category 2 above, the ADR category, this research has demonstrated that ADR can take place within one of a number of different structures. As identified above, the most familiar structure is that of the courts. Mediation as a process or technique can be required or encouraged for claims that are proceeding within the court procedure, or before they start it.[21] A second possible 'structure' for ADR is ephemeral, since there is no reason why any dispute cannot be discussed by the parties merely with the assistance of any third party, such as a mediator. Nevertheless, such dispute resolution attempts do not

[16] Review of the universal service obligation, available at http://stakeholders.ofcom.org.uk/binaries/consultations/uso/statement/statement.pdf (accessed 21 December 2010).

[17] J Davis and E Szyszczak, 'ADR: Effective Protection of Consumer Rights?' 35 *EL Rev* October 2010, available at: www.littletonchambers.com/articles-downloads/adr-effective-protection-of-consumer-rights.pdf.

[18] *Rosalba Alassini v Telecom Italia SpA, Filomena Californio v Wind SpA, Lucia Giorgia Iacono v Telecom Italia SpA* and *Multiservice Srl v Telecom Italia SpA*, (C-317/8, C-318/08, C-319/08, C-320/08) March 18, 2010. See ch 1 above.

[19] See C Hodges, 'The European Approach to Justice and Redress' (2011) 53 *Canadian Supreme Court Law Review* (2n edn), 301.

[20] See C Hodges, *The Reform of Class and Representative Actions in European Legal Systems: A New Framework for Collective Redress in Europe* (Oxford: Hart Publishing, 2008).

[21] Such mediation can be encouraged (eg by court costs rules, as in England & Wales) or a formal part of the litigation procedure.

take place entirely in a vacuum, since it is well recognised that they take place within the 'shadow of the law',[22] in that the state courts are always present in the background and can be fallen back on if necessary.

A third possible dispute resolution structure has its own distinct architecture—that of CADR. In simple terms, it might be described as 'ombudsmen', but that is misleading since some leading examples do not involve ombudsmen and instead might be summarised as 'code-based dispute resolution systems'. In any event, the architecture is not that of courts, but is quite separate from courts and distinct from that of courts. It is a separate universe. As this book has identified, it is this separate architecture that now exists for C2B claims.

Undoubtedly, however, the ombudsmen model that operates in CADR was copied from the pre-existing separate world of public sector ombudsmen. Public sector ombudsmen are traceable to Sweden in the 18th century.[23] The function of public sector ombudsmen is usually wider than providing a dispute resolution option, and typically provides a mechanism of scrutiny and control over public services and authorities. Structurally, an ombudsman would typically be considered to be appointed by Parliament, and therefore ultimately represent citizens in scrutinising the state, even though the office might at first sight to be located more in the public sector than anywhere else. For the citizen wishing to challenge decisions by the state, the ombudsman would offer an alternative to judicial review of administrative action in the courts. Such an alternative has generally become increasingly attractive, partly because of the costs of the litigation route, whereas ombudsmen are free to citizens, and partly because the investigatory power of ombudsmen and their ability to effect systemic change is wider than judicial review. Various parallels can, therefore, be seen between public ombudsmen and CADR ombudsmen—and other CADR systems—in terms of independence from the body being investigated, cost advantages, investigatory power, and ability to affect generic change in the behaviour of the respondent.

Ombudsmen have also mushroomed in the United States since the 1960s inside public agencies, universities,[24] and corporations,[25] spurred initially by a small number of academic enthusiasts.[26] Some landmarks were Resolutions of the American Bar Association in 1969, 1971, 2001 and 2004, the formation of the Corporate Ombudsman Association in 1985 (which changed its name to The Ombudsman Association in 1992) and its adoption of a Code of Ethics and Standards of Practice, the 1986 Defence Industry Initiative on Business Ethics and Conduct, re-enactment of the Administrative Dispute Resolution Act in 1996,[27] Howard notes the wide range of activities of different ombudsmen in America, and categorises their work into three broad areas: communications and outreach; issue resolution; and identification of areas for systemic change and issue prevention.[28]

[22] RM Mnookin and L Kornhauser, 'Bargaining in the Shadow of the Law: The Case of Divorce' (1979) 88 *Yale Law Journal* 950.

[23] SD Anderman, 'The Swedish Justitieombudsman' (1962) 11:2 *American Journal of Comparative Law* 225–38; T Buck, R Kirkham and B Thompson, *The Ombudsman Enterprise and Administrative Justice* (Aldershot: Ashgate, 2010).

[24] See CL Howard, *The Organizational Ombudsman. Origins, Roles , and Operations. A Legal Guide* (ABA Section of Dispute Resolution, 2010).

[25] An early article was I Silver, 'The Corporate Ombudsman', *Harv Bus Rev* May-June 1968, 77.

[26] K Culp Davis, 'Ombudsmen in America: Officers to Criticize Administrative Action' (1961) 109 *Penn L Rev* 1057; W Gelhorn, *When Americans Complain: Governmental Grievance Procedures* (1966); RV Peel, 'Preface' to Symposium, 'The Ombudsman or Citizen's Defender: A Modern Institution' 377 (1968) *Annals Am Pol & Soc Sci*, ix; SV Anderson, *Ombudsman Papers: American Experience and Proposals* (1969).

[27] See 5 U.S.C. § 571(3) (2007).

[28] Howard, above, p 75.

Models of CADR

A wide variation in CADR models exists in EU Member States, across different sectors and countries. In some Member States there is almost no organised CADR, whereas it has developed significantly in other States, stretching back sometimes 40 years. Further, the national CADR systems are frequently dynamic and still developing. Developments are occurring in terms of structures, techniques, operational aspects, and a widening of sectoral coverage.

Broadly, three types of host structures can be identified for CADR systems:

a. **CADR arrangements within public regulatory bodies**. Examples are those within the German Bundesbank and Bundesnetzagentur; in Lithuania, the State Consumer Rights Protection Authority and various sectoral agencies; in France the *Médiateur* of the *Autorité des Marchés Financiers*; in UK, the Financial Ombudsman Service is not within the Financial Services Agency but a subsidiary of it; and in Poland the Trade Inspection and other bodies. In addition, public regulatory or enforcement bodies might not offer a dispute resolution facility, but they may nevertheless receive a substantial number of complaints about traders, such as the UK's OFCOM.
b. **Independent decision-making bodies**, which operate across an individual sector, and might be called Boards (Nordics and the Netherlands), Tribunals (Slovenia) or Ombudsmen (Nordics, UK, Germany). There is a range of models and arrangements. There maybe a supervisory body, which might be private or statutory. Examples of statutory ombudsmen are the UK Financial Ombudsman Service, Pensions Ombudsdman and Legal Ombudsman, and the French Energy *Médiateur*. Examples of private sector CADR providers are the German Insurance and Transport Ombudsmen, the French communications *Médiateur* and his support body AMCE, and the UK bodies Ombudsman Services and the CEDR Disputes Group.
c. **Dispute resolution arrangements sponsored by a trade association in order to resolve disputes arising under a code of business practice**. These structures usually combine stages of initial administration of complaint handling together with informal conciliation between consumer and trader (such as the UK FLA scheme, the UK CCAS schemes, like Motor Codes or the ABTA scheme), and then ultimately an arbitration stage that would be outsourced to an independent body for a decision (in effect to a private sector CADR provider of type b above). The outsourcing function is designed to satisfy the requirement of independence. The first stage might or might not be carried out by a body that is technically independent of the trade association (the Motor Codes structure is independent of SMMT, whereas ABTA does not have an independent body).

Various points can be made about the above arrangements. Firstly, the primary distinction between the above three categories of host bodies turns on whether the host is a public or private entity. An issue arises of the extent to which any of these three structures satisfies the requirement that the CADR provider be independent of the parties: this is discussed below.

Secondly, the above three models can overlap or be combined together in some circumstances, so the above categorisation should not be regarded as exclusive or final. Companies or consumers might have the ability to access two or more different CADR systems for the same complaint, and those systems might be examples of any of the above three models. The models can also involve some intermingling: model c can involve an aspect of model b.

Thirdly, some diversity exists, and hence there is opportunity for confusion, particularly in the minds of consumers. Confusion or experience of poor quality CADR might lead to a lack of trust in the system as a whole, as well as in individual CADR systems or providers.

Fourthly, it is obvious that no single model exists for CADR architectures across Europe. Further, it is difficult to see how the existing models could be rationalised into a single model. That realisation underpins the European Commission's approach to CADR. The Commission cannot insist on or propose a single model. The national models are the structures that must continue and be built on, even if some structures are reformed. Accordingly, the way in which the Commission proceeds to construct a structure for CADR that can operate across borders within the single market has to be by way of requiring that any individual CADR system that might exist has to conform to essential requirements that are sufficiently generalised that they can encompass the majority of existing models, rather than to a specific individual model.

Ombudsmen

There are at least two different types of ombudsmen:[29]

- public sector ombudsmen, who consider complaints about local councils, government departments or other public bodies, and
- private sector ombudsmen, who consider complaints about a range of businesses such as banks, insurers, telecommunication providers and estate agents.

In the dispute resolution context, the primary function of an ombudsman is to issue an independent authoritative decision on the legal merits of a case, even though in many CADR examples the decision might not be legally binding on one or both parties. As a preliminary stage, the ombudsman or a member of his staff might attempt to reach agreement by mediation. The investigative procedure is traditionally an inquisitorial mode of operation, but CADR examples now increasingly involve merely considering the evidence put before the ombudsman by the two parties. The process usually involves considering documentary evidence only, rather than interviewing witnesses or holding hearings. That approach contrasts with dispute resolution techniques that apply under codes (see below), where each side asserts its case. A document-based approach brings the advantages of speed and low cost. The ombudsman will usually have expertise in the relevant area of the dispute.

Ombudsmen who operate in CADR must be distinguished from other types of ombudsmen. The most familiar ombudsmen are probably those who are appointed by Parliament to resolve disputes between citizens and state entities. These exist in almost all European states and, as noted above, their existence has influenced the development of private ombudsmen. They usually have wide ranging investigative powers. Other types of ombudsmen are not primarily involved in dispute resolution at all, but are public enforcement officials. Such officials exist in all Nordic states, such as the Danish Consumer Ombudsman, who is the principal national enforcement authority for consumer and competition law. Thus, there are differences in the powers that different enforcers and ombudsmen have. A contrasting example is the Danish (Parliamentary) Ombudsman, who holds investigative

[29] See *Mapping UK consumer redress. A summary guide to dispute resolution systems* (Office of Fair Trading, May 2010), available at http://www.oft.gov.uk/shared_oft/general_policy/OFT1267.pdf.

powers in relation to 'decisions, acts or omissions' of all Danish public authorities but no enforcement power. His determinations are recommendations and not directly enforceable, but in practice his standing and social authority (he reports directly to Parliament) are such that the recommendations are almost always voluntarily complied with.

The adoption of the name 'ombudsman' or '*médiateur*' for decision-makers who operate in the CADR context has brought with it an aura of independence and hence authority in relation to their office and recommendations or decisions. There is, however, a risk that unless such individuals and organisations are in fact adequately independent or impartial, consumer confidence in them and in CADR in general will suffer. The point is relevant also for in-house *médiateurs*, as discussed below.

CADR With Business Codes of Practice

Although independent dispute resolution may be carried out by a body called an ombudsman or some other name, or under another procedure such as referral to independent arbitration, the context in which many sectoral CADR schemes operate is as the 'back end' of resolving consumer disputes under a sectoral code of business practice. The norms that are being applied are, therefore, those set out in the code, rather than under the law. This model exists widely across European states, notable examples being the Netherlands and UK.

In the Netherlands, the two independent bodies operate to a model (that is slightly different between them) under contract with sectoral trade associations with a single national template, and thereby designed to provide a structure and mode of operation that is transparent, consistent, and satisfies acceptable criteria.

The British model (where it does not involve statutory ombudsmen) typically involves private sector CADR bodies providing contracted dispute resolution services to trade associations where the CADR bodies are either approved by a regulatory body (eg OFCOM and OFGEM for communications and energy respectively) or may operate to an officially approved scheme (hitherto the OFT's CCAS, but possibly moving to approval by a Trading Standards body). The British model also relies on transparency of structures and operations (information on complaints, naming respondents, identifying outcomes, identifying problems, and responses, and on outcomes, duration and cost of the dispute resolution processes), and on governance models in which the committees that oversee codes, dispute resolution functions and sanctioning of members are not composed solely of traders but involve independent personnel and stakeholders.

The objective behind these two national models is to ensure that the schemes satisfy acceptable criteria, notably independence and impartiality in decision-making, and can be trusted by the public. In contrast, equivalent private schemes in France and Germany are not subject to official approval mechanisms, and tend to stress the personal integrity of the chief ombudsman. One measure of the level of public trust in any private system will be the incidence of use by the public. In this respect, it is interesting to note the differing levels of usage of schemes from the data recorded in chapter 14 above.

Are there significant differences between 'ombudsmen' and 'code' dispute resolution models? They seem to be roughly equivalent, in that both can operate well, and are sometimes found alongside each other (the UK communications providers). It is only necessary to have one or the other, but not both. However, one or the other might be more appropriate in particular circumstances. The main difference is that an ombudsman is usually more independent of the trade sector, especially if the provider works across several different sectors. But other private CADR bodies also work across sectors and are regarded as satisfactory. Any difference between the two approaches in this respect may lie more in perception and public confidence than in the reality of independence.

Modes and Techniques of Dispute Resolution in CADR Systems

CADR systems employ one or both of two techniques that are wholly familiar from courts and other dispute resolution systems: *mediation* (or conciliation, and for present purposes these two words are treated as meaning the same)[30] and *adjudication*. The outcome of the adjudication stage might be binding on the respondent company or it might not. If not binding, it would simply be a recommendation.

Negotiation leads to an agreement between the parties themselves, whether the negotiating process occurs direct between the parties or is facilitated by a third party, such as a mediator or trade association. *Adjudication* occurs where an independent party such as an arbitrator, panel or court, makes a determination on the merits of the dispute by applying external criteria such as rules of law to the facts as they appear to the decision-maker. Such techniques can be found in any CADR model and individual techniques, or combinations of techniques, are not specific to particular CADR types.

Thus, on this analysis, there are only two distinctions between *approaches* in dispute resolution, namely between resolutions that are *agreed* by the parties themselves and those that are *imposed* by determination by a third party. Thus, these two paradigms of approaches to dispute resolution represent opposed modes, which give rise to fundamentally different considerations of individual and constitutional determinacy. The negotiation paradigm involves self-determination, based on respect for an individual's personal integrity, and his or her freedom to enter into a contract or not. But, in such a situation, society may raise concerns about an imbalance of negotiating power between the parties, for example through one party's inability to bargain fairly or effectively for various reasons, such as informational asymmetry or some form of disability or dominance. At the other extreme a dispute is determined by a third party, either as a result of acceptance by both parties of such a mode of resolution (eg through agreement to mediation or arbitration) or as a result of the imposition of such a mode by society through the power of the state (ie through the rule that the court process and decision is binding on everyone if it is invoked by any claimant).

However, the distinction between these modes of resolution does not necessarily infer that the two modes can never be combined. For example, a court or an arbitrator, who possesses power to impose a determination, may still possess power, or *de facto* discretionary freedom, to suggest solutions or behave more like a mediator in pointing out views on the evidence or merits of a case, before imposing his or her independent judgment on the parties. By contrast, a mediator is essentially an independent channel of communication between the parties and does not possess power formally to impose a solution. However, in practice some mediators can, through their behaviour or force of personality, significantly influence the views of one or both parties by suggesting views on the merits and likely outcome of how an independent adjudication would turn out, which

[30] Some definitions state that a mediator is essentially a passive go-between, whereas a conciliator is more active in proposing solutions: see *Mapping UK consumer redress. A summary guide to dispute resolution systems* (Office of Fair Trading, May 2010), available at http://www.oft.gov.uk/shared_oft/general_policy/OFT1267.pdf.

will guide the parties towards agreement. Both third party adjudicators and mediators are intended to be strictly independent and disinterestedly neutral between the parties. Whilst any bias in an independent adjudicator (judge or arbitrator) will be condemned, the activities of mediators have divided opinions on whether their function is validly to influence parties based on their experience and independent assessment, or whether such influence may overstep the bounds of acceptability.

Arbitration is sometimes referred to in CADR schemes, but the word is often misleading. It is a form of adjudication, where the decision-maker is a private person or panel, rather than a state official (judge). In its classic meaning, arbitration occurs where all parties consent that their dispute will be heard before a third party arbitrator (rather than a court) whose decision will be accepted by them all as binding (save in limited circumstances). Arbitration has long been used in B2B contracts and practice as the preferred form of dispute resolution, in preference to the courts. The reasons are usually avoiding media interest in disputes, expertise and some flexibility in the procedure, and sometimes cost and speed. However, a consumer contract that includes a term that any dispute will be referred to arbitration would be an unfair term and so illegal: the consumer cannot be bound in advance to an arbitration procedure at the time of purchase. Some CADR systems are based on arbitration models (Spain, the Netherlands) or involve a final, optional, stage in which the consumer may agree that the dispute will be referred to a binding arbitration procedure but that situation appears to be rare and disappearing.

Since the 1980s, there has been a firm downward trend in the number of disputes that UK-based CADR providers handle through arbitration. The rise in the popularity of other dispute resolution mechanisms such as adjudication and conciliation, which provide feedback on issues, is perceived by them to have had a demonstrably beneficial effect in reducing the incidence of consumer detriment across a range of sectors.

Mediation and conciliation are the primary techniques used in many CADR systems. The techniques of mediation and arbitration produce different results over whether the solutions are *binding or non-binding* (see below). Decisions by a court do, of course, have the force of law, and so are binding on the parties. Similarly, where the parties have contractually agreed in advance that a dispute will be referred to arbitration, decisions by the properly constituted arbitrator are, under both contract law and the substantive law of all advanced jurisdictions, binding on both parties, and can be enforced through subsequent court proceedings, without the need for a complete re-hearing of the underlying dispute by the court, often through abbreviated procedures.

In the classic mediation situation, the principle has been that the process is voluntary for both sides, and the purpose of the mediator is to assist communication between the parties, so that they may reach their own agreement, if they wish. One or both may not wish to reach agreement. The mediator is not empowered to impose any solution that could be binding on the parties. If they reach any agreement, it will have the force of a private contract between them, and be enforceable as such. ADR schemes vary over whether the neutral party can suggest a solution.

However, the technique of conciliation/mediation can be used in some ADR systems where the neutral party ultimately has the power to impose a binding solution, whether this power is imposed by statute or by prior agreement of the disputing parties. In this respect, the classic non-binding mediation situation is irrelevant, since the context is one in which a binding solution may be imposed, but the neutral party chooses to adopt a mediation technique as a preliminary to using the power to impose a solution.

Unless the CADR scheme ends in an arbitration stage, where the consumer has to agree in advance to be bound by the outcome, no decision by a neutral ADR provider is binding under any scheme on a consumer. The concerns here partly arise from issues of *asymmetrical power* between trader and consumer, and partly under protecting the human rights of the consumer under Article 6 of the European Convention on Human Rights (ECHR), which guarantees maintenance of the consumer's right to determination of her rights through a judicial process.[31]

In some systems the consumer is required to agree at the time of pursuing the dispute that the outcome under an arbitration system will be binding. This occurs in the Dutch, Spanish, and some UK systems (such as ABTA). It does not technically offend Article 6 ECHR. However, it is less attractive than many other non-binding schemes.

The Sequencing of Dispute Resolution Pathways

Many CADR models involve a *sequencing* or escalation of techniques, starting with direct negotiation, then providing mediation, before ending with arbitration. Such sequencing therefore proceeds from negotiation to adjudication modes.[32] The objective is to achieve efficient outcomes through escalation of formality. The stages, which are illustrated in Table 1, are:

1. Direct negotiation between consumer and trader *always* comes first, and is a precondition of access to almost every ADR scheme.
2. The ADR scheme frequently first employs a *mediation/conciliation* technique: it suggests to either the consumer or the trader that their position in the case has no merit, and thus the consumer need not pursue the issue further or the trader should immediately make a voluntary satisfactory settlement offer. Several ombudsmen comment that many of the cases they handle involve misunderstandings between customers and traders, rather than breaches of rules.[33]
3. ADR schemes then differ on the nature of the next stage depending on whether they have the right to make binding or non-binding solutions.
   i. If they can only offer non-binding solutions, they make a recommendation: this tends to occur in ADR systems that are relatively new, such as in Germany, and almost all in France. The alternative open to the consumer in Germany would be to enter a binding process, such as to make a court claim: only rarely is binding arbitration an option.
   ii. In contrast, countries that have longer ADR histories and experience, such as the UK and the Netherlands, have progressed beyond having ADR bodies that can make non-binding recommendations to allowing them to make decisions that are binding on the business (whether through trade association membership, under sectoral legislation, or voluntarily) but not on the consumer. In effect, this situation is quasi-one-way arbitration.

[31] 'In the determination of his civil rights and obligations …., everyone is entitled to a fair and public hearing within a reasonable time by an independent and impartial tribunal established by law.'

[32] This was first described by I Ramsay, 'Small Claims Courts in Canada: A Socio-Legal Appraisal' in CJ Whelan, *Small Claims Courts. A Comparative Study* (Oxford: Clarendon Press, 1990) 38. The Leuven study suggested a generalised theoretical model that matched amounts in dispute to different types of pathway: theoretically simple as such an approach might be, it is arbitrary, and our findings do not support any such behaviour on the ground based on any monetary categorisations: Stuyck et al, above n 7, p 42.

[33] The French telecoms *médiateur* is one who holds this view.

Figure 15.1: Integrated use of techniques by CADR provider

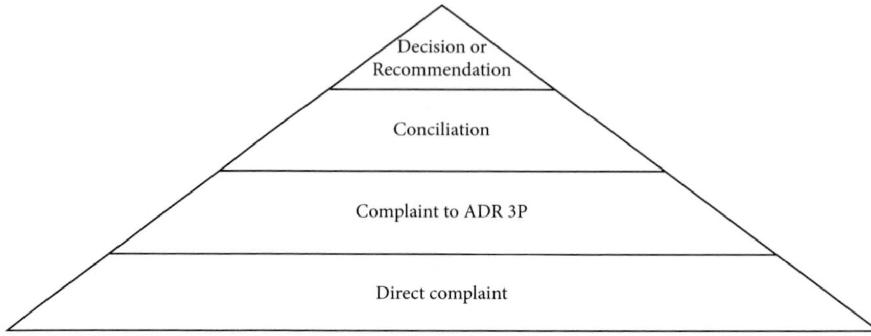

Some schemes employ a more sophisticated series of steps than that shown in Figure 15.1, so as to provide more stages for parties to consider their positions, and hence agree solutions without the matter being referred by a case officer to the Ombudsman for formal decisions. An example, based on the British Pensions Ombudsman's procedures, is shown in Figure 15.2. Complaint systems in some French in-company *médiateurs* require complainants to pass through a sequence of stages within the company's complaint handling process, such as local, regional then national level, before reaching the *médiateur*. The difference between these two approaches is that in the former model the consumer is in touch with the neutral party throughout the process, whereas in the latter model he/she is only in touch with the *médiateur* at the end of the process. Company *médiateurs* argue that their model imposes downward pressure on the company to agree solutions. Conversely, consumer associations argue that the latter model imposes a succession of barriers for the consumer in obtaining satisfaction, and many just give up. Certainly, the statistics of in-company *médiateurs* reveal very low numbers of cases handled.

Figure 15.2: More sophisticated model for escalated use of techniques

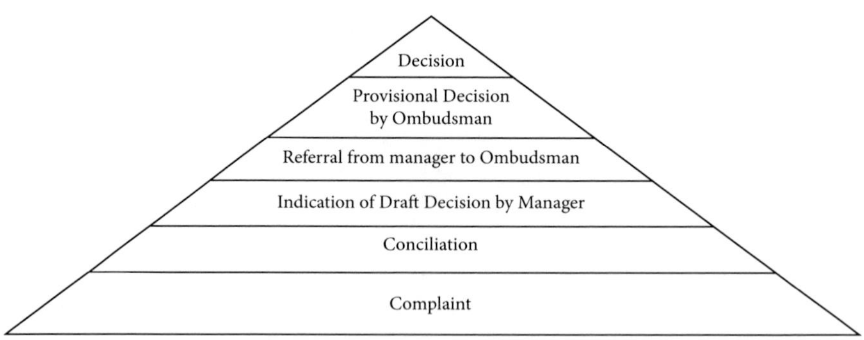

Figure 15.3: Escalation model with an outsourced function of binding decision-making.

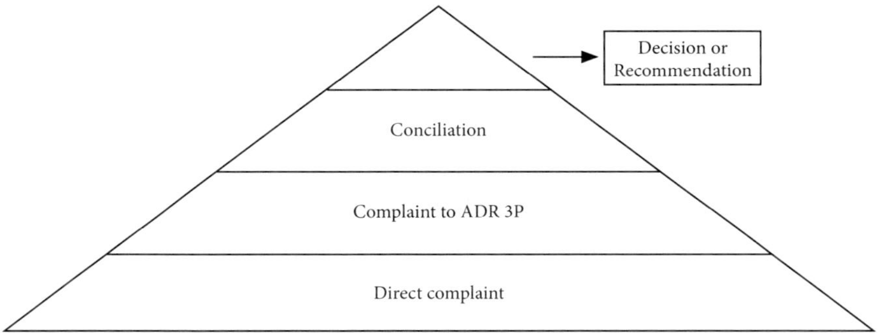

The First Stage: Direct Contact with Traders

Almost every CADR system not only encourages direct contact as a first stage, and many CADR rules require that before they have jurisdiction to consider a complaint. This finding was also made by the Leuven Study, which concluded that direct negotiations between customers and businesses are by far the most popular form in which consumer complaints are made.[34]

As the case studies in Chapter 12 demonstrate, in competitive markets, the best companies now view complaints and complaint handling as integral parts of their goal of improving their products and services, and are part of its quality system. An integrated complaints handling system should make the consumer feel trust in the company. Each sector develops its own culture, and there are some differences in complaints and dispute handling between sectors. The retail sector trades on its attractiveness to customers, and has no great reputational issue as a whole; its brands are respected and it wants to solve disputes.

Direct contact between complainant and respondent has several advantages. First, it can maintain or rebuild the relationship between them. Splitting parents may benefit from maintaining a communicative, as opposed to adversarial, relationship, especially where children are involved. Companies that trade on high reputations may seek opportunities to gain customer feedback for quality improvement reasons as well as pleasing customers, as illustrated by the Customer Care approach at the companies noted in Chapter 12.

Secondly, as with all triage techniques, it manifests an application of the principle of proportionality. An important goal is to provide a pathway that has proportionate cost and time. If the consumer can provide evidence of a valid complaint, and/or the trader is prepared to settle, resolution of the issue without undue delay, transactional cost or formality delivers proportionality.

Thirdly, direct contact may result in communication that either weeds out some claims or enables the respondent to respond in a flexible manner. A consistent message from CADR providers, demonstrated by the statistics in Chapter 14, is that CADR schemes receive many contacts that do not turn into claims (800,000 contacts to the FOS did not proceed in 2010). The evidence from the ABTA scheme is that making consumers focus on the matters

[34] J Stuyck, above n 7, p 9.

that are required to complete the claim form makes them focus on what the dispute is really about, what they want, and a sense of proportionality over what the value really is.

The main disadvantage of requiring direct contact is that it constitutes a barrier to further forms of dispute resolution. Thus, if a dispute is not resolved at the initial stage of direct negotiation, the complainant will have suffered delay and possibly extra cost. The same argument was raised when mediation was introduced as a first step into English civil procedure in 1999.[35]

Evaluation of whether there is force in this 'barrier to justice' argument depends on a number of factors. How much delay and extra cost do claimants generally suffer as a result of the existence of this barrier, as against the percentage of claims that are resolved (filtered out) as a result of it being in place? Note that time limits can be placed on the initial direct contact stage, which forces both parties, especially respondents, to respond quickly, and limits the possible disadvantage of claimants.

It should be remembered that many court processes also include barriers to accessing that dispute resolution pathway, such as fees to be paid to the court, forms to be filled in, lawyers to be found, instructed and paid. These features can involve far greater cost and delay than some ADR techniques, although a Small Claims track usually offers reduced barriers.

Advice, Information and Dispute Resolution

There is a clear finding that many customer contacts to both traders (see chapter 12) and CADR providers (chapter 14)[36] are inquiries for information and not—at that stage at least—complaints or disputes.[37] Initial contacts may turn into disputes if they are badly handled. A number of important consequences flow from this observation.

A national policy of ensuring that consumers and traders have access to accurate information both before and after transactions does seem to reduce the incidence of problems that arise after purchase. This is strongly indicated by the Nordic experience and architecture (see the chapter on Sweden), but similar approaches can be seen in many states (such as the UK's planned reorganisation of a maze of consumer advice bodies into a simpler structure focused on a network of Citizens Advice bureaux).

The ability for consumers to request information and on products and services is clearly beneficial, and should be encouraged. Use of products and services should be safe, appropriate, and effective. Happy customers are good for business. Contact points between consumers and traders can collect useful data on products, services, consumer preferences, trends and market data.

[35] A Zuckerman, *Zuckerman on Civil Procedure. Principles of Practice* (London: Thomson, Sweet & Maxwell, 2ed, 2006); D Dwyer (ed), *The Civil Procedure Rules. Ten Years On* (Oxford: OUP, 2010).

[36] In UK, statistics recorded on consumer contacts to official channels, such as Consumer Direct and Trading Standards, initially indicated a high level of disputes over cars. However, after SMMT established their Motor Codes dispute resolution scheme, to which all contacts to Consumer Direct were referred, it was discovered that a significant number of contacts were merely requests for more information on a product or issue, and not complaints. This information changed the general view of industry standards.

[37] The point is illustrated anecdotally by the experience of Hodges in listening in to customer inquiry calls at a major consumer products company. A significant number of calls in relation to, for example, shampoo were along the lines of 'this colour turns out to be the wrong colour for my hair, what colour should I try?' and not 'the description of colour on the product is wrong' or 'the product has burned my hair' or 'my hair is falling out after I used the product'. Callers who met a friendly, informed and reliable response went away satisfied.

Information can be provided by a number of different sources, such as traders, regulators, consumer associations, or dispute resolution providers (theoretically including courts). It may be appropriate, in some circumstances at least, for consumers to seek information from a reliable source that is separate from a trader, but some consideration should be given to what that source is. The Nordic arrangements, illustrated by Sweden, not only place strong emphasis on providing consumer information but also provide a clear and efficient structure for such provision. Pathways for providing information should be reliable, but should also be efficient.[38] Thus, there should not be too many possible sources, and the attention of regulators and others should not be unnecessarily diverted, since the overall costs would be disproportionate.

Although providing information to consumers is an inherent function of CADR providers, it can become a challenge. Where, as often occurs, a significant proportion of contacts are not disputes to be processed, CADR providers often have to structure effective information and triage filtering systems as their first line, with significant cost. The wastage rare is high for other reasons. Many CADR providers receive complaints that do not fall within their remit (and should be directed to other CADR providers, if they exist) or are made too early. CADR systems can exert some downward pressure on traders to provide full information themselves in user-friendly fashion and to respond quickly to customer contacts of any kind.

Care is needed in classifying consumer contacts. The motor vehicle sector was criticised by the UK authorities over its apparently high number of customer complaints recorded by the official agencies, but when it took over receipt of all complaints after establishing its own code of practice, it found that a high proportion were solely requests for further information (such as 'how do I get a particular feature to work', rather than 'the feature does not work').

CADR and Collective Redress

CADR schemes are designed to attract and process individual consumer disputes with traders. In doing so, all of the current CADR schemes of any size inherently process multiple similar cases, identify cases that raise similar issues, and make internal arrangements so that their processing of mass cases is done efficiently and with consistent outcomes. In other words, CADR schemes are entirely capable of handling collective mass issues.

Such an aggregation process is similar to that operated by some courts, notably the process-driven Group Litigation Order in England. Such CADR systems that operate this way are in general doing nothing unusual or inappropriate.

The largest CADR operation in Europe, the UK Financial Ombudsman Service, has developed specific systems to identify and process mass cases. In recent years around half of its caseload involves a number of mass issues, such as bank overdraft charges or payment protection insurance. It does not have an externally-facing 'collective procedure' that can be adopted by outside agents, such as lawyers or other representatives, but instead operates the 'collective procedures' itself internally. That situation should clearly have advantages in terms of reducing the transaction costs of processing mass claims.

[38] The efficiency consideration is behind the UK government's 2011 proposals to rationalise consumer advice bodies into a 'front line' based on Citizens Advice bodies (and regulators with a front line of trading Standards Services): see ch 11.

The FOS has no formal collective redress mechanisms, but has the flexibility to develop various strategies to address multiple claims. Strategies include, firstly, grouping similar cases so as to identify a lead case that can be resolved as a precedent and lead to formal resolution or voluntary settlement of the other cases, secondly, where cases turn on a point of law, referral of a test case to the court for its binding resolution, thirdly a 'wider implications' procedure where issues may be resolved by a regulator or through some ADR-style procedure.[39] However, cases do not always turn on a single issue.

The signal that a mass issue might arise can come from any external source or internal scrutiny. The selection of the appropriate handling procedure is left to the discretion of the CADR provider. Unlike a collective action in the courts, there is no need for formal procedures for declaration that particular procedures are appropriate, that certain issues or representatives are appropriate, or that certain evidence or hearings or settlements are appropriate: all these features are internalised.

A CADR provider may be very well placed to identify a mass issue at an early stage. Best operating practice in regular scrutiny of the subject matter of contacts, whether they are complaints or not, should enable generic issues to be identified at an early stage. It is possible that such identification may be earlier than that made by traders or regulators. It is clearly better to harness feedback mechanisms so as to reduce the number of complaints before they escalate. This requires regulatory intervention: the telecommunications regulators noted above for Lithuania and the UK are good examples of regulators that watch trends and take positive interventionist action.

The issue comes back to having links with regulators. CADR cannot resolve issues that a court or regulator should resolve. Changing the rules is a matter for parliaments, courts and regulators, not CADR bodies. Systems need to be designed that enable all these levers to work together.

There are two main challenges in dealing with mass issues: maintaining operational performance and ensuring that decisions are sufficiently consistent as between similar cases. Courts face the same problems. By their nature, mass issues concern a large number of individuals, and the sudden arrival of a significant increase in claims can result in an inability by CADR providers (as with courts or companies) in responding within previously set time limits. There is emerging evidence that collective actions in European jurisdictions are not capable of delivering outcomes with sufficient speed or proportionate cost.[40] What represents a 'mass issue' can involve different degrees of magnitude for different sectors. Of course, providers of products and services to mass markets can by definition affect many thousands of customers. On the other hand, holiday and travel companies may only have to deal with a few hundred passengers in an aircraft or guests at a hotel, although food contamination at a hotel can affect many people over time. CADR systems can and should be designed to be able to process multiple cases. Extra capacity can be sought by calling

[39] See ch 11 above.

[40] The experience of product liability cases in England shows that many failed because of poor merits, and lasted several years: see C Hodges, *Multi Party Actions* (Oxford: Oxford University Press, 2001). The largest mass litigation in England in the past decade, over injuries allegedly caused by the MMR vaccine, took 10 years and then collapsed before trial when it was clear that the vaccine was not the cause of the claimants' conditions. The German litigation of Deutsche Telekom investors under the 2005 Capital Investors Class Action Law (KapMuG) is likely to continue for 10 years. In contrast, the Dutch approach in the 2005 Class Action Settlement Law (WCAM), based on incentivising parties to negotiate settlement of their disputes, which are then made binding by the court, has proved to be attractive and largely efficient: see F Weber and WH van Boom, 'Dutch Treat: The Dutch Collective Settlement of Mass Damage Act', WCAM 2005, *Contratto e Impresa/Europa*, No 1, pp 69–79, 2011.

on similar CADR schemes' resources and expertise,[41] perhaps in the same sector in other countries or through EEC-NET and FIN-NET.

Variations in Effect: Persuasive or Binding?

Two issues arise. First, should a trader, or group of traders, be required to belong to a CADR scheme and, secondly, whether the conclusions of the CADR third party are binding or not on the trader and/or on the consumer.

CADR systems vary in the extent to which they are mandatory for traders, and this is often related to whether they are delivered by public and private entities. In relation to the first issue, the models are:

a. CADR is mandatory for all consumer traders, or for a specific sector of traders. The CADR function is usually located within a public body, often a regulatory authority, but sometimes a separate public body (such as the UK Financial Ombudsman Service). There is sometimes no scope for any other type of CADR body to exist, although sometimes public and private CADR bodies co-exist and there may be an element of overlap and competition. The UK FLA scheme tries to attract complaints so as to avoid them going to the Financial Ombudsman Service, and the French in-house energy company *médiateurs* try to resolve complaints that might go to the national *médiateur*.
b. CADR is mandatory for all consumer traders, or for a specific sector of traders, since the relevant traders are subject to a legal obligation to belong to a CADR scheme, but are free to choose which CADR scheme. Here, CADR services would typically be provided by one or more private sector bodies.
c. There is no legal requirement for traders to belong to any CADR scheme. CADR services will always be provided by private sector bodies, either by individual companies in-house (through customer care departments, or French *médiateurs*) or by external providers, often operating on a sectoral basis, and frequently being organised by a trade association.

Overall, C2B ADR schemes are therefore either imposed as binding on all traders in a sector (often funded by a levy on all) or exist with the voluntary support of the majority of traders in a sector, usually involving the relevant trade association.

In either event, decisions by the independent ADR provider may be binding on the trader: in the first case, because decisions are made binding by law, and in the second case, as a matter of prior voluntary acceptance by businesses, usually through their trade association. This prior voluntary acceptance of decisions that are formally only recommendations is a notable feature. The acceptance may be as a matter of contractual arrangements, as in the Netherlands (sequences of contracts between member companies and their trade associations, and then between the trade association and DGS), or as voluntary commitments (some UK and German schemes, again usually involving trade associations and companies). The result is an imaginative means of avoiding contravening Article 6 of the European Convention on Human Rights (see further below).

[41] An example here from England is where the trade association ABTA is able to provide extra resource to member companies that experience unexpected spikes in numbers of claims, for example after a company merger before systems have been rationalised.

This *de facto* one-sided binding effect (on business but not on consumer) is clearly an important aspect not only of the principle of independence but also an important factor in gaining consumer trust in the ADR system, as evidenced by the volume of its use. If consumers do not trust the independence of an ombudsman, they will not use him. These points are examined in greater detail below.

The proof of the effectiveness of a one-sided voluntary acceptance of binding effect is the extent to which traders comply with decisions in fact. Here, the Swedish figures are somewhat surprising: the average compliance rate is reported to be only 75 per cent, although in some sectors it is effectively 100 per cent. The UK figures seem to be higher. The approach that is most consumer-friendly is in the Netherlands, as a result of the trade association guarantee noted above.

Acceptance in advance—or after an award—is, however, not universal by business. The norm in France is that the 'principle of voluntary mediation' is relied on by many CADR schemes to justify the situation that recommendations are not automatically accepted as binding by sectors or companies. Business representatives in France say that even in such cases 90 per cent of recommendations by *médiateurs* are observed by traders.

Looking now at whether CADR is binding on consumers, in those schemes that involve arbitration the consumer has to agree at the time of lodging a complaint that she will accept the decision as binding, thereby waiving her right to raise the matter in court. The classic example is the Spanish arbitration scheme. This also arises under the UK's private code-based schemes. It should be noted that in some schemes, the impact of a consumer surrendering rights to a court claim may be of less impact where there is a preliminary conciliation stage that is, of course, not binding. However, those schemes that require waiver of rights for use of an arbitration process are not the model that is widely used: most schemes do not bind the consumer.

There is another interesting variant on the arrangements, which is found increasingly widely as mediation spreads across national civil procedure systems. This is that access to the courts is not denied but claimants are encouraged to use ADR as a first step. An example is the English Court rule that where a claimant institutes a claim in the courts but should reasonably have used an ADR approach, the claimant may be ordered not to recover his costs from the losing defendant and may also be ordered to pay the defendant's costs.[42] This preserves the consumer's right to access a court whilst encouraging use of CADR.

Conceptual Issues with CADR

The Basis of CADR Decisions: Law and Fairness

A feature on which national ombudsmen schemes differ is the extent to which they apply the law or some other standard. This raises the question: Should decisions be based on law or on some other criteria?

It might be thought that CADR schemes are based on applying standard consumer protection law. However, although all schemes inherently do apply the law, many go beyond

[42] Civil Procedure Rules, r 44.5(3).

the legal standards by applying either the provisions of codes of business practice, and/or by basing decisions on fairness or equity. By definition, codes of business practice should inherently include standards of trading practice that are required by the law, notably the 'UCP' Directive[43] and other measures of the Consumer *acquis*, now including the Consumer Rights Directive,[44] but they may, and usually do, set higher standards. Indeed, that is a major purpose of codes of practice.

The entire Netherlands geschillencommissie system is based on applying codes of practice, as are many CADR schemes in Germany, France and the UK.

The 2011 French Mediation Charter provides that a *médiateur* forms his opinion on the basis of law and equity,[45] and the Charter of FFSA provides that advice issued by the mediator shall be 'prepared taking into account elements of law and equity but also with the aim of achieving an amicable solution which cannot correspond to a judicial approach'.[46]

Including a 'fairness' or equity basis of decisions in the UK is widespread, for both statutory and private CADR schemes. The jurisdiction of the UK FOS is to base decisions on what is 'fair and reasonable' on a case by case basis, and to take into account relevant law and regulations, regulators' rules and codes of practice.[47] This is mirrored in the FLA's private Code. Principle 6 of the FSA's Principles for Businesses requires firms to treat customers fairly.[48] Similar rules on basing decisions on fairness apply to the Legal Ombudsman, the Housing Ombudsman and the Energy Ombudsman, and under the OFCOM requirements (which refer to law and equity).[49]

The banks, in particular, have long objected that the fairness criterion constitutes authority for the FOS to decide a dispute in a way that might differ from how a court might decide it, and possibly from the extensive regulatory rules to which they are subject. In other words, a court applies the law, whereas the FOS decides what seems fair and reasonable. The banks object that that difference produces a situation in which decisions of the FOS establish a 'separate universe' that may be inconsistent with the legal requirements, and one in which decisions can be difficult to predict, and in effect impose requirements retrospectively that can be higher than the legal requirements authorised by statute or by the statutory regulators. Hence cases may also be difficult to settle.

Arguments can be made on both sides of this debate. Firstly, do we not expect that decisions by any court or state-authorised independent decision-maker must be just, and that justice requires that the substance of the decision be fair and reasonable?[50] However, this broad philosophical approach is more difficult to apply when dealing with the minutiae of trading rules and standards. There can, indeed, be a difference between what is required practice under a rule of law and a practice standard, and hence what some might consider to be fair and reasonable at any particular time. Legal obligations on the terms or duration

[43] Directive 2005/29/EC of the European Parliament and of the Council concerning unfair business-to-consumer commercial practices in the internal market.

[44] Directive 2011/83/EU of the European Parliament and of the Council of 25 October 2011 on consumer rights, amending Council Directive 93/13/EEC and Directive 1999/44/EC of the European Parliament and of the Council and repealing Council Directive 85/577/EEC and Directive 97/7/EC of the European Parliament and of the Council.

[45] See ch 3 above.

[46] See p 53 above.

[47] DISP 3.5.4R.

[48] See FOS/FSA/OFT, Consumer Complaints (Emerging Risks and Mass Claims), 10/1 Discussion Paper, March 2010, p 9.

[49] See ch 11 above.

[50] A Sen, *The Idea of Justice* (London: Allen Lane, 2009).

of a manufacturer's guarantee, for example, may be extended beyond legal standards in a code, or voluntarily.

The rule of law, and promotion of predictable and consistent business practice, requires there to be one set of legal rules against which legal disputes should be decided. It may be constitutionally dangerous for a CADR system to decide the rights and wrongs of a dispute other than on the basis of the law. If a particular business, or sector, wishes to apply higher standards to their activities, that should be a matter for their self-determination, having defined what such standards are to be. If it is a legislator or regulator who wishes to apply a higher standard than current law, then the mechanism should be to change the law. Trying to achieve regulatory pressure through a 'fair and reasonable' test in dispute resolution has some attractions but on closer analysis essentially smacks of unfairness and cheating.

It may, however, be observed that the unfair commercial practices are prohibited by EU law, and that recourse to bodies that determine unfair practices under codes are encouraged.[51] Thus, fairness in commercial practice is a legal requirement, although that provision might be obscured by other more detailed requirements, especially in sectoral legislation and rules.

It is interesting to speculate whether there may be a difference in the legal approach between civil law and common law jurisdictions here. The concept of fair trading that emerged in the UCP Directive was based on civil law tradition and caused great concern to common lawyers, although the latter includes principles of equity. Regrettably such an inquiry is beyond the terms of this book.

There are, however, reasons of market policy why a CADR system may be designed to reach decisions that are based on market norms of fairness rather than the lower legal standards. One rationale is to enable prevailing market standards to be upheld if there is a 'legal lag', in other words a delay in amending the lower standards of the law. The dispute resolution system would, therefore, contribute to an objective of raising standards rather than upholding less acceptable behaviour.

Another rationale is based on consciously seeking to balance the well-known asymmetry of power between traders and consumers, in favour of the latter. Marc Galanter famously asserted that 'haves come out better than have nots in courts'.[52] he asserted that the good law is the law that delivers access to justice conceived as a justice that occurs in many rooms beyond the courtroom even when those rooms are rather sealed off one from the other.[53] Mechanisms such as the FOS were designed specifically as integral parts of regulatory systems, so as to frustrate repeat players' advantage and to impose as behavioural pressure on firms.

In summary, the position is somewhat confused, and it is difficult to reconcile the competing arguments of principle and policy. There are obvious good reasons why it is advantageous to be able to apply clear rules to resolve disputes, so as to provide certainty for both traders' behaviour and consumers' expectations. Hence, achieving consensus on

[51] Directive 2005/29/EC, Arts 5 and 10.

[52] 'Courts produce not only decisions but also messages. These messages are resources which parties use in envisioning, devising, negotiating and vindicating claims (and in avoiding, defending and defeating them).' M Galanter, 'Why the "Haves" Come Out Ahead: Speculations on the Limits of Legal Change' 9:1 *Law and Society Review* (1974) 165–230.

[53] M Galanter, 'Justice in Many Rooms', in M Cappelletti, (ed), *Access to Justice and the welfare State* (Alphen aan den Rijn: Sijthoff, 1981), 147; C Parker, *Just Lawyers: Regulation and Access to Justice* (Oxford: Oxford University Press, 1999), chs. 3 and 4; J Braithwaite and C Parker, 'Conclusion' in C Parker, C Scott, N Lacey and J Braithwaite, *Regulating Law* (Oxford University Press, 2004).

the rules that apply to particular circumstances should be achieved by having clear laws and codes. The philosophical conundrum of to what extent a court of CADR body can declare what a rule is, or whether that is a matter for a legislature or regulator, is perennial, and not resolved in the specific circumstances of CADR bodies any more than it is for courts. However, the issue of the relationship between CADR bodies and courts deserves further attention, to which we now turn.

Should CADR or Courts Decide the Law?

The German Insurance Ombudsman is careful to avoid making determinations of law, since that is regarded as the exclusive role of the courts. It is felt that if that Ombudsman were to make determinations that 'clarified' or differed from existing understanding of the law, he would first be acting unconstitutionally and secondly establishing a 'separate universe' of requirements that would affect business and consumers and which might be inconsistent with legal requirements.

The British Pensions Ombudsman can go further, and may refer any question of law to the court for determination.[54]

The logic of this position is that an ombudsman should not decide a dispute in which the law is unclear. Instead, the matter should be referred to the court for clarification, perhaps on a 'reference procedure' similar to that under which the Court of Justice (ECJ) operates. The issue is important if a national Constitution exists that provides for separation of powers of making law (the legislature), applying the law (the courts) and assisting in resolving disputes without trespassing into the other two areas.

The solution that a CADR system should not decide issues of law is supported by the fact that the strength of 'due process' requirements under a CADR procedure are normally less stringent than under the civil procedure of courts. As discussed below, the former may be constitutionally acceptable, but concerns would be higher if the CADR process were used to decide issues of law. Indeed, a major attraction of CADR is that it is appropriate, simple and swift in applying clear law to factual disputes, but it is not designed to deliberate on complex legal questions. The emerging position is that CADR is good for facts whereas courts are good for law. For relatively modest consumer claims, neither forum is particularly good at the other function. This involves a redefinition of roles that may be controversial, but is clearly emerging from current practice.

Our conclusion is, therefore, that a CADR system should not decide issues of law, which should be left for a court. However, if the relationship between CADR and court systems is to operate well, an important design point should be addressed. There is a need for a simple, effective, cheap and speedy mechanism under which a CADR body can refer cases to a suitable court for determination of the law (like the British Pensions Ombudsman). The procedure would be similar to a reference procedure between member State courts and the EU's Court of Justice.

The same logic would point to the need for a mechanism under which regulators or legislators may swiftly amend rules prospectively, so as to ensure clarity of the legal requirements. An example of this is provided by the practice of various regulated sectors, where issues that arise in CADR cases are considered by regulatory bodies, so that rules

[54] Pension Schemes Act 1993, s 105(7).

can be amended. The Lithuanian telecoms agency, for example holds regular meetings with providers for precisely this purpose.

Binding and Non-binding Decisions

Two issues arise here. Firstly, should it be a requirement for one or both parties to have, and use, an CADR scheme? Secondly, should the decisions of a CADR body be binding on one or both parties, or merely non-binding recommendations? The status of debate has partly answered these questions, so that the topical ones are: should a CADR system be binding on all traders, and should the outcome be binding on traders and/or businesses?

In almost all CADR schemes, consumers are not obliged to use a CADR scheme. It would be contrary to the EU unfair contract terms legislation,[55] Article 6 of the ECHR, and the Commission recommendations on ADR,[56] for a trader to seek to bind a consumer to CADR or arbitration before the time of sale. Such provisions are, of course, common in commercial contracts, but banned in B2C contracts because of the unequal bargaining power of the parties. It is only a state's courts that may issue decisions that are binding on any citizens, for which enforcement is backed by the state's exclusive coercive power.

It is legal for a consumer to agree after a dispute has arisen that it be resolved by binding arbitration. This is the position in various CADR arbitration schemes, as noted above. In some schemes, the consumer might access a conciliation function of an CADR scheme free (or at low cost) but is required to agree to binding arbitration if agreement is not reached and a decision is needed that is binding on the trader.

On the other hand, a trader can contractually agree to CADR on a standing basis that will apply to all consumers. This is wide practice in those schemes where the result is not already biding by law. The Netherlands scheme goes further, so payment of any sums ordered by the CADR body to the consumer is guaranteed by the trade association, which has a contractual right to collect it from its member firm.

However, the French Charter maintains that a trader has to be free to refer a dispute to a CADR scheme or not, and will not be bound by any recommendation. The arguments are made that a trader is otherwise locked into accepting every nuisance claim, and that traders accept decisions voluntarily *after* they are made in the vast majority of situations. There is a wide fear amongst some sectors of business that the risk of unjustified consumer claims is significant. However, it is striking that the attitude of the companies discussed in Chapter 12 take exactly the opposite view in their customer care policies, which are designed positively to attract all customer contacts. Their finding is that the incidence of unjustified claims is so low as to be negligible, and not worth bothering with in practice. They do operate some anti-fraud checks, but these are designed to prevent repeat claims rather than to discourage claims *per se*.

The clear majority practice in Nordic states (in Sweden traders are bound unless they object within 30 days), the Netherlands, Germany and the UK is that CADR decisions are not binding on consumers but are binding on traders either by law or by prior voluntary acceptance. Estonia and Portugal consider it is not constitutional for decisions to be binding.

[55] Case C-168/05 Mostazo Claro [2006] ECR I-10421 and Case C-40/08 *Asturcom Telecomunicaciones SL v Cristina Rodríguez Nogueira* [2009] ECR I-9579.

[56] Commission Recommendation of 30 March 1998 on the principles applicable to the bodies responsible for out-of-court settlement of consumer disputes (98/257/EC), principle VI.

Even though decisions may not be binding on consumers, they may, of course, face difficulties in objecting to an adverse decision. If the consumer subsequently takes the claim to court, the courts may well be expected to follow the decision of an established CADR provider, perhaps even imposing a costs sanction on the consumer for bringing the case.

It is sometimes noted that the conclusions of public sector ombudsmen are not binding on the public administration. There is an important distinction, however, between disputes between citizens and the state, and those between public parties. The reasons for the difference is that it is not constitutionally appropriate for the discretion on the executive branch of a state to be subject to external authorities. A state entity should have power that includes a margin of discretion to reach decisions, since many conflicting factors may have to be balanced. The state's exercise of power should only be subject to the confines of its constitutional power, as reviewed by the appropriate court, and should be subject to democratic scrutiny by parliament. Public sector ombudsmen are invariably appointed by, and report to, parliaments, so their recommendations may be adopted voluntarily by the administration, but if not the administration will be answerable to parliament but not to the parliament's investigatory ombudsman. Thus, the functions of public and private sector ombudsmen are significantly different. An argument cannot be made that just because public ombudsmen's decisions are not binding, the decisions of private sector ombudsmen should not be binding. The argument that private sector ombudsmen's decisions should be binding on traders is, indeed, strengthened when part of their function is viewed as being regulatory, in the public interest.

Underlying this debate is the practical issue of whether business wishes consumers to trust CADR schemes, and therefore to use them. Consumer trust may be significantly dented where business does not accept an advance binding effect. The issue is more one of practice than principle. Our findings indicate that there is a clear link between CADR schemes in which traders are bound to accept the decision and the level of consumer trust in the scheme, which is usually reflected in the level of complaints directed to the scheme. This effect can be seen from the statistics compared in chapter 14.

The conclusion is that current best practice in Sweden, Germany, UK and the Netherlands is that decisions are binding on traders, whether this result is imposed by statute or accepted voluntarily. It is open to legislators to impose requirements that membership of CADR schemes by consumer traders, and observance of decisions by properly constituted ombudsmen, is mandatory. That solution would have clear advantages in relation to the use of CADR schemes. If a mandatory legal solution does not emerge, we urge businesses across Europe to adopt this standard, which should assist in building consumer trust and in supporting business.

Compliance

If ombudsmen's decisions are 'binding' on traders, a further practical question is how to ensure that decisions are in fact complied with by business. Various models are found:

a. **Dutch-style trade association guarantees**: the trade association contracts with DGS that it will guarantee all decisions, and contracts with its members that they will indemnify such guarantee. Thus, if, as happens only very rarely, a trader refuses to pay on an adverse decision, the trade association will pay the consumer and claim reimbursement from its member, probably then expelling the member from membership of the association. That mechanism is extremely effective, but does not cover traders who are not members of an association (assuming the association is part of the Geschillencommissie structure, which may be true in the Netherlands but might not be so if the system were to be copied in other states). The answer in the Netherlands is that traders will be 'named and shamed' by the press.

b. **A 'name and shame' technique**, used in Sweden but also elsewhere, again operated not by the ARN but by media take-up of a published list.
c. **Enlisting pressure from a regulator**. This is especially relevant for rogue traders and where there has been a significant and continuing breach of the law.
d. **An intermediary who blocks trading**, such as under a chargeback mechanism, where media decline to carry advertisements banned by an advertising standards body, or a decision on domain name ownership by WIPO.
e. **Fast track enforcement in the courts**. Since ADR telescopes the evidence-gathering process, there could be a leapfrog procedure (leaping the evidence-gathering stage) for enforcement of ombudsmen's non-binding decisions: new evidence and an objective assessment would be guaranteed.

An issue that has arisen in our discussions in several countries is that some traders (and the airline sector was mentioned frequently[57]) do not comply with CADR decisions. In countries such as Spain, such traders do not agree to use the arbitration process. This raises the issue of whether particular sectors need some compulsion, as occurs for example for financial services.

Due Process Issues for CADR

CADR systems *can* deliver speedy, low cost and effective dispute resolution. In this context, courts should not be seen as separate, but as one dispute resolution option, alongside CADR providers. The fact that courts are usually more expensive and slower than CADR systems, as well as being less user-friendly, is a key reason for the success of good CADR systems. This is not to argue for the obsolescence of courts in B2C disputes. Indeed, it is the continued existence of courts that provides an incentive for both the establishment *and the ongoing use* of CADR systems. There is both an element of competition here, and a 'shadow of the law' phenomenon.

The rules of civil procedure (formality of proceedings) that are considered to be a requirement for the acceptable operation of courts give rise to certain levels of cost and duration. Attempts to simplify and avoid such procedural guarantees, such as through Small Claims procedures and use of mediation alongside court claims, can only be taken so far without offending requirements of procedural justice, such as due process.

In contrast, many consumer complaints are of such a nature that they can be resolved through procedures that involve less formality than would be required for courts, and hence deliver advantages of speed, low and proportionate cost, and informality and little effort for those involved. They typically involve well-established rules of law, terms and conditions, or provisions of a code of business practice, and relatively straightforward factual aspects. But CADR systems still need to satisfy parameters of justice: there is a balance to be struck between requirements and efficiency. This raises the issue of what essential requirements

[57] See *ECC-Net Air Passenger Rights Report 2011* (The European Consumer Centres' Network, 2011).

are necessary for CADR systems, in order for them to operate acceptably in terms of the requirements of procedural justice.

It has been found above that some CADR systems have evolved, and that some of the older models are closer to court-style mechanisms, and hence process cases lore slowly than more recent models. There is clear variation in the speed and cost of CADR systems, and their ability to satisfy key parameters, such as independence. The result is a striking variation in the attractiveness to consumers and the uptake and *use* of a system by consumers. Where the key parameters are satisfied, use will be considerable, and the system will be highly effective.

The tension is between procedural guarantees of due process versus customer demands for speedy resolution of their disputes. On one view, due process requirements have been dangerously ignored by some CADR models. On another view, contemporary ideas about how the principles of procedural justice should apply to dispute resolution procedures have clearly evolved. It is no longer the case that the procedure necessarily has to look like that of a court, with an ordered sequence of investigation and presentation of evidence and arguments, and a hearing in the presence of all parties, with rules on admissibility and forms. Indeed, the fact that 'corners can be cut' in traditional civil procedures in the context of CADR is what gives rise to the new processes being able to realise the benefits of increased speed, lower cost, and increased user-friendliness.

However, the question should be asked: what essential requirements of procedural justice and protection of human rights should still apply to new forms of dispute resolution? How many corners can validly be cut?

The procedural steps that occur in consumer CADR systems can be analysed as follows:

a. *Lodging a claim*. An explanation of what the dispute is about needs to be done concisely and clearly. The procedure needs to be user-friendly, and many CADR providers offer on-line facilities. In order to enhance consumer accessibility and trust in CADR, as well as increased knowledge of the availability of CADR generally, we recommend that a standard claim form is agreed at EU level, made available through guidance rather than under law, so it can be adopted to particular types of claim, and evolved, as necessary.
b. *Presentation of evidence*. Many ombudsmen have asserted to us that the evidence and assertions in most consumer disputes are limited and straightforward. The evidence should usually have been identified between the parties during the direct-negotiation phase prior to lodging a claim with a CADR body. Consumers and traders are often able to lodge documents on-line.
c. *Obtaining expertise*. Two approaches are adopted by CADR bodies. In some, the ombudsman (and staff) has the necessary expertise personally: examples are the German Insurance Ombudsman, who is a distinguished professor of law, and who is familiar with almost all issues that arise. In other systems, the ombudsman may have legal training, but it is necessary to obtain external assistance from an independent expert who is familiar with the subject matter: an example of this is under the British motor vehicle code system, where an engineer might be instructed to visit the vehicle, or repair facility, make an inspection and report. The expert may be trained in mediation, and able to assist the parties in reaching settlement on such a site visit. Otherwise, the expert reports back to the ombudsman, and his report is made available to the parties. A comment by one of the British car scheme operators was that in a dispute over whether a repair used new or used parts, an expert can often decide the case simply by looking at a photograph.

d. Evaluation. This function is performed by the neutral party as soon as all relevant information is available. It involves examining the facts and applying the relevant rules (law or code) to the issues that are raised. It is performed in the same way whether that neutral party is subsequently to perform the function of mediator or adjudicator, ie whether the view that he or she takes of the merits of the case are to be binding or not binding on the parties.

e. Enforcement or follow-up. It is not the normal function of neutral CADR parties to provide an enforcement function after they have delivered their recommendation or decision on the merits—unlike a court. However, some CADR systems include a means either of ensuring that traders observe decisions (these means are discussed below in relation to issues over binding decisions), and/or a means of checking whether they do so.

Key features that enhance the efficiency of CADR systems are:

a. a model in which adversarialism is minimised,
b. a lack of formality,
c. use of streamlined and especially online procedures,
d. absence of oral arguments, legal representation, or hearings at which all parties are present, and
e. sectoral expertise.

The Purpose and Nature of CADR

At this point, a strenuous debate should be noted for and against the use of alternative dispute resolution methods, whether generically or individually, as against maintaining the primacy or exclusivity of state courts as the proper forum for deciding issues of law and rights. It is not the function of this book to enter into that debate, but the empirical finding that CADR systems are now so widely used and growing cannot but have an effect on that debate.

The debate involves examination of the function of dispute resolution, and of what outcomes people are seeking.[58] Some of the options are:

- resolution of a grievance
- vindication of rights: rectification of a wrong done in breach of a right
- rectification of loss; restoration of *status quo ante*
- declaration that a respondent has acted contrary to an accepted standard of conduct; 'vindication'
- public upholding of a norm of society
- public imposition of a sanction
- triggering of wider public sanctioning, eg by a regulator
- day in court: being listened to, irrespective of outcome
- exposure of widespread irregularity, with a view to cessation and behaviour modification
- deterrence: of the specific respondent and generally of the actors in the sector

[58] M Galanter, 'Why the "Haves" Come Out Ahead: Speculations on the Limits of Legal Change' 9:1 *Law and Society Review* (1974) 165–230.

An important attack on ADR in general comes from the viewpoint that determinations of civil and human rights recognised and upheld by the state should be the exclusive preserve of state institutions. Some are concerned that the law itself will not be clarified and developed if court determinations reduce in number. Further, privatised resolution procedures can result in outcomes that have little to do with the rights involved, and raise concerns about the risk of abuse flowing from imbalances of power. Debate can polarise around whether enforcement of law should be dominated by concerns of efficiency or of justice, and the constitutional implications.[59]

Different methods of dispute resolution may be more appropriate for different objectives and functions, and discussion has altered the ADR acronym to talk of 'appropriate' dispute resolution.[60] The use of mediation has been strongly criticised by some as an alternative to court adjudication.[61] Mediation has strong advantages in the right circumstances, such as where it is important for the parties to avoid an adversarial confrontation and to restore bilateral relations and communication.[62] Hence, it can be useful in disputes involving families and children. In the C2B situation, it is often the trader who wishes to retain a relationship with its customer, and hence wishing to make the CADR pathway attractive to the customer, rather than the other way around.

Some general points can be made from this study over how CADR compares with the courts. The essential advantages of CADR in relation to courts can be:[63] speed, accessibility, informality, expertise, lower cost to the state (but sometimes internalised cost to the sector), potentially lower regulatory burden, and increased motivation.[64] The disadvantages of CADR can include failure to deliver just outcomes, lack of accountability or transparency, failure to act in the public interest (and even continuation of anti-competitive rents), and lack of performance or inefficiency.

The extent to which CADR offers advantages and disadvantages compared with the courts differs from country to country. One important factor is the extent to which the national courts are speedy and operate with low and predictable costs. It has been noted above that countries that have efficient and low cost courts (such as those similar to the German civil law system) have developed CADR to a lesser extent than countries where the courts are slow and where costs are unpredictable and disproportionate (such as common law jurisdictions like UK). Accordingly, extensive CADR mechanisms have developed more quickly in some jurisdictions, notably the UK, the Netherlands and the Nordic states. Italy also has its own form of CADR, since its courts are hopelessly clogged and slow. Another key consideration is whether legal advice can be given only by lawyers (as in Germany) or also by others (which contributed to historical development of advice and dispute resolution schemes by trade unions and business in the Netherlands and the UK).

[59] See generally C Menkel-Meadow, 'Dispute Resolution' in P Cane and HM Kritzer, *The Oxford Handbook of Empirical Legal Research* (Oxford, Oxford University Press, 2010).

[60] ibid.

[61] R Verkijk, 'Mandatory Mediation: Informal *In*justice?' in A Uzelac and CH van Rhee (eds), *Public and Private Justice. Dispute Resolution in Modern Societies* (Antwerp: Intersentia, 2007); H Genn, *Judging Civil Justice. The Hamlyn Lectures 2008* (Cambridge: Cambridge University Press, 2010).

[62] S Roberts and M Palmer, *Dispute Processes. ADR and the Primary Forms of Decision-Making* (Cambridge: Cambridge University Press, 2005).

[63] CH van Rhee and A Uzelac (eds), *Civil Justice between Efficiency and Quality: from Ius Commune to the CEPEJ* (Antwerp: Intersentia, 2008).

[64] CJS Hodges, S Vogenauer and M Tulibacka, *The Costs and Funding of Civil Litigation. A Comparative Perspective* (Oxford: Hart Publishing, 2010).

ADR as an Essential Aspect of Regulation and Behaviour Control

It has been noted that although some CADR techniques are stand-alone dispute resolution procedures, many CADR schemes operate as an integral part of a wider regulatory scheme. Overall, it is entirely misleading to view many dispute resolution mechanisms on their own, without considering the broader context of how they operate within a system that is primarily intended to deliver control of behaviour and in which resolution of disputes is a secondary consideration, albeit a necessary and desirable one. In simple terms, therefore, the dispute resolution function is the 'back end' of a system of regulation, or self-regulation, that is primarily focused on the 'front end' of maintaining a standard of general business practice, and disputes that arise over such practice are funnelled towards the tailor-made resolution system that accompanies the regulatory system.

Accordingly, it is both misleading and unnecessarily limiting to consider a CADR technique merely in terms of its dispute resolution function alone. Such a function is, of course, important, and it is relevant to ask to what extent a CADR technique is successful in delivering effective, efficient and desirable resolutions to disputes. But it is also important to ask other questions. Does the technique deliver *ex post* controls on the behaviour of individuals, businesses and governments? Does it deliver preventative justice, through reducing the number of disputes that arise, or the number of instances of undesirable behaviour, thereby acting as an *ex ante* control? Does it provide feedback for system operators, or those responsible for external governance of the system or operator, of the quality system and quality control of the operator's activities? Hence, does the dispute resolution system enable quality monitoring, improvement, and compliance?

Further, in designing modern dispute resolution systems, the opportunity to specify a system in which the architecture and functionality can deliver appropriate and reasonable behaviour control outcomes, as well as resolution of disputes, is a crucial goal and design feature that should not be overlooked. Overall, the norm is that CADR systems are now usually designed so as to provide regulatory outcomes.

Some systems appear to be particularly successful at contributing to a low incidence of disputes nationally. Good examples are Sweden and the Netherlands. The Swedish model relies strongly on providing easily accessible expert consumer advice, both before purchase decisions are made and after complaints arise. There is also the collaborative attitude of many traders, and their ability to reach solutions with customers. The general incidence of problems appears to be reduced by these mechanisms, and the number of claims that reach the ARN appears to be low.

In the Netherlands, compliance by traders with agreed standards appears to be achieved by the *ex ante* model of agreeing terms and conditions in advance, thereby being the key that opens the door to the official CADR process. The trade associations function to remind their members of the agreed rules, and this seems to involve a low level of non-compliances and enforcement action. Note it was only recently that the Netherlands saw the need (partly imposed on it by an EU requirement) to create a Consumer Authority. A major function of such a public authority is to use harder enforcement techniques against traders who are *outside* the Geschillencommissie system, or otherwise behave in a manner that takes them 'off the reservation'.

The British model relies on extensive self-regulation involving trade associations and codes. The pressure for compliance exerted on their own members by, for example, ABTA, is striking, and includes imposition of sanctions, thereby avoiding formal enforcement by public authorities, who are in any event involved in the code committees. In contrast, the German *ex post* model operates on the basis that traders work on their own terms and conditions, but the trade practice association and consumer associations are active and speedy in raising non-compliance issues, backed by the right to seek an injunction in case of breach.

Capturing and Using Market Information

A major potential advantage of any dispute resolution system is that it can identify behaviour that requires attention, and set precedents for future behaviour. CADR systems have a particularly strong potential in this respect, arising from their ability to aggregate data from multiple individual inquires and complaints. Their ability to achieve this arises from modern information technology systems. The data that is valuable is not just the nature of issues raised and decided in any decisions (the relatively few that reach the top of the pyramid of the process, for which formal decisions are taken), but also those involved in the mass of contacts that constitute the bottom of the pyramid. Theoretically, courts could disclose their 'entry level' data, and some do, but the focus of courts is on the content of a relatively small number of decisions that reach the top, output stage and provide important legal precedents. In this respect, CADR systems can far exceed the mass regulatory capability of courts, since, as mentioned above, a primary focus of courts is on clarifying the law.

The market has moved from issues about small individual issues to extensive implications about major products that have huge commercial value.[65] This development calls for a re-examination of what forum is appropriate to deal with large and small issues: the legislature, court, regulator, trade association, individual business, committee, consumers and the market?

ADR systems can provide data that provides the relevant behavioural (regulatory) information. Further, they can provide such information cheaply, quickly and efficiently. ADR systems therefore represent major opportunities to reduce the number of legal problems before they proliferate, as well as a means of self-regulation in relation to ongoing behaviour. Designing ADR systems that provide both dispute resolution and regulatory functions can save a great deal of resource on enforcement. What is needed is for them to operate as a Quality Management System for business.

CADR schemes can provide an 'early warning system' that identifies emerging trends and addresses the issues before undesirable effects escalate and proliferate. Such issues may be non-compliance with law (such as excessive bank charges or dangerous products), the need for new or more elaborated rules, or merely changes in behaviour that would improve situations even if no breach of law has occurred. Issues may relate to general trends in a market, or the fact that the operations of individual traders give rise to concern. Many ombudsmen commented to us that many consumer cases involve misunderstandings, and this can be identified and sorted out by better communication.

The mechanism by which CADR systems produce the relevant data is based simply on the principle of transparency. There is a clear trend for CADR schemes to publish data on the issues that arise in their caseloads, and sometimes on individual traders. In order to give a complete picture, of course, such market data need to be aggregated with similar complaint data received by regulators.

[65] N Huls, 'Consumer Bankruptcy: A Third Way between Autonomy and Paternalism in Private Law' (2010) 3.1 *Erasmus Law Review* 7, at www.erasmuslawreview.nl/files/ELR_2010-1_03_Consumer_Bankruptcy.pdf.

Should it be regulators that publish the names of individual companies? This already occurs in some countries, where it is regarded as an essential behavioural tool, which increases pressure on those firms who rely on high market reputations, reducing the need for public authorities to take formal enforcement steps that would be more expensive. The FOS published complaints data that identified individual traders, and this had a profound effect. It showed that 50 per cent of the complaints that it handled came from just four banks out of 100,000. The media publicity and pressure from regulators resulted in the four (and others) paying more attention to improving their complaint handling.

It may be simple for disclosure of companies' names to be made, but this may also be disproportionately costly and even misleading in some circumstances. An example of the misleading effect is that quoted in Chapter 11 where complaint data held by public agencies seemed to indicate a problem with motor vehicles but when the substance of the data was examined it was found that the majority of 'complaints' were requests for information.

We recommend that ADR systems should be designed to operate so as to achieve regulatory outputs. We suggest that the issue of how much information should be disclosed is a matter for consideration in the circumstances of a particular sector and scheme.

The ability to deliver feedback information that can be used to improve regulatory compliance at proportionate cost could be immensely useful for small and medium-sized enterprises (SMEs). SMEs account for 99 per cent of enterprises, of which 92 per cent are micro-enterprises, and provide more than two thirds of private sector employment.[66] It is well-recognised that 'businesses, in particular SMEs, often lack clarity about how to comply with regulation'.[67] A 'Key Finding' of research by the UK's OFT in 2010 was:

> In general businesses seek to treat consumers fairly although they may have a limited understanding of the law. SMEs in particular are likely to have less awareness of the detail of consumer protection laws, and how they can access relevant information to assist compliance. Larger businesses are more likely to understand the detail of the laws but may have different drivers for not complying.[68]

EU studies have found that 'the smallest firms face the greatest costs in complying with regulations',[69] a view echoed in national studies.[70] For example, UK government research into health and safety regulation found that, on a per employee basis, SMEs may be spending almost six times more than larger ones on risk assessment.[71]

Noting SMEs' limited capacities and resource, and the crucial relevance of SMEs in stimulating economic growth, as part of the EU's core economic strategy,[72] the European Commission has proposed:

[66] *Report from the Commission to the Council and the European Parliament Minimizing regulatory burden for SMEs Adapting EU regulation to the needs of micro-enterprises*, COM(2011) 803, 23.11.2011, http://ec.europa.eu/governance/better_regulation/documents/minimizing_burden_sme_EN.pdf.

[67] *Delivering regulatory reform. Report by the Comptroller and Auditor General* (National Audit Office, 2011), available at www.nao.org.uk/idoc.ashx?docId=89f6cf32-eeeb-4f0a-b862-d5a9feec4388&version=-1.

[68] *Consumer Law and Business Practice. Drivers of compliance and non-compliance* (Office of Fair Trading, 2010), OFT1225, available at www.oft.gov.uk/shared_oft/reports/Evaluating-OFTs-work/OFT1225.pdf.

[69] *Report from the Commission to the Council and the European Parliament Minimizing regulatory burden for SMEs Adapting EU regulation to the needs of micro-enterprises*, COM(2011) 803, 23.11.2011, http://ec.europa.eu/governance/better_regulation/documents/minimizing_burden_sme_EN.pdf.

[70] 'micro businesses … can find the cost of regulatory compliance to be disproportionately high, placing additional calls on scarce resources': *Lightening the Load: The Regulatory Impact on UK's Smallest Businesses* (Department for Business Innovation and Skills, 2010), available at www.bis.gov.uk/assets/biscore/better-regulation/docs/l/10-1251-lightening-the-load-regulatory-impact-smallest-businesses.pdf.

[71] *Improving Outcomes from Health and Safety* (Better Regulation Executive, 2008).

[72] Communication from the Commission 'Europe 2020 – A strategy for smart, sustainable and inclusive growth' COM(2010) 2020.

> There needs to be a special effort to promote the development of SMEs, a major source of economic growth and job creation in the Union, accounting for more than 67 % of private sector jobs and providing more than 58 % of total turnover in the EU.[73]

In implementing this policy, the Commission has stated that the regulatory burden needs to be minimized.[74] Further, providing information and advice to economic operators (especially SMEs) is a legitimate function of Member States that needs to be given a greater priority.[75] The approach here exactly mirrors that identified in this book in relation to empowering consumers: finding and effective and efficient means of providing information on appropriate market behaviour and trends to SMEs (as for consumers and traders generally) will assist with regulatory compliance, reduce the need for (and hence cost of) enforcement, and increase customer satisfaction.

What Criteria Should Apply to CADR?

Requirements for CADR systems have been established by EU Recommendations of 1998[76] and 2001.[77] The titles and purposes of these two recommendations are somewhat confusing. They are in fact directed at different types of CADR: the 1998 Recommendation was directed at CADR bodies involved in resolving disputes that were proceeding *within the court system*, whereas the 2001 Recommendation was focused on bodies that handle disputes *outside the court system*. The latter is obviously now more relevant for what has become a separate and distinct world of CADR systems. Nevertheless, the principles applicable to such bodies should overlap to a great extent, if not be identical, not least because the CADR providers often provide both types of service, and there is no reason in principle why the principles applicable to them should differ.

We now seek to review the principles set out in the two Recommendations, and to apply these requirements to the national systems that we have researched, noting major compliances and issues, and other matters that might be relevant to provide as further requirements.

The 1998 Recommendation, which is at Appendix 1, established the following 'principles':

I. Independence: guaranteeing the impartiality of the decision-making body.
II. Transparency: appropriate measures must be taken, including:
III. Adversarial: allowing all the parties to present their viewpoint and to hear the arguments and facts put forward by the other party, and any experts' statements.
IV. Effectiveness.

[73] Proposal for a Regulation of the European Parliament and of the Council establishing a Programme for the Competitiveness of Enterprises and small and medium-sized enterprises (2014–2020), COM(2011) 834 final, available at http://eur-lex.europa.eu/LexUriServ/LexUriServ.do?uri=COM:2011:0834:FIN:EN:PDF.

[74] ibid.

[75] *The future of market surveillance in the area of non-food consumer product safety under the General Product Safety Directive*, (BSI, 2011), *http://ec.europa.eu/consumers/safety/projects/docs/final_report_the_future_of_market_surveillance.pdf*.

[76] Commission Recommendation of 30 March 1998 on the principles applicable to the bodies responsible for out-of-court settlement of consumer disputes (98/257/EC), available at http://eur-lex.europa.eu/LexUriServ/LexUriServ.do?uri=OJ:L:1998:115:0031:0034:EN:PDF.

[77] Commission Recommendation of 4 April 2001 on the principles for out-of-court bodies involved in the consensual resolution of consumer disputes (2001/310/EC), available at http://ec.europa.eu/consumers/redress/out_of_court/adr/acce_just12_en.pdf.

V. Legality.
VI. Liberty: The decision taken by the body concerned may be binding on the parties only if they were informed of its binding nature in advance and specifically accepted this.
VII. Representation: the procedure does not deprive the parties of the right to be represented or assisted by a third party at all stages of the procedure.

The above principles are examples of their historical context. They were written at a time in which the model of dispute resolution that people had in mind was a court, involving well-established constitutional principles of procedural justice, and involving representation by lawyers. In addition, the CADR system that was held in mind was one that operated in a similar fashion to a court. The findings of this study have shown that requirements that CADR systems be adversarial and involve legal representation and hearings with full opportunity to hear all evidence are clearly out of place in relation to CADR systems.

At the present time, however, that context has evolved significantly, driven by market practice. Complaints about the non-involvement of lawyers and various other developments are not heard from consumers or their representatives (although they may be uttered by lawyers, such as the 2010 dispute in Italy in which lawyers went on strike at their exclusion under the proposed implementation of the Mediation Directive. The dispute was settled by requiring lawyers' involvement. That solution may be expected to defeat wide use of the mediation procedure in Italy, and hence be economically self-defeating for lawyers as citizens decline to use CADR.)

The 2001 Recommendation was designed for out-of-court bodies involved in the consensual resolution of consumer disputes: hence, it was intended to apply to 'new forms' of ADR bodies and not courts. The model was that of conciliation and/or mediation, but not arbitration or any form of binding process: 'procedures that … attempt to resolve a dispute by bringing the parties together to convince them to find a solution by common consent'.[78] The principles that apply here were said to be:

A. Impartiality.
B. Transparency.
C. Effectiveness.
D. Fairness.

It will be seen that there is some inconsistency between the 1998 and 2001 Recommendations. In the European Commission's 2011 proposal, the four 2001 criteria were repeated without further elaboration: entities should offer impartial, transparent, effective and fair ADR procedures.[79]

Proposed Essential Requirements and KPIs

We find that society and the market are looking for CADR schemes to satisfy both particular criteria, or *essential requirements*, and also to meet certain performance standards, or *key performance indicators* (KPIs). The former govern the acceptability of the process from the point of view of justice. The latter are more concerned with the performance quality

[78] para I.1.

[79] Proposal for a Directive of the European Parliament and of the Council on alternative dispute resolution for consumer disputes and amending regulation (EC) No 2006/2004 and Directive 2009/22/EC (Directive on consumer ADR), COM(2011) 793, 29.11.2011, Art 1.

of an individual scheme, and would enable performance to be overseen and comparisons to be made between different schemes. It should, however, be recognised that the same performance levels should not be applied to every scheme. Some schemes handle cases that are inherently short and simple (such as non-delivery of goods), and others handle complex and lengthy ones (such as pensions). This is shown from the data collated in Chapter 14. It is also recognised in the UK system that KPIs are agreed annually between some regulators and individual schemes (see Chapter 11).

The Commission's recommendations were drafted over 10 years ago, when CADR was far less developed and there was almost no sign of ODR, and they should be refreshed in the light of the current environment.

Further, the principles applicable to a CADR system should be the same as apply to any other validly constituted legal dispute resolution mechanism—especially a court. *All* DR systems should be evaluatable against their own essential requirements and KPIs—so that CADR systems and courts and any other system can be compared by users, so as to provide information on how to exercise free choice. There has been some discussion of such criteria.[80]

We propose that the following essential requirements should apply to *all* dispute resolution (DR) systems, including CADR and courts:

Proposed Essential Requirements

1. Accessibility

a. The DR system should be visible to potential users.
b. Its procedures, costs and duration should be clear in advance of use, and be proportionate.
c. The service should be free to consumers.
d. It should provide a service in all languages appropriate to the nature of disputes that it purports to handle.

2. Requirements of justice

a. Confidence and trust. Every DR system should maintain the confidence of the public and not attract disrepute.
b. Impartiality and independence. Both those responsible for the DR system and those involved in making decisions should be independent of all who might have an interest in the outcome, and should demonstrably have no conflict of interest. Decisions should be manifestly impartial.
c. Transparent Rationality. Reasons should be given for decisions.
d. Consistency. Decisions involving similar subject matter should be consistent and sufficiently predictable. Consistency should apply both to decisions of the particular DR system and to decisions made by similar DR systems.
e. Fairness. Decisions should conform to principles of justice and fairness. Systems should not attract unmeritorious claims, and should identify them and stop them at an early stage.

[80] See C Hodges, 'Towards Parameters for EU Civil Justice Systems' in S Vogenauer and C Hodges (eds), *Civil Justice Systems in Europe: Implications for Choice of Forum and Choice of Contract Law* (Oxford: Hart Publishing, 2012); C Hodges, 'Public and Private Enforcement: The Practical Implications for Policy Architecture' in R Brownsword, H-W Micklitz, L Niglia and S Weatherill (eds), *The Foundations of European Private Law* (Oxford: Hart Publishing, 2011).

f. Competence. The DR system should not make decisions on issues or cases for which it does not have competence, or for which another DR system would be more appropriate.
g. Confidentiality. Confidential information of the parties should be maintained during the DR process. Once a decision is reached, the outcome should be available. At that stage, parties should be able to assert the continuing confidentiality of facts that are subject to legal obligations of confidentiality.

3. Effectiveness
a. The DR system should deliver outcomes appropriate to its role.
b. The duration of its procedures should be proportionate and acceptable, given the nature of the subject matter.
c. The cost of the system as a whole, and the fees payable in individual cases should be proportionate to the service provided and the disputes for which it is intended.
d. Decisions should be binding on traders.
e. The system should provide for an adequate level of compliance with its decisions.

4. Accountability and verification
a. There should be appropriate and transparent oversight mechanisms, to provide democratic and social confidence in the process and in its outcomes.
b. The ADR provider should publish at least annually data on:
   i. its KPIs (the number of claims received, how they were processed, what resolutions were achieved, how long they took, and what the costs were)
   ii. claims handled, in agreed formats, identifying types of claims, urgent issues, whether the traders complied with any agreements or determinations.

Proposed KPIs

We propose that the following *KPIs* should be applied, so that the performance of ADR providers may have democratic accountability. These are matters of operational data, such as on:

1. Claims data:
a. the number of claims received,
b. how they were processed,
c. what resolutions were achieved,
d. how long they took,
e. whether the traders complied with any agreements or determinations,
f. what type of issues were raised,
g. which companies were involved,
h. what significant issues were raised.

2. The costs of the system.

Architectural Issues

This section addresses the issue of the design of CADR systems at national, or supranational, levels. The starting point is the finding that many of the existing national CADR systems in European States are different, and there is no obvious unified or best national model. The questions therefore arise: what models or features might be best? Is full sectoral coverage necessary? If it is, how can more extensive coverage and use be created? What is the minimum size, and optimal size, for regulatory, CADR and court systems? Can some small Member States, and their businesses, afford or cope with the infrastructure necessary for multi-sectoral CADR services?

Centralised and Sectoral Schemes

No state included in this study has *only* a single, integral CADR scheme that processes every type of C2B claim. In that respect, the architecture of CADR systems differs somewhat from courts: every state has a single court system, effectively operating as a monopoly provider of justice, even if individual courts may have special jurisdictions and be geographically decentralised. There are, of course, national models in which there is a central national CADR body that can accept any type of cases, but this always acts as a residual rather than exclusive body, and its existence does not preclude the existence of other, and hence competing, CADR bodies, which are usually organised on a sectoral basis and sometimes regionally (Spain and France).

The advantages of having sectoral schemes include:

- expertise in the type of dispute and hence less need for technical evidence, and so quicker and more informed decisions, which will be useful for sectors that have a high degree of technicality, that consumers may not posses;
- suitability of the technique to the regulatory architecture of the sector, such as the ability of the CADR body to integrate more effectively with a sectoral regulatory body;
- application of practice or standards that appear relevant for the firms in the sector.

The disadvantages can be:

- the standards of the dispute resolution process, or of business practice in the sector, remain insulated from general standards and are below a required standard: this is a form of 'capture' of the process by the sector;
- the existence of a diverse range of options for redress can confuse consumers and businesses.

The conclusion is that sectoral CADR bodies can be useful and efficient. But their quality needs to be maintained. The architecture of CADR systems at national, EU and global level needs to be consistent so as to provide inter-operative functionality. A clear risk exists that if CADR systems are to proliferate, whether sectorally, nationally or supra-nationally, there is a risk that the options will be unnecessarily diverse in architecture and means of operation. That will be confusing to all, especially to consumers, and tend to chill use of CADR as a means of attracting and capturing consumer issues. There needs to be some order and consistency to the overall architecture. We have found that national architectures of CADR systems are already significantly different, despite the fact that many schemes claim to satisfy the EU Recommendations. There may be virtue in allowing some, or maybe all, elements of the CADR provider system to operate freely within the private sector or freely within national models, since this may lead to design elements that are appropriate to local conditions and tend to encourage innovation. However, some order and consistency needs to be introduced in order to maximise the benefits of CADR within the internal market.

We suggest that the keys to this problem of development of sustainable CADR coverage, whilst avoiding proliferation of systems that are hugely diverse and confusing, are simplicity and having a single portal for all consumer claims, whether it operates as a first- or last-stop. In our view, the considerations favouring a full horizontal coverage outweigh the considerations that argue against.

Maximising Usage: Unified Architecture, Visibility, Consistency and Trust

It is striking that there is a vast difference in usage between different CADR schemes across different countries: see chapter 14. The differences between similar schemes clearly exceed what might be expected, for example for similar sectors in different jurisdictions. The major factors that encourage high usage appear to be high visibility of the CADR scheme, confidence in its impartiality, and the fact that it is attractive in terms of cost and duration. A significant number of CADR schemes fail such criteria and, accordingly, their usage levels are very low.

The Netherlands (see Figure 15.4)[81] shows that if consumers and those who signpost CADR schemes are aware that there must be an CADR scheme for every, or most, sectors, then visibility of all and every CADR scheme will be increased, and this will have a considerable effect on usage rates. Consumers will think there is a suitable CADR scheme that covers the particular sector in which the trader that they have an issue with operates. This perception will increase pressure on traders to establish an CADR scheme in their sectors if one does not exist. Hence, the key is having a comprehensive national umbrella, which provides consistency of operation of sectoral schemes and a perception that most areas will be covered.

The key appears to be that all sectoral schemes should form part of a single umbrella, which provides consistency of operation, and also sufficient simplicity, such that all ADR schemes will have high visibility. After all, high visibility is a feature enjoyed by courts: citizens and businesses know that there is a court system that can handle legal disputes, even if they are not familiar with internal procedures or with internal variations in procedures between different types of courts.

Figure 15.4: The Netherlands Model

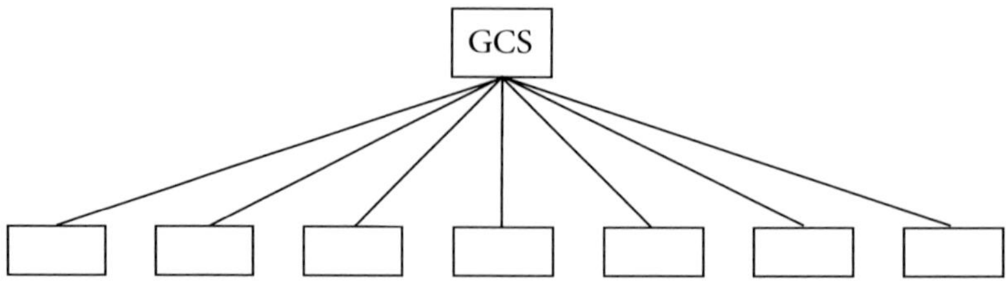

[81] A similar unified national scheme exists in Korea.

The CADR system in the Netherlands has taken four decades to cover virtually every sector, one at a time. But at a certain point of development, critical mass was achieved that accelerated the addition of sectors to the national model. Once a sufficient number of sectors had been covered, businesses in the non-covered sectors concluded that it would be to their commercial advantage to have CADR coverage, and the rate of coverage increased to its current comprehensive state. Hence, businesses wanted CADR systems for their commercial benefit. Once a CADR system is in place, it can, if appropriately designed, provide further and ongoing benefits, and thereby maintain or even raise the standards of commercial practice that prevail in the sector.

Similarly, business leaders in France have made a strategic decision in favour of supporting the growth and use of CADR, but the pre-existing CADR arrangements raise two challenges for building consumer trust and hence usage. Firstly, reliance on in-company *médiateurs* raises issues of their independence and hence does not build consumer trust. Secondly, continuance of a situation in which recommendations will not be voluntarily treated as binding by traders does not build trust.

Having a single national CADR architecture is clearly attractive. But it may not be appropriate for some Member States, either because they are too small to support multi-sectors (such as Slovenia) or because their national CADR systems have already developed to a stage where a single unified model could probably not realistically be imposed (such as the United Kingdom, France and Germany). What, therefore, is the way forward in such situations?

We suggest that empirical evidence for the need for a CADR solution in a country and a sector is needed as a pre-requisite to extension of CADR to a sector. Money should not be wasted on unnecessary systems for disputes that do not need to be included in a comprehensive CADR system merely for the sake of providing 'complete CADR coverage'. Evidence of need could come from business demand, a level of consumer complaints, or evidence of significant consumer detriment or unfair trading in a sector.

Two extremes of where CADR might not be necessary arise. There may be situations in which the level of trade, and the level and type of problems, do not justify a solution other than the courts, or which justify a non-CADR solution, such as action by regulators or of some other type. At the other extreme, although the volume of complaints might be high, companies are capable of resolving a sufficient number through their internal customer care schemes, and should be incentivised to do so. The need for additional CADR coverage in those circumstances would have to be carefully evaluated, since companies are already funding CADR in-house though customer care departments.

On the other hand, a major problem that is reported by almost all CADR providers is that their areas of competence are limited, and that the more successful they are in attracting complaints, the higher is the number that they have to reject because they fall outside the particular scheme's competence. In other words, a significant number of complaints are directed to the wrong CADR provider. As a result, the complaint might have to be redirected to another scheme, or there may be no relevant scheme, or it might be relevant for more than one scheme (such as in transport or holiday issues). Hence the issues are that the width of coverage of some schemes might leave gaps, and that there needs to be some arrangement for deciding allocation or priority whether several schemes could apply.

Taken together, these considerations do indicate a need to fill gaps, and/or to have a general means of catching any complaints, and allocating them to the most appropriate CADR track. It should also be remembered that small countries are unlikely to be able to support multiple tracks, so their most appropriate CADR model may initially be to have a general front-end portal that captures all complaints and then allocates particular types of claims on to such specialist CADR schemes as might exist at a second layer. That means of operation is already how ECC-NET and FIN-NET national offices operate, and the Energy ombudsmen have recently started.

A response to this diversity is for states or pan-EU sectors to adopt a model that provides a general framework and general standards, and for there to be a recognised general brand or access portal for users. Existing examples are the Lithuanian central state authority; the national Board framework in the Netherlands, and more restricted examples are the CCAS scheme in the UK, and France's recent energy ombudsman.

A single point of access for consumers can provide considerable advantages for consumers. The advantages of the Swedish approach of prioritising consumer advice have been discussed above. Another example is the UK's Consumers Direct, which is a service provided by government as a single point of information and access for consumers. Consumers Direct can be accessed online or by phone. Consumers Direct does not itself attempt to mediate or otherwise assist in resolving individual complaints. It provides information on options for procedures that could be pursued by complainants, and refers consumers to relevant dispute resolution schemes. Consumers Direct may be discontinued but the policy of having an easily identifiable advice facility appears to be transferred to the Citizens Advice network.

It is not feasible that a single national architecture (like the Netherlands) should apply to CADR in every Member State. Instead, strong consistency of functions and outcomes can be identified, and could, depending on the state of local development of CADR, be extended further or constructed from scratch. The key is to adopt unified EU-wide and national umbrellas for dispute resolution structures within which individual schemes operate in predictably consistent ways. This should include CADR providers as well as courts.

The objective is to make the CADR options highly visible to consumers. Consumers should be familiar with CADR as a concept, and have the expectation that any valid complaint about any trader in any sector will be able to be raised with the trader and then, if necessary, with an independent ombudsman. The CADR schemes might vary as appropriate between sectors, to take account of the particular type of dispute (such as expert investigation or opinion might be necessary, say in automobile or building disputes) but the basic processes and essential requirements should be the same. But consumers should be encouraged to think 'There must be a CADR for my dispute, and it is one that I can trust.' This in turn generates incentives for traders to create sectoral Boards, and support them so as to ensure that they are trustworthy.

Hence, it is unnecessary that every State should have the same internal architecture of CADR systems. Indeed, some Member States have passed the point at which they could be forced into a single-provider structure like the Netherlands. Small states such as Slovenia could not support, and do not need, an CADR body for every sector, such as is developing in Germany and the United Kingdom.

In those States where it is not feasible to have local CADR providers that cover every type of dispute in every sector, there are two options for development of CADR systems:

a. *Vertical*: some CADR bodies might operate at both national and EU level. An example might be for complaints to be referred by a national office (such as a national generic CADR office, an EEC-NET office, or court, or regulator) to a competent CADR provider for the particular sector, whether operating in another Member State or on a pan-EU basis.

b. Horizontal: some CADR bodies might operate across several (or all) Member States. Existing examples include the EEC-NET; the pan-EU ODR platform being considered by the European Commission; or the global 'jurisdiction' available since 1999 under the Uniform Domain Name Dispute Resolution Policy ('UDRP') of the Internet Corporation for Assigned Names and Numbers ('ICANN') on the recommendation of the World Intellectual Property Organization ('WIPO'). There is no structural reason why CADR providers, especially those with sectoral expertise, could not provide CADR services to consumers and businesses in other countries. Such a system already operates under the EU's New Approach system with notified bodies.

Some national disputes can be resolved by fora in other jurisdictions. For example, all EU disputes involving PayPal, which is based in Luxembourg, are resolved by the UK FOS system. Disputes requiring sectoral expertise could be outsourced to CADR providers in other states.

Filling Gaps to Extend Coverage

The Leuven study recommended that an ADR scheme with general competence and guaranteed geographical coverage is a necessary complement for sector specific mediation and arbitration schemes.[82] Some Member States have universal horizontal coverage of CADR: a CADR body will exist to which consumers may bring any complaint against any trader in that State. Examples are the Nordic states, Spain and CEE states. In contrast, some large Member States do not have full horizontal CADR coverage. Consumer complaints may only be brought to such CADR bodies as exist, and about such traders as are subject to such sectoral CADR schemes. This is the position in the United Kingdom, Germany and France. In the Netherlands, coverage depends on whether the trader belongs to a trade association that has joined the CADR system, or has adhered voluntarily, which many small traders will not have done. It is clear that coverage of CADR schemes is spreading in those States from sector to sector, over time. But it is not comprehensive, as the European Commission's 2011 proposals would require. The example of the Netherlands and the UK show that spontaneous sectoral CADR schemes can eventually coalesce to form an almost universal comprehensive national system.

However there are three drawbacks that arise in considering how a comprehensive national model might be created along the precedent of the Dutch system. First, organic growth takes a long time. It took 40 years for enough individual Geschillencommissie boards to be created, such that a reasonably comprehensive single national model can be said to exist. Secondly, all the sectoral CADR schemes must have sufficient similarity in structure and operation that they can be considered to be sufficiently compatible to form a single national 'system'. If there is too much diversity in sectoral CADR schemes, of whatever kind, consumers would not be convinced that a reliable integral national system with comprehensive coverage existed. Thirdly, if full coverage is desired, by definition there must be no gaps. This means not only the obvious point that all sectors much be covered, but also that *all* traders must belong, or be subject to, a CADR scheme. This

[82] J Stuyck, above n 7, p 114.

is an inherent problem with any voluntary CADR scheme. There may be some traders, especially small businesses, who are not members of a trade association and/or are not members of a sectoral CADR scheme. That is certainly the case in the Netherlands, the UK, Germany and France.

It can be argued that this third drawback can be seen as a strength. In the Dutch system, for instance, there is an incentive for traders to adhere voluntarily to the code and Geschillencommissie board for their sector, since the ability to advertise that fact brings commercial advantage. Nevertheless, not every trader is subject to a Geschillencommissie board in the Netherlands, so although the system has many admirable features, it is not comprehensive, and consumers cannot bring every complaint to a CADR scheme. Gaps in coverage, whether at sectoral or trader levels, can only be filled by making coverage mandatory, and that comes with consequences and a cost.

The European Commission has proposed, and many policy-makers and consumer representatives argue, that there should be full coverage by CADR pathways for every B2C dispute. But how could this be achieved for states like France, Germany and the UK? The issue is not whether ADR is a good idea for consumer disputes (almost every country thinks it is), nor how a central, residual body could be established (a structure that would fit into the national architecture is reasonably obvious in most countries), but how it could be paid for in a time of economic stringency. Governments that are now completely focused on cutting public expenditure will be reluctant to make public funds available to establish a residual CADR scheme: they do not know how much it might cost, since they do not know how many complaints it might attract. They also do not want to impose the cost on businesses, since the overriding economic strategy is to encourage private sector recovery as swiftly as possible. Could these issues be overcome? We believe they can.

The options for making CADR comprehensive across all sectors are:

a. To leave CADR as voluntary and let market forces gradually operate to extend coverage. The problems with this approach are that progress might be very slow, and there is no guarantee that all sectors would eventually be covered, if that is desired.
b. To make it mandatory on traders to offer CADR but without specifying which type of CADR should be adopted. This is theoretically achievable. It has the advantage that the market is left to devise CADR schemes that are appropriate for sectors, to pay for them, and thus to exert pressure on CADR providers to offer cost-efficient and effective services, and to innovate.
c. To create a statutory CADR provider, such as an Ombudsman.

But the problem with options b and c are that they are unattractive in the current economic climate.

Creating a residual CADR scheme would involve two types of costs: the costs of establishment and the running costs in processing whatever volume of claims occurs. Various options arise for establishing a residual scheme, such as:

- Merge existing sectoral CADR schemes, so as to reduce gaps and introduce economies of scale into shared overheads, and reduce wasted costs through the need to reject.
- Encourage more sectors to introduce sectoral CADR schemes funded by the business sectors, which would reduce the number of residual disputes not covered by sectoral schemes.
- Introduce more advice schemes, to reduce the number of disputes that arise.

- Maximise the transparency of complaint data held by CADR schemes and regulatory agencies, so as to reduce the number of disputes by maximising the ability to identify problems and the speed of doing so.
- Reject the CADR approach entirely, and direct consumer complaints at the courts and/or at regulatory bodies. This is a highly unattractive option, which is really the proof of the pudding. The UK's OFCOM receives around 200,000 complaints annually. Most of these should be directed at the CADR bodies, and represents a huge wastage of the regulator's resources. Equally, the cost of maintaining court systems is clearly far higher than that of CADR systems: the whole point is CADR systems is that they are far cheaper than courts. Furthermore, in most countries, courts involve significant public expenditure, whereas CADR systems are mainly privately funded. This option does not make economic sense. The rational economic solution is to transfer C2B disputes away from courts to CADR schemes.
- Persuade or require business to fund a residual CADR scheme.

How many disputes would a residual CADR scheme have to process? The scale of demand in countries may, in fact, be quite limited. This is particularly so in the Netherlands and the UK. The reason is that many sectoral CADR schemes already exist in those states. The demand, therefore, comes from, firstly, those sectors that have no CADR scheme *and* no effective ability to handle disputes through other ways, notably by in-house customer relations departments, and, secondly, traders who are not members of existing schemes, usually because they are not members of trade associations, and usually because they are small traders. There may be many small traders[83] but how many disputes are they likely to give rise to? How many consumers are they likely to affect through failure to deliver, failure to deliver appropriate quality or safety, unfair contract terms, and so on? How significant is likely to be their customers' wish for redress?

It has been argued above that CADR could have advantages for SMEs and the economy in providing an effective but low cost means of bridging the regulatory compliance gap that SMEs face, and in providing effective and low cost regulatory enforcement by public authorities.

In the Netherlands and the UK, private CADR bodies already exist that could provide the infrastructure on which a residual scheme could be built. CEDR already has a residual scheme, its Independent Consumer Redress Service, whose rules are set by CEDR, so do not need to be negotiated with members, although fees are payable by members for caseload. It would appear, therefore, that the establishment and basic infrastructure costs would be limited, and case fees could cover the expanding capacity. There may be a need for some additional initial establishment funding, but it might not be much, given existing structures.

How could case fees be collected? The two options are for fees to be imposed on traders by law, or accepted by agreement. Since the traders involved would probably not belong to trade associations and may be small, they would not be expected to join a residual scheme by agreement. But, in any event, the cost of administering a membership scheme for all traders would be significant and the compliance rate would be questionable. The preferable

[83] The definition of an SME covers all enterprises with less than 250 employees and equal to or less than either €50 million turnover or €43 million balance sheet total. Micro-enterprises are the smallest category of SME, with less than ten employees and a turnover or balance sheet total equal to or less than €2 million: Commission Recommendation 2003/361/EC of 6 May 2003 concerning the definition of micro, small and medium-sized enterprises, OJ L 124, 20.5.2003, p 36.

option seems to be that a residual scheme could be authorised by law to charge case fees to traders who have been given an opportunity to respond to cases brought within clear and fair procedures of the scheme. The determinations would either be binding or would be enforceable in court on a subsequent but fast track procedure, and subject to extra cost penalties unless the trader had good reason for not joining in the CADR procedure, or was able with justification to bring forward further evidence that could not have been brought forward earlier. The cost could be made a debt claimable by the consumer or the CADR scheme. The latter may be preferable.

Thus, a residual CADR scheme could be created with standing procedures by adding it on to an existing, substantial and well-funded scheme. The architecture could also be designed to *encourage* trade associations and traders to establish (a) information facilities and (b) sectoral CADR schemes, thereby reducing the number of claims that would be coverable under the residual scheme. Various incentives could be envisaged. Firstly, there could be cost advantages through lower case fees. Secondly, adherence to an official sectoral CADR scheme could be marketed as having commercial and brand advantage. It might have an officially recognised status, such as the UK's CCAS badge. Thirdly, sectoral schemes might apply higher trading standards than 'normal' CADR or court bodies, through being linked to sectoral Codes of Practice that established higher standards than those required under general consumer protection law. The Netherlands' system is a clear example of such an approach, as is the widely used self-regulatory Code approach adopted in UK. Fourthly, sectoral schemes might be swifter than general residual schemes (and certainly than the courts) since they could take advantage of specialist expertise and innovative information technology processes. The object would not be to undermine existing CADR schemes, but to make them more attractive for traders.

In short, it is arguable that the number of claims of a national residual scheme in the UK and the Netherlands might be relatively limited, firstly because of the wide coverage of existing schemes, secondly because incentives could be designed to encourage traders to handle claims in-house, and to create more or join more sectoral CADR schemes.

In Germany, the situation may be different because of the existing culture that claims can be brought in courts, and are backed by insurance, so the demand for CADR systems may currently be limited, even though it might grow.

A further economic point is that the cost of CADR schemes saves money elsewhere. Firstly, it saves money on courts. CADR schemes replace private enforcement through courts, by functioning as what might be described as 'surrogate private enforcement'. Both the infrastructure and case costs of courts can be reduced if (lower cost) CADR pathways operate effectively. Secondly, CADR schemes that have adequate transparency provide data that can reduce the number of disputes and encourage trading standards to rise. These points are discussed elsewhere. But the cost savings overall of these aspects could be significant, as is shown by the data on the low level of disputes handled in Sweden and the Netherlands. Thirdly, the best CADR systems have strong regulatory components, and hence affect business behaviour and raise trading standards whilst reducing the need for enforcement by public authorities. The nature of public authorities' activities can be altered by the presence of an effective CADR scheme, enabling the authority to alter both its monitoring and enforcement activities, especially by concentrating more on 'rogue' traders whilst relying more on CADR's more self-regulatory effects to police responsible businesses. CADR should not be intended to deal with rogue traders: that is a matter for regulatory enforcement by state bodies.

Best Operating Procedures

In this section, we examine some of the design and operational challenges that existing CADR schemes face. This will consider some of the more important essential requirements and with KPIs with which we have suggested above that schemes should comply.

Confidence and Trust

A conclusion from the empirical data in Chapter 14 is that CADR schemes will not be used where they do not command the confidence and trust of consumers. Further, traders will not support or, where they have a choice, fund such schemes without having trust in them. These qualities are of fundamental importance.

It is difficult to measure levels of confidence and trust in any judicial or similar system that decides on rights. To a large extent, the requirements of independence and impartiality are tests that, if satisfied, themselves produce general confidence and trust in the system, its procedures and outcomes. Requirements of procedural justice (due process) are also important.

Ensuring high degree of confidence and trust in a CADR system is an important requirement precisely because the system is not judicial. The state's judicial system is unique and monopolistic, and its decisions are backed by the coercive power of the state. In contrast, an alternative dispute resolution system is by definition optional for consumers to use. If it is going to be used, and to provide the benefits over courts that are desired, it must be trusted by consumers. It must also be trusted by businesses. Both sides will in practice be subject to its decisions, even if they are not legally binding. Hence, processes and outcomes must be fair and just.

The measures of confidence and trust in a CADR scheme are, therefore, visible in its statistics of use. Assuming its existence is known, if it is not trusted people will not use it. As illustrated in Chapter 14, there is in fact a wide variation in usage rates between different CADR systems in different Member States. That fact should tell us a great deal about whether particular CADR schemes are trusted by one or both sides, and should be a major pointer towards whether the internal arrangements about processes and the independence of decision-makers is perceived as being satisfactory. It is perception that matters here. The fact that a given mediator might be impartial is irrelevant if she is not perceived to be independent. One conclusion is that statistics of usage and performance need to be published so as to support democratic confidence in the impartiality of a system, and give a measure of its level of trustability.

Accessibility

The Leuven study pointed out that the accessibility of ADR directly relates to the sort of society Europe prefers.[84] National CADR schemes use many available techniques to draw consumers' attention to their existence. A holistic approach is to provide consumer education that can be utilised and inform choices at pre-contractual stages; and to provide

[84] J Stuyck, above n 7, p 6.

information about complaint and dispute resolution options that can be utilised later if necessary. Enforcement bodies can run general campaigns to make consumers and traders aware of certain issues.

The current state of development in the UK, Germany and France is that business CADR schemes are likely to continue to be adopted for several more sectors as part of codes of business practice. How codes operate will continue to develop. (Developments in the court systems and rules are also likely, such as over extending court-assisted mediation and imposing lower and predictable costs for smaller cases. These developments will affect the balance of use as between codes and the courts, but non-court mechanisms are likely still to be highly attractive for consumer disputes.) There may be quite a proliferation of CADR schemes in different business sectors. This should be good for consumers and business in theory, but the proliferation will itself bring problems.

Several aspects should be examined. How should experience and best practice be analysed and shared, and improvements made? Should there be a standard for CADR systems? Should there be some centralisation of mediation, conciliation and arbitration functions? If so, should there be multiple entry ports, or just a small number? How can improvements in outcomes (speed, cost, effects) be obtained? How can those in dispute access information about CADR and access its processes? Should there be greater promotion of CADR options?

Sweden has good accessibility because of the simple national structure of advice and ADR bodies. The Dutch system also has the advantage of standardisation, which increases visibility. The UK introduced a national first point of contact for consumer advice, called Consumer Direct, which may be accessed by phone or website, which refers consumers to the relevant high quality specialist advice and redress services (such as code schemes or ombudsmen). This has been a considerable success. The Belgian Belmed takes a considerable step forward in terms of accessibility through the single national web platform, but the current challenge is to build enough sectoral CADR bodies for the system to function with full or adequate coverage.

There are in fact many CADR schemes that are not particularly visible, and have not been notified to the Commission since they do not satisfy every one of the notification requirements. Some major schemes (examples in Sweden, French insurance and other schemes) operate well, but are denied official recognition and publicity. Equally, some less satisfactory schemes may exist and use the name 'ombudsman' or call themselves 'CADR' but not operate well. These issues of quality, use of names, and visibility need to be addressed.

Language

Language is the biggest barrier to cross-border complaints. But larger schemes have the resources to provide translation facilities. The UK FOS is able to work in 49 languages. This points towards the advantages of being able to employ economies of scale. Should CADR bodies seek to pool resources, or might a centralised facility be useful? The language capability of the ECC-Net is a useful resource in this respect. ODR can provide multiple communication platforms: Stanford University is trying to establish a communications standard, related to the B2B Electronic Data Interchange standard.

Access Cost

Should consumers have to pay a fee to access a CADR scheme? The principal argument in favour of this is that every service has to be funded. In particular, the state charges users fees for the dispute resolution services that it provides through the courts (France is one of the few countries where court fees are very limited). Users also have to fund their own lawyers, and the transaction fees, unless exempted through legal aid, are usually transferred to the loser at least in part.[85] There may be an argument that charging a fee would introduce a proportionality check, since a user would review whether the cost justified the sum or issue at stake. There may be a residual argument that some time-wasting or fraudulent claims may be made, perhaps concerning types of issues rather than all. It would be useful to have some empirical evidence on the second and third issues, but this study has not revealed particular evidence of these risks.

On the other hand, the principal arguments would be that the policy is to encourage consumers to use CADR systems, especially if the schemes are designed to produce important feedback information on market issues. Identification of an important market issue may have little relevance to the value of an individual claim, but the mere identification of a dispute, especially where there is a mass issue, will be important. In those systems, especially ODR systems, that may be attractive to SMEs, there is also a similar accessibility point.

A 2005 study on ADR in the EU found that mediation would be more easily accepted by unequal or private parties if it were free of charge.[86] The Leuven study found that only a limited number of arbitration schemes apply loser pays against the consumer.[87]

We have found that the clear majority of CADR schemes are in fact free to the consumer. This is even established as a 'principle' in the French Charter (although the French 'principle' that the courts are fee has clearly influenced this rule). The 'state of the art' (or of the market) is clearly that consumer CADR schemes should be free to consumers.

It should be noted that some ombudsmen believe that the pyramid structure (illustrated in Figures 15.1 and 15.3) assist in resolving disputes, since the downward pressure (akin to 'the shadow of the law' as exerted by courts) focuses minds on problems and induces a sense of proportionality.

Efficiency

Many of the procedures involve paper-based or online procedures only, and are hence quick and cheap. Thus, they tend to have features that look more inquisitorial than partisan, at least on the basis that many schemes do not hold hearings.

A major factor that affects the duration of processes appears to be whether decisions are made by panels of three or by a single person. A panel of three has advantages of balance and expertise. However, how important are these factors in cases where consumers and businesses seek swift solutions, and costs can be cut? Might different models be appropriate

[85] C Hodges, S Vogenauer & M Tulibacka, *The Costs and Funding of Civil Litigation: A Comparative Approach* (Oxford: Hart Publishing, 2010).

[86] A De Roo and R Jagtenberg, 'ADR in the European Union: Provisional Assessment of Comparative Research in Process' in L Cadiet, E Jeuland and T Clay, *Médiation et arbitrage. Perspectives comparatives* (Paris: LexisNexis, 2005) p 185.

[87] J Stuyck, above n 7, p 127.

for different sectors or types of case, on a basis of proportionality? It may be that the level of trust in courts or arbitrators in some Member States is less than in others, which might strengthen the case for decisions by a panel of three. However, where trust in the impartiality and independence of the decision-maker is not an issue, a single individual should suffice.

Many CADR providers report that they receive a significant proportion of complaints that are not within their particular jurisdiction. This can waste a great deal of time on the part of consumers and CADR bodies. There are various reasons for this situation. Firstly, CADR bodies report that consumers have failed to give traders an opportunity (or sufficient opportunity) to resolve the matter directly. Secondly, there may be confusion over what complaints are within the scope of a particular CADR body, either because there may be different CADR bodies with different jurisdictions, or because there may be no other relevant CADR body (hence, a gap in coverage). Thirdly, such a gap in coverage may lead to people trying to contact one CADR body because it is all that exists, even though it cannot handle the case. Fourthly, many consumers may simply be requesting information about a product or service, rather than wishing to raise a dispute. The solutions appear to lie in encouraging higher visibility of CADR generically, and of the fact that in-company and external assistance forms a holistic whole, such that the former should be contacted first.

Independence and Impartiality

We have found a range of arrangements in the CADR systems that claim to satisfy the principles of independence and impartiality: CADR providers are located in regulatory bodies, in traders, in or adjoining trade associations, in independent private bodies paid by firms, or statutorily independent. A spectrum of arguments is used to justify these arrangements.

The concept of impartiality requires that the third party must be neutral between the parties and have no interest in the outcome of the dispute, and so be in a position to be able to form a view that is not improperly influenced by either side and is also seen to be unable to be influenced. Hence, the third party must have no conflict of interest as between the parties. In order to overcome any perception of bias, the third party must also be independent of the parties. A third party might in fact be impartial, even though having some connection with one or other primary party. But in order to guard against the possibility of bias, and to ensure that impartiality is demonstrated, the requirement of independence is added.[88] The concept of 'independence' requires that a party who makes a decision on the merits of a dispute between two primary parties must have no connection, especially any financial connection, with either of the primary parties, and especially not be paid by either of them.

In applying these requirements of impartiality and independence to CADR systems, three aspects arise: the structural position of the third party; the individual characteristics of the third party; and the source of the rules that are applied by the third party. The concepts of impartiality and independence are well understood in relation to judges and arbitrators. The requirements apply both to the individual who makes the decision and to the body that supervises the process.

[88] The Commission's 1998 Recommendation required 'Independence: guaranteeing the impartiality of the decision-making body'. The 2001 Recommendation only specified impartiality. The 2004 European Code of Conduct for Mediators specified both independence and impartiality.

Many of the older CADR models operate on the basis of a balanced panel, based on the arbitration model. The panel in Nordic and Dutch Boards comprises an independent chair (often a judge) and two other members, one appointed by each 'side', usually from a pre-existing list of approved consumer and business nominees. Such a system is intended to create the impression of balance. The independent chair will have a casting vote.

In the more recently-established CADR systems, decisions are taken by individuals. A case may be dealt with by a case handler, who mediates and can make recommendations, and refer formal decisions to a more senior ombudsman. Case handlers and ombudsmen should all satisfy the requirements of impartiality and independence. The reason why these more streamlined systems have evolved, replacing panels of three people, is simply due to the practical reality that ombudsmen systems have become victims of their own success in attracting large volumes of complaints, and such volumes simply cannot be processed within what are regarded as acceptable timescales and budgets by less streamlined systems. The judicial approach, with a panel of three arbitrators, is something of a luxury, and comes at a cost in terms of expense and time. Those who criticise a single ombudsman system from the theoretical perspective have to bear in mind that some such systems have been given a democratic vote of confidence by users, visible through high case volumes.

The presence of nominated experts on a panel can have another function, namely of providing expertise. Some consumers cases may only be resolvable with the application of expertise. The approach of a court system would be to commission external independent expertise, involving cost and time. The CADR solution is based on the fact that many consumer cases can be resolved by locating expertise within the CADR ombudsman or panel. The German Insurance Ombudsman and the many UK FOS ombudsmen have and develop expertise in the complexities of their particular fields. Where necessary, ombudsmen can usually call for external expert help, but this seems to be rare. The Netherlands and Nordic panel models believe that the presence of experts on their approved lists provides sufficient internal expertise on a panel in many cases. For example, in a dispute over whether a garage fitted a new or reconditioned engine in a car, the issue might be resolvable by one or both of the nominated members of the panel simply looking at a photograph.

Independence of the decision-maker is assisted by the personal prestige of the individual. This feature is seen in the German Insurance and Transport Ombudsmen, who are distinguished judges and/or academics. The Chair of the FLA's two panels are distinguished academics. Consumers' confidence is assisted where judges are involved as arbitrators, such as in Denmark, the Netherlands and Portugal.

A possible approach involves accreditation of individual mediators or arbitrators against published standards, irrespective of whichever body organises the process. The technique of accreditation is similar to the process of appointment and validation for judges and professionals. The model has certain similarities to the EU's New Approach to product regulation, which involves accreditation of Notified Bodies prior to their empowerment to exercise certain delegated approval or monitoring functions as services to business entities.

Trade association code schemes

A general feature of most arbitration services is that they involve decision-makers who are independent of the consumer representation or of the business sector. Some mediation schemes involve independent mediators, even if the sponsoring body is a trade association, but some trade associations provide mediation as a preliminary stage, especially where they act in a self-regulatory role in relation to their members (an example of ABTA and its travel companies).

The degree of independence is supported where the substance of the rules being applied by a business code are approved by an independent committee that has a majority of non-business members,[89] or a regulator. The UK's CCAS model includes wider governance and scrutiny than occurs just from business supervision of its code, by requiring the involvement of stakeholders such as regulators and consumer associations on a governing body, which oversees both the substance of the code and the operation of its processes.

The UK CCAS system has overcome the historical objection to self-regulatory systems that business will use the system as a self-serving defence against consumer complaints and the imposition of regulation. The code systems sponsored by trade associations have developed a model in which different functions are exercised by people who have different degrees of independence, depending on their function. In the UK model for CADR schemes, the initial mediation function is carried out by a body that is hosted by the trade association but usually formally separate from it, but any formal 'decision' is outsourced to a CADR body that is completely independent of the sector (such as CEDR Disputes Group and Ombudsman Services). This model is shown in Figure 15.3. The result is that the decision, which is accepted as binding by both parties, is made by a panel or individual that satisfies the principle of independence. There may be an objection that the body that performs the initial stage of mediation is not sufficiently independent. Our anecdotal observation of these systems leaves us with the clear impression that they currently operate satisfactorily and impartially as between consumer and trader, but that should be subject to more empirical analysis.

This example illustrates the point that different functions (mediation, the making of recommendations, or of decisions that are binding on one or both parties) form a continuum in which the degree of independence that is required can legitimately vary. Thus, the Code body may provide conciliation and administration functions, but the outsourcing of formal decisions to independent CADR bodies is intended to provide sufficient independence of the ultimate decision-making.

A further feature is to provide for oversight functions of such a system, with sufficient independent members of a governing board. Such arrangements should be fully transparent, in that all governance structures, affairs and deliberations are published. From the evidence assembled in our study, therefore, surrogate requirements for full independence can be based on principles of governance, transparency and separating functions, which appear generally to operate satisfactorily.

One model, although rare, involves an oversight and appeal function, such as in Sweden, where decisions of the Kundombudsmannen can be appealed to, and the whole complaints function overseen by, a Kundpanelen which includes a majority of external members.

The key to satisfying the requirements of independence and impartiality is to set standards for operating procedures of CADR bodies. If such standards are not imposed on sectors by law (such as in the telecoms or energy sectors), they can be established (as the Office of Fair Trading has done) as official standards, the observance of which brings official approval (by the OFT) of a scheme, and the ability to market such approval and use of the official logo. This has come to be regarded as the 'gold standard' and worth achievement by some sectors in the UK, such as travel (initially) and motor vehicles.

[89] The Chairs of the Finance and Leasing Association's panels, for example, are leading professors of finance and consumer law.

This official scheme not only requires the adoption of operating procedures that comply with the standards, but also auditing of compliance, and transparent scrutiny through publication of performance data (both of the CADR provider and of complaints processed on traders). The publication of such data provides ongoing transparency to the market and to regulatory oversight by regulators. 'Name and shame' techniques can then be adopted by market commentators, such as consumer bodies and the media, thus increasing competition in the sector.

It should not be forgotten that the opposite problem can occur, where the CADR body is too close to a regulator, or even to a consumer association. Examples of close connection between CADR decision-makers and regulatory bodies are the UK FOS, and the German dispute boards that are located within the Bundesbank and Bundesnetzargentur. An example of where the CADR service is located within the consumer association is found in Slovenia, although the association merely provides mediation and representation functions, and not a decision-making function.

It is no surprise that UK banks, for example, have long objected that the FOS is not sufficiently independent of the Financial Services Authority. We think there is force in that objection, and that CADR bodies should not be hosted within a regulatory body. Nevertheless, we consider that the data produced by the CADR body, and its operations, should be fully transparent, whether to regulators, consumers, business, government or the media.

In-house ombudsmen: a misclassification

There are several examples of where companies have built dispute resolution arrangements in-house: notably French *médiateurs*, the rare but intriguing company Swedish Kundombudsmannen and Kundpanelen, and the British Code bodies. Several of these have particular characteristics. For example, in order to access a French company *médiateur*, a consumer usually first has to pass through several internal complaint handling tiers (that raises issues of accessibility and duration, as well as independence). The Swedish model has an 'ombudsman' plus a second appeal tier that includes consumer representatives. The British Code model has an initial mediation function that is increasingly technically separate from the sponsoring trade association, although usually funded by the trade association and sharing the same premises, but with a governance structure that includes independent people and with the function of making formal decisions on cases outsourced to a fully independent CADR body.

These models all grow out of in-house company complaint and customer care functions. But are they sufficiently independent to be considered to qualify as external CADR systems? Some companies' ombudsmen/*médiateurs* ague that they are neutral and *impartial*, and able to make decisions that are independent exercises of their own unbiased judgment. However, consumer and academic commentators are frequently sceptical of such arrangements, and observe that although experts imbedded in companies may be able to apply considerable expertise, thereby assisting speedy understanding of the subject matter of what might be a complex issue, the fact that they are paid by the company manifestly does not satisfy the requirement of independence that is necessary to qualify as a CADR body. The latter view would seem to be correct. Even if an in-house ombudsman is in fact impartial, there remains a perception problem, and the empirical evidence appears to substantiate the fact that consumers have not placed their trust in in-house *médiateurs*. The better way to view in-house ombudsmen is as part of companies' customer care systems and in-house dispute resolution systems, but not as independent external CADR systems. The point is largely one of the use of the name 'ombudsman' or '*médiateur*', in a manner that may mislead consumers, rather than the function of the personnel.

The European Commission clearly has the same view of the status of in-house 'ADR' functions, since they are excluded from the scope of the 2011 CADR proposals.[90] The contrary view may be particularly contested in France. However, the reality is clear: in house dispute resolution is exactly that, and it does not satisfy the independence requirement to qualify as 'CADR'.

Nevertheless, in-house customer care and complaint mechanisms do fulfil a vital and integral function, which is an essential first stage to independent CADR systems, and should in our view also be an essential first stage of almost all court-based dispute resolution. So in-house dispute resolution systems are highly important, and need to be efficient and effective. But they are not a substitute for external CADR systems.

Conclusions on independence

A possible way of looking at the diversity of independence arrangements is to view them as manifestations of evolving models in what is a new and fast-moving field. This reduces the criticism of particular arrangements, as they are viewed in a wider pan-EU comparative context that illuminates the aspects of evolution. However, some current arrangements are not satisfactory and should be reformed. The fact that some arrangements are not *seen* to be satisfactory will limit the effectiveness of an CADR system, and we have found clear evidence of low usage in such cases. The case for full independence, therefore, is not just a theoretical one but also a practical one of whether a particular CADR scheme is going to deliver its full functional potential. Where schemes are reformed, consideration should be given to the reasons why complete independence should not be achieved. Perhaps there may be reasons for taking intermediate steps.

It is important that CADR providers should satisfy the criteria of independence and impartiality, so that civil society can have trust and confidence in the fact that they deliver fairness and justice. Hence, case handlers, ombudsmen or other intermediaries and decision-makers must all have no conflicts of interest, nor any perception of any such conflict.

The criterion of independence is not satisfied by in-company ombudsmen or by ombudsmen who are subsidiaries of ministerial or regulatory agencies. Such ombudsmen are in reality part of the trader's customer care team, and not independent. It is acceptable for conciliation functions to be undertaken by in-company customer care personnel or by code bodies that are paid by, but organisationally separate from, trade associations, provided the formal governance and oversight of such operations is undertaken by a body that is independent of the business sector and on which a majority of members, including the chair, are fully independent and have no connection with the sector.

The tension that emerges is an organizational one. If consumers and businesses demand faster and cheaper performance from CADR systems, illustrated by the European Commission's 2011 proposal that decisions must normally be given within 90 days, are systems involving panels too cumbersome? Is the role of two members on a panel to be partisan? If so, is it only necessary to have a single independent decision-maker, of sufficient personal stature? In which sectoral boards is efficiency of processing enhanced by having a decision-maker with detailed sectoral expertise, rather than obtaining such expertise from an independent expert? In which types of case, and hence boards, can the necessary expertise be located within a single decision-maker? If a single decision-maker is a general judge, will she have adequate technical expertise if she sits alone? Is it preferable for a single decision-maker to be a permanent ombudsman, since she will have a higher level of technical expertise?

In these questions we can see why ombudsman models have developed, replacing panels of three 'arbitrators'. Both models can satisfy the requirements, such as independence and impartiality. The key drivers, however, are cost and duration, and these have driven developments in where expertise is located. This has produced a model that has evolved from looking like a court or arbitration panel to a distinctive expert ombudsman model.

Transparency

How much should be published about the CADR process and its decisions? The publication of details of processes and of decisions is intended to provide transparency, and hence support trust and democratic support for the CADR process. Three aspects arise over what and how much should be published, one relating to the CADR provider, and the other two to the traders and consumers involved.

We have suggested above that the structure, and details of the actual operations of a CADR provider should be published. The KPI targets and actual performance should be published. There has been a clear trend towards publishing such data by many CADR bodies, but not all of them yet do so.

Publication of the details of individual complaints is partly justified as a means of maintaining transparency of the quality of decisions of the CADR body, but more importantly as a means providing the market regulatory functions discussed above. Publication of aggregated data on issues and trends is particularly important. Some commentators argue that every decision should be published. This is currently resisted by some CADR bodies, largely on the basis of cost, especially where there are many cases involved (only important decisions are published in the Netherlands). One benefit would be to have available a corpus of precedents that could guide business behavior, but this is less important where CADR only applies settled law. The use of information technology may make it economically feasible to publish individual decisions online, in a manner that could be searchable, but to highlight the major decisions and aggregate data.

Some traders have no objection to their names being published in relation to every cases processed, but some object. Publishing details of individual claimants and respondents might affect their privacy rights. There is a general trend in the UK towards publication by regulators (Information Commissioner,[91] FSA,[92] OFCOM[93]) and CADR bodies (FOS,[94] Legal Ombudsman[95]).

[90] Proposal, n 72 above, Art 2.2(a).

[91] *Access to information held in complaint files. Guidance for organizations* (Information Commissioner's Office, 2011).

[92] FSA is required to report every six months on the complaints that it receives: see http://www.financial-ombudsman.org.uk/publications/complaints-data.html.

[93] *Telecoms Complaints. Q2 (April to June) 2011* (OFCOM, 2011).

[94] *Transparency and the Financial Ombudsman Service* (Financial Ombudsman Service, 2011), at http://www.financial-ombudsman.org.uk/publications/policy-statements/publishing-decisions-sep11.pdf.

[95] *Discussion paper. Publishing our decisions* (Legal Ombudsman, 2011).

The solutions to these problems involve reaching a balance between different considerations: confidentiality of individual human rights and commercial proprietary information; openness/transparency; free speech.[96] There is also the policy issue of the extent to which the business community wishes to support the CADR system as providing credibility, trust and independence. The central issue is whether the obligations of disclosure are binding or not. Hence, the future may involve introducing a statutory requirement to produce information.

Some CADR providers and ECC-Net offices publish not only whether a determination has been made but also whether the business has complied with it. This practice has developed in those countries and systems where decisions are not accepted as binding. Thus, the Nordic ECC offices and regulators of course have no power to take enforcement measures against individual traders under recommendations by CADR bodies, but non-compliance by individual traders is given substantial media publicity by consumer and general media. Publication and transparency about individual respondents appears to be a practice that is growing.

An issue that concerns EEC offices and CADR bodies is that they sometimes receive information that fraudulent traders are operating, but that if there is delay in giving such information to public regulatory bodies the trader will have disappeared, and any ADR decision or private court enforcement cannot be enforced.

There is an issue over how much to make public of the details of individual disputes *during* the CADR process. Many court processes are open to the public, for reasons of maintaining transparency over the integrity of the process itself. However, there is an issue of whether individuals would be inhibited from raising valid issues if they are concerned about losing anonymity. An opposite concern is whether anonymity would encourage fraudulent claims, and make them more difficult to police. The extent which these issues are relevant would require empirical evidence, and might differ between types of claim.

A matter of concern in the mediation community is whether mediators can be compelled to give evidence in civil proceedings. In Bulgaria, France and Poland, the mediator has immunity and can refuse to testify. In Italy, 'the confidentiality stipulations are more rigorous, while the Swedish mediation rules state that confidentiality is not automatic and a special agreement to that effect is required between the parties'.

Factors Affecting Costs, Efficiency and Incidence

What lessons can be learned about how to reduce the cost of disputes resolution, and of CADR schemes in particular? The costs of a CADR scheme depend on a number of variables, notably:

1. The scope (range) of the scheme, ie whether it is national or sectoral. The lesson here is that economies of scale can be effected.
2. The number of cases that a scheme has to process. The lesson here points towards use of individual case fees, to reduce the incidence of unnecessary cases, which could be resolved at earlier stages.
3. The number of cases that fall outside the scheme's jurisdiction, notably those that should have been directed to some other scheme (if it exists) and especially the

[96] Note Case C-506/08 *P Sweden v MyTravel and Commission*; Case C-71/10 *Office of Communications v Information Commissioner*; Case C-104/10 *Patrick Kelly v National University of Ireland (University College, Dublin)*.

number that are merely requests for information, or that are premature since they should first have been directed to the relevant trader before being sent to the CADR scheme. Redirection has been found to be a significant problem for many existing schemes. The cost of processing large number of 'invalid' cases is considerable for many schemes. The lesson is that attempts to reduce the number of invalid cases will cut case costs.

4. The type of case. Some cases require more work than others. For example, personal injury cases (not the focus of this book, but examples of some relevant schemes are given from Sweden, Germany and France) typically involve the need for examination of detailed records and/or of the patient, and may require complex expert opinions. In contrast, some CADR schemes attempt to build sectoral expertise into the case handler, conciliator or adjudicator, notably for example in financial services or communications cases. The lesson here is that certain types of case have inherent features that make then more or less costly. However, some schemes can build in economies in their processes, as noted next.
5. The efficiency of the scheme's processing process. A major factor, for example, is whether the scheme is based on placing papers before a panel of three decision-makers, who need to be assembled together (such as in the Nordic or Netherlands models), or whether a case officer may handle cases, referring where necessary to a single ombudsman (as with may schemes in UK, Germany and France). Another factor is the ability to cut costs by relying on information technology for lodging and processing claims, which can significantly speed up cases and cut costs. A striking example is the French telecom scheme's refusal to accept complaints by telephone since that mode costs too much to process. Economies may be made in lodging allegations, collecting documents or obtaining expert opinions more quickly and cheaply than if they were done as distinct and sequential operations as in a court procedure.
6. The number of cases that are received by a CADR scheme is heavily influenced by the number of inquiries and complaints that have to be dealt with, and therefore filtered out, at 'lower' levels, by consumer advice systems, in-house CADR systems, or other arrangements. For example, a national 'residual' CADR scheme might not have to handle many disputes if they have been resolved by information systems, by earlier independent advice to consumers, by traders themselves, by earlier independent conciliation facilities, and so on. The Nordic model appears to be exceptionally effective in achieving both avoidance and early resolution of disputes through accessible advice systems on the demand side. The Dutch system of negotiating sectoral terms and conditions as a preliminary stage in establishing a dispute resolution Board also appears to encourage self-regulatory awareness by traders and controls by trade associations on the supply side, which tend to reduce the incidence of non-compliance and hence disputes. The power and effects of these features on the demand and supply sides may be very powerful in reducing the need for dispute resolution mechanisms, and hence their costs.

It is clear that significant economies of scale can be achieved in the supply of dispute resolution facilities. Leading examples of where economies of scale have been achieved are the Swedish national CADR system (the ARN), which handles all types of disputes that are not resolved by sectoral CADR schemes; the UK FOS, which was formed by a merger of a range of voluntary sectoral CADR schemes in 2001; the Dutch *Geschillencommissie* system, where around 50 sectoral schemes are administered on the same model by a single foundation; and the UK's two leading private sector CADR bodies (CEDR Disputes Group and Ombudsman Services), which administer a range of schemes on similar models.

Conclusions

CADR has grown quietly over as long as forty years from individual techniques of mediation and arbitration into an extensive and distinct self-standing matrix of dispute resolution schemes for consumer-to-business disputes. Both individually and collectively CADR schemes now provide effective dispute resolution for a large and growing number of issues. CADR has, in fact, matured into its own universe of dispute resolution that exists independently of the courts, and deserves to be considered on its own terms. CADR systems provide dispute resolution for many situations that have been quietly abrogated by courts. CADR is continuing to grow spontaneously, and has considerable further potential.

In particular, CADR offers considerable efficiency and effectiveness, since it can provide not just dispute resolution pathways but also regulatory and behaviour control of consumer traders and markets. CADR can be designed to integrate with regulatory, and self-regulatory, systems in an effective and cost-efficient manner.

CADR is still in a developmental phase. Experience is still developing with different techniques and structures. Considerable experience is already available of some techniques and general conclusions of them can be drawn. But it is too early to propose binding models that would apply in all circumstances. There needs to be further evaluation of the context in which particular techniques operate, so as to clarify parameters and requirements for best practice. Such context includes the architecture of the national legal system, the regulatory system, and the state of sophistication of regulators and business.

Incentives can be constructed so as to assist development by CADR schemes, especially by the private sector. An example is an official code approval scheme, such as the CCAS. It is almost startling how many CADR systems—and certainly many of the best current examples—are funded by the private sector. This represents privatisation of the cost of dispute resolution that is strongly resisted in terms of 'loser lays' rules, but is accepted when the outcomes can be seen as providing regulatory and commercial benefits. The implications are considerable for saving public expenditure, and redirecting public enforcement resource on rogue operators. Similarly, CADR offers the potential to provide cost-effective collective redress for small consumer claims that is far more effective, swift and cheaper than court-based collective procedures.

This analysis has been limited to C2B contract issues, but similar approaches can be developed for other types of claims such as personal injury cases. The demand for CADR can be expected to continue because:

- The high cost of litigation will force consumers and traders to seek cheaper and quicker pathways;
- CADR will be pushed by more businesses as part of customer care and quality systems;
- wider adoption of enforcement policies of restorative justice will pressure companies to seek quick negotiated solutions to major disputes, especially mass issues that require further restrictions in government expenditure on legal aid and courts will encourage

them and companies (and third party funders) to seek quick and cheap dispute resolution;
- the trend towards greater transparency on governance and wider involvement of civil society will be pursued by more businesses, and lead to adoption of more code-type solutions since they involve more stakeholders.

CADR systems will undoubtedly develop further. Innovation is usually helpful, but the risk is one of diversification within a single market. The key question is what form of external stimulus by governments can assist consumer CADR systems to be developed further.

The major lesson is that structures should be kept simple, so as to be visible and attractive to consumers and traders alike. It will also keep low costs low, since that is an essential feature in the attractiveness of those who have chosen CADR over courts. The lesson from the Nordic and Dutch systems is that structural simplicity is essential.

In short, we are witnessing the advent of a new European civil legal system. It is not based on the paradigm of courts as exclusive purveyors of dispute resolution services, onto which arbitration and mediation have been grafted. Instead, CADR systems have emerged as a discrete and distinct world of their own.

If CADR is to be of use to European civil society and the internal market, it will need nurturing on its own terms. The aspects that deserve particular attention are issues of structure, the independence of CADR providers, the incentivisation of in-house services, the relationship between CADR and courts, and between CADR and regulators. There needs to be a strategy for promoting, and for signposting, and sharing good practice, and encouraging

A Model for a National Consumer ADR Architecture

How would a European state design a CADR system so as to maximise:

a) swift, cheap, trusted dispute resolution of C2B complaints, with full restitution where due;
b) identification of market and trader issues, wide compliance by traders with trading laws and even higher standards so as to prevent problems arising, prevent escalation or spread of avoidable problems?

The principal design considerations are:

1. to maximise effective trade, and thereby minimise the number of C2B disputes, by providing expert, informed and reliable sources of consumer advice, from a small number of trusted and clearly identifiable bodies. There needs to be a unified national network of advice centres, linked to expert sectoral bodies.
2. to provide a similar structure of CADR, designed so that it is inherently more attractive to consumers and traders than the court system as a process for resolving small disputes involving applying established law to factual trading situations. Hence, it needs be more user-friendly, quicker, and cheaper than courts, as well as satisfying the essential requirements for any acceptable means of dispute resolution, such as independence, accuracy and consistency of outputs, and so on.

Almost all C2B cases involve small sums of money. Hence, the dispute resolution system has to be proportionate in terms of cost and duration. Even court small claims tracks are often challenged to fulfil the current standards demanded by modern consumers and markets of cost and duration. Above all, the system for C2B disputes has to be user-friendly: court systems almost always fail that test, whether on their own or especially when CADR systems are available as an alternative. Lodging a claim should be done online, and the case taken forward by the CADR body, acting impartially but providing swift feedback to the consumer and trader over settlement (conciliation, provided by phone or online), followed by delivering a decision. Even a court system that involves lodging papers followed by a decision to mediate, and then setting up a mediation, is too slow for modern consumers and traders, and involves disproportionate cost.

It is suggested that the outline of a CADR system should be as follows.

1. There should be a national CADR system. It should be recognisable as a system, and have a simple and consistent structure that can be easily identified and remembered by consumers and traders. Hence, it should not consist of a multitude of different models or operational arrangements. It is not necessary to impose a single operational model on every kind of sector or dispute, since some sectors might differ, but there should not be too many variations and the variations should be few and rational.
2. A CADR body must satisfy the essential requirements. All dispute resolution bodies (including courts and stand-alone arbitrators or mediators) should satisfy the same essential requirements. (A suggested list of essential requirements is discussed elsewhere.)
3. The extent to which proof that a CADR body or scheme satisfies the essential requirements might vary. The extent to which a certification process (whether granted by the state, or an independent body, or self-certification) depends on the circumstances. In any event, there should be an inspection/audit process, and a power to disqualify.
4. The name 'ombudsman' or 'médiateur' should be reserved for independent CADR bodies that satisfy the essential requirements. Such names should not be available for in-house customer relations of customer complaint functions, or any bodies that do not comply with the essential requirements. It is, of course, wholly appropriate for traders to use mediation functions, whether in-house or outsourced. However, confusion and misleading impressions as to independence etc must be avoided between independent CADR bodies and traders' in-house complaint handling functions/personnel.
5. CADR bodies that have power to make determinations on merits, whether formally binding or persuasive, should be independent of regulatory authorities, businesses and consumers or any other interested parties, and have no conflicts of interest.
6. All individuals acting for CADR bodies as mediators or decision-makers should be independent and have no conflicts of interest. They should have professional certification, obtained after undertaking training courses and refreshers approved by professional bodies.
7. The CADR system should be free of charge to consumers.
8. CADR bodies may be funded by the state, or from any other source, provided there are sufficient safeguards to ensure a satisfactory level of trust in their operational and decision-making independence and impartiality.
9. Funding from business is acceptable provided there are (a) governance arrangements that guarantee a majority of non-business personnel on an oversight board, (b) full transparency of the funding, mode of operation, personnel, and performance of the

body, and (c) the personnel who are involved in mediation and decision-making functions have no conflict of interest and hold professional certification.

10. Consumers should be able to access accurate, independent and comprehensive information and advice, both before making purchases (including on choosing between competing products and services) and afterwards (on how to contact traders, how to complain, and possibly assistance in the complaint process). The purpose of the advice function is to support informed and competitive consumer and trading decisions, and to reduce the incidence of problems that need to be resolved as disputes.
11. Such advice should ideally available from state-authorised bodies, even if funded by business (as on the Nordic model of local Consumer Advice Offices funded by local government, and sectoral State Bureaux funded by business associations).
12. The structure of advice and information bodies, of regulatory and of CADR bodies, should be simple and easy for consumers and traders to understand: a clear national structure is important.
    a. For advice bodies, there should be a national body with comprehensive web information, linked with an appropriate number of local outlets, and with a limited number of national sectoral bodies acting as centres of expertise.
    b. For CADR, there should be an ultimate and residual national CADR body, linked with an appropriate number of sectoral bodies that would be competent for handling all issues within their sectors.
    c. For regulators, there should be an ultimate and residual national consumer authority function, linked with an appropriate number of sectoral authorities that would be competent for issues within their sectors, and with a network of local enforcement authorities.
13. When any issue arises with a product or service that has been sold, consumers should be encouraged to contact (a) the supplier, (b) any appropriate source of independent advice.
14. Traders may if they wish inform consumers of a relevant, approved CADR scheme at any time, before or after purchase.
15. Traders should be required to refer consumers to the relevant CADR scheme, or inform them of their ability to contact it, when a dispute has arisen, pointing out that the facility is not available until the expiry of the time within which the trader may try to resolve the issue, or unless the trader sends a deadlock notification within that period. The cost of this should be kept to a minimum. If the existence of CADR bodies is sufficiently well-known in the country, this notification requirement may be unnecessary.
16. When a dispute arises, consumers should be required to contact the trader first before referring any dispute to court or to a CADR scheme, and to allow the trader an opportunity to respond to the problem within a fixed time. This would not be required where the trader is suspected of being fraudulent or having committed an offence, in which case the enforcement authority should be told as soon as possible.
17. CADR bodies should not be contacted until the trader has been given a reasonable time to respond: the cost to CADR bodies of rejecting premature complaints can be huge. This assumes that the advice function and the CADR function are split.
18. The time that the trader should be allowed to respond and to try to resolve the issue should be fixed, and approved by the regulatory authorities, in consultation with all

stakeholders. Current standards of 8 weeks seem to apply, but this may vary with size of trader and sector and type of problem. However, any variations should be kept to a minimum, since a national standard time would be simple to remember.

19. The dispute resolution system should follow a simple sequence:
    1. Consumer contacts the trader
    2. Consumer contacts the CADR, or is referred by the trader.
    3. CADR tries to conciliate.
    4. CADR makes a formal determination on a fair solution.
20. In diagrammatic form, the consumer should start at the bottom of a pyramid structure. Most disputes would be resolved at the bottom level, and more would be solved at each higher level, leaving a minimal number to be formally resolved at the highest level. (See the pyramid at Figure 15.1, p 406).
21. When a dispute is received by a CADR body, after the trader has been given a reasonable time to solve it, the CADR body should normally first try to reach a solution through conciliation, and if that is not possible within a reasonable time or with reasonable and proportionate effort, should then make a determination on a fair and legal outcome.
22. A CADR body should give a written decision that gives reasons of proportionate length that substantiates the determination.
23. After a CADR body has given a determination, whether it is binding or non-binding, the opponent should be given a reasonable (fixed) time to comply, or provide reasoned objections. The nature of CADR cases is that it would be disproportionate to provide a CADR appeal facility.
24. If a party to a CADR case wishes to enforce a non-binding CADR determination, there should be a fast track court procedure, so as to save costs. The procedure should not require the need to re-examine all the evidence afresh (the case file would be transferred to the court by the CADR), and give a reasonable opportunity for either side to introduce fresh evidence (but subject to a possible cost penalty if the court's time is wasted). The court should be free to make its own determination on the evidence: there should not be a presumption of liability.
25. In principle, the outcomes of disputes, and performance of CADR bodies, should be transparent. Relevant aggregated data should be published by CADR bodies, which can be aggregated with data from public agencies or any other source, so as to give a full picture of market issues that might affect consumer trading. Such aggregated data could inform consumer advice and choice, safety issues, protection issues, and enforcement action. The necessary data includes the number of complaints received, the identity of the traders, the outcomes of contacts (settled by the parties, withdrawn, subject to a decision by the CADR body, complaint upheld or rejected), the nature of the issues raised.
26. However, it may be disproportionately costly to make available the outcome and reasoning in every individual case. Hence, the amount of information made public may vary sector and type of case. The level of information made public should be decided by the oversight agency and stakeholders, in consultation with the CADR's governing body.
27. CADR bodies should publish Key Performance Targets, indicating if these are agreed with regulators or stakeholders, and their outputs on performance achieved against such targets, at least on an annual basis. Matters covered should include total

administrative cost, cost per case handled, number of complaints processed and outcomes, duration of processing.

28. A consumer should be free to bring a complaint in court (thereby complying with ECHR Article 6).
    a. The court would be the correct track if any point of law needs to be decided.
    b. The court would also be appropriate as a safety-net or long-stop for any case where the CADR system has broken down, or for any other valid reason.
    c. However, the court would normally not accept straightforward cases that could be resolved by an available CADR system, unless and until that CADR system had been tried and not produced a result.
    d. Court guidance may provide that a case should not be commenced unless and until appropriate contact and ADR has occurred between the parties.
    e. Court rules may provide that where a case has been commenced before appropriate contact and ADR has not occurred between the parties, the commencing party may or should not be able to recover his costs, and may or should be liable for the opponents' costs.
29. The function of CADR bodies is to apply established law to factual disputes. In principle, CADR bodies should not decide issues of law (although there can be a measure of discretion in cases of little legal importance).
30. CADR bodies should refer issues of law to a court for determination.
31. Equally, courts should refer a case to a relevant CADR body if it involves application of fixed law and it is proportionate for a CADR body to process it. This will usually be the case in mass cases.

Commission Recommendation of 30 March 1998 (98/257/EC)

II

(Acts whose publication is not obligatory)

COMMISSION

COMMISSION RECOMMENDATION
of 30 March 1998
on the principles applicable to the bodies responsible for out-of-court settlement of consumer disputes (*)
(Text with EEA relevance)

(98/257/EC)

THE COMMISSION OF THE EUROPEAN COMMUNITIES,

Having regard to the Treaty establishing the European Community and in particular Article 155 thereof,

Whereas the Council, in its conclusions approved by the Consumer Affairs Council of 25 November 1996, emphasised the need to boost consumer confidence in the functioning of the internal market and consumers' scope for taking full advantage of the possibilities offered by the internal market, including the possibility for consumers to settle disputes in an efficient and appropriate manner through out-of-court or other comparable procedures;

Whereas the European Parliament, in its resolution of 14 November 1996 (1), stressed the need for such procedures to meet minimum criteria guaranteeing the impartiality of the body, the efficiency of the procedure and the publicising and transparency of proceedings and called on the Commission to draft proposals on this matter;

Whereas most consumer disputes, by their nature, are characterised by a disproportion between the economic value at stake and the cost of its judicial settlement; whereas the

(*) A communication on the out-of-court settlement of consumer disputes was adopted by the Commission on 30 March 1998. This communication, which includes this recommendation and the European consumer complaint form, is available on the Internet (http://europa.eu.int/comm/dg24).
(1) European Parliament resolution on the Commission communication `Action plan on consumer access to justice and the settlement of consumer disputes in the internal market' of 14 November 1996 (OJ C 362, 2. 12. 1996, p. 275).

difficulties that court procedures may involve may, notably in the case of cross-border conflicts, discourage consumers from exercising their rights in practice;

Whereas the `Green Paper on the access of consumers to justice and the settlement of consumer disputes in the single market' (2) was the subject of wide-ranging consultations whose results have confirmed the urgent need for Community action with a view to improving the current situation;

Whereas the experience gained by several Member States shows that alternative mechanisms for the out-of-court settlement of consumer disputes – provided certain essential principles are respected – have had good results, both for consumers and firms, by reducing the cost of settling consumer disputes and the duration of the procedure;

Whereas the adoption of such principles at European level would facilitate the implementation of out-of-court procedures for settling consumer disputes; whereas, in the case of cross-border conflicts, this would enhance mutual confidence between existing out-of-court bodies in the different Member States and strengthen consumer confidence in the existing national procedures; whereas these criteria will make it easier for parties providing out-ofcourt settlement services established in one Member State to offer their services in other Member States;

Whereas one of the conclusions of the Green Paper concerned the adoption of a Commission recommendation with a view to improving the functioning of the ombudsman systems responsible for handling consumer disputes;

Whereas the need for such a recommendation was stressed during the consultations on the Green Paper and was confirmed during the consultation on the `Action Plan' communication (1) by a very large majority of the parties concerned;

Whereas this recommendation must be limited to procedures which, no matter what they are called, lead to the settling of a dispute through the active intervention of a third party, who proposes or imposes a solution; whereas, therefore, it does not concern procedures that merely involve an attempt to bring the parties together to convince them to find a solution by common consent;

Whereas the decisions taken by out-of-court bodies may be binding on the parties, may be mere recommendations or may constitute settlement proposals which have to be accepted by the parties; whereas for the purposes of this recommendation these various cases are covered by the term `decision';

Whereas the decision-making body's impartiality and objectivity are essential for safeguarding the protection of consumer rights and for strengthening consumer confidence in alternative mechanisms for resolving consumer disputes;

(2) COM(93) 576 final of 16 November 1993.
(1) Action Plan on consumer access to justice and the settlement of consumer disputes in the internal market, COM(96) 13 final of 14 February 1996.

Whereas a body can only be impartial if, in exercising its functions, it is not subject to pressures that might sway its decision; whereas, therefore, its independence must be guaranteed without this implying the need for guarantees
that are as strict as those designed to ensure the independence of judges in the judicial system;

Whereas, when the decision is taken by an individual, the decision-maker's impartiality can only be assured if he can demonstrate that he possesses the necessary independence and qualifications and works in an environment which allows him to decide on an autonomous basis;

whereas this requires the person to be granted a mandate of sufficient duration, in the course of which he cannot be relieved of his duties without just cause;

Whereas, when the decision is taken by a group, equal participation of representatives of consumers and professionals is an appropriate way of ensuring this independence;

Whereas, in order to ensure that the persons concerned receive the information they need, the transparency of the procedure and of the activities of the bodies responsible for resolving the disputes must be guaranteed; whereas the absence of transparency may adversely affect the rights of the parties and cause misgivings as to out-of-court procedures for resolving consumer disputes;

Whereas certain interests of the parties can only be safeguarded if the procedure allows them to express their viewpoints before the competent body and to acquaint themselves with the facts presented by the opposing party and, where applicable, the experts' statements; whereas this does not necessarily necessitate oral hearings of the parties;

Whereas out-of-court procedures are designed to facilitate consumer access to justice; whereas, therefore, if they are to be effective, they must remedy certain problems associated with court procedures, such as high fees, long delays and cumbersome procedures;

Whereas, in order to enhance the effectiveness and equity of the procedure, the competent body must play an active role which allows it to take into consideration any element useful in resolving the dispute; whereas this active role is all the more important when, in the framework of out-of-court procedures, the parties in many cases do not have the benefit of legal advice;

Whereas the out-of-court bodies may decide not only on the basis of legal rules but also in equity and on the basis of codes of conduct; whereas, however, this flexibility as regards the grounds for their decisions should not lead to a reduction in the level of consumer protection by comparison with the protection consumers would enjoy, under Community law, through the application of the law by the courts;

Whereas the parties are entitled to be informed of the decisions handed down and of grounds for these decisions; whereas the grounds for decisions are a prerequisite for transparency and the parties' confidence in the operation of out-of-court procedures;

Whereas in accordance with Article 6 of the European Human Rights Convention, access to the courts is a fundamental right that knows no exceptions; whereas since Community law guarantees free movement of goods and services in the common market, it is a corollary of those freedoms that operators, including consumers, must be able, in order to resolve any disputes arising from their economic activities, to bring actions in the courts of a Member State in the same way as nationals of that State; whereas out-of-court procedures cannot be designed to replace court procedures; whereas, therefore, use of the out-of-court alternative may not deprive consumers of their right to bring the matter before the courts unless they expressly agree to do so, in full awareness of the facts and only after the dispute has materialised;

Whereas in some cases, and independently of the subject and value of the dispute, the parties and in particular the consumer, as the party who is regarded as economically weaker and less experienced in legal matters than the other party to the contract, may require the legal advice of a third party to defend and protect their rights more effectively;

Whereas, in order to ensure a level of transparency and dissemination of information on out-of-court procedures in line with the principles set out in the recommendation and to facilitate networking, the Commission intends to create a database of the out-of-court bodies responsible for resolving consumer disputes that offer these safeguards; whereas the database will contain particulars communicated to the Commission by the Member States that wish to participate in this initiative; whereas, to ensure standardised information and to simplify the transmission of these data, a standard information form will be made available to the Member States;

Whereas, finally, the establishment of minimum principles governing the creation and operation of out-of-court procedures for resolving consumer disputes seems, in these circumstances, necessary at Community level to support and supplement, in an essential area, the initiatives taken by the Member States in order to realise, in accordance with Article 129a of the Treaty, a high level of consumer protection; whereas it does not go beyond what is necessary to ensure the smooth operation of out-of-court procedures; whereas it is therefore consistent with the principle of subsidiarity,

RECOMMENDS that all existing bodies and bodies to be created with responsibility for the out-of-court settlement of consumer disputes respect the following principles:

I

Principle of independence

The independence of the decision-making body is ensured in order to guarantee the impartiality of its actions.

When the decision is taken by an individual, this independence is in particular guaranteed by the following measures:

- the person appointed possesses the abilities, experience and competence, particularly in the field of law, required to carry out his function,

- the person appointed is granted a period of office of sufficient duration to ensure the independence of his action and shall not be liable to be relieved of his duties without just cause,
- if the person concerned is appointed or remunerated by a professional association or an enterprise, he must not, during the three years prior to assuming his present function, have worked for this professional association or for one of its members or for the enterprise concerned.

When the decision is taken by a collegiate body, the independence of the body responsible for taking the decision must be ensured by giving equal representation to consumers and professionals or by complying with the criteria set out above.

II

Principle of transparency

Appropriate measures are taken to ensure the transparency of the procedure. These include:

1. provision of the following information, in writing or any other suitable form, to any persons requesting it:

- a precise description of the types of dispute which may be referred to the body concerned, as well as any existing restrictions in regard to territorial coverage and the value of the dispute,
- the rules governing the referral of the matter to the body, including any preliminary requirements that the consumer may have to meet, as well as other procedural rules, notably those concerning the written or oral nature of the procedure, attendance in person and the languages of the procedure,
- the possible cost of the procedure for the parties, including rules on the award of costs at the end of the procedure,
- the type of rules serving as the basis for the body's decisions (legal provisions, considerations of equity, codes of conduct, etc.),
- the decision-making arrangements within the body,
- the legal force of the decision taken, whereby it shall be stated clearly whether it is binding on the professional or on both parties. If the decision is binding, the penalties to be imposed in the event of non-compliance shall be stated, as shall the means of obtaining redress available to the losing party.

2. Publication by the competent body of an annual report setting out the decisions taken, enabling the results obtained to be assessed and the nature of the disputes referred to it to be identified.

III

Adversarial principle

The procedure to be followed allows all the parties concerned to present their viewpoint before the competent body and to hear the arguments and facts put forward by the other party, and any experts' statements.

IV

Principle of effectiveness

The effectiveness of the procedure is ensured through measures guaranteeing:
- that the consumer has access to the procedure without being obliged to use a legal representative,
- that the procedure is free of charges or of moderate costs,
- that only short periods elapse between the referral of a matter and the decision,
- that the competent body is given an active role, thus enabling it to take into consideration any factors conducive to a settlement of the dispute.

V

Principle of legality

The decision taken by the body may not result in the consumer being deprived of the protection afforded by the mandatory provisions of the law of the State in whose territory the body is established. In the case of crossborder disputes, the decision taken by the body may not result in the consumer being deprived of the protection afforded by the mandatory provisions applying under the law of the Member State in which he is normally resident in the instances provided for under Article 5 of the Rome Convention of 19 June 1980 on the law applicable to contractual obligations.

All decisions are communicated to the parties concerned as soon as possible, in writing or any other suitable form, stating the grounds on which they are based.

VI

Principle of liberty

The decision taken by the body concerned may be binding on the parties only if they were informed of its binding nature in advance and specifically accepted this.

The consumer's recourse to the out-of-court procedure may not be the result of a commitment prior to the materialisation of the dispute, where such commitment has the effect of depriving the consumer of his right to bring an action before the courts for the settlement of the dispute.

VII

Principle of representation

The procedure does not deprive the parties of the right to be represented or assisted by a third party at all stages of the procedure.

THIS RECOMMENDATION is addressed to the bodies responsible for the out-of-court settlement of consumer disputes, to any natural or legal person responsible for the creation or operation of such bodies, as well as to the
Member States, to the extent that they are involved.

Done at Brussels, 30 March 1998.

For the Commission

Emma BONINO
Member of the Commission

Commission Recommendation of 4 April 2001 (2001/310/EC)

II

(Acts whose publication is not obligatory)

COMMISSION

COMMISSION RECOMMENDATION
of 4 April 2001
on the principles for out-of-court bodies involved in the consensual resolution of consumer disputes
(notified under document number C(2001) 1016)
(Text with EEA relevance)

(2001/310/EC)

THE COMMISSION OF THE EUROPEAN COMMUNITIES,

Having regard to the Treaty establishing the European Community, and in particular Article 211 thereof,

Whereas:

(1) In order to ensure a high level of consumer protection and to promote consumer confidence, the Community should ensure that consumers have simple and effective access to justice and encourage and facilitate the settling of consumer disputes at an earlier stage.

(2) The continuing development of new forms of commercial practices involving consumers such as electronic commerce, and the expected increase in cross-border transactions, require that particular attention be paid to generating the confidence of consumers, in particular by ensuring easy access to practical, effective and inexpensive means of redress, including access by electronic means. The e-Europe Action Plan, agreed by the Feira European Council on 19 and 20 June 2000, recognised that for e-commerce to reach its full potential consumer confidence must be enhanced, in partnership with consumer groups, industry and Member States, by promoting access to alternative dispute resolution systems.

(3) On 30 March 1998 the Commission adopted Recommendation 98/257/EC on the principles applicable to the bodies responsible for out-of-court settlement of consumer

disputes (1). However the scope of that Recommendation was limited to procedures which, no matter what they are called, lead to the settlement of a dispute through the active intervention of a third party, who proposes or imposes a solution. It did not concern procedures that merely involve an attempt to bring the parties together to convince them to find a solution by common consent.

(4) The Council, in its Resolution of 25 May 2000 on a Community-wide network of national bodies for the extra-judicial settlement of consumer disputes (2), noted that those out-of-court bodies falling outside the scope of Recommendation 98/257/EC play a useful role for the consumer and invited the Commission to develop in close cooperation with Member States common criteria for the assessment of such bodies which should ensure, inter alia, their quality, fairness and effectiveness. In particular it indicated that Member States apply such criteria to include such bodies or schemes in the network referred to in Commission working document on the creation of a European extra-judicial network (EEJ-Net) (1).

(5) Article 17 of Directive 2000/31/EC of the European Parliament and of the Council of 8 June 2000 on certain legal aspects of information society services, in particular electronic commerce in the internet market (2) stipulates that Member States should ensure their legislation does not hamper the use of out-of-court schemes available under national law, for dispute settlement.

(6) Electronic commerce facilitates cross-border transactions between business and consumers. Such transactions are frequently of low value and therefore the resolution of any dispute needs to be simple, quick and inexpensive. New technolgy can contribute to the development of electronic dispute settlement systems, providing a mechanism to effectively settle disputes across different jurisdictions without the need for face-to-face contact, and therefore should be encouraged through principles ensuring consistent and reliable standards to give all users confidence.

(7) The Council, in conclusions adopted on 29 May 2000 (3), invited the Commission to draw up a Green Paper on alternative methods of settling disputes under civil and commercial law to take stock of and review the existing situation and initiate wide-ranging consultation.

(8) The European Parliament in its opinion on the proposal for a regulation on jurisdiction and the recognition and enforcement of judgments in civil and commercial matters (4), called for the extensive use of extra-judicial dispute resolution for consumers transactions, in particular where the parties are domiciled in different Member States and in view of the cost and delay associated with going to court. The Council and Commission in their statement for the adoption of the abovementioned Regulation stressed that in general it is

(1) Commission Recommendation of 30 March 1998 on the principles applicable to the bodies responsible for out-of-court settlement of consumer disputes (OJ L 115, 17.4.1998, p. 31).
(2) OJ C 155, 6.6.2000, p. 1.
(1) SEC(2000) 405. See Internet site: http://europa.eu.int/comm/consumers/policy/developments/acce_just/acce_just06_en.pdf
(2) OJ L 178, 17.7.2000, p. 1.
(3) SI (2000) 519.
(4) Opinion delivered on 21 September 2000 regarding Regulation (EC) No 44/2001 (OJ L 12, 16.1.2001, p. 1).

in the interest of consumers and undertakings to try to settle their disputes amicably before resorting to the courts and reiterated the importance of continuing the work on alternative methods of dispute settlement at European Community level.

(9) The principles set out in this Recommendation do not affect the principles laid down in Commission Recommendation 98/257/EC which should be respected by those out-of-court procedures which, no matter what they are called, lead to the settling of a dispute through the active intervention of a third party, who proposes or imposes a solution, usually by means of a binding or non-binding formal decision, upon the parties. The present principles should be respected by any other third party procedures, no matter what they are called, which facilitate the resolution of a consumer dispute by bringing the parties together and assisting them, for example by making informal suggestions on settlement options, in reaching a solution by common consent. The principles are limited to consumer dispute resolution procedures which are designed as an alternative to resolving the dispute in a court. Therefore customer complaint mechanisms operated by a business and conducted directly with the consumer, or where a third party carries out such services by or on behalf of a business, are excluded as they form part of the usual discussions between the parties prior to any dispute materialising that would be referred to a third party body responsible for dispute resolution or a court.

(10) The impartiality of these dispute resolution procedures must be guaranteed to ensure that all parties have confidence in its fairness. Whether it is an individual or a group responsible for the dispute resolution procedure, appropriate measures should be taken to ensure impartiality and to ensure the disclosure of information to the parties demonstrating their impartiality and competence to allow the parties to make an informed choice as to whether to participate in the procedure.

(11) In order to ensure that both parties have access to the information they need, the transparency of the procedure must be guaranteed. The agreed solution resolving the dispute should be recorded and made available to the parties by the body responsible for the procedure to avoid later uncertainty or misunderstanding.

(12) In order to enhance the effectiveness of these procedures in resolving cross-border disputes, they need to be easily accessible and available to both parties wherever they are situated. In particular electronic measures to facilitate this should be encouraged.

(13) If such procedures are to provide a realistic alternative to a dispute going through the courts, they should aim to overcome the associated problems of cost, delay, complexity and representation. Measures guaranteeing proportionate or no costs, easier access, efficiency, the monitoring of the progression of the dispute and keeping the parties informed are necessary to ensure its effectiveness.

(14) In accordance with Article 6 of the European Human Rights Convention, access to the courts is a fundamental right. Since Community law guarantees free movement of goods and services in the common market, it is a corollary of those freedoms that operators, including consumers, must be able, in order to resolve any disputes arising from their economic activities, to bring actions in the courts of a Member State in the same way as

nationals of that State. Consumer dispute resolution procedures cannot be designed to replace court procedures. Therefore use of such procedures may not deprive consumers of their right to bring the matter before the courts unless they expressly agree to do so, in full awareness of the facts and only after the dispute has materialised.

(15) The fairness of the procedures should be safeguarded by allowing the parties to provide any necessary and relevant information. Depending on the organisation of the procedure, information provided by the parties should be treated as confidential unless they expressly agree otherwise, or, if an adversarial approach is used at any stage appropriate measures should ensure its fairness. Measures should be envisaged to encourage and monitor the parties' cooperation with the procedure, in particular by requiring information that may be necessary for the fair resolution of the dispute.

(16) Before the parties agree to a suggested solution on how to settle the dispute they should be allowed a reasonable amount of time to consider the details and any possible conditions or terms.

(17) In order to ensure that procedures are fair and flexible and that consumers have the opportunity to make a fully informed choice, they must be given clear and understandable information in order that they can reflect on whether to agree to a suggested solution, obtain advice if they wish or to consider other options.

(18) The Commission will include in its database of the out-of-court bodies responsible for resolving consumer disputes information provided by Member States regarding the use of such principles by consumer dispute resolution bodies falling within the scope of this recommendation in order to participate in the European extra-judicial network (EEJ-Net).

(19) Finally, the setting out of principles for bodies responsible for consumer dispute resolution procedures not covered by the principles in Recommendation 98/257/EC seems, in these circumstances, necessary at Community level to support and supplement, in an essential area, the initiatives taken by the Member States in order to realise, in accordance with Article 153 of the Treaty, a high level of consumer protection. It does not go beyond what is necessary to ensure the smooth operation of consumer dispute resolution procedures. It is therefore consistent with the principle of subsidiarity,

HEREBY RECOMMENDS:

That the principles set out in Part II are respected by all existing and future bodies providing out-of-court consumer dispute resolution procedures falling within the scope of this recommendation as defined in Part I:

I. **SCOPE**

1. This recommendation applies to third party bodies responsible for out-of-court consumer dispute resolution procedures that, no matter what they are called, attempt to resolve a dispute by bringing the parties together to convince them to find a solution by common consent.

2. It does not apply to customer complaint mechanisms operated by a business and concluded directly with the consumer or to such mechanisms carrying out such services operated by or on behalf of a business.

II. **PRINCIPLES**

A. **Impartiality**

Impartiality should be guaranteed by ensuring that those responsible for the procedure:
(a) are appointed for a fixed term and shall not be liable to be relieved from their duties without just cause;
(b) have no perceived or actual conflict of interest with either party;
(c) provide information about their impartiality and competence to both parties prior to the commencement of the procedure.

B. **Transparency**

1. The transparency of the procedure should be guaranteed.

2. Information about the contact details, functioning and availability of the procedure should be readily available to the parties in simple terms so that they can access and retain it before submitting a dispute.

3. In particular, information should be made available on:
(a) how the procedure will operate, the types of disputes that can be dealt by it and any restrictions on its operation;
(b) the rules governing any preliminary requirements that the parties may have to meet, and other procedural rules, notably those concerning the operation of the procedure and the languages in which the procedure will be conducted;
(c) the cost, if any, to be borne by the parties;
(d) the timetable applicable to the procedure, particularly with regard to the type of dispute in question;
(e) any substantive rules that may be applicable (legal provisions, industry best practice, considerations of equity, codes of conduct);
(f) the role of the procedure in bringing about the resolution of a dispute;
(g) the status of any agreed solution for resolving the dispute.

4. Any agreed solution for resolving the dispute by the parties should be recorded on a durable medium and should clearly state the terms and the grounds on which it is based. That record should be made available to both parties.

5. Information on the performance of the procedure should be made publicly available, including:
(a) the number and types of complaints it has received and their outcome;
(b) the time taken to resolve complaints;
(c) any systematic problems arising from complaints;
(d) the compliance record, if known, of agreed solutions.

C. **Effectiveness**

1. The effectiveness of the procedure should be guaranteed.

2. It should be easily accessible and available to both parties, for instance by electronic means, irrespective of where the parties are situated.

3. The procedure should be either free of charge to consumers, or any necessary costs should be both proportionate to the amount in dispute and moderate.

4. The parties should have access to the procedure without being obliged to use a legal representative. Nonetheless the parties should not be prevented from being represented or assisted by a third party at any or all stages of the procedure.

5. Once a dispute has been submitted it should be dealt with in the shortest possible time commensurate with the nature of the dispute. The body responsible for the procedure should periodically review its progress to ensure the parties' dispute is being dealt with expeditiously and appropriately.

6. The conduct of the parties should be reviewed by the body responsible for the procedure to ensure they are committed to seeking a proper, fair and timely resolution of the dispute. If one party's conduct is unsatisfactory, both parties should be informed in order to enable them to consider whether to continue the dispute resolution procedure.

D. **Fairness**

1. The fairness of the procedure should be guaranteed. In particular:
(a) the parties should be informed of their right to refuse to participate or to withdraw from the procedure at any time and access the legal system or other out-of-court redress mechanisms at any stage if they are dissatisfied with the performance or operation of the procedure;
(b) both parties should be able to freely and easily submit any arguments, information or evidence relevant to their case on a confidential basis to the procedure unless agreement has been given by the parties to pass such information to the other party. If at any stage, the third party suggests possible solutions for resolving the dispute, then each party should have the opportunity to present their viewpoint and comment on any argument, information or evidence presented by the other party;
(c) both parties should be encouraged to fully cooperate with the procedure, in particular by providing any information necessary for a fair resolution of the dispute;
(d) prior to the parties agreeing to a suggested solution for resolving the dispute, they should be allowed a reasonable period of time to consider this solution.

2. The consumer should be informed in clear und understandable language, before agreeing to a suggested solution, of the following points:
(a) he has the choice as to whether or not to agree to the suggested solution;
(b) the suggested solution may be less favourable than an outcome determined by a court applying legal rules;

(c) before agreeing to or rejecting the suggested solution he has the right to seek independent advice;
(d) use of the procedure does not preclude the option of referring his dispute to another out-of-court dispute resolution mechanism, in particular within the scope of Recommendation 98/257/EC, or of seeking legal redress through his own judicial system;
(e) the status of an agreed solution.

THIS RECOMMENDATION

is addressed to Member States in so far as it affects them, in relation to those procedures designed to facilitate the out-of-court settlement of consumer disputes and to any natural or legal person responsible for the creation or operation of such procedures.

Done at Brussels, 4 April 2001.

For the Commission

David BYRNE
Member of the Commission

European Code of Conduct for Mediators

This code of conduct sets out a number of principles to which individual mediators may voluntarily decide to commit themselves, under their own responsibility. It may be used by mediators involved in all kinds of mediation in civil and commercial matters.

Organisations providing mediation services may also make such a commitment by asking mediators acting under the auspices of their organisation to respect the code of conduct. Organisations may make available information on the measures, such as training, evaluation and monitoring, they are taking to support the respect of the code by individual mediators.

For the purposes of the code of conduct, mediation means any structured process, however named or referred to, whereby two or more parties to a dispute attempt by themselves, on a voluntary basis, to reach an agreement on the settlement of their dispute with the assistance of a third person – hereinafter "the mediator".

Adherence to the code of conduct is without prejudice to national legislation or rules regulating individual professions.

Organisations providing mediation services may wish to develop more detailed codes adapted to their specific context or the types of mediation services they offer, as well as to specific areas such as family mediation or consumer mediation.

1. COMPETENCE, APPOINTMENT AND FEES OF MEDIATORS AND PROMOTION OF THEIR SERVICES

1.1. Competence

Mediators must be competent and knowledgeable in the process of mediation. Relevant factors include proper training and continuous updating of their education and practice in mediation skills, having regard to any relevant standards or accreditation schemes.

1.2. Appointment

Mediators must confer with the parties regarding suitable dates on which the mediation may take place. Mediators must verify that they have the appropriate background and competence to conduct mediation in a given case before accepting the appointment. Upon request, they must disclose information concerning their background and experience to the parties.

1.3. Fees

Where not already provided, mediators must always supply the parties with complete information as to the mode of remuneration which they intend to apply. They must not agree to act in a mediation before the principles of their remuneration have been accepted by all parties concerned.

1.4. Promotion of mediators' services

Mediators may promote their practice provided that they do so in a professional, truthful and dignified way.

2. INDEPENDENCE AND IMPARTIALITY

2.1. Independence

If there are any circumstances that may, or may be seen to, affect a mediator's independence or give rise to a conflict of interests, the mediator must disclose those circumstances to the parties before acting or continuing to act.

Such circumstances include:

- any personal or business relationship with one or more of the parties;
- any financial or other interest, direct or indirect, in the outcome of the mediation;
- the mediator, or a member of his firm, having acted in any capacity other than mediator for one or more of the parties.

In such cases the mediator may only agree to act or continue to act if he is certain of being able to carry out the mediation in full independence in order to ensure complete impartiality and the parties explicitly consent.

The duty to disclose is a continuing obligation throughout the process of mediation.

2.2. Impartiality

Mediators must at all times act, and endeavour to be seen to act, with impartiality towards the parties and be committed to serve all parties equally with respect to the process of mediation.

3. THE MEDIATION AGREEMENT, PROCESS AND SETTLEMENT

3.1. Procedure

The mediator must ensure that the parties to the mediation understand the characteristics of the mediation process and the role of the mediator and the parties in it.

The mediator must in particular ensure that prior to commencement of the mediation the parties have understood and expressly agreed the terms and conditions of the mediation agreement including any applicable provisions relating to obligations of confidentiality on the mediator and on the parties.

The mediation agreement may, upon request of the parties, be drawn up in writing.

The mediator must conduct the proceedings in an appropriate manner, taking into account the circumstances of the case, including possible imbalances of power and any wishes the parties may express, the rule of law and the need for a prompt settlement of the dispute. The parties may agree with the mediator on the manner in which the mediation is to be conducted, by reference to a set of rules or otherwise.

The mediator may hear the parties separately, if he deems it useful.

3.2. Fairness of the process

The mediator must ensure that all parties have adequate opportunities to be involved in the process.

The mediator must inform the parties, and may terminate the mediation, if:

- a settlement is being reached that for the mediator appears unenforceable or illegal, having regard to the circumstances of the case and the competence of the mediator for making such an assessment, or
- the mediator considers that continuing the mediation is unlikely to result in a settlement.

3.3. The end of the process

The mediator must take all appropriate measures to ensure that any agreement is reached by all parties through knowing and informed consent, and that all parties understand the terms of the agreement.

The parties may withdraw from the mediation at any time without giving any justification.

The mediator must, upon request of the parties and within the limits of his competence, inform the parties as to how they may formalise the agreement and the possibilities for making the agreement enforceable.

4. CONFIDENTIALITY

The mediator must keep confidential all information arising out of or in connection with the mediation, including the fact that the mediation is to take place or has taken place, unless compelled by law or grounds of public policy to disclose it. Any information disclosed in confidence to mediators by one of the parties must not be disclosed to the other parties without permission, unless compelled by law.

French Charter of Consumer Mediation[1]

PREAMBLE

Created by Law No. 2010-737 of 1 July 2010 the Commission of Mediation of Consumer Affairs (CMC) is responsible for issuing advice and proposes measures of any kind to evaluate, improve, and disseminate best practices for non-judicial mediation in consumer matters.

The Commission of Mediation of Consumer Affairs is an independent body, consisting of one President and five consumer representatives, of which five are professionals and two qualified individuals.

This commission is not intended to address individual mediation cases but to participate actively in the development of quality mediation in consumer matters.

While establishing the Commission on October 20, 2010, the Secretary of State for consumers made it her particular mission to develop a charter of good practice for mediation. The purpose of this charter is to establish principles and rules to be followed by mediators as well as businesses, industries, and governments that implement mediation.

This Charter is part of the European Directive 2008/52/EC of 21 May 2008 "on certain aspects of mediation in civil and commercial matters."

It will serve as a foundation for the evaluation of the practices of mediators by the commission.

ARTICLE 1 - DEFINITION OF CONSUMER MEDIATION

Mediation of consumer matters is a structured process in which the mediator's mission is to facilitate the resolution of a dispute between two parties, one of which is a professional and the other a consumer, an individual acting outside of his profession. Mediation is conducted by an impartial mediator with competence and efficiency.

Mediation is a process freely agreed to by the parties. The parties free to stop at any time, to continue, or not to enter into the mediation. Mediation requires the parties to show loyalty that is characterized by a willingness to work together and to meet information requests from the mediator.

[1] http://www.mediation-conso.fr/charte.html.

The mediation is free for consumers.

Mediation is a confidential process unless the parties agree otherwise.

ARTICLE 2 - THE COMMITTEE ON MEDIATION IN CONSUMER MATTERS (CMC)

The CMC is responsible for assessing good practices in mediation.

In this context, the CMC is to capture or takes notice of any proposed new charter of mediation to ensure that the conditions for its establishment and its operation comply with this Charter. The CMC performs the same evaluation regarding mediation of existing consumer matters. Following this assessment, the CMC invited the *Mediateur* to agree to this Charter. He will then appear as a signing mediator of this charter on the CMC website: www.mediation-conso.fr.

The mediator may mention this listing by stating: "Mediation recognized by the Commission of Consumer Mediation (CMC)."

A consumer can inform the CMC of the misapplication by any mediator who referred to provisions in this Charter. The CMC may remove any mediator from its site who practices or operates in a manner that is inconsistent with this Charter.

ARTICLE 3 – LE MEDIATEUR

Article 3.1 - Guarantees of impartiality and independence

The Médiateur must have the necessary guarantees of impartiality and independence in the exercise of his functions. He must also have the assurance of the parties. For this purpose, he is expected to adhere to the following rules:

- An advisory opinion of the consumer association may be requested to approve the appointment.

- In the case of a commercial mediation, the appointment has to be at the highest level

- On his appointment, the Médiateur agrees to report any inconsistency or conflict of interest that should arise during his term.

- The mandate of the Médiateur has a term which must be sufficient to ensure stability and continuity in cases dealt with: a minimum period of three years, renewable in the same manner as the appointment, is appropriate.

- A Médiateur cannot be revoked during his term of office, except for legitimate reasons. He may not combine his mediation function with other functions within the company or sector.

- The Médiateur must have his own means of operation, including an independent budget and a dedicated team appropriate to his needs. His jurisdiction should be as wide as possible.

- The Médiateur is an identified person. When there is a mediation body, that body is represented by its president.

Article 3.2 - Guarantees competence and efficiency

The Médiateur is chosen for his human qualities and competence. The Médiateur warrants, as applicable, training or experience appropriate to the practice of mediation in consumer matters. He is committed to regularly updating his knowledge. Legal training or specialist expertise is not essential but the Médiateur must be able to call upon people in the event that legal or technical assistance is needed.

ARTICLE 4 - MEDIATION PROCESS

Section 4.1 - Information and communication

A company that has its own Médiateur, or a business using a sectoral Médiateur, has to inform consumers adequately about the existence of the Médiateur's role, scope, free proceedings, referral procedures and possibility for the consumer to be assisted by any person of his choice.

All appropriate contractual documents between the professional and the consumer must include details of the Médiateur.

Information on the Médiateur is communicated via the websites including businesses or sectors concerned and should be easily accessible.

Eligibility to apply to the Médiateur, with contact information and referral procedures is indicated at the negative response of the last level internal appeals procedure.

Communications on the Ombudsman should never be used for advertising purposes.

Article 4.2 – Reference

The Médiateur can only be approached after all other avenues of the consumer service have been taken, or in the absence of a response of the customer services within the deadline of two months.

The existence of a customer service and appropriate quality is essential for the proper functioning of the mediation but cannot be confused with it.

The referral to the Médiateur must be made in writing and sent by mail, email or fax. Any request for mediation results in an acknowledgment.

It is recommended that the Médiateur redirects complaints to the right level if the case was sent prematurely.

If he declines jurisdiction, the Médiateur must inform the consumer in writing. In cases of multiple mediation systems, the consumer is free to enter the mediator of their choice.

Section 4.3 Conduct

The date of receipt of the request for mediation, if it is admissible, is the starting point for mediation.

Each party must be able to hear their views.

The Médiateur and the parties are bound by confidentiality regarding the names of the parties, the information obtained during the investigation of the dispute and the facts they have learned in the context of mediation.

The Médiateur forms his opinions on the basis of law and equity.

He informs the parties in writing of the result of his mediation. His answer should be clear and easily understandable. At that date, the statute of limitations begins to be operational.

The parties are free to accept or reject the Médiateur's proposed solution; however, the refusal to follow the Médiateur's opinion must be substantiated and forwarded to the consumer and the mediator.

The end of the mediation process may be found, at the request of the parties, in a written protocol which states the points of agreement that the parties have decided to. This MOU may be subject to approval by a judge as provided in the Code of Civil Procedure.

If the notice was accepted by the parties, the Médiateur is destined to be informed by them of any difficulties in the implementation of this notice.

Article 4.4 Term

The duration of mediation should normally not exceed two months from the date of acknowledged receipt of the request for an admissible mediation. In the case of complex litigation, mediation can be extended once, for the same period, at the request of the Médiateur.

Article 4.5 Freedom of mediation

Each party retains the right to terminate the mediation at any time. For consumers, the mediation cannot, under any circumstances, be a prerequisite for legal action.

ARTICLE 5 - ANNUAL REPORT AND PUBLIC MEDEATEUR PROPOSALS

Each Médiateur prepares an annual report which is published and sent to the CMC for information.

This report includes an analysis of cases (total number, number of cases rejected, number of positive reviews to the professional or consumer...) and a summary of the main disputes dealt with in the year. It also includes the charter under which the mediator holds office, his career and the means at his disposal to accomplish his missions.

In addition, from the treatment of individual cases, the mediator may make proposals for improvement to prevent the renewal of certain repetitive or significant litigation, and help improve the quality of service sectors.

These recommendations, which follow the implementation, are included in the Médiateur's annual report.

The principles and rules defined in this document must be included in each of the charters establishing a Médiateur for consumer matters.

This Charter refers in particular to the following texts:

- Articles L534-7, R534-11 and R534-12 of the Consumer Code

- Recommendation No. 98/257/EC of the European Union March 30, 1998 on the principles applicable to bodies responsible for the resolution of consumer disputes (JOCEL115 of April 17, 1998).

- European Recommendation No. 2001/310/EC of 4 April 2001 on the principles applicable to court bodies involved in the consensual resolution of consumer disputes (JOCEL109 of April 19, 2001).

- European Directive 2008/52/EC of 21 May 2008 on certain aspects of mediation in civil and commercial matters.

- Opinion of the National Consumer Council (NCC) of 6 July 2004 on mediation in the area of consumer matters (BOCCRF March 1, 2005).

- Opinion of the CNC of 27 March 2007 on mediation in the field of consumer matters and alternative dispute resolution.

- Charter of Médiateur of public services.

- Report of the State Council of July 20, 2010 "Developing mediation as part of the European Union"